CONTEMPORARY CHINA INSTITUTE PUBLICATIONS

ECONOMIC DEVELOPMENT IN PROVINCIAL CHINA

THE CENTRAL SHAANXI SINCE 1930

ECONOMIC DEVELOPMENT IN PROVINCIAL CHINA

THE CENTRAL SHAANXI SINCE 1930

EDUARD B. VERMEER
Sinologisch Instituut, Leiden

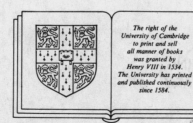

CAMBRIDGE UNIVERSITY PRESS
Cambridge
New York   New Rochelle
Melbourne   Sydney

Published by the Press Syndicate of the University of Cambridge
The Pitt Building, Trumpington Street, Cambridge CB2 1RP
32 East 57th Street, New York, NY 10022, USA
10 Stamford Road, Oakleigh, Melbourne 3166, Australia

First published 1988

Printed in Great Britain at the University Press, Cambridge

British Library cataloguing in publication data
Vermeer, Eduard B.
Economic development in provincial China:
the Central Shaanxi since 1930. –
(Contemporary China Institute publications).
1. Shensi Province (China) – Economic conditions
I. Title II. Series
330.951'17042 HC428.s/

Library of Congress cataloguing in publication data
Vermeer, E. B. (Eduard B.)
Economic development in provincial China : the central Shaanxi
since 1930 / Eduard Vermeer.
p.   cm. – (Contemporary China Institute publications)
Bibliography:
Includes index.
ISBN 0-521-34392-5
1. Shensi Province (China) – Economic conditions.   2. Agriculture-
Economic aspects – China – Shensi Province – History – 20th century.
I. Title.   II. Series.

330.951'17058–dc1987-22499 CIP

ISBN 0 521 34392 5

VN

CONTENTS

v

TABLES

MAPS

GRAPHS

PLATES

INTRODUCTION: SOME PROBLEMS OF REGIONAL ECONOMIC DEVELOPMENT

In the PRC, contemporary history has often been a forbidden and somewhat dangerous field of interest for communist historians. One of the official taboos was, and still is, to recount any display of regional, political or social diversity. Officially, it is always society as a whole which marches forward or is pushed back on the road to socialist progress. It is the entire Chinese nation that suffers from foreign imperialism or from landlord exploitation, that fails in the Great Leap Forward or booms under Deng Xiaoping's liberalization. To a certain extent, this unitary tendency also conforms to older Chinese cultural and political beliefs. As a rule, Western historians or social scientists who would have liked to shatter these uniform images have been denied access to local sources. Until 1978, local publications such as provincial newspapers were not permitted to be carried out of China. The exceptional case of Guangdong province – across the border from Hongkong, with information from a steady flow of refugees, visitors and smuggled-in newspapers – was used to write the one and only provincial history since 1949, Ezra Vogel's *Canton under Communism* (1968). It focused on the successive waves of communist policies sweeping over Guangdong and their local political response. In contrast to Guangdong, much less antagonism and opposition between national and local leadership is evident in Shaanxi province. This may be due not only to the absence of such political discrimination as directed against southerners and against commercially-oriented, clan-dominated or foreign-influenced communities, but also to the very facts of economic life: Shaanxi province received a great deal of direct central government support for its economic development, not only during the 1950s but to this very day.

The focus of my study is not politics, but economic development,

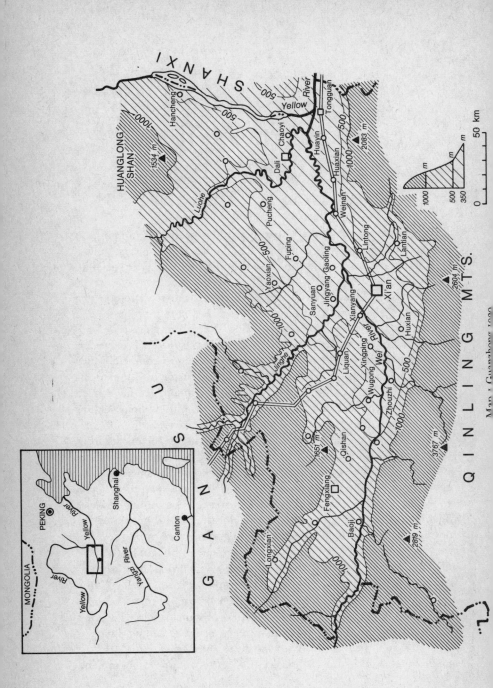

Map 1 Guanzhong 1980

and not the province of Shaanxi, but its core region, the Wei River valley. More so than political ideas, economic development is tied down to a set territory with certain geographical conditions. This is particularly true for agriculture. Using almost exclusively local sources, I have tried to see the process of transformation of the economy and environment through the eyes of local farmers and county officials, while turning a deaf ear to political rhetoric. A detailed survey of 7 counties in 1979 gave me a fair cross-section of the regional economy.

The Wei River valley, which almost coincides with the Guanzhong area of Shaanxi, is a distinct economic region. Its size of some 30,000 square kilometers, and its present population of around 15 million are about equal to Taiwan, or to a small European country, such as Holland. The Qinling mountains separate Guanzhong from south Shaanxi, which is mostly mountainous and where rice grows along the Hanshui – this area is closer to Sichuan than to the rest of Shaanxi. In the north, the transition to the loess hills and mountains of Yan'an is more gradual.

All those who have studied China's economic and social history, whether imperial or republican, have been confronted with large variations between provinces, regions or even villages. Obvious dichotomies between town and country, between mountains and plains, between dry and irrigated agriculture have to be bridged to obtain an integral picture of the economy and society of China or of its major economic regions. At least in this century, there has been no such thing as a 'typical' Chinese region which could reflect the main processes of political, social and economic change. Rather, the many exogenous shocks, internal warfare and political strife have each time made China into a different jig-saw puzzle. At least until 1949, it was too large and too diverse for any government to handle. What one finds in this century is a politically and economically divided China before 1949, and a politically united but still economically very diverse China since the establishment of the People's Republic.

Where were Guanzhong and its capital city of Xi'an positioned along the major dividing lines of modern China's history? First, this was one of the most backward interior areas of China. It did not take part in what Fairbank has called the 'minor tradition of maritime China'. Xi'an was one of the few large cities (Taiyuan was another) which did not receive the 'treaty-port' status. Only after the Longhai railroad had been extended to Xi'an in 1935, outside (but not foreign) investments started to trickle into Guanzhong. Second, after 1930 Shaanxi (at least its central and southern parts) in theory was a Guomindang-controlled area. However, in most of north China, the Guomindang government had only a very feeble influence, and shared its political and military power with either Japanese, semi-independent or hostile groups. The northernmost parts of Guanzhong were bandit territory, and later came under communist control. Third, from 1937 onwards, much of China was occupied by the Japanese. Only the least developed areas in the interior could be sustained (from 1944 these were further reduced) as Free China. The economic history of wartime occupied China, and especially of its links with Free China, still needs a great deal of investigation. Shaanxi, like the province of Sichuan, escaped Japanese occupation. Instead, these interior areas witnessed a sudden influx of Guomindang armies, government officials and fugitives from the east. It is no coincidence, then, that only in 1939–40 the Shaanxi government succeeded in its long-standing opium eradication campaign. One should not over-estimate, however, the degree of administrative control over the countryside during the 1940s. For one thing, the census of 1953 showed a population total for Shaanxi province which was almost a quarter more than had been present in the government's records. Fourth, when China reasserted itself under communism and actively developed its border areas, the Wei River valley and Gansu became the major thoroughfare to northwest China, as they had been under the Han and Tang dynasties. A new element was introduced with the industrialization program of interior cities under the First Five-Year Plan, from which Xi'an benefited greatly. Its rapid population growth, which had already begun during the war (1940: 200,000, 1950: 500,000, 1960: 1,000,000) and the vacillating communist policies towards this urban growth provide us with fascinating pictures of the growing pains of a frontier economy. Fifth, since the 1960s Shaanxi province appears to have been little involved in national politics, but it was usually on the receiving end and 'leftist'. Sixth, while the collectivization drive of the late 1950s aimed at laying a uniform pattern of development over rural China, the introduction of modern technology into farming during the 1960s again split rural China. Electricity, irrigation machinery, chemical fertilizer, tractors and macadam roads were allocated by the State to the densely populated river valleys, but not to other areas. In the 1970s the gap was partly closed, yet it became increasingly clear that some agricultural areas, with flat terrain, good accessibility and irrigation from surface or underground water resources could be modernized, but that many areas hardly could, or not at all. Within the Wei River valley the economic contrast between irrigated plain and dry upland became very distinct. The dividing lines – often loess cliffs or other visible traits of the landscape as observed from the ground or from a satellite – ran right through county administrative divisions. Seventh, the opening-up of coastal China for foreign investors is still of a limited quantitative significance at this date, but eventually might result in more rapid economic growth and considerable qualitative change in the institutional framework of industrial development in coastal China. Shaanxi province increased its foreign exports to 53 million US\$ in 1983, from 12 million US\$ in 1978, still only one-tenth of the per capita average in China, and foreign imports were even less than half that amount.[1] It is too early to say whether interior China will fall behind, or be drawn into the coastal sphere. The record shows that Communist China is not apt to maintain separate economic or political systems within its territory – the recent decollectivization drive gave a clear example of this unitary tendency.

In this study, I rarely touch on the issue of central–provincial government relations. There is a total absence of meaningful inform-ation about the economic decision-making process between these two levels of government, so the little one can say on this is highly speculative. Moreover, we are not dealing with a province, but with a subprovincial region consisting of three prefectures and one large municipality. From 1949 till 1954, Xi'an did not come under the jurisdiction of the provincial government, but was on a par with Shaanxi province under the Northwest (Military) Administrative Commission. The military dimension of the economy has weakened since World War II; however, a number of defense industries were established in Xi'an in the 1950s and later. One may ask in how far this has been due to Xi'an's strategic inland location, not too close to any possible 'front', or to political leverage or military favouritism, but one should not expect an answer. High-level political discussion in China is secret, and political propaganda such as carried by newspapers is usually very uninformative about regional economic problems. Under Deng, this has started to change.

During the 1930s and 1950s political goals for urban and rural development may have been essentially different. Both the nationalist and the communist governments, once in power, held that only on the basis of industrialization and in the urban environment could a modern (socialist) state be built. The urban work force was made subservient to the goal of rapid industrialization, and although social services slowly improved, its wages, living conditions, social life and political freedom were tightly controlled and kept down to a minimum. For the rural areas, with some 85 percent of China's population, nationalist and communist political goals were more limited in one sense but more utopian in another. Modernization through improved agricultural techniques and economic organization, should lead to higher production and to a larger rural surplus, with which to support urban and industrial China. The village population, once put on the right track (for the communists, this was Land Reform and collectivization), should develop by its own force into economically self-sustaining, socially just and equitable and democratic communities. 'Self-reliance' was a broad concept, of which economics was just one dimension. Urban and rural economic policies were so different, because they emanated from different concepts about what urban and rural development should be. Because of these goals, different economic frameworks were set up for the state-owned urban-industrial sector and for the collectively-owned rural-agricultural sector. Rather than striving after economic unity and integration, the communist government created intermediary state organizations, which monopolized or dominated exchanges of products, materials, labour, funds, know-how etc. between the two sectors.

An essential element of collective farming organization in China was the tying-down of the village population to its own soil, with extreme limits on mobility. Because of this, unlike other developing countries, China did not allow for a spontaneous balancing of population and economic resources. There was no movement (also in the sense of 'migration'!) towards more equal opportunities of employment and income. Only the counties near Xi'an and some counties which had to accommodate settlers from the Sanmen reservoir site in 1958–60 took exception to this. The rate of urbanization in most counties hardly rose at all. Between collective villages, only for reasons of marriage were a small percentage of youngsters (usually the brides) allowed to move.

The economic framework sketched out above and its political background apply to China, not just to Guanzhong. Dwight Perkins recently distinguished four central features of China's rural development policies since 1949: the government's capacity to implement village-level programmes on a nationwide basis through bureaucratic and Party channels, commitment to giving the rural poor a larger share of benefits, emphasis on heavy industry but with little benefit to the urban elite as far as housing and other urban infrastructure is concerned, and severe limits to migration to urban areas.[2] One might add one or two more, notably state control of trade and of village industry. All these features were common to Guanzhong. This confronts us with the question, how far local variation (not in institutions, but in economic development) could go and what decided it? An answer should be sought in the local geography, the location of the Wei River valley and Xi'an within China, the historical heritage, the degree of central government support (due to political leverage or other reasons), local economic resources, all adding up to a factor endowment mix peculiar to Guanzhong, or to parts of it. Was there much room for a 'provincial' strategy of development based on local advantages and disadvantages?

A number of questions arise when one observes the economy of this area grow and diversify under population pressure and State control. To what extent did the monopolization of trade by the State since the 1950s reduce or even wipe out previous local differences in marketing opportunities? Did the construction of a highway network, which varied considerably in density between counties, bring significant shifts in economic development and income between counties? And what about the railroad? One wonders also about the economic and social effects of the shift from handicraft industry located in the villages to large-scale industry located in Xi'an, Baoji and other cities in the 1950s. The evident economic gains to the urban economy shown by official statistics may well have been offset by concomitant losses to rural or semi-rural private handicraft industries.

Chinese industrial development policies during the 1960s and 1970s have been portrayed as supporting small-scale industry and the development of small urban centres. One might argue that, in spite of obvious economies of scale in many industries, social and political considerations (such as the provision of local employment, the tapping of local financial resources, and the cult of self-reliance) and also prices and transport subsidies strongly influenced locational decisions in favour of smaller urban centres. Some have gone further than that, and concluded that 'whatever political or social benefits may be achieved, where local resources permit, the creation of these rural, small-scale industries is an obviously rational policy in economic terms alone'.[3] Whether this assessment is correct or not, only more detailed study of various types of industry, and also of opposite centralizing tendencies within State industrial organizations, will be able to tell. Even at first sight, Xi'an stands out as a growth pole where most of Shaanxi's new industrial expansion (planned by national or provincial authorities) was located. In 1983, Shaanxi's second largest city, Baoji, had only one-fifth of the industrial output of Xi'an. For Guanzhong, cement, agricultural machinery, and at a later stage also chemical fertilizers were produced primarily in one or two large-scale factories. 'Walking on two legs' was an elegant political catchphrase; but how long was the other leg and did it produce a smoothly-running economy?

Because of the lack of regional studies many of the problems posed by economic historians and economists of China cannot yet be answered in a satisfactory manner. Let me mention just a few.

The demographic effect of famines in China, and their contributing factors, have been touched upon in a few studies, notably of the famines in Hebei and Henan in 1743, 1878 and 1922.[4] Yet until now the two most serious famines of this century, the Shaanxi–Gansu famine of 1928–31 and the Great Leap Forward famine of 1960–1 have hardly been studied. In both cases, we see local starvation occurring because of a defective national political and economic framework and confiscatory taxation with little concern for peasant life, certainly matters of national historical significance. For the historian, a basically political explanation (such as warlordism and ruthless taxation)[5] has a certain attraction because it connects famine with other events of the same period. However, Guanzhong had experienced two similar famines in the last decades of Imperial government, under quite different political conditions. Possibly, it is only the introduction of modern government and modern means of transportation which create the conditions for averting recurring starvation in regions periodically afflicted by droughts. As the Great Leap Forward showed us, the machinery of modern government may well work in the other direction, too. Even under a unified communist government with several years of experience in nationwide control of grain-purchase, -distribution and -sales, there was widespread starvation in 1960–1, but as a local phenomenon. Vast differences in available foodgrain per capita appeared between provinces, and within provinces, between counties and even villages. To a large extent, local governments, not local weather conditions, were to blame. Kenneth Walker recently tried to bring together provincial data on foodgrain production and consumption and construct a national picture of the 1959 foodgrain shortage and the subsequent famine conditions. However, until now most official data still have been kept secret, and what little has been published is admitted to be inaccurate. At least for Shaanxi province, as indicated by Walker, one of the most severely stricken areas,[6] our tentative conclusions tend in the very opposite direction. In spite of (or maybe because of) the marginality of agriculture in many parts of Shaanxi, from demographic and other evidence Shaanxi seems to have fared remarkably well in 1960–1 (Shangluo Region even became a major exporter of foodgrain). Between 1957 and 1960, the number of pigs increased by a half to 3.5 million, certainly not a sign of a severe foodgrain shortage. Was Shaanxi just lucky with the weather, or is there a political explanation?

The militarization of China in this century has usually been portrayed as having had a negative effect on economic development. It did not stop with Chiang Kai-Shek's establishment of the Nationalist Government in Nanking. 'The trend toward militarization became manifest during 1927–36 as the Guomindang became obsessed with the pursuit of illusive military power, which resulted in ten years of civil wars and the non-implementation of promised revolutionary programs.'[7] Most studies have focused on the Nationalist Government or at least on national goals. For most areas of China an assessment of the local effects of warlord armies and of their negative and positive contributions still has to be made. Destruction of human life and property, requisitioning of labour, crops and animals certainly weakened the national and local economies. For another part, and especially so in Free China during the war against Japan, the military presence served to mobilize and organize local economic resources, to improve transport and communications, to introduce new technology, and to increase demand for food, clothing and many other agricultural and industrial products. Shaanxi province may have had a few significant, uncommon characteristics throughout the period. It was never united under one warlord. All its successive warlords or military commanders came from outside the province (Feng Yuxiang, Zhang Xueliang, Sun Weiru, Mao Zedong, Hu Zongnan), and had little commitment to local affairs but were oriented towards national goals. Partly for that reason, military and civilian government (communist areas excepted) may have been less intertwined than in most of China. The buildup of Guomindang power started under peaceful conditions in 1932–6. From 1927 till 1947, there was very little actual fighting in Shaanxi; Feng was defeated elsewhere, and in 1936 the Xi'an incident showed that Zhang's Manchurian army, the Northwest army and the Red Army preferred not to fight each other. Subsequently, the Japanese chose not to invade Shaanxi, although Xi'an was bombed several times. Thus, Guanzhong profited from being a military base without much actual fighting and from its strategic position in a political tug-of-war for more than a decade. Its population increase from immigration is an indicator of this.

The evidence from wartime Guanzhong suggests that industry and agriculture were stimulated by the war effort at first, but suffered in the final years. As the government tried to strengthen its control over agricultural production and commodity trade in 1942, the peasantry's response was a retreat to more autarchy and to black marketing. Whether the burden of war was quite unevenly and unjustly distributed, as Hsi-sheng Ch'i believes,[8] would be difficult to establish with the available data. Grain taxes and grain procurement and conscription may have been more heavy than in occupied China. But is there reason to believe, with Ch'i, that 'poor peasants were deprived of their livelihood, while the rich peasants and landlords not only evaded taxes but often became hoarders of grain and made huge profits'?

Redistribution of land during Land Reform has varied greatly in scope between regions with different tenancy rates. In Guanzhong, only some 10 percent of all farmland was involved. Rural redistribution of wealth (land, houses, animals, stocks) was of social and political significance rather than of direct economic significance. The poorest 30 percent of the rural population received an average of 1 *mou* ($\frac{1}{15}$ ha) per capita. Communist sources, in contrast, stressed the high degree of inequality in Suide and Mizhi counties in north Shaanxi during the 1930s and 1940s, and the economic improvement after redistribution. Possibly famine, the chances of new economic development and the war effort had had a more egalitarian effect on the crop-growing villages in the plains than on the thinly populated, often lawless, mixed pastoral-agricultural mountain areas.

Some authors (myself included) have addressed the question of the level of per capita consumption in rural China. The answer seems to be that in the 1930s, 1950s and 1970s per capita output value and material consumption did not increase much, but that many non-material services of health care, education etc. vastly improved the quality of life.[9] Guanzhong's rural economy of the 1920s and 1930s was characterized by extreme fluctuations in output and consumption, depending on weather conditions, requisitioning by bandits or armies and interruptions of trade flows. Constructing averages from years of abundant harvests and of large-scale starvation is meaningless. More than anything else, the stabilizing effects of rural safety and economic support for the poor have contributed to the peasants' sense of well-being during the 1950s, although we will see that in some sectors, such as animal husbandry and rural handicrafts, the peasantry was seriously hit by government policies. The extension of irrigation and agricultural modernization have had similar stabilizing effects on Guanzhong's foodgrain production in the 1970s. Nevertheless, the 1979 survey showed substantial income differentials between irrigated and dry farmland areas.

Both during the 1930s and during the 1950s cotton became the leading commercial crop, sustaining the development of cotton textile industry. The effect of China's modern cotton industry on textile handicraft production has been a much-debated issue. Kang Chao concluded that the persistence of the textile handicraft sector was not mainly due to a separate demand, but to the availability of surplus labour with close to zero costs in China's peasant households.[10] We will explore this issue in a separate chapter on cotton production. Right from the 1930s, cotton as the major economic crop received much attention from the State. In the same way as the development of cotton production may be considered as the best indicator of the government's attitude toward agriculture and trade in north China, the development of textile handicraft industry showed its attitude towards village and private industries.

In 1953–4, the communist government saw to it that the State would have total command over raw cotton and other agricultural products, and forbade private trade in and production of cotton goods. The negative effects, economic and social, of the stamping out of rural handicraft production and of the forced transformation to urban industrial production have received scant attention from Chinese or Western writers. Only very recently the Chinese government has taken a slightly less repressive attitude towards village industries. The same goes for the sector of services and trade, for which woefully little data have been collected during the past decades.

There has been some debate over the issue whether or not relative prices, or State mandatory planning of crop acreages, have been most influential in shaping China's agricultural performance. It seems wise to use the word 'shaping' here, rather than 'deciding', because naturally agricultural growth has been sustained primarily by adding new inputs of labour, irrigation water, fertilizer, new varieties and other technological changes. The debate has been fueled by the price increases of 1979 and the condemnation by the present Chinese leadership of previous policies of State mandatory planning and allocation. There is a general consensus now, based on the agricultural performance in the past few years and that of the decades before, that the emphasis on local self-sufficiency in foodgrain production during the 1960s and 1970s has been harmful to rural production and income in China.[11] Because comparative advantages were under-utilized, not only total crop output but also trade and industry have suffered. Whether this policy should be labeled 'Maoist' and be associated with the Cultural Revolution decade 1966–76, as Lardy does, is another matter. Its roots go back to World War II, and administrative convenience may be a better explanation than ideological motives. It appears that already during the 1950s the combined effect of State monopolization of trade and population growth forced previously pastoral areas (such as Yulin Prefecture in north Shaanxi) and cotton areas (such as central Guanzhong) into growing more grain. The traumatic Great Leap Forward experience of severe local grain shortages strengthened the desire for grain self-sufficiency with local governments and peasants.

The problem we have to address is a complex one. At least three different prices (quota-, above-quota- and negotiated prices) were used by State organizations when purchasing cotton and grain. For most of the 1960s and 1970s, there is no data on quantities sold at which price. The economic calculations of county officials and village leaders could be widely off the mark: quantity and quality of cotton output varied greatly from year to year. With high costs of chemical fertilizer and pesticides, it was a risky crop. The cotton mills in Xi'an had a quite different perspective, however. Throughout China, there was a severe shortage of raw cotton. Thus, local and provincial (or rather, agricultural and industrial) preferences in crop choice differed. Moreover, Chinese planning practices hardly allow one to distinguish between price effects and allocative measures, as the two are intertwined. For cotton, the State has always used acreage quotas, not output quotas as it does for grain; this left the rural collectives at some liberty to choose the most economical use of high-quality land, fertilizers, irrigation water, etc. in cotton production. With liberalization after 1980, in spite of price rises the farmers of Guanzhong reduced the cotton-sown acreage as much as they could. Unit yields during 1980–3 sank to only one-half of the national average, which is indicative not only of bad weather, but also of decreased investment in chemical fertilizers, pesticides, and labour. This dramatic trend was exactly the opposite of the cotton boom in the North China Plain. Why? Were maize and wheat more profitable in the eyes of the local farmer, was his primary concern avoidance of risk, or was cotton less 'liberalized' and more difficult to handle individually? The record for China after liberalization has shown that farmers can accomplish what State planning could not, in making use of comparative economic advantages of trade.

Even so, one must realize that between 1978 and 1984 many inputs in agriculture were increased, notably those of chemical fertilizer and improved strains, and agricultural growth has been due to increased inputs and knowhow as well as to policy changes. The growth in the past few years, therefore, has not been a 'one-time shot in the arm', as some observers believe. Even a more rational pattern of crop distribution does not have just a one-time effect; it takes many years of experience in economic decisions, before one is able to fully realize the benefits of liberalization and trade. For Guanzhong, the possible impact of these policies was obscured (and overshadowed) to a great extent by the disasters of 1980 and 1981. Its positive grain production record since then still is too short for final conclusions to be drawn about relative weights of such diverse contributing factors as improved varieties, higher prices, privatization of production, liberalization of trade, increased input of fertilizers and pesticides, and weather conditions. In any case, in a province so diverse geographically as Shaanxi, provincial-level generalizations of the effects of new economic policies cannot be pushed very far. There seems to be no reason why the effects of national policies should not have also varied between regions during earlier decades.

The harmful consequences of the ongoing deforestation of hills and mountains, mainly due to reclamation and the felling of trees for fuel and timber, became most evident in the terrible floods in west Guanzhong and south Shaanxi in 1981. At least for the Qinling mountain range, in recent decades the provincial government seems to have been unconvinced of, or not impressed by, the long-term dangers (for water supply, soil fertility and protection against floods) which specialists had warned about. Only by a concerted political effort and by economic pressure could county and village governments have been persuaded to forego short-term benefits of exploitation. With the Tongchuan–Hancheng coal belt near at hand one wonders why the provincial government could not or would not interfere with felling trees for fuel. For the northern loess hills, the government's record has been somewhat better, after the failure of the giant Sanmen project in the early 1960s. By coincidence, this area as an 'old revolutionary base' was entitled to extra State support anyway. However, in Yan'an Prefecture alone 1.3 million ha of grasslands were destroyed between 1958 and 1978. Between 1971 and 1980, almost every year 700,000 ha or more of Shaanxi's farmland were struck by drought, in 1980 even 2.1 million ha; during the 1950s, both floods and droughts had been far less serious. Because of the sheer magnitude of the water and soil erosion problem of the Yellow River basin, the treatment of the Loess Plateau is of interest to China and the world. For that reason I have devoted ample attention to the slow but widespread soil conservation efforts since the 1960s. Because of a locally perceived severe shortage of irrigation water and the low costs of collectively organized labour, many surface water retention reservoirs (which tend to silt up rapidly) and plateau improvement measures have been undertaken; these measures may be uniquely Chinese. The environmental consequences of agricultural intensification and of extension of farmland in mountain areas deserve further study.

In the Wei River plain, the landscape has changed greatly: straight tree-lined roads and canals, telephone poles, tractors and other modern facilities have sprung into existence. The villages, originally very small, doubled or tripled in size but maintained their nuclear structure. Because of collectivization, the tiny farmplots of some 0.1 to 0.5 hectares were combined into large consolidated plots of 3 hectares or more, managed by production teams which owned some 25 to 50 hectares. In spite of the gains by rationalization of land use, during the 1960s and 1970s an ever-increasing amount of farmland (0.5 to 0.8 percent yearly) was lost to non-agricultural uses. The collective or State ownership of land greatly facilitated this process. With the recent splitting up of land between contracting farmers, land use planning has become much more difficult.

Semi-arid Guanzhong had a long tradition of irrigation projects, which was picked up again by relief agencies and the Guomindang government in the 1930s. The large amounts of silt carried by the

Yellow River and its tributaries create insurmountable technical difficulties for large-scale reservoir projects. Small reservoirs and diversion canals, however, have been constructed with great success. Maintenance was guaranteed by the abundant supply of rural manpower (at least in spring and winter) and by its organization by irrigation district authorities and collectives. Since the 1960s, pump irrigation machinery was introduced to secure irrigation from underground water, and that from greater depths. The effective utilization rate of water was increased. Nevertheless, already during the 1970s many projects ran up against the limits of available water supply. From the 1930s onward, the borderline between the irrigated lowland area and the dry plains north of the Wei River (the so-called *Weibei* area) had been gradually pushed northwards. Did this borderline become stabilized around 1980, and if so, for what reasons? One may point to some problems which were in evidence in other areas of north China, such as alternative water uses, sinking underground water levels, rising electricity costs, but also to essentially political changes in allocation and distribution of irrigation water. After 1980 the irrigated acreage may well have fallen slightly.

After most farm animals had been killed during the famine of 1930, it took Guanzhong's agriculture many years to recover. Pigs (the main source of fertilizer) and draught animals were imported from mountain areas and other provinces. The farm soils, with the exception of small stretches of irrigated land along the Wei River and its tributaries, received very little fertilizer. Yields of wheat remained low and unstable: between 600 and 1,000 kg per hectare, with a five year average of below 800 kg/ha during 1936–40 and below 700 kg/ha during 1941–5 in Guanzhong. These local data confirm the essential correctness of Paul W. Wilm's estimates for the loess area, as noted down in 1947; in contrast, Buck's data were quite off the mark.[12] Between counties, differences were large. Since the 1950s, with population growth, increased irrigation, more pigs and agricultural intensification, the farmland of Guanzhong received increasing amounts of manure. For irrigated areas, chemical fertilizer became available in greater quantities during the 1970s. Wheat and maize strains were improved or imported, and in this way a greater tolerance for drought, cold, or disease was bred into high-yielding varieties. The research done by the Northwestern College of Agriculture and the establishment of popularization and breeding centres during the 1940s laid the basis for higher-yielding wheat varieties. This network was expanded further under communism. Then, every county ran a breeding station, responsible for a rapid popularization of varieties which fitted local conditions. Improved agricultural implements and tractor power could plough the soil to greater depths, and break the ploughpan which previously had impeded root growth. As elsewhere in north China, because of this total package of agricultural technical improvement, yields of wheat and maize have doubled or tripled over the level of the 1950s. How far and with what speed did this transformation process spread over Guanzhong, and to what extent have 'traditional' areas remained outside of it? State organization may have been uniform, but water availability, soils, terrain and climate certainly were not. Yet, within the Chinese context of self-reliance, every village had to feed its growing population and to literally force its farmland into giving higher yields. How was this done, and which low-yield crops were driven out?

During the 1930s and 1950s, most pigs were raised in the mountain areas of Shaanxi, where fodder was cheap. From the 1960s onwards, however, pigs became one of the few sources of private income under collective farming, and Guanzhong farmers everywhere turned to pig-raising on a massive scale. Pigs could be fed with products from the private plot, and with whatever could be had legally or otherwise from the collective. In the 1950s, the number of pigs (live at year-end) had remained below half a million because of the low prices for pork and manure, lack of fodder, and diseases. In the mid 1970s, in Guanzhong pigs totalled three to four million head. Since then, because of a saturation of demand for pork, lower prices for manure and higher feedgrain prices, their number went down by about one-third. The same factors were at work in the rest of China, yet there the number of pigs remained stable since 1979. The downward trend in Guanzhong deserves further explanation. Pig farming has been very sensitive to policy changes, prices and grain harvests, and its increase has demonstrated the growth of the private rural economy during the 1960s and 1970s (contrary to what political statements then and now would have us believe). In contrast, draught animals, which suffered from Land Reform and collective ownership, remained at the level of one animal for every two hectares of farmland since the 1950s; after the recent decollectivization they came to be preferred to expensive tractors and their numbers increased again. Especially for dairy cattle, chickens and milk goats, the post-1978 policies led to sizable increases.

The improvement of varieties in China's modern agriculture is a subject which deserves far more attention from agrarian historians and economists than it has received until now. It is the basis for fundamental changes in yields and cropping patterns. The combination of a rather short growing season, a large amount of heat, and a variable and often insufficient water supply makes growing grain and cotton in north China far from easy. Moreover, a lack of pesticides until the 1970s had made wheat very vulnerable to rust, scab, lodging, smut and other diseases. Irrigated cotton was attacked by aphids, red spiders, bugs etc. and especially in dark and humid years damages were very serious and still are. Much valuable experience has been gained with various local cultivation methods over the past decades. It would appear that the state extension network has been most capable in introducing new techniques and experiences. If pushed too far, however, by national or local self-styled agricultural or plainly political authorities, the reverse side of the coin appeared. Agriculture then was subjected to standard prescriptions which eventually failed because of local conditions. Proper feedback could not always be given. Another danger now looms, that of a breakdown of planning. The recent split-up of large cultivation plots and the greater freedom for farmers to use their own seeds should be watched carefully by local agricultural experts for possible negative effects on seed quality and pest control. The question how far the government should go in guiding agriculture is a difficult one, but in my view it will always have to be answered on the basis of local conditions.

The cooperative movement, which was supported by various banks, played a major role in the rapid increase of cotton production in central Guanzhong during the 1930s. Around 1940, the Guomindang government took more active control of cooperative affairs and increased its financial support. The wave of war refugees, the desire to contain communism, and the necessity for planning a war economy were the main causes for that. In contrast to the rural cooperatives, the industrial cooperatives and defense cooperatives were not very successful, however. Whence the difference? In how far did they differ from the communist cooperatives?

In the spring of 1955, many local cadres voiced doubts about stepping up the pace of cooperativization. At that time, 16 percent of all rural households had entered agricultural producers' cooperatives. A year later, the CCP had forced over 90 percent of the peasants into collectives. Neither in size, nor in speed of this transformation did Guanzhong show any deviation from national trends. During the people's commune movement of 1958–60, however, there is some evidence that Shaanxi proceeded rather cautiously – and therefore had less of a disastrous retreat.

The negative aspects of collectivist policies during the 1960s and 1970s have been highlighted under the post-1978 leadership. In Shaanxi, however, there were 'left' tendencies which made Guanzhong lag behind in the decollectivization drive. Local leaders found it hard to accept that the collectives had outlived their usefulness as organizers of agricultural production. Was this really the case? It is not easy to strike a balance, especially when social and political considerations are also included. If one narrows one's view down to economic performance only, the answer still may be different for major economic functions of the collectives. However, labour incentives seem to have been most deficient, with depressing effects of an economical as well as a psychological nature. What explains the farmers' resentment against so many State organizations, cadres and guidance from above?

In a lengthy chapter, we will follow the vicissitudes of cotton cultivation in Guanzhong over half a century. Political, economic and climatic factors had great effects on sowing acreages and yields, because cotton was the main economic crop in a predominantly subsistence economy. More so than with any other crop, successive governments sought by a range of means to stabilize and raise output of cotton. Large cotton mills were established in Xi'an in the 1930s, and again in the 1950s, and under a persisting national cotton shortage, their demand for cotton had to be met locally as much as possible. Obligatory sales, fixed prices, rationing and finally directive planning of the cotton acreage were meant to secure a regular supply from the farmers to the State and its mills. As elsewhere in China, this bureaucratic system did not produce the desired results. Wartime controls and low prices brought production down, and affected quality. In the 1950s, under the influence of improved varieties, more fertilizer and irrigation, cotton yields had risen from about 225 kg/ha to about 300 kg/ha. After a severe drop, yields climbed to a new level of 400 to 500 kg/ha during the late 1960s. In spite of an increasing and guaranteed supply of chemical fertilizers, irrigation and labour, China's average cotton yields remained at this same level during the late 1960s and 1970s, and the sown acreage did not increase either. Only under the new policies of the 1980s did national yields shoot up, to 750 kg/ha in 1983. However, the Guanzhong picture is different from the national one. Probably because of a continued improvement of cotton during the anti-Japanese war, cotton yields in Guanzhong were considerably higher than the national average in the late 1940s and 1950s. In the mid 1960s, they were about equal; in the 1970s some 10 to 40 percent lower; in the 1980s, even lower by one-half. Why did Guanzhong fall behind?

Organizational changes in rural China understandably have drawn much more attention from social scientists and contemporary historians than quantitative economic changes. The 'Chinese road to socialism' indeed has been a unique phenomenon in this world, and the road back from socialism is perhaps even more unique. These transformations, it should be reminded, have been paved with modern inputs. Between 1965 and 1978, China's agriculture changed beyond recognition. Agricultural machinery increased ten-fold(in terms of horsepower), chemical fertilizer use over four-fold, and electricity use seven-fold. Again, between 1978 and 1983 these inputs rose by 50 to 90 percent. Organizational changes can only be evaluated in a satisfactory manner in this context of physical transformation of agriculture. Therefore, we will follow closely the introduction of modern inputs as a vital part of agricultural history.

In a final chapter, the focus is on the development of economic differentials within Guanzhong, and their natural and man-made causes. The introduction of modern inputs has been a major cause for economic divergence. For the communist period, I draw heavily on a rural survey I undertook in 1979, and on data provided at that time by seven County Agricultural Bureaus for the 1957–78 period. These counties were selected to provide two crosscuts north-south, viz. Chunhua-Wugong and Hancheng-Weinan. For northwest Guanzhong, use has been made of a separate three-county survey. Since the 1930s, the development of transportation, intensification of land use, new agricultural technology and industry greatly changed some areas, while other areas were only slightly affected. Rather little could be done with mountains and slope land, but parts of the dry plain were converted into high-yield farmland. Nevertheless, population doubled or tripled everywhere. In terms of output value and of urban economic change both the state-owned county industries and the collectively-owned county-based industries became economically more important and foci of planning during the 1970s. Their productivity varied considerably, but generally increased quite fast, according to survey data on some forty of the largest local industries in seven counties. *In toto*, industry has contributed rather little to employment for the growing population of Guanzhong. By 1978, within most counties less than 5 percent of the labour force was industrial.

In 1937, even in the plain areas, counties did show considerable variation in agriculture. In extensive farming areas such as Pucheng county, farms had an average size of almost four hectares, and grew wheat or millet, and a little cotton. In traditionally intensive farming areas such as Zhouzhi county, farms averaged only one hectare, and grew wheat, maize, some millet and sorghum, but also cotton and poppy. In a modern farming area, Jingyang county, farms were rather large, with an average size of three hectares; there, cotton was the dominant crop together with wheat; maize and millet came next, and no sorghum or poppy were cultivated. Betweeen these counties, average farmland values differed by a factor of 6 and average indebtedness by a factor of 3. Rich peasants' households had an average size of 10 persons, as against only 4.5 persons in poor peasants' households. After the 1950s, much of the diversified economy, especially that of the mountain areas, was lost. Intensification of agriculture, population growth, and the levelling policies under communism contributed in various ways to the disappearance of most of these differentials. It remains to be seen to what extent local specialization will return under the present policies. Now that food grain has become abundantly available, mountain areas probably will no longer be required to deliver food grain to the State as taxes. To an increasing extent, the artificial situation of the 1960s and 1970s, in which the government guaranteed to purchase food grain from any village at the same price irrespective of transportation costs, is being broken down by market forces. What influence did this equalizing tendency have on regional income differentials over the past few decades?

For the provision and distribution of social services, the government's record for the 1960s and 1970s is very positive. Not only did the welfare system operate well in providing minimum subsistence in calamity-stricken counties and villages, but also poor county governments were allowed to engage in considerable deficit-spending. Teachers and health workers were available to poor and affluent alike; at least, differences in numbers between counties were not correlated to average income levels. Being basically quantitative, our 1979 survey did not go into the quality of services provided.

The themes I shall develop here do not cover all aspects of the local economy. I certainly would have liked to be able to say more on trade, consumption, finance and some other aspects of economic life. Yet I feel the essence of Guanzhong's economic history over the past half a century to be the visible and tangible transformation – beyond recognition – of the urban and rural economic environment. The present oldest generation grew up in an age in which starvation and flight from local disasters was a regular phenomenon. It saw the first railroad coming into Guanzhong and the rise of Xi'an from a sleepy administrative center of 100,000 people to an industrial metropolis. It saw a new government and the Communist Party move into and soon dominate all spheres of life and work in towns and villages. It saw a previously dry plain north of the Wei River change into irrigated farmland, lush with high-yield wheat, maize and cotton. It saw the replacement of domestic animal breeds by foreign ones, of oxen by tractors, of home-made tools by factory products. It saw population triple, because of an unheard-of improvement of health care and material growth. Never before, and probably never after, has change within a lifetime been so total and so rapid.

Our history of Guanzhong starts with the famine of 1928–31. It marked the end of an era characterized by lack of government control, pillaging armies, banditry, and isolation from the modernizing China. Relief measures were insignificant at first, but did bring foreign and Guomindang agencies into the area, and finally helped the strongly reduced population to prosper again. The social and economic structure hardly changed, however, until around 1935, when the railroad reached Xi'an. Communications and transport were the key to drawing Guanzhong into the national economy, and also to economic integration within Guanzhong itself. World War II, the mid 1950s and again the 1970s were periods of rapid expansion of the road network, although for various reasons it was often underutilized. Rather than treating Guanzhong's economic history in a chronological order, I have devoted all but one of the nine chapters of this study to a single sector or topic which covers the entire 50-year period.

In chapter three, I sketch the growth of Xi'an and the development of industry. During the war (and also because of it) the political and economic climate became very oppressive. Urban labour was strictly controlled by the Guomindang, as it would be under the communists. Much less controlled, however, was the influx of people into Xi'an until the end of the 1950s. In an appendix, I have given a survey of the demographic change in Xi'an and Shaanxi province. The build-up, almost from scratch, of Xi'an in the 1950s gives some idea of the problems facing the new government in the urban environment and of its principles of spatial and industrial planning. The Great Leap Forward food shortage and industrial crisis brought a sudden end to the economic boom. On the basis of some assessments of the industrial situation around 1980 and recent new data we try to evaluate past performance and future opportunities for Shaanxi's industry. Also, we go into its professional structure and the level of urban social services and wages. While in Xi'an very little reminds us of agriculture and the country it is supposed to serve and rule, most county capitals are still very sleepy rural towns. There seemingly is little connection between the large-scale industrial development of Xi'an, Baoji and some other centres and the county state- or collectively-owned industries. For that reason, these are treated separately in chapter nine as constituent parts of local economies.

Chapter four focuses on the physical aspects of the transformation of Guanzhong's mountains, loess plateau and river plain. Water and soil erosion, deforestation, degradation of mountains and hills and downstream problems of heavy silt loads have made the national and local governments devise a series of counter-measures. Village collectivization had created a framework for joint protective action but also for efforts directed at reclamation of hills and wasteland and immediate exploitation of their natural resources. In the river plain, particularly along the railroad, much prime farmland was lost to other uses. But also agricultural modernization and collectivization changed farmland use, plot sizes, road patterns etc. The major contributing factor to agricultural change in semi-arid Guanzhong has been the extension of irrigation, which is outlined in chapter five. The management of irrigation districts before and after the communist take-over showed a high degree of continuity, which is worthy of further exploration. An important question here is, to what extent have the limits of possible water use been reached?

Chapter six gives the agricultural history of Guanzhong, and goes into soils, crops and cropping patterns, fertilizers (until recently mainly pig manure), variety improvements, cultivation methods and other agrotechnical changes over the past fifty years. I have concentrated on wheat and maize as the major crops of the region, although of course there are considerable differences between areas. Cotton is treated in a separate chapter (and poppy in chapter one). Although one cannot give exact weight to various factors responsible for the raises of yields, I have tried to describe major changes of inputs and cultivation techniques. For understandable reasons, handbooks and journals have maintained a constant flow of information on these subjects, probably more so than on any other sector of the economy. An agricultural geography of Shaanxi (published for internal use) supplied a complete cross-section of the 1974 agricultural situation. Of great assistance to me has also been the guidance of several professors and the librarian of the Northwest Agricultural College in Wugong. I wish to thank particularly Professor Ma Hongyun, the Agricultural Bureau Chiefs and other local cadres in the counties I visited in 1979 for their efforts to enlighten my understanding of local farming. Since then, mechanization and chemical fertilizer use have continued to progress rapidly. There have been two bad harvest years and three good ones: weather is still an important factor.

The chapter on cooperativization and collectivization which follows sketches first the cooperative movement in the Guomindang period. It mainly concerned cotton-growing farmers. Land Reform and collectivization were introduced by the communists with little or no room for local variations. More than any other subject, collectivization, and its consequences for the local economy, is difficult to evaluate because of the strong political overtones of all Chinese statements on collective organization and because of its uniform application throughout China. Thus, I have looked primarily at the introductory period of the 1950s and at the demise of the collectives in the 1980s. My speculations concerning the stagnation of the collective method of production and distribution are based to a larger extent on information about China than on Guanzhong. Unlike other provinces such as Anhui or Sichuan, Shaanxi has been slow in following the national lead. Therefore, local political statements on the subject have been rather stereotyped. However, local press reports give a fair impression of recent developments, particularly of the boost of specialized production after rural decollectivization.

After the 1950 Land Reform, taxation and state grain procurement were reorganized. Even for the mid-1950s, when data were relatively good, estimations of procurement and consumption levels must remain tentative. For 1974 and again for the early 1980s, we have treated this subject in chapter 6, section g, under food grain output since the 1960s; procurement of cotton is treated in a separate chapter devoted to cotton, chapter eight. It has been so treated because it has been Guanzhong's most important economic crop, grown only in certain parts of Guanzhong, and because it reflects more than any other crop state efforts to influence agricultural production. We will go into the effects of World War II, the demands of cotton industry, variety improvements and expansion or contraction of the cotton area. For some periods, inputs and yields, and costs and benefits will be analyzed, also relative to other crops.

A final chapter explores regional inequality within Guanzhong. Changes in land use, the extension of irrigation, improved communications and the introduction of modern industry (both large- and small-scale) were major factors. We will also evaluate the effects of communist policies regarding self-reliance at the levels of village, county and province. This chapter is not meant to be a summing up of economic change, but rather a display of local variety in the modern economic history of Guanzhong.

Most of the counties in Guanzhong have their own local history, written in the Ming or Qing dynasties, and a few were written in the 1920s and early 1930s. I hope my study will stimulate others to revive this rich tradition of local and regional histories. Within Guanzhong, many relations between areas can be expressed in, and reflect, universal relations between mountains and plains, upstream and downstream, rural–suburban–urban, irrigated and dry agriculture, centre and periphery, and commercial and subsistence agriculture. As such, these relations reflect the underlying economic geography of medium-size river basins. Yet, in any region the mixture of these elements is different and the historical process is unique. If anything became clear to me in the course of my surveys and my study, it is that each county has its particular traditions and current flavour.

What attracted me to the Guanzhong region for an economic history? There were several considerations. It is a rather isolated, medium-sized, geographically distinct river basin. It has seen tremendous changes over the past 50 years, and became linked by railroad to modern China only in 1935. From the 1930s until today it has contained both modern and backward agricultural areas. As a semi-arid region, the impacts of irrigation and crop cultivation stand out clearly on satellite pictures. There is some data on its economic development during the 1930s in the archives of the Nationalist government in Taibei. Although affected by the war against Japan, it escaped the disruptive effects (also data-wise) of Japanese occupation. Both the Guomindang government in the 1930s and the Communist government in the 1950s have tried to build up Guanzhong as a stepping-stone to northwest China. Finally, the area is well-known as

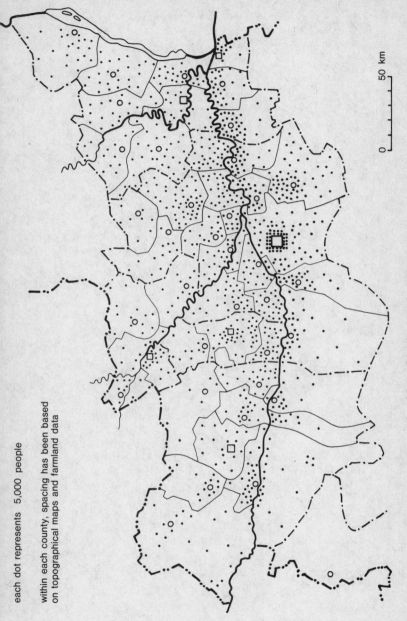

each dot represents 5,000 people

within each county, spacing has been based
on topographical maps and farmland data

Map 2 Distribution of population, 1935

50 km

0

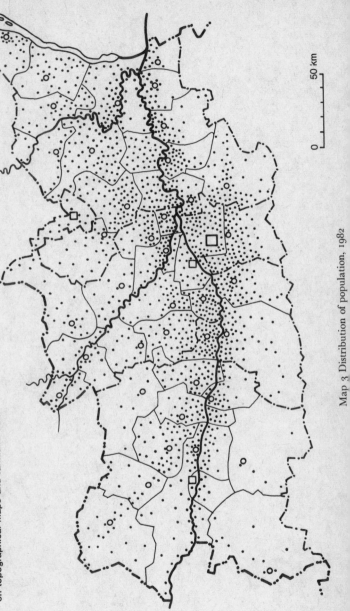

each dot represents 10,000 people

for Xi'an, Baoji, Xianyang and Tongchuan municipalities
only the rural population has been indicated

within each county, spacing has been based
on topographical maps and farmland data

50 km

0

Map 3 Distribution of population, 1982

the heartland of China's early empire, with its capital Changan. Chinese historians and Western tourists were attracted to it and marveled at the remnants of a glorious past, and they still do. And so do I.

Every generation has to use and shape its own economic environment and organization. With population growth, pressures have become greater and the need for change more urgent. The transformation of Guanzhong by its inhabitants, and by outside forces in this century, is the main theme of this study.

GUANZHONG: THE FAMINE OF 1928–31

A. POLITICAL SETTING

The Wei River valley along the middle reaches of the Yellow River was once the cradle of China's culture. Its traditional name, Guan-zhong, 'the land between the passes' refers to its secluded geographical position: the Qinling mountain range in the south, the loess hills in the north, and the Yellow River in the east. Well-protected by these natural boundaries, it became the base area of the first Chinese empire, where Changan with a population of one million was the capital. After the Han dynasty, however, the economic and political centre of the Chinese empire gravitated toward the much larger and better-endowed North China Plain and the Lower Yangzi River region. In subsequent centuries Guanzhong (now part of the province of Shaanxi) remained important as a thoroughfare along the old Silk Road which connected China with Central Asia, and as a buffer zone against attacks of nomad 'barbarians' – the last of which was a Muslim revolt during the drought disaster of 1876–9.[1] In this century, however, natural and man-made disasters have made Guanzhong and the loess hills north of it notorious as one of China's worst places to live, frequently visited by drought and famine, infested with bandits and forever poor. Little attention was paid by the central government, which was very weak anyhow, with two notable exceptions. During the Boxer uprising in 1900 the two Empresses-Dowager fled to the interior and settled in Changan (Xi'an) for some months, just at a time when the area was hit by a severe 3-year drought. With them, extra foodgrain was brought in and relief grants were donated. Even so, according to a Western traveller 30 percent of Shaanxi's 8.5 million inhabitants died of starvation, and the government was not in a position to help them. 'During the winter of 1900–1901 more than

300,000 villagers, desperate and starving, made their way to Sian. Owing to fear of bread riots, the government did not allow them within the city walls . . .'² A second exception, also short-lived, occurred in the mid 1930s. The Longhai railroad was extended from the North China Plain to Xi'an, some large irrigation projects were undertaken with foreign aid, and an attack was mounted on the communists who settled in Yan'an.

Outside political and economic interest (both Chinese and foreign) in Guanzhong was minimal. After the breakdown of the early Republic various warlords occupied parts of Guanzhong at one time or another, of whom only Feng Yuxiang, the 'Christian general' played a national role. When Feng was appointed military governor of Shaanxi province in 1921, after his having defeated several local warlords, his authority did not extend over much more than the immediate vicinity of Xi'an and over the 180 km long Xi'an–Tongguan road built by his soldier-labourers. 'The two words seem incompatible in China' according to a contemporary traveller, but then Feng's army style was somewhat out of the ordinary.³ He left Guanzhong for the more promising province of Henan within a year, and went from there to Beijing. In the meantime, Guanzhong was left to his lieutenants, competing armies of small warlords, outside appointees such as Sun Yo of the third *Guominjun*, and fugitive armies from the neighbouring provinces of Henan, Gansu and Suiyuan – not to mention those bandit leaders whose forces were too small to secure the foothold of a district capital and thereby rise to a warlord status. Feng and his first *Guominjun* marched in from Suiyuan again to relieve a 8-month siege of Xi'an in 1926. This siege had been laid by a former governor of Shaanxi who had recruited an army in Henan, destroyed everything along his way to Xi'an, and then sat down to starve garrison and population within the city walls – deaths from starvation were reported to number 15,000 to 35,000.⁴

Feng sided with the victorious Guomindang and with his 200,000 man army left Guanzhong again in 1927. But when he opposed Chiang Kai Shek in 1930 he saw his army crushed completely, and disappeared for good from the national scene. Guomindang control penetrated Shaanxi province only in the early 1930s.⁵ So at the time of the drought Guanzhong was not integrated in a national political or military framework, but basically left on its own to cope with the disaster.

The severity of the 1928–1931 famine can be ascribed both to natural and to man-made causes. Except for a narrow stretch of land along the river banks of the Wei River, and a number of small patches of land between the foothills of the Qinling mountain range, agriculture in Guanzhong was entirely dependent on rainfall. The amount of precipitation averages some 500–600 mm in ordinary years; of this, 60 percent falls in July–September, often in the form of violent rain-storms. The growing season lasts from April to October. During spring and early summer temperatures are already quite high, and evapor-ation is considerably in excess of precipitation. So every spring, farmers wait anxiously for rain. Without rain, the winter wheat will wither and die, and sowing of spring wheat, millet or other grains is futile. If rain falls no earlier than June, a second crop may make up for the loss of the first one. But when the summer rains are violent, this second crop may be washed away together with the loose topsoil. If the summer rains are late, or if autumn is cold and dark, lacking sunshine, the autumn crop will have no occasion to ripen, and will be killed off by the late October frosts. The porous loess soil that covers Guanzhong is fertile enough, but is not capable of holding water for any length of time. Only in gulleys near rivers and on the Wei River flood plain is there underground water at depths reachable by traditional means; the rivers themselves are rain-fed and carry little water except during the summer flood season, when water is least needed.[6] Severe erosion and porosity of the soil, a heavy silt load of the rivers together with the total absence of rocks or stones as building materials made construction of reservoirs or ponds impossible. So for almost all of Guanzhong the situation was one of dry farming, in an area with marginal amounts of rainfall, on a soil which does not hold water very well. 'Ordinary' droughts of 2 to 2.5 months occur about once every 5 years in Guanzhong, serious droughts lasting most or all of one season occur about once every ten years, and severe drought disasters, it seems, once every thirty years.[7] Floods due to violent rainstorms usually bring damage on a more limited scale to crops planted in river gulleys or on hillslopes; the mountainous western parts of Guanzhong and the irrigated fields along the Wei River are most vulnerable, especially along its lower section. A contemporary newspaper gave the following survey of the immediate causes of the famine in Shaanxi:[8]

Year	Causes of famine, in order of importance
1928	drought, locusts, flood, pests, hail, soldiers, bandits
1929	drought, soldiers, bandits, hail, locusts, pests
1930	drought, flood, bandits, pests, locusts, rats, storm, hail
1931	drought, flood, hail, storm, frost, pests, rats

In all these years, drought was the major cause of famine. As the population moved closer to total starvation, economic support for regular soldiers or even bandits became exhausted. The 1927 autumn harvest was already considerably below normal, but in 1928, there was almost no harvest at all. Drought was not limited to Guanzhong; the whole middle and upper Yellow River basin was struck.[9] Soon, famine started getting serious. The China International Famine Relief Commission found in February 1929 that 80 percent of the population

had not tasted healthy food for 4 months, but were living on pigs' food – husks, straw, dried leaves, bark of trees, cotton seeds and thistles . . . 2 percent had already died of starvation . . . The year 1930 saw the zenith of the famine. Men rose each morning and cursed the sun as their greatest enemy. The earth was a brown hard baked crust. The heavens were like brass . . . One glorious day in August 1930, rain poured down and everyone danced for joy. The farmers said they could just manage an autumn crop, and sowed the precious seeds which they yearned to eat. But alas, two weeks before the harvest a cloud darkened the earth and descended on the waiting harvest. Before night fell locusts had devoured every bit of green leaf and yellow corn.[10]

C. FLIGHT AND DEATH

Few farmers had managed to save enough seed-grain for 1930. In an official report on the famine, it was estimated that by 1930 only one-fifth of the land of Guanzhong was planted, the rest lying fallow for the sole reason that the owners had died or fled or had had no means of planting; it was estimated that only one-half of the original 6 million people of the area were left. The winter of 1930 was extremely cold. 'Its agony can never be described. Along the roads a number of maimed cripples drag themselves, exhibiting stumps of limbs showing frostbite sores'.[11]

A more thorough investigation conducted in 1931 showed that an average of 70 percent of the cultivable area had been abandoned and left fallow. Even in the least seriously affected counties near the provincial capital, the cultivated area had been reduced by over one-third.[12] The least productive fields were abandoned first, and a considerable part of the well irrigated poppy fields and cotton fields were converted back into grain, but even so, there remained a severe shortage of foodgrain well into 1932, especially in the western parts of Guanzhong.[13]

There is no way of establishing the number of people in Guanzhong that died as a result of the 1928–31 famine, as population records both before and after are known to be incomplete. The population decrease was due to several causes:

a people who had left their village and not (yet) returned at the time of the new population count – usually their fate was unknown. Insofar as still alive and within Guanzhong they might show up in population totals elsewhere;

b people who had starved to death or died from famine-related causes (epidemic diseases arising from weakened resistance and concentration of refugees, attacks by wolves etc.);

c people who had been sold, i.e. women sold as servants or in marriage and children sold in adoption;

d a decline in the number of births.

Population figures supplied by all but a few county authorities in 1930 show a mid-time decrease of 700,000 people, or 14.2 percent of their total population. The western counties were most severely stricken; population of the 7 counties west of Xi'an on the Wei River left bank had been reduced by over 30 percent by then, in two of these by over one-half.[14] After another year of drought disaster, the Provincial Relief Society estimated that 900,000 people had died *in situ*, 1,900,000 had left their villages with fate unknown, and over 300,000 women and children had been sold.[15] Subsequent estimates put the total number of victims at 3 million or more.[16] Because official population registration both before and after the disaster suffered from undercounting to varying degrees (but probably to as much as 15–20 percent), these figures did not give a complete picture. Village investigations conducted by several researchers during the 1930s provided more detail on demographic consequences of the 1928–31 famine.

A contemporary demographer, after having conducted an investigation of 219 villages in four representative districts in different parts of Guanzhong in 1936, gave several explanations for the great losses in population:

—outright starvation had killed 13% of the villagers during the famine.

—one-third of the villagers had become refugees, but most returned eventually.

—household size decreased from 6.5 persons in 1927 to 6.1 persons in 1936.

—the male-female sex ratio of 118.5 reflected a discriminative neglect and sales of females during the famine.[17]

Similar conclusions can be drawn from a 1936 survey of some 1300 households in 6 districts:[18]

—between 1928 and 1930, population was reduced by an average of 26 percent; by 1936 population numbers were restored to 86 percent of the pre-famine level, partly by high birth rates (32–48 o/oo) and comparatively low death rates (15–30 o/oo), partly by a return of refugees.

—household size decreased from an average of 5.7 in 1928 to 5.1 in 1930.

—the male-female ratio was 114 for the whole population in 1936, but as high as 1.29 and 1.40 in the age groups 5–9 and 35–39, which were born during the 1928–1930 and the 1898–1901 disasters.

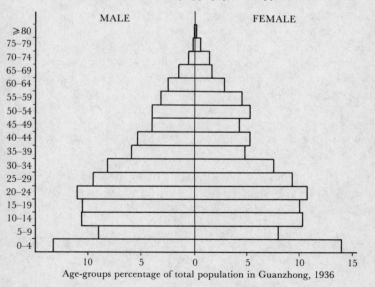

Graph A Guanzhong 1936 population pyramid

Age-groups percentage of total population in Guanzhong, 1936

The population pyramid constructed on the basis of this survey for 5-year age groups in Guanzhong in 1936 shows clearly the effects of these calamities.

From these and other village surveys,[19] too, the western districts of Guanzhong appear to have been hit the worst. Contemporary travellers gave a most appalling picture of life in towns and villages:

According to the prefect of Qishan 72,500 people had died from famine, 30,860 people had fled, so that of the original population, only 20 to 30 percent was left . . . People were not buried anymore. Passers-by stared at the corpses lying along the road, but with eyes that did not seem to see anything.[20]

Only some 500 households still live within the 8 *li* (3 miles) of city walls of Baoji. Trade is gone, people are in a very sad condition. There has not been a harvest for several years, yet taxes are heavy. Many people died or fled. The county population has declined from over 200,000 to 140,000 . . . The city of Fengxiang has almost lost its entire population . . . In the countryside, fields lie fallow, houses are few and mostly in ruins. Beggars along the roads have no clothes or food. There aren't any draft animals left.[21]

Of the calamity-stricken people, those who could be sold, were sold; those who could flee, fled. But the old women that could not be sold, and the old men that could not move, and the too young children, what should they do? Man has a social nature. A village chief in Wugong has ordered that the left-over old people and children were collected to live together, saying 'Otherwise it is too lonely!' . . . Inevitably there was cannibalism.[22]

Peasants from the region west of Xi'an came to the capital to sell their most precious possessions and their very means of survival: doors, beams, millstones, draught cattle, hoes, plows, harrows and other agricultural implements. Of course prices fetched were extremely low. Plow and cordage for mules, hoes and blades sold at some ten percent of their original value.

Villages are mostly denuded, not only of trees but also of everything else that was saleable. All the woodwork is gone – doors, windows and roof timbers having been sold for food.[23]

The slaughter of draught cattle (mainly oxen; horses and mules had been requisitioned by the armies to the extent that few were left) meant a serious setback in cultivation methods, from which it would take many years to recover.[24]

The rural population did not flee to the towns; on the contrary, people left town in search for food. Registered population of the capital of Xi'an increased between 1928 and 1930, but then went down in 1931, and picked up again in 1932–4.[25] Countryside and county cities were described by foreign government advisers in 1934:

> not only the countryside but even 95 percent of the cities we visited are like ruins. Very many of the magistrate's offices look more like deserted temples rather than governmental buildings.[26]

Even before the famine, however, the same description had been valid: the urbanization rate of most districts was only 5 to 10 percent, and repressive government had kept economic development and population numbers down. City walls offered protection against bandits outside, but not against harsh government inside, and shopkeepers often had preferred the former.[27] The fact that refugees did not flee towards the cities of Guanzhong during the famine years serves to show the very limited extent of relief grain distribution by governmental authorities and relief organizations. For most peasants, undertaking the trip to the city was a gamble – so many calories spent on the journey, so little hope of receiving some food in return.

D. RELIEF MEASURES

Relief from the provincial or local governments could not but be insignificant. In 1930, the provincial warlord Feng Yuxiang was definitely beaten, and provincial financial reserves had been exhausted completely. Of the provincial budgetary expenditure in 1931, one-half went to provincial defense, 30 percent to administration, and 10 percent to construction – nothing to outright relief. Even of this meagre provincial budget of 20 million dollars, only one-quarter was sustained by tax receipts, 40 percent by loans from the central government, the remaining one-third was a deficit. Surtaxes of the county governments yielded two or three million dollars, most of which were used in paying police forces.[28] Thus, official tax receipts of the civilian government could hardly contribute to relief – and unofficial taxes collected by non-registered runners and military government taxes only increased the people's burden.

Grain reserves which used to be stored in government warehouses had been emptied during the 1920s, and had not been restocked. 'The armies under general Feng have swept the province bare of grain . . . It is reckoned that 70 million bushels of grain were either eaten or carried away by these military marauders.'[29]

In some county cities in 1929, both government and merchants organized free distribution of food grain, but on a very limited scale. Relief grain became exhausted within months. Many of the soup-kitchens were not managed well, relief funds were squandered, and did not last very long. 'All the famine relief efforts only touch the margin . . . There is grain outside but the difficulty is to get it up. Hundreds of refugees are being fed, but for the great mass nothing can be done. Meanwhile soldiers are going east, commandeering the few remaining carts and animals.'[30] A missionary noted:

Such was the reputation of Shaanxi province for both typhus and banditry that a scouring of both Tianjin and Shanghai for months found no adventurers willing to undertake the field work of supervision (of famine work) usually performed by local missionaries.

Five hundred tons of green beans were imported in 1930. They were the first food supply to reach Shaanxi from the outside.[31] Only from 1931 onwards was more grain brought in from outside the province. Relief efforts of the China International Famine Relief Commission, such as the operation of refuges for children, soup kitchens, and relief-through-labour programs were mainly effective in *redistributing* food to the nearest and poorest people, as most of their relief aid consisted of money which was spent in buying from local grain stocks, and not of net grain imports. The same applies to relief efforts by the foreign missionary establishments in Guanzhong, the Roman Catholics, the British Baptist Society and the Scandinavian Alliance Mission. By May 1929, the Baptist Mission fed 1,400 people daily in Sanyuan, and subsequently opened nine more soup-kitchens in neighboring counties north of Xi'an. The operating funds came from Europe and from the China International Famine Relief Commission. According to their own estimate, these Baptist food-kitchens saved 20,000 people from starvation. But at least partly, one should add, at the expense of the non-Christian poor.

In 1930, other forms of relief were rendered impossible by bandits, four more distributions were made of $10,000 throughout the same 150 square mile area . . . This accounts for the comparatively small death rate in Christian villages . . . At Easter of this year our Chinese leaders suggested themselves that one-third of the money go to the relief of non-Christian neighbours whose condition was desperate.[32]

As the foreign missionaries had pointed out to the Chinese before, in a situation of severe shortage, concentration of relief aid on a selected group of survivors-to-be is the only sensible thing to do. If spread too thinly, relief aid would only postpone starvation for some time, and then be buried along with the victims.[33]

Relief-through-labour projects created better conditions for the future. The Provincial Famine Relief Commission had a dirt road built from Xi'an to the railroad terminal of Tongguan at the Henan border. At first this road mainly served General Feng's military purposes – his Henan campaign and his army provisions, which by 1930 were almost completely obtained from outside the province.[34] But after his defeat at the end of 1930 the road became more widely used for civilian grain transport. The shortage of carts and draught animals, which had been requisitioned by soldiers or eaten, limited transportation capacity severely. Some other roads built by Feng to the north and west of Xi'an were often unsafe because of bandit attacks on grain convoys, and therefore little used. During 1931, five more roads were opened, with a total length of 400 miles.[35] An irrigation scheme, the Jinghui Ditch, was undertaken from November 1930 to June 1932, funded by the CIFRC and the Provincial Government for 400,000 *yuan* each. This scheme was very successful, and irrigated over 5,000 ha of wheat in 1932 and 27,000 ha in 1933. 6,000 wells were dug in 1930, with the subsidies from relief committees, in the areas along the Wei River in Changan, Xingping, Huaxian and Dali.[36] Seed grains were imported, too. One might say that these belated relief efforts did not help the population to survive, but helped the survivors in some areas to regain economic strength.

E. FAMINE AND A DEFECTIVE POLITICAL AND ECONOMIC STRUCTURE

The drought and its terrible consequences revealed many defects of the existing political and economic structures in Guanzhong.

Grain surpluses and trade. Grain output in Guanzhong was subject to strong fluctuations. A normal or good harvest would yield sufficient foodgrain for one-and-a-half or two years – a margin needed to cope with years of harvest failure. Taking grain surpluses away from the peasantry (by taxation, confiscation, robbery or otherwise) is a deadly threat in a semi-arid region where consecutive years of drought may occur. Not so, of course, if the government is able and willing to provide relief grain and seeds in such a situation. And if the population has sufficient savings and income from other economic activities foodgrain might be purchased from elsewhere, inso far as communications are good enough not to make transport costs prohibitive. None of these conditions existed in Guanzhong during the 1920s. Warlord Feng Yuxiang 'happened' to be in Guanzhong during 1928–30 and felt his prime responsibility to his army, not to the civilian population. The civilian government was weak and corrupt. County magistrates showed little concern for anything but collecting a maximum of taxes, legal or illegal, in a minimum of time. Outside the immediate vicinity of Xi'an there was no local administrative network of any sort.[37] Local merchant groups had suffered from Feng's forced sales of military bonds (with a nominal value of 7 million yuan, which became worthless after Feng's defeat), military exactions, government taxes and bandits. Communications with other provinces were blockaded by military strife, and within Guanzhong both road and river transport was poorly developed, especially so in the mountainous western parts.[38]

Thus, the removal of family and village grain stocks by taxation or otherwise, meant courting disaster, because the authorities were in no position to return in bad times what was taken in ordinary harvest years.

I asked both peasants and local officials for a solution of the famine problem. Why didn't they think of a way of relief? Their answers were not the same. Officials would answer: 'communications are bad, one cannot send relief grain to faraway places'. Peasants would answer: 'we had no money, we couldn't buy grain'. . . . Old peasants said: 'formerly, in case of a disaster year each family would have some savings to buy grain with, or it would sell a sheep or an ox, so that it could tide over the disaster year. But nowadays, it is different. Which family still has savings of grain and cash?[39]

Specialization in commercial crops: poppy. During the 1920s irrigated fields in Guanzhong were increasingly devoted to poppy. This crop fetched a very high price, and local warlords stimulated production of it by heavy taxation. On irrigated fields where no poppy was planted a so-called 'laziness tax' was imposed of 80 to 160 *yuan* per ha, or about 100 times as much as on dry land. For poppy fields opium tax had been put at 240 *yuan* per ha per year from 1921 till 1927, and at 160 *yuan* per ha during 1928–32, but actual levies greatly exceeded this amount.[40] These irrigated areas, most of which lay between the Wei River and the Qinling foothills, were densely populated and relied on the northern districts for their foodgrain.[41] After the drought had struck

and grain supply was interrupted, poppy cultivation declined considerably between 1930 and 1933.[42] Judging from tax returns, several
tens of thousands of hectares still were devoted to poppy by then, but
there are no official sown area statistics, as the crop was 'officially
illegal'. Military government had become increasingly dependent on
tax income, or direct income, from poppy cultivation. Apart from the
(unknown) amount of poppy sold to outside Guanzhong, poppy made
a double negative contribution to local economic development: it
occupied irrigated land which was able to produce crops with a much
higher utility to the local population during disaster years, and it
sapped the strength of the labour force.

In a country where about one-fifth of the population are parasites, such as we
find the percentage of opium addicts in Shaanxi, how can we expect it to be
prosperous? We were happy to notice that mostly only the lower class of
labourers for instance the rickshaw-coolie, and the upper-class gentry are
opium addicts, and that the real farmers are very seldom addicts.[43]

The number of opium addicts greatly varied between districts, but also
according to different authors. Official registration numbers, such as
2,000 addicts in Dali county in 1931 or 7,600 addicts in Wugong
county some years later, certainly show only a small part of the
number of users, but the inn-keeper in Wugong who thought their
number to be 'nine out of ten' must have based his estimate on a non-
representative sample of his guests.[44] At the time, the image of the
Shaanxi peasant was one of bad health and laziness owing to the use of
opium.

The peasants of Shaanxi have a low work efficiency and are lazy. This is, no
doubt, the result of past cultivation of poppy which gave high income for little
labour, and a dull mind to peasants who used it. They would not care any
more for agriculture or sideline activities.[45]

Unless the character of the native Shaanxi people changes, they are doomed to
extinction. They are improvident, fond of good feeding when harvests allow it,
and worst of all they are handicapped by opium . . . Opium smokers cannot
eat the coarsest food.[46]

These harsh words of a visiting Reverend in 1931 described a
situation which was to continue until the mid 1930s. A missionary
noted in 1935 that about half of the people who applied for church
membership were addicts.[47] Opium has been described both by
contemporary and by later authors as one of the major evils of warlord
China during the 1920s and 1930s, and rightly so.

Industries. In most areas there were few economic activities outside agriculture. Wheat, the dominant crop, was sown in September–October and harvested in June. Of the autumn grains, millet, maize and sorghum were most popular. Cotton, poppy, hemp, soy-beans, rape and other industrial crops were partly sold, partly processed and used by the villagers for their own needs. The mountainous areas north and south of the Wei River valley produced local specialities widely sold in the region: tobacco, medicinal herbs, wool, fruits, bamboo, almost every district was known for one specialty or another. Coal, sulphur and cement came from the northernmost districts, timber, wood and charcoal from the Qinling mountains. Likewise, traditionally there were local industries producing for larger areas: grain destilleries in Fengxiang, paper-making factories in Pucheng, potteries in Tongguan, linen in Longxian, leather-making in Dali. Generally speaking these industries had declined during the 1920s, not because of competition but because of the general insecurity of the period, and during the famine years they came to a virtual standstill.[48] Cottage textile industry was common in all cotton growing areas, but some centres such as Xingping county had a tradition of manufacturing high-quality goods for wider sales. The same goes for oil-pressing, although its higher capital requirements made it an industry undertaken by rich peasants only. Most industries were seasonal in character, small-scale affairs with a primitive technology, and closely linked with agriculture. Rising and falling with agricultural output and local demand, they offered no economic security when the drought came.

F. THE FABRIC OF THE VILLAGE

Guanzhong villages were small, closely knit and largely self-supporting. Their usual size was 200 to 400 people, somewhat larger in the floodplain and smaller in the loess hills. Villages were mostly well in sight of each other, being so close and in a landscape almost without trees. Peasants worked close to home: the distance to their most outlying plot averaged no more than 1 kilometer. Fragmentation of landholdings due to the inheritance system had resulted in tiny and scattered plots, sometimes less than one-tenth of a hectare and seldom larger than one-half of a hectare.[49]

The sunbaked wall surrounding each village indicated the dangers of rural life. Tucked within, the walled courtyards of each dwelling symbolized the basic cells of society: the households. In the loess hills villages often consisted of tiny groupings of cave homes, dug into the side of a cliff or a cut-in road.

Because most women (especially in the more backward western parts) still had bound feet, very few went to work with the men in the fields. Apart from managing the daily household affairs, women engaged in spinning and weaving, making straw hats, clothes, bamboo baskets, utensils etc. Reflecting the low level of development, there were few commercial and social activities in or outside the village.[50] Clothing and food were extremely poor. According to a 1936 survey

Culture in the Guanzhong villages has stopped at the 18th–19th century . . . A comparison with eastern provinces shows that Guanzhong has very few commercial people, 0.5 as against 2 to 7 percent . . . Education is very backward; during the famine it came to a virtual standstill . . . Hygienic knowledge is conspicuously deficient, sometimes one does not wash for a whole year. Infant death is beyond counting . . .[51]

Less accustomed to stark poverty, Western observers would draw a darker picture of the quality of life, both before and after the famine:

Within the walled cities of Shaanxi . . . black swine were wandering at will, pariah dogs covered with great open sores, human beings in little better condition . . . Smaller towns and hamlets were always filthy and miserable, a few women on crippled feet hobbling about the doors of their caves or mud huts . . . In the depth of winter, both boys and girls between 5 and 10 wear nothing but a ragged jacket of quilted cotton reaching barely to the waist, and wander disconsolately about with the lower half of the body naked, chapped and begrimed . . . Undoubtedly this Spartan treatment makes those who survive less susceptible to cold![52]

There was no order, no security for life, for property, for freedom, for anything. An armed man could do whatever he liked with the poor people . . . The social order is entirely destroyed. Many diseased and suffering persons lying in the public place are passed without notice.[53]

Most parts of Guanzhong were too little developed, too poor and too insecure to allow for the accumulation of wealth. Moreover, the few wealthy landowners and merchants there were would be subjected to heavy exactions by various military units and government officials. As an early visitor to Guanzhong noted 'it is hardly possible for any man to be much richer than his fellows'.[54] Yet both at the top and at the bottom of village society there were groups with a distinctly different economic position. The few richest families usually dominated political, military and commercial contacts with the outside world, these three functions being intertwined and mutually dependent. The village chief, a rotating office, was held responsible for grain tax payments; the village militia chief for public safety, protection of officials and safe transport routes. From the hamlet up there was a hierarchy of village, community (*xiang* or *li*), subdistrict (*ju*), before arriving at the lowest official level of government, that of the county (*xian*). Bearing responsibility for tax collection could be profitable but dangerous. It required harsh treatment of the common peasant but great dexterity in handling those higher up in the hierarchy, the military and officials. These intermediary positions were held mainly by people of merchant origin, in the absence of a class of landed gentry.[55] At the bottom of society there was a perpetual drop-out of the poorest and weakest males. Many poor youngsters could not afford the price of a bride, and would have no land for cultivation anyway.[56] They either stayed with better-off relatives who were willing to put up with them, or left the village to become peddlars, hired labourers, coolies, miners, or worse, soldiers or bandits (the order here is that of social standing). Superfluous girls would be sold off as slaves in rich households or as prostitutes. In a society hovering around the subsistence margin such as Guanzhong was, differences in living standard which seemed small to outside observers were keenly felt and might mean life or death, especially so in years of disaster. Poor households used to borrow grain, in spring, from rich families, to be repaid after the summer harvest with 20 to 30 percent interest. Land was given as collateral, and might have to be handed over in case of default – the start of a downward spiral which could not easily be stopped. During the famine, credit became very tight, and interest rates went as high as 60 percent per mensem.[57] To a large extent the economic position of individual peasant households was determined by the labourer: dependent ratio, which changed according to the life cycle. The famine, by killing off first the eldest, youngest, weakest and poorest, reduced the average household size and improved the labourer:dependent ratio considerably. In a similar way, it brought the population:land ratio down.

G. FAMINE AS A LEVELLER, OR AN AGENT OF NEW ECONOMIC INEQUALITIES?

At first, the famine caused a considerable decline of all economic activities, agriculture, industry and commerce, especially so in the most seriously stricken western districts.[58] Land prices went down until 1934, labour was in short supply and wages consequently went up.[59]

Because prices of land were low, people could easily buy land, and there are not many tenant farmers . . . Land rents are extremely light . . . In the mountains, landlords do not demand rent in case of harvest failure, so there are very few disputes.[60]

Statistics show a slight concentration of landholdings in some areas, and an impoverishment of the richest families in other areas. In 4 villages in Weinan county, where 3 out of 217 households were classified as 'landlords' by the surveyor, their landholding went down from an average of 5 ha in 1928 to 3 ha in 1933. The percentage of outside investment in landholding remained negligible.[61] According to one source, small peasants in the central parts of Guanzhong had sold some 20 percent of their farmland during the famine, which was bought up by the richer peasants who had remained in the village, while all landlords and merchants had fled. Probably referring to irrigated areas in the vicinity of Xi'an, the same source adds that most of the land that was sold during the famine went to military officers, who became opium traders and merchants; many of the old landlords went under.[62] In 1936 only some 5 percent of Guanzhong's peasants were tenant-farmers, 30 percent were partly-tenant, partly owner, and almost two-thirds of the peasants owned the land they farmed.[63] The picture drawn by communist sources and echoed by Mark Selden of a sharp rise in tenancy and of class differentials because of the famine in north Shaanxi does not appear to be valid for Guanzhong.[64]

Yet, after the famine, land sales to new owners and repossession of land by the original owners often introduced more impersonal relationships between landowners and tenants. In the plain areas, contracts increasingly were put into writing, and fixed rents (in money or in kind) gained on sharecropping and other types of rent.[65]

Repossession itself became a public topic in the Xi'an newspapers in 1931. A county prefect had proposed that peasants, who had had to sell their land during the famine, would be allowed to buy their land back with an interest-carrying loan before 1933, on the basis of the price they originally sold it for. Many people wrote to the newspapers in support of this proposal.[66] But it did not result in any official action. Conflicts about repossession were particularly sharp if the landlord had been away for a long time, or the quality and value of the land had increased in the meantime.

Land prices in Moziqiao were 8–10 *yuan* per ha in 1928–9, but in 1932 after completion of the Jinghui Ditch 80–100 *yuan*, and in the past two years they went up to about 650 *yuan*. In the richest stretch of land, of 200 ha, a landlord called Li had fled elsewhere because of the army grain tax levied by Feng Yuxiang. So the tenants had paid instead. Subsequently, after completion of the Ditch, the landlord returned and asked rent, but all tenant families resisted, because the sum of substitute tax payments paid by them by far exceeded the land value at that time. But in 1934 owing to somebody's mediation, Mr Li started granting freedom of rent, and paid water fees on behalf of the tenant families, and then received all his land back. The present agricultural experimental station of the Qinling University is on this land of Mr Li.[67]

In the loess hills of north Guanzhong, there may have been a larger percentage of pedlars and hired agricultural labourers, 20 to 30 percent of the agricultural households.[68]

In this case, as in some others, it seems that large landlords managed to get their landholdings back only because of government support – for which a price had to be paid in the form of a piece of land donated to military officials or a government institution.

In the newly developed Jinghui irrigation district north of Xi'an there was a definite increase of tenancy, and also of short-term labourers.[69] In a few areas large landholdings were created and exploited by merchants, military officers or government institutions.[70] With the building of some large irrigation districts in the 1930s new forms of supra-village organisation were created, new improved varieties of cotton were introduced, and new breeds of domestic animals. The improved population:land ratio gave a breathing space, but did not lead to a significant change in agricultural technology and methods. Lack of draught cattle and manure after the famine, and a weakened labour force, were the main causes for the reduction of land taken into cultivation and for low yields during the early 1930s, apart from the fall of demand for foodgrain. Although more of the sown area was devoted to industrial crops, subsistence farming remained dominant.

Government measures and a new infrastructure changed the face of Guanzhong after 1934. Rural safety, education, credit coops and banks were promoted with more or less success. A railroad was built, which finally linked Xi'an with 'modern' China. Industry and commercial crops were greatly stimulated by the improvement of the road network. Poppy was banned in 1935, and replaced by high-quality cotton. The provincial government doubled its budgetary income and expenditure between 1932 and 1937. The southern and western parts of Guanzhong were increasingly drawn into the modern sector created under Guomindang rule. Regional differences increased as a consequence. In how far were these developments still related to the previous famine of 1928–31? The famine shook the foundations of the local social and political structure. Feng Yuxiang lost his economic support, and the rural elite saw a temporary breakdown of the socio-economic framework and of its position therein. After the famine, Guanzhong was prostrate, exhausted and bare, open to receive outside efforts at building new political and economic structures.

Conclusion. The famine of 1928–31, like its predecessors of 1876–9 and 1899–1901 killed, or at least reduced the Guanzhong population by, two or three million people. A more exact number cannot be established, because of the traditional underregistration of population and the uncertain fate of refugees and people sold or adopted. At that time, Guanzhong was not integrated in a national political framework, but basically left on its own to cope with the disaster. Feng Yuxiang felt that his prime responsibility was to his army, not to the civilian population of Gansu, Shaanxi, Henan or any other province he happened to be passing through. The severity of the famine was due to several causes. The drought lasted for three to four years. Government, armies and bandits had taken away most of the farmers' grain reserves and also the mules and horses needed for transport. Thus, the local population had no means of obtaining foodgrain from elsewhere. Lack of modern communications (the railroad ended at Tongguan – it is no coincidence that the least accessible areas in west Guanzhong suffered much more than east Guanzhong) – would have prevented effective outside help on a large scale in any case. Banditry also hampered transport, or at least raised its costs, but was a consequence of, rather than a contributing factor to famine. Poppy, as a high-value crop, did contribute to the income of the region, but its rewards went mainly to high army officers, and it brought little benefit to the civilian population. Industries and trade were weakly developed, and almost totally dependent on agricultural surpluses. Thus, the region had little or non compensatory sources of income.

Relief measures had only marginal effects, mainly in redistributing foodgrain to the Christians, poor people and the lucky ones. Eventually, however, relief-through-labour schemes of irrigation and road construction helped the survivors survive. As with any famine, the oldest, youngest, poorest and weakest had died, so that far fewer dependents had to be supported by the adult labour force. Yet, owing to a severe shortage of seeds, draught animals, pig manure, carts and other means of production, it took several years before output could regain former levels. Many of the poorest and the few rich households in the villages were swept away by the famine; it seems that 'middle peasants' enlarged their share of land holdings. Thus, the famine did result in a decrease of rural differentials in most areas, rather than in an increase as communist sources would have it for north Shaanxi. By 1936, only 5 percent of Guanzhong's peasants were tenant-farmers. In some areas a new economic elite (military and government officials, and some merchants) had started to acquire highly productive irrigated farmland, often under poppy. The poppy-eradication campaign, therefore, met with considerable resistance.

A major political effect of the famine was that it swept away local power-holders and Feng Yuxiang, the warlord. The region was laid open to outside efforts at national integration and for political and economic change. In the 1930s, the Guomindang military and civilian apparatus moved in, but also some other semi-independent armies and the communists. Possibly most important of all, the railroad, which reached Xi'an in 1934 and Baoji in 1938, drew Guanzhong into modern China.

2

COMMUNICATIONS AND TRANSPORT

A. TRADITIONAL AND MODERN TRANSPORT BEFORE AND DURING THE WAR AGAINST JAPAN

The development of transportation has played an integral role in the economic growth of Guanzhong since the early 1930s until today. Building of roads and railroads received a great deal of attention both by the Guomindang and by the communist central governments and by provincial authorities. Albert Feuerwerker has warned against overestimating the economic effect of modernization measures undertaken during the first half of this century, and rightly so.[1] However, during this period railroads and highways were built for other reasons than economic ones alone. In 1926–8 the warlord Feng Yuxiang wished to be able to move his troops rapidly from the Northwest to the North China Plain. Also, in this way he provided them with meaningful work as soldier-labourers.[2] The China International Famine Relief Commission wanted to combine labour with relief for the victims of the famine of 1928–31. Its road-building and irrigation projects were meant to prevent such drought and large-scale starvation from every happening again. The Nationalist government strove after national integration and economic development of Guanzhong as a stepping-stone to China's Northwest. Also, it wished to encircle the Red bases in north Shaanxi. During the war against Japan, road building was to serve the military buildup in Free China. To that end, connections with Hanzhong and Sichuan were improved. The transportation network had to be expanded in order to accommodate coal, raw materials and finished products of the factories which had been transferred from east China, away from the Japanese invaders. The new Communist government stressed the same goal of integration of the Northwest within the whole of China, but much more forcefully so. Guanzhong and its capital of Xi'an were to profit from their intermediate geographical position between the North China Plain

47

and the northwestern provinces of Gansu, Ningxia and Xinjiang, as in the past. Its main and only artery since the Han dynasty, the Silk Road, was outdone by the new railroad connection Xi'an–Lanzhou–Urumqi.

Modern transportation came to Guanzhong only very slowly, and mainly by outside agencies. In 1921 the first dirt highway was built from Tongguan at the Henan border to Xi'an beside the old haphazard route, with international relief funds. There was a daily bus-service, but its main users were soldiers.[3] In 1927–8, the road to Lanzhou was improved, but in mountainous sections such as Yongshou and Binxian cars still had to be pulled by mules. Until 1931, Guanzhong had no other improved routes besides this 380 km-long section of the old Silk Road. The American engineer O. J. Todd, who worked in China for two decades, described the situation he found in the 1920s as follows:

The sunken roads (in the loess area) have been cut by narrow-tired carts and worn by wind and water. In the rainy season they often become mud-holes. In winter they are blown full of snow. The raised road has a distinct advantage . . . The worst enemy of the dirt road is the narrow-tired two-wheeled freight cart. Road upkeep is not generally organized in China except where motor bus companies hold franchises . . . The majority of peasants think that roads take their land that would normally raise food and leave it idle for the use of merchants, officials and others whose duties are other than tilling the soil. Local officials are frequently of the opinion that they are entitled to profits from all new utilities.[4]

The dirt roads required constant maintenance, as they still do today. Loess itself is an excellent material for road building. The narrow wheels of the traditional carts make deep cuts into the roadbed, and the tracks erode easily. In the dry period, the fine loess is blown away. In the rainy season it is carried away as silt. In the 1930s, the provincial government had ordered that carts should be fitted with rubber tyres to prevent damage to the roads. When wet, however, the dirt roads get slippery and virtually impassable for rubber-tyred carts or motorcars. Transport problems were greatest in the hills of north and west Guanzhong, where roads had very steep sections, in canyons and in places where the road moved from one terrace level to another. Because of erosion, roads sank deeper and deeper, aggravating thereby the difficulties of all transport vehicles. Finally, they had to be abandoned for a new route (sometimes already partly formed) on the side. In the words of Harry Franck:

The narrow canyons were often so congested with beast-drawn traffic that the hundreds of wheelbarrows had to join the pole-shouldering coolies and other pedestrians on the paths along the cliffs high above.[5]

The first wave of road construction came in 1930, with a relief-through-labour program sponsored and directed by the China International Famine Relief Commission. The severity of the famine of 1929–31 had been due to a great extent to the lack of modern transportation facilities to and within Guanzhong, and to its secluded position, which hampered economic and political integration. As for railroads – which had made all the difference between the Great Drought in the North China Plain in 1920–1 and the previous one of 1876–9[6] – Guanzhong still had none. Waterway transport was hardly possible; only small rafts could get up the Wei River to Wugong and up the Yellow River to Hancheng. The road system of 1931, all dirt, consisted of the improved Tongguan–Xi'an–Lanzhou motor road, two narrow motor roads from Xianyang to Fengxiang and to Sanyuan, and a 20-mile web around Xi'an. Also, a 15-feet wide improved cart road led to Pucheng, where it split north to Yan'an and east to Dali and back to Tongguan. The total of motor roads came to 465 miles. Another 432 miles of cart roads could occasionally be used by cars[7] (see Map 2).

Of these connections, the 120-mile Xi'an–Fengxiang road and the Xianyang–Sanyuan road had been graded and widened for car use in 1930–1, as a famine-relief project. In subsequent years, roads were built to connect Xi'an with the irrigation works of the Jinghui project, with the Luohui irrigation project in Dali and with the Weihui irrigation project near Wugong. All these projects were financed with international relief funds. As a famine-relief measure the road building program proved to be very practical. Almost all funds could be spent directly on wages, almost all the necessary materials and labour were locally available, and land was very cheap at that time. 2,500 men could be employed per mile efficiently, which meant one day's work for a road 20 feet wide.[8] Local labourers were organized in labour gangs of 20 to 30 men, which were recruited and led by a foreman as was common practice elsewhere in China. The surveying work, guidance and coordination were done by foreign engineers appointed by the relief organization (such as Todd and Eliassen), but also by local foreigners with an interest in furthering these programs, such as the Swedish missionary Gustav Tornvall who was killed by bandits in 1932.

The most important road built under the relief programs was the highway from Xi'an to Lanzhou in Gansu. The U.S.A. donated $350,000 to rebuild this road in 1931. This used to be a cart journey of 18 days over a road 480 miles long. In the Shaanxi section, major obstacles were the hills at Yongshou, Binzhou and Dingzhou, the crossing of the Dingzhou creek in Changwu, and the crossing of the Wei River at Xianyang. The hill sections had grades of 25–33 percent where loaded cars and carts had to be hauled up by teams of cattle and mules. From 1931 until 1934, the road was reconstructed to become a 24 to 30 feet wide dirt road, with a maximum grade of 7 percent. The National Economic Council took over the project after the Nationalist government had granted another $200,000 for the completion of the road. As a result, the Xi'an–Lanzhou trip could be done in three days by car, except in the rainy season. During rainfall, the clayey stretches in the hills still remained practically impassable; Todd's recommendations to the government to macadamize these sections were not followed. Nevertheless, he could proudly write in 1934:

Should drought again produce famine in this region the Government will be able to move staff and food to the affected areas much more rapidly than in the past. Order can be maintained and bandits will not find it so easy to prey on the travelling public. It has been a source of pride to all donors . . . that it now stands as a monument to constructive altruism. It is lasting and benefits every class of the communities that it serves.[9]

The pace of roadbuilding quickened after 1934. Post-famine recovery, the successful development of irrigation schemes and of cotton production, and expecially the new railroad from Henan which reached Xi'an in 1934 and Baoji in 1938 were great stimuli to local economic development. Roads were built by the national, provincial and county governments mainly in *Weibei*, the plain area north of the Wei River in the eastern half of Guanzhong. Also, connections with south Shaanxi crossing the Qinling mountain range via Fengxian in the west and Lantian in the east were built in 1936. From there Sichuan and Hubei could be reached. The year before, a second link with Gansu starting from Fengxiang to Tianshui or Pingliang had been established.

The war which broke out in 1937 gave extra priority to the building of roads and railroads. Movement of troops and of the many refugees to Free China put a terrible burden on the existing road system and on the scarce means of transportation. Now the main throughfares from

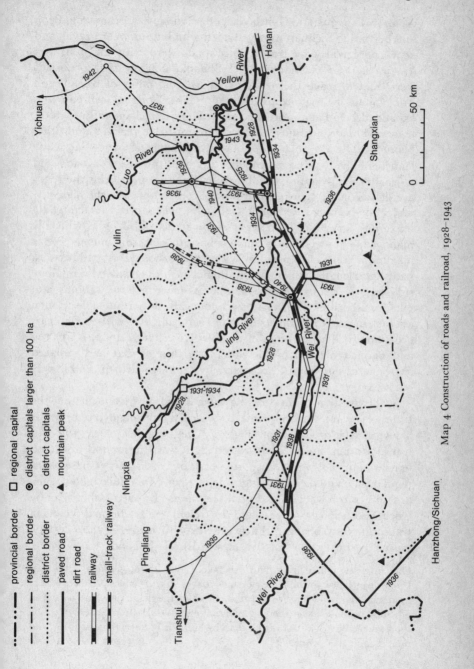

Map 4 Construction of roads and railroad, 1928–1943

Xi'an to Tongguan, to Gansu via Yongshou, and to Fengxiang, Baoji and beyond to Sichuan were provided with macadam or gravel, and kept up regularly by troops. Dirt roads were built to Yulin (via Yan'an) and to Yichuan in north Shaanxi. Narrow gauge railroads were built to reach the newly expanded coal mines of Baishui and Tongchuan in 1937 resp. in 1942.[10] The Longhai railroad was expanded from Baoji westward. Lack of funds, steel and railway stock, however, made it impossible for Tianshui to be reached and other planned railways such as Tongguan–Hancheng, and Sanyuan–Hancheng had to be postponed till after the war.[11] Roads and railroads built by national and provincial authorities during the 1930s are shown on map 4 with their date of completion. For the highways under the National Economic Council, a width of 7.5 meters and a maximum grade of 8 percent were standard. The provincially managed highways had a standard width of 5 to 6 meters and a maximum grade of 10 percent. Within Guanzhong, this road network had a total length of about 2,200 kilometers in 1942. In addition, there still were the old cart roads, maintained more or less by county and village authorities. The best and economically important of these, such as the Liquan–Wugong–Zhouzhi road, might be used by cars occasionally. The crossings of the Wei River, at Weinan, Xianyang and Baoji, remained problematic. The bridges that had replaced ferries here were bombed regularly by Japanese aircraft, and mostly out of order.[12]

Modernization of the road network by no means meant that the transport sector was modernized as well. For civilian use, only the Tongguan–Xi'an–Lanzhou highway had regular truck and bus transportation. From Xi'an, cotton cloth was transported west, and leather and wool were transported east; 65 trucks and 35 buses went regularly up and down this highway in 1936. More bulky goods, such as flour, cotton wool or coal would be carried by carts rather than by trucks. Both for passengers and for freight the traditional means of transport were cheaper.[13] Fuels were expensive, and in short supply, especially during the war. In the words of J. J. Todd:

One rickshaw pulled by a man can take a load of 700 pounds of flour or kerosene or baled cotton. The rickshaw makes 20 to 25 miles per day. Where human labour is low in price and gasoline is high the rickshaw seems to have an advantage. This is true where speed is not essential. Even in passenger traffic thousands go by rickshaw rather than by autobus because the cost is less and more baggage is permitted.[14]

The rickshaws and wheelbarrows had replaced much of the animal-drawn means of transportation during the 1930s. In Guanzhong, oxen were generally used for ploughing, and horses and mules for transportation. The Mongolian horse (and to a lesser extent also the Gansu horse) was 'very small, violent, lazy and difficult to teach' and therefore not well suited for pulling a cart. So the peasants used mules (from crosses with the large Guanzhong donkey) for pulling in the harness, and horses only as an auxiliary. The old carts usually had two to three mules when on longer distance hauls. With the rubber-tyred carts only one mule was used. Because of requisitioning by army and bandits and because of the deaths of many draught animals during the famine the number of horses and mules in Guanzhong had greatly declined. During the second half of the 1930s, it slowly regained the pre-famine level. A 1936 estimate put it at a little over 10,000, or only one-quarter of that of ten years before. There was one oxen to every two peasant households, but of horses or mules only one to every fifty. An economic survey undertaken in 1941 showed that there was one horse to every 25 households. As the number of mules used to be somewhat smaller than that of horses, by that time probably one out of every 15 households owned a horse or a mule.[15] Of the various means of transportation, the coolies with shoulder poles would carry some 70 kg, especially over short distances and in difficult terrain and in towns. Wheelbarrows and pushcarts carried about 250 kg, and were most effective on good roads. Rickshaws carried a little more than that, and were used everywhere. Horses and mules carried about 150 kg, and were more effective when pulling a cart. Two mules could pull over 1,000 kg. 'Whether man or animal, the distance that can be covered on one day can be 60 km'.[16]

Most traditional forms of transportation have persisted until today and still dominate in many sectors. Some have almost or completely disappeared, however. During the 1930s and 1940s flat-bottom ships in sizes varying from 1 to 60 tons were used on Guanzhong's rivers: a 220 km section of the Yellow River, an equally long section of the Wei River up to Xianyang (usually no further upstream than Weinan, but sometimes another 85 km up to Wugong) and a 25 km-long section of the Luo River. The Wei and Luo River waterways could accomodate only very small ships or rafts; cotton and wheat flour were the main cargo downstream. On the Yellow River, transport was more significant. Coal from the mines of Baishui and Hancheng was transported down the Yellow River from Yumenkou to Tongguan, and from there by railroad, or with smaller boats upstream, to Xi'an. Salt from Chaoyi and from Shanxi province went the same way. Altogether the volume of this waterway transportation was not very large.[17] The irrigation projects undertaken since the 1930s took away much of the flow of the Luo and Wei Rivers, which had been very shallow during most of the year to begin with. The railroads, once in operation, superseded all previous forms of long-distance transportation. By the 1950s along the Wei River shipping was as good as finished.[18]

The connection of Xi'an with the Longhai railroad was the beginning of a new economic era for Guanzhong. The line was very successful. The 1936 import volume of Xi'an for major goods such as cotton cloth, kerosene, and iron and steelware was 4 to 5 times as much as three years before.[19] In 1935 it was decided to extend the Longhai railroad from Xi'an westward to Lanzhou. Instead of following the traditional route via Binxian and Changwu to Ningxia, a more southern course was adopted along the Wei River. The main reasons for this choice were that it would avoid the heights of the Liubanshan mountains and would make a future extension line to Sichuan province easier and shorter. A steel bridge was built to cross the Wei River at Xianyang, and Baoji was reached in 1938. West of Baoji, however, construction would become extremely difficult along the tortuous and narrow upper reaches of the Wei River. After the Japanese occupation of north China the Longhai railroad authorities pressed for an extension of the railroad to Tianshui, so as to provide shelter and defense for the railway stock in case Xi'an would be captured by the Japanese. Also, many Longhai railroad workers had fled from the occupied East and needed work. Although in 1941 the central government decided to complete construction of the 152 km-long Baoji–Tianshui section, it gave no priority to it and work came to a halt. Then oil was discovered near Lanzhou, which was badly needed for the war effort. Now construction work was resumed, and at the end of 1945 Tianshui had been reached. The extension to the coal mines in North Guanzhong reached Sanyuan by 1941. Moreover, a 60 km-long narrow-gauge line was built from Weinan to Baishui.[20]

Already before 1937 the State, whether the military or the civilian government, had been greatly involved not only in the construction but also in the operation of railroads and highways. During the anti-Japanese war all modern means of transportation came to the disposal of either the army or the civilian Transport Bureau in Xi'an, and also very many draught animals and carts. This situation of State dominance of the transport sector would continue under communism.

After a brief period of an individual peasant economy, collectivization in the latter half of the 1950s ended most of the private transport and ownership of draught animals and carts. Trade and transport themselves, it seemed, were held in low esteem by the communists, and especially so when not a part of the State sector. Only for transport handled by the nationalized railroads and by the local transport departments of the State were statistical data collected. Only very recently some statistical data have been published, but still the subject receives scant attention. Thus, in the following we have relied on qualitative rather than on quantitative data, taken sometimes from Shaanxi province, sometimes from a few counties in Guanzhong only. A picture of the expansion of the railroad and road network in Guanzhong is shown on Maps 4 and 5.

Under the First Five-Year Plan (1953–7) the national government had planned a rapid industrial build-up of Northwest China. Xi'an, Lanzhou, Baotou and also some smaller regional centers received a great influx of capital goods and people. Between 1949 and 1956 the urban industrial labour force in Shaanxi (most of which was concentrated in Xi'an) grew from 60,000 to 300,000 workers. A giant cement factory (then the largest in China) was set up in Yaoxian in 1956–9. Regional coal mines were developed to serve the increasing regional or even national energy needs.[21] Coal output of Guanzhong's largest mining district, Tongchuan, likewise quintupled between 1952 and 1957.[22] Cotton production, Guanzhong's major agricultural commodity, was considerably increased to serve the newly established cotton textile mills in Xi'an. Within a period of just a few years, the transport volume, and thereby the demands made on the existing network and means of transportation, rose dramatically. As in other parts of China, these demands were met mainly by an expansion of railroad transport. New lines were added, locomotives and wagons were imported from the USSR and their intensity of use was pushed as far as possible. Between 1953 and 1956, the average number of wagon loads on the western section of the Longhai railroad increased by 250 percent. In 1957, 3,830,000 tons of goods and 9,070,000 passengers were moved by railroad, a 92 and 60 percent increase over 1952.[23]

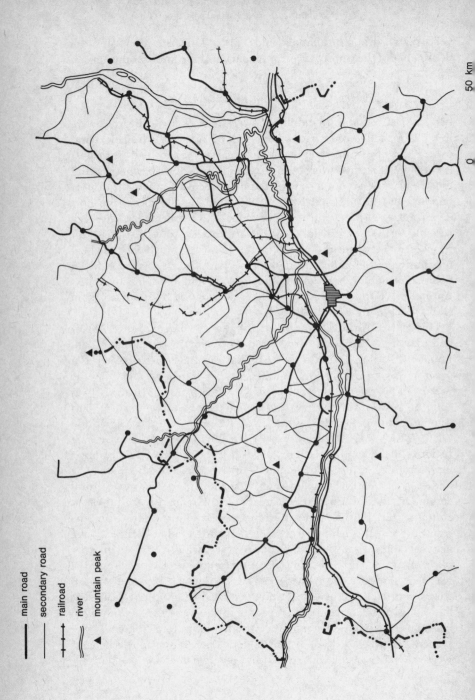

main road
secondary road
railroad
river
▲ mountain peak

0   50 km

Table 1 *Railroad and highways in Shaanxi, 1949–1984*

	1946-9	1952	1956	1966	1974	1978	1980	1983	1984
a1 railroad length (km)	521[a]	451[i]	521[a]	837[i]	1,072[c]	1,732[i]	1,855[g]	1,744[i]	
a2 railroad transport volume (billion ton/km)		0.47[i]		7.6[i]		16.6[i]		19.9[i]	21.6[j]
b1 highway length (1,000 km)	4.4[bf]	3.9	6.4[d]	17.7	25.6[b]	32.7	33.6[g]	33.8[i]	
b1.1 of which macadam or gravel			.8[e]		3.1[b]		10-15[h]		
b2 highway truck transport volume (million ton/km)		40[i]		360[i]		740[i]		770[i]	812[j]

[a] Wu Yuan-li, *The Spatial Economy of Communist China*, NY, 1967, p. 259.

[b] *Shaanxi Provincial Service* 18 Sept. 1974. 35 percent of the highway length consisted of all-weather roads, *Shaanxi Ribao* 30 Dec. 1973.

[c] *Shaanxi Provincial Service* 16 June 1974.

[d] *Shaanxi Ribao* 3 Jan. 1957.

[e] *Shaanxi Ribao* 7 Nov. 1956. Only 15-76% 'could continue traffic in case of heavy rainfall.'

[f] Zhou Yishi, *Zhongguo Gonglu Zhi*, Taibei 1957, pp. 312–20. Figures apply to 1946 and 1947.

[g] *Zhongguo Jingji Nianjian 1981*, p. iv 306.

[h] Estimate based on county data.

[i] *Shaanxi Ribao* 14 and 19 Sept. 1984. Of the 36,832 km of roads in 1983, 24,644 km were up to national standards, viz. 235 km of 2nd grade road, 5,658 km of 3d-grade road, and 18,751 km of 4th grade road. The 34 km-long Xi'an-Sanyuan road (to be built by foreign contractors) will become Shaanxi's first and only first-grade road. The 1990 goal is a highway network of 40,000 kilometers.

[j] *Shaanxi Ribao* 6 Apr. 1985.

The stress on railroad transport remained an essential characteristic in subsequent decades. 'The focus on heavy industry has worked in favour of rail transport technologically and against road transport, as can be seen in the railways' higher research efforts and the outmoded standards of truck manufacture as well as low road design standards.'[24] The railroad connection with Lanzhou was completed in 1957, with Chengdu in Sichuan in 1956. Both were badly needed, because road transport could cope no longer.[25] Also in 1957 a railway bridge over the Yellow River at Tongguan established a direct connection between the Longhai railroad and the north–south railroad of Shanxi province. Within Guanzhong, in 1963 a 45 km-long branch line Xi'an–Huxian–Yuxia was completed, which contributed greatly to the industrial development of Huxian. Most important, however, was the extension from Xianyang to the coal mining city of Hancheng in northeast Guanzhong during the 1960s. This line opened up the agricultural plain north of the Wei River to cheap long-distance transport.[26] At first, all these lines were single-track.

In sharp contrast with the Longhai railroad, which still had considerable overcapacity during the 1950s,[27] the highway transport sector was plagued by bottlenecks and crises because of its inability to handle a rapidly increasing volume of goods and passengers. For Shaanxi province, transport tasks (goods and passengers) in 1955 were 58 percent up on 1954, in 1956 162 percent (volume of goods) resp. 62 percent (passengers) up on 1955, in 1957 again 74 percent (volume of goods) up on 1956, according to official sources. In the year of 1956, road transport carried 1,550,000 tons and 3,170,000 passengers, 5.6 and 4.7 times as much as in 1952.[28] By far, most of this transport was situated in Guanzhong. In 1954, half of the transport was handled by the State organizations, half of it by 'the masses'. In highway transport, basic construction materials, coal, gasoline and diesel constituted 28 percent of the total volume, foodstuffs 35 percent, salt and miscellaneous materials 23 percent.[29] Highway transport suffered from bad roads, lack of trucks, congestion and bad organization.

Our province has over 5,000 kilometers of highways. But quality is low (at present only 15.76 percent can continue traffic in case of heavy rainfall), which severely limits the efficiency of cars. On the rather good roads, speed may exceed 30 kilometers per hour, but on the average bad road, it does not reach 20 kilometers per hour . . . The number of cars is too small, they are too old; the roads are few in number and deficient in quality, and we ourselves have not enough understanding of the business . . . The situation in transport is tense.[30]

All this, of course, reduced possible savings in transport costs. Only along newly-built mountain roads, where human porterage was replaced by truck transport, large cost reductions were realized.[31]

The provincial government took several measures to fight the tense situation in highway transportation. Two serious bottlenecks, the crossings of the Wei River at Xianyang and at Weinan, were removed; highway bridges were built there next to the existing railway bridges in 1953–6. Until 1957, 2,900 kilometers of highways and 5,000 kilometers of cart roads were repaired or newly constructed in Shaanxi province – the distinction between the two categories was not too clear.[32] Although this fell short compared to earlier planning,[33] there was no lack of construction labour or of official optimism.

The Provincial Communications Bureau drew up a 7-year plan (1956–62) for construction of communications, which foresaw the building of 57,500 km of highways.

According to the regulations of the State Council, every adult labourer has to devote 5 days per year to road building (as a corvée duty). With 6 million labourers, Shaanxi should have 30 million labour days. If every kilometer of highway needs 5,000 cubic meters of earthwork we may build over 10,000 kilometers of road a year . . . We must mobilize the masses . . . Carts and draught animals are vital, too. We must make sure that roads are built according to the standards set by the government.[34]

For many reasons, however, this labour potential could not be put into full effect. Technical knowledge was deficient. There were almost no materials for modern roads, such as tar or cement, and only to the south of the Wei River was stone or gravel near at hand. The organization of surveying work, of land acquisition etcetera required much more time than impatient government officials would allow for. Most important of all, there were not sufficient means of transportation, old or modern, and there was no way of rapidly increasing the number of trucks[35] or horses and mules. For the latter, the government realized that one had to rely on the peasantry. In 1956, local leaders had returned many rubber-tyred carts to the newly-formed Higher Agricultural Producers' Cooperatives, presumably for reasons of animal care rather than for organizational efficiency – a decision regretted by higher authorities almost at once.[36] Early in 1957, the province still commanded 4,000 rubber-tyred animal-drawn carts, but the villages had a greater number. These were to be used on good roads, and still constituted a small minority. Of iron- and wooden-wheel carts, which were very slow and damaging to road toppings, Shaanxi's peasants had some 150,000. 'The task which the masses' transport has shouldered in recent years is half as large as that of the whole transportation of Shaanxi province.'[37] The shoulders meant here may have been both animal and human.

The changes in the social and economic organization of China had their effects on the transport sector as well. Land Reform and collectivization made it harder to find human labour for *coolie* work, such as pulling rickshaws, shouldering poles, or pushing wheelbarrows. This work had always been very hard labour, with the lowest possible social standing, performed by bachelors without land or property. On the other hand, the number of draught animals suffered because of collectivization, and their quality as well. At the same time, heavier demands were made on oxen for ploughing.[38] Transport by human labour, therefore, may have increased within the village for short-distance transport, and decreased for longer hauls. This tendency was reinforced by the anti-commercial policies of the government. Trade was increasingly centralized and monopolized by state trade organizations; peasants had to deliver their grain and cotton to central collecting points set up by state purchase agencies in the larger villages.

In spite of these transport problems, there was quite an expansive mood in 1957–9. Guanzhong had truly become part of a national grid of transport and trade. Cotton, coal, industrial products and grain were traded with other provinces in large quantities. The Second Five-Year Plan included goals for 1962 of 30,000 kilometers of motor roads, 2,000 kilometers of riverways, and a railway Xi'an–Hankou across the Qinling, none of which were even remotely realistic,[39] and this was even before the Great Leap Forward started its upward revision of all previous goals. The Sanmen hydroelectric power station project on the Yellow River necessitated the movement of huge quantities of construction materials to the building site and a resettlement of over 100,000 people in Shaanxi. This was the largest construction project during these years, but there were many more. Information on the transport sector indicates a great increase of transport volume, highways and means of transportation, both modern and traditional. In Xi'an it was urged that trucks (660 out of 1,000) belonging to state organizations which only performed transport duties within the municipality should be put to better use; short-distance transport should be taken over by 'the population' with traditional means.

Because of the organization of People's Communes, means of transportation and human labour could be pooled to form large transport gangs within each county and each commune. A serious lack of reliable data, however, impedes any effort toward further analysis.[40]

After the hectic Great Leap Forward years, the transport situation eased and was slowly improved. The policy of economic development centered around agriculture and agriculture-related industries, a substantial decrease of heavy industrial production, the abandonment of many construction projects and a decrease of the urban population all reduced the demands made on the transport network. Most of the responsibility for planning, construction and maintenance of roads fell to the provincial and county authorities. These, in turn, gave emphasis to self-reliance on the part of the People's Communes which were to supply and organize the necessary labour for highway construction. Only trunk roads of national or provincial significance continued to be maintained by the provincial government.[41] The trunk roads had larger widths and higher standards of construction and maintenance. Within Guanzhong, in this category fell the old route Tongguan–Xi'an–Changwu to Ningxia, the roads crossing the Qinling mountains to south Shaanxi, the roads Xi'an–Tongchuan–Yan'an and Xi'an–Hancheng into Shanxi, and the roads on both sides of the Wei River Xi'an–Baoji into Sichuan or into Gansu.

C. REGIONAL, COUNTY AND VILLAGE TRANSPORT IN THE 1960s AND 1970s

In spite of the generally rather poor weather conditions of the 1960s, around 1965 the agricultural economy of Guanzhong started to respond to the new inputs of irrigation, chemical fertilizer, machinery and improved varieties. A modest growth occurred in most industries (cotton textile excepted) and in coal mining, stimulated by the construction of the railroad to Hancheng. As a consequence, the transport volume at all levels increased. A wider range of industrial and agricultural products was transported by the agricultural collectives within their borders, and quantities rose, too. During the 1970s the pace of industrial growth quickened. Coal production tripled, reaching 27 million tons in 1979, and then fell off to 21 million tons in 1983.[42] County Transport Bureaus, which had lost part of their transport tasks to the People's Communes in 1958, saw their transport

Table 2 *Volume of goods moved by County Transport Bureaus, 1957–1978*
(1,000 tons/km)

County	1957	1965	1974	1978	i.e. ton/km per cap. in 1978
Pucheng	2,188	1,355	3,423	9,799	15
Weinan	4,286	2,323	5,196	8,620	13
Liquan	n.d.	380	673	1,030	3
Wugong	90	n.d.	260	400	1
Hancheng	n.d.	n.d.	1,800	3,331	12
Chunhua	n.d.	n.d.	802	1,760	12

Data supplied by county statistical departments. Transport within county borders only, exclusive of railway transport. The low figure for Wugong county may be attributed to its small size, its lack of industry, and its easy access to railway transport.

Table 3 *Relative shares of means of transportation used by County Transport Bureaus, 1965 and 1978*

(percentage of total volume of goods moved)

County	Cart		Truck		Rickshaw		Train	
	1965	1978	1965	1978	1965	1978	1965	1978
Qianxian	70	42	15	40	15	18	—	—
Wugong	65	10	20	50	15	40	—	—
Pucheng	90	10	10	70	—	—	0	20

Data supplied by county statistical departments. Pucheng excluded rickshaws, but included railway transport within its borders.

volume grow again, at an increasing speed, to a still modest average level of about 10 ton/km per capita by 1978. See Table 2.

The Transport Bureaus obtained more trucks, and thereby could reduce their animal-drawn cart transport. They used more human labour pulling rickshaws, however, especially within towns. The agricultural collectives not only started to use tractors for transport from about 1965, but also greatly increased their number of draught animals. Within Guanzhong, the number of horses and mules almost doubled between 1965 and 1975, while the number of oxen (which

Table 4 Draught animals in Shaanxi, 1933–1983

(1,000)

	oxen	horses	mules	donkeys	camels	Total	% of China total	% of China total except oxen [1]
1933	683	92	131	221	–	1,127		
1936	1,001	128	152	445	–	1,726		
1940	752	85	62	–	–	–		
1942	839	84	113	256	–	1,282		
1945	813	87	113	229	–	1,242		
1947	796	81	118	212	–	1,207		
1949	1,065	57	101	263	–	1,486	2.5	2.6
1955	–	–	–	–	–	2,660	3.0	
1957	–	–	–	–	–	2,528[x]	3.0	
1965	1,781	74	101	352	0.3	2,304	2.7	3.7
1975	1,864	135	203	367	–	2,564	2.6	3.0
(1975 Guanzhong only	932	107	157	130	–	1,326)		
1979	1,752	118	234	339	–	2,451	2.6	3.0
1981	1,721	114	238	368	–	2,441	2.5	3.0
1983	1,803	–	–	–	–	2,438	2.4	2.5

[x]Of this number, only 1,910,000 animals 'could really be used'.

Sources: Shaanxi Nongye Dili, Xi'an 1978, p. 22; Zhongguo Nongye Nianjian 1981, p. 49; 1982, pp. 58–62; 1984, p. 119. [1]Fazhan Nongye yu Jianshe Xibei' (Develop agriculture and build up the Northwest), Xibei Ziyuan Vol. I no. 3, Dec. 1940; Shaanxi Provincial 12-Year Plan for Agricultural Development, Shaanxi Ribao 29 Jan. 1956; Shaanxi Government Work Report, Shaanxi Ribao 4 Feb. 1958; Zhongguo Tongji Nianjian 1984, p. 162; Zhongguo Jindai Nongye Shengchan Ji Maoyi Ziliao, p. 301.

were used almost exclusively in the fields) and donkeys (which are less reliable for transport duties) remained about the same.[43] See Tables 3 and 4. So in the State sector and in the collective sector both modern and traditional means of transportation increased considerably during the 1960s and 1970s.

For the state sector, it was most important that during the 1970s both the railway network and the highway network increased in length to a considerable extent (see Table 1). Their quality increased as well. In the early 1970s a major road bitumening program was started. Within the Guanzhong plain, all People's Commune seats were linked up with country roads. Passenger transport was improved by extending bus lines and services. For both goods and passenger transport, the railroad remained the prime means of transportation except for very short distances. The Xi'an–Baoji railway had been double-tracked by 1977. Double-tracking of the Xianyang–Hancheng line was still in progress in 1983. The Baoji–Tianshui section was electrified between 1977 and 1980, as had happened earlier with the Baoji–Chengdu line. In 1972, construction of a northern extension into north Shaanxi was started, which crossed the Wei River in Lintong and connected Xi'an (via Tongchuan) with Yan'an in 1980. In 1983, construction of a railroad Baoji–Ningxia was announced.[44] By 1980, Shaanxi had 1,855 kilometers of railroad, double the length of ten years before; almost all of this was in Guanzhong. Its passenger and road transport was still far behind the average level for China. Although the road network had been expanded to 33,600 km, as yet less than a third had a hard-top surface. By 1983, Shaanxi still had only 1,600 buses, half the all-China average.[45] The relative shares of railroad, highway, waterway and air in transport of goods and passengers by State organizations are shown in Table 5. Guanzhong being the most developed and populous part of Shaanxi, it had a more than proportionate share of transport and highways. In a survey of 7 counties the bitumen-surface highway length quadrupled in Guanzhong between 1965 and 1978, per square kilometer of farmland from 0.06 km to .24 km. Dirt highway length increased from .18 km per square kilometer in 1965 to .42 km in 1978. Even so, it remained well below all-China averages. See Table 6.

The definition of highway used in Table 6 is a very strict one: intercommunal roads designated as such by the county government which have an average width of at least 6 meters and are maintained with county funds. The total road network of village roads is many

Table 5 *Volumes of freight and passenger transport by State organizations in Shaanxi, 1980, and within Xi'an municipality, 1981*

	Shaanxi 1980		Xi'an 1981	
	Freight (million ton/km)	Passenger (million pass./km)	Freight (million ton/km)	Passenger (million pass./km)
railway	17,957	6,288	18.6	14.5
road	1,054	1,623	81.7	96.8
waterway	12	0.7	–	–
air	3	117	–	–
Total	19,026	8,029	100.3	111.3

Sources: Shaanxi Ribao 20 June 1981; *Zhongguo Jingji Nianjian 1983*, v p. 170.

times larger, but no data have been collected according to a uniform standard.

Apart from the provincial highways and the county highways there are *main roads* connecting People's Communes (width 6–7 meters) *branch roads* connecting villages within People's Communes (width 5–6 meters), *production roads* for tractors between the fields (width 4–5 meters) and *production paths* for carts or walking tractors (width 1.5–3 meters).[46] The main and branch roads are usually lined with trees, as part of the official program of one hundred trees per inhabitant, and serve for reinforcement of roadsides, for fuel and for shade.

Construction costs for provincial and county highways have been stated to be 100,000 – 150,000 *yuan* per kilometer, depending on the terrain. With the recent decline of provincial government revenues, Shaanxi had difficulties in sustaining a major roadbuilding effort. Yet such expenditure would seem justified, in several congested areas, when coupled with other measures such as traffic separation, improvement of road sides and an increase of the number of trucks.[47] Road toppings generally are made with coal tar, and rather well-kept.

One problem for Shaanxi's transport sector was and still is its dependence on other provinces for trucks, buses, cars and tractors. In 1980, the provincial output of motor vehicles was only 890, of tractors only 173.[48] The Xi'an Car Factory was the largest loss-making unit in Shaanxi province in 1983.[49] Bicycle production, on the other hand,

Table 6 *Highways, population density, and farmland area in 7 counties, 1965 and 1978*

	Land surface (sq.km)	Population (1,000)	Farmland area (sq.km)	Highway length		Macadam highway length			Population density (inh./sq.km)
				dirt (km)	macadam (km)	per sq. km of surface (km)	per s. km of farmland (km)	per inhabitant (km)	
1978									
Wugong	455	369	339	55	58	.13	.17	.16	811
Weinan	1,088	649	861	237	227	.21	.26	.35	596
Pucheng	1,766	650	1,239	694	323	.18	.26	.50	368
Qianxian	1,275	417	713	360	140	.11	.20	.34	327
Liquan	1,082	345	617	242	102	.09	.17	.30	319
Chunhua	965	145	387	n.d.	120	.12	.31	.83	150
Hancheng	1,869	281[a]	339	164	100	.05	.29	.36	150
Total	8,500	2,809	4,495	1,752 +	1,070	.13	.24	.38	330
1965									
Wugong	455	273[b]	344	39	27	.06	.08	.10	600
Weinan	1,088	489	916	142	59	.05	.06	.12	449
Pucheng	1,766	467[b]	1,320	178	77	.04	.06	.16	264
Qianxian	1,275	309	758	110	100	.08	.13	.32	242
Liquan	1,082	257	692	133	12	.01	.02	.05	238
Chunhua	965	113	453	104	0	.00	.00	.00	117
Hancheng	1,869	190[a]	381	161	34	.02	.09	.18	102
Total	8,500	2,098	4,864	867	309	.04	.06	.15	247

[a] These data may not be consistent
[b] intrapolated according to growth rate in other counties

showed an explosive and profitable growth: from only 20,000 bicycles in 1978 to an output of 167,000 in 1980 and 546,500 in 1982.[50] Bicycles, carts, walking tractors, rickshaws and other forms of slow traffic use the same highway as trucks and buses do, because there are no separate lanes. In the immediate vicinity of cities and on the Tongguan–Xi'an–Baoji highway on the south bank of the Wei River traffic congestion is very serious, and trucks are slowed down considerably. North of the Wei River, there is far less congestion.

Few trucks are larger than 5 tons. Recently some trucks have been bought by peasant household coops, but tractors remain by far the dominant mechanical means of transport for agricultural products. The 1980 stock of large and medium tractors in Shaanxi was 20,000, and 3,500 farm trucks;[51] probably over two-thirds of these were situated in Guanzhong. With decollectivization and trade liberalization in progress, one witnesses a rapid growth, especially of long-haul small-scale transport to collective markets and to the cities, on bicycles, with buses and with the traditional means of carts and shoulder poles.[52] Increasing the number of buses is nowadays seen as a major contribution to the improvement of people's lives.[53]

Management of road transport has been under criticism lately. Between 1977 and 1984, the number of employees of the Provincial Road Transport Management Bureau increased from 1,100 to 1,800 people 'without system and without need'. Two-thirds of the yearly expenditure (of 6 million *yuan*) was used for unclear purposes. It was therefore proposed to decentralize management to the local authorities.[54] Railroad transport procedures were simplified, when the Xi'an Railroad Bureau abolished the transport permits previously required from the Provincial Commercial Bureau, the Grain Bureau and the Foodstuffs Bureau. The provincial government decided that transport of goods over a distance of less than 50 kilometers should be handled completely by trucks under contract, and no longer be included in the railway transport plan. So as to concentrate on long-distance hauls, railway transport over a distance of 50 to 100 kilometers should also be turned over to road transport as much as possible.[55]

Conclusion. The development of a modern road network and of a railway in Guanzhong was the result of the Nationalist governments' effort to integrate Shaanxi and the Northwest with Republican China. Also, it served the military build-up of the Nationalists against the Red bases in north Shaanxi and against the Japanese who had occupied the neighbouring province of Shanxi. Because the railroad followed a new route along the Wei River to Baoji and beyond, the old Silk Road which had been modernized with foreign relief funds in 1931–4 lost much of its trade. Former important political and economic centers, such as Binzhou, Fengxiang and Dali, gradually sank into oblivion, and Baoji, at the railroad junction to Sichuan, developed into the second city of Shaanxi. Railways to Tongchuan and to Hancheng opened up the coal mines of north Guanzhong in the 1940s and 1950s.

Road transport remained very backward. In the 1930s, a severe shortage of draught animals and carts persisted, especially for longer distances. There were very few trucks and buses until the mid 1960s, fuel was always expensive and often in short supply. Wheelbarrows, pushcarts and rickshaws were the preferred means of transport over short and medium distances and mule-carts if the farmer could obtain them. When more water was diverted for irrigation purposes in the 1950s, ships and rafts disappeared from the Wei and Luo Rivers. Long distance transport had become dominated by the government during the war and it would remain so under communism. During the First Five-Year Plan, the transport situation was very tense because of low quality of roads and heavy demands. Private ownership of draught animals and carts was taken over by collectives and by county transport bureaus which also had a virtual monopoly over modern means of transportation until the coming of walking tractors in the 1970s. Transport and trade suffered from centralization and anti-commercial policies. Railroad transport was favoured by the government over other forms of transport; in Shaanxi province, its volume rose 16 times between 1952 and 1966, and again by 2.6 times up to 1983 (for trucks, it rose by 9 and 2.1 times respectively).

It appeared that the major highway-building effort of the late 1960s and early 1970s, which was sustained primarily by county funds and people's commune labour, resulted in a highway network with a more than adequate capacity in most parts of Guanzhong. Traditional transport profited first; between 1965 and 1975, the number of mules and horses about doubled (but can the rubber-tyred cart they pull be called 'traditional'?). Lack of trucks, organizational bottlenecks and the use of roads by pedestrians and slow human- or animal-drawn carts, however, severely limited their use for mechanized medium- and long-distance transport. Between 1974 and 1978, the number of trucks increased quickly and the transport volume of County Transport Bureaus in Guanzhong roughly doubled.

In the seven counties surveyed in 1979, macadam highway length had quadrupled since 1965, to 170 meters per square kilometer of farmland – still only about half the all-China average. Traffic congestion was very serious around cities and on the Tongguan–Xi'an–Baoji highway. In the 1980s, liberalization of trade and the increase of walking tractors and bicycles has congested roads still further. The limited financial resources of the provincial government and the priority treatment of railway expansion to Yan'an and Ningxia leave insufficient room for rapid improvement (the Xi'an–Sanyuan highway and bridge project excepted). Also, with privatization of part of road transport and the need for more careful land use planning and labour mobilization since the demise of the collectives, the county governments may be less inclined to invest in road building. Yet transport improvement should be considered to be an important condition for rationalization, integration of industries and for agricultural specialization.

3

THE GROWTH OF XI'AN AND INDUSTRIAL DEVELOPMENT

A. XI'AN BEFORE AND AFTER THE RAILROAD

It was at a strategic point, where the Silk Road crosses the Wei River from where it continues its way along the Jing tributary, that the Zhou, Qin, Han and Tang dynasties built their respective capitals. The various sites were well chosen. To the South, the Qinling mountains provided a natural barrier for defense, and timber and fuel. The Ba River, Feng River and some smaller streams supplied fresh water. As the power and population of China grew, so did Changan, until the capital had a population of one million within an outer city wall of 9 by 11 kilometers in the seventh century A.D. Then, decline set in. The capital was destroyed in 904, and would never recapture its former status and glory. In the early Ming, the present city walls and fortifications were built, much smaller in scope, but still the most extensive and best preserved in China today.[1] During the Qing and early Republic, the built-up area and population did not extend beyond these walls. Population dwindled down to a mere 100,000. After the Manchu garrison had been chased out in 1911, the military and administrative functions of Xi'an became weaker and weaker. It was a provincial capital in name, but with little power even within Guanzhong. As capital of a poverty stricken, bandit-infested area, without minerals, without access to major waterways or to a railroad, Xi'an remained untouched by foreign capital and the treaty port system. The 1934 railway connection, the war against Japan, and the First Five-Year Plan brought an industrial boom and successive waves of social and economic change to Xi'an. In the past fifty years, the population and built-up area of the city proper increased by ten times.

In origin, then, Xi'an ('Pacification of the West') was neither a mercantile nor an industrial city. Rather it served as an administrative center and sometimes as a military base during succeeding dynasties. As with most other Chinese cities, governmental functions dominated. From here, the countryside was ruled. Within the city, commercial

Plate 1 Gate tower and eastern city wall of Xi'an, inner side. The houses on the left have back rooms dug into the wall.

activities were kept under tight control by State officials, which might be a reason for merchants to take their trade elsewhere, e.g. to Sanyuan.[2] So outside the city, commercial establishments might spring up. The city outlay was planned by the government and reflected its sense of order. 'Traditional cities were walled, in a regular pattern, with great gates from which broad straight avenues ran to the opposite gate. The major streets, fixing the main axes, divided the city into major quarters. Each quarter tended to be functionally specific: warehouses, transport termini, retailing, manufacturing, schools, barracks . . .'[3] The lack of economic growth in Guanzhong and the various disasters of the late Qing and early Republican period had reduced the non-administrative functions and population of Xi'an to a level considerably below that of the early Ming. The walled city was in a very dilapidated state, there were many open spaces, and the number of inhabitants reached a low of 108,000 by the early 1930s. The exceptional visitor was warned against what he might find:

You people in Shanghai are living in luxury and comfort . . . Now you are going to take a trip to the Northwest. I warn you, you may see a lot of unpleasant things there and be terribly depressed by your experience. Our people in the Northwest are leading a very poor and wretched life. Most of them have hardly anything to maintain their existence.[4]

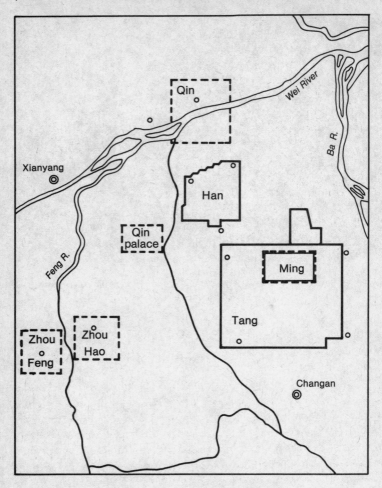

Map 6 City sites of Xi'an, early Zhou till Ming/Qing

Surveys of Xi'an at that time gave a total of 4,000 merchant households, 6,000 labourers in small industries[5] and many civil servants and soldiers, as a young missionary remarked in 1932:

Sent to a big city (Xi'an) to evangelize its people, how would *you* begin? I bought a map, nailed it to the wall of my study, and a friendly official made the map live. He marked the schools, the colleges and the university with their 40,000 students, the barracks and cadet schools with their 20,000 soldiers, seven Government offices with their 15,000 civil servants . . .[6]

When the Guomindang Government took over political power after the defeat of Feng Yuxiang, it could not play a very active economic role. Official provincial and local tax receipts averaged 8 million dollars per year during 1931–3, almost half of which came from land tax.[7] Lack of sufficient income from these and other 'special' taxes (of which the opium fine was by far the largest, with about 4 million dollars a year), coupled with high expenditure for defense and public security purposes, made the provincial administration dependent on loans from the central Government, banks, or other sources. These institutions, however, were very reluctant to lend money to Shaanxi.[8] Political and military control were not very extensive either (although a Political Training Bureau of the Military Council had been set up in 1934), at least until the war against Japan. Mao, Peng, Zhu and Xu joined forces with Liu Zhidan in north Shaanxi in 1935 and the 1936 encirclement campaign failed. Chunhua, Fengxiang but also part of the eastern valley (Sanyuan, Dali etc) was under communist influence for some time.[9] The establishment of a Red basis in Yan'an and Chiang Kai Shek's conflict with Zhang Xueliang and Yang Hucheng (the 'Xi'an incident') made this painfully clear in 1936. No wonder no foreign or Chinese capital was attracted to Xi'an. A provincial governor (himself a Zhejiang man) remarked wrily that 'in many respects government in the Northwest is easier than elsewhere, as the authorities are not handicapped by unwelcome foreign interference'.[10] In 1935–6 the new railroad and the upswing of agricultural production (especially of cotton) brought the first few modern industries to Xi'an, and therewith the beginnings of modern economic growth.

The railroad connection with north China was not just a means of cheap transport. Of course it was important now that Guanzhong products could be traded with eastern goods on a much larger scale, and that heavy machinery could be brought safely to Xi'an. But the railway meant more. It symbolized the determination of the Nanking government to integrate Shaanxi and the Northwest with modern China, military, politically and economically, and made such penetration from the east possible. Within a year or two, land prices in the northern part of Xi'an in the vicinity of the railway station jumped from 600–750 dollars per hectare to about 30,000 dollars per hectare.[11] The Government established a small power station, a water works, a cotton mill, and a machinery factory, founded several new schools and colleges, and opened up the improved highway to Lanzhou.[12] A serious opium-eradication campaign was started, poppy being replaced by improved cotton seeds distributed by the provincial authorities. The provincial tax system was simplified, and many minor local taxes and exactions were abolished.[13] These measures were all meant to modernize Guanzhong and its central city of Xi'an, and to attract the trust of banks and investors from east China, and to a certain extent they did.

In 1936 several new modern industries moved into Xi'an, the largest of all being the Dahua cotton mill, with a capital of 3 million dollars, owned by a firm with cotton mills in Shijiazhuang and Hankou. Its 25,000 spindles and 820 looms were operated by a labour force of 600 male and 300 female workers, most of whom had been brought in from Hubei as no local female workers could be found. The Huafeng and Chengfeng flour mills, with an initial capital of 300,000 and 1 million dollars, were founded with local capital and by a Qinan-based company. Each produced about 3,000 sacks of flour per day. These industries had their own power generators. The Zhongnan match factory had already been established in 1935, and produced 300,000 boxes per year with over one hundred workers. In nearby Xianyang some other industries were set up in 1936: a German-owned wine distillery and an oil-press factory, both of which ended production after two years, and a cotton-packing factory with a labour force of 3,000 during the busy season.[14]

So little time elapsed between this first start of Xi'an's industrialization and the war with Japan, that one can only speculate about how Xi'an's modern economic sector might have developed under conditions of peace. Some positive and negative factors became clear soon, though. Because of the successful completion of the Jinghui and Weihui irrigation schemes the agricultural raw materials basis, especially of cotton, was rapidly expanding. There was a considerable demand for products both from the Xi'an factories and from east China, owing to rising peasant incomes and cheaper transportation via the Longhai railroad. Some of this demand hurt local industry, especially cotton textile handicrafts and coal mining in northern Guanzhong.[15] The national government had made commitments to develop Guanzhong, and the communist presence in Yan'an in north Shaanxi added to the strategic value of Guanzhong. On the negative side, however, the financial weakness of the provincial government and the lack of local capital continued to make Xi'an dependent on outside support for its modern economic development. Although some smaller modern industries, notably matches, chemicals and machinery were established with local capital, the railroad, banking, textile, and flour industries were almost wholly established with outside capital.[16] Shaanxi province had a serious trade deficit, once poppy cultivation was effectively banned. Only cotton and tong-oil exports, almost all to Japan, brought in a significant amount of foreign exchange – 9.6 million and 1.5 million *yuan* in 1937. In that year, imports almost doubled over 1936, while exports (opium excluded) were halved.[17] There was no skilled industrial labour force. The infrastructure was still very weak, and its improvement would take time. Because of its location and size, the Weihe valley seemed to have only a limited capacity for modern industrial growth.

B. WAR-TIME XI'AN; POLITICAL CLIMATE, INDUSTRIAL PRODUCTION AND LABOUR

The outbreak of the war against Japan at the end of 1937 brought Guanzhong and Xi'an in a completely new position, as it did to Sichuan and Chongqing. The economy was placed on a war-time footing, with increasing government involvement and control. Political control of the area was reinforced after Yang Hucheng had surrendered and was carried off to Nanjing. Hu Zongnan, a relative of Madame Chiang Kai-Shek, took over military power with his First Army, which had bravely defended Shanghai. The number of troops in Guanzhong was considerably increased, both for defense against the Japanese who had occupied Shanxi and Henan provinces and for encirclement of the communist Shaan–Gan–Ning area. In 1939 the number of troops was increased from 100,000 to 300,000 for the latter purpose.[18] During the 1939–1940 winter offensive, Chunhua and some other counties up North were captured from the Communists. During the 1940s Hu's military strength increased considerably. His was one of the few Guomindang armies to be spared from the destructive 1944 Ichigō campaign along the Beijing–Guangzhou railway.[19] Foreign observers held that the Japanese could have beaten Hu Zongnan, but thought it wise to leave the Xi'an zone of the conflict between Guomindang and Communists undisturbed – if the two Chinese camps were separated territorially, they might at last compose their quarrels, which would strengthen the war effort.[20] This military presence put quite a burden on the economy of Guanzhong, especially in the provision of grain and draught animals. However, it also contributed to a greatly increased demand for industrial and mining products, which could only be partially fulfilled by increased production. Hoarding and inflation became very serious, which in turn forced the government to institute price controls, rationing and state allocation of vital raw materials and products.

In 1937, Sun Weiru was appointed governor of Shaanxi province. Soon antagonism developed between him and the Guomindang, because of his liberal policies and he had to step down. Under his successor Jiang Dingwen, 'progressive forces have been attacked and conservative forces have been activated', according to a contemporary leftist source. In 1939 and 1940 many magistrates from Sun Weiru times were replaced by 'anti-communist elements and former communist traitors'. Before that time, only 50 out of over 1,000 officials in the administration were really reactionary anti-communists, so no anti-communist measures had been really taken.

By 1940, of the top dozen high officials, eight were from other provinces. The dominant political group belonged to the C.C. clique, with Wang Debu (director of the Shaanxi Provincial Government Committee), Zhou Jiechun (director of Finance), Zhou Baimin (director of Agriculture) and Peng Shaoshi (secretary of the provincial government). Main opposition was centered in the Revival Society (with cliques around Kang Ce and Hu Zongnan), which had its main strength in the army, but also prominent officials such as Wang Jieshan, director of Education and Sun Shaozhong, director of Construction. Moreover there were three youth parties, and still the Northwest Army representatives such as Sun Weiru.[21] The Guomindang pursured a very active policy of recruitment. From a mere 1,000 members in 1934 the Guomindang grew to 12,000 in 1939 and 25,000 in 1940. The C.C. clique suffered a temporary set-back in 1941, when a new governor and party secretary were appointed. From 1943, the provincial party chairman Gu Zhendgding again followed the CC line, but he also sought and received support from general Hu Zongnan.[22]

As the war lasted, the political atmosphere in Xi'an became more and more oppressive. According to a resident foreign missionary, the communists could speak freely in 1937, but were put into a concentration camp from 1939 onwards.

In 1937, the Red Army occupied the towns and villages to the North of Sian. They were well disciplined . . . hard as nails, and cheerful . . . The Communist Political Propaganda Corps was a remarkably efficient organization, composed of young intellectuals . . . What convinced believers! What dogmatic and intolerant preachers! What aggressive evangelists! . . . They stood on boxes and held forth the passers-by on the main streets of Sian. Mass meetings were held daily in the city hall, at which some of the traitors and reactionaries were tried by the People's Court. Barracks, schools, factories etcetera were visited by eloquent speakers. The young students of Sian were swept off their feet by this revolutionary atmosphere.

But a few years later:

The increase in the authority of the State was accompanied by a stricter control of the Guomindang of the life and thought of the people . . . Party Headquarters were multiplied in the army and civil service, in schools and universities. 'One leader, one party, one programme' type of propaganda was conducted. The activities of the Secret Police became apparent . . . The intellectual atmosphere of Sian became oppressive with its sinister activity . . . In 1939, a concentration camp was established in the western suburb of Sian, to correct the thoughts of wayward youths who were interested in communism. In 1942, there were about 3,000 inmates.[23]

Likewise, in 1939 the Guomindang went into organizing labour unions in order to better control the rapidly growing labour force of Xi'an. By 1940, Xi'an had over 50,000 industrial labourers, 55 percent of whom were newly arrived workers from the villages or from outside Shaanxi since the outbreak of the war. The degree of organisation, however, was not high, only about 20 percent. Over one-half of this work force were children and women. The labourers from outside the province (often refugees belonging to a company that had moved to Xi'an) were better trained than the mostly unskilled local labour force. Between these two groups, conflicts occurred regularly, and the labour unions could play an intermediary role herein. Other functions of the labour unions were education, recruitment for membership of the Guomindang, political control against communist tendencies, and curbing wage demands. To this end, also the labour bosses were used and so-called die-hard elements belonging to the Green Society. 'During the war, we shouldn't talk about wage improvement; whoever demands it, is a traitor.'[24] Labour conditions had deteriorated considerably after 1938, notably because of a lengthening of the workday to 10–12 hours, increased demands of production, and inflation. In some vital branches, however, workers appeared to be able to defend their interests much better than in other branches. Especially the workers in the electricity plant, machinery repairshops, highway construction and post office succeeded in maintaining their 8-

Table 7 *Xi'an production labour force, various branches, 1937–1939*

Branch	1937	1939
(Railroad	?	+9000)
Bus transport	130	250
Spinning	1500	3500
Textiles	400	3900
Army blankets	500	1200
Cigarettes	–	450
Paper	20	420
Army uniforms	200	20800
Postal communications	400	750
Electricity works	370	770
Flour	300	900
Rickshaws	3000	6600
Cargo loading and unloading	250	2250
	7070[+]	50790[+]

Source: Kangzhan Zhongdi Shaanxi, pp. 53–7

hour working day and comparatively high wage levels. The tables 7 and 8 show the increase of the Xi'an industrial labour force and the changes in wages and working hours in various branches before and after the outbreak of the war against Japan. Because of inflation, especially in the price of foodstuffs during the second half of 1939, the absolute nominal increase carries little meaning.[25]

Labour conditions may have been worst in the small-scale establishments where army uniforms were made at piece-rate wages. Generally speaking, the few large-scale modern companies would offer their labourers better conditions in terms of working hours, housing and social security than small enterprises did. All companies and labourers, however, suffered from the effects of the war in the east. The first wave of refugees had brought the population number of Xi'an to some 220,000 in early 1938 – an increase of 70,000 people, mostly adults, in less than two years. In Xi'an not enough employment could be created for these people, and both skilled and unskilled labourers had to compete for jobs.

Grain remained cheap until the summer of 1939, and then its price quadrupled within a year. Textiles had suddenly become scarce after the Japanese bombing of the Dahua mill late in 1938, and their price rose

Table 8 *Labour wages and working hours in Shaanxi, various branches, 1937–1939*

Branch	(hours per day)		(monthly wage, *yuan*)		Remarks
	1937	1939	1937	1939	
Textile	10	12	9–10	12–15	Food included
Army uniforms	–	14	–	12–15	Piece wage, food excluded
Chemicals	8	10	10	15	Food included
Postal communications	8	8	18–24	25–30	Food and lodging excluded
Highways	8	8	9–10	12–15	Food and lodging excluded
Railways	8	8	12	12	Food and lodging excluded
Electric power	8	8	25	30	
Ironworks	10	12	24	28	
Machinery repairs	8	8–9	24	28	
Coal mining	15–16	15–16	24–30	30	Pitstays last a fortnight
Coops	–	10	–	15	Lodging included, food excluded
Coolies	–	–	0.2/day	0.5/day	
Drivers	15–16	15–16	12–15	12–15	

Source: Kangzhan Zhongdi Shaanxi, p. 53–57.

six-fold between 1937 and 1940. Some other budgetary items, such as housing rent, rose because of population pressure. Salt became very scarce as well.[26] These inflated prices were to a certain extent compensated by the various employers by wage rises, but belatedly and insufficiently so.

For the factory owners in Xi'an (or Xijing, 'The Western Capital' as it had been renamed in 1932) the war years were bad times as well. Japanese bombers destroyed the Dacheng Cotton Mill and the Shenxin Fourth Cotton Mill, which had just moved to Xi'an from Hankou, before their spindles had been installed in 1938. In winter 1939, the Dahua Cotton Mill was destroyed. These were Xi'an's largest and most modern mills.[27] Because of the repeated bombings, several factories decided to move to Baoji, a hundred miles west at the end of the railroad. Part of Xi'an's population fled in fear as well.[28] During 1938 and 1939 the total population of Xi'an actually went down a little. Other facilities in Xi'an suffered from bombings, too. In March 1939 the BMS hospital (the largest in town, with 100 beds) was destroyed; during the summer many schools were hit. The October raids of 1939 did the severest damage:

Offices and residences and banks were smashed. Cotton and flour mills were set on fire. The electric lighting station was put out of action. Yet there was comparatively little loss of life, since the people were holidaying outside the city. Though air-raids continued with less frequency until 1944, they failed to destroy the spirit of resistance in the Chinese people . . . People became accustomed to nuisance raids.[29]

Another problem for factory owners (including the government) was the unpredictability of transport and trade. In 1938, communications and trade with east China had been severed, demand for and prices of industrial goods increased, so that in Guanzhong local handicraft production flourished as never before. After 1939, the war front stabilized somewhat, and Japanese- and east-China-made goods could flow into Guanzhong again. Although rural handicraft production was affected much less by competition with eastern goods, city handicraft production was. Weaving industries turned to making coarse army cloth, leaving the better class markets to the goods from the east.[30] Because of insecure trade-flows, prices were hard to predict. The rapidly growing demand which resulted from the cutting-off of eastern goods, a swollen city population and army needs usually guaranteed easy sales, but a severe shortage of raw materials and transportation difficulties often hampered regular production. Hoarding was a logical answer to the problems of material supply. In turn, this led to a vicious circle of inflation.

Retail market prices in Xi'an doubled in 1940 and tripled in 1941 – actually a lower rate of inflation than in the wartime capital of Chungking. From 1942 onwards, inflation became rampant, up to 400 percent a year.[31] The prices of manufactures (and especially imported goods) rose much faster than those of raw materials. Coal and cotton remained cheap, while wheat, iron and salt became very expensive. See Table 9.

According to some, until 1940 the rate of inflation was much higher than the increase of the amount of money in circulation, and hoarding of goods was the major cause of inflation.[32] For the early war years, this may indeed have been the case, at least if one goes by money issuance alone. Money supply was greatly increased after 1939, when a dozen major national banks established branches in Xi'an. During 1941–4, the government established eight county banks, mainly in north Guanzhong, but also in Lantian and in Tongguan, of very small size.[33] The provincial government remained in a very difficult financial position. Central government subsidies decreased every year, from 22 percent of the provincial budgetary income in 1937 to 13 percent in 1939 and 9 percent in 1940–1. Income from opium fines went down as well, especially after 1939. Provincial bonds issued during 1939–41 covered about one quarter of the budgetary income. The only solid sources of income, the 'special consumption tax' (a kind of VAT) and the land tax together represented only 30 percent of the budgetary income of 1941. So from here, too, inflationary pressures were strong. There are no budgetary data for the late war years – there may not even have been a budget.[34]

The picture of industrial development in Xi'an during the late war years is rather diverse. It seems that the large cotton textile mills suffered most from the war. The industrial cooperatives, which had been set up with government backing in Baoji, Xi'an and other cities since 1938, flourished during 1940 and 1941, but then declined. Inflation, inability to compete with Japanese goods, capital shortage, lack of funds for procuring raw materials on the black market, and insufficient government support have been indicated as major causes for their demise.[35] However, the number of small factories in Xi'an continued to expand during the war, although not sufficiently to create enough employment for the refugees who kept flowing in. In

Table 9 *Relative prices of some raw materials and manufactured goods in Xi'an, 1937–1942/1943.*
(April 1937 = 100)

Raw Materials	April 1942	April 1943
Iron	8800	26333
Coal	1667	4259
Cotton	1058	5543
Wheat	2875	12917
Wood (fuel)	1800	6111
Tobacco	3442	5870
Salt	3989	9889

Manufactures	April 1942	April 1943
Steel	5517	26897
Iron nails (import)	26667	29778
Cotton yarn	2800	10232
Cotton native cloth	2643	16369
Cotton seed oil	3444	22500
Wheat flour (native)	3381	14238
Paper (Machieh)	4381	11587
Cigarettes (import)	30470	144017
Hydrochloric acid	2667	5337

Source: Yin-yuen Wang, 'Price Margins of Important Raw Materials and Manufactured Goods in Sian, Shensi', *Economic Facts* No. 27 (Dec. 1943), p. 307–13.

1942, there were 64 factories, only 3 of which had a capital of over one million *yuan*. Almost half of these were located outside the city walls in the new eastern city district or near the railway station. The next year, the number of factories had doubled to 135 (not-officially registered factories excluded). Most of these produced textiles or machinery.[36]

Coal consumption in Xi'an, which was mainly by factories and the power station and therefore may serve as an indicator of industrial production, doubled between 1940 and 1941 to 133,500 tons. Production of the Tongchuan coal mines rose from 129,000 tons in 1940 to 232,000 tons in 1941 and 250,000 tons in 1942. There were over 3,000 miners in Tongchuan alone at that time, almost all refugees from Henan province. From 1943 on, however, the Longhai railway wagons became unavailable, transport was halted, and one after another the mines had to stop operation. Xi'an and Xianyang then suffered from a lasting coal shortage.[37]

Compared with industrial development in other provinces of Free China there were similarities and differences. The pattern of growth during the early war years and of decline after 1942 was about the same. Throughout the period, each year Shaanxi province had some 5 to 7 percent of the number and capital of newly registered industries in Free China. This was about as much as Hunan or Guangxi provinces had, almost twice the amount in Gansu, but only less than a quarter of the newly-registered industries and their capital in the Chongqing area. See Tables 10 and 11. There were major differences as well, in branches of industry and in ownership. While Sichuan experienced a great expansion of iron, chemical and machinery industry, in Shaanxi industrial development remained linked to its agricultural bases: cotton and foodstuffs. Lack of minerals, of coal mines and of cheap river transport were the major factors which put Guanzhong at a disadvantage. In contrast with most other areas of Free China, in Shaanxi only a small minority of industrial companies was owned or run by the government, although usually the larger ones. Private industry, with 89 percent of all companies owned 68 percent of the total registered capital during the war period. Government investment in new industries was at its peak during 1939–41, when 29 new public companies were set up in Shaanxi, with a total capital of over 7 million *yuan*. In the subsequent three years, only five industries were set up by the government, with a total capital of less than 100,000 *yuan*.[38]

A survey of the industrial situation in 1945 showed that at the end of the war, Shaanxi's industries – 1905 in all – were still very much

Table 10 *Number of newly registered factories[x] in Shaanxi, 1936–1944*

Until 1936	1937	1938	1939	1940	1941	1942	1943	1944	date unclear	total
21	6	20	69	45	71	72	33	52	6	367

Table 11 *Newly registered factories, capital and workers in some areas of Free China, and transferrals from the East*

	Shaanxi	Gansu°	Sichuan	Chongqing	Free China total	Shaanxi share of total (%)
no. of factories	367	220	1,134	1,518	5,266	7.0
capital (million *yuan*)	316	167		1,408	4,801	6.6
workers (thousands)	31.2	10.4	64.8	90.9	359.6	8.7
no. of factories moved West	26		319		410	6.3
no. of technicians moved West	352		7,311		11,036	3.2

[x] According to the registration rules of the Ministry of Economic Affairs, in order to be registered a factory should meet at least one of the following three conditions: more than 30 employees, mechanized production, capital larger than 10,000 *yuan*. Mines are excluded.

° Oil excluded.

Sources: Li Zixiang, 'A bird's eye's view of the industry in the rear area during the war', *Jingji Zhoubao* Vol. 1 no. 6 (1945), pp. 10–12, 'The great west movement of industry', *ibidem* no. 7, pp. 12–14, and 'The development of industry in the rear area', *ibidem* no. 8, pp. 12–15.

Table 12 *Industrial production in Shaanxi, 1945°*

Branch	Number of industries	Monthly output
cotton textiles	879	3,907 rolls (16–20 feet wide)
woollens	25	166,200 yards (uniform cloth)
wheat flour	13	167,300 sacks (of 20 kg)
metal goods: iron	114	76,722 tons
other	141	–
machinery, tools	210	300 tons
matches	6	8,400 boxes
paper	4	120 tons
breweries	210	–
distilleries	6	89,900 bottles
dyestuffs	4	–
medicine	5	–
cigarettes	13	1,704 boxes
leather goods	60	38,300 ox hides
candles and soap	95	9,600 resp. 21,000 boxes
print shops	32	–
acids	2	108 tons
oil pressing	4	300 tons
cement	1	510 tons
glass	9	60 tons
other	162	–
Total	1,995	

°Communist areas excluded.

Source: Bai Yinyuan, 'Present situation and future of construction of Shaanxi', *Shaanzheng* Vol. VIII no. 1–2 (1946), pp. 12–21.

agriculture-oriented. Cotton textile production was lower than at the end of the 1930s, because of the decline in cotton: the 1945 and 1946 cotton harvests yielded slightly over 500,000 *dan*, half the level of 1936–40. Wheat flour industries had expanded considerably during the war, mainly because of demands created by an increased urban population but also because of a shift to wheat instead of other foodgrains.[39] See Table 12.

In 1943, recommendations were made for post-war reconstruction of Northwest China by an investigation team under Warren Kuo. They concluded that Xi'an lacked too many resources in its surroundings, and could not become a national capital. It would be the major basis for the development of the Northwest, however. One should expect that the skilled people who had gone west because of the war would return to the more affluent areas in the east once the war was over. Therefore, the central government should provide incentives for skilled people (locals included) to stay. As the natural cotton district for the Northwest, Guanzhong should be developed into its centre of cotton textile industry, with a supporting steel industry. Xi'an and Baoji (and Tongchuan for coal and cement) should become major industrial bases.[40]

The war was not over yet, however, and would be followed by civil war. In 1944 and 1945, inflation, taxation, repression, military damage and urban shortages of food and industrial goods got worse. It has been argued that in times of national stress, instability and wartime, Chinese citizens are likely to seek safety and refuge in the countryside.[41] Like the war-time capital Chongqing, Xi'an was exceptional in that its population continued to increase – to 400,000 by the end of 1944.

The various schemes of resettlement in the north Guanzhong mountains had succeeded in accomodating some 70,000 civilians and soldiers by 1943. Then, people started coming back. Agricultural reclamation was slow because of difficult terrain, lack of supplies, and rural unsafety – only to be expected as the sites of the largest reclamation areas had been chosen with the purpose of containing the communist threat from the north.[42] Few city refugees were prepared to move into such areas, or even to leave Xi'an for smaller cities. A growing number of people in Xi'an was unemployed and dependent on state relief. In winter 1943–4, 132,000 people received relief food from the provincial government in Shaanxi; two-thirds of those lived in Xi'an, as against only one or two thousand in the other towns of Guanzhong.[43]

Living conditions in Xi'an suffered from housing and water shortages. The well water in the city became bitter and saline – a phenomenon which had also occurred during the Tang dynasty.[44] Immigrants were particularly vulnerable to some endemic diseases, such as goitre and malaria. Infectious diseases made life in Xi'an unhealthy. Nevertheless, with 300 hospital beds and 80 doctors Xi'an had two-thirds of all modern health facilities in Guanzhong, a medical college, a school for midwives, and a Hygienic Cadres Training Institute.[45] Also, Xi'an was the starting point of public health programs. Both government and missionary organizations made considerable efforts to improve urban health.[46] Because of the presence of so many soldiers, officials, students and temporary labourers from rural areas, the population was predominantly male; in December 1944, there were 248,000 men and 144,000 women.[47] Thus, no 'normal' birth and death rates could be expected. In 1939, with a more normal composition of the population, both birth and death rates had been 20 per 1,000. In 1949, the birth rate was considerably higher (28/1,000) and the death rate somewhat lower (16/1,000). During both years, however, infant mortaility was estimated to be as high as 200 per 1,000.[48] Between 1945 and 1949, health facilities were expanded both by the government and by missionary organizations.[49]

Economic and other information on the final war years and subsequent civil war period in Xi'an is scarce. The bumper wheat harvest of 1944 eased the urban food supply situation, but in 1945 the wheat harvest was a disastrous failure, being only half the size of the previous year.[50] Refugees kept coming in, from Henan after the Japanese offensive in 1944, and from northern Guanzhong during the civil war. While official figures gave a population number of about 500,000 for Xi'an in 1948, local reports went as high as 700,000. Most of the newly arrived refugees lived in shacks or holes built outside the city walls. After the Japanese defeat, part of the refugees (especially intellectuals from the east) left, but many more stayed on. In March of 1947, Chiang Kai-Shek assembled a 230,000-man strong army in Xi'an and recaptured part of northern Shaanxi. Within one year, however, the wheat-producing counties of Hancheng, Chengcheng and Heyang had been lost again, and in the west, traditional wheat suppliers such as Wugong and Qianxian counties had almost returned to autarchy because traffic was unsafe. When the communist troops raided this area in May 1948, wheat prices on the Xi'an market rocketed by 50 percent, then came down, and went up by 70 percent again when Tongguan was closed off.[51]

Local government came into an increasingly difficult position. Even though Xi'an itself was safe enough, the various attacks and counterattacks in the north of Guanzhong led to violent fluctuations in material supplies. The maintenance of the Hu Zongnan's armies (variously estimated as between 200,000 and 400,000) took up most of the provincial budget, and more than it could bear by itself.[52] Inflation was fueled not only by local deficit spending, hoarding and speculation, but also imported from outside: the Nanking government note issue increased by 20 times between 1944 and 1946, and by 100 times between 1946 and 1948. Prices followed suit.[53] In May 1948, Xi'an presented a gloomy picture:

The city has fallen in the grip of hunger. Some old people starved . . . youngsters beg. Faces are somber. Government efforts at price control have been counterproductive. The officially fixed price for flour actually has driven up black market prices; these in turn led the official price. The government is really powerless. Inflation is unprecedented and will probably become worse. Because the war expands, rural production declines and urban industry has a shortage of materials . . . Supply cannot meet demand in any way. Military expenditure of the government is huge, but the area it controls has shrunk and therefore its income decreases every day.[54]

A year later, on 20 May 1949, Xi'an was taken over by the communists. During the civil war, Hu Zongnan's armies had been too strong to be attacked. When Henan province fell to the communist armies, however, Guanzhong was cut off. Hu Zongnan was ordered to draw back across the Qinling mountains to Hanzhong, and from there to Sichuan province. For defense, a 30-kilometer long moat had been dug around Xi'an by conscript labour but the final transfer of power was peaceful, without damage to the city. Communist troops marched in through the north and west gates while Hu Zongnan's troops were still leaving through the south gate.[55]

C. INDUSTRIALIZATION AND IMMIGRATION DURING THE 1950S.

Economic priorities of the new government were restoration of production, control of inflation, organization of labour, and improvement of urban facilities and labour conditions. After a year or two, it had succeeded rather well in most respects. For some unfortunate reason, in measuring economic performance the year of 1949 has usually been taken as a base year by the communists. This was a most unstable year, however, because of civil war, revolution and change of government. Between 1949 and 1952, industrial production output value (inclusive of handicrafts) went up by 115 percent.[56] Most of this increase can be attributed to an increased output per labourer, and not to new production facilities.[57] Anti-inflation measures of the government included the seizure of banks[58] and grain stocks, payments in kind, and re-opening of trade flows. The shortage of wheat in the east coast cities drove up prices in Xi'an as well. In August 1950, a catty of wheat which cost 666 *yuan* in Xi'an would bring 920 *yuan* in Tianjin, so in order to reduce the outflow of foodgrain the official purchase price of wheat in Xi'an was raised to 740–780 *yuan* in October, to 850 *yuan* in early December and to 930 *yuan* and 970 *yuan* in January and February 1951. Black market prices usually were 5 to 10 percent higher than that.[59] Cotton cloth prices had risen sharply in 1950 compared to before the war, in terms of grain by 40 to 70 percent. Its causes were the war damage to industry, high production and sales costs, a breakdown of old commercial networks which the communist government had not been able to replace yet, and the stop of foreign imports of cotton.[60] During the year of 1950, prices of eight daily commodities in the cities rose by 70 percent, but in 1951 prices were basically stable.[61]

Organization of labour was effectuated through labour unions, most of which had existed prior to 1949 and were now transformed in a communist sense. By October 1950, already 40 percent of the 64,000 labourers and employees in Xi'an municipality participated in the labour unions.[62] The government as a rule had not changed the private ownership of capitalist enterprises, although it nationalized the largest cotton textile company in Xi'an, the Yongxing Company, which belonged to the China Bank.[63] Through the Party and labour unions, however, workers were stimulated to demand better treatment – long working hours (usually 12 hours per day), scolding, a ban on attending meetings and payments in kind instead of wages were common complaints[64] – wage demands were out of the question. Early in 1952, the 15,000-odd industrialists and traders of Xi'an were forced in mass meetings to confess to some 25,000 economic crimes – eight that didn't were arrested.[65]

In 1952, both labour conditions and wages of workers in State-owned enterprises were considerably improved. This attracted a swelling number of labourers from the country.

The peasantry say 'you are better off as a vagrant than as a farmer.' A single worker of 40 to 50 years old will be able to receive, apart from food, clothing and lodging, from several *yuan* to ten *yuan* bonus a month. This is several times as much as a peasant in North Shaanxi . . . Too many construction workers have flocked into the city. Until 1951, they would return home in winter. But after the wage raises of 1952 a worker could sustain a family. So workers with a trade took their relatives to Xi'an to live. This resulted in a housing shortage.[66]

In the first few post-war years, although wages were low, workers usually did not have to pay for housing, water, electricity and other services. For regular workers in state-owned enterprises several wage raises adding up to about 30 percent were effected in 1953, 1954 and 1956; part of this was intended to cover rent and costs of increased services.[67] Many 'temporary' workers, however, remained outside this state-employed sector.

> I have been a temporary worker in the edible-oil refinement department of a marketing and sales cooperative for three years. I work all day, with no social activities . . . There is little concern for our education, rest and social welfare. We work 11 to 12 hours per day, sometimes 13 or 14 hours. The wage is low, mostly 15 to 16 *yuan* per month . . . The labourers cannot support themselves.[68]

Urban facilities improved by the municipal government in the early post-war years included a new water-works in 1952 (which added some capacity to the waterworks completed in 1946), an electric power station in 1953, road pavements and sewerage.[69] The big boom in city construction came in 1954, as a consequence of the major economic role attributed to Xi'an in the First Five-Year Plan. Within just three years, state investments in industry, culture and education, city utilities and housing rose tenfold (See Table 13).

It would be a mistake, however, to attribute the rapid growth of population and economy of Xi'an after 1949 wholly to state development policies. At times, refugees and peasants flocked into Xi'an in spite of government measures to stop them. When the war was over, many young soldiers found that their native village offered no satisfactory position to them – which often had been the very reason why they had had to enlist before. Land Reform in 1950–1 made people flee who were not in good standing with the new village leadership, who were dispossessed or vulnerable to communist attacks because of their economic position or previous association with the Guomindang army or government. Also, the Yellow River floods of 1947 and 1949 and the recurrent droughts in western Henan during the early 1950s made Henanese peasants move to Guanzhong and a return home from Xi'an unattractive.

Some state policies pushed villagers to the city, notably the general anti-capitalist attitude against peasants operating small-scale production facilities such as oil-presses, and more specifically, the virtual interdiction of rural grain milling and cotton weaving from 1953–4. The cotton textile handicraft production had especially provided income and employment to tens of thousands of villagers in Xingping,

Table 13 *Completed state investments in capital construction and housing in Xi'an, 1953–1957*

(1952 = 100)

	1953	1954	1955	1956	1957 (plan)	Share of 1953–1957 total (%)
Completed investments in capital construction	109	283	381	915	579	
of which: industry	198	384	648	1,675	1,130	60.2
culture/education	199	239	237	564	313	16.6
urban utilities	75	174	213	504	349	5.2
Surface of housing construction	238	239	705	1,065	717	

Source: Xi'an Ribao 2 and 3 Oct. 1957.

Liquan and Weinan counties and in the Jinghui and Weihui irrigation district areas; this ended when the government ordered in 1954 that cotton-producing peasants should sell all their raw cotton to the state, except for a kilogram or two for their own private use.

Seen in international perspective, since World War II urban growth rates of 5 or 6 percent per year have been quite common in developing countries. Irrespective of governmental policies, the pull effects of large cities have been quite strong. With the foundation of Higher Agricultural Producers' Cooperatives in 1956 an even stronger economic and organizational framework had been created which was able to stop peasants from leaving for the city; by that time also urban social control had been tightened a great deal.

Rhoads Murphey distinguished three main categories of administrative rules by which the Chinese government tried to stop urban immigration. First were population registration regulations, which required the population to carry a form of identity card. Second were regulations governing changes in employment. Third were, after 1954, regulations governing the control of primary foodstuffs. None of these controls were fully effective prior to 1958, because of black markets for papers and food, because of rural cadres desiring to get rid of surplus labour, and because of city employers hiring cheap illegal labourers, not through the Labour Bureau.[70] In the case of Xi'an, controls were further weakened by the stop–go policies of the local government during the years 1957 through 1959, to which we will revert later.

The principles of communist urban planning have been described in several general articles by Western writers. Mao's slogan of 1949 'transform consumer cities into producer cities' was taken from other socialist countries[71] and so was the very centralized state-directed approach to city planning. The geographical dispersal of industries and population and the construction of new industrial cities in interior areas as carried out in the First Five-Year Plan was an imitation of Soviet principles and experiences. Specific to China was the anti-urban legacy left to Chinese communism when the urban communist movement had been completely wiped out in 1927–30. The cities, and especially treaty port cities, came to stand for Western and Japanese imperialism. Guomindang rule also had tainted the urban image. Thus, in the early communist period, the city was seen as the centre of undesirable social and economic forces. Although the Soviet Union approach to socialist construction implicitly favoured large cities, yet from the beginning, Chinese planners have tried to keep city growth down as much as possible.[72]

During the 1950s, this goal was reinforced by the general idea that the east coast cities had grown out of proportion. New industrial bases would have to be set up in interior areas, so as to achieve a more balanced spatial distribution of industry and bring industries closer to their raw materials and energy bases. Also, the growth of small and medium size cities would provide each province with centres of modernization. These centres should be politically and economically capable of fulfilling their roles as 'growth poles' of the socialist economy, and therefore they were put in command of most resources of the surrounding area. As Skinner remarked, Chinese municipalities have largely been the creation of a modern centralizing government, created and enlarged by fiat. Municipal boundaries have been drawn to incorporate the entire built-up area of the city, industrial and residential suburbs included, plus rural areas important to the city's viability and future development.[73] The aforementioned characteristics of Chinese city development were especially strong in Xi'an, which always had been an administrative centre rather than a commercial one, and which never had been a treaty port with commercial quarters.

Xi'an municipality was created in 1944. After the communist takeover, for one year, it was administered by the Shaan Gan Ning

Border Region Government, which established itself in Xi'an. Then it was brought under control of the Northwest Military Region Administrative Committee, and in March 1953 it became a city under direct control of the central government. Only in June 1954, when the Northwest Region was abolished, did Xi'an come under Shaanxi provincial control. The municipal area was enlarged to 567 square kilometers. In November 1958, four neighbouring counties Changan, Huxian, Lantian and Lintong were incorporated into the municipality with retainment of their county status. (See Map 6) Three years later, this incorporation was undone, as part of the restoration of the administrative situation before the Great Leap Forward. In September 1965, the five suburban districts of Baqiao, Yata, Weiyang, Caotan and Afang (Changle had been abolished in 1957) were combined into one surburban district; this was split up again into three districts in 1980. Of these, the Yata district controls 9 People's Communes and Street Committees in the south, the Baqiao district controls 10 People's Communes and Street Committees in the east, and the Weiyang district controls 7 People's Communes and Street Committees to the north and west of the walled city. The three districts of the inner city, Lianhu, Beilin and Xincheng have not changed since 1949, except in name during the Cultural Revolution when they were to carry rather unoriginal names such as Hongwei (Red Soldier) and Dongfeng (East Wind). In 1966, Yanliang district, an airfield and a town at 80 kilometers from Xi'an, was transferred from Lintong county to Xi'an municipality. The incorporation of Xianyang municipality under Xi'an in the same year was undone in 1971.[74] Although we have little information about the reasons for these administrative changes. it seems clear that Changan was slowly absorbed, while sudden enlargements of the administrative area of Xi'an occurred in periods of an expansive mood in politics, only to be undone subsequently.

In 1983 again, several neighbouring counties have been brought under the administrative control of Xi'an municipality.[75]

The population of Xi'an grew by about 80,000 per year between 1949 and 1953. High birth rates (up to 48.3/1,000 by 1956) and low death rates (down to 7.5/1,000 by 1956) resulted in a natural increase of 10,000–20,000 per year;[76] immigrant labourers and their dependents, and villages incorporated in the new city outlay of 1954 made up the major part of the increase. The First Five-Year Plan speeded up the growth of Xi'an even more, especially in the years 1954 through 1956. Of the 156 key projects in this plan, 24 were in Xi'an. Xi'an was meant to become, together with Lanzhou and Baotou, one of the three new industrial centres of northwest China, and a centre of commerce, administration and education as well. The abolition of the Northwest Region diminished Xi'an's supraprovincial economic position to a certain extent, but did not affect its prime position as the supplier of industrial products and the gateway to the Northwest.

New industries set up by the central government under the First Five-Year Plan included a thermo-power station, a building construction company, a textile finishing plant, several cotton mills, a textile printing and dyeing works, oil and fats factories, flour mills and an enamelware factory. Heavy industrial development got even more emphasis: large manufacturing plants making electrical appliances, power generators, diesel engines, electric motors, measuring equipment, dyestuffs, oxygen and many other producers' goods. Altogether 77 nationally-owned industries were founded, of which more than twenty had an employment larger than 1,000 workers.[77] New industries founded by provincial or municipal government generally were smaller in scale, numbered 120, and produced a wide range of both producers' and consumers' goods. Bricks and tiles, metalwares, electric appliances, oxygen, farm implements, boilers, automobile spare parts, chemical products, rubberware, plastic wares, and consumer items such as flour, cotton cloth and pharmaceuticals. Some of these products, notably bed sheets, precision instruments, electric machinery, enamelware, varnish and paint, bone powder and asbestos, were of a quality high enough to be exported abroad. In 1956, the total value of industrial output (inclusive of local State-owned and joint State–private industries and city cooperatives) was already three times as much as in 1952, and 16 percent higher than the original target for 1957. Between 1949 and 1952, Xi'an's gross value of industrial output had increased by 110 percent to about 150 million *yuan*; between 1952 and 1957 it rose again by 220 percent, or by 26 percent per year, to 550 million *yuan*.[78] This growth rate was considerably more rapid than that for the entire province of Shaanxi.[79] See Table 14.

In spite of many calls for restraint, following material shortages during early 1957, investments in capital construction increased by 40 percent over the previous year. This was partly due to the definite shift from central government investments to provincial and local investments which occurred after the decentralization policies of 1957. In

Table 14 *Output increases of some major products in Xi'an, 1949–1956*
(1949 = 100)

1956

Gross Industrial Output Value	786	Cotton cloth	934
Gross value of handicraft production	520	Printed cloth	1796
Machinery	3400	Edible plant oil	1890
Electricity	1978	Flour	314
Spindles	746	Soap	649

Sources: Xi'an Ribao 7 Sept. 1957; *Zhongguo Xinwen* 16 Nov. 1957.

this final year of the First Five Year Plan for Xi'an 60 million *yuan* was invested in local industries (as against only 35 million *yuan* in the previous four years), out of a total industrial investment of 76 million *yuan*. 44 percent of this sum still was financed by the Central Government, the remaining majority of the capital came from the local government, banks and other local sources.[80]

Much more publicity was given to the creation of new State-owned industries than to the gradual breaking-up of existing private industry and handicraft production. Private industries continued to be strong in cotton textiles and food products until 1954. From then onwards, they were gradually converted into joint State–private industries, a process completed by 1956. Lack of orders, shortage of raw materials, lack of qualified manpower, lack of funds, unfair competition by State enterprises and harassment by State and Party officials drove them slowly out of business. Especially the larger enterprises saw their turnover diminish rapidly in 1954 and 1955, while the smaller ones held their ground only in the sectors of foodstuffs and combustibles retail sales.[81]

According to official data, which are likely to be an undercount, in 1954 70 percent of the industrial labour force of Shaanxi province worked as an individual, in private, small industries with less than 10 employees, or in handicraft cooperatives (see table 15). Their total production value was 278 million *yuan*, or 35 percent of the total gross industrial output value. Their average gross output value per labourer was only one-sixth of that in privately-owned large industries and State-owned industries. This may be ascribed, among other

Table 15 *Industrial labour and gross output value in Shaanxi, 1954*

	No. of labourers	%	Gross Output Value (million yuan)	%	GIOV per labourer (yuan) A	B
individual industries (rural included)	139,247	53.4	214.4	27.3	1,540	1,197
private small industries (< 10 employees)	22,168	8.5	35.7	4.6	1,610	1,861
handicraft coops	21,696	8.3	18.9	2.4	870	2,371
(other handicrafts)			9.2	1.2		
private large industries } State-owned industries }	77,839	29.9	507.0	64.6	8,740	—
Total	260,950	100	785.3	100 .	3,009	—

N.B. GIOV per labourer (A) has been derived from other data. The source itself gives quite different figures for 'Output Value' per industrial labourer, which appear in the last column (B). Of the 21,696 handicraft coop members, only 5,530 are stated to be members of *production* coops, the others being also engaged in marketing and sales. This suggests a much higher productivity in handicraft cooperatives. There is not enough data to reconcile the differing figures.

Source: Zhongguo Kexueyuan Jingji Yanjiusuo (ed.), *1954-Nian Quanguo Geti Shougongye Diaocha Ziliao*, Beijing 1957.

things, to mechanized production, economies of scale, and to a higher value of inputs.

Of these individual industries, one quarter (by output value) was located in Xi'an; in metal-work 45 percent and in textile handicrafts 72 percent. Of the private small industries, 81 percent (again by output value) was located in Xi'an.[82]

After the nationalization or cooperativization measures in 1955 and 1956,[83] most individual industries and trades had to be ended or were driven underground. In 1956–8, 8,000–9,000 households continued to operate individually, against growing political opposition. Early in 1957, some people advocated legalization of the small unlicensed retailers and manufacturers still existing in Xi'an, because of their important economic function. In vegetable retail sales, for instance, they constituted 44 per cent of all greengroceries.[84] The anti-rightist campaign of 1957, however, and the high tide of socialist and collectivist fervour during the Great Leap Forward made individual enterprises or handicrafts into economically backward and politically dangerous undertakings. As the mayor of Xi'an, Liu Geng, reported to the People's Congress on 29 May 1958: 'Unlawful activities including black marketing, operating underground factories and speculating which had once made their appearance again were promptly stopped . . . Individual handicraftsmen and peddlers have further realized the dead end of capitalism and hence have voluntarily obeyed . . .'[85]

Of the above-mentioned labourers in Xi'an, non-licensed so-called 'black' families constituted 16 percent in 1954 and 25 percent in 1955, at least according to official statistics which could not be very accurate.[86] In 1956 45 percent of all small traders were transformed into cooperatives, and the remaining 17,000 traders were integrated in 1958.[87]

We may conclude that to a very considerable extent the growth of the labour force in state enterprises during the Five-Year Plan period was drawn from absorption of private industries and trades. The combination of their labour skills and the modern means of production provided by the State was responsible for the sharp rise in production.

At the end of 1956, for the first time the local press printed stories about the problems of rapid urbanization. For regular State employees, working and living conditions had become very tight. A letter to the Shaanxi Daily described the cramped situation of a handicraft management bureau, where 23 employees shared one office of 38 square meters, containing 18 tables and 18 chairs, and a dormitory of

Table 16 *Industrial labour, gross and net output value in three types of industry in Xi'an, 1954 (Sept.) and 1955 (Aug.)*

Type of industry	No. of labourers		GIOV (million yuan)		GIOV per labourer (yuan)		Added Value (million yuan)		Added Value per labourer (yuan)	
	1954	1955	1954	1955	1954	1955	1954	1955	1954	1955
individual	21,433	20,778	39.2	37.9	1,830	1,820	18.8	17.8	878	856
small private	6,030	5,797	16.6	10.8	2,750	2,840	11.2	6.3	1,855	1,653
coops	(1,379)	5,189		(13.9)	—	—	—	—	—	—
Total	28,842	29,764	(71.1)	62.6						

Source: Zhongguo Kexueyuan Jingji Yanjiusuo (ed.), *1954-Nian Quanguo Geti Shougongye Diaocha Ziliao*, Beijing 1957. ( ) = derived figure

13 square meters with 4 beds. 'People go to the railway station in order
to sleep, but it is very noisy there.'[88] New construction workers and
industrial workers had come to Xi'an in such large numbers that there
was nowhere to lodge and feed them. Many boarded out with peasant
households in the vicinity of Xi'an, but that was inconvenient for
transport and gave rise to social tensions. Some slept at their
construction site, in the open air or in temporary shacks. This was
usual for the peasant labour gangs which were fetched from seventeen
counties in Guanzhong to assist with construction work in Xi'an,
13,000 peasants in all, and another 9,300 from the calamity-stricken
provinces of Henan and Hebei, most of them refugees. Thousands of
these temporary construction workers received training on the job,
and were eventually made into permanent skilled workers.[89] Altogether almost 100,000 labourers were needed for capital construction
projects in Xi'an, the nearby towns of Xianyang and Huxian, and
Baoji.[90] Early in 1957, however, the State investment and construction
program was cut back 'because of shortage of supplies' and many of the
temporary construction workers were sent home.[91] People previously
designated as 'cooperative members who assist in construction' now
came to be called 'peasants who flock blindly into the cities'.[92]

The refugees from other provinces were the first to be urged to go:

Our province is a region with good harvests for successive years, and in the past
has already given some aid to outside refugees. We have some capital
construction projects which attract refugees for temporary labour. Before
September last year, we gave them the necessary support, and either sent them
back to their villages or gave them temporary resettlement. After September
. . . we did not resettle them any more. We promulgated two directives to urge
all local authorities to send them back. We founded 'refugee returnment
stations' in Xi'an, Baoji, Xianyang, Tongchuan, Lintong, Weinan and
Huanglongshan. From September last year till 10 March our province spent
820,000 *yuan* in travel fees and economic support. We want the refugees to
return . . .[93]

In the summer of 1957, however, capital construction in Xi'an reached
new peaks, and the send-back campaign was not heard of for some
months. With the winter season coming, again city authorities tried to
make over one hundred thousand temporary workers and dependents
leave. On 18 October the City People's Committee passed a 'Decision
on the population control work of our city', which referred in a very
negative manner to immigrant workers (estimated to number 60,000
at that time), who had no regular occupation, registration or fixed

address. Some were said to sell phony medicines or to trade illegally in State-controlled goods; they fell into thieving and 'directly threatened the safety of people's life and property'. Another 30,000 dependents, relatives of cadres and workers, would be sent to the production front. Population control committees were established at various levels.[94] Eventually about 130,000 refugees, unemployed, dependents and temporary workers were moved out of Xi'an, and in the first months of 1958 the 19 police precincts of Xi'an reported that there were no 'unregistered, falsely reported or unlawful residences' any more.[95] The pendulum swung back again in autumn, with the Great Leap Forward construction drive. In November 1958, the labour shortage was said to be intense, with a need for over 150,000 extra labourers in Xi'an city.[96]

As much as possible, instead of bringing in labour from outside of Xi'an, attempts were made to engage women and old people in productive work. Under the slogan 'Replace men with women' male workers from commercial and food departments were reassigned to steel production or other industrial work, and their place was taken by women.[97] By November 1958, 30,000 women participated in street factories and commercial collectives, 15,000 in State commercial organizations, 24,000 in State industries and 3,000 in State capital construction.[98] Because of the numerous organizational and administrative changes of the years 1958–60, and the very subjective reporting on economic activities, it is hardly possible to establish a valid picture of labour movements and economic growth during the Great Leap Forward. It is clear, though, that the 18 People's Communes formed out of the previous 607 Higher Agricultural Producers' Cooperatives of Xi'an municipality made a very flexible use of their labour force.[99] Both inside and outside their territory, peasants might engage in industry, construction, transport and trade. In how far the temporary extension of the Xi'an municipal authority over four neighbouring counties during 1958–61 (hailed by Christopher Howe, for Shanghai, as 'a major step forward in consolidating the strength of the core urban area . . . enabling the city to plan improvements of its food and raw material supply . . . paving the way for the growth of rural industry . . . lessening the peasants' motivation to migrate'[100]) had positive effects on planning and economic integration must remain an open question. In any case, it was a short-lived experiment.

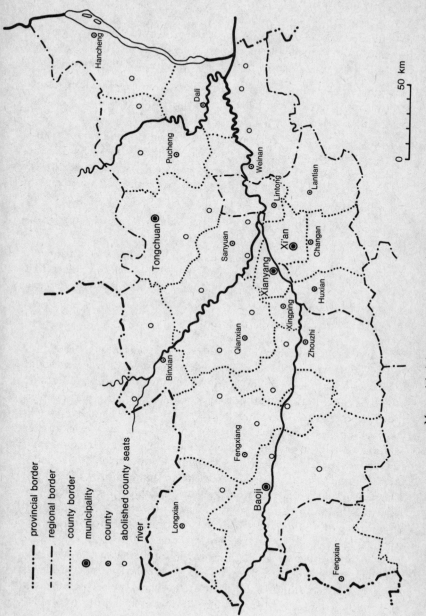

Map 7 Administrative divisions, 1958–1961

provincial border
regional border
county border
municipality
county
abolished county seats
river

Hancheng

Dali

Pucheng

Weinan

Lintong

Lantian

Tongchuan

Sanyuan

Xi'an

Changan

Xianyang

Xingping

Huxian

Qianxian

Zhouzhi

Binxian

Fengxiang

Longxian

Baoji

Fengxian

50 km

0

D. CITY PLANNING

As indicated above, during the 1950s the growth of Xi'an city and its population was partly planned, partly spontaneous. In theory city planning was highly centralized. Major guiding principles were:

a   functional zoning, i.e. relatively homogenous zones of land use in different parts of the city. Industrial, residential, cultural and recreational areas were developed separately;

b   reduction of transportation need between residence, work, and commercial and social service centers. Preferably these should be at cycling distance. This called for a location of some light industries, shopping and servicing centers close to residential quarters;

c   wide, straight intersecting lanes;

d   a spacious setup of industries, with room for future expansion and storage of materials, and buffer zones;

e   three- or four-storied residential buildings, without elevators, with small 1 to 3 room apartments with shared kitchens and toilets. The norm for net living space per inhabitant was only about four square meters, reflecting a low priority for housing;

f   public but no private motorized transportation.

In practice, however, the first two principles might come into conflict with each other. Also, the political 'pull' of large national industries might be too strong for the municipal authorities to handle, especially because their urban planning departments were short on skilled manpower. According to K. I. Fung, several major factors contributed to a disorderly urban sprawl: legislative weaknesses relating to administration of land allocation, squandering of land (which was entirely free), indiscriminate adoption of Soviet regulations for industrial construction, and an acute shortage of urban planning resources. He mentions several examples of squandering of land in Xi'an from Chinese sources, e.g. a university which obtained 90 hectares to accommodate its planned future growth (from 3,000 students in 1957) to 12,000 students. At the end of 1956, there were 260,000 square meters of illegal construction in Xi'an city alone.[101]

During the short liberal period of early 1957, the Industrial and City Construction Bureau of Xi'an indicated several serious problems in city construction, and uttered a plea for more timely, more complete and more integrated planning. It noted that the demand for land had become increasingly greater. Industrial, cultural and educational tasks had been enlarged. The increased amount of construction also necessitated the use of more land for temporary residence.

We do not have good estimates of national and local construction, especially not of light industry, educational facilities and local service enterprises . . . We just blindly limit the development of population and land use, and turn our backs to the rules of economic development.

For housing, more space was used than the national norms allowed for. These had been reduced in 1956 to 6 square meters of living space (4 square meters of *net* space) and 1 square meter of public service buildings per person. The Bureau held that these standards were too low, and that 9 meters per person would be more proper. The housing mixture was wrong, too.

Without regard for the actual conditions of Xi'an, it has been arbitrarily ordained that 60 percent of housing construction should be apartment buildings and 40 percent single-storey houses. Square meter costs allowed for apartments has been lowered to 48 *yuan*, which is too low. For single-storied houses (with thatched roofs) the norm is only 38 *yuan* . . . Green areas of the city have been reduced considerably . . . Schools and factories are built far away, which is inconvenient for transportation.[102]

Several months later some national publications were equally critical of Xi'an's city development. Their criticisms were essentially similar. A Xinhua report wrote that the new city districts had been set up too spaciously. Yet net living space per inhabitant was only 2.6 square meters in 1957, as against 2.94 square meters in 1949. The usual form of constructing buildings along the streets first, leaving the middle area empty, was wasteful of land. The new four-storey buildings were twice as expensive as brick houses, which cost only 25 *yuan* per square meter to construct. His conclusion was that building standards should be adjusted downwards.[103] It was also suggested to raise rents, so as to stimulate upkeep of old houses. For five classes of homes (viz. concrete, tiled roof with brick walls, partly brick/partly mud walls, or entirely with mud walls, and thatched roof with mud walls) rents were proposed ranging from 6 *yuan* per month to 1.5–2 *yuan*. These rents were said to be 40 percent lower than the old rents, but slightly higher than the existing rents after rent reform.[104] In a

Shaanxi Ribao editorial, people were urged to build more private homes:

Xi'an has built 2.8 million square meters of living space since 1949 (at that time it had 2,250,000 square meters). Of this, only 3 percent has been built by private persons . . . With one thousand yuan one can build a two-room 25 square meter-home. If one doesn't need State investment, and moreover solves one's individual problem, this is advantageous both to the individual and the State.[105]

As far as can be ascertained, none of these suggestions had any noticeable effect in subsequent few years. Rents, norms for building cost, for living space per capita, and for building density, remained essentially unchanged.[106]

In line with some of the Chinese criticisms of this period, K. I. Fung has given a negative appraisal of Xi'an's city development policies. He writes that

Xi'an offers a good example of a chaotic and dispersed pattern of development . . . The majority of the factories in this new industrial city were scattered outside the existing built-up areas, because the building sites for these factories had been selected at random in an area to be used for long-term development. The 'textile city' of Xi'an was located at the banks of the Chanhe, about 8 kilometers from the city, and over 20 large State enterprises were scattered over the Northern and the Western suburban areas. As a result, new industrial projects were dispersed in all directions with a radius of between 20 and 30 kilometers from the city . . . It should be mentioned that these were not self-contained settlements like satellite industrial communities that possessed at least the basic amenities.[107]

Quite a different impression was received by Hans Schenk in 1971. He noted that Shanghai had developed new towns outside the former city limit, but that Xi'an had been developed in a different manner:

Xi'an's town extension are really *extensions*. The Ming town gradually spreads, and the surrounding former Tang town comes to new life. This process is deliberate: harmony and symmetry are carefully preserved; the existing gridiron pattern of roads is extended beyond the huge city walls and the city gates.[108]

The judgment passed by K. I. Fung may be considered too harsh. Indeed the situation of a dispersed pattern of industrial construction did create short-term problems of excessive land use; transportation was inconvenient and costly; urban facilities had to be extended further, which took time and also money. For some years, a situation existed of inadequate infrastructure, or as it was called by the Chinese, 'too much flesh but not enough bones'. There was a lack of good roads, of buses, of commercial services and of housing. Especially the housing shortage was very serious. Xi'an had already been overcrowded in 1949. The 2.6 square meters of living space per capita in 1956 was far below any other Chinese city, with the exception of that other fast-grower in the Northwest, Lanzhou.[109] Most facilities and social services had improved, but people's expectations and demands had risen as well. In 1957, less than half of Xi'an's population had running water, many students could not enter primary or secondary school, many sick people could still not enter hospital. In other counties of Guanzhong, however, this situation of insufficient infrastructure was even worse.[110] It was the sheer size of new industrial investment rather than the location of new industries that was responsible for shortages of housing, transportation facilities, material supplies and social services.[111] Such an imbalance was accepted by the Chinese government and Communist Party at that time as a temporary situation, and as an inevitable one if fast industrial growth was to be achieved. The subsequent Great Leap Forward showed that the Communist Party leaders were willing to go even further in sacrificing short-term conveniences to the all-overriding goal of economic growth (although long-term goals did include raised standards of citizens' living conditions).[112]

From a long-term point of view, the location of industries far away from the old walled city of Xi'an has been a fortunate choice of Chinese and Soviet planners during the First Five Year Plan. Of course, the Soviet Union had ample experience in planning new industrial cities, and one of their lessons obviously had been to leave much space for future expansion of industries, housing, traffic and recreational facilities. The location of industries in the vicinity of the East–West railroad but outside of the walled city continued a pattern set under the Guomindang. A railroad branch line in southwesterly direction to Huxian was constructed at considerable distance; it moves away from Xi'an and Changan, and for that reason Xi'an's southern suburbs and Changan have been able to maintain their agricultural character, cultural treasures and luring landscape. An additional reason for locating industries at some distance from Xi'an must have been the demand for easy access to river water for industrial use. The discharged water, most of which is heavily polluted, has been used to raise fish or to irrigate farmland in the northern suburban areas of

Xi'an.[113] Most of the housing and commercial facilities for the new industrial workers and their dependents were built either next to factories (as with the textile city in the east across the Chanhe river) or in the open space between the old walled city and the heavy industry in the west.[114] Thereby, the pressure on the walled city quarters has been reduced. By the 1970s, hospitals and educational facilities had been spread all over the city and its suburbs. Universities with their often spacious campuses have been concentrated in the 'cultural' area of the south (*see Map 8*).

The very wide thoroughfares built in the suburbs (and also, if possible, within the walled city) had elicited considerable criticism in 1957, when the General Engineer of the Xi'an Municipal Construction Bureau had been quoted as saying

Roads are built too wide. The main roads in the suburbs are all over 30 meters wide, and usually over 40 meters. Some even reach 80 to 100 meters' width. My objections to this have not been heeded. Reasons for that are the imitation of the Soviet Union, and the fear that after a number of years one would have to go through the trouble of enlarging them . . . In many places in the city there is a 6 to 9 meter wide green belt between the two driveways. This has no use, because cars do not go fast.[115]

With the value of hindsight, however, one might argue that these early wide roads have saved present and future costs of traffic congestion, and added to safe and pleasant road use by cyclists and pedestrians – still the main users. The fact that the old walled city and its cultural treasures have been well-preserved has become a major asset in attracting tourists.

Key to Map 8 opposite

1 Cars	12 Xinhua Printing	21 Fourth National Cotton
2 Red Flag Watches	13 Flour	22 Fifth National Cotton
3 Shaanxi 11th Cotton	14 Chemicals	23 Sixth National Cotton
4 Mining Machinery	15 High-Voltage transmission	24 Cement Products
5 Metallurgy	and generating equipment	25 Textile Printing and Dyeing
6 Pesticides	16 Transformers	26 Mechanized Brick
7 North West Textiles	17 Machines and Tools	27 Cotton Velvet
8 Textile Printing and Dyeing	18 Electric Power	28 Color Television
9 Cranes	19 Electric Power	29 First Municipal Milk
10 Steel	20 Third National Cotton	30 Minerals exploration
11 Pharmaceuticals		31 Measuring equipment

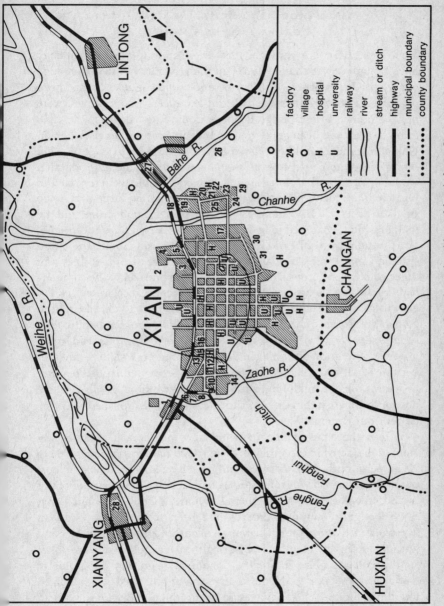

Map 8 Xi'an and surroundings, main factories, universities and hospitals, 1978

E. FOOD SHORTAGE AND INDUSTRIAL CRISIS AFTER THE GREAT LEAP FORWARD

The Great Leap Forward and People's Commune movement may have brought fewer changes to Xi'an than to cities not so accustomed to a frenzied pace of growth. The 300,000-odd peasants, who had been organized in 607 Higher Agricultural Producers Cooperatives, were now combined into 18 large People's Communes. Because the 1958 grain harvest had been good (750 kg per rural capita), as elsewhere in China, free meals could be offered in village mess halls. Creches were set up everywhere so as to enable women to participate in production work.[116] At the end of the year, some 40,000 people were reported to participate in local iron and steel production, in 53 large and 4,500 small furnaces.[117] One wonders where the iron ore came from, and the fuel; in winter, coal used to be in short supply. Vegetables had been in short supply as well, and the general optimism about the grain situation made People's Communes change over to vegetables and other commercial crops. In 1959 and 1960, expansion of the commercial vegetable area around Xi'an city was greatly accelerated. It had grown from 3,100 ha in 1955 to 7,900 hectares in 1958, and rose to 21,600 hectares in 1959 and 29,000 hectares in 1960. Per capita daily supply rose by 18 percent to 0.7 kg in 1960.[118] In 1960 and 1961, however, the grain situation in Xi'an became very tight – whether because of bad harvests in Shaanxi province, excessive exports to other provinces, or to malorganization and disruption of distributive networks, or a combination of these, cannot be established with the data at our disposal.[119]

Within the cities of Shaanxi, and also in Xi'an, a grain saving campaign started in the spring of 1959. 750 tons of grain were saved in Xi'an per month. Methods were publicized on how to make the most out of the reduced foodgrain rations, or according to the jargon of this period, 'revolutionary techniques of preparing food'. In Guanzhong, State foodgrain supply standards had been fixed in 1955 with an average yearly per capita distribution of 205 kilograms of summer and autumn grains to members of agricultural cooperatives. To put it simply, villages were entitled to retain at least 205 kilograms of foodgrain per capita, the necessary amount of seed, and a fixed amount of fodder. Those villages (later: Production Brigades) with an average availability of less than 180 kilograms of foodgrain per capita in a given year would be entitled to receive supplementary foodgrain up to that level.[120] In the 1970s, these minimum standards had been substantially lowered, to 180–200 kilograms per capita as the limit for supplying grain to the State and to 160 kilograms per capita for being entitled to supplementation of foodgrain;[121] it seems likely that these lowered standards were set during the post-Great Leap Forward food crisis. The campaign for saving grain met with considerable apprehension. Peasants and citizens feared that the saved grain would be requisitioned by the State and be distributed to others, that supply standards would be lowered and less would be distributed in the future. Also, by saving they would run the risk of being called capitalists by others.[122] According to official statistics, after November 1959 the rural population reduced its average monthly foodgrain consumption by 4.5 kilograms per capita – or by about one-quarter. Through the mess-halls (of which there were 13,900 in the rural districts of Xi'an and the four counties then under its administrative control, so their size was quite small) foodgrain consumption could be kept under control.[123] In an effort to stimulate peasants to sell foodgrain, in September 1959 the Central Government slightly relaxed the monopsonist position it had held for two years, and allowed again a certain amount of free grain trade.

Although highly speculative, on the basis of some foodgrain production data for smaller areas and population data there is reason to believe that the food crisis did not affect Shaanxi as much as it did China.[124] The effect of the People's Commune organization on people's life and agricultural and industrial production in Xi'an cannot be separated from the larger context of an industrial breakdown, natural calamities and national shortages of foodgrain and cotton. Early appraisals of planning, industrial management, accounting, wage and supply systems and collective social services such as nurseries of the Dongfeng People's Commune in Xi'an were quite positive.[125] At the end of 1959, however, already 'some rightist elements . . . wanted to destroy the collective labour and slandered the People's Commune. They advocated giving land to the peasants.'[126] Whatever the success of large-scale organization in Shaanxi may have been, there is no indication that the national decision to set up People's Communes (within cities as well), their subsequent breakdown, and the eventual decision to scale down rural collectives and to disband urban communes were in any way influenced by developments in Shaanxi province.

According to recently published official data, between 1958 and

1962 (the so-called Second 5-Year Plan period, although there was no such plan) the economy of Shaanxi fared badly in all respects. In 1958, over four times as many capital construction projects had been started as in the previous year. From 1960 onwards, most of these had to be called off, because of shortage of materials, bad quality, inadequate surveying and planning, lack of demand, lack of skilled work force or for other reasons. Over 100 million *yuan* was lost because of abandoned large- and medium-scale reservoir projects, and another 200 million *yuan* because of other abandoned projects.[127] After 1959, agricultural production fell off to an all-time low in 1962. Industrial production increased until 1960, but then plummeted. In 1962, compared with 1958, foodgrain production had decreased by 22 percent,[128] cotton production by 66 percent, oil crops production by 74 percent, and the gross value of agricultural production by 30 percent. The gross value of industrial output in 1962 was 15 percent lower than that in 1957. Cotton yarn production went down by two-thirds between 1959 and 1962, and steel production, which had not reached more than 28,000 tons in 1960, came down to 7,000 tons. As a consequence, in 1962 gross total income in Shaanxi was 31.5 percent lower than it had been 5 years before, and the accumulation rate had gone down to 5.4 percent [129] Peasant purchase power was severely reduced.

For Xi'an, as for many other cities, the industrial breakdown and the food shortages after the Great Leap Forward marked the end of an expansionist period. Immigrant workers from other provinces, temporary labourers from the country, and many recent settlers and cadres were sent back to their place of origin. On the extent of depopulation of Xi'an there is no data. In Lanzhou, which had a similar size and economic position, the municipal population decreased by 156,700 people in 1961 and 1962; in 1962, the number of State labourers and employees was one-third less than five years before.[130] Not only in the provincial capital, but also in the smaller towns of Shaanxi was population reduced. Even before the Great Leap Forward started a run for industrial development and for Xi'an and other cities, the non-agricultural population had risen to 2.5 million, or 14 percent of the Shaanxi total.[131] Within two years, it increased by another million. In 1963, the non-agricultural population had been reduced to the 1957 level again, down to a mere 13 percent of Shaanxi's total population.[132] The margin of rural foodgrain surpluses, necessary to sustain a growing urban population, had obviously become too thin around 1960.

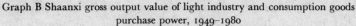

Graph B Shaanxi gross output value of light industry and consumption goods purchase power, 1949–1980

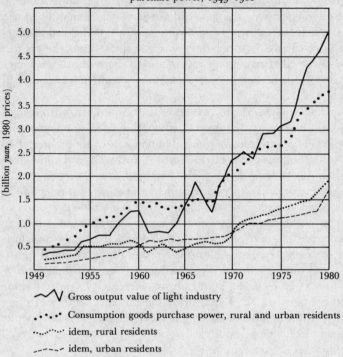

~~~V Gross output value of light industry

••••••• Consumption goods purchase power, rural and urban residents

•••••••••••• idem, rural residents

‒‒‒‒‒ idem, urban residents

Source: *Shaanxi Jingji Tantao*, Xi'an 1984

The small-scale private economy was restored for a short time. Xi'an had about 25,000 licensed households and 10,000 unlicensed workers operating in this sector in 1962. Political and economic pressure brought their numbers down to 3,500 by 1965, to be abolished completely by the Cultural Revolution.[133]

F. INDUSTRIAL GROWTH AND AN ASSESSMENT OF STRENGTHS AND WEAKNESSES IN THE 1980S

The 1960s and 1970s were a period of moderate growth and generally little qualitative improvement of Xi'an. The industrial picture was rather diverse. Cotton textile production, the mainstay of Xi'an's industry and of Shaanxi Province's exports, could not hold its ground against the East Coast cities for a variety of reasons, and slowly declined. The Central Government continued to invest in nationally-owned heavy industries, such as steel, power, machine-building, machine tools, chemicals, mining equipment, textile machinery, farm machinery, defense industries and civilian aircraft. Industrial production was boosted again during 1963–6. Since then, industrial growth has been sustained at an average rate of almost six percent a year until 1976, and 8.5 percent thereafter. 1982 GIOV was ten times as much as in 1957 (see Table 17).

We have no separate data for total industrial output, but for light industry only it appears that gross output value in Shaanxi rose from about 800 million *yuan* in 1961–3 to 1.8 billion *yuan* in 1966, then fell to 1.5 and 1.2 billion *yuan* respectively in 1967 and 1968 and climbed to 2.5–3 billion *yuan* during 1970–5.[134] After 1978, as a consequence of a national shift in priorities to less investment and more consumer goods, in Shaanxi most heavy industries stagnated. A notable exception to this was the airplane industry, which expanded rapidly since 1980 and employed over 100,000 people by 1984. Particularly the machine building industry, responsible for one-third of Shaanxi's total industrial output value, suffered from reductions in national capital construction.[135] In contrast, light industry increased its output value by one-third between 1978 and 1982. Output of sewing machines, watches, cigarettes, and woollen blankets almost doubled, while several completely new industries were set up with great success, notably bicycles and televisions.

In 1983–4, the pendulum swung back again. Many light industries (particularly cotton textiles) declined, and gross output value of light industry rose by 2 percent per year only; heavy industry, in contrast, picked up and its output value rose by 40 percent between 1982 and 1984 to a total of 8 billion *yuan* as against 6 billion *yuan* for light industry (see Table 18).

Forty to fifty percent of Shaanxi's industrial production was concentrated in Xi'an municipality and about 5 percent more if one includes a wider area of Xianyang, Changan and Huxian. Xianyang city is still mainly a textile centre, the textile industry being responsible for two-thirds of its total industrial output value in 1983. Several modern industries were located in Xianyang during the 1970s, however, notably nitrogenous fertilizer, pumps for deep wells, spool thread, typecasting machinery, air compression equipment and, of late, color television sets. The color television plant was set up with the aid of Hitachi, and started production in 1982. In 1984, the State

Table 17 *Gross Industrial Output Value of Xi'an Municipality, 1949–1982*
(1980 unchanged prices)

Yearly percentage change		index (1957 = 100)		
1949–1952	+ 28.3%	1949	15	
		1952	31	
1953–1957	+ 26 %	1957	100 = 469 million *yuan*	
1958–1962	+ 8.4%	1962	150	
1963–1965	+ 24.7%	1966	405	
1966	+ 39.5%	1976	705	
1967–1976	+ 5.7%			
1976–1982	+ 8.5%	1982	1060 = 4,973 million *yuan*°	
1949–1982	+ 13.8%			

°Of which 235 million in Changan county; municipal, provincial and national entreprises accounted for 45.4 resp. 34.1 resp. 20.5%:
Sources: *Zhongguo Jingji Nianjian 1983*, pp. 169–70; *Zhongguo Tongji Nianjian 1983*, p. 87; *Caimao Jingji* 1983 no. 10, p. 60. Index figures and yearly percentage change for 1976–1982 have been derived from other figures.

Planning Committee approved a program for tripling its production capacity to 3 million 14-inch and 22-inch color TV tubes per year by 1988. Xianyang's urban population has reached 180,000 in 1983.[136]

The industrial situation of Shaanxi province and of Xi'an around 1980 showed serious structural weaknesses in its major branches. The textile industry was backward in its production methods and un-competitive within China (let alone internationally), and offered only a small range of specialized products. The capacity of dyeing and printing works, and their quality, were deficient. Out of 25,000 looms, only 6,000 could produce wide cloth. There were no funds for renovation. Moreover, the industry was almost entirely limited to natural fibres. About half of the raw materials of cotton and wool had to be imported from outside the province. Yet cotton products constituted 65 percent of the total export value of Shaanxi.[137] As table 18 shows, Shaanxi was much behind China in its development of chemical industries, of fertilizer, plastics, sulphuric acid, tyres etc. Nitrogenous fertilizer industry had very high production costs, because of the many small plants and the common process of gassing of anthracite – a type of coal that the mines in Guanzhong do not

Table 18 *Industrial production in Shaanxi, 1982–1984, and in Xi'an, 1982 and 1983*

	Unit	Shaanxi 1982	Shaanxi 1983	Shaanxi 1984	of which in Xi'an 1982	of which in Xi'an 1983	Xi'an % of Shaanxi 1982	Shaanxi % of China 1982
Gross Industrial Output Value	(mi. *yuan*)	11,349	12,713	14,142	4,973	5,320	43.8	2.03
of which heavy industry	"	5,546	6,748	8,082	2,175	2,561	39.2	2.01
of which light industry	"	5,803	5,965	6,060	2,798	2,759	48.2	2.06
No. of State-owned enterprises	(1)	2,400	n.d.		464		19	2.8
No. of collective enterprises	(1)	7,800			1,696	2,016	22	2.6
Industrial employment	(1,000)	1,307	n.d.		525		40.2	2.2
(Total employment in State-owned units and urban collectives	(1,000)	3,085			1,028		33.3	(2.7)
Cotton yarn	(1,000 tons)	165	164	145	85.3		52	4.9
Cotton cloth	(million meters)	711	743	627	359		50	4.6
Chemical fibres	(1,000 tons)	2.4	1.5	6			0.5	0.5
Printed and dyed cloth	(million meters)	398	331	274	n.d.			
Woollen blankets	(1,000 pieces)	469	n.d.					1.7
Paper and paperboard	(1,000 tons)	99	115	134				5.6
Pharmaceuticals	(tons)	2,346	2,593	2,800				2.3
Bicycles	(1,000)	546	339	303	380		70	4.7
Sewing machines	(1,000)	602	648	632	270		45	3.8
Watches	(1,000)	1,244	1,207	1,071	1,154		93	1.7
Televisions	(1,000)	98	159	239	52		53	0.6
Radios	(1,000)	108	41	59				
Laundry machines	(1,000)	77	121	172				3.0

	Units					
Lightbulbs	(1,000,000)	38	46	55	n.d.		3.5
Beverages (alcoholic)	(1,000 tons)	47	62	83			1.3
Dairy products	(1,000 tons)	8	8	8			
Cigarettes	(1,000 cases)	395	487	551			2.1
Enamelware	(1,000 tons)	5	n.d.	n.d.			
Coal	(1,000,000 tons)	20	22	24	–	0	3.0
Electricity	(million kWh)	7,437	8,006	9,083	314	4	2.3
Steel	(1,000 tons)	199	287	326	n.d.		0.5
Rolled steel	(1,000 tons)	129	204	225	88	68	
Timber	(1,000 cu.m.)	453	445	466	–		0.9
Cement	(1,000 tons)	2,579	2,795	3,104	75	3	2.7
Sulphuric acid	(1,000 tons)	126	123	125	31	25	1.5
Chem. fertilizer (100%)	(1,000 tons)	224	264	295	14	6	1.8
Plastics	(tons)	6,500	7,649	7,988	9,856	?	0.7
Rubber tyres	(1,000)	76	110	177	n.d.		0.7
Machine tools	(1)	1,143	1,753	2,081	n.d.		0.9
Walking tractors	(1,000)	13	22	26	3		1.1
Diesel engines	(1,000 Hp)	226	301	321		23	4.5
Railway freightwagons	(1)	931	1,792	1,827		100?	0.8
Generators	(MegaWatt)	987	1,114	1,151	816	83	8.8
Transformers	(million Volt-ampère)	2,910	n.d.	n.d.		100?	

N.B. About military industries no information has been published. However, they are known to constitute a major part of Xi'an's heavy industry.

Sources: Xi'an Ribao 27 Apr. 1983, 1 May 1984 and 6 Apr. 1985; Zhongguo Jingji Nianjian 1983; Zhongguo Tongji Nianjian 1983.

produce. Smaller plants could only operate at a loss, which totalled 90 million *yuan* over the 1971–8 period. Small steel works, local farm machinery factories and sugar plants had similar problems. The lack of ore resources makes steel plants uneconomic in any case.[138] The local industries of Xi'an failed to capture the expanding local market for small consumer items such as scissors, locks, cosmetics, toys and plastics. Their market share for these items fell from 30 percent in 1980 to only 18 percent in 1983, because of lack of competitiveness in price, quality and variety with products from other provinces. In 1984, textile and other light industries (such as bicycles, watches and radios) experienced a drop in output. The Nanniwan walking tractor factory suffered from competition with superior models from Henan province, and the black-and-white Petrel television sets were in little demand outside of Shaanxi. The largest single loss-making unit during the early 1980s was the Xi'an car factory, which had been formed out of a merger with several suppliers of spare parts; at the end of 1983 it was closed down by the Provincial Government, which demanded 're-adjustment, improvement of work order and raised quality' before production could be resumed.[139] After some years of readjustment, Shaanxi province reported to have 33 enterprises with profits in 1983 exceeding 5 million *yuan* each, totalling 280 million yuan, and 38 enterprises with losses in excess of half a million *yuan* each, totalling 90 million *yuan*. The net added value in 40 major industrial branches (defense industries excluded) was reported as 1,540 million *yuan*, or 12 percent of their gross output value. Profit and tax together of all State-owned industries amounted to 17.2 percent of their gross output value in 1982 and to 16.6 percent in 1983. Per labourer, gross output value was 8,586 *yuan* in 1982. All these figures indicated a lower-than-average performance of Shaanxi's economy, and improvement was called for. In 1983, profit on state investments was 43% lower than the national average, and productivity per labourer 27% lower.[140]

A similar critical assessment was made of Xi'an's industry only. Although Xi'an was portrayed as having many strong points, '. . . well-located, ample energy resources, a strong industrial base, many scientists, good communications, lively trade and finance . . .', nevertheless in industry, profit per worker was only 940 *yuan* in 1981, one-fifth of that of the Shanghai and one-half of that of the Lanzhou worker.[141]

A very critical macro-level analysis of three decades of investment policies and economic efficiency in Shaanxi's State-owned economic sector published in 1980 showed that economic results of State investments generally had been rather poor. Although, over three decades, per capita investments had been 35 percent higher than the national average, the 1978 average per capita income in Shaanxi was 19.5 percent below the national average, and the budgetary income per capita was even 42.3 percent lower. (In 1983, income would even be 24 percent lower than the national average.) According to the various types of economic performance indicators used by Chinese economists the profitability of investments had declined. The incremental capital:output ratio had become very high, investments took longer and longer to bear fruit, construction costs had increased and capital recoupment periods became extremely long. Although these phenomena were common to all China, in Shaanxi province they generally were more serious[142] (see Table 19).

Whatever the value of such macro-economic performance indicators, they were guides for both Chinese economists and politicians in their thinking and decision-making. The consistently poorer-than-average performance of Shaanxi, therefore, would hurt Shaanxi in obtaining Central Government economic support for economic development.

Various initial measures were taken by the Provincial Government around 1980 in order to cope with the above-mentioned industrial problems. Industrial enterprises were granted more decision-making powers. Large-scale mergers were effected by enterprises which were in the same line of business, but had been subordinate to different departments, regions, levels of government or conglomerates. Investments in new facilities were reduced, and funds were redirected towards improvement of existing facilities. Light industry and commercial development were stressed at the expense of heavy industry, especially machine-building industry which was seriously overstocked.[143] Recommendations were made to increase employment in urban collectives and in commercial and food services and material supplies – at that time only 12 percent of the urban labour force was engaged in tertiary production. 'If we would have the rate of Indonesia or Pakistan, it should be doubled.'[144] Collective urban enterprises were expanded.[145] These measures were all in conformity with national economic policies of the early 1980s. The provincial textile merger (into one enterprise with 93,000 employees, 80 percent of all those employed in cotton and woolen textiles and in printing and dyeing factories) and the electrical equipment merger (into an enterprise with 23,000 employees) were notably successful.[146]

Rationalization and productivity improvement measures were

Table 19 *Economic performance indicators, Shaanxi (and China) 1952–82*

	52–57	58–62	63–65	66–70	71–75	76–78	79–82
1. Incremental investment: incremental national income	2.6	3.7	2.1	5.9	11	5	?[c]
(China)	(1.7)	( )	(0.9)	(2.3)	(3.8)	(3.2)	(3.7)
2. Total investments of completed projects: investments in all added fixed assets (× 100)	77	67	96	44	58	64[a]	78.9[b]
(China)	(83.7)	(71.6)	(87.5)	(60.8)	(61.8)	(69.4)	(80.6)
3. Average construction period of large- and medium-size projects (years)	<5				>10		
4. Capital recoupment period of large- and medium-size projects (years)					27		
(China)	(6)				(11.5)		
5. Construction costs:							
– Investment per additional coal production capacity (*yuan* per ton)		44.6			106.4		
(China)					(119)		
– Investment per square meter of concrete apartments (*yuan*)	55					120	143[d]
(China)	(60)				(>100)		(132[d])

[a] 1978 only. The all-China figure for 1978 is 74.3.

[b] unweighted average of 80.3 (1979), 60.8 (1980), 78.8 (1981) and 95.7 (1982).

[c] Computation of the ICOR for Shaanxi during 1979–1982 is complicated by lack of data and by disasters. National income of Shaanxi province jumped from 7,121 million *yuan* in 1978 to 8,504 million *yuan* in 1979. The drought disaster of 1980, however, brought income down by 5.8 percent to 8,011 million *yuan* (all figures in fixed prices). The flood disaster of 1981 in South and West Shaanxi again caused a low income (not divulged at the time, but the Gross Industrial and Agricultural Output Value remained at 14.3 billion *yuan*) and destroyed a great amount of capital stock; State investments in capital construction during that year were one-third lower than the 2 billion *yuan* of 1980 and still may have included some replacement of destroyed assets. 1981 Shaanxi national income was subsequently stated to have been 8,453 or 8,435 million *yuan* (which seems too high), and 1982 national income has been given as 9,270 or 9,130 million *yuan*. The 1979–1982 ICOR value for Shaanxi probably would be very high.

[d] unweighted average of 1981 and 1982 cost prices per square meter of urban residential building and renewal.

N.B. The first indicator, which is similar to the Incremental (or Marginal) Capital:Output Ratio, is used by the Chinese only in its inversed form, viz. Added national income:Investment in added fixed assets. Problems inherent to this indicator are well-known: it ignores the lag between investment and output increase (which differs according to type and size of a project, from less than one year in small manufacturing facilities to over ten years in large hydro-electric power plants), it ignores technological progress as a factor influencing the capital stock-output relation, and there is no satisfactory way to allow for depreciation. The ICOR values, therefore, should be used only over longer periods of time and for aggregate economies, and with caution. The same applies to the second indicator, which also ignores time lags, as it sets off investments which start to bear fruit in a set period against all investments during that period; the two are directly related only if both initial investment and its completion fall within this set period.

Sources: Lilun Tansuo 1980 no. 3; *Guangming Ribao* 15 May 1980; Erhard Louven, *China Aktuell* Apr. and Aug. 1983; averages for China under 2. have been calculated from *Zhongguo Tongji Nianjian 1983*, p. 343; *Gongren Ribao* 19 Dec. 1983; *Shaanxi Ribao* 20 June 1981 and 27 Apr. 1983; *Zhongguo Jingji Nianjian 1983*, IV p. 105.

hampered, however, by firmly entrenched local interests and by the so-called 'iron rice bowl', which made it virtually impossible to close down factories or to dismiss employees of State-owned enterprises and organizations. During the early 1980s, many heavy industries such as the Xi'an Steel Works and the Shaanxi Diesel Engine Plant were still running at considerable losses. Provincial and municipal authorities blamed this on bad management, lack of orders, with overly high overhead, too low prices, inadequate renovation and incompetent leadership – a wide range of factors not to be remedied easily, if at all. Under the Sixth Five-Year-Plan, Central Government investment priorities laid with energy and transport, particularly in or near the coastal areas, and this left out Shaanxi and Xi'an. The coal fields of Northern Guanzhong have not been included in the national energy development projects.[147]

Yet because of two very large power projects, construction of which commenced already in the late 1970s, Shaanxi province may become an important net exporter of electricity after 1986. At that date, the 1,050 MW Qinling Thermo-electric power station in Weinan will be completed, and two years later, the 800 MW Ankang Hydroelectric power station will also start feeding the Northwest Power Network.[148]

Priority projects financed by the provincial government include polyester fibres and printing and dyeing of textiles, improvement of storage facilities of petroleum and cold storage in Xi'an, the Xi'an railway station, the Shaanxi glass factory and an aluminum factory in Tongchuan.[149] Agriculture-related industries were affected by the continuously downward trend in the sown cotton area in Guanzhong during the 1980s, and by the calamitous grain harvests of 1980 and 1981. In a positive way, output increases of oil crops, fruits, tobacco, sugar beets and of animal products such as goat's milk, wool, pork and eggs stimulated local industrial growth. The 1983 grain harvest was an all-time record, but the cotton harvest an all-time low. Shaanxi's provincial economic performance, although considerably improved after 1978, had lagged behind that of other provinces. The 1983 gross value of its industrial and agricultural production was 31.5 percent up on 1978, against a national increase of 46.2 percent. In 1982, income per capita was 344 *yuan*, as against a national average of 458 *yuan*. Profit on investment had been 43 percent lower than the national average, and productivity per labourer 26.9 percent lower than the national average. Of Shaanxi's 106 counties and municipalities, 73 needed financial subsidies, to a total of 240 million *yuan* in 1983. These

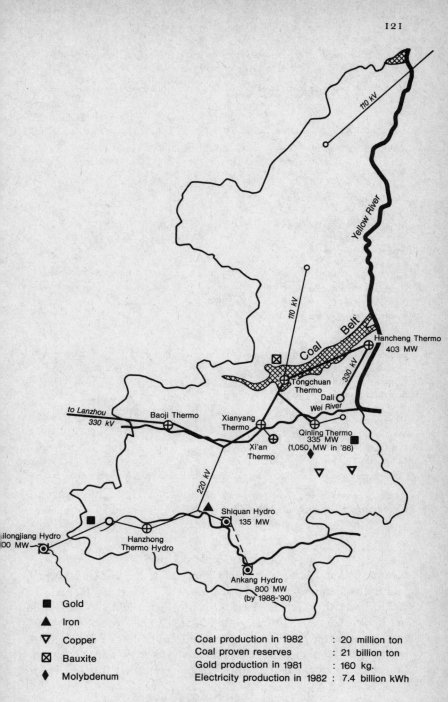

Map 9 Mining and energy in Shaanxi, 1982

Table 20 *Professional structure by major branches, Shaanxi 1982*
(1,000)

	Male	Female	Total	Per millage of China total
Total working population	8,397.3	6,537.3	14.934.7	28.7
Agriculture, Forestry, Animal Husbandry and Fishery	6,089.4	5,375.8	11,465.2	29.9
Mining, lumber industry and transport	123.1	20.0	143.1	17.4
Electricity, gas, water supply	28.9	11.8	40.7	28.9
Manufacturing industry	851.1	555.4	1,406.5	22.8
Geological prospecting and surveying	23.1	3.9	27.0	35.0
Building industry	242.5	61.1	303.6	27.8
Communications, transport and postal services	166.0	42.3	208.3	23.1
Trade, catering, retail trade and storage	199.6	156.7	356.3	23.1
Management of housing and of public utilities, and resident services	31.2	36.2	67.4	27.5
Health, sports, welfare	79.1	56.6	135.8	33.3
Education, culture, arts	297.6	134.7	432.3	35.0
Scientific research and technical services	41.0	23.1	64.1	52.1
Finance and insurance	22.8	9.7	32.5	31.8
State organs, Government-, Party-, and mass-organizations	193.1	44.0	237.1	29.6
Other occupations	8.8	6.0	14.8	59.5

Source: 10 Percent Sampling Tabulation on the 1982 Population Census of the People's Republic of China (computer tabulation), Beijing 1983.

figures given at the Provincial People's Congress in May 1984 were meant to demonstrate Shaanxi's inadequate performance, which politicians blamed on the 'Leftist' spirit still present in Shaanxi.[150]

The lower-than-average level of economic development also shows in the employment structure of Shaanxi. The 1982 Census distinguished not only urban and rural, State and collective employment, but also the number of male and female workers in major economic branches. It should be remembered, however, that this applied to

Table 21 *Non-employed population of Shaanxi, 1982*
(1,000)

	Male	Female	Total	% of total
In school	628.5	398.8	1,027.3	23.8
Working at home	380.3	1,920.3	2,300.6	52.6
Waiting for school entrance	42.0	30.5	72.4	1.7
Waiting for State assignment	2.5	0.7	3.2	0.1
Urban unemployed	30.3	35.5	65.8	1.5
Retired or discharged	146.1	66.4	212.6	4.9
Others	334.1	305.5	639.6	14.7
Total	1,563.7	2,757.8	4,321.4	100

Source: see table 20.

provincial totals. Within Shaanxi, Guanzhong is the most indus-
trialized and best accessible region, with much higher percentages of
non-agricultural employment than those listed in Table 20. As
elsewhere in China, unemployment has become more serious in the
1970s and 1980s. The non-employed population of Shaanxi in 1982
(subdivided into several categories which were not sharply defined)
consisted mainly of housewives and of students; total urban employment was below 100,000 (See table 21).

The professional structure of Shaanxi province, as shown in the 1982
census,[151] was characterized by a somewhat lower percentage of non-
agricultural employment than the China average (23.2 percent of
total employment as against 26.3 percent for China), and by a stronger
male predominance in those occupations. Two-thirds of non-
agricultural occupations were held by men (2,308,000) and one-third
by women (1,162,000), while the all-China ratio was 174:100. Mining
and transport was much less developed than average in China, and so
were to a lesser extent also manufacturing, transport and trade. The
concentration of scientific research and technical services in Shaanxi
reflects Xi'an's position as a regional centre for the Northwest (which
it shares with Lanzhou), and its advanced industries of air-planes,
precision equipment, geological prospecting equipment, and possibly
military industry. In most other major professional branches, the
Shaanxi figures did not differ much from the national average
employment percentages. Male predominance was particularly strong

in the usual male occupations (mining, prospecting, building) but also in the State-, Party- and mass-organizations and in education.

Two recent economic developments deserve special mention. North Shaanxi had been a burden for the provincial economy for many years, as an extremely poor area. Since 1980, the Central Government provided a yearly subsidy to this area of 50 million *yuan* per year, for agricultural construction purposes. Partly because of this support, partly because of decollectivization and agricultural specialization, per capita production and income rose by 30 to 40 percent between 1978 and 1982. The 1982 gross agricultural production value per capita (195 and 255 *yuan* in Yulin resp. Yan'an) and net income per capita (110 and 140 *yuan*) still were much below the Shaanxi average (itself being 20 percent below the 1982 national average rural net income of 270 *yuan*), but they were definitely on the increase.[152] If the subsidy and the upward economic trend continue, Shaanxi province will be less affected by the poverty of the loess plateau area.

Guanzhong and especially Xi'an and surroundings have witnessed a phenomenal growth in the number of foreign tourists since 1978. Responsible for this interest are no doubt the beauty of Xi'an as a traditional Ming/Qing-style city, the excavations of the clay army guarding Qinshi Huangdi's tomb in Lintong, and the many other relics from the past. Far more can and probably will be done to open up (also in a literary sense!) the cultural treasures of Guanzhong for tourism. New archeological discoveries continue to draw the interest of specialists and tourists alike. With the increasing wealth of the Chinese citizens, a growing desire to spend holidays away from polluted cities, and improved railway and road transport Guanzhong may become a major attraction for tourists from other provinces as well.

Between 1979 and 1984, foreign currency receipts from tourists rose 6-fold to 47 million *yuan*, and further rapid growth may be expected. In Xi'an, awareness of the duty to preserve one's cultural heritage has increased. The 1978 construction of the 27 meter high Bell Tower Hotel close to the (36-meter high) Bell Tower has already been openly deplored. A good example of architectural adjustment was the 1981 contest for reconstruction of the Nanda Street district, at the Southern gate of Xi'an. Under the rules passed in 1980, no high buildings may be erected in the vicinity of historical buildings, and within the city maximum heights have been imposed.[153]

Table 22 *Foreign tourism in Shaanxi, 1979–1984*

	no. of groups	total no. of people	of which foreigners	of which overseas Chinese	foreign currency income (*yuan*)	i.e. per capita (*yuan*)
1979	1,702	21,212	18,202	3,010	7,750,000	365
1980	2,747	33,625	29,932	3,693	17,570,000	523
1981	3,830	58,963	55,227	3,736	25,660,000	437
1982	5,705	81,372	76,131	5,241	31,721,000	390
1983	7,700	102,479	89,294	13,185	38,489,000	376
1984		151,300	138,500	12,800	47,120,000	340

Sources: Shaanxi Ribao 4 Apr. 1984 and 6 Apr. 1985.

G. THE QUALITY OF URBAN LIFE

The reduction of the urban population after the Great Leap Forward and the moderate growth during the 1960s and 1970s enabled Xi'an to improve urban facilities and social services for its residents. Underground sewers, electricity and piped drinking water facilities became universal although water supply is still inadequate. City transportation was served by better roads and more buses. Some modern facilities, however, such as telephones,[154] did not advance beyond the level of the late 1950s. Great advances have been made in medical care,[155] and in secondary education. In most respects, the urban residents of Xi'an have received much better access to public services than the remainder of Shaanxi's population have. In 1982, with about 7.5 percent of Shaanxi's population Xi'an had 40 percent of all buses, a quarter of all hospital beds, doctors and nurses, and 13 percent of all secondary school students of Shaanxi province. Average urban income was two or three times as high[156] as in rural Guanzhong. In 1982 consumer durables, with the exception of transistor radios and to some extent bicycles, had not yet penetrated rural areas, but in the cities and towns of Shaanxi one out of 3 households had a television set and an electric fan, one out of 6 a tape recorder, and one out of 18 a washing machine.[157] In most cases, these amenities might be shared by two or three households; the usual arrangement of apartment buildings has shared kitchens and toilets.

In some major aspects, however, city life hardly improved, if anything at all. Housing in terms of available surface per capita only barely kept up with population growth, and remained at the low level of about four square meters per capita – less than half the living space available to rural inhabitants, which rose from 9.5 square meters in 1980 to 12.3 square meters in 1983.[158] Its quality has improved to a certain extent, as traditional loam houses were replaced by 4- or 5-story apartment buildings with electricity and running water, but most apartments can be seen to lack proper maintenance. The extremely low rents (1.20 *yuan* per month in 1957, 2 to 3 *yuan* per month in 1977) may be the cause of insufficient funds for maintenance being put aside by the municipal government and by State enterprises. Recent government efforts to promote private ownership of homes will find little response as long as there seems to be little economic benefit and a fair chance of future political trouble in such an acquisition. In 1981 and 1982, urban residential construction in Shaanxi increased to 2.5 and 3 million sq.m., over twice the 1978 figure.[159]

Table 23 *Some social services in Xi'an city, 1949–1982*

	−1949	1957	1959	1982
Population (1,000)	460	937		2,180
No. of dependents per worker	4.1			0.77
Housing added to stock since 1949 (million sq.m.)	(current: 2–2.2)	2.8	3.7	12.5
Other buildings added to stock (million sq.m.)	(current: 1.5–1.2)	4.3	5.2	16.7
Built-up area (sq.km.)	13	71–85		130
Sewerage (km.)	25	102	188	414
Running water availability (% of all households)	6	76	>80	100
City buses (1)	17	98	140	524
Telephones (1,000)	0.1–1		8.5	16.8
Primary school students (per 1,000 pop.)	64	103		100
Secondary school students (per 1,000 pop.)	16	29		95
University students (per 1,000 pop.)	5	22		20
Hospital beds (per 1,000 pop.)	1.1	3	6	8.6

Sources: Xi'an Lishi Shulüe, 1959; Zhongguo Tongji Nianjian 1983; Zhongguo Jingji Nianjian 1983; Shaanxi Ribao 27 Nov. 1957; Ma Zhenglin, op. cit.

Real earnings (including wages, overtime, bonuses and subsidies) of the urban work force in China did not improve any further after 1956–7. During the Great Leap Forward years, they sank by about one-quarter, then rose again to their previous height around 1965. Since then, average real earnings slowly declined by some 15 percent till 1978.[160] Reasons for this decline were both political, arising from levelling policies of the Cultural Revolution period, and economic. Between 1965 and 1975, the annual rise of labour productivity was close to zero, the workforce of State-owned enterprises increased rapidly (especially during 1970–2), with most new employees starting at the low end of wage scales.[161] For Xi'an, however, this situation was somewhat different. Industrial expansion and urban employment occurred mainly in the heavy industrial sector, notably in chemicals, aircraft, and machine-building, where the average wage compared favourably with wages in light industries such as textiles and food products. Nevertheless, even after the wage raises in 1978–80, the average income in Xi'an was stated to be only 41.60 *yuan* per month in 1980, a nominal increase of 68 percent over 1965. This figure may have been exaggerated by 15 to 20 percent.[162] The increase over 1965, however, can be entirely attributed to a higher labour:dependent ratio. Because of the fuller labour participation of women, and the reduced number of children, one labourer or employee supported 4.1 dependents in 1949, 2.06 dependents in 1965, 0.92 dependents in 1980 and 0.77 in 1983. In this way, the greatly increased labour participation helped to maintain the standard of living.

For Xi'an city, several surveys have shown some slow improvement of income and living standards over the past 25 years. The average wage, when corrected for inflation, has gone down by over one-quarter between 1957 and 1981, but his has been compensated and more than that by a higher rate of labour participation. The most extensive survey has been summarized in Table 24.

As compared with the Xi'an urban averages (see note 153) the 400 households of this sample were slightly above average, for two reasons. All households had employment in the state-owned sector, and already lived in Xi'an in 1957. For the same reasons, their average living space per capita was higher than the average of 4.06 square meters. Around 1980, average wages and incomes in Xi'an were about 10 percent higher than in other cities of Shaanxi.

All in all, urban workers did poorly in improving their wages and income during the 1960s and 1970s. The wage improvements of 1979–80 were long overdue, and the level reached in 1980 was difficult to maintain under inflationary pressures. Only in 1984, the real wage may have increased again. The nominal wage went up slightly in 1982 and 1983. The average wage of employees of urban collectively-owned enterprises remained about a quarter below those paid by state-owned enterprises (see Table 25).

A 1984 survey of households with employment in the State-owned sector throughout Shaanxi province showed that between 1978 and 1983 the average wage rose from 640 *yuan* to 824 *yuan*, and per capita income from 290 *yuan* to 453 *yuan*. Corrected for a 15 percent inflation (the official figure) this would mean an increase of the real wage of 12 percent and of percapita income of 36 percent over this 5-year period.[163] To the political and economic causes for the low wages mentioned above should be added the lack of bargaining power of trade unions, the unlimited reservoir of cheap rural labour, and a persistent orientation towards maximum employment rather than towards productivity and profit gains.[164]

During the early 1980s, these and other societal problems, such as pollution, were discussed more openly than before in the local press. Pollution of water and water shortages in Xi'an could not be remedied in the short term. Air pollution, because of industry, was most serious in Yanliang and Jintai districts. Xi'an city proper had considerably less air pollution than these districts. Baoji and Tongchuan cities, both of which lie in narrow valleys where smog does not spread easily, had equally serious high levels of air pollution, and, according to one writer, high incidence rates of lung cancer as well.[165] The supply system of consumer goods was another area of criticism. In part, shortages were caused by insufficient production with rising urban demand (pork being a notable exception since 1980). Peasants were urged to produce more vegetables and more milk. Because dairy cattle would need much State investment, individual peasants were offered bank loans for raising goats rather than cows.[166] Moreover, the distributional system was deemed inadequate and too inflexible. The rapid increase of individual hawkers and retail sales points did much to remedy these defects.[167] Improvement of marketing channels and economic networks and reducing the number of links in State-run commerce was a major concern of the provincial and municipal government.[168]

When in 1983 the quality of life and services received greater attention from the government, critics of Xi'an's internal economic structure indicated many weaknesses, some of which could not be remedied within just a few years. For urban housing, only 3.8 square meters per capita was available, and many buildings were in disrepair. Roads were too narrow. Water supply was very inadequate, only 400,000 to 500,000 tons per day, but water needs were 600,000 to 700,000 tons. Only 60,000 tons of the discharged polluted water received treatment. There were not enough schools. Xi'an's cultural heritage was not preserved. Cultural and recreational facilities were few – Xi'an had no public library, no radio station, no museum, no youth centre. There were not enough banks, or bank personnel.[169] A list of 'improvements in people's life' presented by the municipal government some months later was not too impressive: 1,500 extra milk cows (Xi'an, as all other Chinese cities, had a severe shortage of milk), 2,100 more retail sales points, 170 extra buses, a 'save water campaign', 2,300 meters of new sewers, 30 public toilets. It was a start, no more. Probably the best achievements of Xi'an's municipal government were in job creation: in 1983 92,000 more jobs were provided.[170]

Table 24 *Income and expenditure of 400 state enterprise workers' families in Xi'an, 1957 and 1981*

	1957	1981	After correction for inflation (62%)
Average wage + bonuses (*yuan* p.m.)	59.87	69.67	−27.5%
Labourer:dependent ratio	1:1.72	1:0.82	+39.6%
Income for living expenses (*yuan* p.m. per cap.)	18.45	37.18	
Living expenses (*yuan* p.m. per cap.)	17.97	36.57	
A purchase of commercial products	14.99	33.49	
B rent, water, electricity, school, transport, mail, culture, medical care, haircut, bathing, repairs	2.98	3.08	

Composition of A	1957	1981
Foodstuffs	68.85%	57.75%
Clothes	12.47%	16.78%
Daily use goods	8.21%	11.35%
Cultural goods	1.67%	8.12%
Fuel	3.8%	2.18%
Medicine	2.8%	0.51%

Actual consumption per capita per mensem	1957	1981
grain (kg)	14.7	13.0
vegetables (kg)	7.3	9.9
plant oil (ounces)	6.8	9.2
pork, meat (kg)	0.5	1.0
eggs (kg)	0.25	0.45
sugar (kg)	0.09	0.2

	1957	1981
Average living space per capita (sq.m.)	3.76	5.57

Distribution of income per capita per mensem, 1981:

above 60 *yuan*	5.75% of population
50–60 "	6.5% of population
35–50 "	45.25% of population
25–35 "	37% of population
20–25 "	4.5% of population
below 20 "	1% of population

Source: Shaanxi Ribao 19 March 1982.

Table 25 *Workers' wages and peasant net income in Shaanxi, 1978–1984*

(nominal, *yuan*)	1978	1979	1980	1981	1982	1983	1984
Average wage of all urban Staff and workers	640	707	785	780	797	824	973
State-owned units only		731	811	812	831	857	n.d.
Collective units only		562	636	609	619	652	n.d.
Net income of all peasants households p.c.	133.1		142.4	177.2	218.3	236.1	262.5
Net income of State employees households p.c.	290				421	453	515.5

Sources: Zhongguo Nongye Nianjian 1982 IV-167 and *1983* V-168; *Statistical Yearbook of China 1981* p. 434 and *1983* p. 488; *Shaanxi Ribao* 22 July 1981, 1, 2, 5 and 10 May 1984, 6 Apr. and 2 May 1985.

The rapid development of a private economy after liberalization policies had been adopted was evident in the urban sector as well, and to a certain extent former distinctions between the rural collective and urban sector were obliterated thereby. The process was sped up in 1983. Particularly individual trade gave rise to new employment.

In Xi'an city alone, there were 22,000 people (half the Shaanxi total) working privately in trade, restaurants, handicrafts, repairs etc. by the end of 1983. This was something of a change over the 1964–79 period, when private work had been banned almost completely. Official figures, which can be reliable only to a certain extent, give the number of privately employed households in Xi'an as 24,600 in 1953, 8,900 in 1957, 14,900 in 1962, 3,500 in 1965 and a mere 281 registered and 110 unregistered households in 1979.[171] Both in terms of manpower and in terms of turnover (2 percent of total retail sales in Xi'an in 1983) the private economy still was insignificant, but its impact on business style and economic behaviour was very evident. Also, it was held out as an example by the authorities in their efforts to raise efficiency in the state-run organizations and enterprises.

Table 26 *Development of collective and private economy in the cities of Shaanxi, 1980–1983*
(number of households engaged)

Year	Collective Industry	Collective Trade	Individual Handicraft	Individual Trade
1980	13,183	2,898	3,051	4,338
1981	13,773	4,235	4,220	8,370
1982	14,173	5,839	6,612	15,323
1983	14,786	7,567	12,189	68,126

Source: Shaanxi Jingji Tantao 1984, p. 261.

Because of decollectivization policies both in the city and in rural areas, and also because of greater freedom of production and trade, during the 1980s Xi'an started to look less austere, more bustling, noisy and crowded, in the way other Asian cities do. However, controls on population movement, industrial production, and trade had relaxed only very slightly, and there was no way of predicting how far the socialist state might go in relinquishing economic and administrative controls and in undoing a well-established urban–rural dichotomy.

Conclusion. Xi'an has been of prime military and economic importance in the Han and Tang dynasties, but at the beginning of the twentieth century it was little more than a regional administrative center without much actual power. Its 100,000 population consisted mainly of soldiers and civil servants. The provincial government, because of the underdeveloped state of the economy, particularly of industry and trade, had only a small revenue from taxes. After the railroad connection had been established, some modern industries moved to Xi'an, notably a cotton mill and flour mills. Local capital was used to set up several other small factories. The province ran a serious trade deficit, which could only partially be compensated with semi-legal exports of poppy until 1939.

The war brought dramatic changes and the beginnings of a state-planned economy. The number of troops in Guanzhong increased to about 300,000, refugees kept flowing in from the east and Xi'an's population swelled to 400,000 by 1944. Their sustenance added to the peasants' burden. In the cities, particularly in Xi'an, the Guomindang tightened its hold on the population. The secret police ended all political opposition from the liberals or the left. Labour unions were organized to control the urban work force and labour conditions generally deteriorated. However, in the early war period the urban economy boomed because of war-created demands for uniforms, transport and construction. The industrial labour force increased seven-fold between 1937 and 1939. When trade with East China was restored in 1939–40, local textile industries started to suffer from competition again. Shortages of raw materials and coal, difficulties in transportation, hoarding and inflation hampered a smooth development of industrial production and sales. Large factories were hurt more seriously than small ones. As the central government subsidies and opium fines decreased after 1939, the provincial government had to rely on borrowing and on all kinds of exactions. After 1942, industrial production stagnated. The maintenance of Hu Zongnan's armies and the campaigns against the communists took more than the provincial economy could bear. During and after the war, inflation was fueled by local and national deficit spending. The Guomindang-controlled area shrunk in the course of 1948 and Xi'an was cut off from its wheat supply areas in the north and west.

Labour conditions and wages improved in the 1950s, especially from 1955 when many new investments came to Xi'an under the First Five-Year Plan. State policies pushed traders and handicraft labourers out of the villages and pulled them to the cities. Only after collectivization of the villages in 1956 was state control of population movement tightened. Until 1960, local authorities sometimes stopped urban immigration but at other times encouraged it. This reflected both seasonal fluctuations of labour need and fluctuations in planning of industrial expansion and urban construction. Xi'an was meant to become one of the three new industrial centres of northwest China and also a commercial and educational center. Seventy-seven national industries were established under the First Five-Year Plan, and one hundred and twenty provincial or municipal industries. Between 1952 and 1957, Xi'an's industrial output rose by 220 percent. Rural and urban private industries (in 1954 responsible for one-third of Shaanxi's industrial output) suffered and most were terminated or driven underground in 1956. Their skilled labourers were absorbed into the new state enterprises. In 1957, 130,000 people were moved out of Xi'an, during a short phase of contraction, but within a year many labourers were pulled back to the city. Also, women were urged to take part in productive labour during the Great Leap Forward.

Under these conditions of rapid growth, city planning was difficult; it also suffered from a lack of qualified personnel and clear authority. There was much illegal construction. State standards for housing were already very low (4 square meters of net living space per capita) but could not be met. The City Construction Bureau had to satisfy or control demands from many competing state organizations. Some people argued that Xi'an's industrial build-up was too dispersed, many industries being located far from the city. Indeed this added to short-term problems of infrastructure, social services and transport. However, in this way room was left for future expansion, and the old walled city has been preserved as a valuable asset in attracting tourists.

In 1960 and 1961, due to the disastrously bad organization of rural and urban production and distribution throughout China, the foodgrain situation in Xi'an became very tight. Already in spring 1959, grain rations were reduced by one-quarter. There are strong indications, however, both from demographic data and from weather and crop reports, that Shaanxi was affected much less than most areas of China. We see no grounds for Walker's assumption that in Shaanxi the area sown to grain was reduced by 7.5 percent in 1958 and by a further 10 percent in 1959, nor for assuming that the 1959 average yield was equal to the lowest annual yield of the 1952–7 period.[172] The major economic crop, cotton, had a smaller sown acreage in 1959 than in 1958 and the food grain shortage had appeared before one had to decide which autumn crops to sow. The Shaanxi farmers and officials had a tradition of being cautious in agricultural production planning and also in consumption; in marginal areas, one is accustomed to large yearly fluctuations of grain output and to local shortages. This tradition may have been a major factor in the hectic Great Leap Forward years. Shaanxi province was the only province in north and northwest China where state procurement of grain in 1959 was below the maximum procurement of the 1953–1957 period. Nevertheless, the industrial and agrarian crisis was severe: the 1962 gross value of agricultural production was 30 percent lower than in 1958, and many industries had been closed down. Cotton output was down to a third of normal. The non-agricultural population shrunk from 14 percent of the Shaanxi total before the Great Leap Forward to about 10 percent after the crisis.

The 1960s and 1970s were a period of substantial industrial growth: about 6 percent per annum. The central government continued to invest in heavy industries: steel, power, machinery, mining, defense industries and aircraft. Textile industry could not hold its ground against the east coast cities. Chemical industry was a weakly developed sector. About half of Shaanxi's industrial production was concentrated in and around Xi'an. Under the new policies, after 1978 heavy industry generally stagnated, while light industry flourished. But this trend has been reversed in 1982–1984. Many light industries, particularly cotton textiles but also watches, bicycles and other consumer goods suffered from competition with other provinces. In contrast, heavy industry (such as steel, machinery, chemical fertilizer and aircraft) experienced new growth.

In the 1980s, Shaanxi and Xi'an's industrial performance was still considerably behind the national average, in terms of technology, output per labourer, profits and growth. A macro-analysis of three decades of investment policies and economic efficiency shows that the economic results of state investments have been rather poor. Rationalization, productivity improvement and commercialization became the catchwords of the 1980s. Large-scale mergers of enterprises, privatization of small enterprises, creation of new trade channels and other reorganizational measures along national lines still have to show their effectiveness. The investment priorities of the central government under the Sixth Five-Year Plan were in energy and transport: none of the national priority projects was located in Shaanxi (apart from defense and aircraft industry, most of which is kept secret). The second half of the 1980s will be different, however. Railroads will be extended, the Qinling and Ankang power stations will generate great amounts of electricity and valuable exploitable ores such as bauxite and molybdenum have been discovered. Also, North Shaanxi has become less of a burden to the provincial economy. Tourism is booming and supplies a growing amount of foreign currency.

The Census of 1982 showed that Shaanxi when compared with China as a whole had a professional structure with little employment in mining, transport and trade and still only 9 percent of its labour force in manufacturing. In non-agricultural occupations there was a strong male predominance.

Urban housing conditions remained crowded and primitive, owing to the lack of investment and maintenance. Only in the 1980s did they receive a greater political priority. Real urban earnings slowly declined (the lack of bargaining power of China's urban labourers is evident), but this was compensated by a rising labour participation ratio and less children per household. The average urban labourer had four dependents in 1949, two dependents in 1965, and less than one in 1980. In this way, real urban income could improve somewhat. Between 1978 and 1984, real earnings improved by about 15 percent, and may have regained the 1965 level. Thus, urban income per capita in 1984 was about half as much as in 1965. Cramped housing, lack of piped drinking water and recreational facilities, pollution and other problems started to receive more public and municipal attention in the early 1980s. Commercial and catering services were expanded by lifting the ban on small private enterprises. The cities lost some of their austere looks and more peasants, hawkers, roadside shops and shoeshine boys can be seen now on the streets of Xi'an. Still, government control of urban population, production and trade are tight and the urban-rural political and economic division has been preserved.

4

PHYSICAL ASPECTS OF A
CHANGING COUNTRY

The visitor to Guanzhong is continuously reminded of being in an ancient center of human settlement and civilization. Many sights will set his mind to work at recalling the area's past history. He may visit excavations of cultural remains such as the neolithic Banpo village (4,000B.C.), the chariot-and-horse pits of the Zhou dynasty (1,000–800 B.C.) or the giant clay army guarding the tomb of Qinshi Huangdi, China's first emperor. Pagodas everywhere cause one to think of the Buddhist expansion during the Tang dynasty, although many have experienced damage by earthquakes and show a lack of proper upkeep both in the past and present. While most of the city walls are dilapidated, they still clearly separate town and country in every district. North of Xi'an along the Wei River, the original 30 meter-high eroded tomb mounds of Han emperors and officials still rise above the alluvial plain, although many have been erased in the past decades. As for the walls and palaces of Changan, built in the seventh century to accommodate a population of perhaps one million people, not much has remained but a few fragments of the 36 kilometer long outer city wall. Traces of ancient canals can also still be found, long ago fallen into disuse and silted up, but still indicating the magnitude of early efforts at irrigation and transportation in the Wei River plain.[1]

There is a stark contrast between this glorious past and Guanzhong's poor conditions during this century. Suggestions for the causes of decline include a drier climate, deforestation, erosion and exhaustion of soil, overpopulation and wars. But all these factors still await further study before their impact can be properly assessed.

Changes in climate, and with these, changes in natural vegetation, appear, from recent pollen analysis, to have been rather minor. Ho Pingdi thought that the sharp increase in *Artemisia* species in the late Pleistocene showed that the climate was becoming cooler and drier, and that the paleo-environment of the loess plateau was a semi-arid steppe, little if at all forested. Pearson and Li Huilin believe, however, that the increase in *Artemisia*, a plant species which is not confined to arid environments and is 'weedy' in nature, indicates the beginning of slash-and-burn agriculture around 5,000 B.C. Climate and natural vegetation may have been not unlike that of the present, with maybe slightly higher temperatures and a little more luxuriant vegetation. This then was a transitional environment between grassland and woodland, with conifer forests growing at high levels, broadleafed trees (willow, walnut, birch, oak etc.) at lower levels, and grasslands with scattered shrubs in the drier northern areas.[2] Although in most places nothing indeed is left of the original vegetation, climate cannot be blamed for this.

A. DEFORESTATION AND AFFORESTATION

Deforestation of Guanzhong started very early. Agriculture and the need for fuel and timber for Changan and other large cities along the Silk Road and the lower reaches of the Wei River led to a complete denudation of the Guanzhong plain and at a later date the northern foothills of the Qinling mountain range also. The higher levels of Guanzhong were affected much later. The northern mountain area was taken into cultivation in the fifteenth and sixteenth century, and rapidly impoverished because of soil erosion.[3] The Huanglongshan mountains (west of Hancheng) were opened up as a reclamation area only in the 1930s, and still have some natural forests at higher altitudes.[4] The Qinling mountain range had been a refuge and a settlement area for many centuries, but received a particularly large influx of refugee settlers during the Drought and the war against Japan, when railroad and roads were expanded. In 1940, it was estimated that the Jianshan area could support 250,000 refugees on its 33,000 ha.[5] During the war many trees were felled by the army for wood and for timber. The price of timber rose, and many tree-felling stations were set up by the local population. Much forest area was reclaimed for grain cultivation. By 1947, the forests of the Qinling natural forest area (Fuping, Ningshen, Zhouzhi and Fengxian counties) had dwindled to 215,000 hectares with 2.2 billion cubic feet of timber.

Provincial tree nurseries were set up from 1935 onwards, and numbered four (with an area of 75 hectares) during 1937–41, nursing about 4 million seedlings a year. Thirty counties had set up three nurseries as well, supplying one to two million seedlings a year. About one-quarter of these seedlings could eventually be supplied as trees.[6] After 1949 the new Government promoted the planting of trees, but management of newly-planted trees was weak. Also, the forest protection work was not well organized, so the burning and cutting down of forests for the creation of farmland continued. In the city of Baoji the price of 50 kg of firewood rose from 0.9 *yuan* to 2.00 *yuan* in 1956. In Lantian, the 1956 wood price was 100 *yuan* per cubic metre.[7] The protection of existing forests was the government's primary concern, and new afforestation came only second. The number of tree seedlings rose to ten million per year. Official figures for 1956 gave 140,900 hectare of forest area in Guanzhong (or 5.1 percent of its surface area), 33,000 hectare of grassland (1.2 percent) and 689,100 hectare of wasteland (25.1 percent); for the Weibei Plateau to the north of Guanzhong, which has a surface area of 3,132,000 hectares, the forest area took 7 percent, usable grassland 10.2 percent, and wasteland 41.4 percent.[8]

During the 1950s, afforestation schemes in Guanzhong were part of the national effort to control the Yellow River and to reduce its silt content. In Shaanxi province afforestation was accelerated in 1956 for that reason.[9] Planning was directed at increasing the provincial forest area from 14 percent of its total surface in 1955 to 34 percent within one decade. Within Guanzhong, forests should cover 28 percent of the middle and lower section of the Luo River basin and 8 percent of the Wei River basin by 1966.

New forests were to serve other uses as well: fuel and timber supply and fruit production. Farmland should be reconverted:

The Qinling mountain area should not be used for agricultural cropping, but for growing useful natural vegetation. After the vegetation cover has increased . . . erosion may be diminished. A policy of reclamation is wrong. We must progressively restore the present cultivated slopes to forest. At the foothills and along the farmland we should plant fruit trees: walnuts, Chinese prickly ash, persimmon, peaches, pears, apples, oil-trees etc.[10]

In 1960, it was reported that the forest cover of Shaanxi province had increased from 10.16 percent in 1956 to 20.87 percent in 1960, but this was a dubious Leap Forward claim. In 1975, it was reported to be 18.24 percent, or 37,300 sq. km, and in 1984, about 30,000 sq. km, 60 percent of which in South Shaanxi.[11]

Although indeed some reforestation has taken place in the past decades (official all-Shaanxi data mention 1.5 million ha of soil conservation forests planted or sown from 1950 till 1982),[12] most of

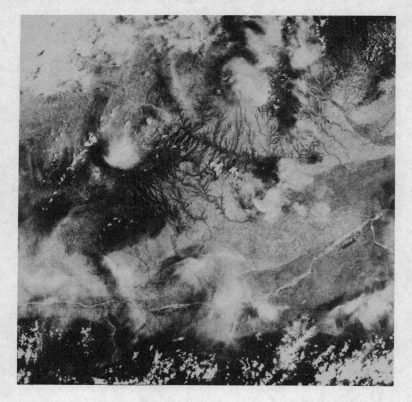

Plate 2 The Baoji–Xi'an section of the Wei River valley. In the Northwest corner, clouds cover Gansu province. In the irrigated plain, white bands of sand indicate river courses. Tones of grey reflect different intensities of crops (as a result of irrigation) and vegetation. Deep black indicates forest and sometimes a reservoir.

these have not survived, and during the same period a considerably larger amount of original forest was lost through reclamation or otherwise. The official forest acreage figures of Shaanxi province have risen above the one mentioned for 1949, but in the area of Guanzhong recent satellite pictures show very little forest left in the Wei River and Luo River basins and on the northern edge of the Qinling mountains. The Wei River basin may have a forest cover of only 3 percent now.[13]

Apart from being vital to the national interest for control of the Yellow River, it appeared during the 1960s and 1970s that forest conservation and afforestation measures were badly needed for regional water conservation as well. After the Sanmen Reservoir

Plate 3 The Wei River valley downstream of Xi'an. The Luohe comes down from the loess plateau in the Northwest. On the other side of the Huanglongshan mountains, the Yellow River descends through Yumenk'ou into the plain, then turns East past Sanmen Gorge. State farms appear at the confluence with the Wei River. In heavily irrigated areas such as Jinghui, villages can be spotted. Note also the sands and salty areas in Dali county.

started impounding water in 1960, its backwash effect and silting of the Wei River bed near its confluence with the Luo River and Yellow River caused considerable problems of drainage in the low-lying areas of Huaxian, Huayin, Dali and Tongguan counties.[14] Reservoirs and irrigation systems had a reduced life-span and high maintenance cost because of increasing silt loads in rivers.[15] The city of Xi'an began to suffer from increasing shortages of water for industrial and human use, due to insufficient replenishment of ground water. By 1980, the Feng and Ba Rivers, which had supplied a one-million city population with water during the Han and Tang dynasties, ran dry for almost half of the year – their upper basins in the Qinling mountains had been completely denuded. Only the Hei River still has a densely forested basin and holds a considerable flow. According to a geographer 'the most fundamental and only way to solve the present water shortage in Xi'an is to restore the forest belt on the north slope of the Qinling mountains.'[16] Both the loess plateau and the Qinling mountain areas became increasingly vulnerable to floods in case of heavy rainfall, a fact which became painfully clear in a series of flood disasters in 1977, 1980, 1981 and 1983, which cost hundreds of lives and great material damage.[17] These floods were attributed mainly to the loss of forest and grass cover because of reclamation by the peasantry.[18] Since then reforestation efforts have been increased.

In the loess highlands in the northern part of Guanzhong during the 1970s the trees most commonly used for reforestation were the Chinese pine (*Pinus tabulae-formis*), the oriental arbor vitae, and the locust (*robinia pseudoacacia*, imported from Germany during the 1960s); the tree of heaven, small-leaf poplar, false indigo, jujube and persimmon were also used in smaller quantities. Shrubs such as buckthorn and oleander were used as well. At the end of the 1970s, experiments with air-seeding trees, shrubs and grasses were conducted by the Wugong Institute of Water and Soil Conservation in Yichuan county; particularly air-seeding of loco (*Astralagus adsurgens*) was successful, if sown immediately after rainfall. Within a year, roots would be over one meter deep. The following year, yield would be 20 tons per hectare. As a legume, it increases soil nitrogen content and creates favourable conditions for planting trees. It also is a good fodder crop.[19]

For trees, lack of surface and underground water is the major barrier to survival. The saplings need many years of careful artificial watering before being able to survive independently. In 1973, Chunhua county was designated as a 'model district'. Through state aid and large-scale efforts by the county population, the forest cover was increased from 3 percent in 1973 to 16.8 percent in 1980 and 18.8 percent in 1981:

From 1949 till 1974, only 10 percent of the labour force in Chunhua county was used in forestry or animal husbandry . . . Only 170 ha of barren land and slopes was afforested per year. In 1974–6 over 40,000 people (i.e. the total rural labour force) took part in afforestation work, creating a total of 16,000 ha of forest . . . There are now 238 tree-farms with 1,776 men personnel, and 2,268 permanent forest protection employees . . . In State-managed afforestation projects, collective labourers receive 105 to 120 *yuan* of compensation for each hectare of afforested area . . . In 1979, average gross income from fruit was 26.6 *yuan* per household in the county.[20]

Not only the income from timber and fruit has considerably increased as a consequence, but also the area under irrigation and the annual output of grain in this county.[21]

Over the past decades there have been successive pleas, plans, government incentives and regulations to curb or stop the ongoing destruction of the forests of Shaanxi.[22] An important element in this effort was the establishment of firm ownership rights after rural collectivization had found a definite shape in 1962:

In forest areas where the ownership right is ascertained, authority and responsibility must be definitely assigned so that existing forests are well protected and nursed. Where it has not been ascertained, this should be done immediately . . . From now on, afforestation must firmly follow the policy that forests which are planted by the State will belong to the State, those by the commune will belong to the commune, those by the production team will belong to the production team, and miscellaneous trees planted by individuals will belong to the individual.[23]

After a leftist deviation during the 1970s, when privately-owned trees were confiscated from peasants in some areas, the latter policy, of ownership belonging to whoever plants a tree, was restored in 1979. In 1981, the peasants were permitted to have individual mountain plots, and also to collectively own mountain plots which were subject to obligatory sales to the State.[24] The effectiveness of regulations appears to have been hampered by lack of control and lack of sanctions. The vagueness and unreliability of past and present official data on forests make an overall quantitative assessment impossible.

Within Guanzhong, the above-mentioned processes caused by population pressure on natural resources had been continuing already for many centuries. The present official data claim considerable increases in the forest area since 1949. The forest acreage figures given for that year (which is commonly used as a base year) are extremely low and cannot be verified. With that caveat in mind, on the basis of official data one may describe the extent of afforestation (inclusive of

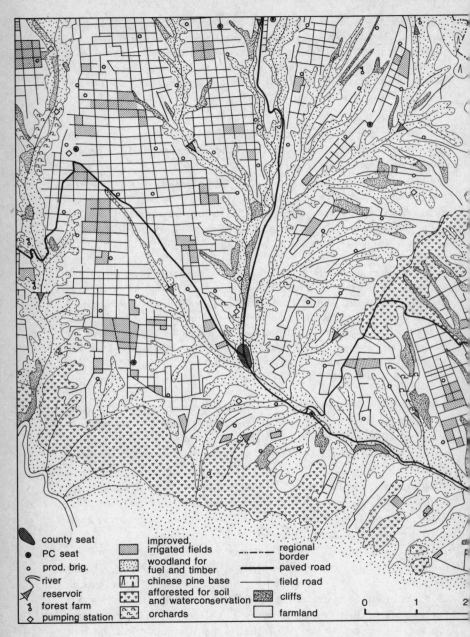

county seat	improved, irrigated fields	regional border
PC seat	woodland for fuel and timber	paved road
prod. brig.	chinese pine base	field road
river	afforested for soil and waterconservation	cliffs
reservoir	orchards	farmland
forest farm		
pumping station		

0   1   2

Map 10 Chunhua county farmland, forests and roads, 1977

orchards and trees along roads etc.) in various geographical areas of Guanzhong as follows:[25]

a the mountainous northwest (Longxian, Qianyang and Linyou counties) had 18 percent of its area under forest in 1978, most of which in Longxian, and an afforestation area of almost half that size.[26] Changwu county had done even better.

b the loess plateau in the northeast (Pucheng, Fuping, Baishui, Chengcheng, Heyang, Yaoxian and Hancheng counties) had 11 percent of its area under forest and trees in 1978, two-thirds of which had been planted after 1949. Of these counties, Yaoxian had the highest percentage, viz. 18 percent, half of which was planted after 1949.

c the river plain area had hardly any forest, either in 1978 or in 1949. However, orchards and trees along roads have been expanded considerably since the 1950s.

d the foothills and mountains of the Qinling have seen an expansion of orchards and a further destruction of primeval forests.

c Deforestation was most severe in the vicinity of Xi'an, and in some counties in the west. E.g. Fengxian lost 71 percent of its adult forest area of 450 sq. km between 1959 and 1976; when the floods struck in 1981, 42 percent of its surface still was covered with mainly scrub forest. Taibai county, however, had maintained a vegetation cover of 77 percent.[27]

Now and in the past the main cause for the limited success in forest conservation efforts has been an inadequate balance of interests. Local short-term exploiters care little about wider long-term goals such as conservation of resources, sediment reduction or flood control downsteam. Over the past decades a growing awareness of these wider interests has been fostered by government propaganda. This was facilitated by the collective framework of rural society. Even so, the poor peasantry has hardly been in an economic position to be able to forego the short-term profits of felling for timber and fuel, or to stop creating additional agricultural land to meet the food grain needs of a growing village population. It appears that sudden organizational changes, such as the formation of the People's Communes in 1958 and the decollectivization of 1979, caused indiscriminate felling on a large scale.[28]

Local leaders and peasants were eager to prove the immediate economic success of the new form of organization, but they were uncertain about how long it would last. This made for a maximal exploitable forest area was reduced by 126,000 ha, or by 28 percent, other years saw forest destruction as well. In the Baoji prefecture, the exploitable forest area was reduced by 126,000 ha or by 28 percent between 1975 and 1979. In the early 1980s every year 700,000 cu. m. of timber was grown, but timber consumption was 1,100,000 cu. m.; 80 percent out of this was felled by villagers, and only 8 percent by State Forest Farms. The permanent cause of forest clearance during the past decades was the continuous growth of the village population under a policy of local self reliance in foodgrain, with a growing need for agricultural land, fuel and timber – a problem recognized again since 1978:[29] 'Through thorough discussions, we have found the basic reason why past efforts to improve water and soil erosion on the Loess Plateau were not successful: . . . undue emphasis on grain production, to the neglect of forestry and animal husbandry and comprehensive management.'[30]

As indicated above, the densely populated plain areas of Guanzhong had already been put to the plow a long time ago. Only the border areas of Guanzhong have been directly affected by deforestation in recent decades, which was made up for by reforestation in varying degrees. Indirectly, the plain areas were affected by the increase of silt loads, of floods and water shortages of the Weihe and its tributaries, and by the limited availability of water from the Yellow River.

B. PROBLEMS OF WATER AND SOIL EROSION

Soil erosion appears under different forms in Guanzhong:

a Most severely affected are the Loess Plateau and the dry upland plain, the *hanyuan*. The principal form of erosion on the plateau surface is sheet erosion by water, while gravitational erosion is very severe in the gullies. Annual soil erosion is about 1,000 to 5,000 tons per square kilometer.

b The Wei River plain is rather flat, with fertile soil and intense cultivation. Soil erosion is relatively slight.

c The Qinling mountain area has thin soils with many rocks. Erosion both by water and by gravitational action is very severe, and annual sediment discharge is about 1,000 to 2,500 tons per square kilometer.[31]

The Wei, Jing and Luo Rivers all carry very high silt loads, and contribute about one-third of the silt load of the Yellow river at Tongguan. The sediment load varies greatly from year to year. Within each year, sediment peaks occur during the flood periods.[32] Soil erosion has caused a loss of soil fertility, silting of reservoirs and canals, rising of river beds and floods destroying bridges, roads, houses etc. These effects have occurred both in the severely eroded gullied loess plateau area and in the flat river plain of Guanzhong. A recent map shows the upper reaches of the Jing and Luo Rivers to be the most severely affected areas, while in Guanzhong itself the severity of erosion descreases as one descends to the alluvial plain; west of Baoji city most of the loess layer originally overlaying the rocky mountains and hills has gone.[33]

C. PLANNING AND THE SANMEN RESERVOIR SCHEME

Although the need for water and soil conservation was recognized already well before World War II,[34] it was only after 1949 that government programs were set up for control of the most seriously affected areas. During the early 1950s both government officials and soil scientists recognized that such programs could be effective only if combined with adequate measures for raising agricultural production The most fundamental solution, that of reconverting agricultural land into forests and grassland, was considered not to be viable for the peasantry concerned, because of their food grain needs. Neither could reclamation of farmland be stopped. However, guidelines were given on how to minimize its negative effects.

In reclaiming farmland one should improve soil structure, soil fertility and its water retention by practicing a rotation system with grass for animal husbandry. . . We should not increase the agricultural area, but strive after an improvement of soil fertility, of plant varieties and insect control, and raise unit yields that way . . . We should create and protect forests, close off mountains as forest reserves and strengthen scientific management.[35]

Under pressure of the Yellow River Water Control Plan adopted by the State Council in 1955 the tempo of water and soil conservation work was considerably stepped up during 1956–1960. It was planned that in a 12-year period (1956–1967) 440 million workdays and 266 million *yuan* of state investment, and an unspecified amount of local investment, would be devoted to this end in the Shaanxi part of the Yellow River basin, i.e. in north Shaanxi and Guanzhong. 42,640 square kilometers of eroding land would be put under control that way.[36] Planning, however, was very hasty and directed at immediate realization of both large and small-scale projects.[37] These included building of dams, afforestation by planting and by aerial sowing, sowing grass and planting reeds in gulleys, building terraces and flood diversion projects. This tendency was pushed to its extreme during the Great Leap Forward (1958–1960).[38] It is difficult to tell to what extent policy statements and plans issued during these years were actually taken seriously and acted upon, especially because early warnings by provincial leaders had been quite explicit.

The 15-year plan for water and soil conservation work of North Shaanxi has been changed into a 12-year plan, and later, because of optimistic estimates into a plan to be completed in 7 years. Now there are only 6 years left . . . Because of failures of dam projects, lack of labour power, and the need for current production and for building roads, according to many local cadres this will cause great problems. We should heed these problems . . . The present way of building water and soil conservation projects by the State is, first build large dams and after that mobilize the masses to undertake small projects. But part of the local cadres feel this is wrong: one should build terraces first, and large dams only after that, in order to guarantee their safety and effectiveness. Large dams have silted up in just three years! . . . Collectivization is still too recent to be fully effective . . . There are not enough local specialists . . . The Yellow River Committee has too little attention for agricultural aspects . . . There is insufficient cooperation between departments . . .[39]

Apart from the general nation-wide frenzy for mobilizing peasants for large-scale farmland capital construction during the initial period of collectivization, national authorities particularly urged the loess area population for water and soil conservation projects. This arose from the necessity to protect the life-span of the Sanmen reservoir and hydro-electric power station, a giant multi-purpose project constructed across the Yellow River downstream of Tongguan in Henan province during 1958–60.[40] In the planning stage it had been suggested that the project would also benefit Shaanxi province: it would prevent flood disasters, supply electricity, increase the irrigated area with 135,000 to 200,000 hectares, improve climate, provide extra income from fish and other aquatic products, facilitate water transport, and anti-erosion projects connected with the Sanmen scheme would stimulate agricultural production.[41]

The Sanmen project turned out to be the largest single engineering failure in post-1949 China. No significant reduction of the sediment load of the Yellow River could be achieved in just a few years, and as it appears now, not even in decades.[42] In 1964, four years after the impounding of water had begun, the amount of sediment deposited in the reservoir had already increased to 4.4 billion tons, almost one-half of the reservoir design capacity at 335 meters above sea level. The backwash effect upstream endangered industrial and agricultural development of the Guanzhong plain and of Xi'an. 'So we were forced to give up the impounding of the reservoir, dismantle the generator just installed . . . and start a renovation program . . . This is indeed a lesson not to be lightly forgotten!'[43] Under the renovation program which was completed in 1971, the discharge capacity of the reservoir was increased to 10,000 cubic meters per second at an elevation of 315 meters, enough to keep Tongguan free from backwater influence during *ordinary* floods. The reservoir is operated at full discharge capacity during the flood season when the sediment concentration is high. In this way in ordinary years a balance can be achieved between siltation and erosion of the Sanmen reservoir.[44]

For Guanzhong, instead of benefits the Sanmen project brought only disadvantages. Of the 300,000 peasants who were resettled in 1957–60, Weinan, Dali, Pucheng and other counties in eastern Guanzhong had to accommodate about one-half. Peasants must have felt they had been cheated, when the low-lying farmland they had left was occupied by 4 state farms, with 25,000 labourers, and was not inundated after all. In 1985, several thousands of illegally returned resettlers were ordered to clear out again by central government and provincial government authorities. 'The income and rights of the state farm workers must be protected.'[45] During the 1960s a considerable rise of the Wei River bed occurred along its lower reaches, which caused drainage problems and salinization in the eastern river plain areas. Because of the reservoir backflow, more than half of Guanzhong's 50,000 hectares of farmland below 335 meters became swampy or saline.[46] In recent years it has been reported that owing to the reconstruction and adjusted use of the Sanmen reservoir the Wei River bed has been sinking again. Because of the necessity to flush sediment through Sanmen, however, less use can be made of Yellow River water for irrigation purposes in Guanzhong. For that reason (but not that reason alone) the central government has turned down provincial requests for a reservoir at Longmenkou,[47] and refused to allocate more water to make possible an extension of the Donglei pumping station in Heyang county, which was designed to irrigate

48,000 hectares of farmland.[48] The only exception to this series of disadvantages may indeed have been the very great attention paid by the Government and the local population to water and soil conservation projects in this area since the late 1950s. Scientific research was stimulated, regulations were passed, political measures taken, and water and soil conservation stations were set up at regional and local levels. Foreign assistance has been given, too.

Engineering measures applied in Guanzhong over the past decades have been adapted to the local situation and improved on the basis of research and experiences.

D. IMPROVEMENT OF SLOPES, GULLIES AND PLATEAUX

Slope improvement. The building of terraces on mountain slopes has been common practice among Guanzhong farmers for many centuries, both on the loess hills and on the rocky Qinling mountain slopes. The level farmland created in this way is better able to retain water, and there is less danger of fertilizer and crops being washed away by rainstorms. Yields on terraced fields are considerably higher than yields on sloping land. During the late 1950s and early 1960s much research was directed towards the questions of terrace construction. Width, length, height, slope, most economical design, access routes et cetera were considered on the basis of local agricultural experiences. On steep slopes, terraces would of course be narrow and have high embankments, and therefore would not be easily accessible and workable. Also, up to a third of the arable surface would be lost. Under such conditions construction and maintenance costs would be high, and even so these terraces would be most vulnerable to rainstorms. During the 'expansionist' period of 1956–60 and again during the Cultural Revolution slopes of up to 30 degrees were considered to be acceptable for terrace-building. The resulting field width, at a maximum terrace embankment height of 3.5 meters, would be less than 4.5 meters.[49] During the 'retrenchment' period of 1961–4 and again since 1970 both state regulations and agrotechnical handbooks have prescribed that no slopes steeper than 25° should be taken into cultivation. In 1985, it was advised to stop cultivation of slopes steeper than 20°. Width of fields should not be less than 3.7 meters, and the embankment height should not surpass 3.5 meters.[50] The main reason for these rules was not concern for economic efficiency, as terraces are built by the local peasantry without government assistance, but rather the concern for water and soil conservation. Many of the steepest terraces were abandoned sooner or later because of recurring water damage, high repair costs and meagre returns. With the original vegetation destroyed, these steep terraces suffer from severe water and soil erosion, even more so when left fallow and in disrepair – a sad sight of misguided human effort.

Large-scale earth-moving projects which caused disturbance of the topsoil may have been a major cause of the low yields and increased susceptibility to floods and droughts which ended the Great Leap Forward. During the early 1960s preservation of surface soil was recommended, and it became common practice in terrace construction to put the fertile topsoil layer aside, to be put back again only after embankments and terraces had been constructed with subsoil with a low organic matter content. More care was also to be given to improving the soil by deep plowing and fertilizer application[51] – but owing to lack of machinery and of chemical fertilizer to this very day the hilly areas have not been able to progress very far in this direction. The water retention capacity of terraces was improved by converting sloping terraces into level ones, and by raising the earthen enbankment on the terrace edge to a height of 20 centimeters above the field level. In this way in some areas with pump irrigation water stable- and high-yield farmland could be created.[52]

For the conservation of barren hill slopes, grasses and trees have been sown and planted. Near villages, narrow strips of sloping terraces have been built so as to provide a good basis for afforestation, and fishscale-like pits for individual tree saplings.

Gulley improvement. Already before World War II diversion dams had been built along the middle reaches of the Jing River, Luo River and other Wei River tributaries in connection with large irrigation projects. In the decades after 1949, in order to accumulate and divert irrigation water for the plain areas of Guanzhong, a large number of reservoir dams were built in the gulleys of northern Guanzhong. These earth dams were relatively easy to build, although during the 1950s and 1960s compaction of earth was done almost exclusively by manpower without machinery.[53] Not much land was lost in the narrow and steep gulleys, and most of it was either unproductive or unsafe because of flood danger anyway. However, major drawbacks were the absence of a reliable and constant river flow, and the rapid siltation of reservoirs. According to official surveys, which apply to the whole of Shaanxi province instead of Guanzhong alone, 32 percent of all reservoirs had silted up completely before 1970, leaving only 23 percent in full use. By 1977, of the total capacity of Shaanxi's 120 medium- and large-scale reservoirs, viz. 720 million cubic meters of water, already 47 percent had been lost through siltation, and 40 reservoirs were no longer in use. Also many reservoirs had become dilapidated and dangerous, with cracks, leaks, or blocked flood diversion channels. In spite of these drawbacks, building of reservoirs has continued on a large scale.[54] Where possible, a 30 to 50 meter-wide tree belt is planted along the reservoir bank in order to reduce the amount of silt washed into the reservoir.[55]

The building of small dams in gullies with the purpose of detaining silt and creating level plots of farmland behind the dam has been common practice in the loess area for many centuries. The resulting fields are fertile, retain moisture well, and may produce yields 5 to 10 times as high as ordinary gully slopeland. During the 1960s optimistic estimates were made about the amount of farmland that could be created in this manner and about its productive capacity.[56] By diverting silt-laden water to flood unproductive land in the gully bottom with a silt layer, fertile new fields could be created.[57] These fields, however, are very vulnerable to floods. The silting method of creating farmland therefore seems to be less useful in the loess gully areas of northern Guanzhong than in the loess hills further up North and West. Recently more 'conservative' measures of gully treatment have been stressed: the cultivation of trees and grasses on gully slopes, and the building of small dams and vegetative structures on the gully bed for its stabilization. Preservation of the plateau surface and the building of gully head works on the plateau is the starting point for stabilisation of gullies. Particular attention is paid to maintenance and repair of field paths and roads, which often run along the gully edge – a breath-taking sight for the Western traveller.[58]

Improvement of the plateau surface. In northern Guanzhong, farm fields on slopes and in gullies represent only a minor part of the agricultural area. Most farmland is situated on the plateau itself, and its improvement has been of great importance both to the local agricultural economy and conservation of water and soil. The levelling of fields and deep ploughing have been the major measures recommended by provincial and local authorities. Both measures contribute to a reduction of run-off and an increase of water retention of the soil; they also raise the efficiency of irrigation water use to a great extent. The newly created level fields may be surrounded by a 15–20 cm high

Plate 4 A reclaimed part of the Jinghe River bed in Fenghuo Brigade, Liquan county. Up high is the loess plateau.

earthen embankment, so as to retain rainfall water or pump irrigation water and to reduce loss of soil and manure. The introduction of pump irrigation in the late 1960s, although by 1980 it had not been extended to more than a few percent of the Loess Plateau farmland area, gave an impetus to the construction of such level fields. This was followed by efforts to build such fields in the rain-fed agricultural areas as well. It has been reported about Chunhua county and elsewhere that the plateau surface with a slope of less than 7° is built into square and level fields, which, after deep ploughing, can retain 100 mm of rainfall within a single day.[59]

Deep ploughing in the plains. Deep ploughing has been propagated by the authorities with varying intensity, at its loudest during the Great Leap Forward and again in the early 1970s. It was one of the eight measures in Mao Zedong's 'Eight-Point Charter for Agriculture' drawn up in 1956. However, it requires much animal labour or tractor power. This was illustrated by the problem of the double-wheel double-shear plow in 1954–8; even in friable loess soil three to four well-fed oxen were needed for its operation.[60] Tractor power became available to most of the river plain area of Guanzhong only since 1970 but not yet to the Loess Plateau area. With the introduction of tractors, plowing depth generally increased from 0.3–0.4 foot to a depth of 0.5–0.7 foot, but with deep ploughing, 1.5 foot or more could be reached. In the early 1970s plowing depths were increased, but a 1975 article noted that about one foot was the most economical depth.[61] The actual benefit of deep ploughing, and how often it should be repeated, is still a matter of investigation and debate. Certainly, the surface crust formed under the impact of rain impedes water infiltration and aeration. The breaking-up of this crust has been a traditional springtime practice in Guanzhong. Ploughpan, or compacted subsoil which usually appears at a depth of 15 to 20 centimeters, hampers percolation of water and penetration of plant roots. Deep ploughing temporarily improves the physical properties of the soil and stimulates root growth. In recent years, however, there are doubts about its long-term effects, and more stress has been placed on increasing the organic matter content of the loess soil in order to achieve a more permanent improvement of soil fertility. 'Unless enough supply of nutrients is given, favourable soil moisture alone would not lead to significant increase in productivity. Unless other appropriate measures are to follow, mechanical methods alone cannot maintain the good soil condition created.'[62] To this end, in counties in the irrigated plain chemical fertilizer use has grown rapidly, from about 10 kg N (counted at 100% effectiveness) per hectare in 1965 to about 50 kg in 1975 and about 100 kg per hectare in 1980.[63] For the dry areas, the *hanyuan* and the Loess Plateau, it has been a consistent policy of the Government not to allocate any chemical fertilizer at all. Instead, green fertilizer (to be sown after the wheat crop) and forage crops have been advocated there already since 1958.[64] In the eroding loess hill areas, rotary cropping of alfalfa and wheat or millet increases production somewhat and reduces erosion by over three-quarters, according to experiments conducted in the early 1960s. However, no more than a few percent of the farmland area was sown to green fertilizer and forage crops.[65] The post-1978 policies of diversification of agricultural production and stimulating animal husbandry in mountain areas, and the replacement of cotton by rape in western Guanzhong have given some substance to the policy of reducing the foodgrain acreage and increasing soil fertility and its vegetation cover. However, in most areas lack of water limits the possible development of green fertilizer and forage crops, and thereby animal husbandry and manure. Opinions about development potentialities of mountain areas differ, and are intricately linked up with the question of how much foodgrain imports the government would allow and be able to procure.[66]

Little has been published about other agronomic practices which help reduce water and soil erosion: contour farming, strip cropping, intercropping et cetera. Their use, however, is mentioned regularly in agricultural journals, handbooks and popular articles. The abundance of rural labour, and its collective organization of production provide ample opportunity for labour-intensive practices of tending crops and conservation of soil. Much depends on local initiative and the insight of village political leaders and agrotechnicians. The Government has stimulated local experiments, especially about intercropping wheat and peas, or maize and soybeans on soils with low fertility.[67] There has been no systematic data collection.

Targets and results. Figures about the area of water and soil conservation where erosion has been put 'under control', or 'under preliminary control' such as used by Chinese officials, carry little meaning. There is no set definition of 'control'. These concepts have been useful mainly in the planning stages, when they indicated the area to be treated with soil conservation measures. Targets were set by provincial authorities for the loess area and for individual counties, and began to rise fast after 1956. A provincial plan drafted in 1956 aimed at bringing the total erosion area of 138,334 sq km under control within 20 years. Water and soil conservation projects completed in 1956 served to protect 11,000 square kilometers, 2.5 times as much as the total of 1950–1955. The Yellow River Water Conservancy Committee planned to control 42,640 square kilometers of the loess erosion area of Guanzhong and north Shaanxi by 1967. In 1958, for the counties in Guanzhong and north Shaanxi by 1967. In 1958, targets of between 100 and 300 square kilometers of controlled area were set per county for the counties in Guanzhong.[68] None of these targets have ever small basins in a far more comprehensive manner. For the loess area as a whole, the present objective is complete control of water and soil erosion within a period of 100 years.

Since 1965, another concept used in official reports on farmland capital construction is that of the 'four fields'. These are made up by level bench terraces on slopes (*titian*), level terraces on the plateau (*niandi*), dam land (*badi*) and flood-siltation land (*yumandi*). By 1965 a total of 120,000 ha of such 'four fields' had been constructed in Shaanxi, and another 450,000 ha between 1965 and 1975.[69]

According to statistics up to the end of 1981, in Shaanxi province 36,800 square kilometers of water and soil erosion area had been improved, or 26.8 percent of the total erosion area. This total consisted of 758,000 ha of level terraces, 1,530,000 ha of soil conservation forests, 370,000 ha of forest land closed off for growth of natural vegetation, 325,000 ha of improved grass land, 512,000 ha of irrigated fields in the loess area, and a small remaining category.[70]

E. ORGANIZATIONAL CHANGE

In water and soil conservation work, methods used by government and village authorities have developed along with the organizational changes of the peasant economy and with technological change. Large-scale organization of labour began after rural cooperativization had led to the formation of Higher Agricultural Producers' Cooperatives in 1956. In subsequent decades, labour input fluctuated strongly between years and between villages. Because of insufficient material incentives, local peasant efforts varied with external pressures arising from political campaigns and with the enthusiasm of commune and brigade leaders for collective undertakings. In 1958, the Provincial Party Committee considered that the average number of labour days per year, which was below 200 at that time, could be raised considerably.[71]

Also, peasants depended on state organizations for the supply of tree saplings and seeds. Although for most construction work local materials could be used, for the allocation of surface irrigation water, irrigation pumps and other machinery villages were dependent on local government bureaus, which, in turn, depended on decisions taken by Prefecture and Province.

The early stage of the People's Communes witnessed a military-style organization of labour gangs for farmland capital construction. These were dissolved after the collapse of the Great Leap Forward. Since the late 1960s specialized farmland capital construction teams have been formed, usually at the level of the production brigade, which work all year round (except in winter). Limits were set to their size, in order to prevent Great Leap-style 'commandism'.[72] Around 1980 about 5 percent of the rural labour force of the Loess Plateau was organized in such professional all-year-round capital construction teams, for construction and maintenance of terraces, roads, dams, forests etcetera. A much larger part of the village labour force, maybe an average of 30 percent but sometimes up to virtually all labourers, has been engaged in farmland capital construction work and afforestation during the slack seasons every year, mainly after thawing in early spring and after the autumn harvest before winter sets in. Whenever possible, these activities have been related to ordinary agricultural activities which contribute to peasant income.[73] Since the decollectivization of 1981 peasants work their family plots again. As yet it is uncertain how this will affect the organization and scope of water and soil conservation work. The scale of such work will probably be reduced considerably, and the total effort as well, unless proper incentives are provided.

Another new element in labour organization was introduced in 1983, when the government permitted People's Communes in the plains to enter into contracts with the People's Communes in the mountains for the exploitation of mountain wasteland for forestry and the grazing of cattle and sheep.[74]

Over the past decades leadership was provided by the Agriculture and Forestry Bureaus of each county, the staffs of which were very small, usually less than a dozen persons. In 1982, new regulations about water and soil conservation work issued by the State Council provided that separate water and soil conservation agencies were to be set up at prefectural and county levels. Shaanxi province had 59 of these agencies at three levels (Bureau, Station and Team), with 918 State employees and 844 peasant-specialists who still were brigade members. About one-quarter of these are engaged in research and extension work at one of the twenty experimental stations through Shaanxi province.[75] In some forest areas, separate state forestry farms have been set up under control of the county government. These provide the People's Communes with saplings. By and large, however, the leadership of water and soil conservation work has rested with the general leadership of agricultural production, both at the village level and above.

Finally, one other characteristic of water and soil conservation work may be mentioned, which developed from practical experience of the 1950s. This is the fosterage of model-type examples for propaganda and for demonstration, and the comprehensive development of small watersheds. In this way, in a situation of very scarce resources (especially technical manpower) and a tiny government apparatus a maximal effect may be achieved. For arousing peasant interest and obtaining political priority, model areas have proved to be very effective. These models, however, have not been without danger. Political careers high and low might become tied up with their immediate economic success. The 'typical' model areas, which had often been selected because of a favourable or special situation from the outset, might draw so much investment and attention that the gap between them and ordinary areas became too large. As a consequence, their credibility and effectiveness as a model might suffer. We lack sufficient data and insight into this question. In Guanzhong, it seems that this perversion of the model-type approach has not occurred to a significant degree. 'Model'-brigades often cited in the press (such as Fenghuo brigade in Liquan county) usually have long-standing connections with the extension network of the Northwest Agricultural College or of the Provincial Agriculture and Forestry Bureau. The 'model'-county of Chunhua has profited from its political status as an 'old-liberated area', which it shares with only a few counties in northern Guanzhong but with almost all counties in Yan'an Prefecture up north. Because of the unhappy experiences with the policy of all-out mobilization of labour pursued during 1956–60, in subsequent decades water and soil conservation work has been focused on small basins as units. This is not to say that provincial and county mass campaigns were not continued in a toned-down version. Propaganda work has remained an important tool in reaching and convincing the local peasantry. Overall comprehensive planning and concentration of efforts, however, have become the new catchwords and more realistic objectives are set for limited areas. In this way, small watersheds have been treated as complete units, which gave greater validity to the concept of model-area and more lasting results. Satellite pictures and travellers' impressions show a piecemeal treatment of the water and soil erosion area, starting with the more densely populated areas.

F. RESHAPING THE PLAIN

Over the past half century the population of Guanzhong almost tripled in number. This rapid growth was predominantly rural; even by 1975, no more than 18 percent of the population lived in cities and towns. If we disregard the city of Xi'an, which stands in a category of its own, and three or four urban centers of secondary importance, a most striking fact is that this population growth by itself brought rather little change to the settlements of Guanzhong. In spite of the new phenomenon of rural safety from bandits and soldiers, farmers continued to live closely together in 'traditional' nucleated villages. No building of isolated homesteads took place, no road-side inns or shops sprang up, and also new villages were extremely rare. Urban sprawl did not occur beyond a narrow stretch of land along the Tongguan–Xi'an–Baoji railway, and even there new construction was situated mostly within the immediate vicinity of county capitals. This persistence of a pre-modern settlement pattern throughout the period of agricultural modernization has been largely due to the socio-economic policies of the Communist Government. Almost total prohibition of private economic activity; agricultural production, and sales planned, and undertaken, by a hierarchy of agricultural collectives which owned most of the land and other means of production; state ownership of modern industry, transport and trade; complete control of population movements – these distinctive features of China's rural development contributed to separate planned spatial arrangements by town and village authorities.

A comparison of rural population densities in the 1930s and in the 1970s shows that population has become more evenly distributed. In the 1930s there was a heavy concentration of population along the Wei River; since the 1950s this has been extended to the plains north of the Wei River. As one leaves the (semi)-irrigated plain and goes north into the dry upland areas, population density suddenly drops by two-thirds, and villages become smaller and fewer in number. The same happens at the transition from the river plain to the Qinling mountain

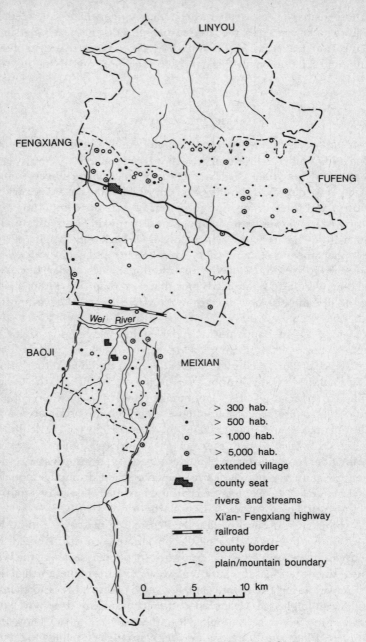

LINYOU

FENGXIANG

FUFENG

Wei River

BAOJI

MEIXIAN

·	> 300 hab.
•	> 500 hab.
○	> 1,000 hab.
◎	> 5,000 hab.
▪	extended village
▦	county seat
～	rivers and streams
—	Xi'an- Fengxiang highway
▬	railroad
- - -	county border
-·-·-	plain/mountain boundary

0   5   10 km

Map 11 Qishan county settlements, 1936

area in the south (See maps 2 and 3: pp. 25–6). Variations in density from county to county reflect mainly the amount of farmland and its productivity, within administrative borders. The map of Qishan county in 1937 shows most large villages to be located at the foothills of the loess plateau and on the Wei River south bank. Forty years later, the People's Communes and Production Brigades were very evenly distributed over the plain. Only a few counties, such as Gaoling and Sanyuan, lie completely in the alluvial plain and used to have a homogenous distribution of villages and rural population. With the exception of the sand area and the saline area in Dali county[76] the quality of the soil in the river plain is fairly even, although the availability of surface irrigation water still is not; the river plain therefore has been capable of supporting very high population densities. Virtually all land was converted into arable land many centuries ago, pastures were rare and tracts of waste or fallow were usually only temporary phenomena resulting from natural disasters and sudden drops in population numbers.[77]

Although land use has therefore not changed very much over the past fifty years, the physical aspect of the countryside has. In the early 1930s the agricultural plain was reported to be almost treeless, dry and dusty:

Except Huaxian and Zhouzhi . . . the whole region we travelled looks like a desert. The effects of deforestation upon the life and prosperity of the people are conspicuous. It is beyond understanding how the people here can work under the scorching sun without ever thinking of having more trees.[78]

Many villages and towns were half-deserted and in ruins:

Often, the city itself seemed half-deserted, with as many ruins and open spaces as occupied mud-dwellings, though its extra-mural outskirts might be densely crowded . . . The smaller towns and hamlets were always filthy and miserable, a few women on crippled feet hobbling about the door of their caves or mud huts, numerous children with running noses and bare buttocks.[79]

This was in the 1920s, but after the Drought the early 1930s were even worse.[80] The country was unsafe. Villages were surrounded by earthen walls. Moreover, at the gate of each house there was a 'ferocious wolflike watchdog.'[81] Dirt roads were primitive, narrow and impassable during rains. Access to the plain was difficult, and transport slow and dangerous. Many steep ascents and descents were the

principal handicap of roads in west Guanzhong. The worst roads were
often those carrying the heaviest traffic. Tracks would erode fast, and
sink deeper and deeper into the soft loess soil. Tiny farming plots were
worked by individual farmers, often without the help of oxen. Graves
dotted the fields in areas where no hills were available for graveyards.
Across the bare plain, from the gate of one village one might see the
walls and low rooftops of several other walled villages. Wooden carts
pulled by a span of mules, rickshaws and wheelbarrows with high loads
moved slowly across the plain, leaving clouds of dust along their trail.
Spots of green indicated the presence of a farmer's well. Only along the
many southern tributaries of the Wei River, at the foothills of the
Qinling mountain range, was vegetation more lush:

The landscape in this section is very beautiful . . . Numerous streams and
canals with clear water, bubbling under the shadow of willow trees and
winding between the rice fields give the weary traveller an alluring feeling.[82]

How different is the picture of the Guanzhong plain today!

Railroads give access from several directions. The treeless dustbowl
north of the Wei River has gone, but so have the bubbling clear
streams of the South. Most water has been forced into straight canals.
Across the Wei River, ferries have been replaced by bridges. Tractors
and bicycles mingle with rubber-tyred carts on the macadam roads.
Between the fields the long, straight dirt roads are lined with poplars.
Land has been reshaped into large rectangular plots, which do not
allow for such oddities as graves or temples. In 1983–4, most plots were
divided between households, and now are very narrow and long. Two
crops a year are often grown, irrigated by pump wells and in tractor-
plowed heavily fertilized soil. Telephone poles and electricity lines and
an occasional chimney of a brick factory or a lime kiln mark the
approach to a village. The village itself and its inhabitants look
uniform, neat and sober, even on market-days. It is evident that the
landscape has been remade and its inhabitants have been reorganized
by a powerful hand.

For most areas and most processes of change there is little data of a
quantitative nature to provide us with more exact information about
the size and speed of this transformation of the Guanzhong plain. Pre-
war surveys either stressed the picturesque, backward aspects of
Guanzhong, the culture of which had 'stopped in the eighteenth or
nineteenth century',[83] or concentrated on the modernization efforts of
the Guomindang government: communications, control of land rent,
irrigation projects, cotton, eradication of poppy, and the promotion of

education, to mention the more important ones. Also, surveys did not cover the plain areas of Guanzhong very thoroughly. The central and southern parts were better represented than the North.

The loss of farmland to other land uses: housing, industry, roads etc. has been most visible in the immediate surroundings of Xi'an and along the East–West railroad from Tongguan to Baoji. As a result of population growth and of the development of the rural infrastructure in the Guanzhong plain during the past decades, it has been a common feature of all rural areas, villages and towns. Land consolidation after collectivization of agriculture in the late 1950s added a few percent to the farmland area by removing unproductive borderstrips between individual plots, by rationalizing field roads and ditches, and by transferral of graves. The subsequent extension of production roads, canals, irrigation and drainage ditches, drying and threshing grounds and other facilities may however have occupied some ten percent of the irrigated farmland area. This is an estimate based on present observation. Statistical data on land use are virtually absent, except for farmland. Both before and after World War II data in statistics and village surveys were biased because of underreporting and this still seems to be the case today.[84] Therefore, although the process of loss of farmland to other uses has been clear enough, it is difficult to give an accurate measure of these changes. According to official figures, the farmland area of Guanzhong was reduced by 358,000 ha (or 17 percent) between 1950 and 1980, most of which was used for capital construction purposes.[85]

In 1956, land use in the Guanzhong plain and in the plateau and mountain area north of it was given as shown in Table 27. The loss of farmland was particularly great in the vicinity of Xi'an.[86]

The process gained speed after 1965, and during the 1970s an average 0.6 to 0.8 percent of farmland was lost each year (see Table 28).

A war-time survey of land use in 17 villages with a total population of 1,339 in Wugong, Weinan and Baoji counties showed that there was very little wasteland. Farmland occupied 93 percent of the surface area. Houses and drying grounds took up 3 percent, graveyards 2 percent, which made the surveyors remark: 'If we assume that in the category 'houses and drying grounds', houses take one-half, then the dead occupy more space than the living!' Almost all farmland was used in dry farming. Vegetable gardens and orchards were a negligible amount.

By 1978, the image of rural land use had greatly changed. Much of

Table 27 *Land use in the Guanzhong plain and Weibei plateau, 1956*

	Guanzhong plain (1,000 ha)	Percentage of total (%)	Weibei Gaoyuan[b] (1,000 ha)	Percentage of total (%)
Agricultural land	1,596.3[a]	58.1	834.5	26.6
Forest land	140.9	5.1	219.9	7.0
Grassland in use	33.3	1.2	316.7	10.1
Wasteland	689.1	25.1	1,298.1	41.4
Non-agricultural use	287.0	10.4	462.8	14.8
(Total	2,746.5	100	3,131.9	100)
(Rural population		7,601,816)		

[a]includes 74,900 hectares of fodder crops (mainly alfalfa)
[b]includes 5 counties in Yan'an prefecture
Source: Qinchuan Niu Diaochadui (ed.), *Qinchuan Niu Diaocha Yanjiu Baogao*, Xi'an 1958, p. 5–6.

Table 28 *Farmland area in 7 counties, 1957–1978*
(1,000 mou)

	1957	1965	1974	1978	percentage reduction 1957–1978
Wugong	546	533[+]	518	509	6.8
Weinan	1442	1374	1331	1291	10.5
Hancheng	575	571	531	509	11.5
Pucheng	1994	1980	1893	1859	6.8
Liquan	1054	1038	958	926	12.1
Qianxian	1170	1141[+]	1103	1070	8.5
Chunhua	721	679	613	580	19.6
Total 7 counties	7502	7317	6947	6744	11.1
	1957–1965	1965–1974	1974–1978	1957–1978	
Yearly percentage of decrease	0.3	0.6	0.8	0.5	

[+] interpolated figure.
Source: data from County Agricultural Bureaus.

Table 29 *Land use in 17 villages in 3 counties, 1941*

	Wugong ha	%	Weinan ha	%	Baoji ha	%	Total ha	%
irrigated fields	2.3	2.2	–	–	10.5	17.5	12.8	3.8
dry farming	93.9	89.5	165.5	96.1	40.7	68.3	300.1	89.1
graveyards	2.1	2.0	2.6	1.5	1.7	2.9	6.4	1.9
houses and drying grounds	2.7	2.5	4.0	2.3	4.1	6.0	10.7	3.2
riverbanks	3.6	3.5	–	–	1.4	2.3	5.0	1.5
wasteland	0.1	–	–	–	1.3	2.1	1.4	0.4
vegetable gardens	0.1	–	0.1	0.1	–	–	0.2	–
orchards	0.1	–	–	–	–	–	0.1	–
Total	104.9	100	172.2	100	59.6	100	336.7	100

Source: Xiong Baiheng and Wang Dianjun, *Shaanxisheng Tudi Zhidu Diaocha Yanjiu,* Wugong 1941, p. 21.

the farmland was irrigated. Graveyards were nowhere to be seen, although not entirely non-existent.[87] Houses and courtyards had expanded considerably, and apparently over the 220 square meter limit per household set by the provincial government in 1958.[88] Next to the village a highly fertilized, well-watered stretch of vegetable gardens was tended carefully by individual households, as part of the private plot. Orchards or at least a few individual fruit trees had been planted in every village. The increase of vegetable gardens, fruit trees, melon fields et cetera may be attributed not only to a rise in the general standard of living in the Guanzhong plain, but also to greatly improved rural safety since 1949. Social control was reinforced by communism, and after collectivization orchards and melon fields were under permanent surveillance by team members during the period immediately before harvest. So thefts gave much less cause for worry.

Plot sizes were very small in Guanzhong, as they were in most parts of China, because of population pressure and the inheritance system. When land was divided among sons, each might want a separate part of the good and the bad land, and the land nearby and the land farther away. Having several pieces of farmland of different quality had the advantage of spreading crop risks and labour. Most peasants were smallholders, owning the land they cultivated. Large landholdings were very exceptional. During the 1930s the average landholding per household was about 2 ha, varying from 0.5 ha in the most fertile irrigated area along the Wei River to over 3 ha in the dry upland area.[89] These differentials reflected different productivity of the soil, and could also occur within the boundary of one county or even one village. In areas with rural industry or near towns, some farms were very small and provided only a minor part of the household income. So farm size was not directly related to economic wealth, although of course poor farmers and small households, on the average, had smaller farms than rich farmers and large households, within the same area had. Wugong county, which had different qualities of land roughly coinciding with its four sub-districts, may serve as an example of different farm sizes.

As Table 30 shows, in the northern First District of Wugong farmholdings generally were between 0.7 and 3 ha, in the Second District, between 0.5 and 2 ha; and in the irrigated Third and South Districts, smaller than 1 ha. Because most farmers owned their land (only 2.5 percent were tenants, 23.5 percent rented part of their land) the size of farmholdings generally was similar to the size of farms. The

Table 30 *Distribution of land ownership in the four districts of Wugong county, 1936*
(percentage of all rural households)

ha	0–⅓	⅓–⅔	⅔–1	1–1⅓	1⅓–2	2–2⅔	2⅔–3⅓	3⅓–6⅔	6⅔–
First	%	5	10	14	13	21	17	7	11	1.6
Second	%	12	24	17	13	15	8	5	7	0.3
Third	%	51	25	11	6	5	1	–	–	–
South	%	40	26	16	4	7	5	1	2	–
Total	%	21	19	14	11	14	9	4	7	0.7
(Farm size	%	20	18	14	10	15	10	5	6	0.4)
(Average household size (persons)		3.8	4.6	5.6	6.0	6.1	6.7	7.8	10.3	15.1

Source: Ma Yulin, *Wugongxian Tudi Wentizhi Yanjiu*, Wugong, 1936, pp. 17 and 32.

Table 31 *Plot sizes in Wugong, Weinan, Baoji and Nanxiong, 1941*

Farm size	Largest plot (ha)	Smallest plot (ha)	Average [+] (ha)
Very small	0.17	0.07	0.12
Small	0.31	0.09	0.21
Middle	0.59	0.13	0.37
Large	1.00	0.13	0.57
All farms	0.52	0.11	0.31

[+]This figure is not a weighted average, but the arithmetical mean.
Source: Xiong and Wang, *Shaanxisheng Tudi Zhidu Diaocha Yanjiu,* 1941

average sizes corresponded more or less with differences in productivity as reflected in land prices. The average plot size, however, was much smaller than this, because most farms consisted of three to five plots.[90] According to a 1941 survey, as shown in Table 31, plot sizes varied from less than 0.1 ha on small farms to 0.6 ha and more on large farms.

Although farmers lived together in nucleated villages, the plain was so densely settled that their farthest field usually was less than one kilometer away.[91] Villages were small, especially in dry land areas. Their size varied from an average 30 households in dryland counties, such as Pucheng, to an average 85 households in irrigated counties such as Huayin, according to a 1936 survey of six counties. The average village in those six counties had a population of 50 households with 293 people, well below average size in the North China plain.[92] The average distance of one kilometer to the farthest plot – and therewith the spacing of rural settlements – had an obvious economic rationale. With increasing distance, a larger labour effort had to be spent in going to and fro, and in transporting fertilizer etc. Rural studies of other developing countries have shown that 'at a distance of one kilometer the decline in net return is large enough to be significant as a factor adversely affecting the prosperity of the farming population'.[93] This is a fortiori the case in the labour-intensive irrigated agriculture which developed in many areas of Guanzhong over the past decades. Intensification of agriculture might have called for further dispersion of settlements. Reasons for *concentration* of settlements, however, have

Table 32 *Villages and administrative divisions of Huxian county, 1932*

Subdistrict	Number of villages	Average population (persons)	Male	Female	Ratio M/F	House-hold size	Farmland area (mou)	Farmland per cap. (mou)	Farmland per village (mou)
Qindu	5[×]	771	2,625	1,230	2.1	5.5	5,691	1.5	1,138
Xianzhong	24[×]	241	3,835	1,947	2.0	5.2	11,263	1.9	469
Dawangzhen	4[×]	551	1,313	893	1.5	4.7	6,197	2.8	1,549
Anshan	17	338	3,153	2,596	1.2	5.4	20,223	3.5	1,190
Taiping(nan)	20	278	2,976	2,586	1.2	5.5	20,262	3.6	1,013
Luoshen(bei)	10	369	1,999	1,694	1.2	5.0	13,514	3.7	1,351
Taiping(bei)	17	375	3,501	2,879	1.2	5.1	23,882	3.7	1,405
Huayuan	20	369	4,012	3,364	1.2	5.7	28,341	3.8	1,417
Huayang	18	390	3,952	3,060	1.3	4.8	27,529	3.9	1,529
Baoyu	17	338	3,072	2,667	1.2	4.5	24,652	4.3	1,450
Xinyang	25	288	3,921	3,293	1.2	5.6	31,509	4.4	1,260
Luoshen(nan)	43	188	4,488	3,584	1.3	4.5	35,277	4.4	820
Xibei(nan)	27	221	3,340	2,614	1.3	6.3	26,588	4.5	985
Xibei(bei)	16	305	2,757	2,119	1.3	5.4	22,909	4.7	1,432
Taofeng	30	253	4,187	3,400	1.2	5.3	37,165	4.9	1,239
Zheng(bei)	55	309	9,442	7,568	1.2	6.4	83,293	4.9	1,514
Wenyi	15	265	2,219	1,763	1.3	4.9	20,154	5.1	1,344
Zheng(xi)	32	256	4,464	3,724	1.2	5.0	46,841	5.7	1,464
Total	395	294	65,256	50,981	1.3		485,471	4.2	1,229

[×]These 'villages' actually are split-ups of the county capital and of two market towns.
Source: Chongxiu Huxian Xianzhi 1933, pp. 97–147.

Graph C Village sizes in Huxian, 1932

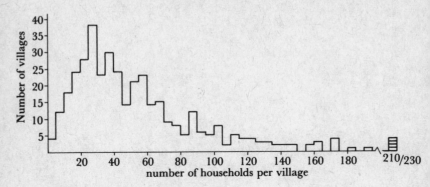

Source: *Zhongxiu Huxian Xianzhi*, 1934

become considerably stronger with the development of social services such as shops, banks, repair stations, and granaries. Since the 1970s, moreover, tractor transport has become more available. Yet no concentration of village settlements has occurred. This is partly due to the labour intensification factor mentioned above, partly also to the collectivization policies which gave every village the status of a separate land-holding unit and a political unit. Also, the rapid growth of rural population after 1949 made most villages more than double in size.

Fragmentation of landholdings was carried even further by the Land Reform in 1950–1951. At the time, Guanzhong had a population of 7 million, almost all rural, and a farmland area of 1,864,000 ha. In the process of Land Reform, 224,000 ha or 12 percent of all farmland was redistributed to 460,000 households. Landlords and 'rich peasants' lost most of their land. Almost all hired labourers, half of the poor peasants and also some 'middle peasants' received some land.[94] So the few large landholdings were dissolved, and many new tiny farms were created. Never meant to be permanent, this situation was fundamentally changed by cooperativization and collectivization.

The formation of collectives was a complex political and social process, which has been described well in the existing literature on China. There have been no studies, however, on the question of what determined the eventual *sizes* of collectives, possibly because of lack of data. National guidelines left considerable latitude,[95] so that provincial and local leadership could and eventually did adopt quite different sizes of People's Communes and production brigades 'in accordance with local conditions' and 'in accordance with the development of production forces'. Production teams as the basic unit of agricultural production and distribution showed less variation in size.

In Shaanxi province, the production brigades established in 1962 fell back to the same size as the Higher Agricultural Producers' Cooperatives which had existed in 1956–7. The sizes of production teams (some 30 households) were either similar to, or smaller than, the Agricultural Producers' Cooperatives of 1955–6.[96] They came close to the size of 20–30 households which had been recommended by the authorities in the 'moderate' period of early 1957.[97]

In Guanzhong the collective farming units roughly corresponded with small natural villages; larger natural villages were divided into two or more units.[98] While the membership of each agricultural collective increased with rural population growth, its available farmland area went down slightly. In the irrigated and dry plain areas of Guanzhong, the size of production teams was 25 to 50 hectares of farmland, with an average population growing from about 150 people in 1962 to over 200 people in 1978 (see Table 33).

The division of cultivation areas among collective farming units meant concentration and pooling of land, labour and means of production within a set territory of 25 to 50 hectares. As a consequence, plot sizes could be greatly enlarged, both in the plain and in mountain areas. On one hand, the new collective farms enlarged the scope of peasant labour, within the village area. On the other, new economic borders were created where they had not existed before. These administrative and economic borders became increasingly rigid, and also difficult to cross. Long-existing movements of labour, both within and outside agricultural occupations, were cut through. Farmland holdings which had been intertwined with those of other villages had to be disentangled. Once or twice certain border corrections were made to the base-level economic units, but after 1962 this possibility was virtually closed. The peasant became tied to the soil owned by his village. Exchange of labour with other villages became rare. An example of initial problems encountered in land division is the case of Wuxing Higher Agricultural Producers' Cooperative in 1956.

Wuxing HAPC had 9 villages. It divided all farmland into 14 units; every production team got one. Some teams received too little land because their labour power had been reported as lower than it was.

Table 33 *Average sizes of production teams and per capita amount of farmland, 1978*

| County | Farmland area (1,000 ha) | Agricultural population (1,000) | Production teams (no.) | Per capita farmland (ha) | Average size of production team | |
					Farmland (ha)	Population (p.)
Wugong	33.9	333	1,452	0.10	23.4	229
Weinan	86.1	570	2,549	0.15	33.8	224
Hancheng	33.9	204	1,220	0.17	27.8	167
Pucheng	123.9	628	2,467	0.20	50.2	254
Liquan	61.7	335	1,701	0.18	36.3	197
Qianxian	71.3	404	1,908	0.18	37.4	212
Chunhua	38.7	140	956	0.28	40.4	146
Total 7 counties	449.6	2,614	12,253	0.17	36.7	213
Percentage change over 1965	−7%	+31%	−3%	−30%	−6%	+35%

Source: data from County Agricultural Bureaus

This was remedied. Then, it appeared that the village tax data, which had served as the basis for farm plot sizes, were incorrect. Also, there was no data on the quality of the soil. So a survey was undertaken to grade land and its productive capacity. After comparison, again the land was redivided. Many team leaders and members were not happy with the results. So . . . 'socialist education' was brought in. A final problem was, that the wheat and cotton area could not be divided evenly. The cotton area was concentrated in the south; the teams living in the north had mainly wheat and little cotton. As a consequence, they could not have as many labour days. The HAPC decided that for the first year there would be labour exchange between teams, for picking cotton and harvesting wheat. The next year, after all land had been measured, one would strive after a general balancing of main crops between teams again.[99]

Mechanization of plowing was a major reason for increasing plot sizes in irrigated areas. Initially, plots smaller than 150 meters by 400 meters were considered too small for the use of tractors.[100] In the 1970s, however, small-size tractors had become common, and these could be used on smaller plots. Rectangular fields were preferred to square ones because fewer turns of the oxen or of the tractor were necessary. For large-size fields, of course, this consideration lost most of its value.

The continuous improvement of irrigation and drainage facilities limited the expansion of field sizes under collective farming. Fields had to be levelled with embankments and be provided with ditches. In most irrigation areas water was in short supply and spread thinly over a great number of villages. The system of rotation irrigation, which arose both from the political goal of 'distributive justice' and from considerations of maximizing total output of crops, extended the infrastructure of irrigation. In semi-irrigated, semi-dry areas collective farms cultivate both dry and irrigated field crops, and have to be able to respond to an often unpredictable amount of irrigation water supply. Small plot sizes contribute to the necessary flexibility.

According to agricultural handbooks of the 1970s, plot sizes should be determined by 'lay-out of the field ditch system, natural slope, soil quality, relative ease of field construction, amount of labour, and convenience to plowing, irrigation and drainage'.[101] On the basis of the exigencies of medium and small-size farm machinery, and with regard to the available animal power and scale of production teams, plot sizes between 100 × 300 meters and 300 × 400 meters were recommended for the plains. In irrigated areas, the smaller size was preferred, in dry areas the larger size.[102] Political propaganda during the 1970s went much further, and showed a clear preference for large size and geometry. Some of this might be attributed to a Maoist political line of 'big is beautiful', some of it also to a traditional Chinese predilection for geometrical plans.

'Xingping county has 38,000 ha of farmland, previously carved up into a myriad of uneven strips and plots of varying sizes. It now has been turned into over 3,000 large squares of level fields, well-ploughed and interlaced by irrigation ditches.'[103]

'The Huxian county CCP Committee has led the people to improve 41,000 ha of farmland . . . It was divided into 60 large sections, with each section subdivided into 2,900 small square plots to increase efficiency.'[104]

Xingping county's large-scale farmland capital construction activities were presented as a model until 1978. Then the county government was severely criticized for major policy errors and economic failures. Later, Xingping was cited as an example of the losses incurred by some intensive farming areas which had too high input costs. In 1979, its production costs for wheat had been 0.38 *yuan*/kg, or 6 cents higher than the listed State purchase price.[105]

More successful land arrangement plans of a smaller scale have been undertaken during the 1960s and 1970s, usually in connection with the creation or improvement of an irrigation network. In the example of the Yaohui People's Commune in Gaoling county, which had a population of 16,000 and a farmland area of 2,400 hectares cultivated by 70 production teams, a new pattern of more evenly spread ditches and roads was created. Resulting field sizes were 8 to 20 hectares. The number of villages and isolated buildings was reduced from 160 to 20. Nonproductive land, which included ditches, roads, houses and cemetries, was to be reduced by half to only 6.5 percent of all farmland[106] (see Maps 12 and 13).

In spite of these examples in the press, from my own observations in 1978 and 1979 and from satellite pictures, it appears that during the 1970s cultivation plots in irrigated areas were rather small, usually no more than two to four hectares. The decollectivization policies of the 1980s have caused a fundamental change in collective farming, the scope of which still is not clear. Most collective farmland has now been given to individual households. This may eventually lead to extreme

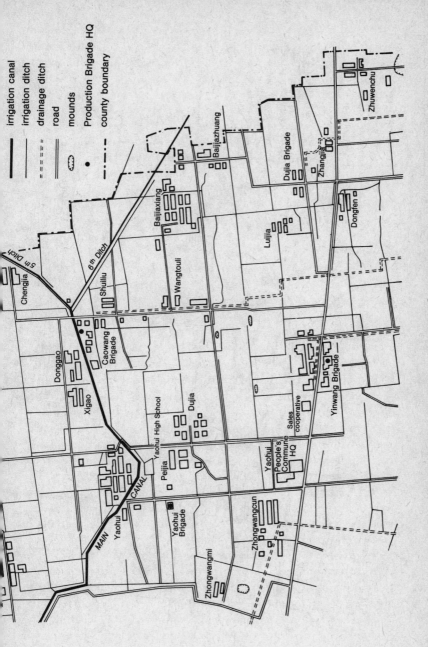

Legend:
- irrigation canal
- irrigation ditch
- drainage ditch
- road
- mounds
- Production Brigade HQ
- county boundary

Map 12 Existing land arrangement in Yaohui PC, Gaoling county, 1975

Labels on map:

5th Ditch

6th Ditch

Chengjia

Shuiliu

Baijiaxiang

Baijiazhuang

Wangtouli

Lujia

Dujia Brigade

Zhangjia

Zhuwenchu

Dongfen

Donggao

Caowang Brigade

Xigao

Yaohui High School

Dujia

Pejia

Yaohui People's Commune HQ

Sales cooperative

Yinwang Brigade

MAIN CANAL

Yaohui Brigade

Zhongwangcun

Zhongwangmi

Zhongwangmi

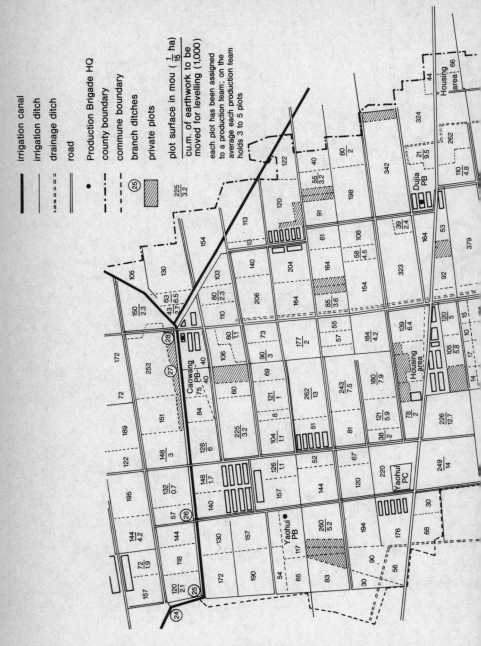

Map 13 Land arrangement plan for Yaohui PC, Gaoling county, 1975

fragmentation, even worse than before 1949. On the average only 0.5 to 1 hectare of farmland is available per household nowadays. A national investigation showed fragmentation to be a real danger, and a threat to modern farming techniques.[107] Also, in conflict with regulations, farmland is diverted to other uses such as housing.[108]

During the 1970s, in the irrigated plain many old villages have been levelled and replaced by neat rows of brick barracks-like homes – a sure sign of progressive government. This saved space, cut down on costs of water and electricity facilities and heating, and showed the virtues of collective living. To a foreign observer, the sight of such a new village is very peculiar, because it is so much like an urban industrial housing area of the nineteenth century – except that there's just one slice of it and in a rural setting.

In the course of constructing new irrigation systems or improving old ones, many roads were straightened or re-laid. Owing to the complete lack of stone or gravel in the loess area and alluvial plain, all field roads, and most inter-village roads as well consist of nothing but compacted loess soil and can be plowed under without difficulty if the need arises. Collectivization and the superabundance of rural labour, especially during the slack season, made it easy to mobilize the peasantry for land improvement schemes. Peasant labour was cheap, both within and outside the collective farm. Considerations of costs weighed heavily in the use of materials, especially of those not locally available, such as tar, cement or steel rods. With land arrangement projects, saving on materials and land was imperative.

Under the collective system, engineers usually got a free hand in laying out completely new irrigation and road systems, without much regard for previous networks, settlements and land-ownership rights. The road map of Weinan county after the construction of the Dongfanghong Irrigation System in the early 1970s may serve as an illustration of this. In its southern parts, the traditional road network still exists; in the north, the new road system is totally unconnected with the location of existing villages (see Map 14, Weinan county road system). Because in the 1980s all farmland has been divided and given into semi-permanent use of individual households, land arrangement plans, road and irrigation canal projects etc. will now take much more time and involve more individual consent. However, with some exceptions, the network of rural infrastructure is quite complete for the time being, certainly as far as irrigation is concerned.

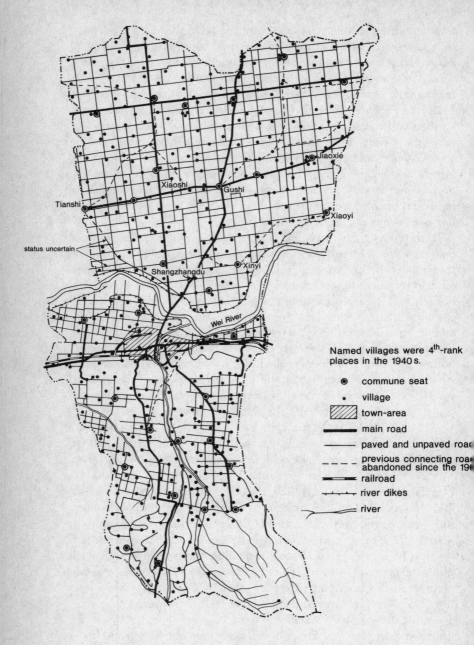

Named villages were 4th-rank places in the 1940s.

⊙ commune seat
• village
▨ town-area
▬ main road
— paved and unpaved road
--- previous connecting road abandoned since the 19·
▬ railroad
⊥⊥⊥ river dikes
⌇ river

Jiaoxie
Xiaoshi
Gushi
Tianshi
Xiaoyi
status uncertain
Shangzhangdu
Xinyi
Wei River

Map 14 Weinan county road and canal system, 1976

Conclusion. Deforestation of Guanzhong started several thousands of years ago. North Shaanxi was taken into cultivation much later, around 1500 A.D., and the Qinling mountains became settled particularly during the 1930s and 1940s. In 1956, of Guanzhong and the Weibei area only 5 and 7 percent were still under forest and 25 and 41 percent respectively were wasteland. Since then, orchards and roadside trees have greatly increased but in mountains and hilly areas most forests have been cut down. As part of the Yellow River control scheme, small reservoirs and protective forests were built at the end of the 1950s and also later but with little success. Reforestation could not compensate for the losses of vegetation caused by farmland reclamation and felling for timber and fuel. Reservoirs silted up almost immediately. The loss of vegetation cover resulted in an increase of the already serious erosion of water and soil and in extremely high silt loads of rivers. Flood disasters have become increasingly serious, as testified by the 1980 and 1981 flood disasters. Generally speaking, successive state regulations and pleas and measures to curb forest destruction have not been effective in stopping local communities and individual peasants who could not afford to care about long-term goals of conservation of resources, let alone about down-stream goals of flood control. The government did not supply sufficient incentives for halting short-term exploitation. Under a policy of local self-reliance, the growing village population just had to fulfill its needs for foodgrain, fuel, timber and money income.

For Guanzhong, the Sanmen project brought many disadvantages. Some 300,000 peasants had to be resettled (as it turned out, most of them unnecessarily so), farmland along the Wei River lower reaches became swampy and saline, and because of the necessity to flush silt through Sanmen, less Yellow River water could be allocated to Shaanxi for irrigation. But it did make clear to anyone, that soil conservation measures were urgently needed. Building steep terraces was prohibited, more care was taken in preserving the fertile topsoil, embankments were built on terrace edges, grass was sown and trees planted on barren slopes. Gully dams were built to create small level fields which were very productive but vulnerable to floods. On the plateau, farmland has been levelled, deep-ploughed and surrounded by earthen embankments so as to retain water, soil and fertilizer. In the plains, ploughing depths were increased to 20 to 25 centimeters by the coming of tractors; the breaking-up of the ploughpan increased moisture retention and benefited root growth. Green fertilizer and forage crops helped to reduce erosion but most hill areas lack sufficient water for such second crops.

Because of inadequate incentives, local peasant efforts varied with external pressures from political campaigns and with the activism of local leaders. The large-scale campaigns of the 1950s were abandoned for more realistic local efforts directed at treatment of small basins in the 1960s. Specialized small teams were formed for that purpose. Around 1980, about 5 percent of the rural labour force on the loess plateau worked in permanent farmland and road construction teams and, seasonally, most of the labour took part in such work. De-collectivization changed all that. Now hillsides have been given over to individual exploitation. Instead of 'model' brigades, we now see 'model' peasants and more so than before the only yardstick is economic success, e.g. in growing fruit trees or keeping milk goats. Now and before, in most places nature is stronger than man and control of water and soil erosion of the Loess Plateau can only be piecemeal.

Because of the socio-economic policies of the communist government, throughout the period of agricultural modernization and population growth the old settlement pattern has persisted. The nucleated villages have become larger and population is more evenly spread across the irrigated plain. Urban sprawl has occurred only along the railroad and few new villages or road-side establishments have sprung up. The landscape itself, however, has changed. The dusty treeless plain is now criss-crossed by straight tree-lined roads and irrigation ditches. Large farmland plots have been created, worked by collectives instead of individuals. Housing, industry and rural infrastructure together may have reduced the farmland area of Guanzhong by about 20 percent since 1950, especially near the cities and along the Wei River. Rural land use changed a great deal between 1940 and 1980, a process which gained speed in the 1960s.

Before collectivization, farm sizes varied with land productivity. In Wugong county, farmholdings averaged 0.5 to 3 hectares in dry areas and were smaller than one hectare in irrigated areas. Most farms consisted of 3 to 5 plots, varying in size between 0.1 and 0.5 hectare. Almost all farmland in Guanzhong was owned by its cultivators. Villages were very small, about 150 to 400 people. Most counties had a few larger market villages, with a population of several thousand people, predominantly male adults. Often, these were strategically located in the plain along trade routes or at the foot of the loess hill area (where the loess cliff would protect their back and the soil was of little use to farming). After collectivization, every village became a self-reinforcing political and economic unit. Large villages were divided into several units. By 1978, the production teams in Guanzhong had an average population of a little over 200 people, with 20 to 50 hectares of farmland. Plot sizes had been enlarged after the pooling of land, labour and means of production in 1956. In the 1970s a plot size of 3 to 12 hectares was recommended for mechanized agriculture in the plain, but most plots were well below that size, partly for reasons of irrigation.

Land rearrangement and large plot sizes appealed to the planners' socialist economic ideals in the 1970s. In the 1980s, all farmland has been divided and given over to semi-permanent use by households. The consequences of the extreme fragmentation for modern farming techniques have already become apparent in the use of tractors and in irrigation. It remains to be seen whether the state regulations forbidding dispersed building of houses (during the 1970s, policy was directed at concentration of settlements in order to improve housing, save space and raise the level of collective production) will be effective. The present rural road and irrigation network is not likely to be expanded in the near future.

5

WATER CONSERVANCY AND IRRIGATION

A. YELLOW RIVER CONTROL AND ANCIENT IRRIGATION PROJECTS

According to Chinese mythology, the Yellow River was first regulated by the Great Yu, who with a big axe cut an opening at Longmenkou (also called Yumenkou. 'The Gate of Yu'). Here the river descends from the plateau and widens into a 5 to 20 km wide flood plain. Its frequently shifting bed forms the border between Guanzhong and Shanxi province. Farmers have tried at times to settle on this 130 km long sandy stretch, but have invariably been driven away by floods. Over the past few decades, repeated consideration has been given to the building of a dam across the Yellow River at Longmenkou, for purposes of flood regulation, hydro-electric power generation and irrigation.[1]

During the 1920s and 1930s, Western engineers and the various Chinese governments made several studies of the Yellow River, mainly concerning themselves with dike repairs in the North China plain after the floods of 1921, 1933 and 1935. There was a growing insight, however, that while flood control was the major objective, soil erosion on the Loess Plateau was the root of the Yellow River problem.[2] Li Yizhi, a German-trained engineer, focused attention on the need for an integrated basin-wide solution for the Yellow River problems, and especially on the silt problem in the middle reaches. He also strove for the creation of a single management agency directly under the central government. In 1933 the Yellow River Water Conservancy Commission was formed, of which he became Director and Chief Engineer until his death in 1938. Neither then, nor after the war, nor under the communist government did the Yellow River Commission develop into much more than a planning organization. It never gained the degree of autonomous authority which its early proponents (and possibly all civil engineers) hoped for.[3] The Supreme Economic

Plate 5 Peanut fields on the Yellow River bed in Hancheng

Council of the Nationalist Government, the Economic Commissioners under the State Council and various departments (notably of Water Conservancy, Electric Power, Agriculture and Forestry) never gave full responsibility to the Yellow River Commission even for plan development. Provincial authority over the development of tributaries remained intact, as long as the Yellow River main stream was not affected. Only at the end of the 1950s did the comprehensive planning of the Yellow River basin affect Guanzhong. Before that time, the plans for flood control reservoirs on the upper reaches of the Wei, Jing and Luo Rivers such as those proposed by Li Yizhi and again after World War II by John Savage (and by John S. Cotton, who differed from his colleagues in stressing the silt detention function of these reservoirs), the hydroelectric stations planned by the Japanese, and navigation improvement projects never progressed beyond the surveying and planning stage.

The Longmen multi-purpose project was included in the plan for control of the Yellow River, drawn up in 1955 with the assistance of Soviet hydraulic engineers. It was to be started only in the second phase, after the first phase projects would have been completed in 1967.[4]

Until today, however, technical difficulties connected with the heavy silt load and extreme variability of the Yellow River, and the projected short life-span of a reservoir (both of which have been amply demonstrated by the Sanmen project) have made the Government decide against any such project. With a projected capacity of 1,500 MW the Longmen hydro-electric power station is the largest station planned in this section of the Yellow River. From its reservoir a canal would divert 240 cubic meters of water per second to irrigate 400,000 hectares of farmland in northeast Guanzhong and fundamentally solve its water shortage. A recent additional consideration against the use of Yellow River water for irrigation of the upland areas of Guanzhong is the increasing water shortage in the North China Plain, where irrigation water has better economic results.[5] Thus, generally speaking, the Yellow River water has been of little use for Guanzhong.

According to another Chinese myth, one of the ancestors of the Zhou tribe called Hou Ji was put in charge of agricultural affairs and conducted grain experiments in the area of today's Wugong county – one of the reasons why the Nationalist Government in 1935 established the Northwest College of Agriculture in Wugong. His great-grandson Gong Liu moved from there to the dry uplands of Changwu and Xunyi where he introduced irrigated farming. This may have been in the eleventh century B.C. By then, irrigated farming was already practised along the southern tributaries of the Wei River.[6] Larger-scale water conservation and irrigation projects, with few exceptions, were only undertaken much later, when the Qin and the Han dynasties created the first Chinese empire in the third century B.C., with Changan as its capital. The Zhengguo Ditch irrigated much of the plain area between the Jing and Luo Rivers – 190,000 ha according to historical sources, but probably only one-fifth of that.[7] A southern irrigation ditch fed from the same source was added in 95 B.C., the Bai Ditch. The 100-km long Chengguo Ditch diverted water from the Wei River in Meixian from A.D. 233 onwards, to irrigate a narrow stretch of farmland along its north bank. On the Luo River, the Longshou Ditch (named 'Dragon Head' because a fossile dinosaur was excavated) was constructed around 120 B.C., with a 6 km-long tunnel through loess hills, dug from deep shafts. It was an outstanding technological achievement, but the tunnel soon caved in owing to lack of lining. The courses of these three irrigation canals were remarkably close to the Jinghui, Weihui and Luohui ditches constructed in the twentieth century.

To secure regular grain transport to the growing capital of Changan, a canal was dug alongside the Wei River to the Yellow River in 129 B.C. It also served irrigation purposes. All canals and ditches in Guanzhong required continuous maintenance and clearing of silt, and fell into disuse in the turbulent centuries after the fall of the Han empire. Under the vigorous Tang dynasty Changan again became the national capital, and transportation and irrigation canals were restored. New irrigation ditches were added in Baoji, in Huaxian, along the lower reaches of the Luo River, and from Longmenkou to Hancheng. After the destruction of Changan (then no longer the capital) in 904, all projects fell into disrepair, to be revived again one thousand years later.[8]

B. CLIMATE AND WATER RESOURCES

Without irrigation, crops are at the mercy of rainfall. In Guanzhong average yearly precipitation varies from 530 mm in the northeast to 700 mm in the west; 50 to 60 percent of this falls between July and September. Annual evaporation is more than 950 mm in eastern Guanzhong and about 100 mm less than that in western Guanzhong.

With the exception of some saline soils along the lower reaches of the Luo River and the 250 sq km of aeolian sand deposits in southern Dali, the Guanzhong plain has nothing but very fertile soil, loose and easy to plough. There is a long season of high temperatures, and many hours of sunshine. Thus the principal constraint for crop growth is water. In spring, temperatures and evaporation are already fairly high, and precipitation often cannot meet the demands for water of winter wheat or of spring-sown crops. In the months of June through August, because of high temperatures in the Guanzhong plain evaporation exceeds rainfall by 35 to 40 percent and water shortage is large. Thus, maize and other summer-sown crops are always under the threat of drought. For the cultivation of two crops a year, supplementary irrigation is indispensable.

In the upland areas and the west of Guanzhong, temperatures are lower and precipitation is higher, so that wheat or other crops (in a single-crop system) are less threatened by drought. The summer monsoon coming into this semi-arid area may bring much rain in one year and little rain in the next year. Every three or four years, Guanzhong experiences a serious drought (defined as precipitation being less than 40 percent of the seasonal average in spring or in autumn, or less than 50 percent of the summer average). Over the past

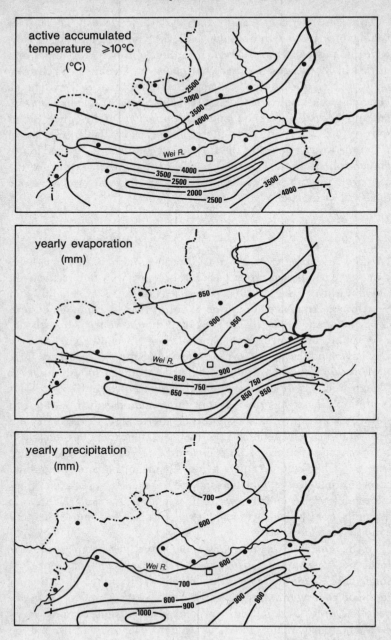

Map 15 Accumulated temperature, evaporation and precipitation

Graph D Xi'an and Yan'an monthly precipitation–evaporation
January–December

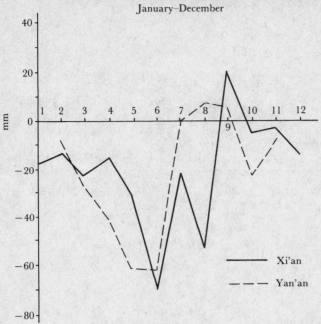

few decades, serious and consecutive droughts have occurred during the Great Famine (in 1928–30 and 1932), during the war against Japan (in 1941, 1942 and 1944), during the Great Leap Forward and its aftermath (in 1959, 1961 and 1963) and in some isolated years (1938, 1950, 1955, 1969, 1977 and 1980).[9] Drought may be defined in other ways as well. The Chinese government has always used definitions based on loss of agricultural production (e.g. harvest being less than 70 percent of normal). A narrow approach from a meteorological point of view, which reflects soil humidity, is the aridity index of *evaporation:precipitation*. When in Guanzhong evaporation exceeeds precipation by 40 percent (K > 1.4) for 20 consecutive days, a slight drought occurs, when it lasts for 30 consecutive days, a medium drought, and when its lasts even longer, a serious drought. Monthly averages of the difference between precipitation and evaporation in Xi'an and in Yan'an show that unlike Yan'an (which may stand for the northern upland areas of Guanzhong) Xi'an suffers from a serious water shortage both in late spring and during the August summer heat[10] (*see graph D*).

Graph E Wei River and Jing River monthly flow averages

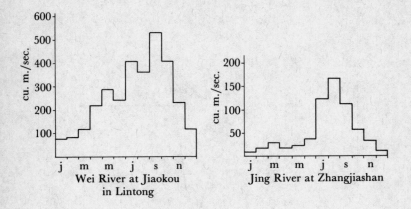

Wei River at Jiaokou
in Lintong

Jing River at Zhangjiashan

Source: *Shaanxisheng Shuiwen Tongji;* J. Humlum, *I Kina.*

Graph F Silt content of the main rivers in Guanzhong and North Shaanxi

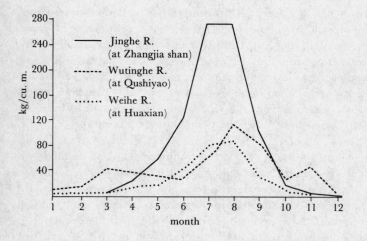

Jinghe R.
(at Zhangjia shan)

Wutinghe R.
(at Qushiyao)

Weihe R.
(at Huaxian)

Source: Nie Shuren, *Shaanxi Ziran Dili,* Xi'an 1981

The rivers of Guanzhong have the irregular regime of rain-fed rivers in a monsoon climate. A small spring flood occurs in March when the snow melts away. The southern tributaries of the Wei River have catchment basins in the Qinling mountains. Their vegetation cover (particularly in the west) is much better than that of the northern tributaries, which descend from the almost completely denuded Loess Plateau of Gansu and north Shaanxi. However, most catchment basins are very small, and heavy summer rains may cause severe floods along the lower reaches. During the 1950s, dikes along the lower reaches of the Wei and Luo Rivers were repaired. Because of reclamation and denudation of mountains and hills in western Guanzhong, the threat of flood has increased again over the past few decades. The terrible floods of 1981, when Guanzhong had 26 consecutive days of rain and dark weather, were deemed 'the severest natural disaster in Guanzhong since liberation' by the provincial governor.[11] Dikes along the middle reaches of the Wei River broke many times during the 1970s, and had to be reinforced. Along the lower reaches, backwash effects of the Sanmen reservoir made the Wei River bed rise during the 1960s, resulting in drainage problems and floods in the Huaxian–Tongguan section.

After reconstruction of the Sanmen dam, this danger subsided, although not completely.[12] Another contribution, albeit small, to flood control has been made by diversion and irrigation projects, and by some small reservoirs on the upper reaches of some small tributaries of the Wei River. One characteristic of the Wei River, and even more particularly of the Jing and Luo tributaries, is an extremely high silt load.[13] For that reason, no reservoirs have been built on their main streams, the inlets of diversion projects have to be continuously cleared of silt, and surface-flow irrigation systems have to be shut down for several weeks a year.[14]

Total surface water resources of Guanzhong are rather limited, unevenly distributed over the area, and very unevenly distributed over the year. Especially from April to June, rivers still carry little water. Underground water resources have been properly surveyed only since the 1970s, when irrigation pumps became more common. The usable amount of underground water (that is, above 100 meters below the surface) in Guanzhong is estimated to be 3.5 billion cubic meters per year. Surface water resources amount to 9.27 billion cubic meters, 2.84 billion of which drawn from outside Guanzhong (See Tables 34A and 34B). Generally speaking, water quality is such that it

Table 34A *River flow resources of Guanzhong*

River	Basin surface		Mean discharge (cubic meter per second)	Yearly flow (million cu.m.)	
	Total (sq.km.)	within Shaanxi (sq.km.)		Total	of which produced within Shaanxi
Jing River[o]	45,431	9,352	67.9	2,140	632
Luo River[o]	26,905	21,691	29.9	943	873
other northern tributaries			±32	±200	n.d.
Hei River		±1,100	±19	1,000	1,000
Ba River	30,000		91.1	600	600
Wei River at Baoji	46,800	17,900	192	2,870	n.d.
Wei River at Xianyang	106,498	n.d.	>254	6,060	n.d.
Wei River at Huaxian	134,777	64,561	337.8	>8,000	n.d.
Wei River at Yellow River				10,653	6,835

[o] At the hydrological measurement stations of Zhangjiashan and Zhuangtou yearly flow of the Jing and Luo Rivers is 2,070 million resp. 890 million cubic meters of water.

Sources: Shaanxi Nongye dili, 1978; *Zhongguo Ziran Dili, Dibiaoshui,* 1981; oral communication at Northwest Agricultural College, 1979.

Table 34B *Balance of water and land resources in Guanzhong (1975)*

	Farmland area (1,000 ha)	Location of water	Yearly flow, (billion cu.m.)	of which from outside area (billion cu.m.)	Area with irrigation potential (1,000 ha)	Project-controlled usable water (billion cu.m.)	Water need (billion cu.m)	Water balance surplus (billion cu.m.)	Water balance shortage
All Guanzhong	2,156	surface	9.27	2.84	1,548	5.23	10.96		5.73
		underground	3.5	–.–	200×	2.36	2.00	0.36	
A. South of Wei River	456	surface	4.0	–.–	250+	2.26	2.19	0.07	
		underground	1.99	–.–	141	1.43	1.20	0.23	
B. North of Wei River:									
1– West of Shichuan River	1,027	surface	4.57	2.57	} 691	2.60	3.69		1.09
		underground	1.11	–.–		0.75	0.62	0.13	
2– East of Shichuan River	673	surface	0.7	0.27	673	0.37	5.08		4.71
		underground	0.4	–.–	80	0.18	0.18	0	0

× Of the total of 1,748,000 hectares of farmland, 235,000 might draw both from surface and from underground water.

+ Of the total of 391,000 hectares of farmland, 138,000 ha might draw both from surface and from underground water.

Source: Shaanxi Nongye Dili, p. 96–97.

can be used well for irrigation, fishery, and industry; only along the Jing and Luo River middle reaches has the water a rather high mineral content.[15]

As Table 34B shows, the over-all irrigation water shortage in Guanzhong is mainly due to a lack of water resources, both from rivers and from underground water, in the plain area which lies north of the Wei River and east of the Shichuan River (Yaoxian–Fuping and further east). If all 673,000 hectares of farmland in this area were to be irrigated, 5.08 billion cubic meters would be needed annually. However, less than 1.1 billion is theoretically available (0.27 billion of which might be claimed by people outside Guanzhong); 0.55 billion cubic meters of water or half that amount were actually under the control of irrigation projects by 1975.

Of the one million hectares of farmland west of the Shichuan River less than 70 percent can be considered irrigable, with a total water need of 4.31 billion cubic meters, three-quarters of which could be provided through irrigation projects. The water need of crops in this area is far lower than in the east.

South of the Wei River, almost 90 percent of farmland is considered irrigable, and overall there is no water shortage, because of ample surface and underground water resources. In the narrow valleys between the foothills of the Qinling mountains, irrigated rice had been cultivated for many centuries, and the marshy plains of Huaxian and Huayin were well-known for bamboo.

C. LI YIZHI AND THE DEVELOPMENT OF IRRIGATION DISTRICTS BEFORE AND AFTER 1949

Early this century, on the so-called Weibei or plains north of the Wei River, there was almost no irrigated farming. Along river banks fields might be flooded in early spring or during the summer; near rivers, water might be drawn from shallow wells. On the left bank of the Jing River, the Longdong Ditch (dating back to A.D. 1737) irrigated some 2,000 hectares, and thus was the largest single project of the Weibei.[16] In 1922–3, the Sino-Foreign Famine Relief Commission had an American engineer, O. J. Todd, survey the area for a possible diversion of Jing River water for irrigation. Together with the Chinese engineer Li Yizhi, chief of the Shaanxi Water Conservancy Bureau and a native of nearby Pucheng, he recommended construction of a 40-feet-high diversion dam on the Jing River and of a new canal with a

2,300 meter long tunnel through rock, to irrigate 90,000 hectares of farmland. Costs were estimated at 1.5 to 1.75 million dollars. To the local warlord General Tian he suggested 'forming a reclamation district for irrigation and calling a meeting of the leading farmers and merchants most vitally interested to get them to pledge financial support by buying reclamation bonds'. Dry land then sold for $150 per hectare, irrigated land would fetch $600. Annual crop production (mainly wheat) would double to 1,500–2,250 kg per hectare;[17] thus the project would have paid for itself very quickly. However, the provincial government and local warlord did not succeed in raising the necessary funds at that time. The project was shelved, but not forgotten, and during the Great Drought the Sino-Foreign Relief Commission decided to undertake this project as a relief-through-labour program in cooperation with the new provincial government and with an overseas-Chinese relief society.[18]

The dire need of the population, extremely low land values, the defeat of Feng Yuxiang which meant a temporary end to the civil war, and the virtual lack of any local authority or organized pressure groups all made it possible that work on the Jinghui project proceeded quickly without any local resistance. By June 1932, a diversion dam with a standard intake of 16 cubic meters per second, a tunnel with headgates, the rock section of canal and main canal to the plain with all bridges and other special structures had been completed. The Shaanxi government, however, failed to complete the work of digging lateral canals on the plains, in part because of the aforementioned problems, which had affected its capacity to raise funds and organize labour. Finally by 1935, mainly through outside funding, eight branch ditches had been finished and 47,000 hectares of farmland were effectively irrigated.[19] Later sources, both from Nationalist and from communist origins, have attributed the successful surveying, construction, fund-raising and organization of the irrigation projects undertaken during the 1930s to the personal qualities and high capabilities of Li Yizhi, who served as Chief of the Provincial Department of Reconstruction. Indeed his record as a professor, planner, writer and political organizer is impressive,[20] especially in view of the fact that most irrigation projects needed outside funding. An important factor in this was the political recognition, after the terrible famine, of the need for Guanzhong's peasantry to be able to stand on their own feet. Irrigation would mean self-help. In 1935, Li Yizhi persuaded the provincial government to borrow from banks, with future tax receipts

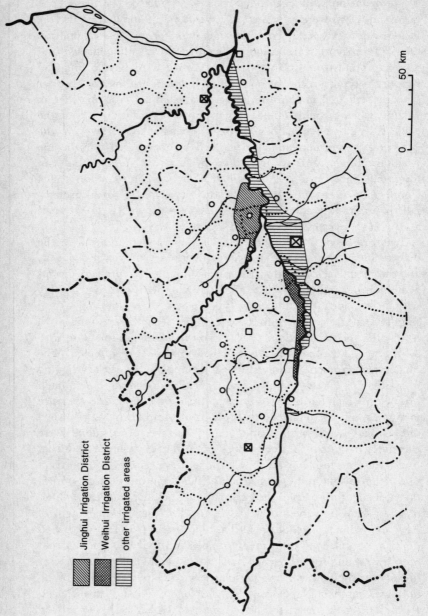

Jinghui Irrigation District

Weihui Irrigation District

other irrigated areas

Map 16 Irrigated area, 1935

50 km

Table 35 *Irrigation ditches constructed in Guanzhong, 1930–1950*

	Height of diversion dam (m)	Intake flow (m³/sec)	Length of main/branch canals (km)	Planned (1,000 ha)	actual 1946	actual 1950	Construction period	Construction cost (1,000 yuan)	Location
Jinghui	9.2	19	274	48.7	44.1	45.9	1930/10–1935/6	1,675	Jingyang to Gaoling
Weihui	3.3	30	178	40	23.7	19.9	1935/4–1937/12	2,300	Meixian to Xianyang
Meihui	1.5	8	122	8.8	5.5	3.1	1936/10–1938/6	216	Meixian to Qishan
Heihui	2.0	8.5	56	10.7	6.1	4.0	1938/9–1942/12	1,800	Zhouzhi
Luohui	16.2	15	84	33.3	–.–	6.7	1934/3–1947/12[+]	3,015	Dali–Chaoyi
Fenghui	1.2	11	48	15.3	–.–	0.7	1941/9–1947/6	426	Huxian to Xianyang
Laohui	1.2	5	22	6.7	–.–	0.8	1943/7–1947/10	1,300[×]	Huxian
Ganhui	3	n.d.	5	0.2	0.2	0.2	1943 –1944/2	n.d.	Liquan

[+] estimated d.d. May 1947.

[×] first phase only.

Sources: Liu Zhongrui, *Shaanxisheng Shuili*, 1947; Wang Chengjing (ed.), *Xibeidi Nongtian Shuili*, Shanghai, 1950; Xibei Junzheng Weiyuanhui Shuilibu (ed.), *Shaanxidi Guangai Guanli*, Xi'an, 1951; Shaanxisheng Renmin Zhengfu Nonglinting Shuiliju (ed.), *Shaanxisheng Nongtian Shuili Gaikuang*, Xi'an 1951; 'Luohuiqu', *Shuili Tongxun* 1948 no. 12.

as collateral. In this way, from 1935 to 1937 the provincial government managed to build another large-scale irrigation project, the Weihui Irrigation Ditch, which irrigated some 20,000–30,000 hectares on the north bank of the Wei River from Fufeng to Xianyang. During the war against Japan, Guanzhong was meant to be a grain and cotton base for Free China. It received financial support from the National Economic Committee for the construction of several more irrigation projects, notably the Meihui Ditch and Heihui Ditch, and also for the Fenghui Ditch and Laohui Ditch which were to be completed only in 1947. The basic concept of all these irrigation projects was the same: a diversion dam, with intake, a main ditch, and several branch canals with headgates. From the headgates onwards, water was distributed to the fields through small ditches operated by local communities. Each irrigation district was to be self-supporting, and was responsible for its own management.

Within the region, there was a certain tradition of irrigation, but only a few percent of the farmland was irrigated. A survey in 1949 of traditional surface-flow irrigation ditches showed a total irrigated area of 20,000 hectares – less than half the area irrigated by the single Jinghui Irrigation Ditch. Data on wells is more scattered – for most low-lying counties this was the main type of irrigation (See Table 36).

Technical management of the large-scale irrigation projects involved managing water, land and people. Water flow had to be measured. Correct standards had to be set for supply and use of it. Waste of water had to be combated. Layout of land and of ditches was improved. Landholdings were measured and recorded. After an investigation of crops, decisions had to be taken about the estimated benefit of irrigation water and about water fees. The rural population was organized to assist in water administration: each village appointed its own Ditch Guardian, who for a one-year period was to be responsible for the good conduct of the water users. The ditch guardians (*qubao*) elected Outlet Officers (*toufu*), and in turn the outlet officers elected Water Elders (*shuilao*). Outlet officers and water elders served a term of two years, and were paid for their work. The Water Elders convened twice a year for a committee meeting with the Irrigation Ditch Management Bureau, where they represented all users of the irrigation district. The largest district, the Jinghui Ditch Irrigation District, had some 60 water elders, over 300 outlet officers and about 1800 ditch guardians (one for every natural village) – a similar ratio existed in the other irrigation districts which had ten to thirty Water Elders. Only healthy farmers who had no criminal record and were not in active civil or military service could be elected as a Water Elder. Their tasks were manifold: execution of measures taken by the Management Bureau, investigation and reporting of water use, assistance in the distribution of water and in settlement of feuds, management of ditch maintenance, overseeing of water fee payment, and guidance of the work of outlet officers and ditch guardians.[21]

Such an elaborate system of irrigation administration and management was completely new to Shaanxi, and after some years it worked remarkably well. The Jinghui Management Bureau described some of the problems met in the early stage of the irrigation project:

1932 was the first year of irrigation. Distribution of water was very unequal. Farmers were not willing to dig ditches as long as the water had not yet reached their village. They thought that all water would be used up by upstream farmers. This passive attitude is still common . . . Moreover, peasants are destitute and weak, because of the Famine . . . Often peasants dig ditches without taking account of geography, and do not follow the courses set by the project technicians . . .

In 1933 farmers grew accustomed to water use, dug more ditches, and started growing cotton. The Northern Main Ditch broke over a length of 9 kilometers, because of a large (11,000 cu.m./sec.) flood of the Jing River, and all sluices and machinery were flooded. During the winter all ditches were repaired and laid out again. In 1934 water distribution became more equal. Management and leadership improved. Because of a lack of rainfall, not enough water could be taken in from the Jing River, less than 13 cubic meters per second. After light rainfall at the end of June, silt content of the irrigation water increased to 30 percent, and the system had to be closed down for a week. The peasants, harried by the drought, forgot all rules and fought every day for each other's water. 'After this experience of drought, we felt that the irrigation burden of this canal was very heavy, and difficult to bear . . . The irrigated area should be reduced. We felt the need for building a reservoir upstream.'[22]

The gradual introduction of consecutive irrigation projects was one of the reasons for their success. Management experiences accumulated, as did insight into farmers' reactions to irrigation projects. Farmers generally had the wrong notion that irrigation suited the summer crop (maize) better than wheat, and would always try for a second crop (maize or cotton) but not apply enough fertilizer to it.

Table 36 *Traditional surface-flow and well-irrigation in Guanzhong counties, 1949*

County	No. of irrigation ditches	Irrigated area (ha)	No. of wells	Area irrigated by wells 1933/1949 (ha)	Irrigated area total 1933
Baoji	15	370			190
Qishan	7	720			1,410
Wugong	12				1,820
Zhouzhi		830			190
Fufeng	18	2,150			190
Huxian					680
Meixian					
Changan } Xianyang }	58	730	29,373	19,330	
Lintong	2/9	150	3,500	1,170	>200
Huaxian	–	–	203	70	180
Huayin	3	170	1,331	180	
Tongguan	–	–	–	–	
Weinan	4	250	188	110	
Lantian	14	1,050	2,170	620	1,590
Gaoling					13,330
Jingyang	7	5,560			
Jianyang	10	320			
Fengxiang	1	50			
Fuping	34/10	1,000	450	250	720
Heyang	–/5	–	n.d.	10	–

					4,800
Sanyuan	9/7	5,670	118	20	
Longxian	10	310			
Chengcheng	5	70			
Chaoyi	3	100	946	440	
Dali	–	–	1,136	640	
Hancheng	46	630/240	251	130	
Tongchuan	8	70			
Yaoxian	10/12	670/290	255	60	
Total	276	20,870			

Sources: Wang Changjing, *Xibeidi Nongtian Shuili*, Shanghai 1950; *Shaanxi Shiye Kaocha* 1933, Tables 4 and 10; Bauer and Liu, *Rural Conditions . . .*, 1933.

They would be lazy in digging earth, and unwilling to participate if the project was outside their own village; therefore contract labour was to be preferred above corvée labour. A farmer would become enthusiastic as soon as the ditch water really started to pass his field, but lose interest if a project took more than 3 years to complete. This kind of experience helped to improve project management.[23]

There were many other reasons for the success of irrigation management as well. In principle, irrigation districts were set up as self-supporting units, all proceeds of the water fees being used to defray management expenses (and to recoup part of the original investment in the Weihui and subsequent irrigation projects). Thus farmers and management bureaux both had reason to be frugal and cut down unnecessary overhead costs. All farmers in the irrigation district had their land measured and assessed at the outset (vagrants and illegal occupants were thrown out), so that each had a well-defined interest at stake.[24] Irrigation water supply paid off, because it was part of a larger framework of rural reconstruction. Government organizations, banks and educational institutions provided improved transportation, superior seeds, loans and know-how – the rural cooperative movement played a useful role in this respect. The newly constructed irrigation systems generally could be completed in just a few years and had been inexpensive and easy to build – the Luohui ditch project being the only exception to that, a major reason for its delayed completion. Because of the delay, when the war against Japan broke out and Shaanxi was cut off from its traditional salt supplies, the salt fields in Chaoyi became very valuable and local merchants and landowners successfully lobbied for a change of the Luohui canal routes.[25] North of the Wei River, farmers had been generally poor and independent, and there was no powerful economic elite to obstruct efforts at democratic management. The few reports about extortion and manipulation of the new irrigation management structures, and about persistent feuds between villages on the upper and lower reaches came mostly from the Heihui Ditch to the south of the Wei River, which used to have more wealth and greater socio-economic differentials. In the words of a later source:

In the Jinghui, Luohui and Weihui Irrigation Ditches serious struggles between downstream and upstream users have been avoided . . . In the Meihui and Heihui Ditch areas feuds were far more serious. There were hate and struggle between village and village, to the point where marriages were broken off. After the irrigation projects had increased water supply, feuds became less frequent. However, the struggle was transformed into struggles between villages and the Management Office. Because of the power of the feudal lords in the Heihui Ditch area, they forced the Management Office to hand over its management to local tyrants . . . The irrigated area shrunk, structures deteriorated and the trees along the ditches were felled.[26]

Neglect of maintenance and deterioration of canals and other structures – which often had not been of good quality to begin with – was a general phenomenon caused by war-time conditions.[27]

After 1949, the communist government reappraised the management situation of the publicly-owned irrigation ditches and decided to let them function in much the same way as before. The Ditch Guardians elected by every village now came to be called Water Conservancy Chiefs (*shuilizhang*). However, general leadership was to be provided by a newly established Provincial Management Office, with a Works Division responsible for control of repairs, water distribution, hydrological recording, land measurement et cetera, and a Water Administration Section which controlled registration of water rights, collected statistics on the actual use of irrigation water, solved feuds about water use and handled water fees. Although each irrigation district was still considered to be a self-supporting economic unit, in this way management of the irrigation system above the head-gate level was centralized. Within the area controlled by each headgate (usually a flow of 0.5 to 1 cubic meter per second, and 500–1,000 ha) maintenance, water distribution and water fees were handled by the irrigation ditch personnel of all levels. The biannual meeting of the elected Water Elders, now called Section Chiefs, (*duanzhang*) was maintained. Standards for water fees were partly revised, although the grading of irrigated land (with the land controlled by each headgate as units) in three categories remained unchanged. It was assumed that water was used for production of cotton in the Jinghui Ditch, of maize in the Weihui and Meihui Ditches, and of rice in the Heihui Irrigation Ditch.

One of the causes of the war-time lack of maintenance of the irrigation systems had been the declining income from water fees. Water fees had risen less rapidly than prices. In 1945, the provincial government had, therefore, stipulated that fees should be set *in natura* (cotton, rice or wheat) by all counties; as a guideline, fees should not surpass 4 percent of the output difference between dry and irrigated land.[28] Four percent appeared to be too little, however, and the 1946

Table 37 *Production and water fees in irrigation districts, 1950*

	production average irrigated	production average dry	production average increase	water fees per ha (kg)		
				1st grade farmland	2nd grade farmland	3rd grade farmland
cotton	450 kg/ha	150 kg/ha	300 kg/ha	18.75	11.25 ×	3.75
wheat	1,350 kg/ha	563 kg/ha	787 kg/ha		not used ×	
maize	1,875 kg/ha	600 kg/ha	1,275 kg/ha	107.5	82.5	45
rice	2,250 kg/ha	-.-	2,250 kg/ha	192	-.-	-.-

× in 1946, the levy standard of wheat had been 180 liter/ha, i.e. 6 percent of the assumed gross production increase.

fees amounted to 6 percent.[29] The communist government raised fee standards still further.

Under the 1950 Regulations for Publicly-owned Irrigation Ditches, each year the standard for water fees and the date of payment was promulgated by the Provincial Water Conservancy Bureau. The standard was 8 percent of the additional gross agricultural production, but if necessary this might be raised. Water fees were reduced in cases of unavoidable calamity or salinization resulting in a reduced harvest, and when no water could be supplied because of insufficient flow during irrigation time. Water fees were not reduced if farmers did not use irrigation water because of sufficient rainfall or for other reasons. The water fees set by the communist government were considerably higher than those set before in the case of the Heihui rice area – which may have been a politically motivated decision to increase taxation in a landlord-dominated area. Households which were very poor or lacked labour power could apply for an exemption.[30]

Besides centralizing the leadership over the publicly-owned Irrigation Ditches in this way, the Government restored neglected dikes and silt-clogged ditches. The Luohui Ditch was completed in 1950. Some 50,000 wells were dug in Guanzhong in 1951.[31]

The success of an Irrigation District is ultimately measured not by its water management, but by its agricultural production. On that score the early 1950s left much to be desired:

In the Jinghui district there is a serious lack of labour power, animal power and manure . . . Crop rotation has received no attention. Irrigation techniques have not been studied. Nutritional power of the soil was neglected. Thus, for successive years after liberation production has declined. An investigation by a Soviet specialist in 1953 has resulted in many proposals for improvement . . .[32]

Although one cannot isolate irrigation from other factors which influence output of crops, from available literature one gets the impression that this decline in output during the early 1950s was due to the new economic framework rather than to a deterioration of irrigation water supply or of irrigation administration. Import of seasonal labour for picking cotton and purchase of fertilizer (mainly pig manure) became more difficult. The cotton price was depressed and 'rich' farmers were disfavoured in many ways. From 1954 onward, however, many measures were taken both to increase and to improve irrigation water supply and its use. The irrigated areas of the Jinghui, Weihui and Luohui Ditches were expanded.[33] Many new irrigation

projects were built by the provincial authorities and by the agricultural cooperatives and collectives. Extension of canals and other
facilities had a positive effect on the utilization rate of irrigation water
in the large state-managed irrigation districts, which still was no
higher than 30 percent in 1956.[34] Of the total irrigated area increase in
Shaanxi province from 224,000 hectares in 1949 to 393,000 hectares in
1955, two-thirds was effected by small-scale projects undertaken by
peasants.[35] Earlier, a subdivision had been given of the irrigated areas
of Shaanxi province in 1953, as follows:[36]

	1953	increase over 1952
(a) large irrigation systems	135,500 ha	5,500 ha
(b) small and medium-scale systems	153,500 ha	8,100 ha
(c) water wheels and wells	90,000 ha	5,200 ha
Total	379,000 ha	18,800 ha

In spring of 1956, 74,000 new wells were dug, many with brick walls,
more than the total built during the 1949–55 period. Many of those did
not function properly, however, because they had not been cleared or
had no equipment whatsoever.[37]

Progress of irrigation work was very uneven. While during 1953–5
qualitative improvement of agricultural production methods as a total
package had been at the centre of all political, administrative and
scientific efforts,[38] in 1956 and 1957 government policy markedly
changed. The Agricultural Development Plan for Shaanxi set a goal of
quadrupling its irrigated area between 1956 and 1967.[39] The 8-Point
Charter for Agriculture, the collectivization drive, and the Great Leap
Forward all made heavy demands on the provincial and local cadres,
technicians, and on the rural population, because they called for a
rapid transformation of agriculture and for a rapid production
increase at the same time. For national reasons which I have described
elsewhere[40] water conservancy and irrigation and organizational
changes became the major means for achieving this transformation
and production increase. As the level of organization and the fervour
for showing how socialist man could transform nature rose, so rose
official irrigated area figures.

In the 8 years since 1949, the irrigated area of Shaanxi province has increased
by 450,000 hectare. This is not enough . . .[41]

In the first ten months of 1957 101,000 ha of irrigated fields were created in
Shaanxi, with a State investment of 3.8 million *yuan*, but in November and

December, 226,000 ha. of irrigated fields were created, with a state investment of only 1 million *yuan*.[42]

In the past two months we have created more irrigated farmland than in the past 2,300 years![43]

During winter and spring, the irrigated area was extended by 1,000,000 ha in 7 months with the state spending only a little money.[44]

Official irrigated area statistics showed a jump in 1956 and again in 1958.[45] This rapid increase was indicative of the great efforts in extending irrigation projects and building new reservoirs and ponds. Some 2,000 reservoirs were built between 1958 and 1961. This still says little about the actual increase of irrigation water supply during those years. More than 100 million *yuan* was lost because of abandoned large- and medium-scale reservoir projects. Two notable failures of large-scale projects begun in 1958 were the Dafosi reservoir, which was meant to irrigate 270,000 ha in Sanyuan, Tongchuan, Pucheng and Weinan, and the Baojixia Water Intake Project. Both were halted in 1961, but the Baojixia project was taken up again in 1969 and completed successfully.[46] Only during the early 1960s were more solid assessments made by the provincial water conservancy organization of the situation of irrigation water supply, its administration and use. By that time, the agricultural collectives had found their definitive organizational form, and the CCP and local leadership had sobered up about what collective organization could and could not do. The main achievements of irrigation administration in Shaanxi province since the early 1950s were considered to be:

— an integration of construction, administration and water use in a single organization. As a result, the irrigated area of the 14 largest state-managed irrigation districts had increased by 163,000 hectares, or double the 1950 area.
—a good use of 'the masses' (i.e. the organized villages) for the rational distribution of water and for irrigation.
—the close links of technical work both with the administrative leadership and with 'the masses'.
—stress on learning by experience. By 1964 there were 11 experimental irrigation stations in Shaanxi. Trials, model examples and promotion campaigns were used to propagate experiences. Training programs had raised the technical level throughout the irrigation district.[47]

After collectivization not only the state-managed irrigation districts, but also smaller irrigation areas had been able to organize their productive activities collectively. The most common form was a seasonal irrigation team, within a production team of several dozen families, which took care of irrigation and of ditch maintenance for all the team's land. Another form was a specialized irrigation team which took care of irrigation work for an entire production brigade or village, and not only maintained existing facilities but might construct new irrigation facilities as well. Finally some of the older irrigation areas had seasonal irrigation teams which were responsible for the area irrigated by one headgate (usually several hundreds of hectares). Organization of such teams and accounting of their work, however, was rather complicated. Before, different irrigation customs had prevailed in various districts of Guanzhong. In the Jinghui irrigation district (the largest and oldest irrigation district, with some 20,000 ha of cotton) and the Luohui irrigation district large plots were flooded by irrigation water. Apart from being wasteful of water this also contributed to salinization of the soil because of rising underground water levels. Particularly the Luohui irrigation district appeared to be vulnerable to secondary salinization. The peasantry of the Weihui irrigation district practised shallow ditch irrigation, and shallow irrigation of small plots at a time; in this way less water was lost by seepage or evaporation, unit yields were higher, and the rate of wilt of young seedlings was much reduced. Experiments showed it to be advisable to apply little or no irrigation at the germinating stage, and to irrigate with small quantities of water through ditches. Rotation irrigation and alternating row irrigation, a maximal use of well water, and irrigation late in the afternoon or at night also were recommended.[48]

Water use was gradually brought under better control. The various administrative units, irrigation bureaus, experimental stations and hydrological stations supplied the information needed to arrange water use in advance for different seasons. Estimation and reporting centres in the large irrigation district gave reports about the soil water content every ten days during the irrigation season. The planned use of water resulted in a more effective utilization, less secondary salinization, an increase of the irrigated area, higher output of crops and lower unit costs. According to a 1964 article, since 1958 the effective utilization rate of irrigation water had been stabilized at 0.4–0.6, or double the 1953 situation. The irrigated area of 17 large irrigation districts had increased from 131,000 hectares in 1954 to 240,000 hectares in 1962. The ten-year average output of various crops (in 31 irrigation districts) amounted to 3 to 4.5 tons/ha for wheat and to 450 to 600 kg/ha for cotton. In addition to the regular Water Use Plan, rotation irrigation plans had been formulated to meet drought conditions. In the case of a too-high silt content of the river water at the intake, or an intake volume of less than 50 percent of normal, the entire system or parts of it would be shut down in a planned manner.

In a summing up of ten years of experience in 1964, the provincial authorities concluded that development of irrigation had been rather uneven. The pre-1958 old irrigation districts were better than the new ones. The large irrigation districts were better than the small irrigation districts, and natural-flow irrigation areas were better than pump-irrigation areas. There was still much room for improvement.[49]

At the end of the 1950s and during the early 1960s secondary salinization became a major problem both in old and in new irrigation areas. The Jinghui, Weihui and Luohui Ditches lost 40 to 65 percent of their water intake volume through seepage, and underground water levels had risen fast.[50] In the Jinghui irrigation district, in 1938, and again during the early 1950s, drainage ditches had been dug; some 7,000 hectares of severely affected salinized soil had been improved this way. In the Luohui irrigation districts, originally a swampy area with several salt lakes, underground water levels had risen since 1955; although drainage ditches were added, water from seepage and from precipitation continued to affect ground water levels. Between 1957 and 1964, average salinity of ground water in the Luohui area (as measured in the drainage ditches) was brought down by one-half, to 5.8 grams per liter, but it was still high enough to reduce output of cotton and wheat by one-third to one-half. With the exception of the Luohui irrigation district, where flooding and flushing techniques were used to reduce soil salinity, and canals were lined with cement, in most other irrigation areas ground water levels went down again during the 1960s and 1970s, because of an increased use of electric pump irrigation water.[51] In the Dongfanghong irrigation district of Weinan county, however, and in the Baojixia irrigation area, history repeated itself. After large-scale irrigation had started in 1971, the ground water table rose, salinity increased, and in 1979 many deep drainage ditches had to be added. An elaborate drainage system also had to be built on 20,000 hectares in North Lintong recently. These drainage ditches took up much farmland and disrupted existing structures.[52]

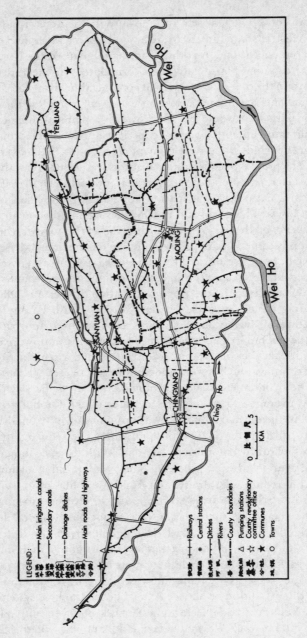

LEGEND:

	Main irrigation canals
	Secondary canals
	Drainage ditches
	Main roads and highways

+++	Railways
●	Central stations
	Ditches
	Rivers
	County boundaries
△	Pumping stations
☆	County revolutionary committee office
★	Communes
○	Towns

YENLIANG

SANYUAN

KAOLING

CHINGYANG

Wei Ho

Wei Ho

Ching Ho

0   5
KM

Map 17 Jinghui irrigation district, 1972

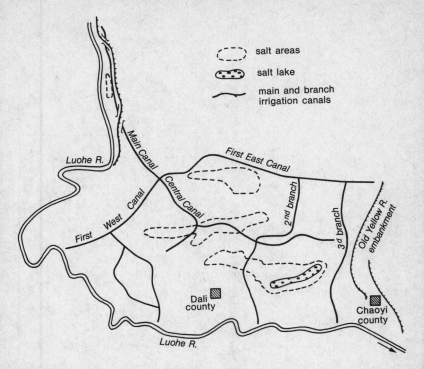

Map 18 Irrigation canals and salinized areas in the Luohui irrigation district, 1965

D. MECHANICAL PUMPING AND THE EXTENSION OF IRRIGATION OVER THE NORTHERN PLAIN

The introduction of pump irrigation in Guanzhong during the early 1960s started a new era of farming, because it added a vast potential of irrigation water which could be supplied regularly (see Table 34). In 1961, the Guanzhong plain had been indicated as one of the priority areas where the central government would start building networks of electric pumping stations. Already 180,000 hectares were irrigated by electrical pumps in that year. Although during the early 1960s the supply of electric pumping equipment was still very modest, in some irrigation districts pump irrigation soon became dominant. In 1964 the Weihui irrigation district used pump irrigation on 52,000 hectares, and natural-flow irrigation only on 12,000 hectares – an expansion mostly due to the Weigao pumping station, construction of which had started in 1958, which lifts Wei River water up 70 meters on to the *hanyuan*.[53] The Jinghui irrigation district started drilling wells in 1964,

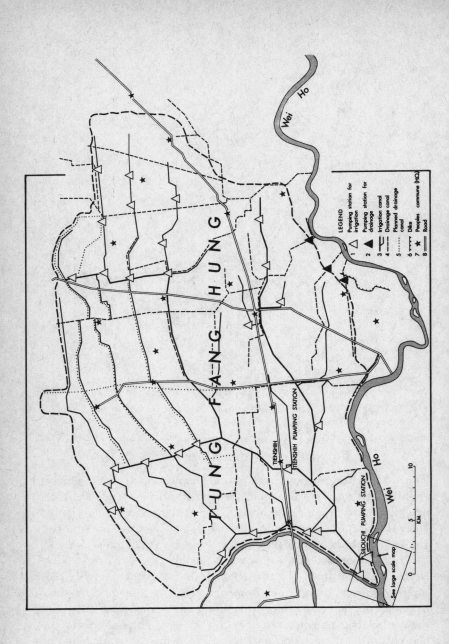

LEGEND

1 △ Pumping station for irrigation
2 ▲ Pumping station for drainage
3 ⊢ Irrigation canal
4 ---- Drainage canal
5 ·········· Planned drainage canal
6 ▿▿▿▿ Dike
7 ★ Peoples commune (HQ)
8 ━━ Road

TUNG   FANG   HUNG

Wei   Ho

Wei   Ho

TIENSHIH

TIENSHIH PUMPING STATION

SHIOUCHI PUMPING STATION

See large scale map

0   5   10
         KM

and by 1972 it drew 40 to 50 million cubic meters of underground water per year from 14,000 pump wells, as against about 400 (*net* use probably came to no more than 200) million cubic meters of water from the Jing River; in summer, 40 percent of its area was irrigated from wells.[64] In 1965, still only 23,000 pump wells (irrigating some 4 hectare each) had been drilled in Shaanxi province, almost all of which were in Guanzhong. Ten years later, their number had increased to 130,000, 90 percent of which were in Guanzhong, irrigating 513,000 hectares.[55] The increase occurred mainly during the first half of the 1970s and took the form of both large- and small-scale pumping and reservoir projects. A minor second 'Great Leap' occurred in 1969–71.[56]

The Dongfanghong project, constructed during 1966–71, could draw 40.8 cu. m./sec. from the Wei River, with a lift of 17 meters, and further northward a secondary station (Tianshui, 32.5 m³/sec. with a lift of 6 meters) and some smaller stations sent irrigation water throughout the northern part of Weinan. In this way, it could irrigate 79,000 hectares of farmland.[57] (See *Map 19: Dongfanghong*). The Baojixia project, constructed during 1969–1971, was expanded further to become Guanzhong's largest irrigation district with an irrigated area of some 160,000 hectares in Fufeng, Wugong, Qianxian, Liquan and Xianyang.[58] In 1971, 41 percent of the farmland of Guanzhong had irrigation facilities, but only 18 percent of this was of a sufficiently high standard (viz. resistance against a drought lasting 60 to 70 days, which occurs once every 5 years in Guanzhong) to have a guaranteed harvest in case of drought or flood. In 1975, it was considered that of Guanzhong's farmland area of 2.1 million hectares, 814,000 hectares or 38 percent was effectively irrigated – an increase of 190,000 hectares over 1971.[59]

Distribution of this irrigated farmland within Guanzhong was very uneven, however. Of the plain areas and the region south of the Wei River, 58 percent of the total farmland of 1.4 million hectares had irrigation facilities. Of the uplands and hill areas in western and northern Guanzhong (14 counties with a total farmland area of 600,000 hectares) only 10.5 percent had irrigation facilities. This stretch of land is generally from 800 to 1,000 meters above sea-level, with underground water at depths of more than 100 meters.[60] In the 1970s many deep wells were drilled here, some even deeper than 170 meters.[61] Also many small and medium-scale reservoirs were built; however, both surface and underground water resources appeared to

Table 38 *Irrigated area in 7 counties, Guanzhong 1957–1978*

	Total surface area (sq.km.)	Farmland area (sq.km.)		Irrigated area (sq.km.)				i.e. percentage of farmland	
		1957	1978	1957	1965	1974	1978	1957	1978
Wugong	455	364	339	110	n.d.	269	298	30	88
Weinan	1088	961	861	43	115	596	654	4	76
Pucheng	1766	1329	1239	43	44	370	498	3	40
Liquan	1082	703	617	35	112	335	372	5	60
Qianxian	1275	735	713	22	n.d.	271	345	3	48
Hancheng	1869	383	339	23	28	51	119	6	35
Chunhua	965	481	387	1	3	7	53	0	14
Total	8500	4956	4495	276		1899	2339	5.6	52

Source: data from County Agricultural Bureaus.

Table 39 *Irrigated area in north Guanzhong, 1978–79 (West→East)*°

County	Farmland area (1,000 ha)	of which irrigated (1,000 ha)	percentage (%)
Longxian ⎱ Qianyang ⎰	95.6	13.8	14
Linyou	34.5	0.5	1
Changwu ⎫ Binxian ⎪ Xunyi ⎬ Yongshou ⎭	150	±15	10
Chunhua ⎫ Yaoxian ⎪ Fuping˟ ⎬ Baishui ⎪ Chengcheng ⎪ Heyang ⎭	321	66	21
Pucheng˟ ⎱ Hancheng ⎰	158	62	40
Total	759	157	21

˟ These counties usually are not considered part of the *hanyuan*
° Clusters based on similar percentages of irrigated area.
Sources: data from County Agricultural Bureaus, and oral communications.

be very limited. After 1975, although the number of pump wells kept increasing in many areas (by the end of 1980 Shaanxi had 150,000 pump wells), ground water levels started sinking and the actual irrigated area could not be expanded much further. Rapid siltation of irrigation reservoirs severely limited their effective life-span. By 1977, 47 percent of the total capacity of Shaanxi's 120 medium- and large-scale reservoirs (which had been 720 million cu.m. of water) had been lost, and 40 reservoirs were no longer in use. Many reservoirs had become dilapidated and dangerous. Yet reservoir building continued, especially of small reservoirs which usually are less effective in case of serious drought. Between 1975 and 1980 total reservoir storage capacity increased by over 60 percent, from 2.4 billion cu.m. of water in 1975 to 3.9 billion cu.m. of water in 1980.[62]

By the end of the 1970s, most areas had realized the slogan 'precipitation, surface water and underground water must all be used'. For example, Pucheng county had 5,352 deep wells irrigating 25,000 hectares, 138 pumping stations irrigating 15,000 hectares, and two

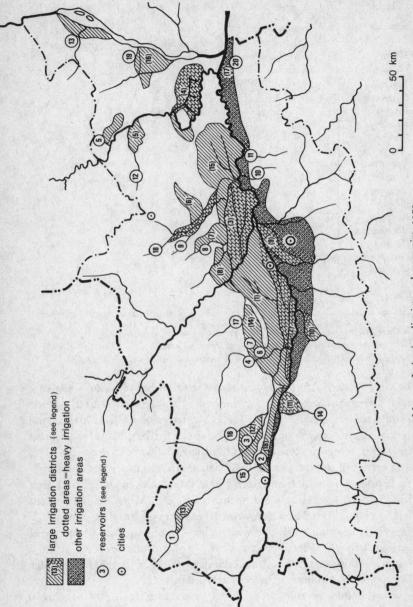

Map 20 Irrigation districts and reservoirs, 1979

gravity flow irrigation districts (Dongfanghong and Yinluo) irrigating 24,000 hectares (one-third of which were also served by pump wells). In Wugong county, three-quarters of its irrigated area used both surface water and well water.[63]

Two very large projects had been started around 1975, in order to relieve some of the water shortage in north Guanzhong. The Donglei pumping station, undertaken by the Yellow River Committee with a 170 million *yuan* grant from the national government, was to pump up 42 cubic meters of Yellow River water per second to various levels (highest lift: 220 meters!) to irrigate 66,000 hectares of farmland in Heyang, Dali and Chengcheng counties.[64] The Shitouhe project would conduct water from a reservoir in the Qinling mountains across the Wei River to the Baojixia Yinwei Main Ditch.[65] As a national geographical handbook remarked in 1980: 'As long as the Longmen reservoir has not been built, irrigation projects drawing water from the Yellow River, and projects leading water from the mountains south of the Wei River to the north must solve the problem of a fundamental water shortage.'[66]

Key to map 20

Main Irrigation Districts and Reservoirs in Guanzhong, 1979

1 Baojixia Yinwei Irrigation District, 158,000 ha. in Fufeng, Wugong, Qianxian, Liquan and Xianyang counties.
2 Weihui Ditch Irrigation District, 87,300 ha. in Fufeng, Wugong, Xingping and Xianyang counties
3 Jinghui Ditch Irrigation District, 85,000 ha. in Jingyang, Sanyuan and Gaoling counties
4 Luohui Ditch Irrigation District, 50,700 ha. in Dali and Pucheng counties
5 Yuejin Ditch Irrigation District, 5,700 ha. in Baishui county
6 Shichuanhe Irrigation District, 1,000 ha. (?) in Fuping county
7 Sanyuan Qinghui Ditch Irrigation District, in Sanyuan county
8 Yeyuhe Irrigation District, in Jingyang county
9 Fenghui Ditch Irrigation District, 1,500 ha. in Xi'an municipality
10 Heihui Ditch Irrigation District, in Zhouzhi county
11 Meihui Ditch Irrigation District, in Meixian county
12 Fengxiang Ditch Reservoir Irrigation District, in Fengxiang county
13 Duanjiaxia Reservoir Irrigation District, in Longxian county
14 Yangmaowan Reservoir Irrigation District, 1,600 ha. (1983: 21,000 ha.) in Qianxian county
15 Dongfanghong Pump Irrigation District, 80,000 ha. in Weinan county
16 Donglei Pump Irrigation District, 48,000 ha. in Heyang county (approx.)
17 Gangkou Pump Station, 15,000 ha. in Tongguan and Huayin counties
18 Fengjiashan Reservoir Irrigation District 46,000 ha. (1981: 75,000 ha.) in Baoji and 7 other counties (approx.)
1 Fengjiashan Reservoir on Qianhe river, 380,000,000 m³
2 Wangjiaya Reservoir in Qianhe river, 75,000,000 m³
3 Dongfeng Reservoir in Qianxian county
4 Yangmaowan Reservoir in Qihe river, 70,000,000 m³ (80,000 ha. irr.)
5 Shibaochuan Reservoir, on Kongzhouhe river. 30,000,000 m³ (1981: 62,000,000 m³) (20,000 ha. irr.)
6 Dabeigou Reservoir, in Qianxian county
7 Laoyazui Reservoir, in Qianxian county
8 Fengcun Reservoir, in Sanyuan county
9 Fengshou Reservoir, in Yaoxian county
10 Linghe Reservoir, in Weinan county
11 Youhe Reservoir, in Weinan county
12 Lingao Reservoir, on Baishui River in Baishui county
13 Panhe Reservoir, in Hancheng county
14 Shitouhe Reservoir, in Taibai county 120,000,000 m³, 30,000 kW (under construction)
15–20 Other reservoirs

Sources: Prof. Zhang and Prof. Li, Northwest College of Agriculture; *Shaanxi Ribao* various issues; Agricultural Bureaus in various counties; *Shaanxi Ribao* Sept. 18, 1984 and Oct. 25, 1984

E. THE LIMITS TO WATER USE IN THE 1980S

Around 1980, however, a definite shift occurred in irrigation development policy. Although the Donglei project would be completed in 1985, it seemed uncertain that the originally planned second phase would be carried through.[67] The Longmen project was shelved indefinitely, and little was heard about the Shitouhe project anymore. The peasantry of the *hanyuan* was encouraged to concentrate on dry farming, and in irrigated areas it was advised to irrigate less.

Some people feel that the standards for irrigation water (300 cu.m. per ha; 460 cu.m. per ha for Stable High Yield Farmland) are too low . . . However, it is dangerous to irrigate too much (a) it decreases the irrigable area (b) it may cause secondary salinization (c) the soil gets stiff and difficult to plow (d) nutritional elements are flushed down to deeper soil layers. It is better to irrigate somewhat less.[58]

Although new wells were still drilled at a rate of some 10,000 a year (for the entire Shaanxi province), more than that number were abandoned. Between 1980 and 1984, the number of wells equipped with electric pumping facilities decreased by 20,000 to 130,800. Reservoir storage capacity increased from 3.9 billion cubic meters of water in 1980 to 4.4 billion cubic meters of water in 1984 – this official figure does not, it seems, take into account the loss of reservoir capacity because of silting. In 1980 the effectively irrigated area of Shaanxi rose by only 6,000 hectares, in 1981 by even less. In 1982 and 1982, by 10,000 and 13,000 hectares.[69] These increases were due to field improvement and to the extension of ditches rather than to increased volume of irrigation water.

On the political level, the reduction of irrigation construction work was explained by pointing to the sudden political and economic changes after 1980.

Before 1979, our province would add about 36,000 hectares of irrigated area each year, but now less than 6,000 hectares. Of course, in order to correct the 'leftist' errors, peasants had to rest a little and farmland capital construction had to be reduced. Why did this situation come about? (1) Many comrades did not know whether to undertake this work or not under the new political line. (2) Owing to insufficient summing up of experiences, capital construction work as such and its errors were mixed up. (3) State investments decreased greatly. (4) Because of decollectivization it was difficult to attract labourers and capital.[70]

There were also some deeper-lying economic reasons for cutting back further exploitation of water resources. Investments in drilling deep wells had always been very costly,[71] some 10,000 to 20,000 *yuan* per well, and the government became more cost-conscious. Falling ground water levels made some wells run dry. Especially in years of drought, there appeared to be an insufficient supply of water and an overextension of pumping facilities and feeder lines. Too many reservoirs, wells and irrigation ditches were competing for scarce water resources.[72] This was due in part to the political system. Although surface water resources had been allocated at an early stage to various localities by the Provincial Water Conservancy organization, a certain sense of 'distributive justice' usually prevailed at all administrative levels, and the higher organization was easily tempted to yield to pressures from below for a larger allocation of water. The easiest administrative and political solution then was to distribute more than a fair share to everybody – and on this basis localities had created an overcapacity of irrigation facilities, which could not be fully used.

At an earlier date, a letter to the editor of the Shaanxi Ribao had described the problem very clearly:

The Qishui River flows through Yongshou, Qianxian, Wugong and other counties. At most, it could irrigate 3,300 hectares, which would be just enough for Wugong. Recently, however, besides Wugong county, also Qianxian county planned to use its water and constructed a 18km. long canal. When the Wugong cadres heard this, they went to inquire. The Qianxian people said they had obtained approval from the Province. However, the Wugong side did not want to abandon their plan either. Now both sides are busily preparing for the use of the water of that river . . . The proverb says: "you cannot cut two heads off one turnip" . . . Now (upstream) Yongshou county also thinks of using the water, which would make both the Qianxian and the Wugong projects in vain . . . This phenomenon also occurs between villages and between cooperatives.[73]

In the 1960s and 1970s, unified planning of surface water use had certainly improved, because of better hydrological data, a raised technical level, better technical training of provincial, county and village cadres, and a greater scarcity of water. Yet local interests and the belief in self-reliant development were quite strong. For underground water resources, however, which still had not been surveyed properly, the situation was much harder to control. Counties and villages usually tried to grab as much water as possible, and the provincial water conservancy authorities had little to stop them with.

At the Provincial People's Congress held in May 1984, it was proposed to establish a water resources management structure, which might also control competition for water between agricultural and industrial users.[74]

During the 1970s, electricity prices for agricultural users had been very low. In Wugong county, 0.02 *yuan* per kWh was charged for irrigation purposes; in Chunhua county, 0.04 *yuan* per kWh for wells with depths over 100 meters, and 0.06 *yuan* for depths less than 100 meters.[75] Although internal electricity prices did not change, rising international prices for energy, and rising internal demand, made the Chinese government more conscious of the need for a frugal use of electricity. Projects with high water lifts, such as the Longdong Jinghui irrigation district project which lifts water 200 meters, now were condemned as uneconomical: additional output covered less than half of electricity costs alone. On the Loess Plateau, dry farming was the future.[76] An investigation of capital investments in agriculture in adjacent Dingxi and Guyuan prefectures in Ningxia and Gansu showed that over the 1949–1979 period state investments in water conservation facilities had been high, but had brought little economic benefit even at heavily subsidized electricity prices (0.03 *yuan* per kWh instead of 0.06 *yuan* was charged for lifts between 100 and 200 meters, 0.02 *yuan* for lifts between 200 and 300 meters, and only 0.01 *yuan* above that). Thus, the high-lift projects planned by the Water Conservancy authorities were rejected on economic grounds; operating expenses alone of irrigation projects were higher than the additional income.[77]

In many irrigation areas of Guanzhong, water fees were collected through the electricity bill. A discussion about water fees was opened in 1983, in order to overcome local resistance to a rise in water fees. This resistance was understandably most strong in the pump irrigation areas with high lifts. New water fee standards were also set for water use on the basis of costs of maintenance, but were not yet sufficiently high to cover costs of necessary renewal of equipment.[78] In 1984, however, the provincial government wanted to raise water fees further:

At present, water fees are too low . . . Installations often date from the 1950s and 1960s and need renewal and transformation . . . The new prices set recently by the Government are based on the principle of costs . . . Water fees in agriculture account only for 2 to 4 percent of the (gross) agricultural production value, and amount to 30 to 45 *yuan* per hectare. They are equal to the 19 kg. of cotton per ha. standard of the early 1950s.[79]

If economic pricing on the basis of actual costs and comparative benefit were to be carried through, as the government said it intended to, an increase in water fees and electricity prices seemed inevitable.

A most important question for the future will be how to overcome the effects of decollectivization on irrigation water management. With the very small and fragmented plots of Guanzhong, irrigation cannot be anything else but a communal responsibility. Decollectivization has led to increased consumption and less investment in capital construction (housing excepted) in People's Communes and brigades.[80] Data on the peasant economy have become more difficult to collect,[81] but one would expect individual farmers to invest in small-scale production means which bring quick returns, rather than in large-scale infrastructural improvements, the costs of which may be difficult to allocate to different users.[82] On the other hand, the increasing level of income resulting from decollectivization and liberalization of production and trade should give greater economic strength. About some policies, such as the contracting out to individual farmers, of exploitation *and* protection of small water basins in mountain areas there is cause for worry.[83] A deterioration of community spirit might lead to neglect or even destruction of irrigation water facilities.[84] A 1983 survey of water conservation management after the implementation of the 'water conservation management responsibility system' (the scope of which had not been indicated clearly yet) showed that irrigation benefits went up by some 20 percent and costs dropped by about 30 percent. 'It raised the efficiency of water conservation investment and guaranteed the continued development even under conditions of reduced investments.'[85]

Agriculture will have to compete for water with urban and industrial users on a much larger scale in the 1980s than before. Industrial expansion, tighter environmental pollution control and rising living standards of the urban population will make great demands on water supply. For Xi'an only, a tripling of the running water supply from a daily 530,000 tons in 1979 to 1,600,000 tons in 2000 will result from the Hei River water drawing project, for which the central government pledged its support in 1984.[86] New legislation was passed to give the provincial government and the Water Conservation Department greater control over rivers and dikes and adjacent land use. Unified planning and protection of existing water conservancy facilities was stressed in the face of encroachment on public land. Cities and villages with responsibility for dike maintenance work were told again of their inhabitants' duty to provide about ten labour days of corvée service per year.[87]

Conclusion. The middle reaches of the Yellow River and its tributaries carry so much silt that the building of large-scale reservoirs is virtually impossible. The lesson taught by the failure of the Sanmen multi-purpose project put an end to central government support for building a reservoir at Longmenkou. In the region, in 1979 there still were hopes for such a project, because it would bring irrigation to 400,000 hectares of dry farmland in northeast Guanzhong. With the growing water shortage in the North China Plain, however, there is little chance that Guanzhong will receive a large share of the Yellow River water.

Without irrigation, the crops of Guanzhong are at the mercy of rainfall. Spring is dry. Of the yearly precipitation of 530–700 mm over one-half falls between July and September but because of high temperatures even then the crops usually are in need of supplementary irrigation. Under traditional agriculture, this was the period of fallow after the wheat harvest, or of less demanding autumn grains. Serious droughts occur every three or four years. When droughts were consecutive, such as in 1928–30, 1941–4 and in 1959–63, the rural economy would suffer greatly. Most rivers carry little water, their high silt loads quickly fill up reservoirs and irrigation canals have to be cleared of silt at least twice a year, or even shut down. The water shortage is particularly severe in the plain area north of the Wei River and east of the Shichuan River; here only 20 percent of the total irrigation water need could theoretically be met, half of which had been realized by 1975.

An outstanding engineer and political organizer, Li Yizhi, succeeded in constructing several large-scale irrigation districts in the 1930s, at first mainly with outside funds but soon also with provincial and local funds. Hereby, the irrigated area in Guanzhong rose from about 25,000 ha in 1930 to 100,000 ha in 1940. Between 1946 and 1950, completion of the Luohui and some smaller irrigation districts added another 10,000 ha of irrigated farmland.

The new irrigation districts were organized as users' communities. Villages appointed ditch guardians, who in turn elected 'outlet officers' who in turn elected 'water elders' (both were paid jobs). The water elders convened twice a year with the Irrigation District Management Bureau, to represent all users. This democratic system worked quite well and was hardly changed by the communists. The extension of irrigation in the 1930s was gradual, part of a larger framework of rural reconstruction undertaken in the absence of a powerful local economic elite who could have usurped benefits – these were main factors in the success of these projects. As self-supporting units, the districts had to be frugal. Under the communists, water fees were raised to 8 percent of the additional produce obtained from irrigation – in this way, the users paid not only for maintenance but also for future extensions.

Between 1950 and 1955, the irrigation area of Shaanxi increased by half to almost 400,000 hectares; then the speed of construction quickened and the pace became frenzied in 1958. When the dust settled in 1961, many projects had been halted or found useless. On the other hand, valuable experience had been gained, and the basic economic framework of collective villages was conducive to specialized management of irrigation and project construction and maintenance. By 1965, the irrigated area had increased to 800,000 hectares, to a large part because of a more effective irrigation water use. Secondary salinization occurred in most new irrigation areas, however, after a decade or so; it was successfully combated by adding drainage ditches and by making more use of underground water. Since the early 1960s, electrical pumps started tapping Guanzhong's underground water resources; by 1975, almost 500,000 hectares were irrigated by pump wells. The Dongfanghong, Baojixia and Donglei pumping stations, built in the 1970s, each drew several scores of tons of water per second from the Wei River and Yellow River. Most irrigation districts now may use a combination of surface and underground water.

Around 1980, irrigation development took a new turn. Underground water levels had been sinking in many areas and the number of functioning pump wells, decreased. The central government became more conscious of costs and shelved large projects in Guanzhong. Reservoir storage capacity still was enlarged somewhat but probably not enough to compensate losses from silting. In a situation of variable and not yet exactly established availability of water, it had been tempting to allocate more water than could actually be supplied. Apparently, in the previous decade local governments and villages had created an overextended network of pumping facilities and irrigation canals, because of an unchecked competition for obtaining water resources. High-lift projects, which had been heavily subsidized through low electricity prices for depths beyond 100 meters, were abandoned first. Water fees were raised to more realistic levels. For much of the Loess Plateau, but also for most of north Guanzhong, irrigation was found to be uneconomical. After decollectivization, existing irrigation facilities have become more difficult to manage, maintain and protect against individual misuse.

6

CULTIVATION PRACTICES, RISING YIELDS AND AGROTECHNICAL CHANGE

A local proverb '*Mai yao hao, di yao dao*' admonishes the Guanzhong farmer to upturn his soil, if the wheat is to grow well. Other proverbs advise rotation of wheat with alfalfa or peas, in order to increase soil fertility, and may be very specific about rotation schemes. Nightsoil mixed with earth (preferably from the toilet floors, stables or living quarters, or even from the stove's chimney) should be applied to the wheat fields before snow in November. '*Jiali tu, dili hu*', 'The dirt of one's home is a tiger in the soil.' Such proverbs reflect conventional peasant wisdom and practices in Guanzhong, and are a valuable source of information.[1] To a very large extent they are valid today, especially for the dryland farming which predominates in Guanzhong.

Proverbs, agricultural handbooks, and description of cultivation practices by agricultural experts or by farmers themselves, however, more often than not describe practices as they should be rather than as they were or are. Generally speaking, our image of 'the Chinese farmer' created by Frank King, John Lossing Buck, communist propaganda and visitors to suburban communes – one might also include fiction, such as Pearl Buck's Wang Lung – has stressed his endless toiling and infinite care for crops and the soil.[2] This may or may not have corresponded with reality. At least for Guanzhong, in the 1930s as well as today, a different or at least a more differentiated picture of cultivated practices applies. In the 1930s, and also later, Guanzhong farmers have been described as lazy for various reasons and their farming methods as backward and labour-extensive.[3] In the 1970s, three-quarters of the fields on the dry uplands (*hanyuan*) of north and west Guanzhong were left fallow after the wheat harvest in June.[4] Thus, two busy weeks, 'Harvesting wheat is like snatching food from the mouth of a dragon' as the peasants have it, are followed by leisure

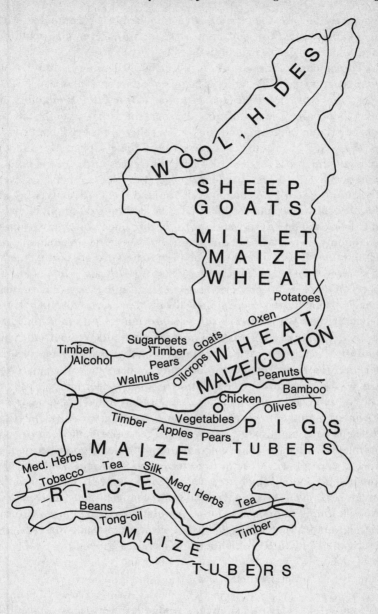

Map 21 Agricultural regions and products, 1980

when and where the summer drought cannot be combated with irrigation water. Frost and snow make for a low level of agricultural activities from December until March.

The amount of labour and fertilizer applied to agricultural plots varied according to a number of factors, most important of which were (and are) distance from the farm or village, the availability of irrigation water, the sort of crop, the economic situation of the farmer or the production team, and (under the collective system) the private or collective ownership of a plot. Often these factors are directly related, which has tended to enlarge differences in the use of labour and fertilizer. Closest to home, vegetable plots usually received irrigation, much care, much fertilizer, and were privately worked, highly productive and well guarded. The farthest plots might often be on poor and infertile terrain, such as hill slopes or sandy gullies, commonly-owned wasteland, and be entirely dependent on favourable rainfall. They might be sown to forage crops or millet, and not receive fertilizer, except for what was left by stray goats or sheep. Of the main crops, irrigated cotton and maize make much heavier demands on the soil and always have received much more fertilizer than wheat or sorghum. Spiked millet and other miscellaneous grain crops often received no fertilizer at all. Without sufficient moisture, fertilizer is ineffective, thus dry fields always will receive less fertilizer than irrigated fields, which may also have more than one crop per year. There is an obvious relation between soil fertility, yields and the cropping system in Guanzhong's dry and irrigated farmland areas. Owing to many centuries of cultivation, there were no natural soils left. All soils were man-made in varying degrees. In the modern period, farmland soils have changed more rapidly than before, because of mechanized plowing, chemical fertilizer, pump irrigation etc. In the premodern period, which in the case of Guanzhong has lasted until the 1960s and even 1970s, farmland soils changed more slowly. Yet fluctuations in human and animal population, resulting from natural or man-made disasters, would greatly affect regional and local soil use, cultivation practices and amounts of fertilizer applied.

A. SOILS

A comparison of Guanzhong's farmland soils in various areas over the past fifty years, which might show how soils have changed under population increase and modern cultivation practices, has to remain tentative. Before World War II, few soil samples were taken. Experimental farms were set up by the provincial government at the end of the 1930s in some irrigated areas, and at the Wugong College of Agriculture, but we have no knowledge of any periodical soil analysis which might have been carried out. At least until the end of the 1970s, various typologies and different local names were in use within Guanzhong for the same soils.[5] The 1958 and the 1977 farmland soil surveys were conducted on a very large scale, but without a sufficiently standardized typology. Yet the 1977 survey represented a giant advance in information about the quantities of nutritional elements in Shaanxi's farm soils.

Now, the scientists have a clear idea of nutrients present in 2,300,000 hectares of farmland. Soil samples have been tested . . . This survey was conducted using a survey of soil types carried out in 1958 as a basis. Some 110,000 rural cadres and peasants were taught basic knowledge of soil surveying and testing at short training courses.[6]

With production brigades and People's Communes as its lowest units, the 1977 survey could serve as a basis for State allocation of chemical fertilizers, and also for crop assignment and other measures guiding agriculture.

Most of the loess in Guanzhong is of aeolian origin, carried by wind from the Gobi Desert for over a million years. In the plain and along rivers, there are secondary deposits of loess, but also of more sandy materials. The texture of aeolian loess is fairly homogenous. About 50 percent consists of fine particles (between 0.05 and 0.005 mm), less than 2 percent of sand and about 20 percent of very fine silt (<0.002 mm). Loess soil is loose and porous, but mostly with very fine capillaries. Therefore its permeability is not very good. Its high content of lime (between 8 and 16 percent) is due to the marine history of the Gobi sands.

The loess deposits are very thick in most places. Under the influence of the semi-arid climate, with heavy summer rains, through a process of erosion, gulleys and ridges have been formed, and loess soil has been carried away. In natural soils, some of the lime has leached out, but the process of concretion has not been much in evidence. In ripened soils, some organic elements occur also in deeper layers, though not many.

As a result of many centuries of cultivation and manuring, the typical *loutu* soil has been formed. Its upper soil layers have a distinct coloring, usually 50 to 60 cm deep, with a higher content of organic

Plate 6 Construction of terraces. Note the distinct top soil layer, which is put aside for future use.

material and nutritional elements. Because of manuring, the lime content of the top soil has increased, and the physical properties and structure of the topsoil have improved. On the other hand, a distinct layer of lime concretions has formed immediately below the topsoil layer. This ploughpan is about 10 centimeters thick. Further down, there is a layer of old cultivated or ripened soil which is rather loose and very porous. Gradually the influence of cultivation becomes less visible, down to the original drab soil.

Guanzhong has five main types of field soils, all of which are loessial (fairly homogenous, with few larger particles), with a high content of calcium. They are called by their Chinese names:

Loutu, stratified old manured loessial soil, is predominant in the plain areas. It has a thick soil layer, rather good porosity, and an excellent water and fertilizer retention capacity. Its field capacity is 19–25 percent. One cubic meter of *loutu* can hold 260 to 300 mm³ of water, of which slightly over half can be absorbed by crops. It is suitable for many different crops. Principal problems are insufficient soil fertility because of a low organic matter content and a low nitrogen content (although slightly superior to the drab soils and alluvial soils of the northern parts of the North China plain), an often not level terrain, and a surface crust which makes ploughing less easy. The richest improved soils, on the second terrace level, are called *heiyoutu*, 'black oily soils'.

Yunitu, 'silt mud soil', well-drained submergic soil developed on alluvial deposits, occurs along the banks of the Wei River and its southern tributaries. Fertility of the soil differs greatly according to the length of its history of cultivation. Near the river, the soils have a rather sandy texture, a thin layer of ripened soil, a low fertility and low yields. Melons, beans and sorghum are common crops here. Farther away from the river, where its cultivation history is longer, the soil has ripened, and suits wheat, maize, cotton, vegetables etc. Usually these soils are irrigated. Flooding with silt and conversion into paddies has created paddy soils with rice production.

Huangmiantu, yellow cultivated loessial soil, with a somewhat coarser texture occurs on the northern loess plateau and loess hills, especially in the Tongchuan–Fuping–Pucheng area and in the gulleys in northwest Guanzhong. It has all the good qualities of loess: loose, easy to plough, good water and fertilizer retention capacity. However, it is subject to serious erosion. It lacks organic materials and has low fertility. The organic matter content of the field layer is only about 0.3 to 0.4 percent. It has a distinct ploughpan owing to shallow cultivation practices.

Heilutu, dark loessial soil, of a clayey variety, covers most of the high plateau areas along the middle reaches of the Jing River, Changwu and Binxian counties. It has a thick humus layer, conserves water and fertilizer very well, and is suitable for wheat or maize. Main problem is its low effective fertility, caused by insufficient ripening of the soil.

Baishantu, 'empty good soil' is the local denomination for the rather unproductive soils on gulley and hill sides and other places where topsoil is or has been removed by natural or human action. This type of 'slope land' (*podi*) used to be of very little value before the 1960s, because of its lack of organic materials, very low fertility, and severe erosion. The building of terraces, however, has created conditions for retaining water and fertilizer better and for soil improvement.

In addition to these major field soil types, three more soil types might be mentioned which occur only on a small part of the farmland area. Drab soils are common to the mountains of west Guanzhong, in Xunyi–Yaoxian and in the Huanglongshan area in the northeast. Sandy soils occur along the Luo River in Dali, and a 250 sq. km. stretch of sand soil at the confluence of the Luo and Wei Rivers is unfit for cultivation. The same county also has saline soils. Under the influence of irrigation, secondary saline soils have formed in some irrigation districts in eastern Guanzhong.

The cross sections of Wugong and Qianxian, where the Wei River valley widens, but its distinct terraces are still retained, may elucidate the relation between the aforementioned field soil types and the geomorphology of Guanzhong. (*See Graph G.*) Soil maps of Wugong

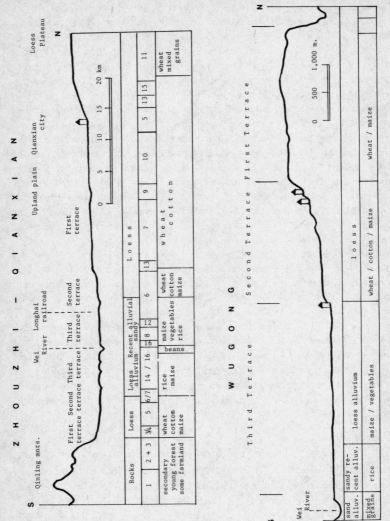

ZHOUZHI – QIANXIAN

Qinling mnts.		Wei River	Longhai railroad	Upland plain	Qianxian city	Loess Plateau

First terrace — Second terrace — Third terrace | Third terrace — Second terrace | First terrace

S ← → N

0 5 10 15 20 km

Rocks	Loess	Loess alluvium	Recent alluvial sandy		L o e s s						
1	2 + 3	3/4	5	6/7	14 / 16	8	12	13	6	7	9	10	5	13	15	11

secondary young forest some farmland	wheat cotton maize	rice maize	beans	maize vegetables rice	wheat cotton maize	wheat cotton			wheat mixed grains

W U G O N G

Third Terrace | Second Terrace | First Terrace

S ← Wei River → N

0 500 1,000 m.

sand alluv.	sandy re- cent alluv.	loess alluvium		l o e s s		
mixed grains	rice	maize / vegetables	rice	wheat / cotton / maize	wheat / cotton / maize	wheat / maize

Graph G Cross-sections of the Wei River Valley, Qianxian and Wugong

Graph H Organic matter content and calcium carbonate content of soils

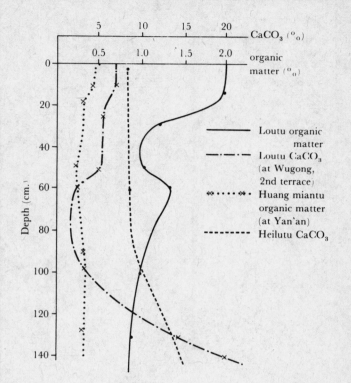

Source: *Zhongguo Turang* 1978, p. 576 and 584

and Hancheng counties give examples of distribution of soils in plain and mountain regions. The Liquan county soil nutritional elements' map shows the relative deficiencies of Nitrogen, Phosphorus and Potassium, as surveyed and mapped by every county in 1976–8 (*see Maps 22, 23,* and *24*).

The organic matter content and the amount of calcium carbonate varies with depth. Heavily manured *loutu* may have four or five times as much organic matter (up to 2 percent) in its topsoil layer as lightly manured *huangmiantu*, and typically it has a second humus-rich layer at 50 to 70 centimers' depth. This same layer is somewhat less calcareous. *See graph H.*

Nowadays the organic matter content of *loutu* and *huangmiantu* is

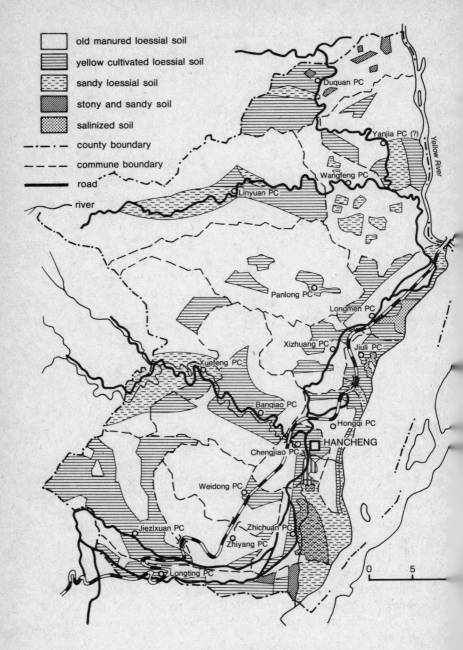

Map 22 Distribution of soils in Hancheng county

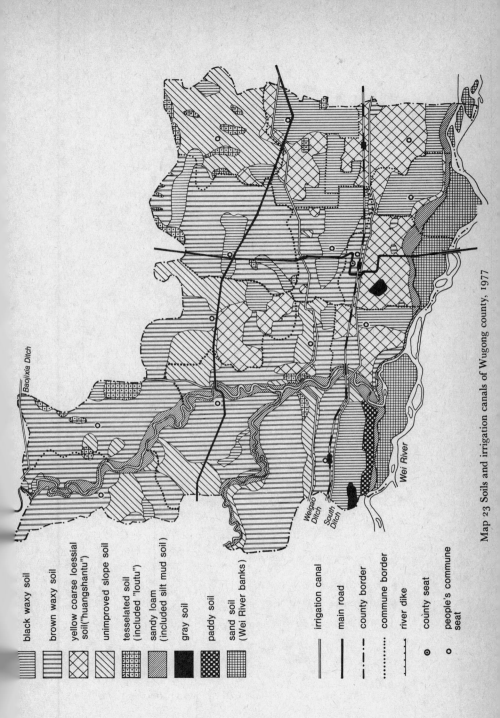

Map 23 Soils and irrigation canals of Wugong county, 1977

black waxy soil

brown waxy soil

yellow coarse loessial
soil("huangshantu")

unimproved slope soil

tesselated soil
(included "loutu")

sandy loam
(included silt mud soil)

gray soil

paddy soil

sand soil
(Wei River banks)

irrigation canal

main road

county border

commune border

river dike

county seat

people's commune
seat

Baojixia Ditch

Weigao Ditch

South Ditch

Wei River

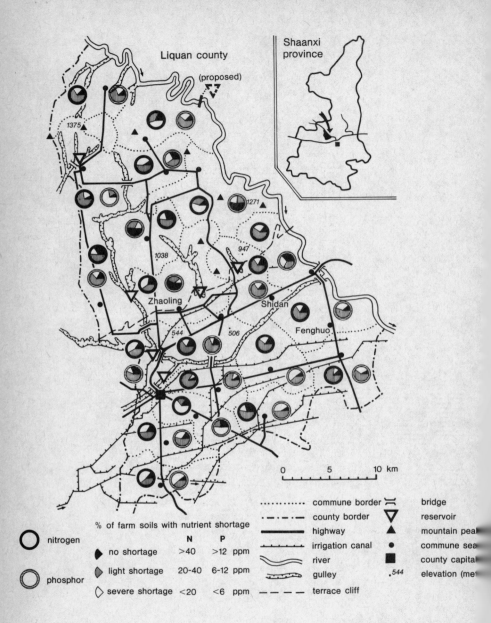

Map 24 Soil nutritional elements in Liquan county, 1977

about one-half to one percent in ordinary soils, and from 1 to 1.8 percent in irrigated heavily fertilized field soils. Whole nitrogen content is in the range of 40 to 70 ppm, and of 100 to 130 ppm in irrigated heavily fertilized soils. Compared with soil samples taken during the 1930s, present maximum values are about twice as high.[7] This shows the effect of agricultural intensification with an increased use of manure and chemical fertilizers. A rise in crop yields could only be achieved by increasing the amount of nutritional elements in the soil. On the average 100 kg of wheat or other grains takes 2.5 kg to 3 kg of whole Nitrogen (N) from the soil (maize somewhat more than wheat), 1 kg to 1.5 kg of phosphate (P_2O_5) and 2 to 4 kg of Potassium (K_2O). On the dry fields in the loess area, without any application of manure average yields of 500 to 600 kg of grain per hectare were obtained. Paul W. Wilm, in his most thorough and extensive study of fertility and yields in pre-war North and Northwest China, estimated that per year 24 kg of N, 18 kg of P_2O_5 and 41 kg of K_2O was added to every hectare of farmland in the loess area by manuring, and that this had resulted in an average grain output increase of 250 to 300 kg per hectare. He concluded that the soil was not exhausted, because more nutrients were added to the soil than were depleted by this yield increase. Fertilization and total withdrawal by crops were in balance.[8] Modern experiments have shown that in wheat fields the utilization rate of manure is about 30 percent, which corroborates Wilm's estimates.[9] On irrigated loess fields, with cultivation of wheat and cotton, three or four times as much fertilizer was applied than the average. Between farms in the same area, Wilm noted a variation in applied quantities by a factor of 3.[10] In irrigated areas, if not enough fertilizer was applied, the soil might be seriously depleted of nutritional elements; or, to put it the other way around, fertilization raised crop yields considerably. Generally speaking, nitrogen lacked most, phosphate much less so, and potassium was abundant in Guanzhong's loess soil. Farm compost, the main source of fertilizer, in comparison with European stable-dung contains less nitrogen, more phosphate, and much calcium (due to the earth with which it is mixed). According to Wilm, average nutrient value of farm compost was 0.39 percent N (range p.23–0.53), 0.32 percent P_2O_5 (range 0.03–0.90), and 0.73 percent K_2O (range 0.29–1.13). In suburban farms, compost mixed with additional nightsoil bought from the city would have nutrient values about twice as high.[11]

Compost fertilizer was prepared mainly from human and animal excrements, mixed with dirt. Animal excrements would be collected every day. All kinds of plant remnants were brought into the pigsties from the farm, or bought or collected from outside the farm. Pig manure together with human nightsoil would be mixed with dirt (to limit the loss of nitrogen), heaped together, and then covered with earth. Water was applied from time to time to maintain the necessary level of humidity. Every few weeks the compost heap was worked over and covered again. The heaps were maintained in this way for the winter period, or for a 3 to 4 month summer period. Before its use, the manure was spread out and dried. Often, again some dirt would be added. Essentially, this process has been the same for ages, and is still used today.

B. PIG RAISING AND GREEN FERTILIZERS

In the early 1930s, because of the Great Famine, most of the pigs (and also many draught animals) had been killed, and human population numbers had declined drastically. Also, a serious decline of purchasing power reduced the amount of manure bought from mountain areas. Lack of labour and draught animals made application of manure very difficult. Instead of manuring their fields, during the early 1930s peasants had more opportunity to rotate grain crops with fallow, beans, or sometimes with green fertilizer crops or fodder crops. With an eased grain situation, more plant remnants and more fodder crops, the pig and draught animal population could be slowly increased. However, according to a 1935 investigation of the plain areas of Guanzhong, in spite of imports from outside the pre-famine level of draught animals and pigs was still far from being reached. It was estimated that there was only one pig for every ten households, and one oxen for every two households. The plain areas heavily depended on outside supplies of pigs and manure.

About 30 percent of the pigs slaughtered in Guanzhong are raised locally, the remaining 70 percent are imported from Gansu . . . The pigs from Gansu need over a month for the 700 *li* walk to Xi'an. They go in flocks of 20 to 40, with 2 or 3 pigherds, by way of Changwu, Yongshou and Liquan. 65,000 pigs are brought to Xi'an each year to be slaughtered.[12]

The plain areas which cultivated wheat, and especially the irrigated areas which practiced a cotton-wheat crop rotation system needed much fertilizer in order to obtain satisfactory yields, but had very little fodder with which to raise and feed pigs. Pig raising was hardly profitable under these circumstances because the feeding costs equalled or surpassed the sales value of its pork – the profit was only in the manure. Moreover, local pig varieties were of an inferior quality. The Luochuan pig which was common in east Guanzhong provided pork with an excellent taste, but its weight reached only 75 kg or so. The Nanshan pig was the common breed in the counties south of the Wei River; it could reach a weight of 150 to 200 kg, but grew very slowly, still weighing only 50 kg after two years. Both its taste and its net pork ratio (pork : body weight) were bad.

In the mountain areas of western Guanzhong the situation was very different. There was more maize, sorghum, oil crops, potato vines, chaff, husks and other plant residuals to feed pigs with. Grain prices were considerably lower than those in the plain areas. The Jingzhou breed was common in the counties northwest of Xi'an, along the road to Gansu (where it originated). It had superior qualities of fairly rapid growth and a lot of pork of excellent taste. The pigs had to be herded down the valley before being sold, so there were some additional costs of transport, but generally speaking the mountain farmers had a considerable advantage over the farmers in the plains.[13] Thus, mountain farmers would sell pigs over great distances. Over short distances farmers with extensive cultivation practices or much wasteland would sell manure or stalks and other plant residuals to areas with intensive cultivation methods or cotton growing. The general shortage of manure was the main cause of low yields even in irrigated areas of Guanzhong.

Other sources of fertilizer, such as oil-cakes and urban nightsoil, were used almost exclusively for irrigated cotton, vegetables and other high-value crops. The availability and price of oil-cakes varied considerably from one year to the next. Unlike in the North China plain, oilcakes were made mostly from cottonseed oil instead of from soybeans, as the high lime content of Guanzhong's loess soil does not suit soybeans well. Cottonseed oilcakes contained about 3.3% N, 1.6% P_2O_5 and 1.4% K_2O, or almost ten times as much nitrogen and about 5 times as much phosphate as manure had. Because they dissolved only slowly, they could be given not only as top-dressing, but also worked into the soil at sowing time.[14] Another advantage was that their application required less labour than that of manure. As described above, the preparation of manure was quite laborious. Fodder had to be collected and fed to pigs. The pigs had to be tended carefully. Pigsties had to be cleaned out regularly. Mixing manure with dirt and composting was a heavy job. Then the manure was carried to the field, or brought to it by cart. For use as basic fertilizer, it was left in little heaps on the field until ploughing. The dry compost was then strewn into the plough furrow, at the same time as the seeds. In April–May, when wheatfields were hoed once or twice, manure was again applied as side- or top-dressing. Local sayings had it that 'whoever does not apply manure to his wheatfields, is like a blind loafer' and 'not applying manure with cultivation of wheat is so bad as to make the Lord in Heaven angry'. However, during the 1930s and 1940s the number of pigs and cattle in Guanzhong was quite small. Many wheat farmers could not apply much fertilizer in addition to their own night-soil; much of the wheat and spring-sown crops did not receive any manure at all. Even by 1965, only 40 percent of the wheat fields in Shaanxi received base fertilizer, and 30 percent top-dressing.[15]

For the dry wheat growing areas, soil fertility and yields were maintained by summer fallow and crop rotation more than by anything else. Most often, wheat was rotated with spiked or yellow millet (*Panicum italicum*, or *Panicum mileaceum*), which had lower yields, but also a lesser demand for nutrients and water. Wheat might also be rotated with spring-sown maize. Sesame, buckwheat and common millet (*Hordeum hexastichum* or *vulgare*) might be included once in a while, or sorghum, a crop which also served as animal fodder, building material and fuel. Forage crops were only secondary, however. From the viewpoint of fertilization of the soil, most important in dry farming was the cultivation of peas and other types of beans (mung beans, broad beans, soybeans). The nitrogen-fixation process at the roots of *leguminosae* had not yet been discovered, but Guanzhong peasants knew that beans made the soil more fertile: 'Wheat is inseparable from beans, and beans are inseparable from wheat.' Peanuts might be grown in sandy soils along rivers in the east, where heat resources were largest. A major barrier for a wider use of forage and green fertilizer crops such as alfalfa, sweet clover and rape was their competition with regular crops for water and for heat – most of the loess plateau area could only meet those needs by devoting the entire growing season to one such crop. In some low-lying areas, however, mung beans or broad beans might be sown immediately after the wheat harvest, and plowed under as soon as the plants started flowering (their nitrogen content was highest then). After some forty days of dissolution, the soil would be ready to be sown to wheat again. In the drier areas of east

Guanzhong, it was more difficult to grow fertilizer crops during the summer fallow or autumn/winter fallow than in the rather moist areas in west Guanzhong.

From the 1930s until the present, agricultural specialists and government organizations in Guanzhong have done their best to promote the use of green fertilizer crops. Not much research had yet been done on the subject, and during the war experimental farms had different, even opposite experiences. Wilm was convinced that alfalfa was a most promising forage and fertilizer crop for dry areas, because with its very deep roots it could withstand drought as no other plant could, and might even serve as human food in case of severe drought. For soybeans, he found the loess area totally unsuitable.[16] Others did not see much future for green fertilizer crops in dry areas, but advocated their use in irrigated areas after wheat. According to some experiments, after a fertilizer crop wheat yields had been higher by 300 kg per ha than after fallow, but other experiments had shown bad results; probably because wheat had been sown too late and been affected by frost.[17] An expansion of the soybean area, in the place of maize, would require less fertilizer and raise soil fertility. A rotation scheme with three crops in two years (wheat + soybeans→fallow + maize→peas + fallow→wheat) would, it was contended, result in a higher output than wheat + maize in double cropping.[18] The Dali experimental farm had obtained good results with mungbeans and even better results with black soybean (*heidou*).[19] In an anonymous official publications of 1942, it was proposed to set up experiments in the application of manure, in green fertilizer crop rotation with wheat, and in the use of oil cakes. At that time, some three percent of the farmland of the Jinghui, Weihui and Changan irrigated areas was sown to beans, two percent to other green fertilizer crops.[20] Thus, both in irrigated areas and in dry areas, peas and beans made a certain contribution to soil fertility, but other green fertilizer or forage crops were little used.

C. WHEAT YIELDS UNTIL THE 1950S

During the war decade, wheat yields fluctuated according to weather conditions, but showed no sign of structural improvement. Even in counties with new irrigation facilities yields were low and unstable. The area sown to wheat rose slowly at first, then jumped in

1942 after the Government had ordered reduction of the area sown to less needed crops in order to cope with increasing urban and army foodgrain shortages.[21] Over the five-year period of 1941–5, the average area sown to wheat in Guanzhong was 1,053, 800 hectares (83 percent of the Shaanxi wheat area), with an average output of 701,600 tons (80 percent of the Shaanxi total output). Thus, average wheat yield in Guanzhong during these five years was 666 kilograms. This was 13 percent lower than the average of the preceding five years 1936–40. In good years such as 1936, 1938 and 1944, average yields reached to 1,000 kg per hectare, but in bad years such as 1937 and 1943 average yields were only about 550 kg and in 1945 only 450 kg per hectare. Between counties, measured over a longer period, yield averages did not differ greatly, and generally were between 500 and 850 kg per hectare. Unit yield distribution over Guanzhong is shown on map 25. Within a single year, variations would of course be much larger. In 1946, for instance, average wheat yield per hectare was 661 kg for all 44 counties of Guanzhong, but 11 counties had average per ha yields below 420 kg, and 8 counties had yields between 900 and 1,280 kg per hectare.[22] The above-mentioned figures should be taken for their relative value rather than for their absolute value. Measures were not standardized yet, and underreporting of output to evade taxation and requisitioning was common among peasants and cautious local officials until the Great Leap Forward.[23] See table 40, Shaanxi wheat area, output and unit yield 1931–1958 and graph I.

The fertilizer shortage was reduced to some extent because of an increase in the number of pigs, at least until 1941. An economic survey held in August of that year showed that for every ten households in Guanzhong there were 4 oxen, 8 pigs and 36 chickens.[24]

Lack of fertilizer was only one out of several causes of low and unstable yields of wheat and other summer grains during the 1940s. Weather was a major factor. Insufficient precipitation in spring, late spring frost, hot winds in May or June, and excessive rains during harvest time all might severely reduce wheat yields. Wheat-stem rust affected all wheat varieties to a greater or lesser degree, especially in irrigated areas; this disease was estimated to cause as much damage as did spring drought. Inadequate ploughing and weeding (a consequence of the lack of animal power) meant that the soil did not weather well and was less capable of retaining moisture. The lack of animal power also dangerously lengthened the harvesting period. Recommendations on how to increase wheat yields, made to the

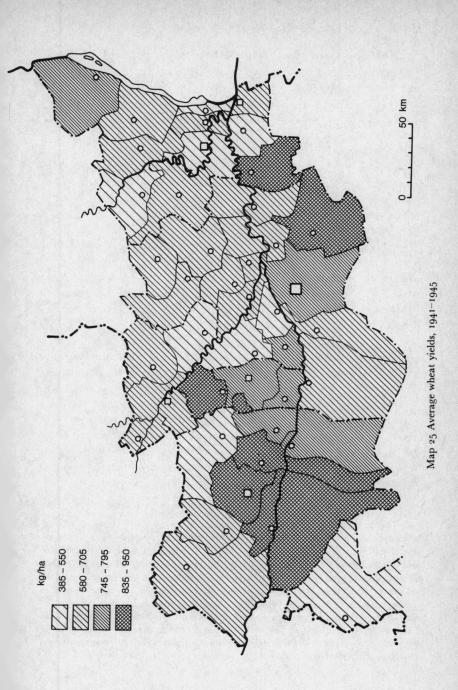

kg/ha

385 – 550

580 – 705

745 – 795

835 – 950

Map 25 Average wheat yields, 1941–1945

50 km

Table 40 *Shaanxi wheat area, output and average yield 1931–1958*

Year	Sown area (1,000 ha)	Output (1,000 tons)	Average yield (kg per ha)
1931	727	595	818
1932	770	427	555
1933	846	546	645
1934	928	1,177	1,268
1935	992	1,206	1,216
1936	973	888	913
1937	910	471	518
1938	990	907	916
1939	1,055	895	849
1940	1,109	853	769
1941	1,136	844	743
1942	1,285	971	756
1943	1,325	789	595
1944	1,273	1,217	956
1945	1,329 (1,298)	589 (917)	443 (706)
1946	1,376 (1,306)	1,349 (1,243)	981 (952)
1947	1,346 (1,319)	1,312 (1,273)	975 (956)
1949	1,465	1,292	834 (882)
1950	1,529	1,357	888
1951	1,561	1,578	1,010
1952	1,579 (1,467)	1,328 (1,233)	841
1953	1,600 (1,525)	1,774 (1,690)	1,108
1954	1,613 (1,572)	2,121 (2,066)	1,314
1955	1,594	1,814	1,138
1956	1,620	2,460	1,479 (1,403)
1957	1,600	(1,883)(2,175)	1,177
1958	1,600	2,500	(1,563)
1960	1,694		

N.B. The 1936–45 data are based on estimates made by the Shaanxi Provincial Agricultural Improvement Bureau. Higher yield estimates (by an average one-third) were given by the National Agricultural Research Bureau, probably on the basis of samples taken mainly from high-yield areas. For 1945–7 these NARB data have been put between brackets. 1952–54 figures between brackets refer to winter wheat only. By preference, local and latest sources have been used for the 1950s. It is not always clear whether secondary crop wheat, which is harvested in autumn, has been included in official figures; this may account for some of the different figures for 1956 and 1957. One picul is assumed to equal 50 kg, and one *mu* $\frac{1}{15}$ ha. According to investigations made in 1957, about 10 percent of the harvested summer grains were not reported to the authorities, but privately distributed.

Government after World War II, included the establishment of draught animal breeding stations, of farmtool factories, promotion of compost manufacturing and of suitable cropping systems, the digging of wells and the breeding of disease-resistant varieties. Chemical fertilizer, it was felt, would greatly raise crop yields but not be available for a long time.[25]

In the first decade under communist rule, wheat yields in Guanzhong were substantially raised. In irrigated areas, yields were about double those obtained during the 1940s, and surpassed 2,000 kg per hectare even in the below-average harvest year of 1957. Irrigated wheat, however, was still rather exceptional. Only 13 percent of Guanzhong's wheat was sown on irrigated land in 1956, but then it produced 23 percent of the wheat output,[26] or twice as much as dryland wheat. In years with less favourable precipitation the difference was somewhat larger. In dryland areas, wheat yields reached about 1,000 kg per hectare, varying with altitude and with precipitation.[27] The all-Guanzhong average was 1,200–1,300 kg per ha in 1953, 1955 and 1957, and rose from 1,500 to 1,800 kg per ha in 1954, and 1958[28] (see table 41 and graph I). During the 1950s, Shaanxi's wheat yields were about 40 percent higher than the national average, and grew at a faster rate.

The increase of wheat yields during the 1950s was due to several factors, most important of which were an increased application of manure, variety improvements, better crop care (both because of more labour and of improved techniques) and extension of irrigation.

Sources: Zhongguo Jingji Nianjian 1934, E52–53; Bai Yinyuan, 'Shaanxi Jianshe zhi Xiankuang yu Jianglai', *Shaanzheng* Vol. VIII no. 2, p. 14; *Shaanxi Xiaomai*, 1947; *China Handbook 1950*, New York, 1950 pp. 537–9; Committee on the Economy of China, *Provincial Agricultural Statistics for Communist China*, Ithaca, 1969; *Dili Zhishi* 1957 no. 8, pp. 339–45; *Shaanxi Ribao* 9 May 1956, 15 June and 15 Sept. 1957, 4 and 6 Feb. 1958. *NCNA* 3 July 1953 and 8 June 1954; *Shaanxi Nonglin* 1960 no. 16, p. 13; *Nongqing Baogao* Vol. 3 to 7 (1931–1938); Xie Huaide, 'Shaanxisheng Wunianlai Xiaomai Zengchan Qingkuang' (The situation of wheat production increase in Shaanxi province in the last five years), *Shaanxi Nongxun* 1955 no. 8.

Table 41 Wheat yields in various counties of Guanzhong, 1940s till 1970s
(kilogram per hectare)

	average 1941–1945	1946	1957	1965	1974	1975	1976	1977	1978	1979
All Guanzhong	666	661	1,169	1,808[a]	1,932	2,329	2,293	1,497	1,528	
7 representative counties	674	622	1,171	2,115	2,327	2,750	2,567	2,212	1,718	
of which Weinan	665	580	1,667	2,048[b]	2,737	3,011	3,470	2,449	3,072	
Wugong	773	620	1,491	n.d.	1,693	1,990	2,192	1,254	1,802	
Qianxian	781	930	946	1,706	2,074	2,392	2,556	1,710	1,794	
Liquan	530	620	1,179	1,987	1,727	2,387	2,060	1,197	1,136	
Pucheng	627	410	1,177	1,649	1,785	1,944	2,129	760	930	
Hancheng	746	960	994	1,091	1,395	1,565	1,480	891	458	1,538
Chunhua	488	480	613	1,091						
3 mountain counties (Northwest Guanzhong)		863[c]							968	
of which Longxian	657	760[c]							1,051	
Qianyang	693	780[c]							1,034	
Linyou	388	300							771	
Heavily irrigated counties:										
Jingyang	702	700		1,815[d]	2,933	3,075				
Gaoling	661	520	2,175							4,612
Huaxian	948		1,763							
Other counties:										
Heyang	581	1,210	1,105[e]			2,475				
Fuping	646	390				2,700				
Jinghui irr. district		1,196[c]	2,346							
All Shaanxi	685	1,177	1,177	1,020	1,508	1,635	1,770	1,463	1,600	2,250
(All China)			855						1,845	2,138

[a] 5 xian average [b] 1966 record figure [c] 1949 figures [d] 1964 figure [e] 1955 figure

Sources: Shaanxi Nongye Xiangai, 1947; Shaanxi Nongye Dili, 1975; data from local Agricultural Bureaus; Zhongguo Nongye Nianjian 1980 and 1981; Wang

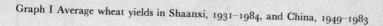

Graph I Average wheat yields in Shaanxi, 1931–1984, and China, 1949–1983

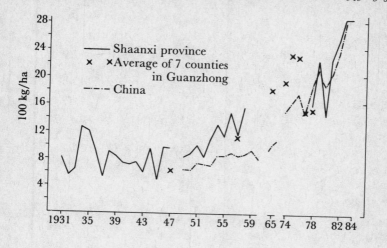

D. PIGS AND MANURE

Application of manure to foodgrain crops had by no means been universal in Guanzhong. There were few pigs, and much of the human nightsoil and animal dung was wasted. 'The masses said in disgust: "the pigs ran through the streets, hardly any earth was strewn into the toilets, and cattle dung was used for fuel." '[29] The bad harvest of 1945 and the economic revolution of 1949 both were responsible for a severe decrease in the number of live pigs. After Land Reform, the number of live pigs in Shaanxi doubled within two or three years to 1.8 million at year-end 1952 – which may have been the level of 1941–2. This rapid increase may be attributed to good grain harvests (also of coarse grains), to little inclination to sell grain (because of inflation) or to pay grain tax, and to high prices for manure. Using foodgrain (especially maize and other coarse grains that do not keep well) for raising pigs seemed to be more profitable. Fertilizer was in great demand, especially in irrigated areas with cultivation of cotton or of secondary crops.[30] After a temporary dip in 1953, caused in part by a lower grain harvest and by the newly introduced grain quota system and fixation of pork purchase prices by the State, the level of 1.8 million pigs was maintained during 1954–6. By that time, however, it was widely felt that fertilizer supply was greatly insufficient to meet the rising demand. Under pressure of government officials, in 1956 the area sown to autumn crops had been considerably expanded in dry areas. Double-cropping led to a reduced grain output, however, which was blamed on the limited amount of fertilizer. In most places one had to return to one wheat crop again.[31] In the rapidly developing county of Wugong, only about half of the demand for fertilizer could be met.[32] Peasants blamed the Government – the only legal buyer – for paying such low prices for pork as to make the raising of pigs quite unprofitable.

The state purchase price of live pigs averaged 32 *yuan* per 100 kg (gross weight), but the sales price on the urban markets was 68–74 cents per kg. The authorities countered by blaming not low purchase prices but other causes:

Real causes of decline in production are: (1) serious pig diseases. More than 100,000 pigs died of sickness, in 18 counties of Guanzhong alone. (2) Lack of fodder. The provincial government had stipulated in 1955, that per live pig 50 kg. of fodder grain might be retained, but in some areas local authorities have cut down this amount. Moreover, after the Higher Agricultural Producers Coops had been formed, cadres stressed cotton and grain production and neglected pig-raising. (3) In Weinan prefecture, where live pig production should increase to 337,000 pigs this year, only 3 percent of the pigs became pregnant. There were not enough sucklings, so the plan was reduced to 220,000. Also, many sucklings died. (4) The price the Coops pay for pig manure to their members is too low.[33]

In order to stimulate pig-raising, the provincial government stipulated that peasants who were short of fodder or cash might receive an advance of 30 to 40 kg of fodder or 10 *yuan* for each pig from the State, to be deducted from eventual sales.[34] In March 1957, acknowledging that fodder prices and peasant wages had risen, it raised state purchase prices by 13.5 percent (and pork sale prices by 6.4 percent).[35] In the meantime, the coops generally had decided to pay higher prices for pig manure supplied by their members. A cartload (of 500–600 kg) now fetched 1.20 *yuan* (as against 0.80 *yuan* before). With a production of 40 cartloads of manure, keeping one pig for a year would give a gross income of 48 *yuan*, and its sale (at 100 kg live weight) 36 *yuan*.[36] An immediate response followed. In June 1957, the number of pigs in Guanzhong had increased by 71 percent over the previous June, to 1,050,000. 'At least 400,000 have no stable, so their dung goes to waste.'[37] At year-end, Shaanxi still had 2,300,000 live pigs. Diseases

Table 42 *Live pigs and draught animals in Shaanxi, 1949–1984*

	pigs (1,000)	draught animals (1,000)	Sources:
1949	745	1,488	*Shaanxi Nongye Dili*, 1978; *Zhongguo Jindai Nongye Shengchan*
1950	1,000		*Xibei Tutechan Gaikuang*, 1950
1952	1,800	2,045	*Shaanxi Nongxun* 1958 no. 1, p. 2
1953	1,614	2,387	*Shaanxi Nongxun* 1955 no. 2, p. 10
1954	1,825	2,586	*ibidem*
1955	1,755	2,668	*Shaanxi Ribao* 29/1/1956
1956	1,756	1,410[a]	*Qinchuan Niu Diaocha Yanjiu Baogao*, 1958
1957	2,300	2,528[b]	*Shaanxi Nongxun* 1958 no. 1, p. 2; *Shaanxi Ribao* 4/2/58
1959		2,520	*Shaanxi Nonglin* 1960 no. 5, p. 35
1960	3,500		*Shaanxi Nongye Kexue* 1960 no. 4, p. 183
1965	3,370		*Shaanxi Ribao* 3/1/78 (derived)
1971	6,000		*Shaanxi Ribao* 26/12/71
1972	8,000		*Shaanxi Ribao* 6/2/73
1975	7,209[c]		*Shaanxi Nongye Dili*, 1978
1976	9,150		*Shaanxi Ribao* 21/12/76
1977	8,425		
1978			
1979	8,223	2,451	*Zhongguo Nongye Nianjian 1981*
1980	7,605	2,473	*ibidem*
1981	6,664	2,445	*Shaanxi Ribao* 27/4/83, 1/5/84
1982	6,398		
1983	6,400	2,425	*Shaanxi Ribao* 24/1/84
1984	6,993	2,420	*Shaanxi Ribao* 6/4/85

[a]Guanzhong only; 83 percent of these could be used, those remaining were calves etc.
[b]Of these, only 1,910,000 'could really be used'.
[c]Of which 46.5 percent in Guanzhong.

and deaths were frequent, especially in areas with busy traffic.[38] Most of the pigs, however, were reared not in the Guanzhong plain but in the mountainous areas especially of southern Shaanxi and the Qinling range.[39]

It is difficult to estimate how much of the pig manure was used on collective fields and how much on the private plots. It is clear though, that in 1957 as well as during the 1960s, there was felt to be a serious shortage of manure. It was estimated in 1957 (probably too high) that 70 percent of the main crops received manure, to an amount of about

30 tons per hectare. This equals some 75 to 100 kg of whole nitrogen. 'From November till March, Shaanxi will need 50 million tons of manure. Sources are domestic animals – every pig can produce 5,000 kg – human nightsoil – this could be about 7.5 million tons, but 30 to 50 percent is wasted – and grasses, mud, stalks, ash, et cetera.'[40] A campaign was then whipped up, at the same time as the Great Leap Forward, in water conservation project construction. Application varied between 20 ton/ha in north Guanzhong and 50 ton/ha in the most productive central areas.

In the light of manure application figures of the next decades, when the pig population was considerably larger, actual levels of application in 1957–8 must have been much lower than reported. Lack of animal fodder (the meagre summer harvest had produced less wheat stalks than usual, and autumn had been too dry for the summer-sown forage crops) prevented a further increase of animal stock in autumn and winter of 1957.[41] The government continued to promote pig production and improvement of pig-breeding techniques.[42] Later, it was reported that the population of Shaanxi had collected 1.4 billion tons of fertilizer in 1958 – zealous reporting during the Great Leap may have carried a few digits too far.[43] A peak of 3.5 million pigs was reported for 1960, and an average of more than one pig per household[44] – both this increase and the subsequent drop during the post-Leap-Forward food crisis are insufficiently documented.

E. DRAUGHT ANIMALS

The development of pig production during the 1950s stood in sharp contrast to that of draught animals. Revolution and Land Reform led to redistribution of farmland, but in plain areas most 'poor and lower-middle' peasants still had to hire an ox from others. In mountain areas, almost every household owned at least one ox, but in the Guanzhong plain maybe only half – data from that period are scarce.[45] Rich peasants secretly slaughtered or sold their cattle, fearing confiscation. Strict government measures were taken against such practices, including an interdiction of private slaughter, a prohibition of bringing cattle to urban markets without permission from the tax bureau, registration and education of butchers, a patrolling of city gates and rewards to informants about illegal slaughter.[46] The large number of deaths, whether by slaughter, disease, or by the difficult to correct neglect of draught animals, was considered to be the number one rural problem.[47]

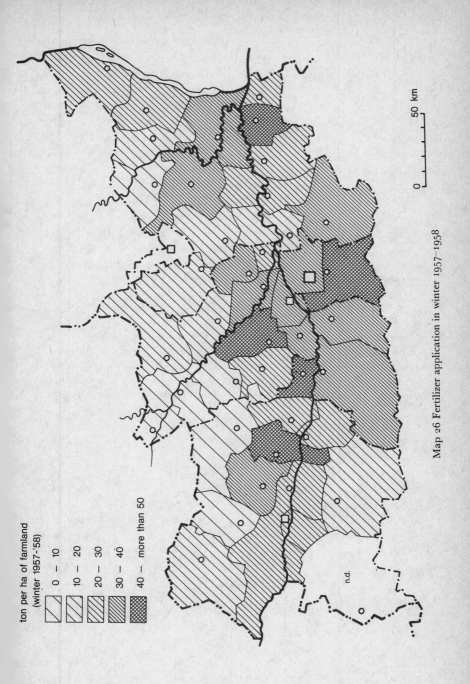

ton per ha of farmland
(winter 1957–'58)

0 – 10	
10 – 20	
20 – 30	
30 – 40	
40 – more than 50	

n.d.

0   50 km

Map 26 Fertilizer application in winter 1957–1958

Subsequent cooperativization and collectivization of agriculture had negative effects on the remuneration of the use of draught cattle and, therefore, on the care taken in feeding and raising animals. Provincial directive did not help. Prices of draught animals went down, and slaughter seemed profitable to many peasant-owners. 'Some cadres consider that the lower the price and rent for cattle given by the cooperative is, the more advantageous it is for the poor peasants who have no cattle.'[48] The coops generally paid 20 to 30 *yuan* less than the market price (which might be about 150–200 *yuan*), according to an investigation of the cattle decrease in Huxian and Xianyang.[49] Sales prices of 6–12 months old calves dropped below 20 *yuan*, thus peasants were discouraged from raising cows.[50] The coops appointed special animal feeding personnel, once the cattle had become collective property, yet many animals died in winter and spring of 1956. In 1956, 5 to 10 percent died, 50 to 60 percent of the draught animals looked emaciated and the reproduction rate was only 1 percent, according to a visitor to several counties in Guanzhong.[51] In the same year, of the 700,000 female draught animals in Shaanxi only 30 percent mated.

Formerly, under individual farming, a draught animal was considered as 'half a family member' and treated lovingly and cared for. After cooperativization, the tasks of the animals became heavier – animals were worked too long and too harshly. Also experience in feeding animals was lacking and management was bad . . . Therefore, many died and reproduction declined severely.[52]

In 1956 and 1957, the number of large animals dropped by 140,000 head. As a result Shaanxi had one draught animal to every 2.3 hectares of farmland, while 2 hectares was considered the maximum.[53] The all-Shaanxi numbers, which are shown in Table 42, do not indicate great changes. However, the all-Shaanxi data do not reflect the shortages felt in Guanzhong, and the large variations between villages. In a survey of draught animals in 12 representative villages in Guanzhong in 1956, there appeared to be between 1.37 and 3.35 hectares of farmland per draught animal, with an average of 2.1 hectares. For the entire 2,311,500 hectares of farmland of Guanzhong in 1956 (of which 19,750 ha of paddies and 208,300 ha irrigated) there were 1,410,400 draught animals, of which 75.5 percent were oxen, 3.3 percent horses, 13.5 percent donkeys and asses, and 7.7 percent mules; 2 hectares were to be ploughed per draught animal. Asses and mules were used mainly for transport, and horses and donkeys were kept for breeding purposes. The conclusions of the 1956 Guanzhong survey were (a) more Qinchuan cattle should be bred (Qinchuan was the dominant breed,

Table 43 *Draught animals in 7 counties in Guanzhong, 1957–1978*
(absolute numbers, and per 100 ha of farmland)

	1957 (1,000)	per 100 ha	1965 (1,000)	per 100 ha	1974 (1,000)	per 100 ha	1978 (1,000)	per 100 ha
Weinan	51	53	46	50	55	62	46	53
Wugong	24°	70	n.d.		26	70	21	60
Qianxian	41.6	53	n.d.		38.9	53	33.8	50
Liquan	30	43	27	39	35	55	31	50
Pucheng	61	46	54	41	60	48	57	46
Hancheng	29.1	76	26.9	71	31.1	88	28.8	85
Chunhua	18	37	17	38	16	42	15	39
Total	254.7	51	225[+]	47[+]	262	57	232.6	52

°The Wugong figures given to me were lower by a factor 10; I have assumed this to be a
miscalculation. The large number of cattle in Hancheng reflects the presence of
extensive forage areas in the Huanglongshan mountains.
[+] Based on interpolated figures for Wugong and Qianxian.
Source: data from County Agricultural Bureaus, 1979

other breeds accounted for only 20 percent), (b) selective breeding
should be carried out by breeding stations, (c) the maize and alfalfa
areas should be expanded (the fodder area, mostly alfalfa, in
Guanzhong was 74,900 ha, 3.24% of the farmland area; maize
occupied 15.6% of the sown area, its grain was used almost exclusively
for human consumption) to alleviate fodder shortages (d) breeding
programs should be directed at increasing the pulling strength but also
the meat content of the Qinchuan oxen.[54]

In eastern Guanzhong and in irrigated areas, where labour
requirements were greatest, the draught animal shortage was felt most
seriously. A survey of Pucheng county showed that the required fodder
was short by one-third. In Weinan county, people were reported as
saying

The oxen have become emaciated, the pigs [privately owned! EBV] have
gotten fat, oxen and horses are protesting. The coop cattle feeders steal fodder,
coop cadres do not care and close their eyes.[55]

Comparison of the 1957 draught animal figures in Table 42 with the
aforementioned 1956 survey shows a decline of 17 percent between
1956 and 1957. There is a difference in samples, however.

In view of later figures, the quality of the draught animals during the collectivization period may have been a more important cause of insufficient animal power than their quantity. Animals were worked harder, not only because of a change of ownership and organization, but also because of the increased requirements for ploughing depths. Under the Maoist '8-point charter for agriculture', deep ploughing was prescribed as a major means for raising production. Until then, shallow ploughing (3.5 to 4 inches deep) had been common practice in Guanzhong. The improved ploughs sold to the peasants could attain greater depths, but then of course required more animal power. The notorious example of the double-wheel, double-shear plough, which was thrust upon the peasantry by the State organizations, but very little used, indicated the limits of animals power. Three to four strong draught animals would be needed for its use, and most cooperatives could not provide this.[56] Although greater depths were propagated occasionally, most experimental farms and successful models ploughed their fields to a depth of 5 inches once a year, during the summer heat or in early spring, and ploughed shallowly several times.[57] At that time peasants feared that deep ploughing would reduce soil moisture, which indeed it would, if at the time of ploughing soil humidity was low. The innate quality of the breed itself was, unlike that of pigs, not a problem. The Qinchuan oxen of Guanzhong were strong and had many other good qualities which could be further developed.[58] As one of China's superior breeds, it is now offered for foreign export.

F. VARIETY IMPROVEMENTS

Of all measures to increase yields of wheat and other grains, variety improvement was most fundamental. Efforts were directed chiefly at wheat, the dominant foodgrain crop, and at a later stage at maize. Other grains such as millets, barley, buckwheat and sorghum received little attention, and the area devoted to such crops was slowly reduced. The primary goal of breeding was high yield. Wheat and maize were mostly cultivated as a single crop, but increasingly crop rotation systems came to be used with 4 or 5 crops in three years.[59] Because of the rather short growing season (the Guanzhong plain has 190 to 210 frostfree days) shortening of the growth period was essential for multi-cropping. Another goal, initially most important, of variety improvement was resistance against diseases. Stripe rust in particular, and yellow dwarf viruses used to inflict great damage upon the wheat crop.

Plate 7 Draught cattle and tractor, Chunhua county. Storage rooms have been dug into the loess walls of a sunken road.

Wheat and maize were seriously affected by aphids, wheat stem maggots, gelichiid moths, red spiders and by corn-borers. Locusts would occur only in very dry summers.[60] Although the local varieties of the 1930s and 1940s had good resistance against frost, the demand for this quality was raised because of the tendency to push the time of harvest to a later date (maize) or to sow later (wheat). Resistance against drought and cold was often good in low-yield varieties, but weak in high-yield strains. Thus, different varieties had to be bred for irrigated and for dry areas. Since World War II, four main new wheat varieties have successively been popularized in Guanzhong: *Bima no. 1*, *Xinong no. 6028*, *Fengchan no. 3* and *Apo*. Roughly, each one raised yields by 20 percent above its predecessor.

Variety improvement work began at the Agricultural School established in Wugong in 1935 and in the Jinghui irrigation district. In 1938, two agricultural experimental farms were established in Jingyang and Dali along with six cotton experimental farms and twelve popularization centers (9 of which in Guanzhong), all subsidized by the central government. Early breeding achievements included *Lanmang* wheat, *Mazha* (Grasshopper) wheat and *Shaannong* no. 7, which were higher-yielding varieties developed from local strains, with good resistance against cold and frost. In 1941, some 30,000 hectares were already sown to these varieties.[61] During the latter part of the war, *Lanmang* was succeeded by *Jinghui* no. 60, which was bred until 1947, and by several other new strains developed from *Mazha*. A provincial crop improvement and breeding station was set up in 1941. It used 50 hectares of irrigated and dry fields of the Agricultural College in Wugong, and had a branch station of similar size in Gaoling. Wheat improvement was its main objective. In 1946, its scope was enlarged and its name was changed into the Northwest Popularization and Breeding Station, with as main goals: (a) support of grain production, (b) preparation of material for popularization and (c) establishment of an agroscientific basis for the other provinces of northwest China.[62]

A striking success was obtained by the Northwestern Agricultural College with a new wheat variety with resistance against stripe rust called *Bima no. 1*. It was bred during 1942–1947 by crossing *Mazha* with *Biyu* 'Jasper' wheat. After trial production in 1950–1952 had shown that its yield was one-third higher than existing varieties, it was popularized throughout Guanzhong and also in west Henan. By 1957, more than 70 percent of Guanzhong's wheat area was sown to it, and yields averaged 2,250–3,000 kg/ha. Its good qualities included a strong stem, which reduced the damage by lodging (toppling over of the ripe crop) in May or June. In fertilized, irrigated areas insufficient air and light at the root of the stem would weaken the stem base, which then would not be able to support a heavy awn, especially when the monsoon winds were strong. Also it had a fairly short period of growth (230–235 days). Most important of all, however, was its resistance against stripe rust, a disease which affected 30 percent or more of Guanzhong's wheat. After 1957, it slowly lost its resistance[63] and production suffered, but it continued to be used for many years in non-irrigated areas.

From *Jinghui* no. 60 was developed a new variety *Xinong no. 6027* which had some superior, but also some inferior qualities. Just as *Bima no. 1*, it had a strong stem, and loved water and fertilizer. It had a high tolerance of midges (which *Bima no. 1* did not) and against stripe rust and smut, but was seriously affected by leaf rust and had no resistance against wheatstem maggot. Also, it did not endure drought and spring frost well, and dropped its kernels easily. It was introduced in areas seriously affected by midges in western Guanzhong in 1950–2, and became more widespread after 1957 as a successor to *Bima no. 1*. In the early 1960s, it was the main variety in irrigated plain areas.

In dryland areas, a shorter (90–95 cm) variety called *Jinghui no. 30*, with high tolerance of drought and cold, and resistance against smut and stem black mildew was popularized during the early 1950s. On dry fields, its yields were 5 to 7 percent higher than those of *Mazha* and *Bima no. 1*. In the early 1960s, it was the main variety on the *hanyuan* in west and north Guanzhong.[64] Around 1960, *Shaannong no. 9* and *no. 1* were trial-produced, and for some years *Shaannong no. 9* was the main variety popularized in areas with good conditions of irrigation and fertilizer.

During the early 1960s, stripe rust damage became more serious again as *Bima no. 1* deteriorated.[65] A decade later, a visiting American delegation was told that 1964 had seen the last major epidemic of wheat in Guanzhong, and that involved stripe rust.[66] The years 1963 and 1964 were dark and rainy during the period of wheat growth, and wheat yields were very low. Apart from stripe rust, two other major causes were responsible: the phenomenon of missing or dead sprouts, and lodging. An estimated 15 to 25 percent of the wheat fields yielded no sprouts; recommended measures were seed treatment, the use of insecticides (mainly benzene-hexachloride '666') against wireworms, grubs and mole crickets, better seed selection (over 30 percent of the seeds were noted to carry wheat scab disease), and better ploughing and sowing methods.[67] Stripe rust and lodging were indicated as the main problems which Guanzhong had not solved yet, which breeding programs should address as their main goals. In 1957, the central government had assigned *Apo*, an Italian wheat variety imported from Albania, to Shaanxi province for trial. This became the dominant variety during the latter 1960s, because it had 'a strong stem, good resistance against stripe rust, tolerance of dark, wet weather, a somewhat shorter straw than *Bima* (about 100 cm) which helped against lodging and facilitated mechanical harvesting, and high productivity with water and fertilizer'.[68] Later, the American Wheat Delegation seemed to question the wisdom of this choice.[69]

It is not quite clear, to what extent villages were free to adopt their own choice of varieties. It seems that, as every county established a popularization center, usually the options were prepared by the local Agricultural Bureau. Many older, local varieties remained in use however, and peasants might revert to those if there was a general feeling of dissatisfaction with a new variety.[70] Some of this might, of course, reflect peasants' resistance to change and be overcome by patient education and demonstration, but some worries might be well-founded in knowledge of local conditions or in different priorities. Peasants, for instance, set great store by the amount of fodder material which could be fed to their private pigs, but State breeding programmes usually moved to less foliage.

Collectivization of agriculture had made it possible for every People's Commune and production brigade to appoint special personnel for selection and popularization of good seeds, whether obtained from outside or locally bred. At the other end of the extension network, research institutions grew in size and number during the 1950s, and built up regular contacts and exchange with selected villages. During the Great Leap Forward period, 30 to 40 percent of all agricultural scientific and technical personnel stayed for over one year in various experimental and popularization units in 30 counties throughout Shaanxi.[71] Again, during the Cultural Revolution, most of the researchers were 'sent down' to villages connected with their original institutions. Because most publications had ceased, there is little information on variety improvement during the latter 1960s. It is clear, though, that the extreme 'monoculture' of one variety was replaced by a great number of different varieties, some of which imported from outside (such as *Apo* and *Afu*, and *Zhengyin* from Henan), other ones bred by crossing with local strains. This may have increased problems of adulteration (which were already serious in 1964)[72] but reduced vulnerability to epidemics. Local breeding was also necessary because the quantity of good seeds supplied by provincial institutions fell far short of the demand.[73] In the early 1970s 'a high level of stripe rust resistance must be incorporated into all new wheat varieties. In some years leaf rust reaches epidemic proportions. Leaf spots severely attack many varieties' according to American visitors.[74]

During the late 1960s and 1970s, *Fengchan no. 3* (a cross of *Danish no. 1* and *6028*) became a dominant wheat strain both in irrigated and in dry, well-fertilized areas. Subsequently, in irrigated areas *Apo* was popularized. It had a somewhat better resistance against lodging and scab than most other varieties. It was further developed to eliminate some defects: susceptibility to lodging, lack of resistance against stem rust, and inferior grain quality. Lodging, according to a 1978 handbook, was 'the greatest obstacle to obtaining high yields of wheat, after soil fertility has been raised. Losses vary between 5 and 60 percent.'[75] This may have been due in part to an application of too much nitrogenous fertilizer with too little phosphate and potash, but certainly also to very dense planting and to still too long stems of the wheat varieties in use. In dry upland areas of Guanzhong various cold-resistant local crosses continued to be used. Most of these were further developed on the basis of *Bima no. 4*, or some other local strain, crossed with superior varieties from Henan province or from outside China.[76] A shorter variety, *Xiaoyan no. 5*, was considered to be most promising at the end of the 1970s; in irrigated areas *Apo* was still dominent then.[77] Because of its early ripening, *Xiaoyan no. 5* was particularly suitable for west and north Guanzhong. In the dry areas of east Guanzhong, *Weimai no. 4* has been bred and popularized by Weinan prefecture since the late 1970s, because of its resistance to drought and high yield.[78]

Apart from technical instructions in handbooks, there is little data on quantities of pesticides used and on the scope of other means of disease control. Hardly any insecticides were available during the 1950s. In the 1960s irrigated areas and during the 1970s also dry areas of Guanzhong seem to have had no difficulty in obtaining DDT, 666, 1605, later also DVP, Paymid etcetera. However, cost considerations may have deterred peasants from using sufficient quantities. Only in 1983 was the use of DDT and 666 ended. Biological control methods (ladybugs, 'red eye wasp' (trichogramma) etc.) have been mentioned, but could hardly be effective in larger areas. Mechanical means (picking insects by hand, using light traps) may have been used rather often, because of the abundance of rural labour. Cultivation practices probably were most effective. Intensification of land use, destruction of border plants and increased plot sizes destroyed most of the habitat where insects used to hibernate. Shallow ploughing immediately after the wheat harvest and deep ploughing during the summer heat brought up eggs and insects to the surface, where they were killed by exposure.[79]

Around 1980, Shaanxi province had more than one hundred seed breeding stations, with 3,000 hectares under direct control by the Provincial Agricultural Bureau. Wheat strains from outside the province were tried first at the experimental stations in Wugong, Sanyuan and Heyang; hybrid maize strains in Qishan. At the various levels of province, prefecture and county, about 100,000 hectares of seed popularization bases were maintained. New forms of cooperation between scientists and peasants were introduced by the contract system in 1983. The largest 'contract' no doubt was the one concluded by the Northwestern College of Agriculture with Heyang county: the College undertook to raise Heyang's average wheat yield by 14 percent per year above the 1981–3 average of 2,033 kg per ha.[80]

G. CROP PATTERNS AND OUTPUT OF FOOD GRAINS SINCE THE 1960s

After the early 1960s, food grain production in Guanzhong rose to far higher levels. We have no provincial food grain output data for this period, except for 1964, 1966, 1972 and 1974. In 1966, provincial output was 5.9 million tons, or only 10 percent higher than in 1956; two years before, there was a record output of 7,460,000 tons, or 359 kg of food grain per capita. 1972 was below average, with 6,270,000 tons or 245.5 kg per capita, and 1974 was an average harvest, with 7,500,000 tons or 283 kg per capita.[81] Within Guanzhong, responsible for output increases were not only higher wheat yields, but also the rapid growth of maize production, both as a second crop and as a single crop. Maize output doubled between 1957 and 1965, and doubled again in the next decade, and continued to rise thereafter. Unlike wheat, maize showed very stable yields, as it had to suffer far less from drought. Maize often made up for a bad wheat harvest. A 7-county survey shows average yields of over 1,000 kg per ha in 1957, about 2,000 kg/ha in 1965 and 2,500 kg/ha in the 1974–7 period (see Table 44). For the entire Shaanxi province, top yield years were 1958 with 1,437 kg/ha, 1973 with 1,770 kg/ha, 1975 with 2,258 kg/ha and 1979 with 2,775 kg/ha.[82]

Between the 1950s and the mid-1970s, Shaanxi's maize area increased by about one-quarter. Official data, which are rather sparse, indicate that maize took 16.7 percent of the foodgrain area in 1955, 17.9 percent in 1971, 19 percent in 1975 and 25 percent in 1980. For Guanzhong only, percentages were 15.6 in 1956, 19.5 in 1971, 20.5 in 1975 and probably about 25 in 1981.[83] The rise in maize acreage and output was due to several factors. First, the extension of irrigation made it possible to plant maize as a second crop in irrigated areas with enough heat. Second, the adoption of higher planting densities and increased fertilization, and other more intensive cultivation techniques, with improved varieties, continuously raised unit yields. Third, on the upland areas of north Guanzhong, maize proved to be capable of obtaining higher yields than other autumn grains such as sorghum. It was cultivated there either as a spring-sown crop, or with wheat in

Table 44 *Maize yields in 7 counties, area and output, 1957–1978 (kg/ha)*

	1957	1965	1974	1975	1976	1977	1978
Weinan	1,277	1,957	2,632	2,850	2,184	2,442	2,734
Wugong	1,781		3,165	2,830	3,011	3,596	3,420
Qianxian	1,050		1,315	2,333	2,594	3,037	3,362
Liquan	833	1,850	2,741	2,557	1,644	2,672	2,820
Pucheng	1,739	1,681	2,566	2,706	2,510	2,756	2,832
Hancheng	1,639	2,049	2,176	2,487	2,543	1,661	2,415
Chunhua	1,047	2,056	1,760	2,297	1,761	1,616	1,860
Total area (ha)	49,135	57,135	88,760	98,200	106,785	115,445	120,255
Total output (1,000 ton)	56.5	109	214.5	258.2	250.9	308.7	356.8
Average yield 7 xian (kg/ha)	1,150	1,908*	2,417	2,629	2,350	2,674	2,967

* 5 xian
Source: data from County Agricultural Bureaus.

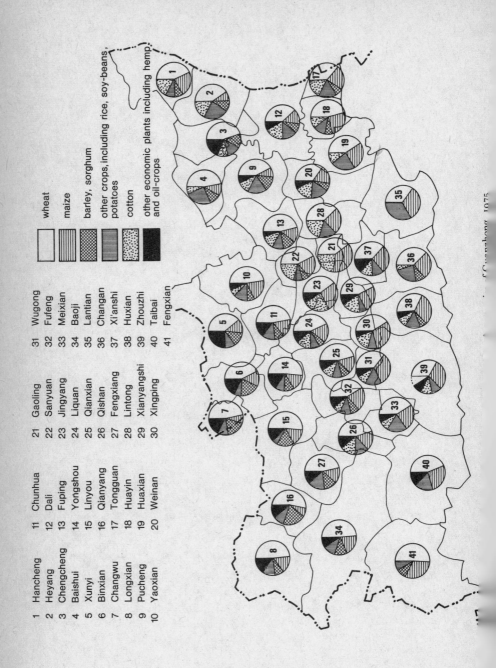

wheat

maize

barley, sorghum

other crops, including rice, soy-beans, potatoes

cotton

other economic plants including hemp and oil-crops

1	Hancheng	11	Chunhua	21	Gaoling	31	Wugong
2	Heyang	12	Dali	22	Sanyuan	32	Fufeng
3	Chengcheng	13	Fuping	23	Jingyang	33	Meixian
4	Baishui	14	Yongshou	24	Liquan	34	Baoji
5	Xunyi	15	Linyou	25	Qianxian	35	Lantian
6	Binxian	16	Qianyang	26	Qishan	36	Changan
7	Changwu	17	Tongguan	27	Fengxiang	37	Xi'anshi
8	Longxian	18	Huayin	28	Lintong	38	Huxian
9	Pucheng	19	Huaxian	29	Xianyangshi	39	Zhouzhi
10	Yaoxian	20	Weinan	30	Xingping	40	Taibai
						41	Fengxian

intercropping. In the warm irrigated areas along the Wei River, two maize harvests might be obtained in one year. However, most high yield varieties in use around 1975 were medium- or late-ripening, and when the wheat harvest was late the season would be too short for a second maize crop. Medium-ripening maize hybrids in use during the 1970s still needed a growth period of 90–105 days after being sown at the end of June.[84] Wheat-maize intercropping appeared to be conducive to diseases, but the often-practiced interplanting with beans helped to meet its fertilizer needs. Since 1978, the bred-in resistance of imported varieties against the corn-borer, smut and black spots and the increased need for fodder for pigs gave further impetus to maize production.[85] The area and output of maize jumped as a consequence.

The crop pattern underwent only marginal changes. Specialization decreased somewhat compared to the 30s. Basically agriculture has been directed at foodgrain production. Within grain crops, the share of wheat and maize has increased. The area devoted to cotton rose to 320,000 ha (the 1936–7 level) in the late 50s, but subsequently fell and stabilized at about 260,000 ha during the 60s and 70s. Of the sown area, cotton took about 11 percent in Guanzhong plain areas (25 percent in some irrigation districts) and about 5 percent in the *hanyuan*.

The possible range of crop specialization for Guanzhong was both limited by the amount of foodgrain imports the central government would allow (either as relief, as in 1981, or in exchange for pork, goats, peanuts, milk powder and other products as in 1982[86] and by the other regions of Shaanxi province. Generally speaking the poor regions of north Shaanxi became an ever-increasing burden during the 1960s. After the mid 1950s their sheep stock hardly increased any further, and grain output remained low and unstable. After 1972, however, grain production developed fast; yet they often were in need of relief grain.[87] Since the 1950s the amount of grain supplied to the State went down from over 20 percent of Shaanxi's total output to about 15 percent. Between 1963 and 1981, the number of people dependent on consumption of commercial grain (roughly speaking, the urban population) increased by 1,980,000 people, and the foodgrain rations assigned to them doubled from 501,000 tons to 978,000 tons. In this period, foodgrain use for industrial and sideline production increased from less than 100,000 tons to 265,000 tons.

In the average harvest year of 1974, the peasants of Shaanxi paid as taxes or sold to the State 17.6 percent of the total foodgrain output; in

Table 45 *Crop pattern in Shaanxi 1949–1983 (% of sown area)*

	1949	1957	1965	1975	1980	1983
food grain crops	88.8	87.2	86.7	85.1	84.2	85
economic crops	8.1	9.0	7.4	8.2	8.1	9.7
other crops (green fertilizer, vegetables, fodder)	3.1	3.0	5.9	6.7	7.7	5.3
multicropping index					133	127

Sources: Shaanxi Nongye Dili, Xi'an, 1978 and Zhongguo Nongye Nianjian 1981 and 1984.

Table 46 *Crop distribution in Shaanxi, Guanzhong plain and* hanyuan,
1971, 1980–3
(percentage of sown area)

	Guanzhong plain 1971	*hanyuan* 1971	Shaanxi province 1971	Shaanxi province 1980	Shaanxi province 1981	Shaanxi province 1983
A. Foodgrain crops	83.1	86.4	86.4	84.2	84.3	85
1. summer grains	48	50.8	39.2		38.1	40.4
1.1. wheat	37.9	46.7	29.6	31.2	32.0	35.2
2. autumn grains	35.1	35.6	47.2			
2.1. maize	19.5	13.0	17.9	20.3	20.8	19.8
2.2. millet	4.1	2.9	5.4	4.7	4.7	4.4
2.3. soybeans	3.0	3.9	5.3	3.8	4.1	4.4
2.4. tubers				7.7		7.1
B. Economic crops	12.7	7.7	7.4	8.1	10.1	9.7
1. cotton	11.2	5.4	5.1	4.9	5.4	5.3
2. oil crops	1.2	2.0	1.9	2.6	4.1	3.7
C. Other crops	4.2	5.9	6.2	7.7	5.6	5.3
1. green fertilizer				2.7	2.5	0.6
2. fodder crops				2.9	1.0	2.6
3. vegetables				1.7	1.8	1.8
4. gourds				0.4	0.3	0.2

Sources: Shaanxi Nongye Dili, Xi'an, 1978 and Zhongguo Nongye Nianjian 1981, 1982 and 1984.

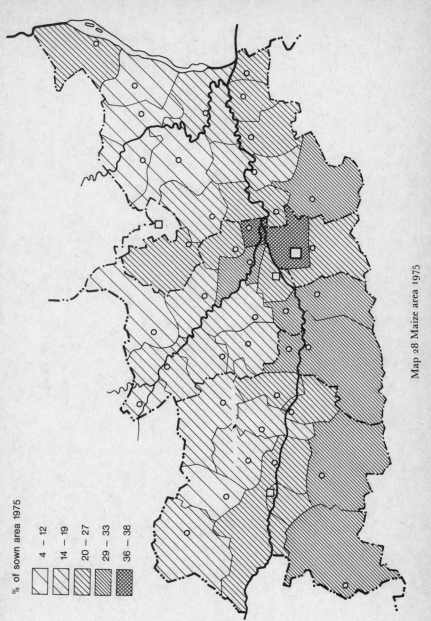

% of sown area 1975

4 – 12
14 – 19
20 – 27
29 – 33
36 – 38

Map 28 Maize area 1975

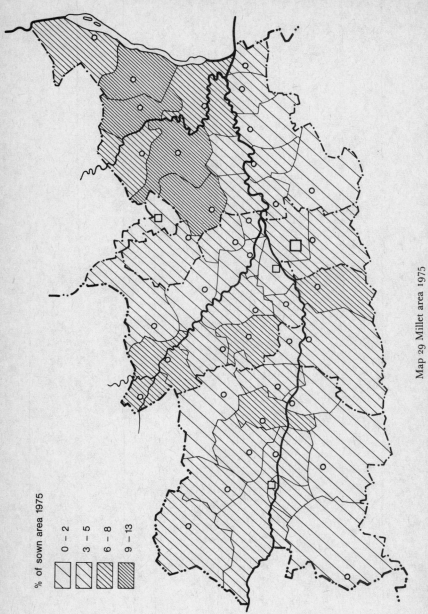

% of sown area 1975

0 – 2
3 – 5
6 – 8
9 – 13

Map 29 Millet area 1975

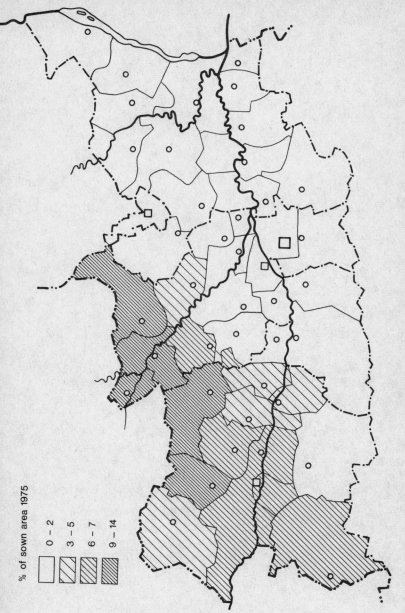

% of sown area 1975

0 – 2
3 – 5
6 – 7
9 – 14

Map 30 Sorghum area 1975

Graph J Food grain output and sheep stock in North Shaanxi, 1949–1982

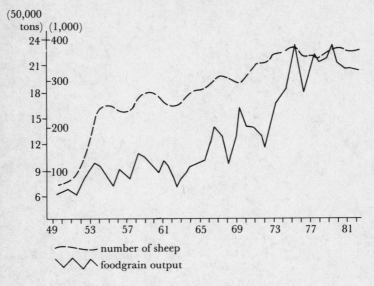

Source: *Shaanxi Jingji Tantao*, Xi'an 1984

Guanzhong only this was 20.1 percent. In 1976, Guanzhong delivered 19.64 percent of its foodgrain output of 4,692,000 tons to the State; in 1979 16.27 percent (of 5,423,000 tons), but in 1980 only 11.9 percent. In the disaster years of 1980 and 1981, foodgrain was imported. In the all-time record harvest years of 1982 and 1983, of total foodgrain output 15 and 19 percent respectively were collected by the State. 1984 again had a record harvest.[88] If this trend continues, the burden of the poor regions in Shaanxi on the agriculture of Guanzhong, which was so heavy during the 1960s and 1970s, may become a thing of the past.

A comparison of foodgrain yields within Guanzhong showed large differences between county averages in 1974. In the least productive eight counties, with 20 percent of Guanzhong's total foodgrain acreage, output averaged 1.6 ton per hectare, with a range from 1.4 to 2 tons. In the most productive quintile, output average was 5 tons per hectare, with a range from 4.3 to 7 tons. The middle one-third of the foodgrain acreage showed an average output of 2.9 tons per hectare,

Table 47 *Food grain supply to the State, 1974*

	All Shaanxi	Guanzhong		Hanzhong	North Shaanxi, Qinling mnts., Daba mnts.
		plain	*hanyuan*		
Agr. pop. (million)	22.71	9.77	2.39	2.1	8.45
Grain area (1,000 ha)	3,135	1,033	469	164	1,480
Grain output (1,000 tons)	7,500	3,765	873	768	2,095
i.e. per cap. (kg.)	330.5	385.5	365.5	366.5	247.5
Grain supplied to the State (1,000 tons) ×	1,328	756.2	154.4	163.5	234.6
i.e. per cap. (kg.)	58	77.5	64.5	76.5	27.5
i.e. % of production	17.6	20.1	17.7	21.3	11.2

× Some of which was 'resold' to indigent collectives.
Source: data from *Shaanxi Nongye Dili*, pp. 200–3.

with a rather narrow range of 2.6 to 3.3 tons. Output per rural capita averaged only 380 kilogram, of which 75 kg was delivered to the State. See table 48, graph K, and map 31.

Since 1979 Shaanxi has followed the national (somewhat contradictory) policies of planning specialized crop zones for grain, cotton, rape, animal husbandry etc. and at the same time allowing peasants to decide for themselves where to cultivate which crop.[88] The foodgrain shortage after the 1980 and 1981 disasters, however, temporarily forced the provincial government to stick to grain production. Village grain stocks had fallen to a dangerously low level of 25 kilogram per capita.[90] Moreover, under the new political circumstances the government had difficulties in maintaining the cotton acreage in low-productive areas. The area sown to fodder crops, green fertilizer, vegetables, tobacco and peanuts considerably increased.[91] In 1984, again regional (per county) specialization was indicated by the provincial government. (See Map 32).

Around 1980, wheat and secondly maize were responsible for most of Shaanxi's foodgrain production; within Guanzhong, where little rice was grown, their position was even more dominant. Gaoliang and millet still played a minor role in west and north Guanzhong. See also maps 25 to 29, and table 46 for 1971 and 1980 crop distribution. As table 49 shows, maize production was about 2.8 million tons in four out of the five years 1979–83. This was almost twice as much as the annual output during the decade 1965–74, and already considerably larger than the 1975 record yield of 2,130,000 tons.[92] Wheat harvests were influenced to a greater extent by weather conditions, and broke all records in 1982, 1983 and 1984. Within just three years, Shaanxi province changed from a situation of severe grain shortage to one of abundance, even though its foodgrain area had been reduced somewhat. This was completely new and unheard of – the State purchased and collected more grain than before, yet local storage facilities were very inadequate. An investment programme was set up by the central and provincial governments to create additional storage capacity of 400,000 tons of grain, in 134 grain silos in 83 counties, to be completed in 1987. Foodgrain was diverted to other uses, such as alcohol and fodder.

This seemed to indicate that grain abundance was expected to stay.[93] Diversification of agricultural production and local specialization was encouraged again by the government in 1984. However, the government urged farmers not to relax grain production. The

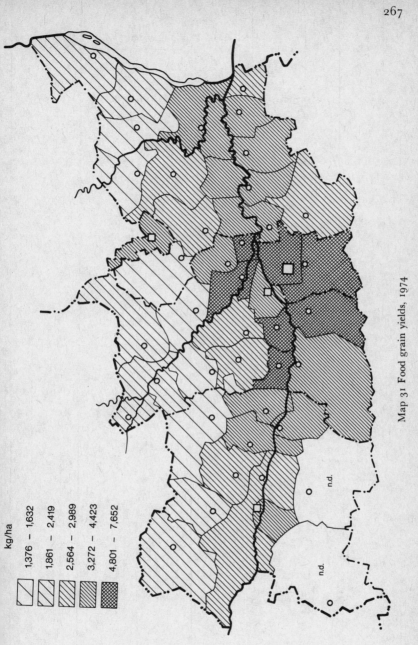

kg/ha

1,376 – 1,632
1,861 – 2,419
2,564 – 2,989
3,272 – 4,423
4,801 – 7,652

Map 31 Food grain yields, 1974

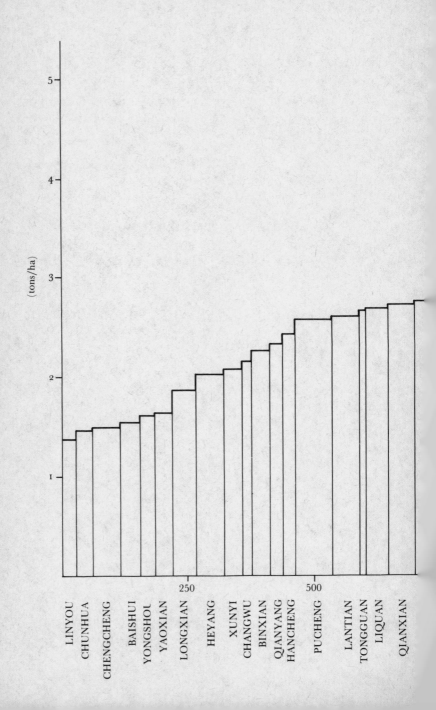

Graph K Food grain acreages and average yield in the counties of Guanzhong, 1974

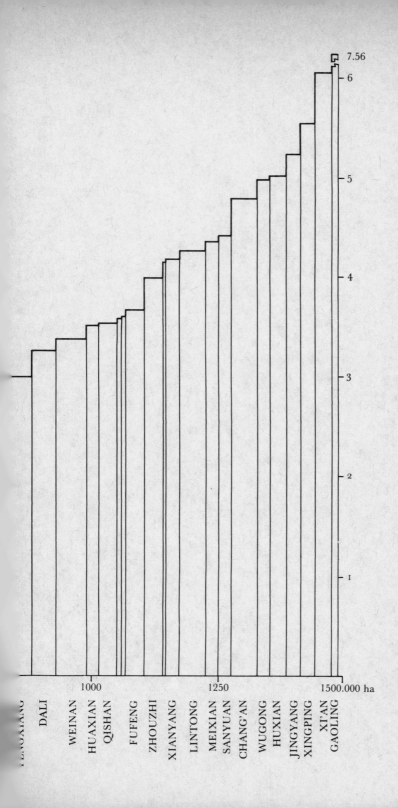

Table 48 *Cultivated and sown area, food grain area and output, and rate of commercialization in Guanzhong counties, 1974*

County	Cult, area (ha)	Sown area (ha)	Multi-crop i.	Foodgrain acreage (ha)	Output (tons)	Yield (kg/ha)	Output per rural cap.	Commercial rate (%)
Xi'an	47,350	77,330	1.63	32,933	200,825	6,098	374.5	15.3
Changan	62,510	103,330	1.65	52,867	253,805	4,801	392	18.8
Xianyang	37,410	51,200	1.37	25,067	104,900	4,185	412.5	21.0
Xingping	37,650	55,730	1.48	25,533	142,165	5,568	423.5	20.0
Huxian	41,480	69,330	1.67	31,333	157,685	5,033	400.5	17.1
Zhouzhi	50,710	77,330	1.53	38,333	153,615	4,907	346	18.1
Gaoling	20,650	32,530	1.58	12,667	95,785	7,652	611	31.6
Jingyang	50,130	72,670	1.45	29,133	153,180	5,258	464	22.5
Sanyuan	38,910	54,670	1.40	25,400	112,335	4,423	443.5	23.5
Fuping	84,240	108,000	1.28	60,533	167,430	2,766	315	20.0
Lintong	76,930	112,670	1.46	54,000	231,050	4,279	429.5	20.2
Weinan	88,110	116,000	1.32	60,600	204,870	3,381	373	20.7
Huaxian	30,060	42,800	1.42	24,200	85,300	3,525	353.5	14.7
Huayin	12,630	17,530	1.39	8,933	32,010	3,583	286.5	15.7
Tongguan	13,680	18,200	1.33	9,467	25,300	2,673	277	18.2
Dali	73,860	106,670	1.44	49,800	162,930	3,272	345	19.5
Hancheng	34,730	46,200	1.33	25,600	61,915	2,419	278	11.6
Heyang	76,420	85,330	1.12	55,067	111,645	2,027	337.5	17.4
Chengcheng	67,990	78,670	1.16	54,333	80,680	1,485	303.5	20.5
Baishui	45,970	54,800	1.19	39,000	60,050	1,540	329.5	16.6
Pucheng	125,510	155,330	1.24	76,067	195,010	2,564	348	21.5
Yaoxian	44,450	51,730	1.16	37,667	61,465	1,632	326	14.5
Lantian	57,630	82,670	1.43	54,733	142,540	2,604	294	13.8

Liquan	63,110	79,330	1.26	45,267	121,170	2,677	389	16.3
Qianxian	72,980	88,000	1.21	51,400	139,540	2,715	371	14.6
Wugong	34,510	53,870	1.56	25,867	129,260	4,997	411.5	18.2
Fufeng	52,010	70,670	1.36	39,000	143,015	3,667	424.5	21.8
Meixian	30,340	45,330	1.49	23,333	100,990	4,328	463.5	24.8
Qishan	44,730	61,400	1.37	36,133	127,535	3,530	401	26.5
Fengxiang	62,300	81,330	1.31	49,667	148,435	2,989	392.5	25.2
Baoji	85,310	109,330	1.28	71,267	211,215	2,964	401.5	22.3
Baoji city	10,000[a]	15,000[a]	1.50	6,533	23,580	3,609	328.5	22.4
Longxian	55,310	55,130	.99	44,933	83,605	1,861	444.5	24.9
Qianyang	39,060	34,400	.88	23,333	54,245	2,325	529	29.4
Linyou	37,290	38,070	1.02	28,067	38,370	1,376	536	27.4
Yongshou	37,300	37,930	1.02	29,800	48,000	1,611	369	19.5
Chunhua	39,740	42,200	1.06	33,600	49,070	1,460	364	14.3
Xunyi	39,200	48,930	1.25	32,067	66,790	2,083	346	10.4
Binxian	50,710	52,930	1.04	37,600	85,060	2,262	390	13.8
Changwu	26,070	30,000	1.15	20,933	45,010	2,150	351	12.6
Tongchuan	10,000[a]	12,000[a]	1.20	6,533	27,230	4,168	311.5	17.1
Total	2,008,980	2,626,570	1.31	1,491,270	4,638,610	3,111	380	19.6

[a] Estimates by this author.

N.B. 1. Some figures, notably the Guanzhong totals, have been corrected by this author.

2. Output per rural capita includes also non-foodgrain producing farmers.

3. The low rates of commercialization in Chunhua, Binxian, Xunyi and Changwu are related to the special tax status of these 'old-liberated areas'. The rate of commercialization is based on taxes, obligatory sales and above-quota sales to the state, and does not take into account so-called 'resold grain', a means by which the state waives grain tax and grain supply obligations of collectives. It therefore overstates actual sales. Partly for this reason, partly because peasants may divert their surplus to other uses, this rate has only a weak correlation with output per rural capita in a single year, but a stronger one with average output of many years.

Source: Shaanxi Nongye Dili.

Table 49 *Output of various foodgrains in Shaanxi, 1979–1984*
(1,000 tons)

	1979	1980	1981	1982	1983	1984
Total foodgrain	9,095	7,570	7,496	9,250	9,650	10,237
Wheat	3,595	2,300 [x]	3,541	4,210	4,445	4,495
Maize	2,875	2,750	2,030 [o]	2,823	2,882	3,131
Rice	795	755	530 [o]	796	844	933
Other grains	1,830	1,765	1,395	1,421	1,479	1,678

[x] suffered from serious spring drought.
[o] suffered from summer floods and dark and rainy autumn.
Sources: *Shaanxi Ribao* 27 Apr. 1983, 1 May 1984, 17 Feb. and 6 Apr. 1985; *Zhongguo Nongye Nianjian 1980* and *1981*.

average output per capita was still only 345 kilogram (as against 400 kg for China), insufficient to support the desired rapid expansion of animal husbandry and food processing industries.[94] In 1985, foodgrain production was 9,519,000 tons, just below the 1983 level.

H. FERTILIZERS

Going back to the original question of the contribution of various inputs to foodgrain yield increases in Guanzhong, in the 1960s and 1970s we have already outlined development of irrigation and variety improvements. Both created the conditions for higher yields, but only with additional amounts of fertilizer could production increase be effectuated. Green fertilizer crops made a certain contribution in dry land areas, and were promoted by the state organizations as being cheap and effective in raising soil fertility, just as they had been during the 1950s.[95] In irrigated and double-cropping areas, however, there was no room for them. Pigs became a more important source of manure during the 1960s, with their numbers doubling between 1965 and 1975. In 1978 at year-end there was an average of 1.5 to 2 live pigs per hectare. After 1978, however, their number stabilized and even declined, as pork prices fell and chemical fertilizer became more easily available (see Tables 42 and 50).

In 1981 and 1982 many pigs were slaughtered because of lack of fodder. One-quarter of Shaanxi's pork production was sold outside the

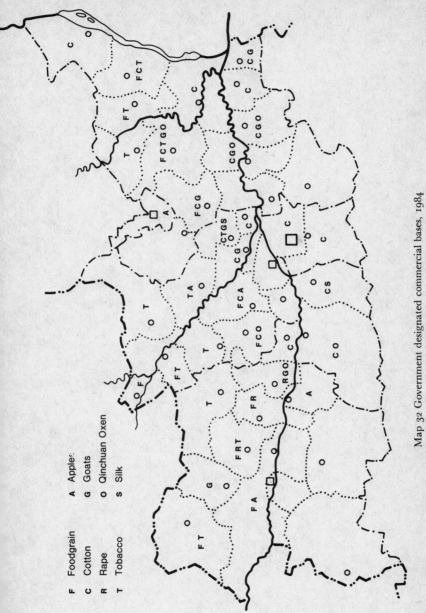

Map 32 Government designated commercial bases, 1984

F Foodgrain   A Apples
C Cotton   G Goats
R Rape   O Qinchuan Oxen
T Tobacco   S Silk

Table 50 *Pigs and chemical fertilizer use in 7 counties, 1957–1978*

	No. of pigs killed per 100 ha of farmland				alive at year-end	Chem. fertilizer used per ha of farmland resp. per ha of irrigated farmland only° (kg. of standard fertilizer)							
	1957	1965	1975	1978	1978	1957	irr.	1965	irr.	1975	irr.	1978	irr.
Weinan	2	15	37	53	(n.d.)	23	511	81	642	444	641	718	945
Wugong	41	n.d.	162	245	(n.d.)	46	151	n.d.		220	275	648	738
Qianxian	n.d.	n.d.	n.d.	31	(137)	–	–	n.d.		123	299	252	522
Liquan	14	22	40	63	(184)	1	29	33	205	124	226	263	436
Pucheng	3	7	26	44	(161)	–	–	36	1,068	157	467	232	577
Hancheng	44	58	52	91	(248)	31	521	74	1,000	203	912	578	1,654
Chunhua	2	8	11	13	(105)	–	–	5	634	45	627	64	463
Total average	10	17	37	63	(153)	10	201	46	575	201	447	376	722

° assuming chemical fertilizer to be used on irrigated farmland only.

Source: data from County Agricultural Bureaus.

province to pay for the grain imports of these years. Internal consumption had also increased. In 1983, however, the State refused to buy more pork from the peasants.[96] Since then, more attention has been directed towards pig improvement work and feeding techniques, in order to raise the quality of pork. Industrial production of fodder increased from 13,500 tons in 1981 to about 50,000 tons in 1983, still an insignificant amount.[97]

Estimating the total contribution made by pig manure to soil fertilization in Guanzhong since the 1960s is complicated because of a scarcity of data on the pig population (see Table 38) and because of differences in manure production and nutrient content related to age, fodder, preparation methods, etc. A local handbook estimated that one pig produced 4.6 kg of N, 2.45 kg of K and 9.35 kg of Ph per year. In terms of the standard chemical fertilizers, this equalled 23 kg of nitrogenous fertilizer, 13.6 kg of superphosphate and 18.7 kg of potash fertilizer.[98] Thus, in 1975, 3,352,000 pigs alive at year-end in Guanzhong have supplied the equivalent of 77,000 tons of nitrogenous fertilizer, 46,000 tons of superphosphate and 63,000 tons of potash fertilizer. During the 1960s and earlier, this was still a sizeable contribution, but by 1975 output of chemical nitrogenous fertilizer was already several times as much, and during the 1980s over ten times as much. The population of Guanzhong, with its nightsoil, added more nitrogen to the soil than pigs did, especially so during the 1960s when pigs numbered only 1.5 to 2 million.[99] As a source of potash fertilizer, however, and also of phosphate, pig manure remained of prime importance. Most beneficial of all, no doubt, was, and still is, the effect of the application of manure mixed with earth on the field soil. Its structure, humus and air content are much improved by the regular working of organic materials into the soil.

During the 1960s and 1970s a clear distinction has developed between fertilizer application in irrigated areas and in dry areas. Almost all chemical fertilizer is applied to irrigated farmland, and virtually none to dry farmland. Pig manure and human nightsoil were applied to both, but mainly to fields near home and private plots, both because of labour requirements and because of the ownership situation. Pigs and nightsoil were mostly private, not collective property, while chemical fertilizer could only be obtained from the State by the collective.

Chemical fertilizers were introduced in Guanzhong not much earlier than in 1957.[100] Phosphate fertilizers were mainly locally produced from lime.[101] Nitrogenous fertilizers were imported from outside the province, until the early 1970s. Annual production capacity was enlarged in 1975 to 736,000 tons of standard fertilizer, both by increasing the number of small-scale factories (producing a few thousand tons a year) from 12 to 40, and by the establishment of the large-scale Shaanxi Chemical Fertilizer Plant, which had a capacity of 60,000 tons of synthetic ammonia and 110,000 tons of urea.[102] By 1977, Shaanxi had 77 nitrogenous fertilizer plants, and also a number of phosphate plants and mines.[103] Only a few of these were large-size, and most produced only 3,000 to 5,000 tons a year. In 1978, 600,000 tons of standard nitrofertilizers (21% N) were produced within Shaanxi, and another 500,000 tons had been allocated by the central government. The central government then decided to build a large-scale plant with an annual production of 300,000 tons 82% N (i.e. 1,200,000 tons of standard equivalent nitrogenous fertilizer), which would triple Shaanxi's production capacity.[104] This decision, however, must have fallen victim to the readjustment policies of 1980, and eventually a smaller plant, with a capacity of 50,000 tons, was set up in Xingping.[105] As a consequence, from 1979 until 1983, Shaanxi's dependence on imported fertilizers decreased. Average application (at 100 percent effectiveness) per hectare of farmland rose from about 10 kg in 1965 to 50 kg in 1975 and 110 kg in 1984. Because of the fact that the irrigated area where it was applied was extended at the same time, average actual application levels rose less, having been rather high from the start (see tables 50 and 51).

I. MECHANIZATION OF AGRICULTURE AND PLOUGHING DEPTHS

Mechanization is generally considered a major, if not the most important, part of agricultural modernization. In Guanzhong, however, the overabundance of rural labour gave little impetus to labour-saving devices except in heavily irrigated areas with double-cropping. Machinery, then, was most essential and most sought after if it created new opportunities and tapped resources unavailable to traditional animal and human labour. In three major areas of agricultural activities this was clearly the case. More drainage machinery was introduced since the 1960s, both for wells and for pumping stations. In most plain areas, and in parts of the uplands, a regular supply of irrigation water from underground water or from rivers was secured.

Table 51 *Chemical fertilizer output and use in Shaanxi, 1979–1984*

	Used amount (at 100% effectiveness)		Output (at 100% effectiveness) (1,000 tons)			Imports as percentage of use (%)
	(1,000 tons)	i.e. per ha (kg)	Total	of which N	of which Ph	
1979	287	75	168.0	154.7	13.3	41
1980	296	77	196.6	168.8	27.8	34
1981	265	70	203.1	170.3	32.7	23
1982	313	83	224.4	187	37.8	28
1983	359	95	263.8	227.8	35.8	27
1984	415	110	294.6	260.6	33.9	29

Sources: Shaanxi Ribao 20 June 1981, 27 Apr. 1983, 1 May 1984, 6 Apr. 1985.

Thus, mechanization of irrigation removed the major constraint for raising agricultural production. Mechanization of transport (train, truck and tractor) opened up new opportunities for cheap long- and short-distance transport. Peasants now could break away from traditional self-sufficiency and began to exchange agricultural and industrial products with cities on a much larger scale than before. The developments of irrigation and of transport have been outlined separately in chapters 5 and 2. More than anything else, however, the socialist symbol of agricultural mechanization since Lenin had become the tractor. During the 1970s, the Chinese considered the area ploughed by machinery as the prime yardstick for agricultural modernization. Only after 1970 were tractors, power tillers, threshers and other machine-powered farm implements introduced in Guanzhong in greater quantities. Table 52 gives totals for Shaanxi province. Probably two-thirds of this machinery was located in Guanzhong. By 1973, Shaanxi was able to produce 80,000 water pumps yearly, and by 1977 26,000 walking tractors yearly.[106]

The first tractors arrived in Guanzhong in 1954, in Xingping, Dali and Fufeng. By 1957, 21 state tractor stations had been established, with a total of 6,700 Hp.[107] At the end of 1962, their number had increased to 61, with 1,256 tractors (and 32,130 Hp.). Most stations operated at a considerable loss, owing to bad management, high fuel expenditure, inferior quality of the tractors, and lack of experience and technical know-how.

This year, only 153,000 hectares were ploughed, instead of the 267,000 hectares which might be possible. Total losses were 1,106,000 *yuan* . . . Problems were (1) ineffective use of labour time, with much travel, (2) incomplete work, (3) bad management and accidents, (4) lack of maintenance of tractors.[108]

Tractor stations were overstaffed, with two well-paid drivers to every tractor. Costs were about 28 *yuan* per standard hectare until 1963, but then dropped to about 20 *yuan*. The provincial government had set a norm of 19.80 *yuan* per standard hectare to be charged to the peasants, and had to cover the deficits incurred by the stations.[109] In 1965, the Pucheng station, which was a model unit, managed to plough an average 300 to 400 hectares with each of its 110 tractors, at a cost of 17 *yuan* per hectare, and made a profit.[110]

Shaanxi province at that time still had only 1,800 tractors, and five years later, in 1970, only 3,000, most of which had been handed over to

Plate 8 Wooden and iron ploughs, Weinan county.

Table 52 Agricultural machinery in Shaanxi, 1962–1984

	Irrigation and drainage machinery (1,000,000 Hp)	Tractors large or middle-size (1,000)	Hand tractors (1,000)	Threshers (1,000)	Machine-powered farm implements (1,000)	Trucks (1,000)	Total motive power (1,000,000 Hp)
1962		1.1			4	0.01	
1965		1.8		0.5	5.1	0.2	
1970		3.0	1.2	11	6.4	0.2	
1975		10.2	18.7	46.4	20.8	0.6	
1978		15.3	48	69	25	1.0	
1979		18.9	63	69	30	1.9	
1980	2.6	20.4	69	74	32	3.5	6.4
1981	2.5	21.0	75	76	32	4.6	6.7
1982	2.6	22.2	91	–	–	6.0	7.2
1983	2.3	22.6	113	87	31	7.7	7.3
1984	2.2	21.4	137	–	–	8.6	7.6

Sources: Zhongguo Nongye Nianjian 1980, 1981, 1982 and 1984; Shaanxi Ribao 20 June 1981, 27 Apr. 1983, 1 May 1984 and 6 Apr. 1985; Zhongguo Jingji Nianjian 1981 IV, p. 306.

People's Communes. Then take-off started. By 1975, there were 10,000 tractors in Shaanxi (almost all in Guanzhong), and five years later, 20,000 tractors, all of which were imported from outside the province. Production of a local power tiller 'walking tractor' had started around 1970, the 12 Hp *Nanniwan* which was produced in Fuping. Two small 12 Hp four-wheeled models *Yanhe 12* and *Yan'an 12* were produced for a few years in Xi'an, but then discarded.[111] The Nanniwan was quite successful, and Shaanxi had already 18,700 'walking tractors' in 1975 and 63,000 in 1979. Actually, one could sit on this walking tractor and use it for transportation as well.

Tractors were, and are, primarily used in irrigated plain areas. In 1974, still only 10 to 20 percent of the dry upland areas was ploughed by machinery.[112] A survey of *hanyuan* counties in 1978 showed that for their 932,000 hectare of farmland there were 3,850 tractors and 7,500 power tillers. In the eastern, less elevated, areas 60 percent of the farmland was stated to be ploughed at least once a year, and in the western, more mountainous areas 30 to 50 percent (see Table 53). This may have been a slight overestimation, in view of subsequent official data. The irrigated areas generally were ploughed two or three times per year, depending on the cropping system. Cost of machine-ploughing (operating expenses only) then was about 23 *yuan* per hectare. Most current practice was one annual deep-ploughing (about one foot) and two shallow ploughings (3 to 6 inches).[113]

Ever since the 1958 guideline of the central government had unequivocally stated that deep-ploughing should be promoted,[114] ploughing depths have been a matter of interest and debate in research institutes and villages alike. Although depths to one foot were possible, the lack of sufficient animal power usually made ploughing depths stop at 5 to 7 inches.[115] Tractors, however, might go much deeper, and around 1960, usually went to 6 to 9 inches according to some, and to 10 to 12 inches according to others.[116] If one goes by the amount of diesel-oil used per hectare in 1962, average ploughing depth may have been 8 to 9 inches.[117] Deep ploughing raises production, because it increases the air pockets in the soil and its water retention capacity, it promotes ripening of the soil and root growth to greater depths. In this way, crops may draw water and nutrition from deeper layers.

Summing up a number of experiments in different areas in Guanzhong, an authoritative article concluded that deep-ploughing raised production both in irrigated and in dry areas, but that ploughing deeper than 14 to 16 inches in some cases actually decreased

Table 53 *Tractors and hand tractors on the* hanyuan *and along the Wei River,*
1978

	Farmland (ha)	Tractors (1)	Hand-tractors (1)	Farmland per tractor (ha)
I. Dry upland mountain areas *(17 counties)*				
a. Longxian, Linyou, Qianyang	132,000	452	990	92
b. Qianxian, Liquan, Binxian, Changwu, Xunyi, Chunhua, Yongshou	320,000	1,499	2,419	91
c. Pucheng, Fuping, Baishui, Hancheng, Chengcheng, Heyang, Yaoxian	470,000	1,900	4,100	78
II. Wugong county	33,900	409	1,090	23
III. Four state farms at the *Wei-Huang River confluence*	18,000	203	n.d.	88

Source: interviews with Regional Agricultural Bureaus.

production. The most effective depth was about one-and-a-half feet. However, the cost of animal and human labour was 2.5 times as much as with 1.2 feet and 5 times as much as with 0.6 to 0.8 foot. If one used a 75 Hp tractor, ploughing 1.4 feet deep instead of 0.7 foot deep would reduce ploughing speed to only 0.2 hectare instead of 1.7 hectare per hour, and increase gasoline use almost 4 times. The most economical ploughing depth therefore was considered to be 0.8 to 1.2 foot. On fertile soils, on the uplands, and on heavy clayey soils, one might plough somewhat deeper than that. On poor soils, on irrigated fields and on rather loose soils, one might plough more shallowly. Deep ploughing should by preference occur during winter- or summer fallow, but near sowing time ploughing should be rather shallow.[118] A few years later, when more tractors had become available, there was still a consensus at the Northwest College of Agriculture that generally 0.8–0.9 foot was the most economical depth for ploughing. Some handbooks advocate greater depths.[119] For breaking the ploughpan of Guanzhong's *loutu* soil, 1 to 1.2 foot generally was sufficient.[120]

After 1979 the number of tractors and power tillers continued to increase, albeit more slowly than before.[121] However, less farmland was ploughed by machinery every year. According to official data referring to Shaanxi province, the percentage of machine-ploughed area was 37.2 in 1979, 33 in 1980, 28 in 1981, and only 23.8 percent in 1982.[122] This anomalous nationwide trend calls for an explanation. The liberalization of trade after 1979 greatly increased the flow of goods and the peasants' need for transportation means. Thus, many tractors and 'walking-tractors' were taken off the fields and used for transport. Decollectivization policies reduced the use of commune- or brigade-owned tractors, either because some individual peasants now became unwilling to use them or pay for them, or because the village cadres ran into organizational problems. Tractors and power-tillers which were handed over to individual peasants or newly bought by them[123] may have been under-utilized. In any case, where farmland was divided into very tiny plots, machine-ploughing outside the fallow period became more difficult and less economical.

In 1978, the agricultural development plan of Shaanxi set various goals for 1985. More irrigation and more chemical fertilizer were considered to be the major means for achieving a rise in foodgrain output from 8 million tons in 1978 to 11 million tons in 1985. Improvement of varieties was mentioned third, mechanization fourth, forestry and animal husbandry last.[124] This order was still reflected in the government's priorities of the early 1980s, but by 1985 the rural economy had taken a rather different turn. Grain production still was stressed, but partly for animal feed. Both irrigation and machine-ploughing had been reduced for reasons of economy – decisions in these respects were taken by individual farmers to a large degree. Chemical fertilizer use rose rapidly, as planned, and variety improvement also kept receiving priority attention. The state slowly withdrew itself from direct involvement in planning agricultural production, and from part of its marketing and distribution.

Conclusion. The loess soils of Guanzhong, under the influence of many centuries of cultivation, have developed into several subtypes with considerable variation in organic matter content and fertility. Only the small stretches of irrigated farmland were worked intensively. Until the 1970s most wheat areas practiced summer fallow, and sometimes crop rotation with millets or peas. For a second fertilizer or forage crop such as alfalfa, water supply generally was insufficient. Pig manure and nightsoil were the main sources of fertilizer.

In the 1930s, most pigs slaughtered in Guanzhong were brought in from Gansu. Local pig varieties were inferior. The mountain areas could raise pigs more cheaply because of low fodder costs. Manure and forage could be transported only over short distances, and most farmers in the plain (especially in irrigated areas) were very short of manure. Ploughing and weeding suffered from the shortage of draught animals. Yields, therefore, remained low. After 1935, experimental stations started with research into crop rotation systems and the use of green fertilizer. In the 1950s, wheat yields were raised considerably, due to an increased application of manure, irrigation, variety improvement and better crop care. The demands for fertilizer stimulated an increase in pig rearing, even though the state paid low prices for pork and collectivization was a disincentive. When the state raised its purchase price in 1957, and coops raised their price for manure, the number of pigs increased by 70 percent within one year to one million. From this source and from night soil, possibly up to 100 kg of whole nitrogen per ha was supplied to irrigated crops and less than half that amount to dry crops. In the late 1960s and 1970s, application levels more than doubled, because of population growth and a tripling of the number of pigs over the late 1950s. In the non-irrigated areas, manure still is the main source of fertilizer.

More so than pigs, draught animals suffered under Land Reform and collectivization. Because of the Famine and World War II, the Guanzhong plain had few draught animals to begin with – in Weinan prefecture, one oxen to every three households in 1949. Rich peasants secretly slaughtered their cattle. Formerly, a draught animal was considered as 'half a family member', but the cooperatives took little care in feeding their animals and worked them very hard. The rate of reproduction went down severely and numbers and quality declined. In east Guanzhong and in irrigated areas the shortage of draught animals was keenly felt, especially since after 1955, with improved ploughs, greater ploughing depths were demanded. The dominant local breed, the Qinchuan oxen, was greatly improved during the 1960s and 1970s, and became one of China's superior breeds.

Variety improvements on a scientific basis started at the Agricultural College in Wugong and in the Jinghui irrigation district. Then and later, efforts have been directed mainly at (apart from cotton) wheat and maize. The main goals of breeding were to obtain high-yield and resistance against diseases. The earlier local varieties possessed good resistance against drought and frost – precisely the qualities which new high-yield varieties lacked most. Breeding programs therefore were based on crossing imported superior varieties with local strains. Shortening the growth period (the Guanzhong plain has only 190 to 210 frost-free days) was essential for multi-cropping.

Since World War II, four wheat varieties have been successively popularized in Guanzhong, each of which raised yields by about 20 percent. The first of these, *Bima no. 1*, had good resistance against stripe rust; by 1957, it was sown in over 70 percent of Guanzhong's wheat area. In irrigated areas, it was succeeded by *Xinong no. 6028*, and in dry areas by *Jinghui no. 30*. Lodging, stripe rust and also wheat scab were the main factors negatively affecting wheat yields in the 1960s. *Fengchan no. 3* and in irrigated areas *Apo* became the dominant strains of the 1970s; they had good resistance against most diseases and gave high yields. All these varieties were rather tall and weak strawed. During the 1950s, all counties established seed popularization stations, research institutions increased, and most important of all, the collective villages could devote specialized personnel and special plots for these purposes. With centralized management and larger plots, there was less occasion for adulteration of seeds; on the other hand, the state purchase system hardly stimulated regard for quality of food grain. Insecticides were introduced since the mid-1960s. Before but also after that, cultivation practices were directed at reducing damage from insects.

Food grain production continued to dominate Guanzhong's agriculture, accounting for over 80 percent of the sown area. Wheat, the main summer grain, and maize slowly drove out millets, gaoliang and other coarse grains. Between 1955 and 1980, maize increased by about one-half to almost 25 percent of the sown food grain area, owing its popularity to its stable and high yields; in irrigated areas in the plain it was the main second crop. Maize output doubled between 1957 and 1965, and doubled again in the following decade; its per ha yield average rose from about 1 ton in the 1950s to 2.5 tons in the 1970s. Provincial average wheat yields were about 40 percent above the national average during the 1950s, and rose from about 900 kg/ha to 1,200–1,400 kg/ha; except for three bad harvest years (1977, 1978 and 1981) yields have been well above 2,200 kg/ha since 1975. During the late 1970s, the national wheat yields caught up with Shaanxi. Because of population increase and because of recurring food grain shortages in North Shaanxi, there was little grain surplus. In the 1970s, the Guanzhong farmers could supply about 20 percent of their food

grain output to the state (the sole buyer). The rate of commercialization varied from 10 to 20 percent in north Guanzhong to 20 to 30
percent in the irrigated plain and the mountains of northwest
Guanzhong. The disasters of 1980 and 1981 made it necessary to
import food grain from outside the province. Subsequently, successive
good harvests seemed to bring Shaanxi and Guanzhong finally into a
position where increasing quantities of grain might be diverted to
other uses, such as animal husbandry.

Within Guanzhong, in 1974 food grain yields averaged from 1.4 to 2
tons/ha in its least productive counties in the north, to 5 tons and more
in the counties in the plain around Xi'an. The difference had become
much larger than in the 1930s or 1940s, mainly due to double-
cropping. For yields of wheat, county averages differed by a factor
of 2 to 2.5, throughout our period, at least in ordinary years. In years of
drought, however, yield differences between irrigated and non-
irrigated counties became much larger. The guarantee of mechanical
water supply and the vastly increased amounts of fertilizer (between
1975 and 1985, chemical fertilizer use on irrigated farmland rose from
100 kg N to well above 200 kg N per hactare) were the main factors in
ensuring high yields.

With the abundance of rural labour, agricultural mechanization
was useful mainly not as a labour-saving device, but as a creator of new
opportunities. Irrigation and drainage machinery supplied underground water from greater depths than before, and secured a more
regular and vastly increased quantity of irrigation water from rivers.
Mechanization of transport gave new opportunities for short- and
long-distance trade. Tractors were capable of ploughing at greater
depths and with greater speed than before. They had already been
introduced in Guanzhong in the 1950s, but only spread slowly.
Shaanxi had no tractor industry of its own and in this early phase all
tractors were managed by state tractor stations. Only in the 1970s,
especially from 1975, did tractors become more generally used. Once it
was produced within Shaanxi, especially the walking-tractor became
popular; it surpassed the 100,000 mark in 1983. Ordinary tractors
increased 7-fold between 1970 and 1980, to 20,000, but then their total
number went down slightly, because of decollectivization.

At the end of the 1970s, tractors still were rare in dry upland areas,
but quite common on the irrigated plain. Wugong, for example, had
one tractor for every 20 hectares of farmland. With oxen, ploughing
depths were 5 to 7 inches, but generally tractors ploughed to a depth of

10 to 12 inches. Occasionally, breaking the ploughpan, one might go to greater depths but this was expensive. After decollectivization, most tractors were sold to individuals and used for transport more frequently. For his tiny plot, the farmer now prefers an oxen or a walking tractor. Here as in other aspects, the state and the village collectives withdrew from direct involvement in agricultural production.

APPENDIX TO CHAPTER 6

Guanzhong climate

Month	1	2	3	4	5	6	7	8	9	10	11	12
Average temp. (°C)	-1--4	0-3	6-8	12-15	16-19	22-25	24-27	21-25	17-20	11-14	4-7	-1--1
Average high (°C)	2-4	7-9	12-15	19-22	22-26	29-32	30-33	26-30	22-27	16-21	8-12	4-7
Average low (°C)	-5--9	-1--5	1-4	7-9	10-14	15-20	20-23	18-21	12-15	5-9	0-3	-2--6
Precipitation (mm)	6-11	5-12	20-27	35-55	42-69	51-91	96-178	99-179	32-98	37-60	22-39	3-10
Other				Frost							Frost	Snow

Source: *Nongye Kexue Jishu Shouce* 1973, p. 32–37

Agricultural calendar of Guanzhong, 1970s

January Accumulate fertilizer, heap manure on wheatfields
Repair irrigation systems
Clean orchards, prune fruit trees

February Accumulate fertilizer, rake the wheat fields to preserve soil moisture, intertill, top-dressing
Apply base fertilizer to cotton fields
Repair irrigation systems
Prepare the soil of nurseries, prepare for afforestation

March Intertill and apply top-dressing to wheat and other summer crops
Prevent and control plant diseases and pests and frost
Select cotton seeds
Nurse seedlings, plant trees

April Intertill and apply top-dressing to wheat and miscellaneous summer grains
Plant and cotton and spring maize
Afforest

May	Guard against frost
	Intertill and loosen the soil of cotton fields, inspect seedlings and fill gaps
	Prevent and control wheat diseases and insect damage
	(Second half) Harvest rape and barley, nurture young trees
June	(First half) Harvest wheat
	Manage cotton fields
	(Second half) Sow late autumn crops
	Graft fruit trees
July	Thin out and single summer maize seedlings, apply top-dressing
	Prune cotton plants, irrigate, intertill, prevent and control diseases and pests
August	Remove old cotton leaves, control pests, irrigate
	Irrigate maize, intertill, apply top-dressing
	(Final three weeks on the uplands) Sow rape
	Repair irrigation systems
September	Pick cotton
	(Mid) Harvest maize
	Fertilize fallow fields, shallow-plow and harrow to preserve soil moisture
	(On the uplands, final ten days) Sow winter wheat
	(Final three weeks) Harvest millet
October	(First three weeks) Sow winter wheat and miscellaneous summer grains
	Pick cotton
	(Final three weeks) Harvest sweet potatoes, continue to harvest maize
	Plant trees, collect tree seeds
November	Apply base fertilizer and deep-plow fields for cotton and early autumn crops
	Repair ditches and roads, prepare for winter irrigation
	Take care of winter fodder for cattle
	Plant trees, deep-plow and fertilize orchards
December	Hoe and heap manure on wheatfields, give winter irrigation
	Repair irrigation systems
	Manage cattle
	Prune fruit trees

Source: Nongye Kexue Jishu Shouce 1973, pp. 32–7

7

COOPERATIVES, LAND REFORM
AND COLLECTIVIZATION

A. COOPERATIVES UNDER THE GUOMINDANG

Cooperatives were a creation of banks and government. Spurred by a favourable price development of cotton and by a strengthening of governmental and commercial institutions from 1934 onwards the national government took an active part in the promotion of cotton growing through cooperative societies. In Shaanxi province the cooperative movement was the responsibility of the Department of Civil Service and the Department for Reconstruction. Under the leadership of Li Yizhi, the Department for Reconstruction directed its efforts mainly to irrigation schemes – reservoirs, canals and wells. Banks took the lead in the promotion of cotton cooperatives. The government-sponsored Provincial Bank of Shaanxi lent out small sums to coops, usually through a merchant, on the guarantee of the county magistrate. This bank would see to it that the merchant would not demand interest rates higher than they were supposed to be. The Bank of China worked closely together with the county magistrate, did not always ask for a guarantee, but only lent to cooperative societies of cotton producers. The Shanghai Commercial and Savings Banks, more cautious, would lend only through the Provincial Bureau for Cotton Improvement and would have nothing to do with the local government. The Sino-foreign Famine Relief Commission worked independently, and by 1934 had limited its activities to cooperative societies in Liquan, Xianyang and Changan counties. Generally speaking the banks were very reluctant to invest for longer periods, and to provide loans to the bandit-ridden poor areas of west Guanzhong. Two foreign experts advised in 1934 that the provincial government, the National Economic Committee and the banks should jointly participate in providing capital for the promotion of the cooperative movement, with a 1:1:3 ratio in poor districts, but no such joint venture was decided upon.[1]

In August 1934 there were 113 coops established in Guanzhong, most of them in the counties around Xi'an. 94 of these were cotton coops (usually cooperating as to production, transport and sales, some only as to insurance of production). Total membership was 33,000, with a working capital of 1 million *yuan*. Table 54 shows their distribution in more detail.

Besides having access to cheap loans, benefits of coop membership generally included receiving more and better cotton seeds, paying less dues when selling cotton, and selling at a better price.

Between 1933 and 1939, various banks supplied 11.7 million *yuan* in agricultural loans to cooperatives in Shaanxi. Most of this sum went into cotton production and sales cooperatives.[2] The central government enlarged the scope of the coop movement after the beginning of the war against Japan. The Shaanxi Provincial Coop Committee, which had succeeded the Agricultural Coop Affairs Bureau in 1937, resorted directly under the Department of Affairs (*Shiyebu*) and the provincial government. It outlined policy, supported promotion of coops, and administered and distributed funds allocated by the government for coop work. By 1940, it had surpassed the banks as a lender. Following central directives, in March 1940 the Committee was changed into the Shaanxi Cooperative Affairs Bureau, which was brought under direct control of the Construction Department. Its staff was about a dozen employees. After the promulgation of tighter rules in November 1941 the Bureau came directly under the provincial government, which made its major decisions. During 1938 through 1940 cooperative funds had been set up in each county, but without much success. Therefore from 1940 onwards each county had an official designated as responsible for the guidance of coop work.[3]

During the 1930s different factors gave impetuses to the movement for the promotion of coops: disaster and relief during 1930–1934, the construction of irrigation projects (both wells and canals), the expansion of the cotton acreage and introduction of new seeds, and the wave of war refugees after 1938. Also, the desire to build up a defence-line against the communists in north Shaanxi played a significant role – after all, the first rules on coops had been promulgated by the Guomindang Government after the retrieval of communist-held territory in 1933. By the end of the 1930s most rural coops went under the name of 'credit coops' without specifying the nature of their business. Only some smaller categories of coops are singled out in official data, of which the most important were the individual coops

Table 54 *Cooperatives in Guanzhong, August 1934*

County	No. of coops	Cotton coops	Credit coops	No. of members	Capital (1,000 yuan)	Provenance of capital
Changan	29	19	10	7,657	186.7	FPAB, BS, BC, SFRC[+]
Lintong	18	14	4	5,078	212.1	BS, BC, SFRC
Jingyang	21	21	–	7,921	389.7	BS, BC
Sanyuan	19	19	–	3,050	89.0	BS, BC
Liquan	3	–	3	75	0.9	SFRC
Gaoling	13	13	1	2,783	96.0	BC
Xianyang	1	–	1	22	0.3	SFRC
Huayin	1	1	–	415	9.5	BC
Weinan	7	7	–	6,300	101.0	BC, BS
Wugong	1	–	1	70	n.d.	FPAB
Total	113	94	20	33,380	1,085.2	

[+] Four Provinces Agricultural Bank; Bank of Shanghai; Bank of China; Sino-Foreign Relief Committee.

Source: Zhongguo Jingji Nianjian 1935, R41–2.

favoured by Mme Chiang Kai-Shek among war-refugee labourers[4] and the 'defence coops' established to promote agricultural credit in the reclamation areas of Hancheng and some other counties bordering on communist- and/or Japanese-held territory. In November 1941, Guanzhong had 5,400 registered coops with a total membership of 315,000 people, and a registered capital of almost one-and-a-half million *yuan* and some 12 million *yuan* in outstanding loans. Because of the current inflation, money figures lost much of their significance, but there was a striking variation between various counties in the amount of loans extended to coops over the 1935–41 period, or still outstanding.

The number of coops and membership in each county was more or less in accordance with rural population figures in Guanzhong in 1941, with some notable exceptions: the border county of Hancheng with its Huanglongshan reclamation area, the county of Wugong where the Northwest Agricultural College was based, and Changan county next to the provincial capital, all of which had a large coop membership. As for the amount of loans extended to coops during 1935–1941, there was a large difference between the three cotton counties Gaoling, Jingyang and Sanyuan with an average of about 20 *yuan* per capita of the *total* rural population, some intermediate counties averaging 5 to 10 *yuan*, and the easternmost counties (Huaxian, Chaoyi, Tongguan etc.) and the northern counties where coops had received very little, both in absolute and in relative terms. The provincial government urged all banks to extend loans, but in view of the communist threat and the poverty of northern Guanzhong banks were unwilling to direct funds to the northern areas. Thereupon, in 1941 the provincial Government lent 1,850,000 *yuan* in relief to eight border counties; the largest recipients were Chunhua county and Xunyi county which had been retaken from the Communists.[5] At the end of 1943, the number of credits coops in Shaanxi had further increased to 10,970, with 550,000 members. Of the outstanding loans total of 124 million *yuan*, 91 million had been given to agricultural production coops, 10 million to transport and sales coops, 12 million each to irrigation coops and agricultural improvement coops, and 1 million to sidelines coops. After the war, however, most coops had ceased to exist.[6]

The coop movement, although eventually reaching no more than a quarter of the rural households, made a significant contribution to the agricultural development of Guanzhong. During the 1930s, especially cotton production and irrigation projects were stimulated by the extension of cheap credit and the cooperative organization of

Table 55 *Loans, membership and capital of cooperatives in Guanzhong, 1935–1941*

	Loans extended to coops 1935 (March)–1941 (Nov.) (1,000 yuan)		No. of coops in 1941	Membership in 1941	Capital in 1941 (1,000 yuan)
	extended total	still outstanding			
Changan	2,936	921	575	41,596	193
Xianyang	1,057	434	212	8,841	31
Xingping	858	181	298	17,316	47
Huxian	969	608	131	12,530	28
Zhouzhi	698	394	109	8,511	18
Gaoling	1,044	133	168	7,326	19
Jingyang	2,316	448	321	14,062	60
Sanyuan	1,704	453	220	8,727	43
Fuping	655	287	132	4,479	29
Lintong	1,824	746	215	15,673	38
Weinan	1,939	693	216	15,499	43
Huaxian	203	47	100	7,716	24
Huayin	99	26	70	2,655	6
Tongguan	69	4	28	1,078	3
Dali	391	137	83	6,433	13
Chaoyi	173	31	66	2,137	5
Pingmin	53	8	10	587	1
Hancheng	647	535	175	18,278	118
Heyang	215	68	76	2,854	6

Chengcheng	212	46	89	4,281	23
Baishui	408	136	87	3,607	8
Pucheng	815	185	118	4,396	17
Yaoxian	226	73	99	6,003	21
Lantian	304	156	102	4,191	11
Liquan	1,095	507	196	7,999	21
Qianxian	861	327	129	8,408	20
Wugong	302	130	223	14,787	35
Fufeng	1,739	823	108	12,311	75
Meixian	656	425	74	5,206	16
Qishan	332	71	71	4,168	12
Fengxiang	1,237	624	143	10,991	60
Baoji	797	568	192	6,408	199
Longxian	548	77	86	3,368	45
Qianyang	640	561	59	2,192	8
Linyou	199	97	61	2,382	6
Yongshou	130	21	54	1,839	9
Chunhua	16	7	57	3,630	34
Xunyi	11	4	75	5,631	56
Binxian	359	269	85	3,106	14
Changwu	71	41	51	2,028	8
Fengxian	1,120	1,039	57	1,635	27
Guanzhong Total	29,928	12,341	5,421	314,865	1,450

Source: Shaanxisheng Hezuo Shiye Gaikuang, p. 21.

production and sales. Different banks had different rules, but generally speaking the following conditions applied:

(1) support and often a guarantee was given by the local government
(2) interest rates charged to the coops were low (about 0.8 percent per mensem); the coops could charge a little more to their members (about 1.2 percent) using the difference as a public fund, for management expenses or for schools etc.
(3) there was a maximum amount each coop could borrow, and a maximum loan per member
(4) loans had to be used for productive purposes, not for consumption, and ran for a short period of 6 to 12 months.

Contemporary communist criticisms of the coops complaining about bad management, high interests, 'dominance of local bullies and evil landlords who use the coops for anti-communist activities and enrich themselves at the cost of the State and fleece the peasants'[7] seem rather unjust. The small size of his farm and commercial production, his poor access to capital and to knowhow for agricultural development, and his weak bargaining power *vis-à-vis* merchants and officials all hampered economic progress of the individual farmer. A cooperative organizational framework of any kind, which provided cheaper capital and greater official support, did help him to improve his weak economic position.

B. LAND REFORM

During the civil war of 1946–9 there was not much fighting in Guanzhong. Shaanxi province had become a backwater by then; the real battle was fought in northeast and east China. The nationalist troops abandoned Xi'an quietly, still leaving through the South Gate while the Communists marched in through the North and West Gates. The first political priority of the new government was to establish control in the countryside. Between December 1949 and May 1950, 12,651 'bandits' were put to death, a category which included active resistants, left-behind Guomindang agents, landlords' militia, highway robbers and other active criminals.[8] A people's militia under communist control was built up rapidly, to 300,000 members (of whom 80,000 in the previously-held communist territories) by November 1950.[9] Organized resistance against economic measures of the new Government has rarely been described.[10]

Land Reform does not seem to have met with much organized opposition in Guanzhong. The most common way of defense by rich peasants and landlords, who saw Land Reform coming, was to secretly split up their holdings among relatives, or even openly sell them. Cattle and other goods were likewise transferred to relatives or tenants, or sold. From the beginning the Communists realized that making revolution in the village would not be easy.

In Guanzhong, the amount of land rented out by rich peasants constitutes only 1 percent of all farmland. Landlords occupy only 5 percent of all farmland. Therefore, together with common land and temple land, little can be distributed. Sometimes there is no landlord at all in a village. So we must concentrate on production.[11]

The endebtment of the peasantry was not very high, either. Most loans were short-term only. Their purposes were manifold: to tide over a few months of living before the harvest, to buy seeds, cattle or other means of production, or to pay for marriage and funeral were the most common uses of loans. A survey of endebtment in a Changan district showed a decline of lending after the communist take-over in May 1949.[12] The serious inflation of this period and of the preceding years had made long-term loans and interest rates difficult to handle. Loans and repayment were in kind more often than not, and between relatives. The prospect of revolutionary redistribution of wealth, of abolishment of all debts and the stigmatization of lenders as usurers and landlords made merchants and rich peasants hesitant to engage in money-lending. On the other hand, under the circumstances it was wise not to hang on to goods and money. One would expect, therefore, that many goods and money changed hands secretly between relatives, and official data on loans may have been much too low. Nevertheless, agricultural production and trade suffered seriously from the sudden decrease of money supply and from the general political and economic insecurity. The State agricultural taxation measures, which weighed heavily on landlords, had similar negative effects.[13]

During spring 1950, some 700,000 people were calamity-stricken, 2,160,000 people did not have enough foodgrain. Moreover, there were refugees from north and east China. In order to get the economy moving again, the government announced that it was permitted to hire labourers and to lend money, and that anybody who sowed would be entitled to the harvest.[14] This, of course, did not help to maintain the revolutionary spirit:

Some people say: the landlords didn't lend much money before liberation; after liberation they didn't lend any more at all, it is pointless to abolish all loans . . . Other people say: it is possible to make revolution after clearing debts, without redistribution of land.[15]

In the winter of 1950, the provincial government started implementing the Land Reform law passed in June. By then, the apparatus of government and Communist Party cadres in Shaanxi consisted of some 50,000 people: 2,000 cadres at the provincial level (exclusive of Xi'an), 200 to 300 cadres at the various Special Districts (prefectures), 200 at the county level, and within each county about 20 cadres at the sub-district level and 2 cadres in every *xiang*. In Guanzhong alone, 12,000 cadres had been assigned to Land Reform.[16]

In the course of time, a more leftist line was taken up in early 1951. There is no reason to assume, or data to prove, that this move to the left originated from Guanzhong itself. Statistical data were now made to show that not 5 percent, but 8 percent of all farmland in Guanzhong was held by landlords. About 10 percent of all farmland was to be confiscated, including the property of temples, churches, schools and societies. Eventually, about 12 percent of Guanzhong's farmland (224,000 ha) was redistributed to 460,000 households with 2,020,000 people (about 30 percent of the population). As a consequence, the bottom 44.2 percent of the rural population then held 34.6 percent of all farmland in Guanzhong.

Between the three Administrative Regions, Land Reform showed certain differentials (see table 56).

In Baoji it appears that a higher percentage of farmland was transferred than in the other two regions. Xianyang region in central Guanzhong had the largest percentage of land recipients, maybe also because its landlords owned comparatively more land than the landlords in the other Regions did. In Xianyang Region, the top 2.97 percent of the rural households owned 11.67 percent of all farmland.[17] Generally speaking, we may conclude that even if Guanzhong did not have much of a landlord class (some 2 percent of the population[18] with 8 percent of the farmland), Land Reform still gave a sizeable increase of about 1 *mou* per capita, or 30 percent, in the individual landholding of the poorest segments of the rural population.

There is no data on the quality of the land transferred, but landlords generally owned above-average quality farmland. The economic value of the land transferral, therefore, may well have been twice as

Table 56 Redistribution by Land Reform

Region	No. of xiang	Poor peasants and labourers (% of pop.)	Percentage of farmland owned by them			
			before Reform (%)	i.e. per cap. (mu°)	after Reform (%)	i.e. per cap. (mu°)
Xianyang	697	51	30.3	2.5	39.0	3.2
Weinan	864	39.4	25.6	2–2.8	32.0	3.5
Baoji	766	45.7	–	2.8	–	4.15
(Xi'an)	–	–	–	–	–	(–)
Guanzhong	2,522	44.2			34.6	

° one mu equals 667 sq.m.

Source: Shaanxisheng Tudi Gaige Ziliao Huibian, 1951.

large as indicated by their surface alone. Transferral of houses, oxen, implements, grain stocks etc. was of a very limited significance economically,[19] but because of its ostentatiousness of great importance politically and psychologically.

In most areas of Guanzhong, Land Reform gave rise to discontent with communist cadres for their high-handedness 'cadres decide everything' and for their arbitrary classification of peasants in political/economic categories[20] – but then insecurity about possible classification was a functional part of the revolutionary process itself, the outcome of which the CCP wished to control and decide. Cadres themselves expressed their disappointment afterwards:

About 30 percent of the peasants have joined the peasant unions by now. But when looked at more carefully, the mobilization of the peasantry has been far from sufficient. The unions have expanded, but that does not mean to say that the true power of the peasants has increased. The "struggle meetings" generally saw just a few people making accusations about their sufferings, but the majority would be bystanders . . . The follow-up was often lax, there was no thorough investigation or education of the masses.[21]

Land Reform was of the greatest concern to the poorest (especially the landless) and to the richest segments of the village population. The so-called 'middle peasant', however, preferred to stay squarely in the middle and not to show his interest[22] – although, as elsewhere in China, he could become the leading force in subsequent rural transformation.

C. TAXATION AND GRAIN PROCUREMENT UNTIL 1957

During the first few years, proper assessment of the grain tax (by far the major tax) was a continuous problem. In 1950, the 35 counties of Guanzhong sent over 100,000 tons of wheat to the city, and over 20,000 tons of rapeseed. The tax duty had been increased by four percent to 75,500 tons.[23] Central government regulations had specified that middle peasants should not pay more than 15 percent, and poor peasants not more than 10 percent, and official statistics (quite understandably) showed the tax burden of these categories to have been just below these percentages.[24] However, in some areas where the land/farmer ratio was favourable, rates were somewhat higher. Different rules in neighbouring districts gave rise to dissatisfaction among the peasants, and disputes also arose about the grading of land.

Essentially, taxation of individual peasants was based on the assessed 'average' production of his fields and on his class status.

'Very often, out of the last five years, three years were chosen as average, rich and poor harvests, and the output average of those three years was taken to be the "many years" average.' This is not right. Furthermore there were the following problems:

(1) in some areas too many land categories were distinguished, e.g. 19 in Huaxian and 18 in Huayin; other areas made too little distinction or none at all;
(2) some lightly taxed areas contented themselves with a low output;
(3) in areas where bordering fields of a similar quality were classified differently, discontent would arise.[25]

The Weinan Special District authorities were seriously criticized because of their standards for calamity-stricken areas entitled to tax exemption. Subdistricts or *xiang* with an output of 20 to 50 percent of normal were considered lightly stricken, and with an output of less than 20 percent, severely stricken.

All this is very wrong. If the harvest is only 50 percent of normal, it is already a severe calamity. Also, it is wrong to take subdistricts or *xiang* as a unit; some peasants in such a unit may well be able to pay grain tax. Furthermore, no distinction was made in these guidelines between rich and poor peasants. This is a grave political error! These guidelines had not been passed on for approval by higher authorities, which is against the principle of one system.[26]

Erring on the side of leniency, however, was more common. Local cadres often could not, or would not, resist pressure from peasants for a lower assessment of 'average' output, of actual output and of the tax to be paid. Also, recovering tax arrears (especially from those classified as poor peasants) was a difficult and unpopular job for local cadres, who usually preferred to let the past be.[27]

More detailed grain tax regulations were passed after Land Reform had been completed. Stabilization of land ownership and of production, an increased number of trained cadres at the local level and experience gained in assessing farmland and output made the application of more sophisticated tax measures possible.[28] The subsequent agricultural cooperatives, which kept detailed records on their production, made tax perception for the authorities much easier and more equitable, but also part of a negotiating process between more equal partners than before. The 1951 grain tax amounted to 480,000 tons, or 11.5 percent of the total Shaanxi harvest. Because of increases in grain output during the following years, this percentage dropped to 9.8 percent in 1952, a little over 9 percent during 1953–1955 and to 7.5 percent in 1956. Rural foodgrain consumption was essentially stable at 244–8 kg per capita during 1954–6.[29]

According to computations made by Kenneth Walker for Shaanxi province's grain production and state grain purchases, during the First Five-Year-Plan period Shaanxi province exported grain to other provinces. However, provincial average urban and rural per capita consumption dropped to very low levels in 1955 and again in 1957. Although his figures apply to provincial totals and not to Guanzhong (for which separate data is not available) the matter is of importance because it bears on the ability of Shaanxi to provide Xi'an with foodgrain and because the vast majority of Shaanxi's urban population lived in Guanzhong and especially in Xi'an (see Table 57).

For the years 1953 and 1954, the data from Chinese sources are fairly complete, and the figures of urban and rural grain consumption of 230–40 kg per capita are reasonable. For the years 1955–7, however, data are less complete, and both urban and rural grain consumption figures in Table 57 are very likely to be wide of the mark; moreover, they differ from figures mentioned above from Chinese sources. Probably, one should also distinguish between annual figures of actual consumption and of newly available foodgrain. Changes in stock are likely to occur which have an equalizing effect on large fluctuations in the latter.

Only for B and C (taxes and gross procurement) Chinese data can be accepted; 1957 output data (A) may have been subject to 10 percent underreporting according to a local source; the estimate of urban population growth (F) is too low (Xi'an's population *alone* increased by about 200,000); it is not certain whether the 1953–7 total grain export figure is net (as Walker assumes) or gross (from which imports into Yulin and other grain-short areas should be deducted). There are some other uncertainties as well, e.g. the fact that only in 1954 did Xi'an become part of Shaanxi province and the distinction between urban and rural population. However careful the methods of computation may have been, the resulting figures for Shaanxi in 1955–1957 are contrary to reason. 1953 and 1954 consumption figures were stable; why would consumption wildly fluctuate *after* the introduction of urban rationing? The 1957 figure of 180 kg is extremely low, in fact the lowest one for all Chinese provinces during the years 1953–7; other provinces in north and northwest China have consump-

Table 57 *Summary of Shaanxi provincial grain output -taxes, -procurement, -resales, -surplus and -consumption 1953–1957, according to K. Walker*

	1953	1954	1955	1956	1957	Average 1953–7
A. Output p. c. of total population (unhusked kg)	294	302	263	308	249	278
B. Collected as taxes by State (1,000 tons)	446	454	417	406	441	433
i.e. % of output	9.4	9.1	9.3	7.5	9.8	8.9
C. Gross procurement by State (1,000 tons)	944	1,294	1,054	989	1,050	1,066
i.e. % of output	19.9	25.8	23.4	18.2	23.2	22.0
D. Rural resales by State (1,000 tons)	208	289	324	237	449	301
i.e. % of procurement	22.0	22.3	30.7	24.0	42.8	28.3
E. Net procurement by State (1,000 tons)	736	1,005	730	752	601	765
i.e. % of output	15.5	20.1	16.2	13.8	13.3	15.8
F. Estimated urban population (millions)	2.43	2.47	2.51	2.55	2.63	
G. Estimated urban grain sales (1,000 tons)	623	645	571	708	515	612
H. Procurement surplus	113	360	159	44	86	152
Estimated grain consumption						
I. per urban capita (unh. kg)	236	240	209	256	180	224
J. per rural capita (unh. kg)	242	229	206	261	206	229

Kenneth R. Walker, *Food Grain Procurement and Consumption in China*, Cambridge 1984, various tables.

Sources: A: *Fourth Session of the First NPC*, Beijing, 1957; *SXRB* 4 Feb. 1958

B: *Shaanxi Ribao* 18 July 1957 and 5 Aug. 1958.

C: *Shaanxi Ribao* 29 Aug. and 4 Sept. 1957; 5 Aug. 1958.

D: 1953–6 construed, 1957 estimated.

E: 1953 *Xi'an Ribao*; rest construed.

F: Estimates by Ernest Ni, *Distribution of the Urban and Rural Population of Mainland China: 1953 and 1958*, US Census Bureau IPR P-95 no. 56, Oct. 1960.

G: 1953 *Xi'an Ribao* 3 Nov. 1955. Other years construed.

H: 1953–1957 total export was 690,000 tons, *SXRB* 4 Sept. 1959. 1953–7 individual years construed (= E-G).

D + G (i.e. total sales): 1954 and 1955 *Shaanxi Ribao* 10 May and 4 Sept. 1957. 1953 and 1956 construed. 1957 estimated to be 2 percent up on 1956, according to plan, *Shaanxi Ribao* 1 Oct. 1957.

I: construed from G and F.

J: construed from output, minus B and E, minus feed, and provincial population minus F.

tion figures of 220 kg or higher. Yet, even in the 'liberal' period of 1957, no fall in urban consumption levels was mentioned in the press, and people kept flocking to Xi'an and to other cities.

We conclude that the 1955 and 1957 foodgrain conditions in Shaanxi were less grim than Walker's estimates show.

D. COOPERATIVIZATION AND COLLECTIVIZATION

Early in 1953, the CCP Provincial Committee, in line with national policies, decided that within three years some 70 to 80 percent of rural labour should have been organized in mutual-aid teams or in cooperatives. At that time, Shaanxi had 300,000 mutual-aid teams and 120 cooperatives.

In 1953 and 1954, the number of agricultural producers' cooperatives increased slowly to 983 in mid-1954. Then, within 2 months the number of APC's was doubled to 1,970 with 40,898 households, still only 1.32 percent of the rural households. The mutual-aid teams did not show much development either, still numbering 330,000 by the end of September 1954, of which only 57,000 were perennial.[30] In December 1954, the CCP Provincial Committee decided to set up another 21,000 APC's in 1955, and to send down many cadres to the villages so as to gain experience and to guide peasants to operate cooperatives.[31]

In subsequent spring, however, many local cadres were hesitant to step up the pace of cooperativization. The Dali county committee decided to dissolve a co-op itself.[32] An article in the provincial newspaper reproached cadres for not exerting themselves enough to keep people from leaving co-operatives, but added that people should be convinced, not commanded, to stay in their co-operative, and not be attacked for it.[33] A newspaper editorial stressed the principles of voluntariness and mutual benefit, and listed violations of these:

Some cadres do not start from the production benefit, but subjectively stipulate that 'no more than x percent may retire from the co-ops'.

Some cadres do not dare to talk to co-op members about the principle of voluntariness (afraid that members might retire). Some cadres do not investigate the concrete reasons why coop members want to retire, but scare those people off with 'removal', 'thought examination' and 'exposure'.

Some cadres make it difficult for those who want to retire by not returning the production materials entered into the cooperative.

Some cadres have not shown the guidelines of the Provincial CCP committee dated March 20 about 'voluntariness and mutual benefit as the principle' to the coop members, afraid that they might want to retire.

All this is wrong and adversely affects production, and only serves to increase problems![34]

The newspaper added that only 16 percent of all rural households had entered cooperatives, while over 50 percent participated in mutual-aid teams; which proved that the mutual-aid team still was the main force of agricultural production, which should not be neglected.[35]

The early Agricultural Producers' Cooperatives were organized in the most developed areas, with activist and generally better-off farmers. In many areas there was a reluctance to accept poor peasants for entry into one's coop. The government tried to rectify this tendency, but gave no rule on how large a percentage of poor peasants should be included in each coop.[36]

Then came Mao Zedong's famous July speech on the need for rapid cooperativization. Within less than a year, 90 percent of rural households had been organized into a total of 51,000 APC's, 62 percent of which in 24,000 so-called Higher Agricultural Producers Cooperatives.[37] There was no room for critical evaluation by provincial or local cadres – let alone peasants – of the content or speed of this transformation. While critical assessments of cooperatives were rare already from the start, after August 1955 they were entirely absent. That and the lack of any local traits in subsequent guidelines and articles on cooperativization[38] makes a description of cooperativization and collectivization in Guanzhong little rewarding.

The process of collectivization and its successes (and sometimes also its setbacks) in Guanzhong were part of a national political movement which portrayed collectivization as an historical necessity and as progress towards the ultimate Good. Of course, certain local variations in speed and method of implementation had to be permitted. For example, early in 1956 all counties and subdistricts were called upon to make their own agricultural production plan for the 12-year period until 1967, but were warned against being too conservative. Although the Draft Rules for Agricultural Cooperatives had been laid down by the central government, each cooperative still had to elaborate on these rules in its own statutes. At least they should stipulate the amount of land which was to remain privately-owned, the retribution method for land and labour brought into the cooperative, the management method of private cattle and implements, and the shares to be set aside for public accumulation and public welfare funds.[39] However, the Rural Work Department subsequently ruled that Higher-stage coops should distribute at least 60 percent and at most 70 percent of the coop income to their members; thus coops were free only within limits.[40]

Before the spring sowing of 1956, 88 percent of the rural households in Shaanxi had been organized into coops, 54 percent of which in the Higher-stage Agricultural Coops.[41] Also, 40,000 private traders were socialized, out of an estimated total of 150,000 traders and service-men (including food business and services). Many gave up their trade and returned to agriculture or found employment in the city – which caused considerable stagnation in trade flows and in the provision of services.[42] Also, as coops concentrated on agriculture, many subsidiary undertakings were abandoned. In the plain areas, these had previously accounted for over 15 percent of rural income, and in some mountain areas for over half. Problems arose with material supplies, with outlets, with unreasonably low state purchase prices, with cadres' discrimination against such undertakings etc.[43]

Cooperatives were meant to fulfill political and social functions, too. The Provincial CCP Committee decided that every coop should have at least 3 to 7 propaganda workers, and every village one reporting official. Village schools, much to the chagrin of teachers who feared a lowering of their salaries and of educational standards, were turned over from the State to the coops.[44] Four categories of households deserved special attention of the coops: the 5-protected households, who received aid for food and clothing, oil and salt, cotton, firewood and burial etc., the households with insufficient labour power, the professional people such as soldiers and teachers, and the lazy ones.[45]

Investigation of economic problems of newly-formed cooperatives usually resulted in policy recommendations to improve accounting work, organization of labour, and to find remedies for shortage of draught animals and of fertilizer. 'Commandism' and 'blind advance and unproductive management' were always criticized as an aberration and not seen as an integral part of the collectivization process itself.[46] Early in 1957, the process was temporarily halted and reassessed, especially as to the best size of cooperatives (somewhere between 10 and 50 households).[47] Mao Zedong's speech 'On the problem of correctly handling of contradictions between the people' which was splashed across three pages of the Shaanxi Ribao on June 19, ended all discussion. 'Rightist' critics of further cooperativization were severely attacked, and the few remaining independent farmers were forced to enter into coops.[48] The right average size of a HAPC was still to be found, but at the end of 1957 a size of 300 households still was condemned as too large.[49]

A year later, the average People's Commune in Guanzhong would have a size of 4,000 households, over ten times as large. Agricultural labour, it seemed, could be organized on a very large scale.

In October 1958, rural Shaanxi was organized into 1,673 People's Communes, with an average size of 1,930 households. In Guanzhong, the average size was over 4,000 households, in North and South Shaanxi 1,200 households. Basically, the People's Commune units corresponded with the previous *xiang* administrative unit.[50] In 1959, a merger of People's Communes resulted in a total of 681 enlarged People's Communes.[51] However, already in December 1958 the CCP leadership had decided to restore the production brigade as an economic unit. Thereby, economic functions of the People's Commune were reduced in favour of smaller collectives, the production brigades. Early in 1960, the Shaanxi provincial governor stated that the People's Commune still had had very little economic power in 1959: it had less than ten percent of the total collective income (public accumulation included) of the three levels of People's Commune, production brigade and production team.[52] In neighbouring Henan, the People's Commune was said to account for 16.4 percent of the total production value, which may have been twice as large a percentage as in Shaanxi.[53] Thus, in the commune movement the Shaanxi peasants had advanced less – and subsequently had to retreat less.

One of the main aims of collectivization was to increase the number of labour days as such and to divert agricultural labour to industrial undertakings. 'The average number of labour days in agriculture in Shaanxi is less than 200, and it should be raised to over 90% of the year.'[54] Another aim was labour specialization. In an example of a People's Commune in Dali county, 52 percent of the labour force was permanently assigned to agricultural work, 34 percent was assigned to various permanent undertakings (10 percent to industry, 19 percent to collective services, 5 percent to animal feeding, and 0.6 percent to management), and 14 percent of the labour force was mobile and used in railroad construction, irrigation works, county industries etc.[55] With existing data it is hard to establish to what extent additional inputs and specialization of agricultural labour did have lasting economic results. Nationwide, results were disastrous. In late 1959 and early 1960, resistance against large-scale labour mobilization and collective organization increased, both within and outside the Communist Party.

The few rich peasants and those cadres who have serious rightist ideas and represent the interests of those peasants vigorously oppose the People's Commune, the free supply system, the mess halls, the Great Leap Forward and the general Party line. They advocate signing contracts with individual households, returning land to the peasants and dissolving the mess halls . . . Events of the past few months show that they have put up a stubborn resistance and launched frantic attacks.[56]

The national food crisis and industrial crisis of 1960 and 1961 forced the CCP again to reconsider the collectivization drive. In 1961 and 1962, the production team was designated as the prime collective unit in the country, with just several dozens of households. The size of the average People's Commune was cut down by two-thirds. Also, farmers were entitled to private plots and some trade restrictions were lifted. Thus started a slow climb out of the 1960–1 crisis.

During the Great Leap Forward and the People's Commune movement of 1958–60 the Shaanxi leadership had to follow the national political trend. There is no indication, however, that at any time the Shaanxi provincial or local communist leaders tried to be in the vanguard of the collectivization drive. In the few cases where Shaanxi communes were held up as examples in the national press, it was for sound reasons, e.g. for flexibility in running a mess hall.[57] If one considers the sad fate – over one million dead of starvation – of the neighbouring province of Henan, which had been a trend-setter, Shaanxi had no reason to regret its cautiousness. As indicated in paragraphs 3 and 6, both demographic and grain production data for these years seem to show that Shaanxi suffered much less from the post-Leap-Forward food crisis than most other provinces. One can only speculate about the causes for that. Were leaders and peasantry more realistic because of their pre-1949 experience with collectives and starvation? Was provincial leadership so much occupied by the already very great demands of industrial buildup that it was less active in reshaping rural society and in extracting grain from the peasantry? Did the presence of 'old-liberated areas' with their favourable tax regime constitute a barrier against excessive extractions of grain? Or was Shaanxi just lucky with its weather conditions? We lack the kind of information needed for an answer to these questions. It is clear, though, that the food shortages of 1959 arose from extravagant consumption and distribution problems, and not from a drop in production. They may have served as an early warning.

In a survey of economic research on China, Dwight Perkins has remarked that the question remains as to the relative importance of modern inputs in agriculture versus institutional reform and labour mobilization as explanations for the rise in farm output after 1960.[58] The growth of modern (and of traditional) inputs in Guanzhong has been outlined elsewhere in this book. In the absence of local economic appraisals of the three-tiered collective system created in 1961–2 after the Great Leap crisis, much could be said about its merits and demerits for agricultural development, but little of a quantitative nature. The present refutation of collectivist agricultural policies has associated them with egalitarianism, self-reliant stress on grain production, lack of crop specialization, lack of incentives, stifling of trade and sideline undertakings, megalomania of cadres, state interference, a too high tax burden and too low agricultural prices, overstaffing of rural cadres and many other evils. These criticisms are more than justified as far as the commune movement of the Great Leap Forward is concerned, and to a considerable extent also as to the system as it functioned during the mid 1970s. This is not to say, however, that the same negative judgment on all accounts necessarily applies to the latter 1960s and early 1970s. During that period, chemical fertilizers, machinery, irrigation pumps, new varieties and many other modern inputs in agriculture were readily absorbed by the Guanzhong villages, within a framework of state rural organizations and of village agro-specialists with the know-how, funds and political power to make good if not optimal use of the scarce modern inputs. In this area of agricultural production it is unlikely that individual farming would have been capable of realizing a similar level of utilization of newly-introduced modern means of production.

The reverse side of the medal appeared only several years later. Specialization of agricultural labour into managerial, technical and commercial functions created a dichotomy between a growing professional elite on one side and a majority of 'dumb' peasants reduced to simple manual work on the other.[59] This gulf widened with the introduction of modern means of production and with the severe restriction of trade activities since the latter 1960s. For many, the fun went out of farming. Peasants lost their interest in work and resentment grew against their station in life. It seems to this author that this psychological process seriously affected rural economic performance during the 1970s. It may have been a more serious disincentive than the egalitarian distribution policies within the collectives now blamed by the present Government. Job satisfaction is the most powerful incentive, and based on more than material rewards alone.

E. BACK TO INDIVIDUAL FARMING

In winter 1977–spring 1978, a year or so before new national policies would start on the road towards decollectivization, in Shaanxi an opposing movement occurred towards enlarging the scale of rural economic accounting units. Because of the subsequent national political changes, this movement has received very little publicity. As explained by local cadres in 1979, the movement was a try-out conducted in the more developed areas of Guanzhong. The transition to brigade-level economic accounting (which meant that not the production team but the usually 10 times larger production brigade would direct production and share its profits) was a clearly egalitarian measure. However, three conditions had to be met before production teams could successfully apply to the county government for an economic merger: production methods had to be rather advanced, average income levels between production teams should not differ more than 20 percent (in 1979, this was changed to 10 percent) and the people involved should be willing. What this last condition meant is not quite clear; in any case no separate procedure for consulting peasants' opinions was to be followed, the consent of the existing organs of representation sufficed. In Wugong, which had 238 production brigades, of which only 6 served as an economic accounting unit, in 1977 and 1978 16 additional production brigades were elevated to that status. In 1979, these mergers were undone again. Political correction came from Beijing.

The *People's Daily* published a letter from a peasant in Fuping county, entitled 'Look at the harm done by making the transition to brigade accounting in a state of poverty'. The letter mentioned five problems to which this transition gave rise: (1) Rich teams stopped working, while poor ones simply awaited the coming of communism. (2) Heavier procurement burdens were imposed on relatively better-off teams. (3) Great losses occurred of draught animals and tools, because of covert sales, insufficient care and too hard working of the animals. (4) Brigade cadres were ineffective leaders. (5) Serious losses occurred in production. Even after the political wind had changed,

cadres urged people to maintain the status quo, babbling 'we have already made the transition, so we might just carry on happily'. The masses objected to this, but did not care to say anything. This situation exists today in Guanzhong, and great harm has been done.

The Provincial CCP Committee acknowledged the correctness of this criticism. Its action, however, still was half-hearted. Newly elevated brigades were allowed to continue to operate as such, 'if they are run well and the masses support the arrangement'. Only if the majority of the peasants were to demand scaling down to the production team again, then the county committee would be obliged to comply.[60] More direct criticism from Beijing followed:

For many years, policies in Shaanxi were overly 'left'. When most of the country was striving to eliminate chaos and restore order, there were disorders on top of chaos in Shaanxi, as the Provincial CCP Committee instituted some wrong regulations concerning the transition of ownership, private plots, household sideline occupations, village fairs and rubber-tyred carts which were not in conformity with the rural economic policies for the current stage.[61]

In subsequent years, provincial leaders reluctantly followed the national drift towards decollectivization and privatization of production and trade. Also, landlords, rich peasants and merchants were rehabilitated, either as a category or individually as victims of past political campaigns.[62]

Local or national publications about the qualities and defects of the three-level economic organization of the rural collectives in Guanzhong (People's Commune, production brigade and production team) give nothing but the standard picture for China. The collective organization was blamed for leading to 'commandism' – the blind giving of orders by the People's Commune leadership (sometimes the production brigade leadership is blamed for the same), and for 'egalitarianism' which seriously affected production owing to lack of incentives to work. Also, the lack of separation between Party, governmental and economic functions led to politization (always 'Leftist') and bad management of the economy, both agricultural and industrial.

In the early 1980s a formal division was made between the

administrative function and the economic functions of the People's Commune. The People's Commune CCP Committees were dissolved, and reestablished at the same time as *xiang* (community) CCP Committees. Its Management Committees were set up separately as *xiang* governments and *xiang* economic organizations. Basically, in Guanzhong it was found that very little changed but their names. In most counties, also the brigade CCP branches were reestablished as village CCP branches. The *xiang* economic organizations went by various names: United Agricultural-Industrial-Commercial Company, Economic Committee, Economic Management Committee and the like. Some places still called them People's Communes. In most places, the economic affairs simply were handed over entirely to the *xiang* economic organization, and the *xiang* and village (*cun*) governments did not concern themselves at all with economic questions. This, of course, would bring up the question whether these governments have complete governmental powers, as every economic regulation would have to pass through the economic committee.[63]

In many examples given in the local press during the early 1980s, individual peasants met with stiff opposition from local cadres. Cooperative and collective industries, however, were always shown as competing very successfully with state enterprises, by offering higher purchase prices, lower processing fees or other advantageous conditions to the farmers. Whether this last picture is correct, cannot be established without corroborative data. It is true that peasants had the best command over agricultural products such as raw materials; however, government regulations still limited the possible use of many products. Also, trade, money supply, machinery and many other inputs depended on state allocations.

In January 1982, the CCP Provincial Secretary Ma Wenrui stated that the plain areas of Guanzhong should adopt the *lianchandaolao* system (which connects productive labour for the collective more closely with income) and the most backward areas, the *baogandaohu* system (which is almost equal to household farming).[64] In the previous year, the *lianchan daolao* system had met with much resistence from cadres high and low. It then was practiced by only about 15 percent of the production teams of Guanzhong. The mining county of Hancheng was the first to apply this system for almost all wheat cultivation in the county, with apparent success. Under the same name of *lianchandaolao* somewhat different systems had been applied in the irrigated plain, dry upland plain and in the mountain areas, but their common characteristics were a certain degree of unified management of production planning, cultivation, investment and allocation of labour, draft animals, large and medium-size farm equipment and water conservation facilities. Also, they all had the '5-fixed and one reward' with a stipulated amount of labour, State quota, output, investment, and work points, and reward of penalty for surpassing or failing to meet the stipulated output.[65] The *lianchandaolao* system as applied in mountain areas came closer to the *baogandaohu* system, because there collective management of machinery, chemical fertilizer, and seeds etcetera was much weaker or totally absent.

An investigation of 24 production brigades in Changwu, Liquan and Xianyang (respectively a backward, intermediate and highly developed agricultural district of Guanzhong) showed the *baogandaohu* or *dabaogan* system (under which both collective production and distribution on the basis of workpoints were abolished) to have been very successful in boosting agricultural output and animal husbandry in Changwu. In 1981, 70 percent of the production teams of Changwu county had applied this system. In areas with a higher level of agricultural development, it had been successful as well. In the medium-developed county of Liquan the *baochanziren* system (which allocates the tilling of farmland to labourers or to households, but maintains collective planting plans and fixed amounts of output, investments and labour points) had been equally successful. In the most developed area of Xianyang and in Fenghuo brigade in Liquan and Wulibu brigade in Changwu the *lianchanziren* or *zhuanyechengbao lianchanjichou* system had been applied. It was characterized by contracting out specialized agricultural and non-agricultural activities, but under unified collective management of production and distribution. The investigators found it suitable only for highly developed areas with a strong and diversified rural collective economy. A fourth system, *baogongziren*, which applied fixed labour points for agricultural labour differed little from the old system, and was rejected as egalitarian and too cumbersome for rural cadres. From this investigation, the conclusion was drawn that the first three systems could all be used.[66]

In September 1982, however, Hu Yaobang pointed out to the local cadres what the official Party position had to be: in all places where the peasants wanted to apply the *dabaogan* system, it should be permitted, and he added that local cadres should not be afraid that this would be considered a transgression or mistake.[67]

From 1981 onwards, particular attention was paid both by the Government and by the local press to the so-called rural 'specialized households' and 'keypoint households', *zhuanyehu* and *zhongdianhu*. These households distinguished themselves from ordinary peasant households because of their commercial production, a certain degree of specialization, and high income. Generally they operated in the politically most sensitive area of rural reform, notably in commercial production of goods not subject to price control, in trade or processing of agricultural products, and in handicraft production. Although the concept of these 'two kinds of households' was applied throughout China, it was not sharply defined. Some provinces did apply uniform criteria for distinction, but were criticized for this in an economic journal.[68] At least until 1984, production remained on a household basis, with a small scale of management with an exceptional two or three hired hands. If the scale of operation was larger, the enterprise would be a cooperative venture. In Shaanxi province, at least four different types of criteria were still under discussion in 1983: income, enterprise size, the use of outside labour, and origin.[69] Indeed the 'two kinds of households' had sprung from very different sources. Although they had made their appearance as early as in 1979, only from 1981 (after the CCP Central Committee document no. 13) did their scope and numbers increase, from 7.6 percent of all rural households in Shaanxi in 1982, to 10.6 percent in 1983 and 12.9 percent by June 1984.[70] Their numbers were largest in the mountain areas with a tradition of commercial production and in the economically most advanced areas. More and more, they became models of rural progress.

F. SUCCESSES AND SOCIAL PRESSURES UNDER THE NEW SYSTEM

One of the earliest and most successful undertakings was garment manufacture in Qianxian county. Apparently, there the tradition of this handicraft had survived all State efforts since 1954 to stamp out the village textile industry. When commercial production of garments (*not* of cloth) was made legal again, the garment industry in Qianxian sprung up immediately. It was clearly competitive with the clothing produced by state factories, which had a record of low productivity, low quality and little variety.[71] The village industries managed to make clothes to order rapidly, and at lower prices. Customers would come from Xi'an and select from magazines which showed the latest

Shanghai trends in color and design. By 1984, further specialization had occurred between and within villages. Some households would buy the cloth, others would cut, again others would sew, seam or fix buttons, and handle sales. Usually a village would operate as one economic unit in this fashion. In 1983, 25 garment-making villages in Qianxian with 2,759 households produced three million pieces of clothing, with a production value of 17 million *yuan* and a profit rate of about 40 percent. Income was high, and there were no unemployed.[72] The 'specialized villages' of Qianxian became a provincial model of organization of both industrial and agricultural production, and later also of marketing.

In Qianxian, 'specialized villages' (*zhuanyecun*) have been designated as such under three conditions: 1) over 60 percent of the households have the same line of enterprise; 2) in this specialty net income is more than 50 *yuan* per capita; 3) its rate of commercialization is higher than 95 percent . . . In 1983, Qianxian had 121 such villages (out of 830 natural villages), with specializations in crops such as vegetables, fruit, tobacco, in animal husbandry such as chicken, pigs, or cattle, in industry such as garments, stitching or lime, and also in transport and building . . . Average per capita net income was 190 *yuan*.[73]

Another sector in which specialized households were successful was in raising chickens, pigs and other animals and in eggs and milk production. This was an extension of the traditional household sideline production. An investigation of household sidelines in Changan *xian* in summer 1981 had shown various forms of production: individual, family-wise, cooperative and collective. Sometimes households would supply semi-finished products to the collective, sometimes they would market their products directly. In 1980, net income from sidelines in 125 surveyed households was 62 *yuan* per capita, one-third of the total net income. Most of this was from pig-raising, but chicken-raising was growing fast. From ten hens the same net income could be obtained as from raising one 100 kg pig.[74] A year later, an investigation of fifty keypoint households in Xianyang prefecture and in Changan county revealed that over one-half were engaged in raising chickens and eggs, and only eleven in the cultivation of crops. The cultural level of these households was far superior to that of ordinary peasants, and they were deemed to be the more 'capable' ones. Three-quarters of these households had a CCP member or base-level cadre.[75] Thus, the new rural economic elite sprang in part from, or was joined by, the previous politico-managerial elite.

Milk provided another example of a boost in production due to liberalization, government support, and improved prices. For over two decades, Xi'an had suffered from a severe shortage of milk. Until the early 1980s, its urban residents needed at least 50 tons of fresh milk a day, but actual supply was no more than 20 to 25 tons. Fresh milk was rationed, and distributed only to infants below one year of age and to seriously ill people with gastric ulcers or esophagus cancer. Even so, in June 1982 fresh milk demand still exceeded 120,000 bottles, i.e. 1.5 times as much as the supply capacity. But within a period of a year and a half, in the eyes of a journalist

a miracle occurred. In April 1984 the Milk Company supplied almost 50,000 kg per day to the market, and the 190,000 subscribing households had milk every day. How come? Some people told me: go and see the dairy cow villages! . . .

In 1979, four peasant households in Tielumiao village privately bought four dairy cows. They were reported to the People's Commune. The People's Commune convened a meeting of all cadres of the production brigades and of the production teams together with the four peasants. Criticism was very severe. 'If everybody would raise dairy cows like you, who would tend the crops?' 'If we develop private business, what about the collective?' 'Keeping a dairy cow means an income of 200 *yuan* per month, this is pure money-making!' But one of the peasants, Li Janhua, took a newspaper from his breast and said: 'This is the written document of the Third Plenum. It says clearly: under certain conditions one may raise dairy and meat cattle privately. What you say does not count, I listen to the CCP Central Committee!' . . . The PC-leader could not bear it and said angrily: 'Dispose of these cows immediately!' However, no one moved . . . and the four peasants kept their cows. Other courageous people followed suit . . .[76]

At a more modest pace, the State farms in Xi'an municipality showed considerable increases in milk output and in profits, too. Between 1978 and 1983, their milk production doubled to 9,450 tons, about as much as what was supplied by private and collective farmers in 1983. A third source of supply, especially of milk powder, was goats.

In October 1982, the Xi'an Municipal Government took a decision to support private dairy farming with loans, a subsidy for feed (2.4 cents for every kg of milk sold to the State) and with technical support. The Municipal Red Flag Milk Factory established fresh milk purchase stations, to facilitate peasants' sales. Early in 1984, there were 4,800 dairy cows in these villages.

The huge fodder market for these cows has been conquered at an early stage by specialized traders' households. Some of it comes from several hundred *li* away. The 'negotiated price' (used by the State for purchasing maize in excess of the quota and above-quota planned purchase) is 34 cents per kg, but here maize sells for less than 24 cents per kg. Long-term contracts have been made with the cattle-raising peasants, with guaranteed delivery date and quality. . .

Most peasants do not raise calves, but sell calves to outsiders before their birth. One female calf sells for 800–900 *yuan*, a male calf for 50 to 60 *yuan*. These calves are raised by outsiders using cheap goat's milk, and the bulls are mostly used as draught cattle or for meat. When the female calf is fully grown, it is sold back to the milk villages for 2,000 to 3,000 *yuan* . . .

More than half of these villages used to be rather poor, with sloping farmland without good irrigation conditions. The value of a labour day would be only 30 to 40 cents, and the household income before 1980 averaged 200 to 300 *yuan* per year. But this has changed. Now families make over 3,000 *yuan* . . . In the milk villages, people say: 'In 1949 we had political revolution, now, with the dairy cows, we finally have economic revolution . . .'[77]

Goat's milk still plays a minor role in China, although in some mountain areas it may be the only type of milk available. Shaanxi province was singled out by the Ministry of Agriculture in 1979 for expansion of its goat's milk industry. In 1978, it had 410,000 dairy goats, or almost half the national total. In subsequent years, their numbers increased to 750,000. In spite of local breeding programs and imports of Saanen goats from Switzerland, by 1984 milk yields were still low. Most goats averaged 250 kg of milk per year, or only one-third of the yield of the superior Saanen breed. About one-half of the goat's milk produced was sold. Between 1978 and 1984 in Shaanxi province, 53 goat's milk powder processing factories were established, with a total production capacity of over 16,000 tons of goat's milk powder per year. Because of insufficient supply of goat's milk, however, actual production in 1983 was 7,100 tons. This was about two-thirds of China's total output. Besides supplying other areas of China with milk powder, Shaanxi also has exported milk goats to other provinces at a rate of about 50,000 head per year. Possibly because of the enclosure of wasteland and mountain areas which resulted from the 'responsibility system', goats and goat's milk production increased more slowly in 1983.[78]

Specialized and keypoint households were and still are politically vulnerable, because of the nature of their business, their high income, or both. A comparison of 700 of these households with 604 'ordinary' households in Zhouzhi county in 1982 showed that the commercialization rate of their production was 69 percent, as against 25 percent for ordinary households. Their average income was 4,839 *yuan*, 2.8 times as much as that of ordinary households.[79] In January 1984, possibly under the influence of the leftist campaign against 'spiritual pollution', the provincial leader Dong Jichang would only support the *healthy* development of the 'two kinds of households'. His was a carefully balanced assessment:

> Some cadres because of 'left' thinking are afraid that the 'two kinds of households' would enlarge rural income differentials and lead to polarization. In some places, these households do not feel safe because of political opposition and jealousy . . . At present, there are two kinds: contracting specialized households and self-managing specialized households. The first are certainly a part of the collective economy. The second, which have usually evolved from household sidelines, are a necessary supplement and component part of the collective economy. They show other peasants the way to become rich . . . These households thus are an organic part of the socialist economy and are the mainstream. However, there also is a 'branch-stream' of crooked people who only care about themselves and not about the State or the collective.[80]

The tone was positive, but cautiously so, and a fall-back position was built in. Indeed a great deal of political opposition from cadres and jealousy from fellow-peasants was understandable, after more than two decades of anti-commercial and egalitarian economic policies. These feelings had to be reckoned with, and new lines of work had to be found for many rural cadres. They were told that 'being a grain chief is not enough', and that they should grasp both industry and agriculture. From agricultural duties, many were transferred to the management of collective enterprises.[81] Even those 'specialized households' which had specialized in foodgrain production, the sector dearest to the Maoists, still suffered from lack of political support in mid-1984. For them, chemical fertilizers and loans were hard to obtain. Also they had difficulties in selling maize and sweet potatoes (which do not keep well) and in storage of grain.[82] A newspaper article entitled 'We must first cure the jealousy of the cadres' described how rich households were pressed by cadres to share some of their wealth with them, and an accompanying cartoon showed how rich peasants were pressed from all sides to pay 'fees', 'subsidies', 'loans' etc.[83] More than anything else, the 'Rules on the protection of legal rights and interests of the rural specialized households', adopted by the Shaanxi Provincial CCP Committee and People's Government on August 28, 1984, read like a list of personal and institutional means of harassment:

  1. The collective and private property used under the contracts . . . may not be violated by any unit or individual.

2. As for specialized households who have left the soil to engage in other undertakings, and after the transferral of the originally contracted land wish to retain the right of contracting, this should be allowed and supported . . .

3. One must allow and support specialized households to go to the city for work . . . For those who wish to engage in industry, transport commerce and food services, the departments concerned must issue business licenses, driving licenses, etc. on time and according to the rules. One household may have more than one license . . . Apart from the issuing agency, no other unit or individual has the right to take these licenses over or to revoke them.

4. Contracts are legal and effective and binding . . . and cannot be changed by one side of its own will.

5. Specialized households should not be harassed or fleeced . . .

6. All departments must strictly observe the Party and State policy rules when supplying production materials, earnest money, loan support etc. They may not withhold capital, supply second-rate products, inflate prices, dump unwanted materials on the specialized households, and depress quality rating or the price when purchasing from them.

7. Banks and credit coops may not . . . arbitrarily freeze management funds of the specialized households or impose illegal charges.

8. Departments for water conservation, electricity, agricultural machinery, commercial and public utilities may not interrupt electricity, water, gasoline etc. without cause.

9. The departments of Finance, Industry and Commerce, Agricultural Machinery, and Communications must not . . . wildly increase taxes. The specialized households may reject illegal and non-unified taxes or fees.

10. . .–17 . . .[84]

Indeed the peasant-entrepreneur had to reckon with a hostile environment. The newly established household contracts for the cultivation of set plots of land were equally subject to egalitarian pressure. In mid-1984, contracts had to be renegotiated because of the lengthening of the contract period. An investigation of the relevant issues in four counties in Weinan prefecture showed that most collectives had demanded major adjustments, involving some 70 percent of all households. This was motivated by the feeling that the original land divisions had been unfair, that plots were too fragmented, and that subsequent changes in population number should be incorporated. Most areas preferred division of land on a per capita rather than on a per labourer basis. On this point the investigators felt differently: in this way households without labour power would also receive land contracts, and land would thus be fragmented further. Most of the rural cadres supported the retaining of a certain percentage of 'machinery land' (5 percent in Huayin, 7 to 15 percent in Pucheng), to pay for agricultural machinery use, but whether the peasants felt the same way was not made clear. Because of lack of experience, assessment of farmland was difficult – yet this was the basis for stipulating the land price.[85]

For China, the 1979–83 period witnessed a sharp rise of agricultural production and of rural income. By a variety of liberalization measures, the Government released the pent-up energy of the peasantry. Price rises for State purchase of cotton, foodgrain and oil-crops were given in 1979. Liberalization of trade by enlarging the scope of collective markets and releasing price control of certain products such as pork, was gradually extended. When cotton and grain had become abundant in 1984, the cumbersome and progressively unjust system of quota prices, above-quota prices and negotiated prices (which had necessitated State control of movements of these products from one brigade to another) could be abandoned for a more simple system. More freedom was given to villages and farmers to choose themselves which crop to cultivate. Last but not least, the collective organization of labour, and distribution of its rewards, has been progressively abolished in favour of individual contracts, *cheng bao*, between farmer's households and the village government. The contracts are either for the cultivation of an allotted piece of farmland, or for the operation of certain undertakings within or outside the village. Although some peasants in this way may have found employment outside of their village, they are still tied to their social and taxation obligations in their village: *litu buli xiang*, they left the soil but are not separated from their village. These various measures were taken within a period of five years, shortly after one another or concurrently. Therefore it is not possible to evaluate the economic effect of each of these measures separately. In the case of Shaanxi, the 1980 drought and 1981 flood disaster annihilated the positive effect of the price rises and liberalization of trade in 1979–80. Only in 1982 did agricultural production and rural income rise sharply. Because of wet weather, in 1983 the cotton harvest failed and the net rural income per capita in the traditionally poor old-liberated areas of north Shaanxi even surpassed that of Guanzhong.[86]

Especially since the 1984 decision of the CCP Central Committee to lengthen the period of household land leases to 15 years or longer, the question might be asked inhowfar China's agriculture was still based on collective farming. Already in 1983 Du Runsheng described the by then uniformly imposed 'responsibility system with payment linked to output', *lianchan chengbao*, no longer as a collective, but as a cooperative system. As far as income was concerned, 'after giving the State its due (the purchase quota and tax) and giving a sufficient amount to the collective (the common fund), all the remainder belongs to ourselves'. Du affirmed that 'for the deployment of machinery and the scope of services, the collective system is a fundamentally advantageous condition', although machine-ploughing and some other services were to be contracted out to individual workers. As far as production was concerned, 'the responsibility system does not mean individual farming. One can see now that the masses are happy to undertake jointly water conservation projects, seed breeding, pest control, unified cultivation and planting plans, a joint public fund etcetera, and they have put these joint activities down in contract form.'[87]

It remains to be seen to what extent the village government or collective will retain economic power. At least, it will continue to direct the exploitation of resources, production plans, the State purchase quota and farmland irrigation. Most important of all, as the land remains publicly owned, it may continue to negotiate and renegotiate the contracts it has concluded with households, in an effort to remedy differentials in income which seem unjust – even though such action might not conform with national policies. More than before, village government may witness a clash of economic policy and economic interests between peasants who have been successful in or outside farming and those who, for whatever reason, lag behind.

Conclusion. In the Guomindang period, various banks moved into Shaanxi and started promoting credit coops and cotton producers' coops. County magistrates took part in providing guarantees. Most loans were for one season only and given out in the most productive cotton areas near Xi'an. From the beginning of the war against Japan, the government's involvement grew rapidly. By 1940, it had surpassed the banks as a lender; each county had one official designated as responsible for cooperative work. Various factors contributed to the growth of the coop movement: relief measures, the introduction of cotton, the war refugees and the desire to contain the communists in north Shaanxi. Both the industrial coops for war refugees and the defense coops in north Guanzhong were very much government creations, and (partly for that reason) largely failed within three or four years. At their height in 1943, the credit coops in Guanzhong had half a million members, or one-quarter of all peasant households. Their contribution to rural economic progress and security of the average, and above-average, farmer was considerable.

Land Reform did not meet with much organized opposition in Guanzhong. Landlords and rich peasants (of whom there were few) secretly split up their holdings. There were negative effects on trade, money-lending, hiring of labourers and production. Eventually about 12 percent of all farmland changed hands. Yet hereby the average landholding of the poorest 30 percent of the rural population was increased by almost one-third.

Proper assessement of the grain tax was a source of much dispute, as average output, land quality and class status of the peasant all played a role. The subsequent cooperativization greatly simplified tax perception and other administrative measures. Because of output increases, the Shaanxi grain tax dropped from 11.5 percent of total grain output in 1951 to 9 percent in 1953–7. Gross procurement of grain by the state varied between 18 and 25 percent in this period.

Cooperativization and collectivization toed the official line prescribed by Beijing: a slow growth of Agricultural Producers' Cooperatives in 1953 and 1954, a retreat in early 1955, and a vigorous campaign to include all peasants into cooperatives during July 1955–February 1956. The early APC's were organized mainly by activist and better-off farmers – often poor peasants were left on their own. After Mao's 1955 speech on the need for rapid cooperativization, almost all rural households were included in coops, and after that, in Higher Agricultural Producers' Cooperatives from which withdrawal was no longer permitted. There was no room for provincial or local variation or independent critical evaluation.

The organization of large-scale economic units was advantageous to production, planning of State investments, development of infrastructure, provision of social services and to greater equality of income within each village. However, trade, individual handicrafts and material incentives were affected negatively. Also, organizational problems (both of agricultural production and of new industrial activities) were seriously under-estimated. This was the painful lesson of the Great Leap Forward crisis. The People's Commune in Guanzhong initially had an average size of more than 4,000 households, much too large to be effective as a unit of production. Very soon, its functions were reduced and its economic weight in Shaanxi in 1959 was considerably less than in Henan province.

In the absence of local economic appraisals of the three-tiered collective system of production teams, production brigades and People's Communes created in 1962, it is difficult to take a firm stand pro or contra the national post-1980 total condemnation of collective policies. Both positive and negative aspects are in evidence but the balance was different in successive periods. For Guanzhong, it would seem that the collective framework was readily accepted as useful during the introductory period of modern means of production, from the mid-1960s till the mid-1970s. In the previous decade, negative effects on trade, on freedom of production and on rewards for individual labour had made many peasants hesitant or outright negative towards the collective economy. During the 1970s, resentment built up against the growing rural professional elite of cadres, the severe restrictions of trade, and egalitarianism. Consequently, many ordinary peasants lost interest in work. Some functions of the collectives, notably irrigation, money supply, transport, distribution of seeds, treatment of pests, benefited from large-scale organization and still do. The major weaknesses of the collectives were in the maintenance of adequate incentives and morale, in efficient organization of production, and in the economic evaluation of productive activities. Local cadres were slow in winding down collective organization after Beijing had told them to – the leftist tradition in Guanzhong was strong.

Liberalization policies led to a vigorous growth of some village industries, such as garment manufacturing, chicken and goat raising, and vegetable milk and fruit production. Some households, more daring, capable or better-connected than others, took the lead in commercial production and were praised for it by the authorities. Within the village, however, they are politically vulnerable because of their high income, and outside it, because of their need for all kinds of official permits. In how far the long-term contracts concluded with individual peasants in 1983 and 1984 will stand the test of time, and price changes, remains to be seen. The village government is likely to become a political battlefield between the well-off and the malcontents.

8

COTTON AND COTTON TEXTILE
PRODUCTION

A. BACKGROUND, CLIMATE AND SOIL

Of Shaanxi's cotton, 90 to 95 percent is grown in Guanzhong.[1] On the loess hills of north Shaanxi the frostfree period is too short, generally less than 180 days. South of the Qinling mountains the climate of the Hanshui valley tends to be too moist and lacks sunshine (only 40 to 45 percent of all days are sunny, as against 45 to 55 percent in Guanzhong). Within Guanzhong the cotton area is concentrated in the low-lying areas along the Wei River and its tributaries, because of their favourable conditions of temperature and water.

Cotton is sown no earlier than the first half of April and harvested before the end of October.[2] The varieties planted during the 1930s had a growth period of 180 days or more; recently introduced varieties have a shorter growth period of 130–150 days. The main weather hazards are spring droughts, summer floods, dark autumns with insufficient sunshine and autumn frosts. In non-irrigated areas sowing of cotton has to wait for spring rain. When the spring is dark, and low temperatures (15–20°C) and high humidity (>90%) persists for more than 5 days, the cotton seedlings are severely affected by insects and die.[3]

Cotton loves sun and heat. The most suitable temperature for the period from sowing to sprouting is 14–18° C, with a lower limit of 10–12° C; for the flowering period 22–25° C, with a lower limit of 15–18° C; for the bolling period not lower than 10–13° C. The present early ripening varieties need an accumulated temperature (≥10°C) of at least 3,200° C, the late ripening varieties about 4,000° C. Therefore the areas above 1,000 metres altitude are not suitable for growing cotton.[4] Cotton needs some 400–500 mm of water during its growth period, most of which is in summer.[5] Yearly precipitation averages 500 to 600 mm in Guanzhong, most of which falls during the summer months. Spring is generally dry, and summer rains are very irregular. Therefore Guanzhong and north Shaanxi more often than not have a water shortage. Cotton is cultivated preferably on irrigated land – by 1975, about 70 percent.[6] On dry fields yields are low and unstable.

The roots of cotton go deep, and like thick layers of soil which are loose and well-drained. If properly managed, therefore, the alluvial and loessial soils in Shaanxi are very suitable for cotton growing. Yields, however, generally are not high. One of the reasons is the traditional practice of shallow plowing, which has formed a hard underfield layer, the ploughpan; the top layer has a thickness of only 10 to 15 cm. This makes for bad porosity and shallow root growth, so that the roots cannot absorb water and nutritional elements from deeper layers.

The war period excepted, since the 1930s the area of Guanzhong under cotton has been some 250,000–300,000 ha, or about 12 to 15 percent of its cultivated area. In irrigated areas, this percentage has been about twice that high. So cotton has been by far the most important economic crop in this region.

B. INTRODUCTION OF COTTON

Chinese cottons tended to be short and wiry of staple, and very white. This latter quality was a big point in their favour. However, yields were considerably lower than those of newly-introduced American varieties. The import and distribution of American seeds in China, officially by various governments, unofficially by various officials, privately by mill owners, cotton enthusiasts, cotton merchants and relief organizations continued throughout the first third of the twentieth century. American seed would produce well for a year or two and then deteriorate rapidly because of crossfertilization and mixing of seed with that of other farmers.[7] The cotton acreage in China expanded considerably, from an average of 3.7 million ha during 1923–9 to an average 4.5 million ha during 1932–1936. This was due both to a rising price ratio cotton:wheat (caused partly by a tripling of factory demand) and to stimuli from the national government.[8]

In Shaanxi this upturn of cotton acreage and production has been much more pronounced. The 1929 famine had reduced the cotton area to virtually nil, and the impact of subsequent government measures was very great.

The cotton acreage of Shaanxi, after a period of growth during the early Republic, declined during the 1920s, mainly because of the

Table 58 *Shaanxi cotton acreage and output, 1923–1939*

Year	Acreage (1,000 ha)	of which in Guanzhong (1,000 ha)	Production (tons)	of which in Guanzhong (1,000 ha)	Average yield (kg/ha)
1924	109		23		214
1925	88		39		440
1926	96		19		192
1927	96		18		186
1928	86		13		155
1929	12		2		138
1930	86		7		79
1931	107	104	17	16	159
1932	91	86	7	6	82
1933	137	121	27	23	196
1934	243	226	50	47	204
1935	243	231	40	38	166
1936	283 (284)	265	47 (46)	44	166 (168)
1937	312 (322)	285	55 (53)	53	177 (165)
1938	253 (255)	235	52 (53)	50	208 (214)
1939	186 (178)	175	49 (46)	47	261 (260)

Sources: data compiled from Li Guozhen (ed.), *Shaanxi Mianchan* p. 2; figures between brackets from *Shaanzheng* Vol. 8 no. 1–2 (1946), pp. 12–21.

extension of poppy, to a level below 100,000 ha. It shot up after 1933 and reached a maximum of 312,000 ha in 1937. Cotton output also more than doubled over the level of the 'twenties, to an average of some 50,000 tons per year during 1934–9. A closer inspection of the cotton acreage shows rather different growth rates between counties in Guanzhong. In comparison with the 1932–3 situation, the average cotton acreage during 1934–1938 doubled or tripled in the counties around Xi'an, but increased even more in the outlying counties farther west (Baoji, Qianxian, Fufeng), North (Chengcheng, Baishui, Hancheng) and East (Dali, Huayin, Huaxian). In 1938 the cotton acreage went down considerably in the 'traditional' cotton areas near Xi'an, but shot up in a number of outlying counties, especially in the west.[9] Several factors have been responsible for these regional differences.

The 1929–31 Famine struck the whole of Guanzhong, but its western districts most severely. Because of the concomitant reduction

Graph L Unit yields of cotton, Shaanxi and China, 1926–1983

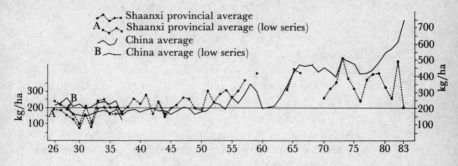

Source: *Shaanxi Mianchan*, 1948; *Zhongguo Mianchan Tongji*, 1948; *Zhongguo Nongye Nianjian* 1980–1984; *Shaanxi Ribao*

of rural population, less area had to be devoted to foodgrain. The commercialization rate went up, with cotton as the major economic crop.

Poppy cultivation, a crop in competition with cotton which likewise is best sown on irrigated fields, had been stimulated by warlords during the 'twenties. During the early 'thirties it was gradually cut back by the Guomindang Government. The campaign for the eradication of poppy started in the eastern and central counties of Guanzhong in 1933, and had become effective there by 1936. It was combined with the issue of cotton seeds by the Government.

'The present Government has put more than 30 districts under ban (out of Guanzhong's over 40) and in these practically no poppy can be seen. The policy is to start with regions where poppy is less cultivated. As a compensation, cotton seeds are distributed to the poppy farmers almost free . . .'.[10]

In newly irrigated areas developed by State efforts and relief organizations since 1931, it was strictly forbidden to cultivate opium. Offenders saw their plants destroyed and were cut off from irrigation water supply by the Irrigation Water Bureau – measures which proved to be very effective.[12]

In 1934 considerable parts of the old irrigated areas at the foot of the Qinling mountains in the south were still cultivating poppy. In Changan county (outside the Xi'an city walls) eradication was effectively carried out in that spring. It had been planned to eradicate 7,000 hectares, but because the farmers had previously seen prohibition and relaxation, in succession, as paper measures they just went ahead. Thereupon a large acreage of poppy was eradicated, and cotton seeds were issued to make up for the losses.[12]

A second campaign directed at Xianyang, Hancheng, Xunyi, Linyou and several counties in south Shaanxi was started in 1935 and became effective some two years later. According to a missionary's view, the Government was 'fully determined to eradicate the opium evil within 3 or 4 years. This year the growth of opium is prohibited. Next year the sale and consumption of the same will be prohibited. The following year the death penalty will be enforced for offenders.'[13]

The third and last campaign was started in 1937 and directed at a dozen counties[14] west of Xi'an, the most productive poppy region. By 1939 there still was a certain amount of illegal cultivation there.

The opium habit, however, was difficult to shake and its *use* continued to be widespread, even in model counties such as Dali or Wugong.[13] Official surveys show 295,175 registered opium users in 1936, and 281,105 of such users in 1939.

In most parts of Guanzhong, however, because of the strict anti-opium policy pursued by the new provincial governor, Jiang Dingwen, *cultivation* of poppy had been eradicated in general. Although planting, transport, sales and smoking of poppy were illegal, yet there still was some trading condoned by high officials. This served the officially registered smokers who had not yet broken the habit and also those people who had not registered. There is little data on the sources of this illegal trade, which was mainly in the hands of high officials. As late as 1951, a vice-chancellor of the People's Court of Justice in Wugong county was discharged because of secretly selling 14 carts of opium.[18]

In 1935, there were 205 opium trading firms and 1,780 opium shops. Their number was gradually brought down. A state monopoly on opium production and supply, the Opium Bureau, was established in 1939, with 3 state factories in Changan, Nanxiong (south Shaanxi) and Yulin (north Shaanxi). All shops and all factories operated by county officials were closed down as a consequence. The Changan factory was meant to serve 52 counties in Guanzhong and the area immediately north of it. Nine distribution stations were set up in Guanzhong,[17] from which sales points, under control of and operated by county governments, were served in each county. From there, opium was distributed to *baojia* heads in the villages.

The commercial stock of opium and the opium stock held by consumers totalled 618,000 *liang* (about 20,000 kg) according to an investigation held in the winter of 1939. Of this stock, the Government bought 462,000 *liang* or about three-quarters. During an eight-month period of clamp-down on opium, over 1,100 verdicts were pronounced on offenders against the anti-opium laws. Addict treatment hospitals were set up in all counties with more than one thousand users, with a total capacity of 14,000 people per month.

The poppy eradication campaign brought a net income of over 5 million *yuan* to the provincial government in 1940, of which two-thirds was donated to the county relief granaries.[18] As poppy became progressively illegal, official reports on it became less reliable, a fact which was aggravated further by the war situation. For the 1930s, however, we have seen that the change-over from poppy to cotton started in east and central Guanzhong, at the same time as the construction of the Longhai railroad to Xi'an. The final campaign of 1937–9 conducted in west Guanzhong coincided with the extension of the railroad.

The increase of the cotton acreage in west Guanzhong between 1936 and 1940, in the face of a downward trend of the provincial cotton acreage (which fell by about one-third during these years), should be attributed not only to the reduction of the poppy acreage,[19] but also to the improvement of transport facilities and to different price elasticities. Central and east Guanzhong as the main centres of the cotton trade suffered considerably from the falling cotton prices, while west Guanzhong cotton production mainly served local markets. During 1934–1937 American cotton prices were fairly stable, at about US$10–11 to US$13–14 per pound. But from 1937 prices fell to US$8–9 in 1938–1939.[20] Also, because of the war export of cotton to the textile mills in Zhengzhou, Qingdao and Shanghai was hampered. We will revert to prices and trade as a single topic later.

The introduction and popularization of improved varieties of cotton in Guanzhong had started at the end of the 19th century, with the import of Chinese varieties from Henan province. During the early 'twenties, deteriorated American varieties were imported. In 1926, Xi'an had two Cotton Experimental Farms, with a total area of 60 ha. Because of man-made and natural disasters, lack of skilled manpower and economic problems, they had no success.[21] Trice varieties were first imported, following the Great Famine, by relief organizations. These gave 10 to 20 percent higher yields, and had much longer filaments. Subsequently seeds were distributed mainly through the Shaanxi Provincial Bureau for the Improvement of Cotton, which was founded in 1934. This Bureau directed two 'institutes for the guidance of cotton planting' in Dali and in Jingyang, each with a cotton farm, and three breeding stations. The Jingyang farm (with some 35 ha) supplied Stoneville seeds, the Dali farm (with some 65 ha) Delfos no. 719 seeds. The breeding stations concentrated on popularizing Stoneville no. 4. In 1937, near the Jingyang farm, a separate 700 ha large Stoneville no. 4 Cotton Seed Management District was set up. The acreage sown to Stoneville no. 4 increased rapidly afterwards: from 30 percent of Guanzhong cotton acreage in 1940 to 80 percent in 1947. Its characteristics were a short stem, luxuriant growth, early ripening, large bolls, long staple length, a cloth element of 33–35 percent, and resistance against wind and rainstorm. A comparison with earlier varieties shows its superior qualities:[22]

Variety	Popularized since	Average yield (kg/ha)	Filament length (inch)	Cloth element
Common Chinese	end 19th century	270	>1	29
Deteriorated				
American	early Republic	324	>1	29
Trice	1931–	378	1	30
Stoneville no. 4	1936–	450	$1\frac{1}{16}$	33
Delfos (Mississippi)				
no. 531	1943–	405	$1\frac{1}{8}$	33

After 1938, the number of cotton experimental farms was increased to six; besides those in Changan and Jingyang counties, such farms were established in Weinan, Xianynag, Baoji and Yonglezhen, with subsidies from the Central government.[23] In spring 1941 the provincial government set up the Shaanxi Provincial Crop Improvement and Breeding Station, which used 45 ha of irrigated and dry land of the Northwest Agricultural College in Wugong, and also a branch station with an area of 55 ha in Gaoling county. Although its main object was the improvement of wheat, cotton improvement was undertaken as well. In 1943 it was reorganized as the Shaanxi Popularization and Breeding Station; cotton breeding was coordinated with the Northwest Agricultural Improvement Bureau in Jingyang. In 1946 its scope was further expanded and its name changed to the Northwest Popularization and Breeding Station. The main goals set were (1) support of grain production, (2) preparation of popularization material, (3) establishment of a permanent agricultural foundation for the Northwestern provinces. The breeding results (mainly directed at Stoneville no. 4) have been indicated above. Quantities of cotton seeds produced by the Shaanxi provincial station increased sharply in 1946.[24] Prospects for expansion of the scope of its work were hampered by lack of financial support, and by the return to the East of many refugee employees, which made this station (as many other organizations in Shaanxi) lose most of its qualified personnel.

Varietal improvements did not show immediately in the provincial average yields. During most of the thirties county yield averages remained at a level of 170 to 200 kg per hectare, not very different from the level of the twenties. A definite rise began in 1939, and for the next decade a new level of about 260 kg per hectare was established.

During the mid thirties, quality and yields of cotton were still very uneven in various areas. Quality and yields were highest in the newly irrigated areas of the Jinghui irrigation district (some 40,000 ha built in 1930–5) and the Weihui irrigation district (some 20,000 ha built in 1935–7), and in Changan county. In the eastern counties the situation varied. The rather wet counties of Huayin and Huaxian, near the Wei–Luo–Huang confluence, were little developed; no attention was paid to seed selection, cotton was usually planted very closely together in narrow rows, picking was hasty because of fear of thieves.[27] Yet because of good irrigation conditions their yields were above-average. The cotton fields north and south of the Wei River in Weinan and Lintong counties were already sown to Trice varieties to some extent; in spite of good soil and gentle climate, yields were limited by the absence of sufficient irrigation water. To the west the generally well-irrigated cotton fields south of the Wei River in Huxian and Zhouzhi counties also showed good yields. Finally, the non-irrigated areas north of the Wei River in Liquan, Qianxian, Heyang, Chaoyi and Hancheng (to mention only the counties with an average production above 1,000 tons) suffered from cold and drought, and received little attention from banks or government organizations. Yields fluctuated greatly, and averages were only in the range of 100–150 kg per hectare.

Damage from insects was a major factor which kept yields low. In dry years, most serious damage was caused by the cotton aphid (*mianya*, Aphis gossypili Glover). It made the plants ripen late and affected production; if affected seriously, the leaves would wither and wilt, and the plant would die. In wet years, most damage was done by the *xiaozaoqiaozhong* (Anomis xanthydima Boisdual), the larvae of which ate cotton leaves in August. The bollworm ('red bell insect' *honglingzhong*, Pectinophora gossypiella Saunders) affected the cotton boll and seeds and the 'large soil tiger' (*dadilaohu*, Agrotis sp.) ate the young shoots in June. The roots of cotton, especially of young shoots, were affected by the mole cricket (*lougu*, Gryllotalpa unispina Saussure), the larvae of the 'golden needle insect' (*jinzhenzhong*, Agrotis sericeus Caud.), and by the white grub (*tucan*). Locusts were not a serious threat, as Guanzhong, because of its height, is not a suitable breeding ground for locusts, and generally too moist and cold in summer and autumn. The Taihang mountains serve as a natural barrier, which usually prevents locusts from the North China plain from migrating to Shaanxi.[26]

Until the introduction of pesticides in the 1950s and 1960s, there was little the peasants could do about pests. Lime was applied, or ashes from grass or wood; insects were also picked by hand.

The dominant factor in production was irrigation: cotton yields in irrigated areas were 300 to 400 kg per hectare, two or three times as high as the yields obtained on dry fields. During the war, the irrigated area was further expanded with the financial support of the National Economic Committee.[27]

Most cotton areas suffered from the rapid deterioration of seed quality noted by Richard Kraus. 'The Chinese peasant's plot was very susceptible to cross-fertilization from other cottons. His tiny production was often thrown in with other people's crops to be ginned, the seeds becoming mixed. The man who gave him new, pure seed last year or the year before no longer had any . . .'[28]

C. COTTON TRADE AND INDUSTRY UNTIL THE WAR

During the 1930s, the cotton market in Xianyang county became the standard for Guanzhong. Because of its position immediately north of Xi'an at the opposite side of the Wei River it had become the natural collection point for the cotton produced in the Jinghui and other irrigation districts. Smaller markets existed in the neighbouring counties of Jingyang and Sanyuan, where local farmers brought their cotton; prices usually were one to one-and-a-half *yuan* lower per bale than on the Xianyang market. For eastern Guanzhong, Weinan county had become the main regional market center since the construction of the railroad. Because most cotton was exported eastward to the North China plain until the war against Japan, cotton prices on the Weinan market were somewhat higher than in Xianyang because of lower moving costs. In the border town of Tongguan, where the railroad crossed the Henan border, the cotton price was higher still, by about 2 *yuan* per bale. Away from the railroad in Chaoyi, a regional market north of the Wei–Luo–Huang river confluence, the cotton price was about the same as in Xianyang.[29] In outlying counties, where communications were bad and cotton production was small-sized and subject to large variation, prices fluctuated greatly between areas and between years.[30]

From 1932 till 1937 acreage, production and export of Shaanxi cotton continued to increase, under the stimuli of increasing demand from coastal factories and from Japan and cheaper transport because of the railroad.[31] During 1934–5, raw cotton accounted for three-quarters of the total value of Shaanxi exports. It was balanced by imports to Guanzhong, as a comparison between 1932 and 1936 the Longhai railroad and the improving economy greatly stimulated imports to Guanzhong, as a comparison between 1932 and 1936 shows.

In 1936 and 1937, 39,000 and 14,000 tons of cotton were exported to foreign countries; the export value of cotton raw materials (inclusive of cotton seed and cotton seed oil) from Shaanxi in 1937 was 9.6 million *yuan* or 17.5 per cent of the national total export value of these products.[33] This was almost double its share in the national cotton output, which shows the export-oriented, 'colonial' character of cotton cultivation in Shaanxi province at that time.[34] The only modern cotton textile mill, the Dahua cotton mill established in 1936 in Xi'an, with its 22,000 spindles and 200 looms used only a fraction of the marketed cotton.[35] Cotton prices were rather stable during this period, at about 0.60–0.80 *yuan* per kg.[36] The war would change all this.

Cotton usually was bought up from the farmers by merchants who transported it, in bales of 150 kg, to a railway station on horse-drawn carts. Before and even after 1934, some transport took place by way of the Wei River, mostly from Weinan downstream.[37] Cooperatives or individual peasants also brought their crop to the local markets on their own carts or on their own backs. Next to the markets of Xianyang, Weinan and Tongguan there were large cotton packing factories, employing seasonal labour.[38] A local sales tax of 5 percent (to

Table 59 *Imports before and after the Longhai railroad reached Xi'an*

		1932 June–Dec	1936 Jan–June
Chinese cloth	(1,000 rolls)	180	839
Chinese gauze	(1,000 rolls)	3	9
cotton thread	(1,000 kg.)	36	60
foreign shirts	(1,000 pieces)	26	51

be paid by buyer and seller each one-half), and in some counties a small transportation tax was demanded by local governments. The provincial tax on locally-made cotton cloth was abolished in 1934, the county cotton tax the following year.[39]

Until the opening-up of Guanzhong by the extension of the Longhai railroad in 1934, most cotton cloth and cotton yarn was home-made. Among various traditional centers of cotton cloth production Xingping county, some 20 miles west of Xi'an, was the largest and most renowned. Xingping never had much cotton cultivation of its own, and possibly owed its cotton weaving industry to its geographical location at the west end of the Guanzhong cotton area. From there, cotton cloth was transported west and sold in Gansu province 300 miles away. Gansu merchants would deposit money with local 'cloth shops' for the purchase of cloth; these shops received a 3 per cent commission both from the merchants and from the sellers. Almost every family in the county had a wooden loom. During the 'thirties much of the spinning was still done at home, but also cotton yarn was bought from outside the county. The spinning was often done by old women or young girls, who spun 6 to 7 ounces (about 200 gram) of coarse yarn or 4 ounces of fine yarn per day. With a wooden loom, in one day a woman could produce 18 to 20 feet of cloth of the regular 'sales cloth' type: a coarse yarn, only 9 inches wide, mediocre-quality cloth, with a length of 100 feet per roll. Weaving one roll would take almost a week, and if one person had to do both the spinning and weaving, about one month. Improved iron looms which were gradually introduced during the thirties could produce three times as much. In 1933, the local market value of such cloth was 3.50 *yuan* per 100 feet, double the value of the 1.3 kg of cotton thread that went into it, but on the Gansu markets it would bring about 5.00 *yuan*. The weaving women in this way earned some 0.30 *yuan* per day.[40] A second type of cloth, of a better quality, was produced for own use. This type had a width of 1 foot and 5 inches, was made from fine cotton yarn, and was much stronger.

Smaller cotton cloth handicraft production centers had existed throughout Guanzhong, but suffered greatly from the increase of imported factory-made cotton cloth after 1934. In most areas rural women gave up handicraft weaving, or only wove for household consumption. Part of the traditional dowry was 6 pounds of cotton, with which to make clothes for the new household; mending, repairs and remakes would make this amount of cotton go a long way.[41] Clothes traditionally were black, or dark blue, so that there would be as little need as possible for washing. For the same reason, and to limit wear and tear, trousers were short and people went barefoot or wore straw sandals. A towel was wrapped around the head. As elsewhere in China, coats and blankets were padded with cotton wool.

Cotton hardly had any competition from other textiles. Some northeastern counties of Guanzhong produced woolens, notably Hancheng (woolen coats), Changwu and Dali. These were too expensive for general use. The wool came from small flocks of sheep kept in the Huanglongshan mountain area and in southern Dali, a sand area long inhabited by Muslims who engaged in animal husbandry.[42] Also, wool was imported from north Shaanxi and Gansu. In some northwestern counties, notably Longxian, but also in Changan and Hancheng, linen was produced from locally-grown flax. Production methods were extremely backward and apart from in Longxian, quantities were insignificant.[43]

In 1937 export of raw cotton and import of machine-made textiles from eastern China was interrupted because of the war. Handicraft industry started to flourish again as a consequence. But its character had changed: apart from handicraft production with old-type wooden looms by women at home, there also was small-scale factory production with iron looms situated in towns and cities.

D. COTTON PRODUCTION, TEXTILES AND STATE INTERVENTION DURING THE WAR AGAINST JAPAN

The war against Japan brought a radical change in the economic situation of Guanzhong. Complete factories were moved inland from the east China coast, and later from Hankou to Sichuan or Shaanxi to

Table 60 Cotton acreage, output and yields in Shaanxi during wartime, 1937–1947

	Shaanxi province			Guanzhong			South Shaanxi		
	acreage (1,000 ha)	prod. (tons)	yield (kg/ha)	acreage (1,000 ha)	prod. (tons)	yield (kg/ha)	acreage (1,000 ha)	prod. (tons)	yield (kg/ha)
1937	312	55.5	178	285.3	52.7	185	27.2	2.8	104
1938	253	52.5	208	234.9	49.6	211	17.9	2.9	164
1939	186	48.6	261	177.2	46.8	264	9.1	1.8	196
1940	175	41.0	234	169.5	39.7	234	6.1	1.3	210
1941	133	38.3	288	125.3	36.6	292	7.7	1.7	222
1942	89	15.4	173	79.7	14.4	181	9.3	1.1	118
1943	97	23.4	241	80.5	20.2	251	16.0	3.2	197
1944	128	19.4	152	107.5	15.4	143	20.3	4.0	199
1945	126	25.9	205	111.8	23.2	208	14.0	2.7	193
1946	158	35.5	225	141.1	34.2	242	16.7	1.3	79
1947	178	48.3	271	158.2	43.6	276	19.8	4.7	238

Calculated from data in Li Guozhen, *Shaanxi Mianchan*, p. 2–14. A slightly different set of acreage figures is given in Bai Yinyuan, 'Present situation and future of the construction of Shaanxi', *Shaanzheng* Vol. VIII no. 1–2 (1946), pp. 12–21, viz. (1,000 ha) 1938:255, 1939:178, 1940:182, 1941:139, 1942:92.

prevent their installations from falling into Japanese hands. Trade with Japanese-occupied eastern and central China was interrupted. Free China had to become economically self-supporting, and create its own bases of raw materials and industry. In Guanzhong, moreover, new outlets had to be found for its cotton production once the eastern and foreign (mainly Japanese) markets had been lost. As the only remaining cotton area in Free China, it received a great deal of attention from the Chinese government, and several modern textile mills were moved to Xi'an. Yet for several reasons Guanzhong was unsuccessful in coping with this new situation. Cotton acreage and production went down within 4 years to about one-third of the pre-war average. Perhaps for strategic reasons, however, official data supplied during the war showed a much less serious decrease.[44] The area under cotton fell below 100,000 ha and production fell below 20,000 tons.

The non-irrigated areas north of the Wei River in particular reduced cotton planting but their yields went up to somewhere in the range of 150–200 kg per hectare. In the main cotton areas in Central Guanzhong, the irrigated fields in Jingyang, Gaoling, Sanyuan and Changan counties saw their irrigation water supply further increased (although many canals fell into disrepair); their cotton acreage and production decreased less severely, and average yields went up to levels of 250–400 kg per hectare. Statistics show very low yields in 1942 and 1944, which is due not so much to weather hazards as to neglect of and underreporting of production – at the time official prices for cotton were kept considerably below market value. The general rise in yields during this decade can be attributed to the variety improvements discussed above and to the extension of irrigation water facilities in central Guanzhong.

The reduction of the cotton acreage during the war had an upward effect on average yields, too, as the least productive fields were the first to be changed over to grain crops. In 1945 almost 40 percent of Shaanxi's cotton was produced in the Jinghui irrigation district, where yields under ordinary conditions would reach 450 kg per hectare.[45] During 1941–47, the Jinghui and Weihui irrigation districts together produced one-third to one-half of Shaanxi's cotton.

In 1938, because of the restoration of the Beijing – Hankou – Guangzhou railroad, Shaanxi cotton could be transported to Hongkong. But after the 'Xuzhou crisis' the international cotton price fell drastically, so that Guanzhong's cotton farmers reduced the sown acreage in 1938 by about one-third. Although some cotton mills were

Table 61 Cotton area, output and yields in four central counties, 1934–1947

	1934–1938 average			1941–1945 average			1947		
	1,000 ha	1,000 tons	kg/ha	1,000 ha	1,000 tons	kg/ha	1,000 ha	1,000 tons	kg/ha
Jingyang	25.1	5.6	223	15.4	4.4	284	19.1	8.2	427
Sanyuan	13.7	2.3	165	7.8	1.8	234	11.6	3.0	260
Gaoling	11.5	2.9	248	8.0	2.0	253	10.6	3.3	307
Changan	21.9	5.4	248	8.8	2.2	250	16.7	6.8	405
Total 4	72.2	16.1	223	39.9	10.4	261	58.1	21.2	366
Total Guanzhong	248.4	46.3	187	103.3	22.1	214	159.1	43.5	274
i.e. percentage of Guanzhong	29%	35%	119%	39%	47%	122%	36%	49%	134%

Based on data in Li Guozhen, *Shaanxi Mianchan*. All figures have been rounded off after computation.

Table 62 *Cotton output in large irrigation districts in Guanzhong, 1935–1949*
(100 tons)

	1935	1936	1937	1938	1939	1940	1941	1942	1943	1944	1945	1946	1947	1948	1949
Jinghui	63	120	90	85	143	89	106	65	91	51	103	103	145	131	78
Weihui				4	8	5	30	15	6	6	25	35	26	17	9
Meihui				1	1	–	1	1	–	–	–	–	–	–	–
Heihui								–	3	3	2	5	4	4	1
Ganhui											1	1	–	–	–
Fenghui														3	2
Laohui														–	–
Total 7	63	120	90	90	152	94	137	81	101	61	131	144	175	155	89
Shaanxi total	404	469	550	525	486	410	383	154	234	194	259	355	483		437?
i.e. percentage of Shaanxi	16	26	16	17	31	23	36	53	43	31	51	41	36		20?

Sources: Shaanxidi Guangai Guanli, Xi'an 1952. *Shaanxi Ribao* 1 Oct. 1957 and 12 Dec. 1957. *Shaanxi Nongxun* 1957 no. 2, p. 3.

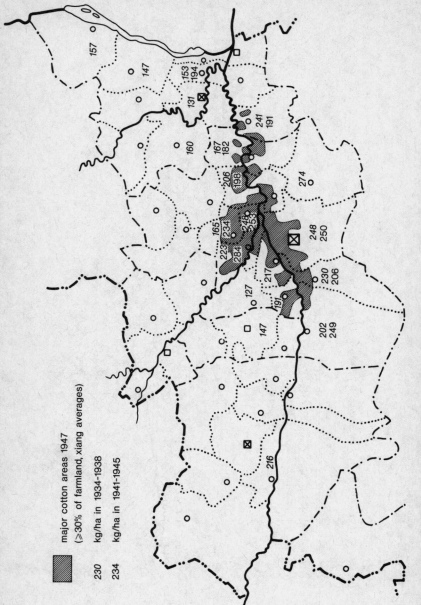

major cotton areas 1947
(≥30% of farmland, xiang averages)

230 kg/ha in 1934-1938

234 kg/ha in 1941-1945

Map 33 Average cotton yields 1934–1938 and 1941–1945

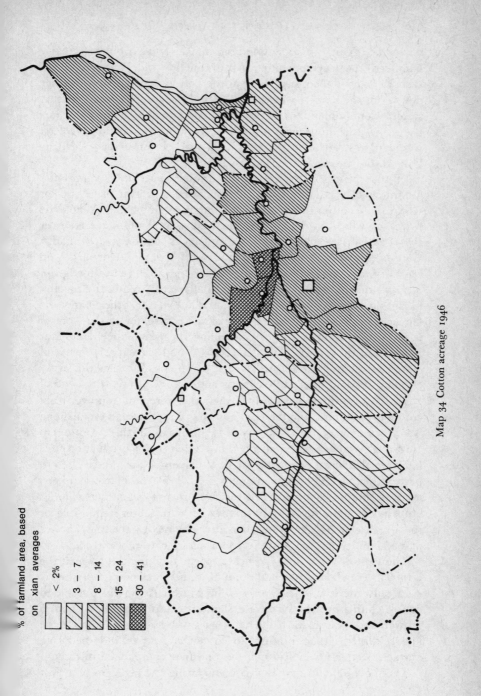

% of farmland area, based
on xian averages

< 2%

3 – 7

8 – 14

15 – 24

30 – 41

Map 34 Cotton acreage 1946

moved to Xi'an, Japanese bombing and internal problems greatly hampered the development of their production and, consequently, of their demand for cotton. In 1939 the cotton acreage went further down, but the harvest was very good and the cotton price remained stable. Communications between Shaanxi and Sichuan were improved so that it became possible to transport Guanzhong cotton westward instead of to the east. The 1940 cotton acreage held its ground, but production went down.

In the spring of 1941, the Government purchased very large quantities of army grain, which stimulated a violent price rise for wheat. The cotton price, however, remained far behind. Wholesale prices of wheat in Xi'an in 1942 and 1943 had increased over the 1937 prices over twice as much as cotton prices had.[46] Cotton growing areas which had always depended on outside grain, and individual farmers, too, now had to buy foodgrain at very unfavourable prices. That is, if after army requisitioning any foodgrain was left on the market at all. On the other hand the Government instituted a price and market control for cotton – one of its unsuccessful measures for controlling the war-induced rampant inflation of these years. The Government both as a (part) owner of cotton textile mills and as the largest consumer of textiles (for army clothing) had an interest in keeping cotton prices low. At the end of 1941 and in spring 1942 many farmers therefore changed over from cotton to foodgrain, and the 1942 and 1943 cotton area in Guanzhong was down to 80,000 ha. A survey of 153 farms in the three counties in Jingyang, Weinan and Xianyang showed that cotton production costs had exceeded income from it by 20 to 30 percent in 1941 and by 7 to 10 percent in 1942. The competing crops of wheat and maize had been more profitable. The worsened relative price of cotton versus other crops and commodities was shown to be the main factor responsible for the decrease in the cotton sown acreage.[47] Moreover, the 1943 harvest was a complete failure, so that a shortage of cotton occurred.

The Cotton Wool and Cloth Management Bureau, to which the farmers were obliged to sell, did not heed the black market prices but paid only the low official price. The Materials Bureau purchased cotton cloth from the farmers at half the market price. So cotton growers and weavers started to hide their production from official eyes, and re-directed their product to cottage industries and the black market. Merchants, mill-owners and farmers complained bitterly.

The Government had been contemplating the problem of a 'just price' for cotton for some time, but had to take action now. It took a set of measures, both political and economical. At the request of the Economic Committees of the various cotton counties, in 1943 a conference was organized of all related organizations, but no significant price rise was decided upon. The provincial government issued regulations on promoting cotton production; performance on this score was put into the local magistrate's record. A Cotton Loans Committee was formed to promote cotton planting. This Committee contracted loans with the five cotton districts into which Shaanxi province had been divided; to an amount of 60 million *yuan* in 1943 and 400 million *yuan* in 1944. According to estimates 70,000 ha of irrigated land and 32,000 ha of dry land were covered by these loans. However, with the rising prices, the loan standards (3,000 *yuan* per ha of irrigated land, for dry land half that amount) were so low as to bring little relief. Moreover, the loans were given after, not before, cotton sowing, so that at best they gave the cotton farmers something to live on for a while. The nominal amount of cotton loans increased to 1.5 billion *yuan* in 1945 and 3 billion *yuan* in 1946 (30,000 *yuan* per ha of irrigated land, for dry land half that amount) – at that time a not inconsiderable subsidy, covering about one-third of production costs per ha.[48]

In 1946 the war-time price controls were abolished, which led to an immediate increase of the area sown to cotton, from 110,000 ha in 1945 to 140,000 ha in 1946 and 160,000 ha in 1947. Cotton production increased much faster, and doubled between 1945 and 1947 – to some extent, no doubt, this increase reflects previous underreporting. Once left free, in 1946 the cotton price rose to 4,000 *yuan* per kg and fell back to 2,600 *yuan*. This price was insufficient to give farmers a fair return.[49] In December 1947, the cotton price fell (from 2 million *yuan* per 50 kg in October) to 3,150,000 *yuan* (inflation!), which was insufficient to cover costs. The State then fixed prices at that level.[50] In the summer of 1948, again the cotton price was fixed by the Government at a price which did not bring growers a fair return. Production costs included 300 labour days (at 6 *yuan* per day) per hectare for weeding (4 ×), irrigation (4 ×), picking and topping, and 1,500 oilcakes (made from cotton oil) per ha (at 0.2 *yuan* apiece). It was to the disadvantage of growers in these years of inflation that many had to sell immediately after the harvest, when prices were low, in order to pay the land tax which was collected at this time of the year.[51]

A situation not easily remedied was the deterioration of the quality of Guanzhong cotton which had occurred during the war. Cotton harvesting and ginning practices had suffered. Because the Government paid such low prices, the farmers were almost forced to adulterate clandestinely their cotton. The Government being badly in need of cotton bought anything offered to her, regardless of quality, at the same price. The peasants of course would sell their lowest quality cotton to the Government, and keep the good quality cotton for their own use or sell it clandestinely. Cotton was being mixed with lime, salt, sand etc. by crafty pedlars, and merchants soaked it with water. Sales suffered as a consequence. After the war many factories turned away from Shaanxi cotton because of its low standard, and fetched their cotton from far away Hebei. In 1946, a Cotton Improvement Association was founded, which included representatives from the Institute for Agricultural Improvement, all large cotton mills, the merchants' union, and from the cotton unions of each county. As its first task it considered the strengthening of inspection, the establishing of standards and the strict grading of cotton in Guanzhong, so that it might regain its prewar quality and trust. However, the problem of funding and organizing this work was not solved easily, and the cotton unions felt that the Government should pay because it had been responsible for the deterioration of Guanzhong cotton.[52]

After the outbreak of the Japanese war, the coastal textile industry suffered a great deal of destruction, and the Longhai railroad transport was disrupted. The price of machine-woven cloth went up greatly, so the Guanzhong population had to use locally-made cloth again. As it turned out, this new demand was met best by small-scale local textile factories (using simple iron looms) and by cottage handicraft production. Their total output was several times as large as that of the large mechanized cotton mills which had been set up in Guanzhong. Several factors were responsible for the lack of economic success of the mechanized mills. In 1938 and 1939, and also later, Japanese bombardments destroyed part of the industrial installations in Xi'an. The factories that were moved to Xi'an from Hubei lost much of their equipment during transport. Valuable technical experience in maintenance of equipment got lost. Guanzhong had no experienced industrial labour force comparable to that of east China. As it was stated in 1936, when the first modern cotton mill was established in Xi'an 'the mill has a problem in finding local labourers, especially women. All female workers are from outside the province, especially from Hubei. Local male labourers are scarce, and the women do not like to work either. They sometimes leave their job after a few days.'[53] The wages offered by textile mill owners were comparatively low (9 to

10 *yuan* per month; chemical factories paid 10 *yuan*, the railways 12 *yuan*) while working hours were long, viz. 10 hours, as against a usual 8 hours in other branches. After 1938 working hours were lengthened to 12 hours a day.[54] So jobs in the textile mills were not attractive.

Another important negative factor was the close official supervision of the city-based mechanized mills. The cotton mill established and owned by the Construction Bureau since 1935, with the employees producing mainly flour sacks, has been characterized as 'pitifully immature'.[55] The largest cotton mill, Dahua, saw its products placed under the control of the military headquarters after the start of the anti-Japanese war, before it was bombed out of production in the winter of 1939 (and again destroyed in spring 1941). The large mills were scrutinized much more closely in matters of taxation than was possible with small handicraft industries. Their owners and their capital came wholly from outside Shaanxi. In their purchase of cotton raw materials and with sales there was less room for circumventing the Cotton Bureau and officially regulated prices. As a consequence, the mechanized mills were offered and had to accept the lower quality cotton.

For all these reasons, the productivity of the mechanized textile mills was not nearly as high as that of the pre-war coastal mills; the quality and price of their wovens were not competitive with the handicraft cotton industry in Guanzhong. Therefore they concentrated on production of yarn.

Between 1936 and 1939 the Dahua cotton mill in Xi'an was considerably expanded by its owners (a family which owned mills in Shijiazhuang and in Hankou as well), from 900 labourers to almost 3,000 labourers. The number of spindles increased from 22,000 to 35,000, the number of looms from 200 to 800. In 1940, at its maximum capacity, it could produce 45,000 bales of yarn and 45,000 rolls of (mainly coarse) cloth per month. Six other small mechanized textile factories in Xi'an, with several dozen labourers each, produced mainly flour sacks, carpets or coarse cloth. In Xianyang a cotton mill which had been moved there from Wuchang in 1938 started operating with only 5,000 spindles in 1940. The Shenxin Fourth Cotton Mill was moved to Baoji from Hankou in 1938. This factory had 20,000 spindles and 400 looms; after the destruction of its spindles it set up again 5,000 spindles in summer 1939. At Qishan, on the Longhai railroad between Baoji and Changan, the Chajiapo Cotton Mill was established; it started producing cotton yarn in 1943. Also in Baoji, which was safer from bombing than Xi'an, three smaller textile mills, named

Yeqing, Taihua and Minkang, with a total of 4,500 spindles and 650 looms, had been established in 1938 and 1943.[56]

In contrast, the number of small handicraft textile factories in Shaanxi rapidly increased during the war. In 1943 there were 106 registered textile plants. Most of these were located in Xi'an, Baoji, Xianyang and Sanyuan.[57] In addition, in smaller cities and rural districts besides Sanyuan and Xingping textile handicraft production flourished, both in small factories and in cottages. As a traveller reported in 1941:

Liquan's commerce has greatly developed since the outbreak of the war. Shops sell mainly cotton textiles . . . Since 1937 local cotton textile production has developed again. There is an industrial textile production of 3,400 rolls of cloth per year, 1,800 of which are produced by women in the villages with old-fashioned looms . . . The rural economy of Qianxian is thriving. 2,500 rolls of cotton cloth are locally woven per year. There are two textile factories in the city, which produce 250,000 feet of cloth a year and 2,700 kg. of cotton yarn. The local economy has improved because of the textile business, which also provided employment to jobless persons . . .[58]

During wartime the total output of cotton textile handicraft industry was several times as large as that of the mechanized cotton mills. In 1946 it was shown to be concentrated in four areas: (1) Xi'an with 110 factories, with 2,220 looms, producing 60,000 rolls per month, (2) Sanyuan with 55 factories with 700 looms, producing 18,000 rolls per month, (3) Baoji with 45 factories with 682 looms and 17,000 rolls per month and (4) Nanxiong (in south Shaanxi) with 6 factories, 160 looms and 5,000 rolls per month. The seven modern mechanized mills mentioned above in 1946 had a total of 80,000 spindles and 2,500 looms.[59] We may conclude that the war helped to create a strong basis of mechanized spinning industry and a wide basis of local and rural textile handicraft production. The predominant position of Xi'an continued after the war. In 1954, 72 percent of cotton handicraft production (by value) was produced in Xi'an, and 21 percent in other cities and towns.[60]

E. RESTORATION, EXPANSION AND IMPROVEMENT DURING THE 1950S

Under the new communist government after three years the pre-war cotton acreage of about 300,000 ha in Shaanxi had been restored.

Further growth was stunted. Annual production during 1951–6 fluctuated between 70,000 tons and 100,000 tons. 1957 was a record year, both in acreage and output: 317,000 ha and over 110,000 tons of cotton. Such a cotton acreage was never to be reached again in Shaanxi. Only twice, in 1973 and in 1982, record harvests have surpassed the 1957 output record.

During the early 'fifties, Guanzhong was viewed by the central government as a region which should provide cotton not only for the 30-odd million population of the provinces of the Northwestern Region, but also for the cotton mills of north China. With a projected annual production of 75,000 tons (80 percent of which by Shaanxi), one-third of this amount would be needed in the region itself, and two-thirds could be exported elsewhere.[61] The main problems with cotton production were considered to be of a 'technical' nature: the lack of skilled labour and of good agricultural implements, insufficient technical progress, insect damage etc. In view of the inadequacy of irrigation facilities, water management should be improved and conflicts over distribution and water use should be resolved.[62]

From 1953 onwards, new elements were introduced in government policies. Compulsory delivery of grain was instituted in order to keep grain prices low, while stepping up the flow of grain to the cities demanded by the industrialization program of the First Five-Year Plan. Extraction of other agricultural products was stepped up as well – at low prices, so that agricultural goods and textile exports might finance Soviet machinery and equipment, and contribute to capital formation. In order to achieve these ends, major changes were carried out in the organization of production and trade, within the framework of a central policy of cooperativization of agriculture. Cotton sales and trade were first dominated, then monopolized by state trade organizations. Cotton cloth industry was concentrated in large state-owned factories built in 1956 through 1959. Some other factors influenced the development of cotton as well: improvement of seeds, extension of irrigation, changed cultivation techniques, and most important of all, the hazards of weather. Early summer rains and a sunny autumn would bring a good harvest; with the exception of 1950 and 1955, the 1950s were generally blessed with favourable weather conditions. For the Great Leap Forward years 1958–60, there are no reliable data about acreage and production, or, for that matter, on weather conditions. There are indications, however, that the 1959 drought and the food crisis in 1960 and 1961 made peasants abandon cotton in favour of foodgrain – nationwide, the cotton acreage fell from 5.5 million ha in 1959 to a low of 3.5 million ha in 1962.

Prices. From 1949 to 1952, China's national cotton acreage and production almost tripled to a level surpassing the pre-war record. By 1953, the national government deemed output 'sufficient to meet the needs of China's textile industry and of the people, thus changing the former situation in which cotton was imported . . . The national cotton acreage this year therefore will be maintained at the 1952 level. Now the former price ratios between foodgrains and cotton have come to show new defects: cotton prices are relatively too high, and there are no national seasonal price differentials.'[63] So the cotton price was lowered.

In terms of wheat, in 1950 the State had fixed state purchasing prices of cotton at about 9:1, close to the pre-war average level.[64] The upward pressure on cotton prices can be explained by its greater relative fall in output compared with the pre-1949 peak figure. In Shaanxi province, the 1950 cotton harvest was a complete disaster. The rainy autumn of 1949 had not only damaged the 1949 harvest (especially in irrigated areas) but also spoilt the cotton seeds. Spring and early summer in 1950 were dry, so that in the non-irrigated areas one could not plant cotton in time. The cotton fields along the Wei River banks were washed away by the summer floods.[65] The 1950 harvest was by more than one-quarter lower than expected, and prices rose as a consequence. A 'reasonable' price ratio, according to local authorities, was 1 kg of standard quality cotton to 7.3 kg of wheat. But in late August 1950 the actual ratio was 1:10. After the harvest and in subsequent spring it still was 1:8.5, but on instructions from the central government local agencies decided to lower their purchasing prices to 1:8 in March 1951. It was further lowered to 1:6.25 in April, 1953.[66] The Shaanxi cotton acreage figures show that the peasants reacted very strongly to the relatively high prices of cotton during 1950–1952, but also to the state purchase price reduction of 1953. Till the 1970s cotton prices were held at this low level.

Slightly different prices were maintained by state purchasing agencies for different districts of Guanzhong. This might make it worthwhile sometimes for the peasant to take and sell his cotton outside his own district, although such action was illegal. Also, cotton was sold directly to customers on the black market in the city.[67] The communist authorities in their efforts to bring about a 'socialist transformation of commerce' gradually spread the state commercial network to below the county level. But primitive transport conditions and local fluctuations in supply and demand caused quite large differentials in local scarcities and therefore in local prices. Effective central price control could not be established in such a situation. Moreover, for the cotton farmer, several prices operated at the same time: the official price for cotton paid as tax in kind, the official price obtained for compulsory sales quota since 1954 (both might be expressed in grain), the price on the free (sometimes illegal) market, and last, but not least, the 'attributed price' for cotton retained by the farmer for handicraft yarn and cloth production and for his own family use. Differentials in cotton quality were a further complicating factor. The official standards of grading cotton might not always be applied in a uniform manner; the farmer could not be certain which price his cotton would fetch once offered to the purchasing agency. When his cotton was offered without distinction together with that of his fellow coop members, he had to be careful not to lose money by supplying higher-grade cotton than his fellow members. A one-grade difference might mean 5 to 10 cents per kg, and the worst qualities (grade 11 or 12) fetched only half the price of the medium (3rd) grade cotton.[68] State price control and cooperative sales were not conducive to quality improvements in varieties, cultivation and processing – we will come to this problem later.

In contrast with the low official purchase prices for cotton, the State established high prices for cotton cloth. In this way, maximal revenues derived from state-owned textile factories could contribute to state capital formation. The average exchange rate of white cotton cloth with cotton was about 7 feet of cloth to one kiliogram of cotton during 1930–6, but it was 5.6 feet during 1950–5, a drop of 20 percent.[69] In order to make this extractive system work, the Government put great effort into controlling the market supply of cotton and in extinguishing rural handicraft production.

State planning of marketing and acreage. After the introduction of state-planned 'unified purchase and sales of grain' in November 1953, many Guanzhong peasants feared that not enough grain would be left for their own consumption, so they expanded the grain area.[70] This and the lowered official purchase price for cotton threatened to lead to a reduction of 15 percent, or well over 40,000 ha, in the area sown to cotton in early 1954.[71] Remedial measures were taken by local cadres: propaganda, more fertilizer, better care for the crop. These fitted well

Table 63 *Shaanxi cotton acreage, output and average yield, 1945–1960*

Year	Acreage (1,000 ha)	Output (1,000 t)	Average yield (kg/ha)	Sources[1]
1945	125.9	25.9	205	*Shaanzheng* Vol. 8 no. 1–2, pp. 12–21
1946	157.8	35.5	223	*Fangzhi Gongye* 1947; pp. 1 11–13
				Shaanxi Mianchan, 1947
1947	178	48.3	271	*Shaanxi Mianchan*, 1947
1948	196.6			*Qunzhong RB* 17/2/51
1949	186.6	44	(236)	*Zhongguo Nongbao* Vol. 1 no. 6 (1950), p. 470; *Shaanxi RB* 1/10/59
	(185.6)	37.5	202	*Shaanxi Nongye Dili* 1978, pp. 8, 38
	(215.8)	43.7	202	*Zhongguo Jingji Nianjian* 1981, pp. 306–9
1950	227	40 (est.)[2]	(176)	*Qunzhong RB* 19/10/50, 11/2/51.
1951	256.7	80	(312)	*Qunzhong RB* 14/6/51
				Shaanxi RB 1/10/59
1952	301	72.5	241	*Qunzhong RB* 9/1/54; *Dili Zhishi* 1957 no. 10, p. 467
1953	296	86.4	292	*Qunzhong RB* 9/1/54
		85.6		*Shaanxi Nongxun* 1955 no. 2, p. 10
1954	290	90.7[3]	(313)	*Shaanxi Nongxun* 1955 no. 2, p. 10 and 1957 no. 2, p. 3.
1955	282	74.7	266	ibidem and *Shaanxi RB* 8/1/56, 23/9/56
1956	320[4]	99.5	(311)	*Shaanxi RB* 23/9/56, 6/12/57, 18/7/57;
	(254)	96.2	379	*Shaanxi Nongxun* 1957 no. 2, p. 3; *Dili Zhishi* 1957 no. 10, p. 467
1957	317	116	(366)	*Shaanxi RB* 9/7/57, 4/2/58
	320	110.5	(345)	*Shaanxi Nongye Dili* 1978, p. 8; *Xinhua Banyue Kan* 1958 no. 6, pp. 53–4
1958 ?	343	217		*Renmin Ribao* 27/9/58; *Shaanxi Nongye Kexue* 1959 no. 5, p. 169;
[5]	313	167		*Renmin Ribao* 27/9/58

1959 ?[5]	300	(133.2)	444	*Shaanxi Nongye Kexue* 1960 no. 1, p. 13. *Shaanxi Nonglin* 1960 no. 7, p. 2
	304	127.5	(419)	*Shaanxisheng 1959-nian Mianhua Fengchan Jishu Jingyan Huibian* 1960, pp. 1–2
1960 ?	300(pl.)	150 (pl.)		*Shaanxi Nonglin* 1960 no. 7, p. 2

[1] By preference the latest provincial sources available have been selected. Derived figures are between brackets.

[2] In 1950 the Northwestern Region produced 48,000 tons of cotton. Shaanxi's output at that time amounted to more than 80 percent of this.

[3] Possibly too low, since 82,900 tons were purchased by the State, *Shaanxi Ribao* 28/12/57.

[4] Possibly too high, since 1957 has been mentioned as having the all-time cotton acreage record, *Shaanxi Nongye Dili* 1978, p. 38.

[5] These figures were too high and have been revoked later.

with the first cooperativization campaign of spring 1954. Producing cotton for the State was depicted as a civic duty and economic benefits (loans, seeds, fertilizer) were to accrue to cooperatives which planted cotton. The remedial measures proved to be fairly effective: the cotton acreage eventually sown in 1954 was almost as large as in the previous two years, and the harvest was even better. The same, however, could not be said of the *national* cotton harvest of 1,065,000 tons in 1954, which was 10 percent lower than in 1953 and 30 percent lower than in 1952. The government in Peking decided action was necessary.

In September 1954, the national government instituted compulsory quotas for cotton growers. According to Chuyuan Cheng, the purpose of this directive was different from that for grain. 'Where the purchase of grain could increase supply by raising the marketing rate, cotton purchases could only be increased materially by an increase in output. By 1953, the marketing rate of cotton had already reached 80 percent of output. The main purpose . . . was to ensure that cotton acreage would not be reduced because of the increasing demands for grains'.[72] Nicholas Lardy quite rightly adds to this another motive for, and consequence of, the compulsory cotton sales to the State, namely the suppression of rural handicraft cotton cloth production. 'Having survived several decades of competition from . . . modern factories, it was suppressed by the price and marketing policies adopted in the mid-1950s, substantially curtailing the income earning opportunities traditionally open to peasants in cotton-producing areas. The state simultaneously became the monopsonist purchaser of raw cotton and the monopolist seller of cotton textile products. Moreover, the state set the prices of raw cotton and of finished textile products in such a way as to further tax the farming sector which was . . . the major market for textile products. State pricing policy quickly established the state-run textile industry as the single most important source of government revenue.'[73]

At the same time as the institution of compulsory quotas, which for the farmers abolished free sales of cotton, a rationing system was set up with per capita quotas (in the form of coupons) for cotton cloth which strictly limited consumption both for the urban and the rural population. Cotton growers at first still were entitled to retain a small per capita amount of cotton wool for their own use (or for private sale) but finally this privilege was abolished as well.

From 1955 onwards, the State instituted the complete advance purchase of cotton. Before, purchase had been after the harvest. No distinction was made between coops, mutual-aid teams or individual cotton farmers, all had to sell in advance. Earnest money was paid on a selective basis because it was meant to aid only those with difficulties in production, not as relief or as a loan for living expenses. Moreover, 'the principle of paying much to organized cotton growers (coops, mutual-aid teams), paying little to individual growers, and paying nothing to the rich peasants is right. Payments to organized peasants are larger in size, and more concentrated, and therefore easier to provide'. In view of this stand, maximum advance payment was put at 12 per cent for coops, 10 per cent for mutual-aid teams and 8 percent for individual peasants. The cotton left-over from last year in the hands of the peasants, it was stipulated, might not be sold to private merchants or other people, but only to the trade corporations.[74]

These restrictive measures, together with the uncertainty about their own food grain supply, made many cotton farmers switch over to foodgrain crops in 1955. The Government urged the grain supply departments to do a good job.[75] Also, pressure was applied by local cadres to conform to the State-planned sown acreage for cotton, and effectively so, according to the official newspaper, Shaanxi Ribao. 'The cotton growers of all areas have, in accordance with the exigencies of the state plan, restricted the area of melons, vegetables, local tobacco et cetera and planted cotton instead.' And it confidently added 'This year we will not have the phenomenon of 'hidden fields' and 'hidden production' of cotton. Patriotic cotton growers will respect all regulations concerning the advance purchase of cotton'.[76] There is no information on the size of this illegal cotton production. In view of the fact that most of the Guanzhong cotton areas were easily accessible and that the political and administrative network of local control had steadily built up since 1950, illegal cotton production on a major scale could be carried on only with the connivance of local cadres responsible for reporting official acreage and production figures to the purchasing agencies. These agencies, on the other hand, tried to squeeze as much cotton as possible from the peasantry.

An additional problem arose with a severe shortage of cotton seeds in 1956, caused not only by the poor quality of the 1955 harvest, but also by the coop movement and the campaign for close planting advocated by agroscientists and backed by the authorities. Peasants who entered the coops often had sold or hidden their seeds beforehand, with the idea of relying simply on the coop. Thus seeds were in short supply, and peasants were urged to bring forward their hidden seeds and not to press oil from cotton seeds anymore.[77]

On the basis of the 1954 regulations on the purchase and sales of cotton, cotton growers were entitled to retain a certain amount of cotton per capita, to be decided once a year by the provincial government before the harvest. This retainable amount at first was put at 1.25 kg, and in 1955 and 1956 at 1.5 kg per capita. However, many farmers retained considerably more cotton, either on their own initiative or because the cooperatives distributed low-grade cotton which would not fetch a good price anyway to their members.[78] Various categories of retained cotton could be distinguished: with the agricultural producers' cooperative (legal or illegal, since coops might have cotton wool legally retained as raw material for handicraft production) and with individuals (legally assigned, illegally assigned, last year's leftovers, and production from their own private plots).[79] Part of the cotton retained in this way was indeed used by the cotton growers themselves, another part was sold on the black markets which flourished in Xingping (the main handicraft textile center) and Jingyang, and to a lesser extent in Huaxian, Lintong and other counties. Prices on these markets were 30 to 40 percent above the state-listed prices at the end of 1956 – which may be indicative not only of depressed state prices but also of the relatively small size of the illegal market.[80] Private cotton pedlars were reported to be able to earn as much as about 100 *yuan* per month, for a 6-hour workday.[81] The Government thereupon decided to allow state-controlled free markets in the countryside, where cotton could be sold legally by cotton producers who could prove they had fulfilled their obligations under the state purchase plan.[82]

F. THE RISING DEMANDS OF THE GOVERNMENT AND STATE TEXTILE INDUSTRY

For China as a whole, the 1956 cotton harvest was bad. Although Guanzhong had a record cotton harvest, it was to feel the national cotton shortage and the remedial measures taken by the national government just as well. The cotton-growing peasants had their retainable amount of cotton lowered by one-quarter to one-half of a kilogram per capita, so that they were allowed to retain only 1.25 kg per capita in 1957.[83] The rations for cotton cloth were cut by 4 feet and one inch, or to about 20 percent below the level of 1956. Cotton cloth

Table 64 *Cotton textile output and sales (exclusive of peasant handicraft production) in Shaanxi 1936, 1949–1957*

	Production (million rolls)	Sales in Shaanxi (million rolls)	of which to private persons
1936	813	687	636
1949	551	429	409
1950	735	570	526
1951	892	780	712
1952	1175	934	870
1953	1473	1303	1194
1954	1566	1287	1172
1955	1329	1289	1178
1956	1749	1737	1582
1957 (planned)	1499	1511	1336

Source: Shaanxi Ribao 21 Apr. 1957. 1 roll weighs 6.35 kg. Dresses are included.

rationing – which was to last for three decades – had started in 1954. State-issued coupons were needed for any purchase of cotton goods. At first, they were provided for one year (September to August), later for shorter periods. The objective of rationing was, of course, to maintain price stability and a more equitable distribution. It was permitted to give one's coupons away to relatives or friends, but illegal to make a business out of buying and selling these coupons. In Shaanxi, the per capita amount of cotton cloth available this way was 21.15 feet in 1955–6; the 1956–7 coupons were valid for 23.45 feet at first, but reduced in spring 1957 to below 20 feet, as stated above. Peasants received a slightly lower amount of coupons than the city population did.[84] This cut in cotton cloth rations, in a situation of abundant supply of cotton wool in Guanzhong, gave a boost to local handicraft cloth production, legal or illegal.

The State cotton textile mills were in an uncomfortable position early in 1957. Their capacity was continuously being expanded, but cotton supply fell short. Since 1949, 5 new cotton mills had been built in Guanzhong and 3 more were under construction. In 1956, because of the bad quality of the Shaanxi cotton harvest, more than 40 percent of the raw cotton used by the Shaanxi cotton mills had to be imported from outside the province. The 32 and 40 count cotton thread was completely made out of imported cotton, because of the insufficient length and ripeness of the local cotton wool.[85] Early in 1957 cotton supply still fell short by about 11,500 tons, and this time it could not be bought from outside the province, so the mills could not work at full capacity.[86] Production plans for 1957 were revised downward, and fell back to the 1953 level. Exports were no longer possible.

As part of the first and second five-year plans, which aimed to construct inland industries near to raw material bases, several modern cotton spinning, textile and dyeing mills were built in Xi'an.[87] The size of these mills averaged 100,000 spindles and 3,500 looms. In 1959, two more mills were scheduled to start producing in Xianyang. In order to meet this rising factory demand, local raw cotton production would have to amount to over 150,000 tons by 1961 – 60 percent more than the 1953–7 average production.[88] The cotton mills in Guanzhong were to provide for the needs not only of the Northwestern provinces, but also meant to supply Sichuan and other provinces with thread and cloth.[89]

Raw cotton supply fell short not only in quantity, but also in quality. The quality of Guanzhong cotton has decreased (since 1946), its staple is not long enough, it is not ripe enough and contains too much dirt. Therefore, it cannot be spun into finer thread than 32 count . . . The cloth made from it is not strong. Our cotton industry, under the principle of getting one's materials from one's own area, for a number of years has been able to produce only medium-grade yarn, which constituted over 92 percent of total production . . . The cotton mills for high-grade goods, which will be built here now and in the future, will need about 20,000 tons of high-grade cotton each year. If we do not raise the quality of our own cotton, we will have to import all this from outside. There are two reasons why quality is bad. First of all, variety improvement has not been carried further. Since 1936 Shaanxi has popularized the Stoneville no. 4 and also bred the *Jingsi* no. 51. Their length is 15/16 to one inch, without much variation. Before 1949, Shaanxi's cotton was rather good, and commanded a market price 5 percent higher than that of outside cotton. But after 1949, varieties in other provinces have been improved quickly, for instance the *Daici* (Delta) no. 15 which has a staple length of $\frac{1}{12}$ inch . . . Secondly, selecting, picking . . . storing, drying and processing management are not good either. Of the 13 cotton-producing provinces, after Xinjiang, Shaanxi has the highest percentage of dirt in it, almost double that of other provinces.[90]

Many cotton bales sent to the factories contained 3 percent and over of impurities, making extra processing necessary and increasing expenses. This may have been due, in part, to the insufficient remuneration received by peasant women for ginning.[91] Although it was not explicitly stated at the time, it seems likely that the state organizations suspected the cotton growers of keeping the best cotton for their own use.

In spring 1957 official policy still supported a certain latitude for peasants' private initiatives in production and trade. However, because the textile mills stood partly idle, pressure was mounted on the cooperatives to abandon their own handicraft production. It was suggested that coops should not retain cotton for coop industrial uses (such as the making of sacks, saddles etc.). 'Many do not need it for that purpose every year, and anyway it could be bought from the State.'[92] Calculations were presented to prove that it was disadvantageous to spin or weave one's own cotton.[93] Later in 1957, however, the political drive for collectivization was vigorously resumed, and private economic activities were limited as much as possible. For cotton, this new line was laid down in a provincial government directive of September. The cotton purchase quota was raised. The retainable amount of cotton was limited to 1 kg per capita, and 1.25 kg in cotton districts 'if it is really difficult to restrict it.' Peasants and coops who sold cotton on the free market were to be criticized severely. In order to encourage selling to the State, an extra 5 feet of cloth were promised for every 50 kg of cotton sold above the norm. Local cotton cloth and cotton yarn produced by peasants could no longer be sold freely.

Those farmers who weave local cloth must sell to the commercial departments designated by the State. It is strictly forbidden to sell local cloth, cotton wool or cotton yarn on the free market . . . First-time small offenders will have their goods bought up (by the State) at the listed price, recidivist profiteering merchants . . . will have their stock confiscated and be severely punished.[94]

This prohibition of handicraft cloth sales was explicitly founded on political reasons:

Last year we did not buy all the cotton we should have bought, so there was a serious black market. A few textile mills had to close down due to cotton shortage. If we do not buy as much cotton as possible, there will be a development of native spinning and weaving, with as a result not only a waste of cotton, but also, even more important, an effect on the application of the policy of unified purchase and unified sales. It might even lead to speculation by rich peasants and to the development of capitalism. We must look at this from the political side as well as from the economic side.[95]

The tension between the quantitative and qualitative limitations of cotton supply on one hand, and the urgent industrial need and rising expectations on the other hand, was resolved in a temporary flight from realism. The Maoist planning of the Great Leap Forward period picked up again the mood of the Twelve-Year Development Plan for

Agriculture proclaimed in early 1956 (which had a 1967 cotton production target for Shaanxi of 500,000 ton).[96] Its optimism was sustained by the bountiful 1957 cotton harvest, which was ascribed to 'collectivization, party leadership, and the labour of the masses'. The quality of this harvest was good, too, 2 to 3 grades higher than average, which meant a considerable increase in the cotton farmers' income.[97] In Guanzhong, as well as in China as a whole, the 1958 and 1959 cotton crops were reported to be very large, but the exact size is difficult to establish. The same lack of reliable data exists for the famine years 1960–1, when due both to a strongly reduced sown acreage and to low yields, cotton production fell to about one-half of the level of previous years.[98] During the early sixties therefore, the newly-built cotton textile factories in Guanzhong had to leave the larger part of their capacity (by then 850,000 spindles and 20,500 looms[99]) unused – a tremendous economic waste. Because this same excess capacity has continued ever since, no new investments have been undertaken in the cotton textile industry in Shaanxi, which has fallen considerably behind the mills in coastal areas.[100]

G. TECHNICAL MEASURES FOR RAISING COTTON OUTPUT

During the 1950s a number of technical problems in cotton cultivation required the attention of cotton growers and of agrotechnicians in the Provincial Agricultural Bureau. Major impediments to raising unit yields were a general lack of fertilizer, serious insect damage, and crude field management and cultivation methods.

The lack of fertilizer was due to insufficient pigbreeding. In the central areas of Guanzhong this was a long-standing problem. In a cotton-wheat crop rotation system there are not enough mixed grains with which to feed pigs. The irrigated areas were not accustomed to pig-raising, and always lacked manure.[101] Cotton fields were reckoned to need 50 cartfuls or so of manure mixed with earth per hectare.[102] Chemical fertilizer has only been generally used since the early 70s, and then with obvious success.[103]

Insect damage became more and more severe during the 50s, especially in the warmest and irrigated areas. Dry areas were hardly affected – a major reason for expanding cotton cultivation in non-irrigated areas. The bollworm affected 2 percent of the kernels in 1947, but during 1954–8 as much as 11 percent of the kernals, 8 percent of the flowers and 63 percent of the young bolls in the irrigated areas of Jing-yang. It was the major plague by then, causing production losses of 10 to 20 percent per year.[104] Dead seedlings (usually due to cotton aphids) were another major cause of production losses; during 1955–9 losses due to this factor alone were 15 to 20 percent of total production, and the dark and humid climate of the sixties increased the aphid damage to levels of 20 to 30 percent.[105] Red spiders (*hongzhizhu*) and cotton bugs (*mianmangchun*, Miridae) were major plagues as well. In the Jinghui irrigation district, 68 percent of the cotton area was affected by aphids, 52 percent by Miridae, and 35 percent by red spiders to different degrees in 1953. DDT, '666', and lime were used to combat these insects.[106] A few years later, all major cotton districts were affected by bugs for over 60 percent of their area, and the outlaying districts in west and north Guanzhong for 35 to 60 percent.[107] Apart from the application of insecticides, such as 666, which were available only in very limited quantities, cultivation habits were corrected in order to limit the occurrence of insect damage. The area around the cotton fields would be thoroughly cleaned of weeds. The habit of cultivating beans and other low crops between the rows of cotton plants (by which soil fertility was increased) was warned against, so that the habitat of the insects might be destroyed. Peasant women were urged to participate in agricultural work and to organize cotton field management teams. During the growing season, ploughing and hoeing between the rows was recommended, in order to remove weeds. Practical experience had shown that after 4 years of continuous cotton cultivation, production would drop severely, (by 45 to 75 percent), owing to increased yellow wilt and dry wilt, so farmers were counselled not to plant cotton for many years in succession.

Planting densities used to vary a great deal between districts. In western Guanzhong, densities were very low, from 30,000 to 45,000 per hectare. In the extreme east of Guanzhong, densities were only little higher. In the low-lying, irrigated areas of central Guanzhong (Changan, Xianyang, Xingping etc.) densities used to be very high, up to 100,000 seedlings per hectare.[108] Except in the latter area, planting densities were considerably increased on the advice of the Provincial Agricultural Bureau (and that of Soviet advisers). In 1953, 15 to 20 percent more seed was used.[109] In the following years, ever higher densities were advocated, or rather imposed, by the authorities. Farmers showed their discontent about the rigidity of the new instructions on cultivation, when local cadres tried to enforce the guidelines developed by agroscientists too mechanically.[110] Some people warned against high densities: 'Planting density used to be

3,600 stems per *mu* ($\frac{1}{15}$ ha) in the past. During the past years, close planting with 6,000 stems per *mu* has been promoted. This is too much, the sunlight cannot pierce through. It must be no more than 4,000!'[111] More flexible and differentiated guidelines were given in early 1957:[112]

dry fields in western Guanzhong	75,000–90,000 stems per ha
irrigated fields in Weihui and south of the Wei River	52,500–67,500 ,, ,, ,,
irrigated fields in Jinghui and Luohui	75,000–90,000 ,, ,, ,,
dry fields in northeast Guanzhong	60,000–75,000 ,, ,, ,,
dry fields in southeast Guanzhong	67,500–82,500 ,, ,, ,,

During the Great Leap Forward high planting densities were imposed. Since the dark sixties planting densities have been left to the collectives to decide, and generally they have decreased again in irrigated areas. Recommended planting densities for irrigated cotton fields were somewhat higher again during the 70s. Variation was from 67,500–82,500 stems per ha in western Guanzhong to 97,500–112,500 stems per ha in plain areas of east and central Guanzhong.[113] In high yield areas plants are pruned two or three times a year, non-fruiting branches are removed, and the plants are eventually topped.

The expansion of irrigation facilities was vigorously resumed after 1949. Irrigated cotton was expected to reach an average yield of 450 kg per ha, as against only 150 kg per ha for dry land cotton. Between 1954 and 1962, in the 17 large irrigation districts, irrigated area increased from 131,000 ha to 240,000 ha. Rotation irrigation was applied, with priority given to the crops in most urgent need of water – often the young cotton plants in June.[114] The management network was based on, and similar to, the pre-1949 large irrigation district organizations, and strengthened because of increased state power.[115]

Water fee standards had been set by the Provincial Irrigation Bureau in 1946 and again in 1951 for three different grades of cotton land, depending on the quality of the land (especially its water retention capacity) and the guaranteeable amount of irrigation water. The fees were based on assumed production increase within each irrigation unit owing to irrigation, as follows:

	Prod. per ha	Increase owing to irrigation	Standard fee per ha
1st grade cotton land	450 kg	262.5 kg	18.75 kg
2nd grade cotton land	337.5 kg	150 kg	11.25 kg
3rd grade cotton land	262.5 kg	75 kg	3.75 kg

The fees constituted about 7 percent of the cotton gross output increase on first- and second-grade land, and 5 percent on third-grade land. Within the lowest irrigation units (below the *tou*, or headgate, usually 1 to 2 m³/sec., irrigating 200 to 300 ha) fields might be graded differently by the people of the area. Because of physical limitations, no such grading within the *tou* had been undertaken by the irrigation authorities. Irrigation water fees were set at a high enough level to defray all operating expenses and repairs of the irrigation system, under the principle of 'water pays for water'. The standard set for water fees was 8 percent of the additional agricultural production benefit, but this might be raised if necessary.[116]

Cotton irrigation techniques were slowly improved, on the basis of practical experiences and the results of experimental farms. Winter irrigation proved to be effective in raising production, because it increased soil humidity at sowing time. It was given in December, before the soil froze. In early spring the soil was harrowed, in order to reduce evaporation. Sometimes irrigation had to be given before sowing in April, but generally speaking there was no conflict between the irrigation needs of wheat (which was harvested end May) and cotton. Summer irrigation of one inch of water was given twice, in cases of drought three times, from early July till August.[117]

A complicating factor, then and now, was the heavy silt load of the Wei River and its northern tributaries, during summer. Intake of water had to be stopped for two to three weeks on the average, when after heavy summer rains the silt load of rivers surpassed a level of 15 percent, so as to avoid clogging of irrigation facilities and ditches. The first-grade fields (making up about one-third of the irrigation area in case of the Jinghui irrigation district) had priority in receiving irrigation water in situations of water shortage. A more economical use of water was essential for achieving higher output levels of cotton, and both technical and management measures were directed at achieving that effect.[118]

H. EXPANSION OF THE COTTON AREA

In spite of state efforts, the cotton acreage was not enlarged much further in irrigated areas after the early 50s. In dry areas, however, a considerable expansion occurred, encouraged by state cadres and under the influence of cooperativization. The improvement in cotton seed supply (quantitative and qualitative), and the promotion of

Table 65 *Cotton sown acreage data 1934–1975*

District	area '34-'38 average (ha)	area '41-'45 average (ha)	area 1947 (ha)	area 1975 (ha)	index ('34-'38 area = 100)			
					'32-'33	'41-'45	1947	1975
Xi'an	21,893	8,783	16,690	4,640 x	37	40	76	21
Changan	11,204	4,111	10,698	5,167	29	37	95	46
Xianyang	2,818	1,895	8,381	8,704	11	67	297	309
Xingping	4,493	3,468	4,774	8,360	20	78	108	186
Huxian	5,135	2,101	4,006	6,933	43	41	78	135
Zhouzhi	11,540	8,022	10,610	8,506	27	70	92	74
Gaoling	25,109	15,352	19,149	6,831	46	61	76	27
Jingyang	13,698	7,752	11,628	15,261	46	57	85	111
Sanyuan	7,374	1,325	1,088	12,027	14	18	15	163
Fuping	19,600	9,103	10,987	19,440	56	46	56	99
Lintong	25,492*	11,661	16,623	18,027	104	46	65	71
Weinan	10,440	3,604	6,057	21,400	20	35	58	205
Huaxian	2,556	1,595	1,383	3,852	23	67	54	151
Huayin	1,359	425*	1,875	1,753	46	31	138	129
Tongguan	6,712	1,809	1,442	3,276	11	27	21	49
Dali	10,471	2,547	3,348	⎱ 18,134	54	24	31	80
Chaoyi	5,482	1,388	3,296	⎰	18*	25	60	
Pingmin					12			
Hancheng	6,427	2,142	4,117	7,400	57	33	64	115
Heyang	13,897	2,601	5,618	15,359	7	19	40	111
Chengcheng	2,640	512	896	7,867	37*	19	34	298
Baishui	1,988	496	603	3,288	25		30	165

Pucheng	4,107	1,213	2,058	16,400	4	30	50	399
Yaoxian	1,787	416*	—	2,587	14	23	—	145
Lantian	2,989	836	202	2,480	29	28	7	83
Liquan	11,093	1,756	1,574	10,667	50	16	14	96
Qianxian	7,155*	675	1,155	10,267	3	9	16	143
Wugong	1,532	1,044	2,222	4,800	32	68	145	313
Fufeng	1,387	1,017	2,001	4,240	12	73	144	306
Meixian	1,009	1,115	1,481	4,080	89	111	147	403
Qishan	959	391	657	2,456	26	41	69	256
Fengxiang	746	426	597	2,440	30	57	80	327
Baoji xian	} 3,493	919	2,911	3,280	6	26	83	94
Baojishi		—	—	—				
Longxian	192	74*	—	—	15	39	—	—
Qianyang	275	104*	—	344	22	61	76	61
Linyou	—	—	—	—	—	—	—	—
Yongshou	71	49*	—	—	35	69	—	—
Chunhua	723	359*	—	—	6	50	—	—
Xunyi	—	—	—	—	—	—	—	—
Binxian	357	75*	—	—	10	21	—	—
Changwu	45	3*	—	—	52	7	—	—
Tongchuan	193	104*	—	—	7	54	—	—
Fengxian	—	—	—	—	—	57	80	327
Total	248,441	101,268	159,127	260,266	—	41	64	97

* Less than five years.

Table 66 *Cotton output data, 1934–1957*

District	production '34–'38 average (1,000 kg)	production '41–'45 average (1,000 kg)	1947 (1,000 kg)	estimated 1957	average yield '34–'38 (kg/ha)	average yield '41–'45 (kg/ha)	yield 1947 (kg/ha)
Xian				3,640			
Changan	5,443	2,196	6,766	4,381	248	250	405
Xianyang	1,992	893	4,038	4,169	178	217	377
Xingping	537	437	3,143	2,516	191	231	375
Huxian	1,021	716	1,557		230	206	326
Zhouzhi	1,035	523	1,360	2,758	202	249	339
Gaoling	2,860	2,026	3,252	5,837	248	253	307
Jingyang	5,588	4,367	8,184	10,462	223	284	427
Sanyuan	2,263	1,811	3,028	8,718	165	234	260
Fuping	1,057	205	192	4,071	144	155	176
Lintong	4,933	1,805	1,426	8,643	206	198	130
Weinan	4,255	2,120	1,672	9,272	167	182	101
Huaxian	2,520	690	858	2,519	241	191	142
Huayin	428	366	219	2,611	167	229	158
Tongguan	236	91	267		174	214	142
Dali	881	314	206	4,630	131	174	143
Chaoyi	1,602	495	469	6,803	153	194	140
Pingmin	848	279	482		155	201	146
Hancheng	1,007	412	1,099		157	192	267
Heyang	2,038	436	1,435	4,734	147	168	255
Chengcheng	287	65	121	1,150	109	127	135

Baishui	292	69	82		147	139	136
Pucheng	656	146	360	4,845[1]	160	120	175
Yaoxian	213	67	–		119	161	–
Lantian	818	183	15	388	274	219	74
Liquan	1,413	289	354	3,869	127	165	225
Qianxian	1,053	84	260	1,241	147	124	225
Wugong	257	185	429	1,220[2]	168	177	193
Fufeng	276	177	394		199	174	197
Meixian	190	143	557	8,326	188	128	376
Qishan	136	64	111		142	174	169
Fengxiang	115	71	125		154	167	209
Baoji xian	756	178	977		216	194	336
Longxian	30	16	–		156	216	–
Qianyang	44	20	–		160	192	–
Linyou	–	–	–		–	–	–
Yongshou	9	10	–		127	204	–
Chunhua	90	79	–		124	220	–
Xunyi	–	–	–		–	–	–
Binxian	44	9	–		123	120	–
Changwu	6	0.1	–		133	33	–
Tongchuan	27	21	–		140	202	–
Total	46,336	22,059	43,438				

[1] actually produced. [2] amount sold.

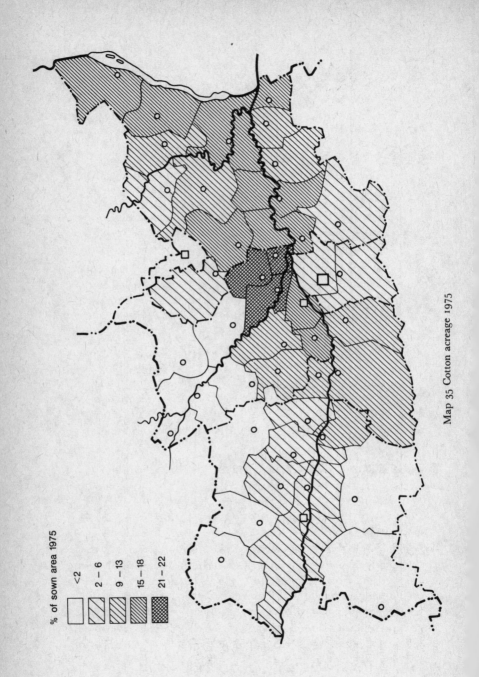

% of sown area 1975

<2
2 – 6
9 – 13
15 – 18
21 – 22

Map 35 Cotton acreage 1975

cotton cultivation through model farms, by county technical stations and by coop-agrotechnicians, were major factors in this. Another factor may have been the gradual official clamp-down on trade in cotton and cotton cloth between the traditional cotton areas and the outlying counties which left the latter with an unsatisfied demand for local cotton cloth. The dryland cotton acreage of Guanzhong amounted to about 160,000 hectares in 1954, or slightly over one-half of the total cotton acreage, most of which was in eastern Guanzhong.[119] Three different dryland areas could be distinguished:

—the lowlands along the Wei River, from Huxian to Huaxian. These had fairly good moisture conditions, and possible access to surface and underground water. Yields were above 375 kg per ha in 1954. Cotton acreage was 10 to 15 percent of the farmland area.

—the western part of the terrace north of the Wei River, from Baoji to Xianyang. Here rainfall was rather good, but because of altitude the growing season was shorter, with frost danger. Cultivation methods were primitive. Yields were 300 to 375 kg per ha in 1954, or even lower. Apart from Liquan county, cotton acreage generally was about 5 percent of the farmland area.

—the eastern part of the terrace north of the Wei River, from Sanyuan to Hancheng. Rainfall was less here, but the climate was somewhat milder than in the west. Cultivation methods were more advanced. Yields were about 375 kg per ha in 1954. Cotton acreage averaged 5 to 10 percent of the farmland area.

In all these 3 dryland areas, but especially in the dry uplands north of the Wei River (the so-called *hanyuan*), during the 50s and 60s the cotton acreage considerably increased. In 1951, the cotton area in the dry uplands occupied only 7 percent of the cultivated area; by 1958 this percentage had doubled.[120] In the years 1961–2, because of the post-Great Leap Forward food crisis, the cotton acreage was considerably reduced, but by 1965 the cotton sown acreage in the dry uplands had reached again the 1957 level. In the following few years it increased some more, but since 1974 the cotton acreage in the *hanyuan* has remained stable. Although our data for the 1960s are spotty and much less complete for this period than for earlier and later periods, some representative counties in the western and eastern parts of the *hanyuan* may illustrate this development. See Table 67.

Table 67 Cotton acreage in some counties on the dry uplands north of the Wei River 1934–1975

	1934–1938 average (ha)	1947 (ha)	1957		1965		1974		1978	
			(ha)	(% of farm-land area)	(ha)	(% of farm-land area)	(ha)	(% of farm-land area)	(ha)	(% of farm-land area)
Wugong	1,523	2,222	3,135	9	4,065×	12	4,670^A	14	4,735	14
Fufeng	1,387	2,001	n.d.	–	2,770	n.d.	4,240	8	n.d.	–
Liquan	11,093	1,574	11,865	17	9,935	14	10,400	16	9,200	15
Qianxian	7,155	1,155	4,730	6	n.d.	–	10,265	14	10,135	14
Hancheng	6,427	4,117	9,700	25	8,010	21	7,400	21	7,335	22
Pucheng	4,107	2,058	10,020°	8	14,070	11	16,000	13	15,665	13
Total	31,701	13,127					52,975	14		

× 1966 figure.   ^A 1975 figure.   ° 1956 figure.

Sources: *Shaanxi Mianchan* 1947 (1934–1947 data); *Shaanxi Nongye* 1966 no. 3, p. 25–30 and *Shaanxi Nongye Dili*, Xi'an 1978 (Fufeng data); *Shaanxi Ribao* 9 Dec. 1957 (Liquan 1957); remaining data from local Agricultural Bureaus.

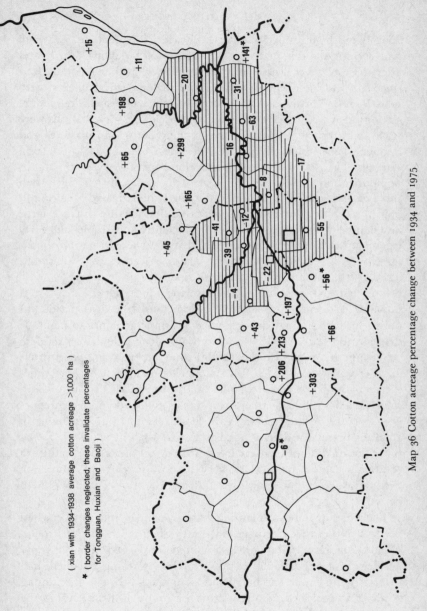

(xian with 1934-1938 average cotton acreage >1,000 ha)

* (border changes neglected, these invalidate percentages
    for Tongguan, Huxian and Baoji)

Map 36 Cotton acreage percentage change between 1934 and 1975

I. VARIETY IMPROVEMENT

Mainly on the basis of the American variety Stoneville no. 4, which had become the dominant cotton strain in Guanzhong during and after the war, several new varieties were developed and popularized since the mid '50s. The provincial and regional governments, with help from the Northwest Agricultural College, established a number of stations for variety trials. Breeding and popularization stations were set up with brigades or communes, under continuous guidance and frequent supervision by agrotechnicians from local Agricultural Bureaus. The period between the development of a new strain and its popularization thereby could be very short, usually no more than three or four years. For cotton in the low-lying irrigated areas major objectives of breeding programs were resistance against diseases, large and many bolls, high cloth element, sufficiently long staple, and early ripening. In the more elevated dryland areas, where irrigation often is insecure and the climate is colder, major objectives were resistance against drought and cold, and early ripening.

The first and very successul early ripening variety was *No. 517*, popularized during 1954–6 all over Guanzhong. Its growth period was only 140 days. It had a fairly good resistance against drought. It deteriorated fairly rapidly, and its staple length had decreased to 27–29 mm by 1958. In the Jinghui and other irrigation districts another variety developed from Stoneville no. 4 had become widespread by 1956, *Jingsi* cotton; it had a growth period of 150 days. Both these varieties still had rather short staples and a low cloth element of 33–4 percent. A late ripening variety introduced from Hanzhong in 1956 and popularized in irrigated areas after 1958, called *Daici (Delta) no. 15* cotton did not last very long. Although it had good qualities of resistance against drought, a very high cloth element, and high production, after 1960 its area was restricted because of its long growth period.[121]

The technique of transplanting cotton seedlings from seedbeds had been introduced from Hubei and south Shaanxi in the late 1950s. Although much extra labour was required (100 to 180 labour days per hectare of cotton) experiences proved to be rewarding. Seedbeds had to be irrigated very carefully, and some days before transplanting fertilizer was applied. Transplanting was done by hand, late in the evening, to avoid desiccation. It was advised not to shake the seedling and its roots with the soil clinging to it, and even to plant it facing in its original direction.[122] The major advantage of transplanting was to advance and lengthen the maturing period of cotton before the autumn frost occurred. It also saved seeds, and sped up dissemination of superior strains. With a shorter growth period, there might be more time for other crops.

Xuzhou 209 and, thereafter, *Xuzhou 1818*, were the most widespread cotton varieties during the 60s. They had a staple length of some 30 mm, a cloth element of 38 to 40 percent, and a growth period of 140 to 147 days. Later Xuzhou 1818 continued to be used only in non-disease areas, with fertile soil; Xuzhou 209 remained popular in west Guanzhong. An important break-through came with the development of varieties with resistance against dry and yellow wilt. *Shaanmian no. 4*, a locally developed fairly short-ripening variety was the first step in this direction; it had become widespread since 1975. *Nos. 401* and *1155* were trial-produced from 1978 onwards, and showed characteristics of both high production and of good resistance against dry and yellow wilt, which had been so damaging to cotton yields in the irrigated areas of Guanzhong. All these varieties have short staple lengths. Heat resources remain a major limiting factor.[123]

J. PRODUCTION INPUTS, COSTS AND BENEFITS

After cotton cultivation became part of the State plan and after agricultural cooperatives and collectives were put under the obligation to devote a certain part of their farmland to cotton, its economic profitability could not very well be assessed any more. The low prices of cotton did not make it attractive for the farmers to devote more collective land to cotton than the acreage assigned by the State. Probably this same reason accounts for the fact that little was published on the economic aspects of cotton cultivation, the costs of various inputs and their benefits. The few articles there were invariably tried to show the profitability of growing cotton in comparison with growing other crops. However, the declining cotton acreage during the 60s and 70s and the fact that no cotton was sown on private plots indicate that the peasantry felt otherwise, for several reasons.

The wheat:cotton exchange rate dropped from 9.6 to 1 in 1957 to 7–8 to 1 during the 60s, and further down to 6.9 to 1 in 1970. Although the cotton price was successively raised in 1975, 1978, 1979 and again in 1980, it still remained at a level very low by world standards. This

Table 68 *Cotton: food grain exchange rates in China, 1952–1983*
(*yuan* per 100 kg)

Year	Grain price	Wheat price	Cotton price	Cotton:grain exchange rate	Cotton:wheat exchange rate
1950	9.82		155.90	15.87	
1952	11.92	16.30	173.56	14.56	10.65
1957	13.32	17.86	171.34	12.86	9.59
1962	18.02	23.48	170.04	9.44	7.24
1965	18.48	22.12	184.04	9.96	8.32
1970	21.64	26.86	185.58	8.58	6.91
1975	21.76	26.86	211.60	9.72	7.88
1978	21.28	27.22	230.48	10.83	8.47
1979	25.72	32.96	265.52 $^\times$	10.32	8.06 or 8.47
1980	25.77		297.23 $^\times$	11.53	
1983	26.91		297.23	11.05	

$^\times$ 5 percent higher in North China.
Sources: Zhongguo Nongye Nianjian 1980, 1981, p. 6 p. 380 and *1984*, p. 176. Grain price is an average price of 6 different foodgrains, viz. wheat, maize, rice, millet, sorghum and soybeans. Cotton price is for standard cotton 3rd grade with a staple length of 27 mm. Both are state purchase listed prices.

unfavourable development of the relative price of cotton affected both the sown acreage and material inputs in cotton cultivation.[124]

In Guanzhong, cotton prices were similar to the national prices mentioned in Table 68, albeit somewhat lower in 1965. Local wheat prices (and those of maize) rose much faster than cotton prices between 1957 and 1965. The unfavorable cotton:wheat exchange rate persisted in subsequent years, quite a contrast with international prices.[125]

Secondly, while cotton yields did not rise much in Guanzhong since the late 1950s, production costs per hectare did. Modern inputs of chemical fertilizer, pesticides, machine-ploughing and electrical irrigation came into common use in irrigated areas. These inputs helped to maintain or expand production, but caused a considerable increase of production costs. The use of fertilizers and pesticides was especially costly. Eventually the phenomenon occurred of so-called 'highly productive poor collectives' which did achieve high yields but at such great expense that no profits could be realized. A nation-wide survey of 302 cotton-producing collectives in average yield areas showed that production costs of cotton had risen from 62 *yuan* per 50 kg

Table 69 *Cotton, wheat and maize State purchase prices in Guanzhong,*
1957–1978
(*yuan* per 100 kg)

	wheat	cotton	maize	cotton:wheat exchange rate
1957	17.80–21.00	176	13.00–16.60	9.8–8.4
1965	23.60–23.80	176	15.40–18.60	7.5–7.4
1972	27.60	205	19.20	7.4
1978	27.60	230	19.20	8.3
1979	33.60	265	19.20	7.9

Source: data provided by Agricultural Bureaus from seven counties.

to 92 *yuan* in 1975 and about 106 *yuan* in 1976–7. They were then an average of 2 percent higher than the income from sales. Between 1965 and 1975, average list prices went up slightly, from 92 *yuan* to 107 *yuan*.[126] The increase of inputs and production costs of cotton occurred throughout Guanzhong, both in high-yield and in low-yield areas. According to an economic analysis of cotton growing in Wugong county, conducted in 1962, the profitability of cotton cultivation depended mostly on the level of output, which fluctuated greatly between villages and between years. Input costs varied much less. In 1962, the break-even point was reached at an output level of about 300 kg of cotton per hectare. Cotton became more profitable than wheat only if cotton yields rose above 375 kg per hectare.[127] For Shaanxi province as a whole, this level was reached, or surpassed, only in one out of three years, notably during 1965, 1966, 1973, 1976–8 and 1982.[128] Generally speaking, farmers appeared to prefer wheat or maize to cotton, especially after short-ripening varieties had been introduced. In this way, in dry areas wheat could be followed by autumn grains, buckwheat or green fertilizer; in irrigated plain areas wheat would usually be followed by maize, sometimes by beans. This combination of two crops within one year also had the advantage of providing fodder for pig-raising, which became increasingly popular as the need for fertilizer became more urgent but chemical fertilizer prices remained very high. Manure mixed with earth was cheaper in terms of nutrient value, and superior in improving soil structure; for most farmers these advantages outweighed the extra burden of labour.[129] In high-production areas, chemical fertilizer was used along with manure and oilcakes. In spite of high levels of application of fertilizer (up to 500 kg N per hectare in high-yield areas) and of insecticide (up to an expense of 150 *yuan* per ha) the hazards of weather and insects still could severely affect cotton production, much more so than maize or oil crops.

Thirdly, the government policy of expanding or at least maintaining cotton production by prescribing a minimum sown cotton acreage each year could be effective only to a certain degree. Although People's Communes and production brigades had to comply with the assigned acreage, theirs was the choice of particular plots and the decision about material inputs and labour to be devoted to cotton growing. When cotton, as often was the case, was held to be less profitable than other crops, farmers were likely to be reluctant in allocating prime land and scarce material resources to it. More important still, stressing grain production and self-reliance became national policy during the 60s and 70s. In view of the rapid population increase in Shaanxi Province since 1949, and its very narrow margin of subsistence, a policy of self-reliance for province, counties and individual communes could not but be detrimental to commercial crops, of which cotton was by far the most important. On the other hand the outlying counties in west and north Guanzhong were urged to try to cultivate their own cotton. Only from 1979 onward, was local and regional crop specialization encouraged again.

Fourthly, with the exception of mountainous counties in the west and north, farmland acreage in Guanzhong was considerably reduced after the 1950s. Roads, housing, industry and other land uses, were expanded, especially in the irrigated plain areas near Xi'an and along the east–west railroad – the two traditional cotton areas. As a consequence, much prime land was lost.

Looking back at the unfavourable development of China's cotton production during the 1960s and 1970s, a Chinese writer mainly blamed low state purchase prices. 'It is true that since 1958 the cotton planting plan was realized as it should be, was still a question which this was of a guiding nature, not a command. Whether the cotton planting plan was realized as it should be was still a question which had to do with prices. Cotton being unprofitable, peasants were not willing to plant much . . . In Hebei, Shandong, Shaanxi and other old cotton areas, cotton production declined heavily . . . There has been a tendency for the cotton area to scatter more and more . . . towards unproductive areas. So cotton has deteriorated, insect pests are serious, productivity is low and quality is bad . . . We must adjust the cotton price.'[130] This judgement holds true for Guanzhong even more than for China as a whole, because in Guanzhong cotton yields remained particularly low and the cotton area is widely scattered.

K. SHIFTS AND DECLINE IN THE 1980s

The price rise and other government measures undertaken in 1979 which were so effective in increasing cotton production in China did not have the same effect in Guanzhong. Table 70 shows the development of cotton acreage and production during the 1970s and early 1980s; the data apply to Shaanxi province as a whole. The Guanzhong acreage constitutes 90 percent of this.

Except for the year 1973, during the 1970s unit yields of cotton were lower by 10 to 40 percent in Shaanxi than the national averages. Over the 1980–3 period, Shaanxi's unit yields were only one-half of the national averages. Only the 1982 harvest showed satisfactory results. In Guanzhong policies with regard to cotton have been somewhat contradictory since 1979. Disappointing yields in 1975 and 1976 had convinced agricultural specialists that the cotton acreage should be reduced, especially in the too cold or too dry areas of the uplands in western and northern Guanzhong. But the Government preferred to hold on to the same acreage it had prescribed since 1971 (between 260,000 and 265,000 hectares). Three consecutive good harvests (1977–9) and the price hikes for cotton in 1978 and 1979 should have stimulated the agricultural collectives to expand the cotton acreage. With few exceptions, however, no such expansion occurred.[131] The 1980 drought almost halved the summer grain harvest, and hailstorms and low temperatures affected the autumn grains and cotton crop, so that only 75 percent of the cotton quota was met.[132] The 1981 floods and storms inflicted heavy damage to the autumn crops of western Guanzhong and south Shaanxi – the 'severest natural disaster in Guanzhong since liberation'.[133] The resulting scarcity of foodgrain and low cotton yields dissuaded the farmers from extending the cotton acreage even with raised purchase prices. The climate seemed to corroborate again the views of those who held much of Guanzhong's farmland area to be unsuitable for cotton cultivation. The 1983 cotton harvest was an outright disaster.

During 1979–81, the provincial authorities hesitantly followed the

Table 70 *Cotton acreage, output and yield in Shaanxi, 1964–1984*

Year	Area (ha)	Production (tons)	Yield (kg/ha)	(National yield average[e]) (kg/ha)	Source
1964	±260,000[g] each year	70,000–80,000	±330	(338)	estimate based on regional data[b]
1965		114,500	±450	(420)	*Shaanxi Nongye Dili*, p. 8
1966		112,000	±430	(473)	*Shaanxi Ribao* 1 Sept. 1984
1970		about 70,000	±265	(458)	estimate based on regional data[b]
1971		about 85,000 (20% up on 1970)	±325	(428)	*Shaanxi PS* 26 Dec. 1971
1972	263,330	94,000	357[c]	(397)	NCNA Ch. 12 May 1972, and 27 Nov. 1973
1973	260,000	132,500	510[c]	(517)	*Shaanxi Nongye Dili*, p. 8
1974	±260,000[a]	about 100,000 (2.5 × 1949 figure)	383[c]	(495)	*Jingji Daobao* Jan. 1976
1975	260,000	85,000	327	(480)	*Shaanxi Nongye Dili*, pp. 8, 172; *Shaanxi PS 9 June 1975*
1976	264,000	60,000–65,000	±250	(420)	*Shaanxi PS* 21 Aug. 1976 estimate based on regional data[b]
1977	263,330	100,000	380	(420)	NCNA Ch. 13 Apr. 1977; SWB no. 928 5 Nov. 1977
1978	252,000	105,000	418	(443)	FB 4 Feb. 1979. p.T.1
1979	250,400	102,450[d]	409	(488)	*Zhongguo Nongye Nianjian*, p. 107
1980	247,000	80,850[d]	327	(548)	*Shaanxi RB* 20 June 1981
1981	256,700	67,500	263	(570)	*Shaanxi RB* 7 Jan. 1982
1982	253,300	125,500	495	(617)	*Shaanxi RB* 7 Jan. and 3 Mar. 1982, 19 Apr. 1983

| 1983 | 200,000 (pl.) 251,200 (real.) | 40,150 | (752) | *Shaanxi RB* 28 Jan. and 1 May 1984 *Zhongguo Nongye Nianjian* 1984, p. 90 |
| 1984 | ?[f] | 73,900 | 160 | *Shaanxi RB* 6 Apr. 1985 |

[a] interpolated figure.

[b] data for smaller areas have been used here as the basis of an estimate of total production and yield in Shaanxi province.

[c] According to *Zhongguo Nongye Dili Zonglun*, Beijing, 1980, p. 208, the average yield in Guanzhong in 1973 was 383 kg per ha. I consider this to be an erroneous use of the 1974 figure.

[d] This figure is also given in *Zhongguo Jingji Nianjian 1981*, pp. 306-9. Subsequently, the provincial newspaper gave a higher figure, viz. 83,500 ton, *Shaanxi Ribao* 7 Jan. 1982.

[e] *Zhongguo Nongye Nianjian 1980*, p. 36, *1981*, p. 31, *1982*, p. 39, *1984*, p. 90. *Zhongguo Jingji Nianjian 1983* IV 1; *Beijing Review* 1984 no. 20.

[f] The 1984 cotton acreage had been reduced by some 43,000 ha.

[g] The cotton acreage was 'basically stable' at 4 million *mou*, *Shaanxi Nongye Dili*, p. 38.

newly formulated national policy of de-emphasizing local self-sufficiency in grain and of promoting instead crop specialization and
concentration on the basis of the natural conditions of each area. In
western Guanzhong the assigned cotton acreage was reduced, and the
cultivation of oil crops (especially rape) was promoted instead,[134]
especially on the uplands. Wugong county which in spite of low yields
had expanded its upland cotton acreage in 1979 reduced it again the
following year, in favour of rape and foodgrain.[135] Its northern
neighbour Qianxian county, which because of its lack of water and
heat resources used to have very low yields, reduced its cotton acreage
by one-third in 1980, despite the good 1978 and 1979 harvests.[136] On
the other hand the cotton acreage in the low-lying, well-irrigated
counties of eastern Guanzhong was to be expanded. The reasons for,
and general traits of, this plan adopted by the provincial government
in fall 1980 were summarized as follows:

At present Shaanxi province is not self-sufficient in grain, nor in cotton, nor in
edible oil. The major reason for that is that crop distribution is not rational, so
that unit yields are too low, and the rate of commercialization is not high. On
the basis of Guanzhong's natural conditions, soil, labour and other socio-
economic factors, in the eastern parts the relative value of grain versus cotton is
16 to 1, but in the western parts it is 6 to 1 . . . Therefore we must establish
production bases for cotton in the east, for grain and cotton in the centre, and
for oil crops and grain in the west and the dry uplands. So cotton fields should
move from west to east, from north to south and from dry areas to irrigated
areas. There are now almost 67,000 ha of dispersed low-production cotton
fields which should be moved to the 18 counties below 500 meter which have
been designated as commercial cotton bases . . .[137]

In 1981 the provincial government reallocated 27,000 hectares of
the above-mentioned low-production cotton acreage from Baoji
prefecture and from the dry uplands to the irrigated areas of five high-
production counties in the east.[138] In order to support this expansion, a
well-drilling program was set up, irrigation and drainage canals were
dug, large quantities of pesticides and good seeds were supplied, and
technical training classes were held.[139] As it turned out, however, it
appeared to be very hard to convince the farmers in central and east
Guanzhong to grow more cotton.

In the Xianyang prefecture . . . cotton production because of the weather fell
to the lowest level since 1949. This has created an ideological problem between
the cadres and the masses. Some people feel we shouldn't grow cotton here
anymore . . . In the past, the prefecture would reduce its cotton area by some

5,000 ha each year. This will be exceeded this year, because many collectives reduced the cotton acreage, some even by one-half. We must make the peasants realise that the state plan combines the interests of the State, the collective and the individual, and convince them not to consider their interests alone. We should try to fulfill the handed-down assignment of 93,000 ha.[140]

In the Weinan prefecture the 1981 cotton acreage had been enlarged slightly to 138,000 ha; the summer floods destroyed some 10 percent of it.[141] The 1982 assigned acreage was smaller, 130,000 ha, but certain measures were thought to be necessary against those counties which would not fulfill their assigned acreage. These would receive correspondingly less grain subsidies, and would have to deliver correspondingly more grain to the State.[142] This seems reasonable enough, since grain subsidies had been instituted in order to enable counties to concentrate on non-foodgrain commercial crops. After two bad harvest years, the 1982 harvest was excellent. However, as soon as the responsibility system had given peasants far greater freedom in their choice of crops to be cultivated, cotton cultivation was reduced in most areas of Guanzhong. The 1983 harvest was down to an all-time low of only 40,000 tons – less than half the average of the preceding few years. How much of this decrease was due to a reduced acreage is not clear. As a result, 80 percent of the raw cotton for Shaanxi's cotton mills had to be purchased from other provinces. Storage and quality had given rise to problems as well.[143] Thus, during the early 1980s, Guanzhong's cotton situation was the reverse of the national trend of fast production growth (viz. 3.0 million tons in 1981, 3.6 million tons in 1982 and 4.6 million tons in 1983); correspondingly, its share of national output had fallen. The future of cotton was bleak, both in agriculture and in industry.

Conclusion. Throughout this century, cotton was a high-risk crop in a rural economy which operated close to subsistence levels. As the main commercial crop it provided cash to the farmer and also was used to meet the government demand for tax and raw materials from agriculture. Production and demand were greatly influenced by market forces until the 1950s. Since then, cotton was controlled heavily by the government and suffered from low purchase prices. Except for the World War II period, Guanzhong's cotton acreage has been about 250,000–300,000 hectares, or 12 to 15 percent of the cultivated acreage. Most of it was concentrated in the low-lying river plain.

Poppy cultivation was eradicated in three campaigns from 1933 to

1937, and finally effectively so in 1940. Cotton seeds were issued by the government to make up for the farmers' losses. In the newly developed irrigation districts government and relief organizations had forbidden poppy cultivation right from the start. In south and west Guanzhong eradication took longest – there remained many users of opium. Cotton seeds were mainly distributed through the Provincial Cotton Improvement Bureau, which operated several breeding and popularization stations. Mainly American varieties (Trice, Stoneville, Delfos) were used. In the 1930s, quality and yields were very uneven in different areas. After the acreage was reduced in 1938, yields started to rise to about 260 kg/ha on the average, partly due to constriction of the sown area to fields with good irrigation conditions, partly because of variety improvements. Until the 1960s, however, damage from insects kept yields low and peasants could do little about it without pesticides. On irrigated fields 300 to 400 kg/ha could be obtained, on dry fields 100 to 200 kg/ha.

The persistence of the textile handicraft sector after Xi'an had been reached by the railroad was not due to lower rural wages; actually industry flourished in the districts north of Xi'an which were comparatively affluent and labour-short, and in Xi'an itself. The 'traditional' handicrafts were to a large extent urban-based. Large enterprises apparently suffered more from material shortages, bureaucratic malpractices, power cuts and insecure trade flows. Until 1937, demand from coastal factories and from Japan stimulated production. Raw cotton was Shaanxi's major export item. Local handicraft felt the impact of textile imports, even though improved iron looms came into use. The war created a new situation: trade with east China and Japan was interrupted, several textile mills came to Xi'an and the relative price of cotton went down. As a consequence cotton acreage and output fell by more than one-half. Only in the Jinghui irrigation district were acreage and output maintained. In 1942, however, prices of wheat and maize rose so much higher than those of cotton that the cotton acreage went down to only 80,000 hectares; moreover, the 1942 cotton harvest was a failure. The Government now took political action and provided loans. Yet only after the abolishment of state price controls in 1946 did the cotton sown acreage and production increase again, but without coming near to the pre-war level. In 1948, price controls were reinstated.

During the war, the equality of cotton deteriorated seriously. Peasants kept the best qualities for themselves, or sold them illegally to small handicraft industries. The modern mills lost their competitive edge in this way and were also more vulnerable to Japanese bombs and Chinese government exactions; they turned to production of yarn and left the local cloth market to the handicraft industries which sprang up around Xi'an, Sanyuan and Baoji.

The communist government first dominated, then monopolized purchase and sales of cotton. Prices were lowered, to a low of 6.25 kg of wheat to one kg of cotton in 1953. Because of very high expectations for cotton production in Guanzhong, and also because of the idea that Xi'an should supply cotton textiles for other provinces as well, a number of large state mills were established in Xi'an from 1956 to 1959. Since 1954, peasants were no longer allowed to operate their own handicraft industries. In this way, the state guaranteed that it would be able to buy cotton at low prices, and sell textiles to the population at high prices. Although acreages for sowing have been prescribed by the government since then, there has been no further expansion from the 300,000 odd hectares of the 1950s. With collectivization, political and economic control of the villages became very strong and illegal production and marketing of cotton was driven out almost completely. A rationing system of cotton cloth coupons was instituted in 1954 and remained in force for three decades. Because of the cotton shortage throughout China, in the 1960s and also later the cotton mills in Guanzhong could not operate at full capacity.

The increases in cotton output in Guanzhong since the 1950s were due to improvement of varieties, increased inputs of irrigation water, manure and chemical fertilizer and improved cultivation techniques. Insect damage had become particularly severe in the irrigated areas in the 1950s; insecticides became available in limited quantities only during the 1960s. Planting densities and other cultivation methods at first were rigidly imposed by administrators. After the Great Leap Forward crisis, they sobered up and left this type of decision to the village collectives which, by then, had trained a number of specialists.

Within Guanzhong, the cotton acreage actually shrank in the traditional irrigated areas but expanded considerably in dry areas. Between 1951 and 1958, their cotton acreage doubled to 14 percent of their farmland. As the counties of the dry plain received more and more irrigation facilities, they could expand cotton cultivation. Different varieties were developed for the usually somewhat colder upland areas: resistance against drought and cold and early ripening were important. Even in the plain, it is doubtful whether the heat resources are sufficient to ensure high yields except under the most favourable weather conditions. All varieties have short staple lengths.

To a certain extent, the unfavourable cotton: wheat exchange ratio, which had dampened peasants' incentives for cotton production for so long, was improved in 1975 and 1978. In the previous decade, production costs of cotton had risen much faster than yields, because of subsequent high costs of fertilizers and pesticides. Price rises were off-set by other unfavourable developments in Guanzhong: 1980 and 1981 were years of disaster and food grain received top priority. Limited by lack of heat and water, yields in west and north Guanzhong came nowhere near the yields obtained in the North China Plain. The agricultural authorities had decided in 1980 that the cotton area should be reduced and shifted towards the low-lying irrigated areas of east Guanzhong. Conflicting figures on the sown acreage since then, and, very low yields, indicate a lack of political control and consensus over cotton cultivation now and in the future.

9

AN EXPLORATION OF REGIONAL
INEQUALITY

The concept of regional inequality implies a value judgment on the existence of differentials in development level, income, political influence, and in the availability of other relevant 'social goods', between regions within a given spatial unit. Most often this unit is the nation-state, the central government of which commands great power and vast resources to reduce inequalities between individuals, economic sectors and regions. With the increased role of the modern state and its public sector, nations have become single units of taxation, currency, law, government policies, and citizens' loyalties. Sub-national 'regions', therefore, are increasingly hard to define,[1] but as a subject of study they still do serve some purposes: (a) comparison of different factor-endowments of distinctive geographical, economical or political units; (b) generalization about different impact of government policies and external change; (c) understanding of interdependent relations between regions, and between region and centre.

Economic differentials between regions are the result of many natural and man-made causes. Agriculture, mining, industry, transport, and other economic activities have always tended to utilize the natural resources of any area according to its comparative advantages. These relative advantages and disadvantages may change rapidly with changes in technology, capital, labour, prices, and so forth. In an ideal situation, locational decisions are continuously taken at all levels of society in accordance with the optimal benefit as perceived at each level: household and village, administrative levels from district upward, individual enterprises, banks and other economic organizations. The range is from the peasant who decides to have his vegetable garden close to his house, to the central government which decides to cut down sugar imports and to promote sugar beet cultivation instead. These locational decisions influence not only economic growth, but also development (in a qualitative sense) of each area. The introduction of new goods, new production methods, and new organizations, the exploitation of new sources of raw materials, new markets and new services bring about qualitative changes in society, which by their very novelty are limited in scope at first, and spread only gradually and unequally. Regional differentials in level of development may be enhanced as a consequence.

Some writers have argued that regional economic growth depends heavily on its resource endowment, location, initial regional exports, and the differing capability of such exports to generate diversification within the region.[2] Friedmann has pointed out that 'regional convergence will not automatically occur in the course of a nation's development history. Impressive evidence has been collected to show why the equilibrium mechanism that has been posited in theory will, in fact, break down. Even . . . advanced economies continue to be preoccupied with problems of depressed and backward regions inside their own national territories. Although the government can make use of technological possibilities and changing demand structures in order to promote development of peripheral economics, this is clearly a matter of deliberate planning. On the whole, unrestrained forces of a dynamic market economy appear to be working against convergence of the centre and the periphery.'[3]

For most of the past fifty years, Guanzhong's economy was very much 'deliberately planned'. During the 30s and again during the 50s, the Wei River valley was expected by many to develop from just a stepping stone to a jumping board, a basis for the development of China's northwestern provinces. These high expectations have not materialized. Over the past half century, Guanzhong has been connected more closely by road and by railroad with other parts of Shaanxi and with other provinces, and Guanzhong has been integrated politically and to some extent also economically with the nation. Economic development and technological change were largely brought in from outside, helping the region to sustain economic growth. However, internal and external dependencies have increased. The policies of 'self-reliant development' should be critically evaluated for their long-term effects on regional economic development, convergence and social inequality.

The resource endowment of Guanzhong in most respects is superior to other regions in Shaanxi province and in northwest China, notably in climate, soil, terrain and accessibility. Within Guanzhong, some natural resources with major importance for economic development are distributed unevenly. Water, heat, forests, coal, and flatland fall in this category. Some human or man-made resources, such as population, railroads, administrative or military centres et cetera, likewise are spread over Guanzhong in an uneven way. Over the past fifty years population growth, political revolution and technological change have brought about significant shifts in the economic potential of the various areas of Guanzhong, and also in the use of land and other resources mentioned above.

A. LAND USE CHANGE

Land use changes have resulted from a variety of factors. Agricultural land has been lost because of erosion (in mountain areas), desertification (owing to sand deposits along rivers or to withdrawal of water), salinization (in the low-lying areas near the Wei–Huang river confluence, and in the Luohui irrigation district)[4] and submersion (near the Sanmen reservoir below 335 m above sea level and along the shifting river channel of the Yellow River and Wei River). This happened sometimes gradually, sometimes suddenly, because of deliberate action or natural disaster. Examples of the latter are the flooding and eventual abandonment of Pingmin county, which was 'wiped off the map' by a Yellow River flood in 1942,[5] and the landslides in southwestern Guanzhong in 1981.[6] Some agricultural land was lost because of improvements of land (terracing), of water supply (irrigation and drainage ditches) or of transport to and from the fields (dirt roads). Most agricultural land, however, was lost to non-agricultural uses: housing, industry, roads, et cetera. Between 1949 and 1980, Shaanxi province suffered a loss of 739,000 ha of farmland, half of which (358,000 ha) was in Guanzhong. Because of reclamation, there has been a somewhat lower net loss of 570,000 hectares of agricultural land, 13 percent of Shaanxi's farmland area. 70 percent of this was used for construction purposes, mostly prime land.[7]

Before the war in several instances state-induced land use changes had a great effect on regional differentials. The construction of the east-west railway from the Henan border to Xi'an in 1934, and to Baoji in 1938, drove up land values in the vicinity of railway stations[8] and diverted trade and industrial activities away from traditional regional centres. The construction of large irrigation projects such as the Jinghui Ditch in 1931–5 greatly raised land values, production and income of the farmers in the Sanyuan–Gaoling–Jingyang area immediately north of Xi'an[9] – thereby creating a rich bufferzone against incursions of bandits and communists from the north. The prohibition of poppy cultivation which become gradually effective during 1935 through 1940 was a severe economic blow to the farmers in the irrigated areas along the Wei River and its southern tributaries, even if the Government softened its impact by free provision of cotton seeds.[10]

The anti-Japanese war brought changes in land use and crops under the influence of government and market forces. Xi'an, Baoji and some border towns increased rapidly in size, because of soldiers, fugitives and newly established modern cotton mills. Local handicraft industries and mines, which since the opening of the railroad had suffered competition from goods from north and east China, flourished again, because of the war blockade and increased demand.[11] State price controls severely depressed the income of cotton-growing farmers who had to sell to the new textile mills.[12] The simultaneous occurrence of an increased demand for wheat and cotton, a lower production owing to losses of labour and animals, and low official prices had quite different effects on commercial cropping in various areas: some areas increased trade, partly through black markets, while other areas witnessed a general return to self-subsistence.[13]

The above-mentioned changes in land use and its profitability had a general effect on the economic prosperity of the population of each area, but only to a certain degree. For one thing, excess labour could move to labour-short areas, for seasonal work in the newly established irrigation districts or for temporary or permanent jobs in the nascent modern economic sectors of industry or in government or army occupations. They would bring home their wages or in any case reduce the imbalance of employment and income between poor and rich areas. During the '30s both landowners and mill owners complained about the difficulty to attract local labour,[14] but that was a boom period; in earlier periods and in wartime, there had been considerable mobility of labour. During the drought of 1929–31 almost 2 million people had fled their villages, many of whom did not return.[15] War refugees were resettled in the reclamation areas of Huanglongshan (Hancheng county), of Baoji–Meixian, in the Jianshan area (Longxian–Linyou),[16] or in the cities of Xi'an, Baoji, etc. When in

1957, in connection with the construction of the giant Sanmen reservoir, 147,000 people were resettled, many of these went to Pucheng, Heyang and other counties with a favourable population: farmland ratio.[17] Until the establishment of the People's Communes in 1958 there were several waves of migrants from mountain and plain areas who 'blindly wandered out' to Xi'an[18] – attracted by new labour opportunities or pushed out by anti-commercial and anti-industrial communist policies regarding the private sector. In all above-mentioned cases, peasants 'voted with their feet' and in that way partly redressed imbalances in employment and income differentials. During the 60s and 70s, with the exception of the *xiafang* and *huixiang* movement,[19] within the collective framework no such population movements were allowed to take place any more. Thereby one corrective factor on regional differentials was outlawed.[20]

Recently, the diversion of agricultural land for other uses has been constrained by new provincial legislation. The 1958 rules had stipulated a compensation to the collective of 2 to 4 times the annual production value; in practice this meant that only about 750 *yuan* was to be paid by the State for each hectare it acquired from the collectives. As this was far below the 'market value', collectives around growing cities such as Xi'an began to rent out their land instead – at an annual rent to 15,000 to 30,000 *yuan* per hectare. 'In this way peasants could make an easy living, and were corrupted.' The new rules were meant to curb these easy and substantial profits for suburban communes.[21] However, as with many Chinese rules, no precise sanctions were indicated. Urban land shortage led to corruption with some officials of the powerful Municipal Land Acquisition Office in 1980 and 1981.[22]

New technology also changed agricultural land use and the income derived from it in various areas of Guanzhong. Mechanical ploughing and chemical fertilizer helped to develop sandy or marshy stretches along the Wei River. Most important were technical developments in irrigation. In fact, this changed geographical boundaries between agricultural regions. Traditionally, Guanzhong could be divided into three parts:

(1) The plains and terraces adjacent to and south of the Wei River were partly irrigated by the Wei River itself and by the many small southern tributaries coming down from the Qinling mountain range, or by shallow wells.

(2) The dry plains to the north of the Wei River, the so-called *Weibei pingyuan*, were sparsely settled and relied on rainfall.
(3) The northern mountain areas with sloping land and gullies engaged in extensive farming with animal husbandry.

Overall and within smaller areas this division corresponded with three types of land: *chuandi* (riverland), *pingdi* (plains land), and *podi* (slope land), of which only the first type was able to produce stable harvests and the third type had almost no value at all. Because of the construction of several large gravitational-flow irrigation systems during the 30s and 50s, the drilling of many electrical wells and the construction of pumping stations during the 70s the irrigated area of Guanzhong tripled to about 45 percent of its total farmland. The dry land border has shifted northward by an average 30 kilometers, to the so-called *hanyuan*, the dry uplands where underground water is 70 to 100 meters deep. Even at state-subsidized electricity prices water from such depths is expensive to lift. The distinction between these areas may be indicated with table 71;

This table is based not only on agrogeographical considerations, but on administrative borders as well; counties have been put as a unit into either one of the categories. In fact, however, an agrogeographical demarcation line would run right through a number of counties such as Pucheng or Yaoxian. Within each county, much finer distinctions can be made.[23]

The use of administrative units as data bases is unavoidable, but always softens up differentials between regions. Even so, the table shows clearly that because of geographical conditions, agriculture in the plain areas can support much higher population densities than the dry uplands can. Within this irrigated farmland area, a further distinction might be made between (1) areas with sufficient irrigation water under ordinary conditions (mostly stable high-yield farmland), (2) areas with irrigation facilities but with insufficient irrigation water, so that rotation irrigation must be applied (the largest of these systems are the Dongfanghong district in Weinan and the Baojixia which serve a.o. Wugong, Liquan and Qianxian), (3) areas on the *hanyuan* with irrigation water drawn from underground water at depths of 70 to 100 meters and more. Satellite pictures indicate that the first two categories each constitute a little over one-third of the 45 percent of Guanzhong's farmland now called 'irrigated'. The second and third categories have depended on state-subsidized provision of capital

Table 71 *Agrogeographical characteristics of* hanyuan *and plain, 1975*

	Weibeihanyuan	Guanzhong plain
surface (km²)	17,300	30,400
elevation (m)	800–1200	360–700
average year temperature (°C)	9–12	12–14
precipitation (mm)	500–600	540–750
acc. temp. (⩾10°C)	2700–3500	3500–4500
frostfree days	160–180	190–210
population,	2,580,000	12,450,000
of which agricultural (%)	93	80
cultivated area (ha)	597,000	1,405,000
i.e. per rural capita (ha)	0.25	0.14
density of population (pop/km²)	149	410
irrigated area (% of farmland)	10.5	58
average grain yield in 1974 (kg/ha)	1,860	3,680

Source: data from *Shaanxi Nongye Dili*, pp. 120, 164.

outlay and overheads, and on low prices for electricity. For that reason they are economically vulnerable nowadays.

The introduction of new crops, usually through state organizations, also affected land use and the income derived from it in various regions. Guanzhong used to be a one-crop-a-year area. Since the '50s, because of early ripening varieties of wheat, cotton and maize, the irrigated plain areas were enabled to cultivate two successive crops in one year (e.g. wheat and maize) or three crops in two years. Regional differentials in output, gross income and employment opportunities were widened as a consequence. Higher output and higher gross income because of double-cropping could be realized only at the cost of increased labour, more inputs of chemical fertilizer and irrigation water, and a greater vulnerability to the hazards of weather. Spring drought and early autumn frost have become great worries to the low-lying areas, but do not bother the dry uplands as much as some decades ago.

During the past few years the provincial and local authorities have paid much attention to the possibilities and desirabilities of agricultural zoning and crop specialization. Some foodgrain areas on the *hanyuan*, especially its high and mountainous parts, have been converted to pastures or fodder areas (for pork and pig manure).[24]

Cotton areas were shifted eastward and to lower altitudes, where heat and water resources are more favourable. In the west of Guanzhong, oil crops and tobacco were promoted instead.[25]

Finally, a factor in regional differentials not to be overlooked is the localized technological modernization efforts by State agricultural agencies. Over the past 50 years, the State gradually built up a network of agrotechnical stations in selected areas. Variety trials, popularization of good seeds, afforestation, irrigation techniques, pest control, cultivation techniques, etc. have been developed by what until today still is a rather limited number of agrotechnicians linked to research centres. The Northwest College of Agriculture, founded in Wugong in 1934, has established links with many villages (later: brigades) in its immediate vicinity or in nearby counties.[26] These experimental stations had an immediate positive effect on the technology and production of its host village and surrounding villages – production would be higher by 10 to 30 percent, according to one source.[27] It seems that the 'model' type approach to promotion of agricultural development has had a certain self-reinforcing effect on successful communes and counties: success brings state support and therefore breeds more success.[28]

B. ACCESSIBILITY CHANGES

Politically, socially, and economically the improvement of communications in Guanzhong over the past half a century has been of the greatest importance to human life and development. During the Great Famine of 1929–1931 almost no grain could be brought in from outside of Guanzhong.[29] The few roads built by Feng Yuxiang to the north and west of Xi'an were little used because of bandit attacks on grain convoys.[30] When the Drought struck and lasted for two successive years, the authorities were in no position to return to the rural population the foodgrain that had been taken from them during the previous years of ordinary harvest.[31] In the western parts of Guanzhong, which were least accessible and farthest away from the North China Plain, the death toll was much higher than in eastern Guanzhong, about 30 to 50 percent of the population. By 1936 most counties in west Guanzhong still had no more than 70 percent of their original population number, while in the east population was almost back to the 1929 level.[32]

During the anti-Japanese war the road system was further extended, especially the connections with south Shaanxi and from there with Sichuan province and the rest of Free China.[33] The new railroad and road systems (on Guanzhong's shallow rivers, waterway transport never amounted to very much) redirected the existing trade flows. Some traditional market centers lost much of their trade. Along the ancient silk road Fengxiang, which had not fully recovered yet from the Famine, sank into oblivion as the hitherto insignificant city of Baoji was built up as a trade and industrial center during the war and the First Five-Year Plan period. The completion of the Chengdu-Baoji railway in 1956, further reinforced Baoji's position as a link between Guanzhong, Hanzhong (southern Shaanxi) and Sichuan province.[34] In the east, Dali lost much of its function as a regional market to Tongguan, both because of the railroad and the war.[35] Sanyuan had been the second largest city of the province. 'Commercially it is an annex to Xi'an, much of the commerce which really belongs to the latter being transacted here to avoid the official exactions of the provincial capital. For the same reason most of the trade to and from Gansu passes through Sanyuan.'[36] During the 1930s a considerable government and Christian missionary effort went into Sanyuan county, but it lost most of its trade to Xianyang, and was left out when industrialization started.

The railway lines to the mines of Hancheng and Tongchuan built in the 1960s improved communications in northeastern Guanzhong and stimulated the agricultural economy and trade.[37] On the northwestern side of Guanzhong, however, the traditional trade routes through the mountains via Fengxiang or Changwu to Gansu and Ningxia dwindled into insignificance.

Already during the war, and still so at present, there is an obvious correlation between the level of income and economic development of the various counties in Guanzhong and the presence of railroad communications.[38] Contrary to expectations, however, no such correlation can be established between the level of income and development and highway network density.[39] This may be due partly to insufficient and/or incomparable data, partly to the influence of geographical factors. A possible explanation may also be found in the fact that the highway network which has been created since the mid-sixties was grossly underutilized, because of lack of trucks and tractors, congestion by carts and pedestrians and because of institutional barriers to trade – such an underutilization is apparent from data on transport volumes and from my own observations in Guanzhong in 1979. In table 6 a comparison has been made between 7 counties, two of which are densely populated and mostly flat (Wugong, Weinan), two of which are thinly populated and mostly mountainous (Hancheng) or heavily intersected by gullies (Chunhua), and three of which are somewhere in between (Liquan, Qianxian and Pucheng).

Few conclusions can be drawn from combining the data in tables 6 and 70. The 1965 and 1978 figures show a correlation between highway length per square kilometer and population density, which is little surprising. Correlation with income figures is very weak.[40]

The economic effect of proximity to trade centers and roads is reduced by State subsidizing policies. State sales prices are generally fixed without regard to differentials in transport costs, and so are State purchase prices for cereals and some other main agricultural products. After the harvest, temporary grain purchase stations are set up by the State in rural towns and at the village level. In the 1970s, those peasants who had to transport their grain over a distance longer than 15 km were recompensed for extra transport costs. So at least for collective production, differentials in transport costs are kept down by the State – an essential part of the policy of self-reliant development, by which every village is meant to have equal opportunity. The liberalization of trade and decollectiviation policies of recent years have again given greater weight to the marketing and transport factor, and thereby to differentials due to location.

C. INDUSTRIAL CHANGE AND LOCATION: A COMPARISON OF THE 1940S AND 1970S

Modern industrial development was brought to Guanzhong only in the late 30s after the extension of the Longhai railroad to Xi'an and Baoji. The anti-Japanese war, by cutting off imports into Guanzhong from occupied China, led to a rapid increase both of modern and of traditional industries. By 1943 there were 247 registered industries in Shaanxi, with 7000 Hp of motive power. Cotton textile plants came first, machinery plants second. 55 percent of these were located in Xi'an, 20 percent in Baoji, and the remaining one-quarter in smaller towns such as Xianyang, Weinan and Tongguan. Most of the factories were of a very small scale; the larger ones all had been established with capital from outside the province.[41] Most factories were closely connected with agricultural production.

Improved iron looms which were gradually introduced during the

30s had helped the traditional weaving industry to survive. But its character changed: apart from village handicraft production with old-type wooden looms, many new small-scale factories with several scores of iron looms were set up in the towns. The few large modern textile mills had much to suffer from Japanese bombings, government supervision, technical failures and lack of qualified personnel; although they maintained their dominant position in spinning, they could not compete well in weaving. After the war four regional centres of small-scale textile production had emerged: Xi'an with 110 factories, Sanyuan with 55 factories, Baoji with 45 factories, and the Xingping–Liquan–Qianxian area with a flourishing cottage industry.[42]

In response to the demands of a rapidly increasing city population during the war, Xi'an and Baoji became major centers of the flour industry. By 1948, of the 16 flour mills in Shaanxi province 9 were located in Xi'an. The largest two of these produced 70,000 sacks of flour per month each, the other seven together produced about 100,000 sacks. Total employment was 980 people.[43]

Cotton packing factories had been established near the production centers, in Xianyang, Weinan and Tongguan in 1935–7. The first two each had a packing capacity of 700 bales (of 300 kg) per day, using modern machinery, and a labour force of over 3,000 people during the busiest season.

Oil pressing was mostly a sideline activity of village landlords and spread all over Guanzhong. Installations were very simple: a millstone, a kettle, and a wooden press. At least 8 kinds of vegetable oils were produced in Guanzhong, most of which were edible as well as combustible. A large-scale modern oil press factory was established in Xianyang in 1936, but it failed after two years.[44] The same fate was suffered by a modern wine-distillery.

Wine-distilleries (using sorghum) were a traditional industry of Fengxiang in mountainous west Guanzhong. Other northern counties produced linen (Longxian), woolens and leather (Dali) and paper (Pucheng and Fengxiang). These industries generally were of a seasonal character, and of a private (family) type.[45]

In the large towns, industries not related to agriculture often had been set up or backed by the Government: the electrical works in Xi'an and Baoji, the pharmaceutical factory in Hancheng (greatly expanded because of the war), the match factories (also in Xi'an and Baoji), the acid factory, the cement factories in the Baishui–Pucheng region, the tobacco factory (which used tobacco and paper from outside Shaanxi), all of which were established between 1935 and 1939. The coal mines in the Hancheng–Baishui–Chengcheng–Tongchuan belt and the small Yaoxian Iron Works also had a large State involvement.

By 1949 the modern industrial basis of Guanzhong still was very weak, very much dominated by the government, and very concentrated in Xi'an and Baoji. Handicraft industry was well developed and spread throughout the region, but with local specialization on the basis of the presence of raw materials or locational advantages. For that matter, processing industries sometimes added little to the agricultural product, e.g. in the case of bamboo (Huaxian), medicinal herbs (Qinling mountains) or peanut oil (Dali). By far the largest employment and labour-added value was in cotton textiles, where large-scale modern industry, small-scale industry, and cottage industry co-existed, each with its own products and markets.[46]

When we contrast this pre-1949 industrial situation with the one found in the 1970s, it is not immediately clear what had happened in some industries, and what effect industrial growth or decline may have had on regional differentials in production and income. Statistical data on the contribution of industry to local employment and income are scarce, except for large-scale state-owned industries. Some major developments can be outlined:

—industrial activities were increasingly concentrated in the cities and towns of Guanzhong. This has been due both to technological development (within industry itself and because of infrastructural needs such as energy supply) and to state industrial and trade policies inimical to cottage industry: the state cotton monopoly in 1953, the forced collectivization and nationalization of 1956, the concentration of rural industries in People's Commune seats in 1958–1960 and the interdiction of home handicraft production since the Cultural Revolution. Even in the 1980s, many economic activities still were not allowed to individuals or enterprises not controlled by the state – notably cotton spinning and weaving. In 1981, the Xi'an municipal government stipulated that peasants could engage in private business in 8 fields, but not in 'mechanized transport work, buying presses etc. to carry on processing, opening up hotels, selling large livestock, peddling industrial products without permission from the industrial and commercial departments, and masquerading as labour contractors'.[47]

Plate 9 Blacksmiths repairing a blade.

—modern industrial expansion was concentrated in Xi'an and a few other cities. By 1983, the second largest city, Baoji, had only one-fifth of the industrial output of Xi'an. Coal mines in Tongchuan and Hancheng and a cement factory in Yaoxian took exception to this. This concentration was due to the war, state industrial planning policies and limited transport facilities.

—the gross value of industrial production in Shaanxi increased greatly. Between 1949, 1970 and 1980 output value rose 19-fold and 39-fold, respectively, and its share of the total gross production value increased from 17.8 percent to 66 and 76 percent, respectively.[48] Since the 50s, with some exceptions, industrial development has slowed down because of under-investment and lack of raw materials such as cotton. By the end of the 70s, technology and productivity had fallen behind other industrial areas of China.[49]

—Since 1965, in the towns of Guanzhong the growth of county-managed collective industries has been more rapid than that of county-managed, state-owned industries. In the seven counties mentioned in tables 72 to 74, with a total city population of 195,000 people in 1978, total employment in state-owned industries rose from 9,300 labourers in 1965 to 14,600 labourers in 1978 and in urban collective industries from 4,700 people in 1965 to 15,200 people in 1978.[50] During the 1974–8 period employment in the former category had been surpassed by the latter. Thus, it appears that employment in state-owned industries was concentrated in the larger cities, while the smaller towns had to develop their own collective industries. Wages and other labour conditions were definitely better in state industries. Between counties differentials in employment, productivity and growth rate were large.

At first sight, it would seem that state-owned industries had a far higher productivity than urban collective industries, because their average gross output value per labourer was three times as high. However, this was not necessarily so, as the primary difference lay with branches of industry, from 2,000 *yuan* in cement to 35,000 *yuan* in textiles. In foodstuffs and edible oil, the added value is very little; in textiles, the prescribed profit rate is very high; with building materials, in contrast, the output value is made up almost completely of labour costs. Within the same branch, more often than not the largest few collective industries, with an average size of about 100 labourers, would have a considerably lower gross output value per labourer than the state-owned industries, which were four times as large on the average. However, the gap was closing; between 1974 and 1978, the collective industries saw their GOV per labourer increase by 45 percent – more than twice as much as the state industries. Since 1979, official Chinese publications invariably cite examples of collective industries being superior in productivity to state industries.[51] Many small-size industries were privatized.

—within the towns of Guanzhong there has been a fluctuating labour force of peasants with temporary employment (legal or not). In 1978, the size of this labour force (whose wages and living conditions were always open to negotiation, but never on a par with town residents) almost equalled the two categories mentioned above.[52] Most of their income reverted to the suburban communes of which they were members.

Table 72 *All county industries in seven counties, 1974–1978*

	State-owned				Collectively-owned			
	Labour force (1,000)		Gross ind. output value (million yuan)		Labour force (1,000)		Gross ind. output value (million yuan)	
	1974	1978	1974	1978	1974	1978	1974	1978
Weinan	3.6	3.5	40.5	55.7	5.5	9.8	9.4	21.2
Pucheng	3	3	18.2	33.2	1	1	3.9	16.7
Hancheng	2.4	3.2	7.6	22.2	0.7	0.8	2.1	3.7
Wugong	1.4	2.3	6.0	11.0	0.4	0.5	4.1	8.0
Qianxian ×	–	0.6	–	0.4	–	0.1	–	0.3
Liquan	1	1	12.4	15.2	1.5	2.4	2.3	5.0
Chunhua	0.6	1	2.7	4.1	0.2	0.6	0.6	1.1
Total	12	14.6	87.4	141.8	9.3	15.2	22.4	55

× data possibly corrupt.
Source: data from county statistical bureaus.

—collective enterprises (a wider concept than industries) run by People's Communes and brigades steadily increased in number, labour force and income. In Shaanxi province in 1979 and 1980 552,000 and 601,000 peasants respectively were employed in these enterprises (some 5 percent of the rural labour force). Total production value was 630 million *yuan* in 1978, 930 million *yuan* in 1980 and 1,300 million *yuan* in 1983.

These enterprises are heavily concentrated in the rural areas of Xi'an and its neighbouring counties of Changan and Huxian and in other counties in the irrigated areas of Guanzhong.[53] In the case of Changan county, their output value rose tenfold between 1971 and 1982.[54]

By 1983, however, the profitability of these enterprises had declined to 18.5 percent of their turnover (before taxes), down from 26.5 percent in 1978. 'Expenses have increased abruptly. Wages and bonuses have risen fast, 1.6 times as much as the taxes and profits handed over to the government and to the collectives. The quality of

Table 73 *Largest state-owned industries in seven counties, 1974–1978*

A. State-owned industries (largest four in each county)	County	Number of labourers		Gross output value (1,000 yuan)		Gross output value per labourer (yuan)	
		1974	1978	1974	1978	1974	1978
Foodstuffs	Weinan	402	407	10,497	13,930	26,112	34,226
Spinning/weaving	Weinan	457	439	15,513	15,080	33,945	34,351
Machinery	Weinan	929	956	4,586	6,941	4,936	7,260
Chemical industry	Weinan	871	846	6,460	15,029	7,417	17,765
Spinning/weaving	Pucheng	199	218	1,824	1,598	9,166	7,330
Chemical fertilizer (N)	Pucheng	433	666	1,049	3,240	2,423	4,865
Coal	Pucheng	154	428	28	952	182	2,224
Transformers	Pucheng	–	359	–	4,640	–	12,925
Chemical fertilizers	Hancheng	276	409	425	2,029	1,540	4,961
Cement	Hancheng	167	194	213	408	1,275	2,103
Cokes (?)	Hancheng	1,223	1,109	2,435	2,382	1,991	2,148
Cotton goods	Wugong	230	273	926	1,334	4,026	4,886
Agricultural machinery	Wugong	308	320	1,125	1,011	3,653	3,159
Chemical fertilizers	Wugong	–	465	–	1,787	–	3,843
Pesticides	Wugong	199	254	1,159	2,660	5,824	10,472
Edible oil	Qianxian	–	66	–	1,954	–	29,606
Agricultural machinery	Qianxian	–	158	–	580	–	3,671
Electrical machinery	Qianxian	–	280	–	1,051	–	3,754
Printing	Qianxian	–	100	–	431	–	4,310
Foodstuffs	Liquan	130	109	3,220	2,560	24,769	23,486
Textiles, leather, sewing	Liquan	340	129	6,352	8,570	18,682	66,434
Machinery	Liquan	341	387	1,359	1,640	3,985	4,238
Building materials	Liquan	357	333	706	1,270	1,978	3,814

		Work force				Gross output value per labourer (yuan)		Percentage change
		1974	1978	1974	1978	1974	1978	
Machinery	Chunhua	205	262	577	722	2,815	2,756	
Building materials	Chunhua	70	129	166	441	2,371	3,419	
Cokes	Chunhua	153	314	400	1,052	2,614	3,350	
Total of 27 (21 in 1974)		7,540	9,766	60,161	94,389			
Average		359	362	2,865	3,496	7,979	9,665	+21%
Weinan only		2,659	2,648	37,056	50,980	13,936	19,252	+38%
other six counties		4,881	7,118	23,105	43,409	4,734	6,098	+29%

B. Industrial branches (15–19 industries of A)	No. of factories	Work force		Gross output value per labourer (yuan)		Percentage change
		1974	1978	1974	1978	
Foodstuffs and edible oil	3–4	628	738	23,660	26,478	+12%
Spinning, textiles, leather	3	1,006	786	23,548	32,122	+36%
(Agricultural) machinery	4–6	1,783	2,636	4,289	5,055	+18%
Chemical fertilizer	2–3	709	1,540	2,079	4,582	+120%
Building materials, cement	3	449	656	2,416	3,230	+34%

Source: data from county statistical bureaus.

Table 74 *Largest collectively-owned industries in seven counties, 1974–1978*

Collectively-owned industries (largest three in each county)	County	Number of labourers		Gross output value (1,000 yuan)		Gross output value per labourer		% change
		1974	1978	1974	1978	1974	1978	
Towels	Weinan	240	297	902	1,274	3,758	4,290	
Clothing	Weinan	192	214	1,294	2,493	6,740	11,650	
Copper	Weinan	94	154	558	823	5,936	5,344	
Wood processing	Pucheng	58	59	182	329	3,138	5,576	
Ceramics	Pucheng	81	122	378	495	4,667	4,057	
Agricultural implements	Pucheng	96	76	320	288	3,333	3,789	
Paper	Hancheng	38	64	139	610	3,658	9,531	
Printing	Hancheng	62	71	379	563	6,113	7,930	
Ploughshares	Hancheng	70	67	151	326	2,157	4,866	
Irrigation	Wugong	133	147	701	1,479	5,271	10,061	
Agricultural implements	Wugong	90	72	255	463	2,833	6,431	
Daily utensils	Wugong	39	51	72	329	1,846	6,451	
Sewing	Qianxian	–	50	–	342	–	6,840	
Assemblage	Liquan	62	65	346	500	5,581	7,692	
Tannery	Liquan	41	43	149	200	3,634	4,651	
Textiles	Liquan	–	40	–	350	–	8,750	
Handicrafts	Chunhua	24	24	176	350	7,333	14,583	
Printing	Chunhua	20	37	86	115	4,300	3,108	
Bricks	Chunhua	59	125	135	172	2,288	1,376	
Total of 19 (17 in 1974)		1,399	1,778	6,223	11,501	4,448	6,469	+45%
Weinan only		526	665	2,754	4,590	5,236	6,902	+32%
other six counties		873	1,113	3,469	6,911	3,974	6,209	+56%

Plate 10 Chalk factory in a Weinan village.

the products is not good enough, there is much hoarding, too much capital is tied up for too long.'[55]

More narrowly defined, collective industries, run by People's Communes and within towns, numbered 7,800 in 1982; they employed 390,000 people and had an output value of 1,550,000,000 *yuan*, 23.4 percent up on 1978.[56]

—rural households, after collectivization in 1956, were still allowed to make some industrial products, to be sold through the collective. Recently more liberal policies have allowed private persons to engage in commercial and certain industrial activities. The so-called 'keypoint households' (*zhongdianhu*) and 'specialized households' (*zhuanyehu*), however, are mainly engaged in specialized agricultural production (pigs, chickens, fruits etc). In a 1982 survey of household sidelines in Changan county, weaving and matting (using stalks of wheat, rice etc.) and other handicrafts accounted for 20 percent of all sideline production.[57] Most of the household industry is for own use (house repairs, furniture, utensils, agricultural tools etc. and does not compete with agricultural labour; it does not for that part enter into official statistics on production and consumption. It should be taken into account, however, when one compares rural living conditions between regions, and with city life – particularly housing.

—industry has contributed rather little to employment for the growing population of Guanzhong. According to official statistics, in 1940 about 7 percent of the working population of Guanzhong was employed in handicraft industry, and 1.1 percent in transport. Only a part of this industry has remained in the villages, most of it was transferred to the towns and cities. Urban industrial labourers numbered 58,000 in 1949 and 284,000 in 1956, most of which in Guanzhong.[58]

Around 1975, in most counties of Guanzhong the urbanization rate was between 3 and 12 percent, only little more than before the anti-Japanese war. On the *hanyuan* (13 counties, 1 *shi*) 93 percent of the population was agricultural in the Guanzhong plain (24 counties, 3 *shi*) 80 percent. The industrial labour force in those counties was only one to five percent of the total labour force. Even a well-developed agricultural county with railroad access, such as Wugong, had almost no industry.[59]

—the low-wage policy of the national government; the low productivity in state enterprises and the growing employment in collective urban enterprises, with below-average wages, all led to a stagnation and real decline of urban wages during the 1960s and 1970s. Only because the labourer: dependent ratio was raised could real incomes improve somewhat. Between 1978 and 1982, the average nominal wage of labourers and employees in the urban sector of Shaanxi rose from 654 *yuan* to 797 *yuan*, or by 22 percent, not all of which was eaten up by inflation, and the dependency ratio went further down from 1.06 to 0.7. The national improvement of the urban:rural income gap (from 2.36:1 in 1978 to 1.85:1 in 1982) occurred in Shaanxi as well, although because of relatively low rural incomes the urban average income of 456 *yuan* in 1982 still was more than double the average rural income of 222 *yuan*.[60]

The data in a Xi'an survey[61] show a somewhat larger increase of income than subsequent provincial data do for the urban population as a whole. 58 percent of the nominal increase between 1957 and 1982 was realized between 1978 and 1982.[62] The improvement of the food basket is evident also in expenditure on tobacco, liquor, tea, fruit, milk and preserves, which rose from 12 percent of food expenditure in 1957 to 24 percent in 1981.

Other cities and towns in Guanzhong may have rather different patterns of income and expenditure, and also of housing. Especially for the contract labour category, there have been serious complaints about the lack of facilities.[63] One gets the feeling that the industrial revolution starts over and over again, and that the process of adaptation to industrial life has not yet gone very far in the smaller towns of Guanzhong. Poor working conditions from which the Xi'an and Xianyang industrial workers wer liberated in 1949[64] have now arisen elsewhere in the area. Differences between the way modern and backward companies treat their workers are still just as great as they were before the war:

The treatment of coal miners in the mechanized mines in Baishui and Tongchuan is rather good. Miners who get injured at work receive support and medical treatment from the companies. Food and drink during the rest period are provided by the companies . . . They do not have to pay rent for the caves they live in, and also have washing facilities. However, local mines elsewhere do not have this kind of facilities. Some even raise food prices to extort the miners. Their life is miserable . . . There is insufficient light and air, sometimes they are not allowed to come up for several days. Child workers are hired, there is arbitrary flogging . . .[65]

Also, the composition of the population in small towns resembles the pre-1949 situation of Xi'an: a very high M:F ratio because of the presence of many temporary male labourers from the countryside. Urban facilities of education, communication and health have improved beyond recognition, but that goes for the countryside as well.

D. LANDHOLDING AND SOCIAL DIFFERENTIALS IN THE 1930S

The Famine of 1929–31, contrary to the convential picture drawn by communist sources,[66] further reduced the already modest levels of inequality of landholding and income in the villages of Guanzhong. West Guanzhong was hit most severely; in some counties the population was reduced by over one-half. Access to outside help was a matter of life and death, but owing to lack of communications and to the political and military isolation of Feng Yuxiang, no help had been forthcoming. Land prices dropped to almost nothing and for several years much agricultural land was left fallow. Because of the economic

Table 75 *Class differentiation in Fengxiang county, 1928 and 1931*

	Before disaster (1928)	After disaster (1931)	Percentage change
Landlords (households)	129	56	−43%
farmer-owners (households)	25,552	18,643	−27%
tenant-farmers (households)	1,048	843	−20%
hired labourers (persons)	3,532	1,932	−45%
unemployed (persons)	4,009	10,399	+259%
total rural population (p.)	204,183	139,134	−32%
average household size (p.)	5.96	4.37	−27%

Source: investigation by the Shaanxi army, *Zhongguo Nongcun Jingji Ziliao*, p. 787.

breakdown, there was a temporary increase in the number of unemployed. An example from western Guanzhong is shown in Table 75.

The decrease in the number of landlords as shown in Table 76, and in their average amount of landholdings, is testified by several surveys. The remaining, comparatively well-to-do, farmer-owners bought up much land after the landlords and the poor had fled. Also the other surviving peasants eventually could profit from the lowered population:farmland ratio after the Famine had killed off the oldest, youngest, weakest and poorest. It took several years, however, to regain economic strength in most areas;[67] eastern Guanzhong was less afflicted, but landholding by landlords declined there, too. In the four villages of Weinan county in Table 76 the landlord families rented out about 40 percent of their land, both in 1928 and in 1933. Rich peasants rented out nothing in 1928 and 6 percent of their landholdings in 1933. Middle peasants rented 1 to 2 percent. Poor peasants rented 7 percent of their land in use in 1928 and 11 percent in 1933.

From these and other data for Guanzhong for the '30s it appears that the main social and economic distinction and potential conflict was at the bottom of village society, not at the top. The poorest peasants and hired labourers often could not afford to marry and were the first to be hit by disaster. For many of them, this was only a temporary phase linked to their age (85 percent of the hired labourers was between 15 and 35 years of age), but some were on the brink of starvation and banditry for their whole lives.[68] Landownership and

Table 76 Landholding per household and per capita of different classes in four villages in Weinan county, 1928 and 1933

	1928			1933		
	(no. of households)	per household (mou)	per capita (mou)	(no. of households)	per household (mou)	per capita (mou)
Landlords	3	81	16	3	55	11
Rich peasants	15	80	9.8	14	54	8.7
Middle peasants	67	34	6.9	57	32	6.6
Poor peasants	114	15.6	3.0	136	13.4	2.9
Others	5	–	–	7	–	–
Average		27			21	
Total farmland		5571 mou			4744 mou	
Of which owned by outsiders		44 mou			167 mou	
Percentage of farmland given into pawn		5.3%			15.2%	

$(mou = \frac{1}{15} ha)$

Source: Nongfuhui, Shaanxisheng Nongcun Diaocha, Nanjing 1934.

wealth may have been much more equally distributed than in the Suide and Yanan area, which dominated communist history writing. However, the difference between middle peasants and poor peasants was substantial, similar to the one in Long Bow village described by William Hinton.[69]

Between various regions in Guanzhong there were great differentials in population density, amount of farmland per capita, land prices, crops and indebtedness of the peasantry. These differences were mostly linked to farmland productivity and to proximity to urban markets. Differences in population densities between counties appear from map 2, which shows high concentrations in the low-lying areas along the Wei River. Two surveys held in 1937 of eight counties throughout Guanzhong gave some indications of differentials between counties. Apart from averages and highest and lowest values, I have presented separately Wugong county in west Guanzhong and Pucheng county in east Guanzhong separately in Table 77.

Between wealth, household size and farm size a high degree of correlation existed *within* each county in this survey. Between averages of counties, there was no such correlation or even a negative one. The most backward counties had the largest farms and households.[70] In the six counties of Table 77 'rich' peasants (5.9 percent) had an average household size of 9.97 persons (11.03 if labourers and distant relatives were included). The 'poor' peasants (38.5 percent) had an average household size of 4.47 persons, and the middle category (55.6 percent) had an average household size of 6.25 persons. Per capita amount of farmland was smallest in irrigated areas along the Wei River and near cities, and largest up north on the *hanyuan*.

Most peasants owned the land they cultivated. Only a few percent were tenant farmers. 10 to 20 percent were semi-owner, semi-tenant. More detailed surveys of single counties during the 30s show a small farm size and comparatively high rate of tenancy only in the most productive farming areas, e.g. in Sanyuan and Xianyang. In Wugong county's irrigated south, three-quarters of the peasant farms were smaller than 10 *mou*, but in its dry north, 80 percent were larger than 15 *mou*. The average farm consisted of three scattered plots.[71] There were no large landholdings. Landlords generally were farmers themselves, very few were merchants or had other professions. Landlord–tenant agreements were orally made, for a non-fixed time. Baoji county still had a share-crop rent system. In Wugong, fixed rents (paid in kind) averaged 34 percent of agricultural output value or 11

Table 77 *Rural economic data for 6 counties, 1937*

		Average 6 counties	Highest value	Lowest value	Wugong	Pucheng
farmland area	per household (*mou* = $\frac{1}{15}$ ha)	29.4	57	12.3	22.5	57
	per capita (*mou* = $\frac{1}{15}$ ha)	5.0	9.7	2.3	3.7	9.7
Landownership (%)	owners	83	91.4	67	90	81.7
	semi-owners	14.8	5	26.9	9	17.3
	tenants	2.2	1	5.4	1	1
land prices 1927	(*yuan per mou*)	16.3	30.3	6.4	22.7	6.4
1937	(*yuan per mou*)	17.0	28.9	6.1	20.5	6.1
average debt per household (*yuan*)		104	169	57	68	169
population density (p. per sq. km)		277	595	143	374	143
average village pop. (p.)		293	447	163	292	163
crops	wheat (% of farmland area)	36.3	50	23.4	23.4	50
	maize (% of farmland area)	15.0	28.7	0	21.8	0
	millet (% of farmland area)	18.2	38.0	6.7	10.2	38
	cotton (% of farmland area)	12.4	30.4	0	17.1	6.3
	poppy (% of farmland area)	2.6	9.5	0	9.5	0
	sorghum (% of farmland area)	9.7	39.9	0	7.3	2.1
family size 1927	(p. per household)	6.95	8.56	6.03	8.56	6.03
1937	(p. per household)	5.78	6.23	5.25	5.94	5.77
population 1930	(% of 1928)	73.8	98	60.2	47.7	81.3
1937	(% of 1928)	85.8	123.1	64.5	64.5	94.4

Sources: Nan Bingfang, 'A preliminary analysis of rural financial problems in Guanzhong in Shaanxi', *Xibei Nonglin* Special Issue, 1938; Jiang Jie, 'An investigation of rural finance in Guanzhong', *ibidem*. 1012 Households were surveyed in Wugong, Zhouzhi, Fengxiang, Jingyang, Pucheng and Huayin counties.

percent of the land value; in Weinan, money rents amounted to 23 percent of the output value and 4 percent of the land value. These may be considered moderate rents. Tenant-farmers moreover were expected to present gifts at festivals and to assist the landlord with marriages and funerals.[72]

E. RURAL ECONOMIC IMPACT OF GUOMINDANG GOVERNMENT

We have noted above agro-geographical differentials between mountain areas in northwestern Guanzhong, the Qinling mountain valleys, the low-lying irrigated stretch of land along the Wei River and the dry upland plain north of the Wei River. Since the 30s two other important differential factors made themselves felt, one cultural, the other political. Both arose from the modernization and build-up of state organizations by the Guomindang Government and were closely connected with the improvement of communications, construction of railways and irrigation systems and credit extension. Western Guanzhong and also the northernmost counties (mountainous and close to the communists) remained almost unaffected by these developments, while the rural areas of central and eastern Guanzhong, especially those near the railway, caught up with modern times. Contemporary sources described the western areas as exhausted by the Famine, very backward and unsafe.[73] Footbinding was common in the west but already rare in the east. The male/female ratio was higher (1.16 in the west, 1.10 in the east), death rates were higher (21.3/1,000 as against 16.6/1,000) and less education was received (49.6% of the men and 2.9% of the women in the east, as against 44.4 resp. 0.1% in the west). 'Culture in the Guanzhong villages has stopped at the 18th–19th century.'[74] Xi'an newspapers ran stories such as this:

There was a case in Tongzhuang (in Longxian county) of a landlord who killed some people. This was not reported according to law to the authorities by the public or the *baojia* chief. Instead they held a public village meeting which took away this landlord's property and sold it for 600 *yuan*, which became public property of all villagers. Thereupon the public ate and drank on a big scale, and spent over 300 *yuan*. This kind of illegal conduct is thought to be very normal by the people of this area . . .[75]

Quite in contrast with this, a modern efficient rural bureaucracy was created in the newly developed irrigation districts in order to manage distribution of water, maintenance of canals and ditches and collection of water fees. It survived war and revolution and even the People's Commune.[76]

Within the framework of the cooperative movement promoted by the Guomindang Government after 1934, loans were extended both by banks and by government agencies to the rural areas. Most of the bank loans went to the three cotton counties next to Xi'an and very little to the northern counties. (see page 292–4). In 1941, the Government decided to supply extra relief loans to counties bordering on or taken from the communist area.[77]

There were darker sides to government official activities as well. Military and political power was commonly used to private ends. The construction of new roads, railroads, irrigation projects etc. gave ample opportunities to the powerful to get rich by land speculation.

Acquisition of land is mostly by military men, or merchants . . . Factors are economic (high interest on loans, which peasants cannot repay) or political. Private gangs of those with political or military power, together with local evil gentry, force peasants to sell. Official organizations, such as the Agricultural College, and the North China Relief Society (which during the Famine bought land on a large scale, on which it has built an orphanage now) have also forced people to sell their land. The Longhai Railroad Bureau, the Weihui Irrigation Ditch Bureau, the Xi'an–Fengxian Highway Bureau etc. all have done the same . . . A certain VIP from Xi'an bought cheaply over 2,000 *mou* of farmland after the Famine in 1933. Nowadays part of this has been rented out, the other part is worked by several dozen of hired labourers and sown to poppy.[78]

Thus, the modernizing areas in central and eastern Guanzhong could not but undergo both the benefits and the burdens of economic and political development and of integration with Republican China. During the war, the peasants' burden in Guanzhong and other areas of Free China was certainly heavy, even without the horrors of Japanese occupation. The tax burden and military exactions took away most of the peasants' surplus and often even more than that. During the last year of the war (Oct. 1944 till Sept. 1945) the average tax burden of the Guanzhong rural household was about 200,000 *yuan*[79] (enough to buy 50 kg of cotton). Although few data have been presented to that effect, it is likely that military exactions bore most heavily on the population near transportation routes and on the rich.

The military burden of war became heavy as well. By 1939, over 200,000 soldiers had been recruited by the Guomindang Government from Shaanxi. More than half of these deserted. Trading in recruits was widespread, and prices for recruits rose fast. The highest prices were fetched in counties near to possible battlefields (Hancheng, Heyang) and in affluent counties such as Sanyuan.[80]

The negative effects of wartime price controls and inflation on the commercial crop areas (especially the cotton districts) have been touched upon above. A survey of living expenses in 24 counties in Guanzhong between 1936 and 1941 showed that foodgrain and fuel expenditure increased by 8 and 6 times, respectively. Together, these items took 61 percent of the average rural household budget in 1936, but as much as 73 percent in 1941. Expenses for medicine, education and religion suffered most (see table 78).

F. REGIONAL DIFFERENTIALS UNDER COMMUNISM: SELFRELIANCE AND DEPENDENCY

In which way did Chinese agricultural development policies affect regional differentials in Guanzhong?

Before the war the mountainous areas of west Guanzhong and the Qinling used to have an economy rather different from the dry land farmers of the *hanyuan*. Over the past 30 years, much of the diversified mountain economy has been lost, for many reasons. The mountain population has more than doubled. Extension of grain cultivation and ruthless exploitation of forest resources have led to large-scale erosion and loss of natural vegetation cover. Exchange of products with the plain areas was made more difficult after collectivization reduced private trade. The rising prices of foodgrain worked against the mountain farmer, too.

Foodgrain prices used to be very low in the mountain areas, but by 1965 prices were on a par with those in plain areas. During the early 50s, as before, most of the pigs were raised in mountain areas: therefore the massive slaughter of animals which followed early collectivization drives and the Great Leap Forward especially hurt the mountain village economy.[81] The formation of very large People's Communes in 1958, which often included both plain and mountain areas, meant a temporary connection, if not equalization, between the two which was broken off because of the 1960–1961 famine. It also meant the end of migration from mountain people to the plains. Only very recently has direct economic cooperation between some villages in the mountain and plain areas been reestablished. Data on mountain areas are of a considerably lesser quality than those on the plain areas,

Table 78 *Average living expenses of a rural household in 1936 and 1941 (yuan)*

	1936	1941	Increase		1936	1941	Increase
foodgrain	170.1	1408.6	8.3	medicine	8.2	33.5	4.1
fuel	26.1	153.6	5.9	education	31.2	125.0	4.0
meat,							
vegetables	26.5	125.5	4.7	religion	5.1	16.7	3.3
clothes	29.4	151.4	5.1	amusement	2.9	19.7	6.8
other food	9.5	44.9	4.7	miscellanea	12.9	60.6	4.7

Source: Survey undertaken by the Northwest Agricultural College in August 1941, Northwest Agricultural College (ed.), *Shaanxisheng zhi Nongye Jianshe*, Wugong, 1942.

so one should be very cautious in the interpretation of the very low income and production figures commonly supplied by mountain villages.[82] Nowadays, both because of individualized production and because of freer marketing policies for their products (pork, goat milk, etc.) mountain areas experience more than other areas the ups and downs of market demand and prices.

The 'suburban' regions of Guanzhong can no longer be defined in the same way as during the '30s. Because of improved transportation they have a longer radius, maybe 25 kilometers by road instead of 10. Also their scope has been considerably increased because of the growth of the cities of Xi'an–Xianyang to a population of 1.6 million, of Baoji to 300,000 and of Tongchuan to 200,000. However, still no more than 12 percent of Shaanxi's population lives in cities and county capitals.[83] Most county capitals in Guanzhong have only 5,000 to 30,000 inhabitants. In county capitals it appears that the urban-rural symbiosis and exchange of labour and products have not changed so much since the '30s. The contribution of collective enterprises to suburban rural income has been referred to above. The sales of vegetables and pork and more recently of chickens and eggs are major sources of income for suburban farmers. Less opportunities are available to farmers living away from cities.

Until 1982, in most areas rural income did not show much increase over the 1930s. However, living conditions had improved beyond comparison. Health, education, relief, a rural infrastructure of roads, electricity and telecommunications were not always tangible, yet these are vital parts of the quality of life. In the provision of these social services, the socialist state took great care to provide an equal distribution to all. In the private sphere, however, social and economic distinctions between rich and poor could not be obliterated. Weddings, for instance, remained costly and ceremonial affairs, and very hard to afford for a young mountain farmer.

'From betrothal to marriage, one generally must spend more than one thousand *yuan* . . .'

'Youngsters have to work for ten years, kill themselves or flee or go stealing . . .'

Those in the mountains want to marry someone outside the mountains. Those in the village want to marry someone in town. Manual workers want someone working with his brains etc . . . Money, power and position lead the mind astray. This is all very unsocialistic!'[84]

For an appraisal of regional differentials, net income from production is only one yardstick out of many. During the '70s it is suggested by available data that regional income differentials in Guanzhong had increased somewhat over the 30s and 50s, and amounted roughly to 1 (dry upland plain, *hanyuan*): 2 (partly irrigated plain): 3 (suburban irrigated areas near Xi'an). Historical data on income development in seven counties are presented in Table 79. Most fall in the middle category; Chunhua in the first. In 1978, the weighted average income of 17 counties of the *hanyuan* was 55.5 *yuan* from collective work only (in the 7 counties of Weinan prefecture it was 56.8 *yuan*, in the 7 counties of Xianyang prefecture it was 50.4 *yuan* and in the 3 counties of Baoji prefecture it was 73.4 *yuan* per capita). In irrigated counties in the Wei River plain average per capita income from the collective was about twice as high. In Jingyang county, for instance, peasants received an average of 107.60 *yuan* in 1978 and 95.5 *yuan* in 1977 in cash alone.[85]

Four years later, income differentials (on the basis of *total* net income) had narrowed down considerably. Average p.c. rural income was stated to be 189 *yuan* in 23 counties of the *hanyuan*, and 254 *yuan* in Xi'an municipality; the provincial average was 222 *yuan*.[86] Only part of this may be ascribed to underreporting of income on the *hanyuan*, before decollectivization. Most of the income increase was genuinely obtained from greater freedom of production and trade and better incentives.

Both in 1957 and in 1978, the rural income differentials can be explained mainly from different crop yields in dry and irrigated areas. On the basis of the traditional distinction between irrigated land, riverside land, plateauland and mountain land, in Fuping county the

Table 79 *Rural income data 1957–1978. Distributed collective income and private income per capita in 7 counties (yuan)*

		1957	1965	1970	1974	1975	1976	1977	1978
Wugong	coll.	35	42	46	64	58	70	76	82
	priv.	25	27	25	25	29	25	25	25
		60	69	71	89	87	95	101	107
Weinan	coll.	56	67	52	60	58	59	67	60
	priv.	15	28	38	45	45	45	45	45
		71	95	90	105	103	104	112	105
Hancheng	coll.	65	70	63		71			78
	priv.	–	–	10		15	–	–	20
				73		86			98
Pucheng	coll.	58	60	52	62	72	69	56	62
	priv.	30	33	31	–	38			42
		88	93	83		110			104
Liquan	coll.	45	50	49		51	56	60	64
	priv.	12	26	28	–	37	35	34	44
		57	76	77		88	91	94	108
Qianxian	coll.	–	–	–	54	51	53	39	52
	priv.				–	16	–	–	18
						67			70
Chunhua	coll.	30	26	25	42	47	36	32	35
	priv.	19	17	15	22	23	22	22	22
		49	43	40	64	70	58	54	57
Average	coll.	48	53	48	56	58	57	55	62
	priv.	20	26	25	–	29	–	–	31
		68	79	73		87			93

N.B. Official figures for 1978 for Shaanxi province were 133 resp. 137 *yuan* of *total* net income, and 68 *yuan* of distributed collective income alone. The figure for distributed collective income is quite compatible with my survey data, but the total net income figures are not. The difference may be explained by the money value of services provided by the People's Commune and production brigade, an understatement of private income in my survey, or both; it is too large to be caused by real differentials between these 7 counties and Shaanxi province.

Source: data collected from County Agricultural Bureaus, 1979.

average value of a labour day in four representative Higher Agricultural Producers' Cooperatives on each of those categories of farmland was 2.7 *yuan*, 1.55 *yuan*, 1.36 *yuan* and 0.99 *yuan* respectively in 1956. So here net income in irrigated areas was about double that on the plateau (*hanyuan*).[87]

The short-term effects of the agricultural price-hikes of 1979, of the liberalization of trade in pork and some other products, and of the privatization of agricultural production in Guanzhong have been a net increase of rural incomes. According to a rural household survey in Shaanxi, average net income per capita rose from 133.1 *yuan* in 1978 to 177.2 *yuan* in 1981, and 218.3 *yuan* in 1982. Assuming an inflation of 18 percent, this still leaves a net improvement of almost 40 percent.[88] In 1983, because of a calamitous cotton harvest, rural net income rose barely to 236.1 *yuan*, quite in contrast with the national upward trend, and in 1984, to 262.5 *yuan*, one-quarter below the national average. In 1983 in Guanzhong, average grain production per capita was only 446 kilogram, and income from animal husbandry only 33.60 *yuan*.[89] The long-term effects remain to be seen. It is already clear, however, that both quantitatively and qualitatively labour input has improved. The change-over to non-foodgrain crops, intensification of cultivation, the increase of household sidelines, the development of processing, animal husbandry and private trading have all increased employment and income in areas neglected or stifled under previous policies of self-reliant development.[90]

Some indicators of development, which I selected from the 1979 survey, have been presented in Table 80. I left out those indicators which appeared to have no discriminate value between counties in Guanzhong (such as birth and death rates, reclaimable wasteland, number of schools and theaters, number of 5-protected households), or subdivisions of agricultural and industrial production, or data which seemed to be corrupt. Nevertheless, the selection of the 18 indicators in Table 80 is a rather arbitrary one and there is no sequential order.

Among the 7 counties, Chunhua was clearly the least developed, which shows in income, relief, electricity, chemical fertilizer etc. However, this had had no effect on health and education personnel. Five counties ran budget deficits, most of them very considerable. The gross agricultural production value per capita and the rural distributed collective income per capita were hardly correlated. The percentage of collective accumulation seemed to be established independent of production and income levels. Chemical fertilizer use differed greatly and appeared to be related with the percentage of irrigated farmland and the urbanization rate. The 7 counties belong neither to the most developed nor to the most backward areas of Guanzhong, but are in the 'somewhat below middle' category. Even so, in 1978 (and the same goes for the early '70s) differentials between these counties were considerable, and larger than in 1965.

Table 80 *Economic and social indicators of 7 counties, 1978*

	Weinan	Hancheng	Wugong	Pucheng	Liquan	Qianxian	Chunhua	Average
1. Population increase 1957–78 (%)	74.5	63.6	70.0	103.8	62.0	61.6	66.7	71.7
2. Rate of urbanization (%)	12.2	12.8	9.8	3.4	2.9	3.1	3.4	6.8
3. Industrial labour force (% of total population)	2.0	1.7	0.8	0.6	1.0	0.2	1.1	1.1
4. Gross ind. prod. value p.c. (*yuan*)	118.6	138.0	51.6	76.7	58.4	10.5	36.3	70
5. Gross agr. prod. value p.c. (*yuan*)	166.5	218.0	160.5	131.5	170.8	115.6	98.9	151
6. Commune-level share of rural collective prod. value (%)	15	14	11	15	7	9	8	11
7. County budgetary income: expenditure	2.23	0.81	1.08	0.77	0.43	0.65	0.13	0.87
8. Peasants on state welfare (%)	15	6	9	5	11	6	89	–
9. Teachers per 10,000 population	9.6	14.5	3.2	9.8	4.6	8.6	11.7	8.9
10. Health workers per 10,000 population	4.8	3.4	1.4	4.4	0.9	1.0	2.1	2.6
11. Rural distributed collective income p.c. (*yuan*)	59.5	78	82	62	64	52	35	62
12. Rural private income p.c. (*yuan*)	45.5	20	25	42	44	18	22	31
13. Distribution of gross collective income, (%) of total								
– tax	5.1	4.2	3.0	4.6	4.3	3	1.5	3.7
– accumulation	5.5	6.3	6.3	5.0	6.9	6	3.6	5.7
– foodgrain rations	19.2	51	41.5	38.1	24.4	40	47.3	–
– workpoint pay	23.6	–	9.7	9	23.3	12	0.7	–
14. Production teams with electricity supply (% of total)	94	79	97	95	97	95	24	–

15. Farmland acreage per rural capita (ha)	0.15	0.17	0.10	0.19	0.18	0.18	0.28	0.18
16. Chem. fertilizer use (kg/ha) (20%N)	717	579	649	232	263	252	64	394
17. Agr. machinery in use (Hp/ha)	1.6	2.1	3.1	1.3	1.4	1.5	1.0	1.7
18. Volume of retail sales per capita (*yuan*)	141	213	140	132	106	91	108	133

N.B. A short explanation is due for some items:

1. Pucheng figure reflects immigration of Sanmen reservoir resetlers.
2. Hancheng figure excludes workers in provincially-owned mines.
4/5. Total values have been divided by the *total* county population.
7. The difference between budgetary income and expenditure is made up by the provincial government.
8. Those on state welfare have a substantial *part* of their income supplied in the form of relief grain from the state.
12. Rural private income figures are not very reliable.
13. Remaining percentage constitutes production cost and welfare fund.
14. Does not necessarily include private homes.
18. Mostly urban and therefore strongly correlated with the rate of urbanization.

10

CONCLUDING OBSERVATIONS

In the economic history of Guanzhong, seven main periods may be distinguished since 1930.

The post-famine recovery of 1931–5 was characterized by a return of refugees to their original villages, and by the introduction of outside agencies of government, relief organizations and banks in the central part of Guanzhong. Politically, Guanzhong became part of National-ist China. Also, the road network was improved. The tremendous losses of labourers, tools, pigs, draught animals and houses during the famine years depressed the level of inputs and agricultural technology, especially in west Guanzhong.

The modernization boom of 1935–42 saw a rapid expansion and transformation of all aspects of the economy. Xi'an and Baoji were connected by railroad with North China, and the road network within Guanzhong, and communications with south Shaanxi and Sichuan were vastly improved. Modern industries were established, with outside capital, to process cotton and other agricultural raw materials. Irrigation schemes, variety improvements and investments by banks and cooperatives started to bear fruit. After the Japanese occupation of North and East China and the communist settlement in Yan'an, the strategic and economic importance of Guanzhong was greatly en-hanced. Factories, capital, know-how, government institutions and armies moved into the interior, where Free China had to be built up. Demand for, and supply of, industrial and agricultural products increased more rapidly than ever before.

Wartime stagnation and problems of organization dominated the decade 1942 till 1952. Inflation, material shortages, a break-down of transport and trade, an increasing tax burden and tax evasion and failure of state control over production and trade hit especially the modern, large-scale 'official' economy. Agriculture recovered in 1946–8, with good harvests of wheat and cotton, but suffered from Land Reform, slaughter of animals, interruption of trade and lack of money supply and hired labour in the 1949–52 period, with low yields except for 1951. Industry received positive impulses from the restoration of agricultural production after the war and from the growing demand of the rapidly increasing urban and rural population. However, Guanzhong lost its priority attention by government institutions after the war and some of its modern industries and skilled labour force returned to East China.

Beginning with the First Five-Year Plan in 1953 up until 1960, Guanzhong, and especially Xi'an, was developed as the major industrial and educational center for northwest China. Many new large industries and coal mines were established by the central government. Agriculture was organized in collectives of increasing size, as elsewhere in China, which directed rural efforts at agricultural production and investments in rural infrastructure, such as irrigation projects. There was a great influx of semi-skilled rural labour into the cities, also from outside the province. The state monopolized industry and trade. Thus the economy was basically divided into a state-owned urban industrial and commercial sector and a collectively-owned rural agricultural sector.

The post-Great-Leap-Forward depression lasted for almost a decade. As the central government lost much of its financial and organizational powers, Shaanxi's industry and agriculture were left to their own devices. Urban income remained stationary at best. Nationwide and in Guanzhong, harvests and industrial output went up considerably in 1964 through 1966, but dropped again in the turbulent years 1967 and 1968. In the central parts of Guanzhong, the basis was laid for mechanized irrigation and ploughing.

From 1969 till 1979 the economy of Guanzhong experienced a steady growth on all fronts, but particularly in heavy industry (with central government investment) and in agriculture. A macadam road network was created. Industry supplied ever-increasing quantities of chemical fertilizer, pesticides, irrigation pumps, tractors and other machinery to agriculture. In the early 1970s, both collective investments (in small-scale industries and in rural technical and social infrastructural facilities) and private investments (in pig-raising) grew rapidly. With the use of modern inputs and a growing rural labour force, agricultural production costs rose as well. As a consequence, there was little room for improvement of peasant income. Industrial expansion, with few exceptions, occurred without much qualitative change. Under full employment policies, the labour force of state- and collectively-owned industries grew steadily and productivity remained low.

With the liberalization policies of the 1980s, and the 1980 and 1981 drought and flood disasters in Shaanxi, national and local planners were confronted with the structural weaknesses of Shaanxi's economy. The irrigated area could no longer be expanded, but because of greater fertilizer use, better incentives and improved varieties, foodgrain yields rose again after 1981, although not as fast as the China average. A succession of disastrous cotton harvests affected rural income and brought into question the possible degree of commercial specialization in agriculture. Light industry fell back after a few successful years, but heavy industry was reinvigorated after 1982; a proper balance still had to be struck. Almost all farmland was leased to individual households. The end of collective production reduced the demand for collective- and state-directed rural economic and social services.

In the above-mentioned periods, weather conditions played a crucial role in 1929–31, in 1959–61 and in 1980–1, by severely affecting the local economy and triggering political change. For the Great Leap Forward crisis, it is debatable in how far it was caused by political factors (notably a breakdown of planning and distribution), economic factors (an over-heated economy without sufficient resources) or climatic factors. In any case, the causes of the crisis lay mainly outside of Guanzhong. Major national political impulses were given by the war against Japan and by the build-up of Xi'an as the stepping stone to Northwest China in the 1950s. Both led to a large influx of people and investments. Land Reform, the creation of People's Communes in 1958–60, and their demise in the early 1980s, each time shook the political and economic foundations of rural society. None of these impulses came from Guanzhong itself. Agricultural growth was largely self-sustained, but industrial expansion and modernization depended heavily on the national government.

The below-average performance of Shaanxi's industry and agriculture after the 1950s can be explained by the natural constraints of crop-growing and the economic and political constraints of a small, resource-poor, divided, and not easily accessible, province in the Chinese interior. The agriculture of Guanzhong, and this goes even more for other regions of Shaanxi, is under the constant threat of insufficient rainfall or heat. By relieving the first of these constraints, irrigation projects boosted yields to well above the China average in the 1930s and 1950s. The limits of water use were reached in the mid-

1970s and since then, not only have average yields of cotton and wheat fallen behind the China averages, but they also have been more unstable and disaster-prone. Also, the problems of soil erosion were more serious than elsewhere. Due partly to political pressure from local authorities, and partly to inadequate surveying and the variability of surface water resources, too many reservoirs, pumpwells and irrigation canals were built, which contributed to a substantial rise in irrigation costs. Around 1980, the central government apparently concluded that an expansion of irrigation in Guanzhong should no longer be supported. In the Yellow River basin, urban and industrial water use demanded priority and agricultural use in the North China Plain was considered to be more productive. Basically, Guanzhong has become permanently divided into four crop-growing regions: the heavily irrigated lowlands, the plain irrigation districts with insufficient water supply, the dry upland plain and the mountain areas. During the latter 1970s, the dry upland plain accounted for more than half of the yearly fluctuations in the provincial output of grain.[1]

For cotton, some additional causes for its disappointing yields after the 1950s may be indicated. The traditional cotton area was located in a rather narrow band of irrigated farmland along the Wei River downstream of Xi'an. Due to the expansion of industry, transport and other land uses, much of this prime land was lost during the 1960s and 1970s. The newly-irrigated districts north of the Wei River suffered from water shortages and the more elevated areas from cold (temperatures in the 1970s were slightly lower than in the 1950s and much lower than in the 1940s.[2]) Often, and especially after bad wheat harvests, farmers diverted fertilizer and other inputs to maize. Finally, Guanzhong cotton had been renowned for its high quality in the 1930s but it deteriorated during the war. In the 1950s, while other provinces improved their cotton, Guanzhong still stuck to (at that time rather high-yielding) short-staple varieties. Only at the end of the 1970s was good resistance against yellow wilt achieved. Careless picking, storage and processing resulted in often unripe and dirty cotton. Thus, quality and prices paid for Guanzhong cotton did not improve – even for average-quality cotton the state had fixed relatively low prices. Contrary to expectations, the cotton mills established in the 1950s have had to import a substantial part of their raw cotton from outside the province.

For Shaanxi's industry and other economic sectors owned by the state, growth and performance were very much linked to national economic trends and especially to investments and allocations by the central government. In the 1960s, there was an over-capacity in cotton textiles and some other industries such as cement, the central government budget' and investments had been drastically reduced and agricultural results were poor.[3] Some national machinery and defense industries were established in Xi'an around 1965 but, generally speaking, outside investment was much reduced. Lack of iron ore and of cheap energy put Xi'an at a disadvantage as against Lanzhou, Baotou and Taiyuan. Apart from its location within China, some other factors hampered a self-sustained development of Shaanxi as well. The small size of its population and therefore of its economy (this it had in common with Gansu and Shanxi provinces), gave it little political and economic muscle against other provinces. For its imports of steel, energy, chemical fertilizer, trucks, cotton, and in bad years, food grain, it was dependent on the central government and other provinces, but it had few high-quality exports. Both North Shaanxi and South Shaanxi contributed little to the provincial economy; in fact, the 'old liberated areas' of North Shaanxi were in need of support during most years (the early 1950s and the latter 1960s excepted) and South Shaanxi used up huge national investments for the construction of the railway along the Hanshui River, without immediately giving economic returns. Its development of tea and two-crop rice production was rather unsuccessful and precious forest resources were squandered by the local population, with disastrous ecological results.[4] Summing up, decisive factors in Guanzhong's economic development have been the marginality of its agriculture, its extremely low level of development before World War II, its position as a core region in a province with poor and mountainous areas which could not form an economic unity and the importance attached by the central government to Guanzhong as an essential link for the opening up of Northwest China. The combination of these factors gave Guanzhong the characteristics of a frontier economy, partly private but mostly pushed forward by the state: Go West, State Plan!

Under these conditions, was there much room for a provincial strategy of development, based on local advantages? The answer is no. The passivity of provincial leadership is striking. Shaanxi had no warlord of its own, in the 1930s its modern sector was developed by outsiders, the Xi'an incident was the only political act (by the military!) of national political significance, Hu Zongnan took no military or political initiatives during World War II and after, and the

Red Base was taken over by communist outsiders. After 1949 Shaanxi seems never to have taken the national lead in anything. It lost its prominent position in Northwest China. It did not go to extremes during the Great Leap Forward or Cultural Revolution. Few provincial leaders were attacked or purged, but none were promoted to leading national positions. National trends were followed at a safe distance, though somewhat to the left, as Shaanxi stood to profit by policies of redistribution and support for underdeveloped regions. Political cautiousness was still evident in the ritual condemnations of the 'left', and in the social science journals, as of 1985. Shaanxi gratefully accepted the science institutes, defence industries and advanced technical industries allocated by the central government to Guanzhong. It also put up with the failure of the Sanmen project and its refugee problems, the slow development of railroads and coal mines since the 1960s, the belated and reduced allocation of large-scale chemical fertilizer plants and the lack of investment in chemical industries, printing and dyeing, and artificial fibres. Its above-mentioned economic dependency on the central government, the diversity of problems posed by each of its three separated regions (one of which as an 'old liberated area' was subventioned by and in reverence of the authorities in Beijing) and the energy-absorbing internal expansion of agriculture and build-up of industry, almost from scratch, within a few decades may partially account for Shaanxi's lack of vigour in national politics. A 'provincial' strategy of development, under the national policies of self-reliance, had to direct its efforts towards supplementing provincial shortages, such as existed in cotton and foodgrain, chemicals, chemical fertilizer and walking tractors. In many of these efforts, results were rather poor, as of 1980. Also, the provincial government could try to meet local demand for expensive consumer durables such as watches and bicycles, and make some profits. However, being totally dependent on national allocations of basic commodities, such as steel, and with little bargaining power, Shaanxi could make few independent choices in industry and mining. In agriculture too, choices were limited. Guanzhong had been divided into three administrative regions, basically along North–South lines. Baoji controlled the mountainous upstream Wei River basin, Xianyang controlled the middle area and the Jing River, and Weinan controlled the lower reaches of the Wei and Luo Rivers and the plains. Under the communist regime, until the early 1980s, each region gave little sign of using its geographical advantages for developing agricultural specialization. Thus, self-reliance and autarchy were promoted for regions and within regions for counties as well.

Paradoxically, since the mid 1950s the physical conditions for local specialization and exchange of products were vastly improved: an extensive road system, a railroad across the plain to Hancheng, state trade organizations with purchase stations in all major villages, allocative planning of crops, financial institutions, safety from bandits etc. Yet these were underutilized because of the essentially political preference for local self-reliance and collectivism and aversion to trade. The government and communist party, it seems, set limits to rural development rather than directly stimulating it by economic means (apart from providing technological support). The state usurped all modern functions, paid much attention to some sectors such as variety improvement, irrigation and food grain production but neglected others, such as trade, protection of forests and animal husbandry. The raising of pigs was developed privately, in spite of, rather than supported by official policies. It sounds frivolous, but one feels tempted to say that the authorities hated the mobility of people and animals but loved the simple earth-bound food crops. The desire for administrative control stood and still stands in the way of the development of a market economy. The preference for foodgrain crops also resulted from the governments' obligation to supplement villages which were short of foodgrain.

Since 1979, specialization has become a national policy. Within Shaanxi province, the crop pattern underwent changes that varied in its three main agricultural regions. On the dry loess plateau of north Shaanxi, a shift away from foodgrain cultivation to animal husbandry and forestry has been advocated by experts and supported by Central Government allocations of foodgrain and funds for such a shift. Indeed animal husbandry and forestry, after a long decline during the 1960s and 1970s, have regained some of their importance, but foodgrain production increased even more. The official sown acreage figures in this area show a slight decline of the foodgrain area, but are not very trustworthy. In Guanzhong there has been a shift from cotton to oil crops and to maize, especially so in its western parts, and an increase of specialization in cotton, peanuts, tobacco, fruits, dairy goats etc. in other parts. Also, because of increased chemical fertilizer and irrigation water use, in more areas a second crop (often maize) was grown after wheat. In south Shaanxi, the picture did not change that much.

A 1982 article on the evils of the pre-1978 State crop allocation policies in Shaanxi mentioned ill-advised double cropping of rice. It also stressed the comparative advantage of varnish trees over tea, and advocated increased planting of the former. Significantly, for Guanzhong the authors came up with very little: tea and bamboo allegedly had been pushed up too far north.[5] Actually, only very little of these crops have ever been grown, on the slopes and river valleys of the Qinling mountains. It seems that at present, as in previous decades, in most of Guanzhong, wheat and maize have the greatest comparative advantage, and, apart from feeding Xi'an, they can also be exported to western China.

With interrupted trade flows and high grain prices, because of a very slow recovery of grain output in most areas of China, grain and especially maize became a far more attractive crop than cotton to the Guanzhong farmers in the early 1960s. Moreover, the wet, dark and cold climate of those years did not suit cotton at all. In the second half of the 1960s, however, with a higher cotton price and a better climate, cotton acreage and output all went up again. In the early 1970s, despite some good production years, the cotton acreage stabilized; increasing production costs (of chemical fertilizer and pesticides) were not fully compensated by price increases, and cotton became less rewarding than wheat and maize, which realized higher yields with a smaller increase of inputs. The government had difficulty in maintaining the cotton acreage target against unwilling collectives – spreading this burden over more villages and regions thus became a logical administrative outcome, but average yields suffered from the dispersal to less suitable areas. Also, even after several bountiful grain harvests and after the abolition of the state unified purchase system, early in 1985, farmers still were obliged by county authorities not to reduce their grain acreage too far. Crop choice is not free, yet.[6]

The relation between agriculture and industry has many economic aspects, some of which should be treated on a national rather than a regional level. Whether agriculture has been 'exploited' by the state for industrial development, through extraction of the agricultural surplus, taxation and quotas and by unfair price-setting for agricultural versus industrial products, seems to be an academic question for a province such as Shaanxi which received so many central government investments in industries (many of which were totally unrelated to Shaanxi's resource base) which it would never have been able to finance on its own and which produced so few agricultural surpluses. In the 1950s, when Shaanxi still was able to export foodgrain, rural taxation became more equitable. With an annual output of 4.5 to 5.5 million tons of foodgrain, Shaanxi gradually reduced its annual grain tax from 480,000 tons in 1951 to 406,000 tons in 1956. Gross procurement of grain hovered around one million tons, except for the peak year of 1954. State resales to villages in need of foodgrain showed an upward tendency and may have reached 400,000 tons in the poor harvest of 1957. The total burden of grain tax and procurement decreased in the 1960s and 1970s, because of low output and rural population growth. As for relative prices, for almost all major commodities prices were set by Beijing and not locally. Indeed, as a cotton-growing region, Guanzhong was hurt by the low prices paid for cotton. On the other hand, the transport subsidy implicit in the system of paying the same farmgate price throughout China benefited the less accessible areas in the interior.

At the county and village level, the problem of industrial develop-ment was posed differently. In the logic of provincial, socialist economic planning there was little, if any, competition or overlap with large-scale state-owned industry. Small-scale industries were based primarily on command over certain local resources, local political pride, lack of alternative possibilities for investment, low labour costs and protected or guaranteed sales. The collective framework has facilitated the squeezing of agriculture, but also the development of crucial small-scale rural industries.[7] Of the 'five small industries' (N fertilizer, Ph fertilizer, farm machinery, cement and hydro-electricity) in the 1970s the first two had been developed on some scale as local industries in Guanzhong. Lack of local resources, funds and know-how limited possibilities for expansion. Whether this has been a good thing or a bad thing for Guanzhong is difficult to tell. Rural small-scale industries have been viewed in a very positive, or cautiously positive light by Western economists during the 1970s, but with more and more reservations in the 1980s.[8] High costs, squandering of resources, wasteful use of energy and low product quality are nowadays seen as major disadvantages. However, agricultural processing and local consumer goods industries have proven to be competitive and responsive to local demand. As the State relaxed its administrative grip on small-scale industry, economic results became a more decisive factor in local development. The revamping of village and township enterprises has been seen as the main means of improvement of the disastrous financial situation of county governments. At the end of

1983, 72 out of Shaanxi's 105 counties were subventioned, their total budgetary receipts being only one-half of their total budgetary expenditure (243 as against 484 million *yuan*). 'This is rarely seen in other provinces.'[9] In the same way as in the pre-communist period, small-scale and handicraft industries have started to flourish in the areas near Xi'an; the fact that then and now these areas are comparatively rich and short of labour refutes the idea that their competitiveness is mainly based on extremely low wages. Their consumer-orientation, more direct relation between profit and wages, greater personal responsibility for the quality of purchased raw materials and finished products may have been decisive advantages against large bureaucratically-run state enterprises.

The difference in economic development policies before and after the establishment of communist rule shows most clearly in the cooperative movements. The rural cooperatives under the Guomindang eventually included one-fourth of the Guanzhong farmers, but were never meant to embrace the entire population. Between 1934 and 1941, the average coop size doubled from 30 to 60 members. Unlike the communist coops in the north during the same period, they were mainly concerned with production, and they were small-scale and not dominated by officials. Cheap credit added to the farmer's private economic strength, to his ability to diversify and to his income. The communist coops and collectives, in contrast, curtailed private income and restricted the scope of extra-agricultural activities. The underlying motive for the commercial banks and for the Guomindang, was promotion of commercial production; for the CCP, it was economic control and equity.

How could the collective system become so unpopular and crumble so quickly in the early 1980s? Apart from the reasons mentioned previously, it would seem that it had inherent bureaucratic tendencies which negatively affected trade, product quality, labour incentives and micro-economic efficiency. Egalitarian pressures, for example, drove the average number of labour days up to unrealistic figures of 380 to 400 per year – in a situation of underemployment obvious to everyone. The fostering of village technical and managerial specialists, however useful and necessary first, was perverted into the formation of a new rural elite wielding an unnecessary and unacceptable amount of power and privilege. Especially disagreeable was their domination of all contacts with the outside world and their virtual monopoly of decision-making about agricultural production. In many sectors (l have used garment-making and milk production as examples) there were oppressive effects. The decollectivization policies were for these reasons not only based on economic considerations; they enjoyed great emotional support as well. Now the peasant became his own master again. However, the by now long-standing traditions of state interference and egalitarianism within the village, and the negative image of commercial activities and of hired labour are not easily eradicated. Successful enterprises, whether owned by the state, collectives or individuals, are under great pressure from many sides to assist the weak and less fortunate, and to give 'voluntary' donations to schools, hospitals, road-building and other social services. With greater and often not well-defined economic freedom, corruption was bound to increase. By 1984, both economic crimes and irregular demands by governmental organizations had become daily subjects in the Shaanxi newspapers. Inevitably, liberalization brought its problems, but the over-all record is very positive.

For state organizations, there are still many economic functions to be fulfilled in a situation of private farming: variety improvement and popularization, pest control, irrigation, veterinary care, the provision of storage facilities, road improvement, technical and commercial information services, protection of land resources are some of the obvious ones. There may be one important political function, too, namely to guard against the formation of monopolies and the abuse of economic power by village governments.

Over the past 50 years, agricultural output of Guanzhong's farmland has roughly tripled. Which factors have been the sources of this growth and which weights should be assigned to factor productivities? For China as a whole, quite different assessments have been made owing to scarcity of data and definitional problems. Within the same publication, for the period 1957–78 one author assigns 35 percent to labour, 36 percent to land (of which 24 percent to sown acreage and 13 percent to irrigation), 9 percent to capital (following Antony Tang) and 20 percent to current inputs, but another author's estimates of the same are 55, 25, again 9, and 11 percent respectively, while the editor states that 'by the mid-20th century, most of China had exhausted the possibilities for future agricultural growth using traditional inputs'.[10] Although, as Guanzhong is a smaller area, less divergent estimates should be possible and the preceding chapters have tried to quantify input changes in the various regions of Guanzhong over time, a final assessment can only be very tentative and non-conclusive. First of all, it is quite clear that until well into the 1970s agricultural growth was achieved mostly by what most people call 'traditional' means: an increasing labour input into agricultural production and labour investment in agricultural capital construction, increasing amounts of nightsoil and pig manure, improved ploughs, an increased and more rational use of surface water resources, and more intensive cropping patterns. Most of these 'traditional' inputs carried a certain modern component as well. Irrigation canals were lined with cement, more intensive cropping patterns might use imported short-ripening varieties, pigs could receive modern veterinary care, etc. Variety improvement (both of crops and of animals) is based on traditional as well as on modern techniques and extension work (at least) calls for 'modern' types of organization. The steady increase of the pig population has been made possible in part by the spread of maize as a second crop, which in turn depended on new early-ripening varieties and mechanical irrigation. Between 1957 and 1978, the farmland area of Guanzhong decreased by about 10 percent, the multicropping index increased by about the same percentage; thus, output increases were solely due to raised yields and shifts to higher yielding crops. We have shown how maize has driven out other autumn grains; to a lesser extent, wheat did the same to millet. Unit yields of food grains in this period about doubled. In assessing the factors contributing to this increase, I consider labour to be less of a constraint because of permanent underemployment. Assuming a 50 percent increase of necessary labour, one-half of which is derived from fuller use of available labourers (250 days per year instead of 200 days) and one half from new labourers, a 20 percent increase of the number of labourers between 1957 and 1978 would have been sufficient (following that line of reasoning, the 70-percent increase of the rural labour force between 1957 and 1978 led to 30 percent unemployment – a conservative estimate; however, there was a peak labour need in two-crop areas and little exchange of labour between areas). Very tentatively then, one might estimate factor productivity in Guanzhong as follows: labour 20 percent, irrigation 18 percent, variety improvement 18 percent, chemical fertilizer 14 percent, manure 12 percent, mechanical ploughing 10 percent and pesticides 8 percent. In heavily irrigated areas, labour and chemical fertilizer would account for more, in dry areas for much less.

More than half of the farmland of Guanzhong today still has no irrigation, no machine-ploughing and no chemical fertilizer and is not likely to have them in the near future. Traditional crop rotation patterns persist here, again with maize gaining on other foodgrains.

Has the gap between these traditional areas and the modernized areas widened in the past decades? In the 1930s, Guanzhong's farmland could be divided into three regions: the mixed pastoral/agricultural mountain area, the dry plains north of the Wei River, and a narrow band of irrigated lowland along the rivers and around Xi'an. For the 1970s and 1980s, I have distinguished (above) four different agricultural regions by adding an intermediary category of partially irrigated farmland. Population growth, stress on foodgrain production, self-reliance and loss of private trade profoundly changed the mountain economy into a poor replica of the agricultural plain, albeit sometimes with a fringe of economic forests and special mountain products. In the plain areas, the main differences were as a result of whether or not there was access to irrigation water. Irrigated areas could use chemical fertilizer, plough with tractors, select high-yielding early-ripening varieties and grow more than one crop per year. Both output and modern inputs greatly increased and changed farming techniques and the face of the country. Non-irrigated areas still hardly receive any chemical fertilizer, but apply large amounts of manure. They grow different varieties of maize, coarse grains or peas etc.; rape, not cotton, is their major 'economic crop.' Even within the same county, foodgrain yields and population density may vary with a factor of three between areas. Between counties, differences may be even greater. In comparison with the situation of the 1930s and 1950s, yield differentials between extremes are still in the same order of magnitude; however, the high-yield area has become many times as large and the high end of the yield curve has become much flatter. Also, there is a far greater stability of output throughout the years. Provincial policies had spread available resources thinly and by 1980, had pushed up the limit of the irrigated and well-developed plain northward about as far as it might go. The egalitarian policies of the 1966–78 period may be viewed as a compensatory reaction to the introduction of modern technology such as irrigation pumps, tractors and chemical fertilizer in rural areas, which created fundamental economic differences. Some areas were served first, other areas came second and about one-half of all farmland lacked the natural conditions for such a modernization. On the dry uplands there is room for specialization, but not for substantial increases in yields. Nevertheless, population growth continued and will continue in all areas, also in those without opportunities for productive employment.

Differences in accessibility became less important economically after trade had been monopolized by the state – our survey showed no correlation between the level of rural income and the density of the highway network.

By the 1970s, regional income differentials in Guanzhong seemed to have increased slightly over the 1930s and 1950s. Both in 1957 and in 1978, the level of income in irrigated areas was about twice as high as in dry areas. In particular the dry plateau areas in north Guanzhong fared badly. Between 1978 and 1982–3, however, rural income differentials between these regions narrowed down considerably. This may have come as a surprise to the communist authorities, who already had prepared public opinion for the opposite tendency, with slogans such as 'let some areas and some peasants prosper first'. The inescapable conclusion is that in Guanzhong the egalitarian policies of the 1960s and 1970s, because of their depressing effect on rural income and trade, were less successful in reducing regional income differentials than the liberalization policies of Deng Xiaoping have been. At least until 1984, one may note a slightly U-shaped curve of increase of rural income. Both the poorest and the most affluent regions have had sizable income increases, while the middle areas have profited less. One might speculate that this will be a temporary phenomenon only, which should be ascribed to a political time-lag of two years or so. Private farming was introduced first in poor areas, and opposition to it was strongest in the middle areas. Suburban and specialized farming areas with a tradition of trade were able to profit immediately from liberalization and increased urban demand.

APPENDIX A:

DEMOGRAPHIC DATA FOR

SHAANXI AND XI'AN

Demographic developments during and after the famine of 1928–30 have been discussed in chapter 1. The population pyramid of Guanzhong in 1936 on page 33 shows the devastating effect of this and previous famines on certain age-groups. From 1932 till 1948, official provincial figures recorded hardly any growth of Shaanxi's population, although from local sources it is quite clear that at least Guanzhong witnessed a considerable increase. Wartime records were complicated by the political division of Shaanxi, with a communist area in the north, by movements of soldiers and refugees and by the traditional evasionary habits of the peasantry. The degree of undercount may well have been in the order of 10–20 percent. Only with the 1953 census could a sufficiently reliable figure be brought forward. In 1950, the provincial government held its population to be 12,142,848 people, itself already a 20 percent increase over the official June 1948 figure of 10,011,201.[1] On the basis of the 1953 census, however, the 1950 population total was revised upwards by another 12 percent to 13,584,000.

Great demographic changes occurred in Shaanxi over the past few decades. After 1949, birth rates remained high until 1972. With the exception of the years 1958–1961 and 1963–4, births numbered between 30 and 35 per thousand. Death rates went down rapidly to somewhat above 10 per thousand. As a consequence, natural increase rates went up to 20 to 25 per thousand during the 1960s. This notwithstanding the fact that countervailing measures were taken by the Government. Population policies followed the national guidelines which called for late marriages in the 1950s (itself part of women's liberation) and for the use of contraceptives. However, only since 1972 birth control measures became very strict and since 1978 extremely so.

During the 1930s, Guanzhong men generally married at 17 to 19 years of age, and women at 15 to 17 years. In 1950, still only 14 percent of marrying women married after the age of 20. The Marriage Law of 1950 set minimum ages at 18 for women and 20 for men. From 1957, late marriages (at an age of 23 or 25, or even older) were advocated, most effectively so in the cities. By 1978, the average marriage age for women was 24.8 years in the cities, and 22.5 years in rural areas. In 1980, 93.6 percent of marrying women married after the age of 20, one-half of them after 23.

Average household size fell from 5.9 in 1936 to 4.9 in 1964 to 4.5 in 1982;[2] it remained somewhat above the average for China.

As tables A and D show, the population of Shaanxi increased very fast during the early

---

[1] *Qunzhong Ribao* 11 Oct. 1950.
[2] Jiang Jie, 'Guanzhong Nongcun Renkou Diaocha', *Xibei Nonglin* Vol. III, July 1938; *Shaanxi Ribao* 28 Apr. 1957 and 20 June 1984; *Renkou Yanjiu* 1982 no. 2, pp. 36–40.

Graph M Population of Shaanxi and China 1949–1983

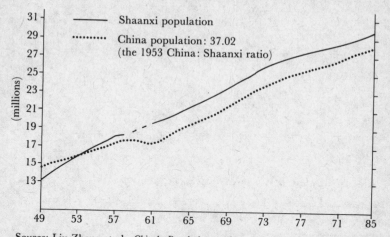

Source: Liu Zheng et al., *China's Population: problems and prospects*, Beijing 1981; Jiang Zhenghua et al., "The prospects for population and socio-economic development of Shaanxi Province", *Renkou yu Jingji* 1986: 3; *Shaanxi Ribao* March 7, 1986

post-1949 years, by 20 percent between 1949 and 1953. This was mainly due to immigration of labourers and refugees from other parts of China. At that time, as a consequence of the 1928–30 famine, the number of Shaanxi people coming into marriageable age was particularly small (see graph A, Chapter 1, p. 33). Under the First Five-Year Plan, although to a much lesser degree, Shaanxi's population growth still was clearly above the China average; this should also be attributed to immigration. The expanding city of Xi'an had a particularly high birth rate. Only from 1956 onwards, supply and use of contraceptives became more general.

The Shaanxi Pharmaceutical Factory started producing contraceptives in 1954. These were supplied mainly to the capital Xi'an and medium-size cities such as Baoji and Hanzhong, but . . . very few were sold. The stockpiled contraceptive creams and suppositories (for abortion) turned bad . . . So the 1956 planned production was 10 percent lower than in 1955. However, after the discussion in the Health Journal was started on birth control, more and more people wanted to use contraceptives . . . Now the medical supply companies also extend to the smaller cities. The number of contraceptive devices has been increased to 316,000, 73 percent more than in 1956. Prices of suppositories for abortion have been lowered to 0.9 yuan.[3]

In stark contrast to the all-China trend, the Great Leap Forward and subsequent food crisis appears hardly to have affected Shaanxi's demographic development. Its population continued to grow by an average of 2.3 percent per year (as against 0.5 percent for China). There is no data to distinguish between the effects of natural increase or immigration, but one would surmise that the abrupt end of so many central government-led construction projects in Xi'an resulted in a net emigration rather than net immigration in Shaanxi. The lower-than-average birth rate of Shaanxi in 1963 also

[3] *Shaanxi Ribao* 12 Mar. 1957.

Table A *Population growth in Shaanxi and China, 1949–1982*

Period	Shaanxi	China	Shaanxi	China
	(percent)		(percent per annum)	
1949–53	20.6	8.5	4.8	2.1
1953–8	15.3	12.2	2.9	2.4
1958–62	9.6	2.0	2.3	0.5
1962–72	27.2	29.5	2.4	2.6
1972–82	13.2	16.5	1.2	1.5

Sources: See Table C.

Table B *Percentage of Shaanxi population residing in Xi'an, 1932–1982*

	Xi'an[o]	Shaanxi	percentage
1932	114,389	9,752,015	1.2
1940	218,044	9,052,988	2.4
1944	392,259	9,374,844	4.2
1949	472,646	13,170,000	3.6
1953	787,300	15,881,281	5.0
1957	937,000	18,130,000	5.2
1970	1,310,000	24,000,000	5.5
1977	2,000,000	27,500,000	7.3
1982	2,180,000	28,904,123	7.5

[o]Changan excluded, agricultural population of Xi'an included.

Table C *Shaanxi population 1928–1984*

	Population	Sources:
1928	11,802,446	1928 Provincial Census
1932	9,752,015	*Shaanxi Dili Yange*, p. 103
	10,624,000	*The Chinese Yearbook* 1944–45, p. 79
1933	9,328,803	Shaanxi Civil Administration Bureau (manuscript)
1935	10,112,230	*The Chinese Yearbook* 1936–7, p. 106
1940	9,052,988	*Shaanxisheng Tongji Ziliao Huikan* no. 1, 1941
1941	9,388,797	*The Chinese Yearbook* 1944–5, p. 73
1944 (Dec.)	9,374,844	„　　　„

Table C (cont.) *Shaanxi population 1928–1984*

	Population:	Sources:
1945	10,634,000	*Xibei Jianshelun*, Shanghai 1945
1947	9,492,489	*Shaanxi Xiaomai*, p. 29
1948 (June)	10,011,201	*China Handbook*, N.Y. 1950, p. 60
1949 (end)	13,170,000 [x]	
1950 (mid)	13,584,000	*Xibei Renkou* 1981 no. 1, p. 107
	13,414,649 [o]	*Shaanxi Dili Yange*, p. 103
1953 (mid)	15,881,281	National Census
	15,054,021 [o]	*Shaanxi Dili Yange*, p. 103
1954 (mid)	16,333,000	*Xibei Renkou* 1981 no. 1, p. 107
(end)	16,510,000	*Xibei Renkou* 1981 n. 1 p. 107
1957 (end)	18,130,000	*Issues and Studies*, 1968 no. 2, p. 25
1958 (end)	18,317,000	*Shaanxi Dili Yange*, p. 103
1960 (end)	19,442,000	Private communication
1962 (end)	20,078,000	*Shaanxi Dili Yange*, p. 103
1963 (mid)	20,319,000	*Xibei Renkou* 1981 no. 1, p. 107
1964 (mid?)	20,766,915	National Census
1971 (mid)	24,601,000	*Xibei Renkou* 1981 no. 1, p. 107
1972 (mid)	25,230,000	*Xibei Renkou* 1981 no. 1, p. 107
1972 (end)	25,535,898	*Shaanxi Dili Yange*, p. 103
1974 (mid)	26,328,000	*Xibei Renkou* 1981 no. 1, p. 107
1978 (end)	27,779,000	*Xibei Renkou* 1981 no. 1, p. 107
1979 (end)	28,070,000	*Shaanxi Ribao* June 20, 1981
1980 (end)	28,310,000	*Shaanxi Ribao* 20 June 1981
1981 (end)	28,650,000	?
1982 (mid)	28,904,123	National Census; 17,694,209 in Guanzhong
(end)	29,040,000	*Zhongguo Tongji Zhaiyao*, 1983
1983 (end)	29,309,000	*Shaanxi Ribao* 1 May 1984
1984 (end)	29,657,000	*Shaanxi Ribao* 6 Apr. 1985

[x] the 1949–53 figures have been revised upwards after the 1953 census, while the pre-1949 figures have not.

[o] Possibly, these figures excluded Xi'an municipality, which until 1954 resorted directly under the central government and not under Shaanxi province.

Table D *Urban and suburban/rural population of Xi'an, 1924–1983*

Year	Urban	Suburban/Rural	Total	Source
1924	120,000			Chen Gengya, *Xibei Shichaji*, p. 438
1926	200,000			Ma Zhenglin, *Fenggao-Changan-Xi'an*, p. 111
1926 (end)	150,000			Ma Zhenglin, *Fenggao-Changan-Xi'an*, p. 111
1931 (June)	108,000			Chen Gengya, *Xibei . . .*, p. 438
1932 (end)	114,389			Chen Gengya, *Xibei . . .*, p. 438
1933	121,583			Chen Gengya, *Xibei . . .*, p. 438
1934	125,141	234,040	(359,000)	*Shiyebu* official figure
1936	150,000			*Zhongguo Jianshe* Vol. xiv no. 4 (1936)
1938 (Jan.)	221,000			*Shaanxisheng Tongji Ziliao Huikan* no. 3
1939 (end)	218,044			*Xibei Ziyuan* Vol. 1 no. 4. p. 170
1942 (Oct.)	270,000			*Shaanxisheng Tongji Ziliao Huikan* no. 5
1944	374,229			*Shaanxisheng Tongji Ziliao Huikan* no. 5
1944 (Dec.)	392,259			*Shaanxisheng Tongji Ziliao Huikan* no. 5
1947 (June)		628,449		Lan Mingbo, *Xi'an*, p. 88
1948	503,000			M. B. Ullman, *Cities of Mainland China*
			700,000	*Jingji Zhoubao* Vol. vi no. 22 (1948)
1949	460,000[a]	(210,000)	710,000	*NCNA* 5 Jan. 1953; *Qunzhong Ribao* 11 Oct. 1950
	500,000[a]			*Shaanxi Ribao* 10 Sept. 1957 *Jianshe Yuekan* 1957 no. 12
1950 (end)	559,127			*Renmin Shouce* 1951
1951		230,000		*Qunzhong Ribao* 2 Feb. 1951
1952	(566,000)			*Xi'an Ribao* 30 Sept. 1957
1952 (end)	700,000			*NCNA* 5 Jan. 1953
1953 (mid)	787,300		1,110,000	Census; *Xibei Daxue Xuebao* 1984 no. 4
1956	950,000[o]	(277,586)		*Jianshe Yuekan* 1957 no. 12 *Shaanxi Ribao* 8 Jan. 1956
1957	(937,000)		(1,359,000)	*Xi'an Ribao* 7 July and 30 Sept. 1957

1958 (1,068,000(300,000 1,368,000[b] M. B. Ullman, *Cities* . . ; *Xi'an Ribao* 5 Sept. 1958

Year	Urban/suburban/rural	Total	Source
1962		1,400,000	*Zhongguo Fensheng Ditu* 1963
1965	(distinction not clear)	1,600,000	Nagel, *Chine*, 1977, p. 969
1970		1,310,000	C. S. Cheng, *Geographical Review* Vol. 63 no. 1 (Jan. 1973). Hans Schenk, *Eastern Horizon* Vol. no. 3 (1973), p. 35.
1971		1,300,000	

Year	Xi'an proper urban (1,000)	rural (1,000)	Changan county urban (1,000)	rural (1,000)	Total urban (1,000)	rural (1,000)	Total	Source
1974	1,151[e]	536[d]		647[d]		1,183[d]		*Shaanxi Nongye Dili* 1975, p. 200
1977	1,290[f]	730[g]					2,634	*Rural Health in the PRC*, 1977
1979			740				2,760	*Zhongguo Baike Nianjian* 1980, p. 78 and 1982, p. 98
1981	1,575	570[d]	742				2,887	*Zhongguo Jingji Nianjian* 1983, v pp. 169–70
1982 (end)	2,180				1,660	1,273[d]		
1983	1,640	580[d]	760				2,940	*Zhongguo Tongji Nianjian* 1983, pp. 87, 108
							5,350	ibidem 1984, pp. 86, 48

( ) derived figures

[a] Difference between the 1949 figures represents transients (a.o. soldiers).

[b] I assume that the 1953 census figure included urban residents only, while the 1958 figures included rural population as well. According to Yuan Ke 'We love Xian', Xi'an's total population was 710,000 in 1949 and 1.4 million in 1958. The municipal area of Xi'an in 1956 was 566.8 sq.km., as against 234 sq.km. in 1949, *Xi'an Ribao* 7 Sept. 1957; it was 861 sq.km. in 1979.

[c] Of which 382,000 in the 3 walled city districts, *Xi'an Ribao* 9 July 1957.

[d] People's Commune population only.

[e] Three urban districts of the city proper only.

[f] Four city districts (157 sq.km.); the total non-agricultural population of Xi'an (861 sq.km.) was 1,468,300, Li Zhongfan et al., *Chengshi he Jingju*, Fuzhou, 1984, p. 433.

[g] Three suburban districts (704 sq.km.).

Table E *Vital statistics of Shaanxi and Xi'an, compared with national data, 1949–1984*

Year	Birth rates (1/1,000)				Death rates (1/1,000)				Rates of natural increase (1/1,000)			
	All China	Shaanxi	All cities	Xi'an	All China	Shaanxi	All cities of China	Xi'an	All China	Shaanxi	All cities of China	Xi'an
1949	36	–	–	28	20	–	–	16	16	–	–	–
1950	37	34	–	–	18	10[a]	–	–	19	24	–	–
1954	38	35	42	–	13	11	8	–	25	24	34	–
1956	32	28.1	38	48	11	10	7	8	20	18.1	30	40
1960	20.9	27.7	28.0	–	25.4	12.3	13.8	–	-4.6	15.4	14.3	–
1961	18.0	21.1	21.6	–	14.2	8.7	11.4	–	3.8	12.4	10.2	–
1963	43.4	38.7	44.5	–	10.0	11.5	7.1	–	33.3	28.2	37.4	–
1964	39.3	40.2	–	–	–	15.6	–	–	–	24.6	–	–
1971	30.7	30.4	21.3	24	7.3	7.2	5.4	5	23.3	23.2	16.0	19
1972	29.8	30.2	19.3	21	7.6	8.4	5.3	5	22.2	21.8	14.0	16
1973	27.9	–	17.4	18	7.0	7.7	5.0	5	20.9	–	12.4	13
1974	24.8	24.4	14.5	16	7.3	7.7	5.2	5	17.5	16.7	9.3	11
1975	23.0	21.7	14.7	15	7.3	–	5.4	6	15.7	–	9.3	9
1976	19.9	19.0	13.1	15	7.3	8.0	6.6[b]	6	12.7	11.0	6.5	9
1977	18.9	18.2	13.4	16	6.9	7.4	5.5	6	12.1	10.8	7.9	10
1978	18.3	–	13.6	–	6.3	–	5.1		12.0	–	8.4	–
1979	17.8	17.0	13.7	–	6.2	6.9	5.1	–	11.6	10.2	8.6	–

1980[c]	20.9	–		17.0	6.4	7.1	5.1	–	11.9	7.2–?	–
1981[c]	21.1	20.4	16.5	18.0	6.6	6.7	5.3	–	14.6	9.7–13.1	11.3
1982	18.6	19.0	18.2	–	7.1	6.6	5.9	–	14.5	12.4	13.0
1983	17.5	16.0	16.0		6.7	6.1			11.5	9.4	10.1
1984		16.6							10.8	10.5	–

[a] figure seems too low.

[b] peak due to Tangshan earthquake.

[c] 1981 figures from the national census were much higher than the previously reported rate of natural increase for 1981, viz. 13.25 as against 9.7. As this margin of difference is very large, the 1980 rate of increase probably has been considerably higher than the official figure of 7.2 as well, and previous years may also have had official undercounts of births.

Sources: Xi'an Ribao 9 July 1957; *Zhongguo Tongji Nianjian 1983*, p. 105; *Rural Health in the PRC*, 1980, p. 123; *Xibei Gesheng Renkou Wenti Lunji*, 1981, pp. 106–9 (*Xibei Renkou* 1981 no. 1); *Shaanxi Ribao* 27 Apr. 1983, 9 March and 26 Feb. 1982; *Renkou Yanjiu* 1982 no. 2, p. 38; *Beijing Review* 19 March 1984, p. 29; *Zhongguo Jingji Nianjian 1983*, v p. 169; *Zhongguo Disanci Renkou Puchadi Zhuyao Shuzi*, 1982; *Shaanxi Ribao* 20 June 1984, 1 May 1984 and 6 April 1985; private communication.

suggests that the drop in births in the previous years had been less severe than in the remainder of China. Death rates reportedly remained at about 10/1,000.

It appears that since the 1960s the rate of natural increase in Shaanxi has been consistently lower than the China average, due both to lower birth rates and to higher death rates. County data from my 1979 survey of Guanzhong confirm this lower rate of natural increase, although the difference is rather small.

Birth rates in Xi'an municipality have been consistently higher than the average for China's municipalities. This can be attributed both to a young population of many immigrant workers and to a comparatively large proportion of rural population, which used to have less reduced birth rates during the 1960s and 1970s. In 1977, for instance, the birth rate in Xi'an's three urban districts was 10.9, but in the suburban districts 19.9 per thousand.[4]

In 1978, 68 percent of women of reproductive age practised birth control. Birth rates were much higher in rural areas than in the urban areas, viz. 17.9 as against 11.2 per thousand, and had been so for many years. In the age-bracket of 30–34 years, 38 percent of urban married women had 3 or more children, but 72 percent of rural married women; in the age-bracket of 35 to 39, however, 63 percent as against 86 percent. These figures indicate both later and fewer births in urban areas and the effect of the anti-natalist policies since 1972. Female infanticide was in evidence in rural areas, where the male/female ratio of reported births was 1.10.[5] According to the Shaanxi authorities, from 1971 through 1981 birth control resulted in a lesser population increase of 2.9 million people.[6] The 1982 census results, however, showed that there had been considerable underreporting of births; the 1981 birth figure had to be revised upward from 9.7 to 13.25 per thousand.[7]

After 1978, anti-natalist policies became extremely harsh, using a combination of economic, social, political and legal sanctions to force parents into a one-child family.[8] In 1984, almost 600,000 parents had accepted the one-child certificate.[9] One wonders how long this campaign can last, particularly now that the rural economy is booming and village control has slackened. Anyway, around 1985 large generations of people coming into marriageable age are bound to push up birth rates again.

Summing up, in spite of the lower-than-average rates of natural increase in Shaanxi province since 1963, over a thirty-year period the population of Shaanxi has increased considerably faster than the all-China average. From 1949 to 1979, Shaanxi's population rose from 13,170,000 to 28,070,000, or by 113 percent, i.e. 2.61 percent per annum. China's population during the same 30 years rose by 78 percent, which is 2.06 percent per annum.[10] This faster growth was entirely due to the 1949–1962 period, as the breakdown in table A shows:

Xi'an's population growth was faster than that of Shaanxi province, because of immigration, high birthrates during the 1950s, and extension of the municipal area. Even so, in relation to the total population of Shaanxi, it remained a capital of moderate size. Some 2 percent of Shaanxi's population lived in Xi'an during the 1930s, 5 percent during the 1950s, and 7.5 percent around 1980. See Table B.

[4]*Rural Health in the PRC*, 1980.
[5]Feng Zhonghui 'Shaanxisheng Yuling Funü Hunyin yu Shengyu Zhuangkuang', *Renkou Yanjiu* 1982 no. 2, pp. 36–40.
[6]*Shaanxi Ribao* 26 Feb. 1982.
[7]See Table C and also John S. Aird, 'The preliminary results of China's 1982 census', *China Quarterly* no. 96. (Dec. 1983), pp. 613–40.
[8]Legal sanctions could be carried out under the new marriage law of 1980 and under the 1981 Draft Parenthood Regulations, *Shaanxi Provincial Service* 3 May 1981.
[9]*Shaanxi Ribao* 20 June 1984.
[10]Ju Xiuzhen and Liang Naizhong, 'Shaanxisheng Renkou Xianzhuang yu Kongzhi Tujing', in *Xibei Gesheng Renkou Wenti Lunji*, Shenzhou Press Hong Kong, 1981 (originally carried in *Xibei Renkou* 1981 no. 1).

APPENDIX B

WEINAN COUNTY
Surface area 1,088 sq.km. People's Communes: 34. Production brigades 509 in 1965 and 500 in 1978. One state farm with 16 ha and 89 labourers.Of the production teams, in 1978 85% had electricity (56% in 1965), 1 percent had running water, 25,5 percent had tractors. 1978 Gross Production Value of the rural collectives was: production teams 59.1 million yuan (1965: 53.2), production brigades 22.6 million yuan (1965: 5.7) and People's Communes 14.7 million yuan (1965: .4).

	Population Total	City	Gross Ind. Agr. Output Value mln. ¥	No. of Prod. teams	Rural Labour force	Farmland Area 1,000 ha	of which irrigated	Wheat 100ha	Wheat 100tons	Maize 100ha	Maize 100tons
	1,000										
1978	649	79	185	2,549	209	86.1	65.4	430	740	278	760
1977	642	75	187.8	1,556	206	86.9	64.9	416	920	258	630
1976	634	73	166.8	2,555	212	87.5	64.1	350	900	174	630
1975	623	72	177.8	2,556	214	88.1	61.1	407	1,120	214	380
1974	612	70	158.2	2,557	209	88.7	59.6	404	940	201	610
1965	489	41	116.4	2,614	178	91.6	11.5	355	750	184	360
1957	372	3.6	66.7	--	158	96.1	4.3	402	670	94	120

	Millet 100ha	Millet 100tons	Beans 100ha	Beans 100tons	Rape 100ha	Rape 100tons	Sorghum 100ha	Sorghum 100tons	Chemical Fertilizer Use 1,000tons	Slaughtered Pigs 1,000
1978	26.7	31	32	29	3.3	1.2	0.7	1.3	61.8	46
1977	30	27	24.7	24	6	3.7	0.7	1.5	29.6	47
1976	32.7	23	28	23	0.7	5.6	2.7	4.1	27.5	41
1975	45.3	39	46	38	4	3.7	10	19.7	39.2	33
1974	49.3	64	24	29	4	2.3	10	23.8	23.1	45
1965	22.7	23	40	44	10	7.8	0.7	2.4	7.4	14
1957	46.7	34	78.7	73	11	1.9	--	--	4.8	2

	Draught Cattle 1,000	Agricultural Machinery 1,000 hp	Gross Value Agr. Output mln. ¥	Rural Net Income p.c. yuan	Commercial Retail Sales mln. ¥	Transport Volume mln. ton/km.
1978	46	142	108.1	105	91.7	86.2
1977	47	120	120.5	112	83.3	4.2
1976	50	111	123.8	104	76.6	4.1
1975	53	86	126.8	103	77.7	5.1
1974	55	79	108.4	105	71.6	5.2
1965	46	8	99.1	95	34.9	2.3
1957	51	1	58.8	71	29.9	4.3

WEINAN COUNTY
STATE OWNED INDUSTRY

| | G.I.O.V. | LABOUR FORCE | OUTPUT VALUE AND LABOUR FORCE IN MAJOR BRANCHES | | | | | | | |
| | | | CHEMICALS | | MACHINERY | | FOODSTUFFS | | SPINNING/WEAVING | |
	mln. ¥	1,000	1,000 ¥	lab.	1,000 ¥	lab.	1,000 ¥	lab.	1,000 ¥	lab.
1978	55.7	3.5	15,029	846	6,941	956	13,930	407	15,080	439
1977	49.1	3.7	10,115	839	6,089	976	13,403	444	15,610	472
1976	42.9	3.6	8,495	873	4,636	930	11,050	421	14,810	436
1975	39.2	3.6	8,171	873	5,095	926	10,189	398	12,250	436
1974	40.5	3.6	6,460	871	4,586	929	10,407	402	15,513	457
1965	14.5	1.4	1,839	150	872	151	6,654	212	7,680	810
1957	1.1	0.1	--	--	--	--	--	--	--	--

COLLECTIVELY OWNED INDUSTRY

| | G.I.O.V. | LABOUR FORCE | THREE LARGEST ENTERPRISES | | | | | |
| | | | TOWELS | | CLOTHING | | COPPER | |
	mln. ¥	1,000	1,000 ¥	lab.	1,000 ¥	lab.	1,000 ¥	lab.
1978	21.1	9.8	1,274	297	2,493	214	823	154
1977	18.2	9.3	1,158	289	2,088	212	859	133
1976	14.3	8.4	1,109	276	1,921	212	810	113
1975	11.9	6.9	1,035	253	1,627	208	748	105
1974	9.4	5.5	902	240	1,294	192	558	94
1965	2.8	1.1	--	--	--	--	--	--
1957	2.2	0.8	--	--	--	--	--	--

A. Stable High-Yielding Farmland area (ha)

	1965	1975	1978
	13,580	20,436	22,370

B.

Forest area (ha)
Grassland area (ha)

	1950	1957	1978
Forest area (ha)	3,067	3,912	8,504
Grassland area (ha)	--	--	--

C.

	1965	1978
Prod. Value of private plots (1,000 yuan)	5,749	8,050
Percentage of total farmland area (%)	7,54	7,92

D.

	1965	1978
Average number of labour days per year (10-point = 1 day)	376	392
Average value of a 10-point labourday (yuan)	0,35	0,35

E. Per cap. average net income

	1957	1965	1970	1975	1978
- from collective (yuan)	56	67.14	52.32	58.39	59.54
- form private (yuan)	15	28	38	44.61	45.46

F. Foodgrain shortage

	1965	1978
No. of teams with insufficient foodgrain and/or poverty-stricken (with population)	471	319
	(135,530)	(95,030)
Resold stategrain (tons)	4,570	3,000
People's Commune subsidy (yuan)	680,000	440,000
No. of 5-protected housholds (with persons)	123(125)	182(187)

WEINAN COUNTY

G. Distribution of gross collective income (%)			1965	1978
costs			27.3	44.8
management			0.5	0.6
tax			7.1	5.1
accumulation			7.0	5.5
welfare			1.7	1.2
paid in grain			16.9	19.2
paid in cash			39.5	26.6

H. Shares of rural gross production value (%)		1957	1965	1978
Agriculture and animal husbandry,		39	88	86
Industry and collective sidelines				
Household sidelines		61	12	14

I. State purchases, quantities and prices	1957	1965	1972	1978
Wheat (tons)	25,135	19,275	10,715	13,330
- price per kg (yuan)	-0.21	-0.24	-0.28	-0.28
Cotton (tons)	8,932	7,850	4,865	7,763
- price per kg (yuan)	-1.76	-1.70	-2.04	-2.30
Maize (tons)	6,390	8,230	6,505	3,696
- price per kg (yuan)	-0.15	-0.17	-0.19	-0.19
Sorghum (tons)	--	5	30	5
- price per kg (yuan)	--	-0.15	-0.18	-0.18
Pork (tons)	616	2,414	5,470	5,755
- price per kg (yuan)	-0.88	-1.00	-1.00	-1.00
Chicken (tons)	--	6	20	17
- price per kg (yuan)	--	-0.82	-1.00	-1.00

J. Share of retail sales within the county handled by	1957	1965	1978
State (%)	49.8	88.3	95.2
Collective organizations (%)	39.7	11.53	4.7
PC members (%)	10.5	0.2	0.1

K. No. of PC members working temporarily in the city	1965	1974	1978
	1,107	2,820	4,506

L. Employment	1950	1957	1964	1972	1978
Employees of state-managed enterprises	--	--	--	--	--
Employees of state organizations	508	620	968	1,275	1,674
Teachers	906	1,396	2,951	5,284	6,247
Health workers	185	568	644	2,270	3,109
Intellectuals	99	526	1,025	1,175	1,342
Party members	309	4,928	8,179	13,347	19,381

M. Education	1950	1957	1965	1974	1978
No. of primary schools	285	402	553	--	390
No. of secondary schools	4	6	77	--	200
No. of students (1,000)	--	63	118	163	135

N. Transport	1950	1957	1965	1978
Public roads (km)		71.6	152	201	464
Dirt roads (km)		71.6	152	142	237
Share in state transport (%)				
cart		--	--	--	--
truck		--	--	--	--
rickshaw		--	--	--	--

O. Finance	1965	1972	1978
County budgetary income (1,000 yuan)	7,160	19,030	32,930
County budgetary expenditure (1,000 yuan)	4,800	8,740	14,740

PUCHENG COUNTY
Surface area 1766 sq. km. People's Communes: 35. Production Brigades in 1965
and 400 in1978. One state farm with 38 ha and 132 labourers. Reclaimable wasteland: 15,000 ha in 1950 14,000 ha in 1957 and 223 ha in 1978. Reclamation costs
rose from 9,000 yuan per ha in 1957 to 15,000 yuan per ha in 1978. Of production
teams, in 1978 95% had electricity (1965:30%), 4% had running water and 25% had
tractors (1965: 2%). 1978 Gross Production Value of the rural collectives was:
production teams 79.3 million yuan (1965: 74), production brigades 14.4 million
(1965:8.9) and People's Communes 16.1 million (1965:10.6).
The area can ba subdivided in plains(37%), mountains (20%) and plateau (31%).

	Population		Gross Ind.	No. of	Rural	Farmland		Sown area and output			
	Total	City	Agr. Output Value	Prod. teams	Labour force	Area	of which irrigated	Wheat		Maize	
	1,000		mln. ¥			1,000 ha		100ha	100tons	100ha	100tons
1978	650	22	135.4	2,467	229	123.9	49.8	634	720	191	540
1977	648	21	141.4	2,468	223	124.4	49.1	635	760	189	520
1976	636	21	141.4	2,469	223	124.9	45.6	655	1350	159	400
1975	627	20	144.6	2,469	219	125.5	42.3	649	1550	129	350
1974	616	20	113.8	2,469	213	126.2	37.0	643	1110	101	260
1965	467	17	104.7	2,467	192	132.0	4.4	659	1310	77	130
1957	319	15	96.0	--	151	132.9	4.3	671	790	46	80

	Millet		Beans		Rape		Sorghum		Chemical Fertilizer Use 1,000tons	Slaughtered Pigs 1,000
	100ha	100tons	100ha	100tons	100ha	100tons	100ha	100tons		
1978	107	140	35	36	30	2	5	10	28.8	55
1977	123	130	23	15	22	3	5	7	20.8	56
1976	119	80	26	14	27	9	6	7	24.3	44
1975	136	110	28	15	19	12	8	13	19.7	33
1974	136	140	21	9	17	4	8	12	14.9	45
1965	111	90	40	30	27	15	2	3	4.7	9
1957	85	37	79	30	42	6	2	1	--	4

	Draught Cattle 1,000	Agricultural Machinery 1,000 hp	Gross Value Agr. Output mln. ¥	Rural Net Income p.c. yuan	Commercial Retail Sales mln. ¥	Transport Volume mln. ton/km.
1978	57	161	85.5	62	86.1	9.8
1977	58	161	85.4	56	83.9	6.5
1976	59	125	92.4	69	76.1	4.8
1975	59	136	101.2	72	63.2	4.5
1974	60	76	80.9	62	53.7	3.4
1965	54	7	92.0	60	26.6	1.4
1957	61	0.6	94	58.5	8.2	2.2

PUCHENG COUNTY
STATE OWNED INDUSTRY

	G.I.O.V.	LABOUR FORCE	OUTPUT VALUE AND LABOUR FORCE IN MAJOR BRANCHES							
			N.FERTILIZER		TRANSFORMERS		COAL		SPINNING/WEAVING	
	mln. ¥	1,000	1,000 ¥	lab.	1,000 ¥	lab.	1,000 ¥	lab.	1,000 ¥	lab.
1978	33.2	3	3,240	666	4,640	359	952	428	1,598	218
1977	43.0	3	3,085	460	3,621	301	658	154	1,797	209
1976	30.6	3	2,246	435	3,705	299	442	158	1,762	205
1975	25.7	3	2,170	431	2,448	293	107	157	1,554	194
1974	18.2	3	1,049	433	--	--	28	154	1,824	199
1965	10.5	2								

COLLECTIVELY OWNED INDUSTRY

	G.I.O.V.	LABOUR FORCE	THREE LARGEST ENTERPRISES					
			TIMBER		CERAMICS		AGR. TOOLS	
	mln. ¥	1,000	1,000 ¥	lab.	1,000 ¥	lab.	1,000 ¥	lab.
1978	16.7	1	329	59	495	122	288	76
1977	13	1	225	54	406	90	265	62
1976	8.6	1	236	55	348	90	396	94
1975	5.5	1	216	56	331	85	377	98
1974	3.9	1	182	58	378	81	320	96
1965	2.2	0.3						
1957	2.0	0.1						

A. Stable High-Yielding Farmland area (ha)

	1965	1975	1978
	3,333	13,333	16,087

B.

	1950	1957	1978
Forest area (ha)	28	319	6,867
Grassland area (ha)	3,000	2,667	2,533

C.

	1965	1978
Prod. Value of private plots (1,000 yuan)	4,300	4,000
Percentage of total farmland area (%)	6	6

D.

	1965	1978
Average number of labour days per year (10-point = 1 day)	370	364
Average value of a 10-point labourday (yuan)	0.39	0.45

E. Per cap. average net income

	1957	1965	1970	1975	1978
- from collective (yuan)	58.5	60	52	72	62
- form private (yuan)	30	33	31	38	42

F. Foodgrain shortage

	1965	1978
No. of teams with insufficient foodgrain and/or poverty-stricken (with population)	130	220
	(15,000)	(32,500)
Resold stategrain (tons)	2,000	6,500
People's Commune subsidy (yuan)	--	4,990,000
No. of 5-protected houshold (with persons)	263(355)	351(453)

PUCHENG COUNTY

G.	Distribution of gross collective income (%)				1965	1978
	costs				40	41.4
	management				0.2	0.2
	tax				5	4.6
	accumulation				4.5	5
	welfare				1.5	1.6
	paid in grain				43.8	38.1
	paid in cash				5	9

H.	Shares of rural gross production value (%)		1957	1965	1978
	Agriculture and animal husbandry,		75	77	80
	Industry and collective sidelines				
	Household sidelines		25	23	20

I.	State purchases, quantities and prices	1957	1965	1972	1978
	Wheat (tons)	23,000	27,500	20,500	7,500
	- price per kg (yuan)	-0.188	-0.238	-0.276	-0.276
	Cotton (tons)	4,845	4,020	2,302	3,772
	- price per kg (yuan)	-2.06	-2.06	-2.06	-2.30
	Maize (tons)	1,000	2,500	3,500	4,500
	- price per kg (yuan)	-0.13	-0.164	-0.192	-0.192
	Sorghum (tons)	--	--	75	115
	- price per kg (yuan)	--	-0.138	-0.176	-0.176
	Pork (tons)	520	2,849	3,780	6,235
	- price per kg (yuan)	-0.96	-0.96	-0.96	-0.96
	Chicken (tons)	--	1	20	33
	- price per kg (yuan)	--	-0.90	-0.90	-0.90

J.	Share of retail sales within the county handled by	1957	1965	1978
	State (%)	60.5	80	80.5
	Collective organizations (%)	30	17.5	18
	PC members (%)	9.5	2.5	1.5

L.	Employment	1950	1957	1964	1972	1978
	Employees of state-managed enterprises	--	--	--	--	--
	Employees of state organizations	--	--	--	--	--
	Teachers	600	1,100	2,300	3,950	6,400
	Health workers	20	950	1,250	2,310	2,834
	Intellectuals	1,520	3,820	6,920	9,173	16,000

M.	Education	1950	1957	1965	1974	1978
	No. of primary schools	70	95	200	--	987
	No. of secondary schools	3	4	25	--	104
	No. of students (1,000)	--	43	82	125	139

N.	Transport	1950	1957	1965	1978
	Public roads (km)	126	175	255	1,017
	Dirt roads (km)	126	126	178	694
	Share in state transport (%)				
	cart	--	90	50	10
	truck	--	10	50	70
	train	--			20

O.	Finance	1965	1972	1978
	County budgetary income (1,000 yuan)	6,090	8,200	11,870
	County budgetary expenditure (1,000 yuan)	6,500	9,330	15,370

HANCHENG COUNTY
Surface area 1868.7 sq. km. People's Communes: 17. Production brigades in 1965 and
1978: 267. One state seed breeding station. Of the production teams, in 1978 79%
had electricity (1965: 20%), 5% had running water and 40% had tractors (in 1965
none). In 1978, Gross Agricultural Production Value of the rural collectives was:
production teams 22.7 million. Production brigades 15.7 million and People's
Communes 6.4 million yuan.
Population of the county increased by immigration from the Samen Reservoir site
in 1957-1960.

	Population Total	City	Gross Ind. Agr. Output Value	No. of Prod. teams	Rural Labour force	Farmland Area	of which irrigated	Sown area and output Wheat		Maize	
	1,000		mln. ¥			1,000 ha		100ha	100tons	100ha	100tons
1978	234	30	83.3	1,220	80	33.9	11.9	198	184	117	398
1977	232	29	70.5	1,244	79	34.6	11.7	197	150	110	182
1976	229	27	64.1	1,244	80	34.7	9.7	200	426	100	254
1975	226	25.5	56.5	1,248	79	35	7.8	201	390	93	232
1974	222	23	54.2	1,248	80	35.4	5.1	167	351	90	195
1965	179.8	10	30.6	1,261	76	38.1	2.8	227	375	72	147
1957	143	8	18.0	--	71	38.3	2.1	220	217	49	80

	Millet		Beans		Rape		Sorghum		Chemical Fertilizer Use 1,000tons	Slaughtered Pigs 1,000	Barley	
	100ha	100tons	100ha	100tons	100ha	100tons	100ha	100tons			100ha	100tons
1978	26	54.2	12	13.1	2.1	0.3	0.5	1.4	19.7	30.9	1.7	1.6
1977	35.1	62.6	8	11	5.6	3.0	0.9	1.4	9.1	36.3	2.0	1.2
1976	23.9	32	7.3	5.2	2.9	1.5	0.7	0.8	7.5	31.2	2.2	3
1975	24.3	27.6	5.3	5.4	0.3	0.1	1	1.9	7.1	18.2	2.5	6.1
1974	25.3	20	9.3	4.5	0.3	0.1	1.2	2.1	6.1	20.4	2.7	4
1965	26.5	28	18	10.8	0.7	0.6	0	--	2.8	22	7.5	8.4
1957	26.5	18	20	20.2	2.3	0.5	0.1	0.1	1.2	17	6.8	5.9

	Draught Cattle 1,000	Agricultural Machinery 1,000 hp	Gross Value Agr. Output mln. ¥	Rural Net Income p.c. yuan	Commercial Retail Sales mln. ¥	Transport Volume mln. ton/km.
1978	28.8	70	51.0	88	49.8	3.3
1977	28.2	55	42.8	76	49.2	2.2
1976	28	48	41.6	86	42.2	2.0
1975	29.2	52	38.3	76	40.1	2.0
1974	31.1	62	34.3	82	38.9	1.8
1965	26.9	4	25.5	70	12.7	--
1957	29.1	--	15.9	65	8.2	--

HANCHENG COUNTY
STATE OWNED INDUSTRY

	G.I.O.V.	LABOUR FORCE	OUTPUT VALUE AND LABOUR FORCE IN MAJOR BRANCHES					
			COKES		CHEM. FERT.		CEMENT	
	mln. ¥	1,000	1,000 ¥	lab.	1,000 ¥	lab.	1,000 ¥	lab.
1978	22.2	3.2	2,613	1,109	2,029	409	408	194
1977	10.6	2.4	2,613	1,167	1,250	312	427	158
1976	16.0	2.4	2,748	1,200	984	295	303	165
1975	14.1	1.8	2,912	1,246	1,074	286	318	170
1974	7.6	2.4	2,435	1,223	425	276	213	167
1965	4.0	0.6	1,400	700	--	--	--	--
1957	1.1	0.4	--	--	--	--	--	--

COLLECTIVELY OWNED INDUSTRY

	G.I.O.V.	LABOUR FORCE	THREE LARGEST ENTERPRISES					
			PAPER		PRINTING		PLOUGHSHARES	
	mln. ¥	1,000	1,000 ¥	lab.	1,000 ¥	lab.	1,000 ¥	lab.
1978	3.7	0.8	610	64	563	71	326	67
1977	3.3	0.8	590	58	502	65	284	70
1976	2.9	0.8	400	41	478	65	240	72
1975	2.5	0.7	233	38	424	65	195	74
1974	2.1	0.7	139	38	379	62	151	70
1965	1.1	0.6	--	--	--	--	--	--
1957	0.7	--	--	--	--	--	--	--

A. Stable High-Yielding Farmland area (ha)

	1965	1975	1978
	2,067	5,293	6,100

B.

	1950	1957	1978
Forest area (ha)	13,333	16,000	31,067
Grassland area (ha)	29,333	26,667	11,333

C.

	1965	1978
Prod. Value of private plots (1,000 yuan)	2,322	2,954
Percentage of total farmland area (%)	9.28%	8.62%

D.

	1965	1978
Average number of labour days per year (10-point = 1 day)	341	395
Average value of a 10-point labourday (yuan)	0.58	0.56

E. Per cap. average net income

	1957	1965	1970	1975	1978
- from collective (yuan)	--	--	63	71	78
- form private (yuan)	--	--	10	15	20

F. Foodgrain shortage

	1965	1978
No. of teams with insufficient foodgrain and/or poverty-stricken (with population)	104	207
	(15,300)	(14,500)
Resold stategrain (tons)	185	415
People's Commune subsidy (yuan)	400,000	2,536,000
No. of 5-protected housholds (with persons)	351(425)	281(302)

HANCHENG COUNTY

G.	Distribution of gross collective income (%)			1965	1978
	costs			35.2	36.3
	management			0.2	0.2
	tax			6.1	4.2
	accumulation			8	6.3
	welfare			2.5	2
	paid in grain				
	paid in cash			48	51

H.	Shares of rural gross production value (%)		1957	1965	1978
	Agriculture and animal husbandry		74	69	64
	Industry		4	12	18
	Collective sidelines		7	8	8
	Household sidelines		9	6	5

I.	State purchases, quantities and prices	1937	1965	1972	1978
	Wheat (tons)	--	4,135	3,335	605
	- price per kg (yuan)	--	-0.238	-0.276	-0.276
	Cotton (tons)	--	3,850	1,691	2,376
	- price per kg (yuan)	--	-1.76	-2.06	-2.30
	Maize (tons)	--	--	1,376	3,790
	- price per kg (yuan)	--	-0.186	-0.192	-0.192
	Sorghum (tons)	--	--	155	440
	- price per kg (yuan)	--	-0.164	-0.188	-0.188
	Pork (tons)	420	1,212	1,300	1,920
	- price per kg (yuan)	-0.80	-0.92	-0.96	-0.96
	Chicken (tons)	2	5	5	6
	- price per kg (yuan)	-0.60	-0.60	-0.82	-0.82

J.	Share of retail sales within the county handled by	1957	1965	1978
	State (%)	41	49.7	62.7
	Collective organizations (%)	47	46	37.2
	PC members (%)	12	43	0.1

K.	No. of PC members working temporarily in the city	1965	1974	1978
		--	--	--

L.	Employment	1950	1957	1964	1972	1978
	Employees of state-managed enterprises	--	--	--	--	--
	Employees of state organizations	220	710	785	694	772
	Teachers	500	850	1,400	1,891	3,482
	Health workers	90	194	277	615	795
	Intellectuals	--	--	--	--	--
	Party members	--	--	--	--	--

M.	Education	1950	1957	1965	1974	1978
	No. of primary schools	291	357	420	--	389
	No. of secondary schools	1	4	5	--	87
	No. of students (1,000)	--	17.7	28	53.5	64.8

N.	Transport		1950	1957	1965	1978
	Public roads (km)		61	70	195	264
	Dirt roads (km)		6	38	161	164
	Share in state transport (%)					
	cart		--	75	40	9
	truck		--	25	60	21
	train		--	--	--	70

O.	Finance	1965	1972	1978
	County budgetary income (1,000 yuan)	2,074	3,949	7,526
	County budgetary expenditure (1,000 yuan)	2,154	6,770	9,237

WUGONG COUNTY

Surface area 455 sq. km. People's Communes: 14. Production brigades 238 in 1965 and in 1978. One state farm with 25 ha (seed breeding). Of the production teams, in 1978 97% had electricity (1965: 60%9, 5% had running water and 60% had tractors (1965: 10%). The Northwest College of Agriculture has its own experimental farms. 1978 Gross Production Value of the rural collectives was 47.4 million yuan for production teams, 11.6 million yuan for production brigades and 7.4 million yuan for People's Communes. Agricultural loans extended to People's Communes and brigades amounted to 1.1 resp. 4.6 resp 9.3 million in 1965, 1974 and 1978.

	Population		Gross Ind.	No. of	Rural	Farmland		Sown area and output			
	Total	City	Agr. Output	Prod. teams	Labour force	Area	of which	Wheat		Maize	
			Value				irrigated				
	1,000		mln. ¥			1,000 ha		100ha	100tons	100ha	100tons
1978	369	36	78.3	1,452	103	33.9	29.8	195	60	205	70
1977	361	31	70.9	1,423	99	34	28.9	196	48	195	70
1976	355	31	66.5	1,470	102	34.1	28	179	62	186	56
1975	351	32	63.1	1,480	106	34.5	27.5	186	56	177	50
1974	345	32	64.0	1,480	103	34.5	26.9	183	50	158	50
1965	--	--	--	--	--	--	--	--	--	--	--
1957	217	22	27.3	--	93	36.4	11	215	32	107	1.9

	Millet		Beans		Rape		Sorghum		Chemical	Slaughtered
									Fertilizer	Pigs
	100ha	100tons	100ha	100tons	100ha	100tons	100ha	100tons	Use 1,000tons	1,000
1978					5	1.2	22			83
1977					3	0.6	10.1			63
1976					5	0.7	11.5			56
1975					16	3.0	7.6			56
1974					33	8.6	7.7			55
1965					--	--	--			--
1957					2	0.3	1.7			15

	Draught	Agricultural	Gross Value	Rural Net	Commercial	Transport Volume.
	Cattle	Machinery	Agr. Output	Income p.c.	Retail Sales	mln. ton/km.
	1,000	1,000 hp	mln. ¥	yuan	mln. ¥	
1978	2.1	105.6	59.2	107	51.7	400
1977	2.1	89.1	55.9	101	47.1	360
1976	2.3	87.7	53.8	95	40.5	310
1975	2.4	72.1	53.3	87	36.6	280
1974	2.6	57.1	53.8	89	34.4	260
1965	--	--	--	--	--	--
1957	2.4	0.2	25.9	60	9.7	90

WUGONG
STATE OWNED INDUSTRY

| | G.I.O.V. | LABOUR FORCE | OUTPUT VALUE AND LABOUR FORCE IN MAJOR BRANCHES | | | | | | | |
| | | | PESTICIDES | | CHEM. FERT. | | COTTON GOODS | | AGR. TOOLS | |
	mln. ¥	1,000	1,000 ¥	lab.	1,000 ¥	lab.	1,000 ¥	lab.	1,000 ¥	lab.
1978	11.0	2.3	2,660	254	1,787	465	1,334	273	1,011	320
1977	8.2	2.2	1,279	233	1,073	427	1,157	271	711	261
1976	7.7	1.9	1,190	216	920	364	1,110	249	510	227
1975	5.7	1.5	458	158	524	300	976	235	990	305
1974	6.0	1.4	1,159	199	--	--	--	--	--	--
1965	--	--	--	--	--	--	--	--	--	--
1957	0.7	0.3	--	--	--	--	--	--	--	--

COLLECTIVELY OWNED INDUSTRY

| | G.I.O.V. | LABOUR FORCE | THREE LARGEST ENTERPRISES | | | | | |
| | | | PUMPS | | AGR. TOOLS | | UTENSILS | |
	mln. ¥	1,000	1,000	lab.	1,000 ¥	lab.	1,000 ¥	lab.
1978	8.0	0.5	1,479	147	463	72	329	51
1977	6.8	0.5	760	190	300	95	120	65
1976	5.1	0.4	758	140	253	90	124	60
1975	4.2	0.4	652	135	250	81	84	44
1974	4.1	0.4	701	133	255	90	72	39
1965	--	--	--	--	--	--	--	--
1957	0.7	0.4	--	--	--	--	--	--

A. Stable High-Yielding Farmland area (ha)

	1965	1975	1978
	5,600	9,387	11,733

B.

	1950	1957	1978
Forest area (ha)	--	--	--
Grassland area (ha)		--	--

C.

	1965	1978
Prod. Value of private plots (1,000 yuan)	5,234	6,281
Percentage of total farmland area (%)	7.81	8.23

D.

	1965	1978
Average number of labour days per year (10-point = 1 day)	275	275
Average value of a 10-point labourday (yuan)	0.47	1.14

E. Per cap. average net income

	1957	1965	1970	1975	1978
- from collective (yuan)	35	42	46	58	82
- form private (yuan)	25	27	25	29	25

F. Foodgrain shortage

	1978
No. of teams with insufficient foodgrain and/or poverty-stricken (with population)	173 (34,600)
Resold stategrain (tons)	--
People's Commune subsidy (yuan)	--
No. of 5-protected housholds (with persons)	72(102)

WUGONG COUNTY

G.	Distribution of gross collective income (%)			1978
	costs			36.5
	management			2.1
	tax			3.0
	accumulation			6.3
	welfare			0.9
	paid in grain			41.5
	paid in cash			9.7

H.	Shares of rural gross production value (%)		1965	1978
	Agriculture and animal husbandry		75.6	71.7
	Industry		5.0	9.0
	Collective sidelines		7.9	5.9
	Household sidelines		11.5	13.4

I.	State purchases, quantities and prices	1965	1972	1978
	Wheat (tons)	10,500	11,480	13,210
	- price per kg (yuan)	-0.24	-0.28	-0.28
	Cotton (tons)	2,115	2,280	2,530
	- price per kg (yuan)	-1.60	-1.60	-1.80
	Maize (tons)	5,505	5,220	13,780
	- price per kg (yuan)	-0.17	-0.19	-0.19
	Sorghum (tons)	--	521	101
	- price per kg (yuan)	--	-0.18	-0.18
	Pork (tons)	1,568	2,576	5,216
	- price per kg (yuan)	-1.04	-1.04	-1.33
	Chicken (tons)	--	--	24
	- price per kg (yuan)	--	--	-1.20

J.	Share of retail sales within the county handled by	1957	1965	1978
	State (%)	66.5	93.9	90.9
	Collective organizations (%)	27.0	3.2	2.0
	PC members (%)	6.5	0.9	7.1

K.	No. of PC members working temporarily in the city		1965	1974	1978
			260	300	2,350

L.	Employment	1950	1957	1964	1972	1978
	Employees of state-managed enterprises	202	1,849	948	3,491	5,476
	Employees of state organizations	585	607	601	715	927
	Teachers	312	515	1,002	1,062	1,244
	Health workers	55	135	246	209	451
	Intellectuals	--	--	--	--	(684)
	Party members	--	--	--	--	(2,717)

M.	Education	1950	1957	1965	1974	1978
	No. of primary schools	110	160	209	--	153
	No. of secondary schools	1	4	11	--	103
	No. of students (1,000)	--	29	--	72	89

N.	Transport	1950	1957	1965	1978
	Public roads (km)			66	113
	Dirt roads (km)			39	55
	Share in state transport (%)				
	cart			65.0	10.0
	truck			20.0	50.0
	rickshaw			15.0	40.0

O.	Finance		1977	1978
	County budgetary income (1,000 yuan)		6,770	9,320
	County budgetary expenditure (1,000 yuan)		6,110	8,620

QIANXIAN COUNTY Surface area 1275 sq.km. People's Communes: 25. Production brigades 306 in 1978. No state farm. Of the production teams, in 1978 95% had electricity (1965: 40%), 2% had running water and 11% had tractors (1965 none). Gross Production Value in 1978 of the rural collectives was: production teams 33.5 million yuan, production brigades 4.9 million yuan, and People's Communes 3.9 million yuan. The area can be subdivided into plain area (50%), hilly area (23%) and plateau area with gullies (27%).

	Population Total	City	Gross Ind. Agr. Output Value	No. of Prod. teams	Rural Labour force	Farmland Area	of which irrigated	Sown area and output Wheat		Maize	
	1,000		mln. ¥			1,000 ha		100ha	100tons	100ha	100tons
1978	417	13	--	1,908	126	71.3	34.5	377	680	155	520
1977	412	12	--	1,908	126	71.8	32.1	399	500	161	490
1976	405	10	--	1,916	126	72.2	30.7	399	870	177	460
1975	395	10	--	1,916	124	73.0	30.0	402	800	150	350
1974	387	10	--	1,919	124	73.5	27.1	378	640	141	185
1965	--	--	--	--	--	--	--	--	--	--	--
1957	258	--	--	--	121	78.0	0.2	444	420	67	70

	Millet		Beans		Broomcorn Millet		Sorghum		Chemical Fertilizer Use 1,000tons	Slaughtered Pigs 1,000
	100ha	100tons	100ha	100tons	100ha	100tons	100ha	100tons		
1978	30	60	6	10	1.5	28	11	24	18	22
1977	--	--	--	--	--	--	--	--	12	20
1976	--	--	--	--	--	--	--	--	12	18
1975	--	--	--	--	--	--	--	--	9	--
1974	--	--	--	--	--	--	--	--	7	--
1965	--	--	--	--	--	--	--	--	--	--
1957	--	--	--	--	--	--	--	--	--	--

	Draught Cattle 1,000	Agricultural Machinery 1,000 hp	Gross Value Agr. Output mln. ¥	Rural Net Income p.c. yuan	Commercial Retail Sales mln. ¥	Transport Volume mln. ton/km.
1978	33.8	107	48.3	44	38.1	
1977	33.7	81	56.0	39	35.3	
1976	36.2	75	56.2	53	31.2	
1975	37.5	68	--	51	32.1	
1974	38.9	70	--	54	28.1	
1965	--	--	--	--	--	
1957	44.6	--	--	--	--	

QIANXIAN COUNTY
STATE OWNED INDUSTRY

| | G.I.O.V. | LABOUR FORCE | OUTPUT VALUE AND LABOUR FORCE IN MAJOR BRANCHES | | | | | | | |
| | | | EDIBLE OIL | | AGR. TOOLS | | PRINTING | | ELECTR. MACH. | |
	mln. ¥	1,000	1,000 ¥	lab.	1,000 ¥	lab.	1,000 ¥	lab.	1,000 ¥	lab.
1978	4.0	0.6	1,954	66	580	158	431	100	1,051	280
1977	--	--	--	--	--	--	--	--	--	--
1976	--	--	--	--	--	--	--	--	--	--
1975	--	--	--	--	--	--	--	--	--	--
1974	--	--	--	--	--	--	--	--	--	--
1965	--	--	--	--	--	--	--	--	--	--
1957	--	--	--	--	--	--	--	--	--	--

COLLECTIVELY OWNED INDUSTRY

| | G.I.O.V. | LABOUR FORCE | SEWING | |
	mln. ¥	1,000	1,000¥	lab.
1978	0.3	0.05	342	50
1977	--	--	--	--
1976	--	--	--	--
1975	--	--	--	--
1974	--	--	--	--
1965	--	--	--	--
1957	--	--	--	--

A. Stable High-Yielding Farmland area (ha)

	1975	1978
	7,033	9,927

B.

	1950	1957	1978
Forest area (ha)	14	390	3,250
Grassland area (ha)	--	--	--

C.

	1965	1978
Prod. Value of private plots (1,000 yuan)	3,280	5,280
Percentage of total farmland area (%)	8.5	8.5

D.

	1965	1978
Average number of labour days per year (10-point = 1 day)	270	275
Average value of a 10-point labourday (yuan)	0.45	±1.00

E.

Per cap. average net income	1972	1973	1974	1975	1978
- from collective (yuan)	50	52	54	51	52
- form private (yuan)	--	--	--	16	18

F. Foodgrain shortage

	1978
No. of teams with insufficient foodgrain and/or poverty-stricken (with population)	242 (26,720)
Resold stategrain (tons)	--
People's Commune subsidy (yuan)	--
No. of 5-protected housholds (with persons)	567(645)

QIANXIAN COUNTY

G. Distribution of gross collective income (%)

	1978
costs	36
management	2
tax	3
accumulation	6
welfare	1
paid in grain	40
paid in cash	12

H. Shares of rural gross production value (%)

	1965	1978
Agriculture and Animal Husbandry	72.3	70
Industry	4	6
Collective sidelines	7.5	6.8
Households sidelines	16.2	17.2

I. State purchases, quantities and prices

	1965	1972	1978
Wheat (tons)	122,000	135,000	170,000
- price per kg (yuan)	-0.24	-0.28	-0.28
Cotton (tons)	2,400	3,200	3,600
- price per kg (yuan)	-1.60	-1.60	-1.80
Maize (tons)	2,500	5,200	6,500
- price per kg (yuan)	-0.17	-0.19	-0.19
Sorghum (tons)	68	120	109
- price per kg (yuan)	-0.18	-0.18	-0.18
Pork (tons)	200	2,800	3,000
- price per kg (yuan)	-1.04	-1.04	-1.35
Chicken (tons)	--	--	--
- price per kg (yuan)	--	--	--

J. Share of retail sales within the county handled by

	1957	1965	1978
State (%)	55	82	85
Collective organizations (%)	25	10	5
PC members (%)	20	8	10

K. No. of PC members working temporarily in the city

	1965	1974	1978
	322	644	1,846

L. Employment

	1950	1957	1964	1972	1978
Employees of state-managed enterprises	162	197	245	1,344	1,488
Employees of state organizations	287	346	624	724	--
Teachers	751	1,821	2,093	3,485	3,586
Health workers	20	75	226	348	352
Intellectuals	--	--	124	224	328
Party members	--	--	--	--	2,312

M. Education

	1950	1957	1965	1974	1978
No. of primary schools	175	249	309	--	352
No. of secondary schools	2	6	7	--	27
No. of students (1,000)	--	41	--	83	93

N. Transport

	1950	1957	1965	1978
Public roads (km)	70	100	210	500
Dirt roads (km)	1,200	5,200	8,200	15,000
Share in state transport (%)				
cart	--	--	70	42
truck	--	--	15	40
rickshaw	--	--	15	18

O. Finance

	1977	1978
County budgetary income (1,000 yuan)	4,140	4,540
County budgetary expenditure (1,000 yuan)	7,070	6,960

LIQUAN COUNTY
Surface area 1,082 sq. km. People's Communes: 20. Production brigades 405 in
1965 and 396 in 1978. One state Popularization station with 51 ha and 58 labourers. Of the production teams, in 1978 97% had electricity (76% in 1965),
6.5% had running water, 23.5% had tractors, 88% had telephones (1965 65%). 1978
Gross Production Value of the rural collectives was: production teams 41.7
million yuan (1965: 33.7), production brigades 6.6 million yuan (1965: 2.9) and
People's Communes 3.8 million yuan (1965: .4).

	Population		Gross Ind.	No. of	Rural	Farmland		Sown area and output			
	Total	City	Agr. Output Value	Prod. teams	Labour force	Area	of which irrigated	Wheat		Maize	
	1,000		mln. ¥			1,000 ha		100ha	100tons	100ha	100tons
1978	345	10	79.1	1701	129	61.7	37.2	357	640	177	500
1977	340	10	70.5	1714	127	61.9	36.3	333	570	165	440
1976	335	10	68.3	1717	125	62.3	35.2	325	830	195	320
1975	327	10	65.5	1747	124	63.1	34.7	343	820	145	370
1974	321	9	64.2	1747	122	63.9	33.5	333	690	131	360
1965	257	5	61.8	1787	110	69.2	11.3	363	620	151	280
1957	213	3	42.4	--	101	83.6	3.5	365	430	72	60

	Millet		Barley		Rape		Sorghum		Chemical Fertilizer	Slaughtered Pigs
	100ha	100tons	100ha	100tons	100ha	100tons	100ha	100tons	Use 1,000tons	1,000
1978	17	20	15	20	19	4	3	10	16.2	39
1977	19	10	13	20	41	8	1	1	6.1	41
1976	17	3	13	20	36	20	1	1	5.2	33
1975	24	12	16	30	11	6	6	8	7.8	25
1974	24	16	17	30	19	10	19	30	7.1	28
1965	27	16	47	40	20	10	13	15	2.3	15
1957	--	--	--	--	22	4	--	--	0.1	10

	Draught Cattle 1,000	Agricultural Machinery 1,000 hp	Gross Value Agr. Output mln. ¥	Rural Net Income p.c. yuan	Commercial Retail Sales mln. ¥	Transport Volume mln. ton/km.
978	31	89.3	58.9	108	36.7	1.0
977	31	78.2	51.6	94	34.7	1.1
976	33	79.1	52.8	91	31.3	0.8
975	34	72.7	52.5	88	28.7	0.8
974	35	65.9	49.5	91	27.8	0.7
965	27	13.2	51.3	76	21.3	0.4
957	30	0.4	41.2	57	12.4	--

LIQUAN COUNTY
STATE-OWNED INDUSTRY

| | G.I.O.V. | LABOUR FORCE | OUTPUT VALUE AND LABOUR FORCE IN MAJOR BRANCHES | | | | | | | |
| | | | MACHINERY | | BRICKS | | FOODSTUFFS | | TEXTILES/LEATHER | |
	mln. ¥	1,000	1,000 ¥	lab.	1,000 ¥	lab.	1,000 ¥	lab.	1,000 ¥	lab.
1978	15.2	1	1,640	387	1,270	333	2,560	109	8,570	129
1977	14.4	1	1,649	385	1,335	346	4,174	115	6,193	132
1976	12.4	1	1,555	374	1,137	353	3,399	138	6,193	132
1975	10.4	1	1,502	349	931	339	2,664	127	4,498	128
1974	12.4	1	1,359	341	706	357	3,220	130	6,352	340
1965	9.2	0.8	690	250	345	287	2,610	120	3,247	130
1957	--	--	--	--	--	--	--	--	--	--

COLLECTIVELY-OWNED INDUSTRY

| | G.I.O.V. | LABOUR FORCE | THREE LARGEST ENTERPRISES | | | | | |
| | | | ASSEMBLAGE | | TANNERY | | TEXTILES | |
	mln. ¥	1,000	1,000 ¥	lab.	1,000 ¥	lab.	1,000 ¥	lab.
1978	5.0	2.4	500	65	200	43	350	40
1977	4.5	2.3	454	65	190	43	--	--
1976	3.1	2.3	381	63	172	41	--	--
1975	2.6	2.1	355	62	123	41	--	--
1974	2.3	1.5	346	62	149	41	--	--
1965	1.3	0.4	217	40	137	39	--	--
1957	1.2	0.3	130	30	78	27	--	--

A. Stable High-Yielding Farmland area (ha)

	1965	1975	1978
	1,333	5,333	7,867

B.

	1950	1957	1978
Forest area (ha)	1,333	2,000	4,667
Grassland area (ha)	--	--	--

C.

	1965	1978
Prod. Value of private plots (1,000 yuan)	2,600	7,800
Percentage of total farmland area (%)	7.7	8.6

D.

	1965	1978
Average number of labour days per year (10-point = 1 day)	364	387
Average value of a 10-point labourday (yuan)	0.37	0.44

E. Per cap. average net income

	1957	1965	1970	1975	1978
	45	50	49	51	64
- from collective (yuan)	12	26	28	37	44
- form private (yuan)					

F. Foodgrain shortage

	1965	1978
No. of teams with insufficient foodgrain and/or poverty-stricken (with population)	682	301
	(71,760)	(37,500)
Resold stategrain (tons)	4,750	--
People's Commune subsidy (yuan)	300,000	300,000
No. of 5-protected housholds (with persons)	201(201)	17(17)

LIQUAN COUNTY

				1965	1978
G.	Distribution of gross collective income (%)			42.6	39.8
	costs			0.2	0.2
	management			5.5	4.3
	tax			6.3	6.9
	accumulation			1.3	1.1
	welfare			25.3	24.4
	paid in grain			18.8	23.3
	paid in cash				

			1957	1965	1978
H.	Shares of rural gross production value (%)				
	Agriculture and animal husbandry		80	84	85
	Industry and collective sidelines		20	16	15
	Household sidelines				

		1957	1965	1972	1978
I.	State purchases, quantities and prices				
	Wheat (tons)	12,000	9,500	10,000	7,500
	- price per kg (yuan)	0.236	0.236	0.276	0.276
	Cotton (tons)	2,200	3,901	2,975	3,850
	- price per kg (yuan)	2.20	2.20	2.20	2.20
	Maize (tons)	3,300	8,000	8,500	8,000
	- price per kg (yuan)	0.192	0.192	0.192	0.192
	Sorghum (tons)	--	1,500	1,000	--
	- price per kg (yuan)	--	0.15	0.15	--
	Pork (tons)	--	762	1,220	1,504
	- price per kg (yuan)	--	1.56	1.56	1.56
	Chicken (tons)	--	19	15	1
	- price per kg (yuan)	--	1.40	1.40	1.40

			1957	1965	1978
J.	Share of retail sales within the county handled by				
	State (%)		69	96	96
	Collective organizations (%)		23	1	1
	PC members (%)		8	3	3

			1965	1974	1978
K.	No. of PC members working temporarily in the city		2,000	2,300	2,996

		1950	1957	1964	1972	1978
L.	Employment					
	Employees of state-managed enterprises	0	367	1,420	2,156	2,696
	Employees of state organizations	130	213	534	769	1,124
	Teachers	389	684	1,080	1,276	1,619
	Health workers	32	56	313	438	330
	Intellectuals	--	30	182	358	380
	Party members	100	2,200	6,280	6,500	10,000

		1950	1957	1965	1974	1978
M.	Education					
	No. of primary schools	300	410	415	--	426
	No. of secondary schools	1	1	3	--	12
	No. of students (1,000)	--	18	53	73	81

		1950	1957	1965	1978
N.	Transport				
	Public roads (km)	12	12	145	344
	Dirt roads (km)	--	135	320	840
	Share in state transport (%)				
	cart	--	93	24	5
	truck	--	--	72	95
	rickshaw	--	7	4	--

		1972	1978
O.	Finance		
	County budgetary income (1,000 yuan)	3,680	4,412
	County budgetary expenditure (1,000 yuan)	3,885	10,354

		1950-59	1960-69	1970-79
P.	Immigration and outmigration			
	No. of immigrants	3,530	13,400	38,500
	No. of emigrants	3,200	11,200	37,500

CHUNHUA COUNTY

Surface area 965 sq. km. People's Communes: 19. Production brigades 221 in 1965 and 219 in 1978. One state seed breeding and experimental station with 357 ha.Of the production teams, in 1978 24% had electricity, 2% had running water and 48% had tractors (1965 all zero %). Gross Production Value of the rural collectives in 1978 was: production teams 10.2 million yuan, production brigades 0.8 million yuan, People's Communes 1.1 million yuan. Grassland area was 30,000 ha in 1950, 28,000 ha in 1957 and 10,000 ha in 1978.

	Population		Gross Ind. Agr. Output Value	No. of Prod. teams	Rural Labour force	Farmland Area	of which irrigated	Sown area and output			
	Total	City						Wheat		Maize	
	1,000		mln. ¥			1,000 ha		100ha	100tons	100ha	100tons
1978	145	5	19.6	956	41	38.7	5.3	201	92	81	150
1977	144	5	17.3	948	39	38.7	4.8	203	180	77	125
1976	143	4	20.1	938	39	39.2	3.2	199	295	77	135
1975	141	5	22.3	988	39	39.7	2.9	201	315	74	170
1974	139	5	24.4	988	38	40.9	0.7	190	265	65	115
1965	113	4	11.0	1,000	44	45.2	0.3	215	235	83	170
1957	87	4	9.5	----	27	48.1	0.1	245	150	57	60

	Millet		Barley		Rape		Sorghum		Chemical Fertilizer Use 1,000tons	Slaughtered Pigs 1,000
	100ha	100tons	100ha	100tons	100ha	100tons	100ha	100tons		
1978	2.6	4	11	5	20	6	11	21	2.5	5.1
1977	1.7	1	12	7	21	2	9	12	1.2	6.4
1976	1.1	1	13	10	24	10	11	110	1.9	6.2
1975	2.0	2	15	16	22	6	23	45	1.8	4.5
1974	3	3	17	14	38	12	36	70	1.8	4.8
1965	--	--	38	25	34	13	--	--	1.3	3.8
1957	8	6	15	12	41	4	111	15	0.2	1.2

	Draught Cattle 1,000	Agricultural Machinery 1,000 hp	Gross Value Agr. Output mln. ¥	Rural Net Income p.c. yuan	Commercial Retail Sales mln. ¥	Transport Volume mln. ton/km.
1978	15	30	14.3	57	15.7	1.8
1977	15	33	12.0	54	15.8	1.9
1976	16	32	15.5	58	15.8	1.5
1975	16	15	18.1	70	12.9	1.0
1974	17	10	21.1	64	10.5	0.8
1965	17	1	10.4	23	4.6	0.0
1957	18	--	8.9	29	3.8	0.0

CHUNHUA COUNTY
STATE OWNED INDUSTRY

	. G.I.O.V.	. LABOUR FORCE	.	OUTPUT VALUE AND LABOUR.FORCE IN MAJOR.BRANCHES							
				COKES		MACHINERY		BUILD. MAT.		FOODSTUFFS	
	mln. ¥	1,000		1,000 ¥	lab.	1,000 ¥	lab.	1,000 ¥	lab.	1,000 ¥	lab.
1978	4.1	1		1,052	314	722	262	441	129	1,097	156
1977	4.0	0.6		859	140	758	199	373	41	1,182	92
1976	3.7	0.6		533	155	639	206	331	45	1,168	100
1975	3.6	0.6		284	150	694	202	358	69	1,161	93
1974	2.7	0.6		400	153	577	205	166	70	1,141	96
1965	0.5	0.1		--	--	--	--	--	--	--	--
1957	0.1	--		--	--	--	--	--	--	--	--

COLLECTIVELY OWNED INDUSTRY

	. G.I.O.V.	. LABOUR FORCE	THREE.LARGEST ENTERPRISES					
			HANDICRAFTS		PRINTING		BRICKS	
	mln. ¥	1,000	1,000	lab.	1,000 ¥	lab.	1,000 ¥	lab.
1978	1.1	0.6	350	24	115	37	172	125
1977	1.3	0.6	274	25	103	29	239	110
1976	0.9	0.2	251	24	93	28	188	105
1975	0.6	0.2	231	24	95	19	98	60
1974	0.6	0.2	176	24	86	20	135	59
1965	0.3	0.2	--	--	--	--	--	--
1957	0.6	0.3	--	--	--	--	--	--

A. Stable High-Yielding Farmland area (ha)

	1965	1975	1978
	247	693	2,027

B.

	1950	1957	1978
Forest area (ha)	1,110	1,458	4,105
Grassland area (ha)	30,467	28,000	10,000

C.

	1965	1978
Prod. Value of private plots (1,000 yuan)	2,764	3,102
Percentage of total farmland area (%)	8.1	8.4

D.

	1965	1978
Average number of labour days per year (10-point = 1 day)	332	380
Average value of a 10-point labourday (yuan)	0.3	0.26

E.

		1957	1965	1970	1975	1978
Per cap. average net income						
- from collective (yuan)		30	26	25	43	35
- form private (yuan)		19	17	15	23	22

F.

	1965	1978
Foodgrain shortage	503	1,127
No. of teams with insufficient foodgrain and/or poverty-stricken (with population)	62,500	128,900
Resold stategrain (tons)	1,750	6,650
People's Commune subsidy (yuan)	200,000	350,000
No. of 5-protected housholds (with persons)	270(270)	220(220)

CHUNHUA COUNTY

G. Distribution of gross collective income (%)		1965	1978
costs		42	45.5
management		0.2	0.3
tax		2.5	1.5
accumulation		4	3.6
welfare		1	1.1
paid in grain		40.3	47.3
paid in cash		10	0.7

H. Shares of rural gross production value (%)	1957	1965	1978
Agriculture and animal husbandry, Industry and collective sidelines	80	83	88
Household sidelines	20	17	12

I. State purchases, quantities and prices	1957	1965	1972	1978
Wheat (tons)	4,680	5,000	5,940	50
- price per kg (yuan)	-0.178	-0.234	-0.276	-0.276
Cotton (tons)	--	--	--	--
- price per kg (yuan)	--	--	--	--
Maize (tons)	100	2,315	2,500	500
- price per kg (yuan)	-0.166	-0.154	-0.192	-0.192
Sorghum (tons)	50	1,750	2,500	225
- price per kg (yuan)	-0.148	-0.148	-0.176	-0.176
Pork (tons)	--	520	800	600
- price per kg (yuan)	--	-0.156	-0.156	-0.156
Chicken (tons)	--	7	1	7
- price per kg (yuan)	--	-1.40	-1.40	-1.00

J. Share of retail sales within the county handled by	1957	1965	1978
State (%)	63.5	82	82.5
Collective organizations (%)	28.4	15.5	16.5
PC members (%)	8.1	2.5	1.0

K. No. of PC members working temporarily in the city	1965	1974	1978
	95	213	1,600

L. Employment	1950	1957	1964	1972	1978
Employees of state-managed enterprises	918	1,430	1,794	2,523	3,165
Employees of state organizations	380	415	346	444	452
Teachers	239	411	637	1,329	1,748
Health workers	26	64	157	154	339
Intellectuals	--	15	30	100	180
Party members	1,473	1,832	3,000	3,709	5,662

M. Education	1950	1957	1965	1974	1978
No. of primary schools	171	241	336	--	461
No. of secondary schools	1	2	4	--	36
No. of students (1,000)	--	10	17	31	39

N. Transport	1950	1957	1965	1978
Public roads (km)		--	104	1,885
Dirt roads (km)		--	104	1,765
Share in state transport (%)				
cart		80	35	5
truck		10	60	95
rickshaw		10	5	0

O. Finance	1965	1972	1978
County budgetary income (1,000 yuan)	898	827	1,212
County budgetary expenditure (1,000 yuan)	1,516	4,598	9,316

P. Immigration and outmigration	1950-59	1960-69	1970-79
No. of immigrants	9,555	12,023	18,520
No. of emigrants	7,668	10,296	18,433

Notes

INTRODUCTION, SOME CONCLUSIONS AND PROSPECTS

1 *Zhongguo Duiwai Maoyi* 1985 no. 3, p. 24.
2 D. Perkins and S. Yusuf, *Rural Development in China*, World Bank, 1984.
3 Dwight Perkins (ed.), *Rural Small-Scale Industry in the People's Republic of China*, Berkeley, 1977.
5 James E. Sheridan, *Chinese Warlord. The career of Feng Yü-hsiang*, Stanford, 1966.
4 Pierre-Etienne Will, *Bureaucratie et Famine en Chine au 18e Siècle*, Paris, 1980; Deng Yunte, *Zhongguo Jiuhuang Shi*, Shanghai, 1937; Paul R. Bohr, *Famine in China and the Missionary*, Harvard, 1972; Andrew J. Nathan, *A history of the China International Famine Relief Commission*, Cambridge, 1965.
6 Kenneth R. Walker, *Food grain procurement and consumption in China*, Cambridge, 1984.
7 Hsi-sheng Ch'i, *Nationalist China at War: Military defeats and political collapse, 1937–1945*, Ann Arbor, 1982, p. 3, 159.
8 *ibidem*, pp. 156–9, 179–180.
9 D. H. Perkins (ed.), *China's Modern Economy in Historical Perspective*, Stanford, 1975, p. 125–6; E. B. Vermeer, 'Income differentials in rural China', *The China Quarterly*, March 1982, p. 1–33; Nicholas Lardy, 'Consumption and Living Standards in China, 1978–1983', *ibidem* Dec. 1984 p. 849–50.
10 Dwight H. Perkins (ed.), *China's Modern Economy in Historical Perspective*, p. 180.
11 Nicholas R. Lardy, *Agriculture in China's Modern Economic Development*, Cambridge, 1983. It was harmful from the point of view of longterm preservation of natural resources as well, Eduard B. Vermeer, 'Agriculture in China: a deteriorating situation', *The Ecologist* Jan. 1984.
12 Paul W. Wilm, *Die Früchtbarkeit und Ertragsleistung Nordchina's*, Wiesbaden, 1968; John L. Buck, *China's Farm Economy*, Shanghai, 1930 and *Land Utilization in China*, Nanking, 1937.

1 THE FAMINE OF 1928–1931

1 According to official figures, the drought and the Muslim 'fury' reduced Shaanxi's population from 11,973,000 in 1875 to 8,094,000 in 1884, or by almost 4 million people. The drought struck mainly the Wei River valley, He Hanwei, *Guangxu Chunian (1876–79) Huabei di Dahanzai*, Hongkong, 1980, p. 124.
2 F. H. Nichols, *Through Hidden Shensi*, p. 230.
3 Feng Yuxiang, *Wodi Shenghuo*, Harbin, 1981; James E. Sheridan, *Chinese warlord – the career of Feng Yü-hsiang*, Stanford 1966; Zhou Mengxian, 'Feng Yuxiang he Zhongguo Gongchandangdi Guanxi (The relations between Feng Yuxiang and the Communist Party). *Huazhong Shiyuan Xuebao* 1982 no. 3, p. 110–118; Harry A. Franck, *Wandering in North China*, New York 1923, p. 367.

4 A recent author puts the figure at 50,000, or one-quarter of Xi'an's population within and outside the city walls. Ma Zhenglin, *Fenggao–Chang'an–Xi-an*, Xi'an, 1978, p. 112.

5 Guomindang members numbered 1,076 in Shaanxi in 1929, and just as few in 1934, or less than one-half percent of the All-China total. Hung-mao Tien, *Government and Politics in KMT China 1927–1937*, Stanford, 1972, p. 30.

6 The Wei River has an average yearly flow of 90 m³/sec at Baoji, and of 190 m³/sec. at Xianyang. 65 m³/sec. is added by the Jing River tributary. The second largest tributary, the Luo River, has an average yearly flow of 28 m³/sec. All other tributaries have a flow of less than 1 m³/sec.

7 Severe drought disasters occurred in 1878–1880, 1898–1900, 1928–1931, and recently in 1960 and in 1980.

8 *Dawan* Oct. 10, 1934

9 In 1928, the Yellow River recorded at Shaanxian the lowest average yearly runoff of the 1920–70 period; only 635 m³/sec., or less than half of the 50-year average of 1,350 m³/sec., *Zhongguo Ziran Dili, Dibiaoshui*, Chinese Academy of Sciences, Peking 1981, p. 97.

10 George A. Young, *The Living Christ in Modern China*, London 1947, p. 63, 69–71.

11 Report by G. F. Andrew of the China International Famine Relief Commission dd. 22 March 1930, *The Herald* of the Baptist Missionary Society, 1930, p. 170.

12 Deng Yunde, *Zhongguo Jiuhuang Shi*, Shanghai 1937, pp. 181–182; *Dagongbao* 8 Jan. 1931.

13 The shortage is reflected in the wheat price indexes of each district for 1931–1933, see *Laodong Nianjian 1933*, pp. 625–39; between Jan. 1931 and Oct. 1933, prices dropped by 50 to 100 percent.

14 *Zhongguo Nongcun Jingji Ziliao* II Vols, pp. 774–7.

15 *ibidem*, p. 773, based on an investigation of 37 counties (out of 40). Contemporary newspapers gave higher but unlikely figures for women and children sold. 'During the disaster, even the sales of children were taxed, with 5 *yuan* a head. From this single item, the Finance Bureau collected 2 million *yuan*' (*Shishi Xinbao* Jan. 20, 1931). 'The Government perceived a tax of 10 percent on sales of humans. In this way it collected 2 million *yuan*' (*Tianjin Dagongbao* Jan. 20, 1931). There is no confirmation of this tax from other sources.

16 According to *Shaanxi Nongye Dili*, Xi'an 1979, p. 5, 3 million people died from starvation and 780,000 people fled to other provinces; these figures, however, include the thinly populated areas north of Guanzhong.

17 *Zhongyang Ribao* Jan. 27 and 28, 1937. Districts represented were Fengxiang, Wugong, Sanyuan and Pucheng.

18 Districts represented were Fengxiang, Wugong, Pucheng, Huxian, Sanyuan and Huayin, Jiang Jie, 'Guanzhong Nongcun Renkou Diaocha' (An investigation of the rural population of Guanzhong), *Xibei Nonglin*, Vol. III, July 1938.

19 See a survey of 7 districts (Weinan, Pucheng, Tongguan, Heyang, Huaxian, Fuping and Lantian) held by the Joint Committee on Rural Reconstruction, *Shaanxi Sheng Nongcun Diaocha*, 1934. In 5 villages surveyed in Fengxiang district, of the original 633 households of 1928, only 276 were still there by 1933, in much reduced size (p. 42).

20 *Shaanbao*, Feb. 10, 1930; the local history of Qishan mentions 75,600 deaths from starvation and 3,670 households which fled out of the county, *Zhongxiu Qishanxian Zhi*, Xi'an, 1935, p. 418.

21 He Jingyun, *Shaanxi Shiye Kaocha* and *Shaanxi Shiye Kaochaji*, Shanghai, 1933, p. 59–61.

22 *Shanghai Xinwenbao*, July 30, 1929.

23 *Tianjin Dagongbao*, Jan. 12, 1931; *Shaanbao Yuekan*, Vol. I, no. 6 (Dec. 1932), p. 805. *Letter* of Rev. H. Payne to Miss Bowser, 23 Jan., 1932. BMS Archives, London.

24 Sha Fengbao, 'Report of a preliminary investigation of animal husbandry in the Wei River region in Guanzhong, Shaanxi', *Xibei Nonglin*, Special issue on animal husbandry, n.d. (1936?).

25 Chen Gengya, *Xibei Shichaji*, Shanghai 1936, and *Xin Shaanxi* Vol. 1 no. 2, give the following figures for the population within the city walls: 99,895 (1928), 112,172 (1930), 108,000 (June 1931), 114,389 (1932), 125,141 (1934).

26 Bauer and Liu, *Rural Conditions and Cooperative Movement in central Shensi*, Economic Council Manuscript, 1934, p. 25.

27 Harry A. Franck, *Wandering in Northern China*, New York 1923, p. 400, found in 1922 that 'within the walled cities of Shaanxi, shops are often poorer and less energetic, while those outside the walls still have the activity of youth . . . Often the city itself seemed half-deserted, with as many ruins and open spaces as occupied mud-dwellings, though its extramural outskirts might be densely crowded.'

28 *Caizheng Nianjian*, Shanghai 1935, p. 1993, and *Xibei Ziyuan*, Vol. 1 no. 2, p. 16–18. Total provincial and local government tax receipts were 6,250,000 dollars in 1930 and 7,975,000 dollars in 1931, most of which from land tax. Military taxes and exactions greatly exceeded these amounts. Because of the squeeze and illegal practices at all intermediate levels (village, area and district) peasants paid more than triple the official tax, *Shaanbao Yuekan* Vol. 1 no. 6, p. 804–6; Bauer and Liu, *Rural Conditions*, p. 36–8.

29 *Letter* of Rev. H. Payne to Miss Bowser, 23 Jan., 1932, BMS Archives, London. 70 million bushels would be enough to feed Guanzhong's entire population for a year. 'Before the Republic, Shaanxi had all kinds of relief granaries: provincial, prefectural and district granaries, privately managed village granaries, cooperative granaries, temple granaries were everywhere. But all these were plundered and destroyed by the warlords', *Zhongguo Nongcun Jingji Ziliao* p. 768. The fate of the warehouse of Chaoyi county is described in Bauer and Liu; see also *Xuxiu Huxian Xianzhi* 1933 p. 267; *Binzhou Xin Zhigao* 1929, pp. 118–19 and *Dalixian Xinzhi Cungao*, p. 86.

30 Letter by Rev. E. W. Burt from Xi'an, *The Herald* 1930, p. 142; p. 470.

31 *China Christian Yearbook 1931*, Shanghai 1931, p. 292–300.

32 George A. Young, *The Living Christ in Modern China*, London 1947, pp. 64–8; Letter by G. A. Young, *The Herald*, London 1930, p. 208.

33 W. H. Mallory, *China: Land of famine*, New York 1926.

34 *Xin Shaanxi* Vol. 1 no. 1, pp. 9–10. The CIFRC undertook to extend this motor-road to Lanzhou, the capital of Gansu province, in 1931.

35 Li Qinfen and Song Zheyuan, *Xibeijun Jishi (1924–1930 nian)*, HK 1978 (reprint), pp. 34–5, 447–52; *Xibei Ziyuan* vol. 1 no. 4, pp. 78–9.

36 Shaanxi Jinghui Guanliju, *Jinghuiqu Baogao Shu* Dec. 1934; Shaan Xi Bei 16 Sept.–3 Oct., 1936; Longhai Tielu Guanliju, *Shaanxi Shiye Kaocha*, Shanghai 1933, Table 7.

37 The average term of county magistrates was less than a year, Hung-mao Tien, *Government and politics in KMT China 1927–1937*, Stanford 1972, pp. 132, 109.

38 The Yellow River carried 35,000 tons in 1930, mainly coal. The Wei River carried 5,000 tons, mainly cotton. The Luo River carried 4,000 tons, mainly flour and wheat. 'Roads are very inconvenient, so that transport and sales of agricultural products is difficult', *Shaanxi Shiye Kaocha*, pp. 86, 91, 301–2. Even in ordinary years, grain prices varied with a factor of 2 or more between districts, *ibidem*, p. 99, and *Laodong Nianjian 1933*, pp. 635–9.

39 Luo Linzao, 'Xibei Nongmin Fuyedi Zhongyaoxing' (The importance of the sideline occupations of the peasantry of Northwest China), *Shi Huang* vol. 11 no. 3 (1934), p. 25.

40 *Laodong Nianjian 1933*, pp. 551–2; *Zhongguo Nongcun Jingji Ziliao*, p. 146; *Shaanbao Yuekan* vol. 1 no. 6 (Dec. 1932), p. 806.

41 See e.g. Ma Yulin, *Wugong Xian Tudi Wenti Zhi Yanjiu*, 1936, pp. 6–8.
42 *Laodong Nianjian 1933*, p. 552.
43 Bauer and Liu, *Rural Conditions . . .*, p. 35.
44 *Xibei Xiangdao* June–Dec. 1936, p. 374. 'To judge from the opium sales of over 10,000 ounces per month, there are much more users than officially registered in Dali.' In *Xibei Nonglin* Vol. III, July 1938, Wugong's officially registered number of opium addicts in 1936 is stated to be 7,597 out of a district population of 100,000. According to an innkeeper in Wugong 9 out of 10 people smoked opium. 'When the drought came, they had no opium anymore, they became restless, could not walk or move and died of hunger', Zhang Yangming, *Dao Xibei Lai*, Shanghai 1937, pp. 102–5.
45 *Xibei Ziyuan* Vol. 1 no. 6 (1940), pp. 72–9.
46 *Letter* of Rev. H. Payne to Miss Cowser dd. 23 Jan., 1932, BMS Archives, London. He and other missionaries often contrasted the Guanzhong peasants with the industrious Shantungese peasants (often Christians) who had settled in the Sanyuan area some 40 years before. Some Chinese sources do, too. 'Because of opium, the common peasant is weak and lazy. According to labour statistics on the Weihui Ditch a Shantungese can dig 6 cubic meters of earth a day, but a local labourer only 2 meters', *Jiang Jie*, 'Guanzhong Nongcun Renkou Diaocha', (An investigation of the rural population of Guanzhong), *Xibei Nonglin* Vol. III, Jan. 1983.
47 *Letter* of F. S. Russell to Miss M. E. Bowser d.d. 3 Aug., 1935, BMS Archives, London.
48 Fu Anhua, 'The industrial situation in the Northwest', *Xibei Ziyuan* vol. 1 no. 1 (Oct. 1940), pp. 43–58; Jiang Jie, *Xibei Nonglin* Vol. III, p. 53; *Laodong Nianjian* Vol. 1 (1933), pp. 56–8, p. 348.
49 See below, Chapter 4.f.
50 'North Shaanxi peasants do not go into teahouses. Processions have been prohibited; moreover, because of the disastrous years, one cannot afford to hold them. Other activities such as jugglery or martial arts I have not seen once . . . The peasants have no amusement at all', *Shaanxi Shiye Kaocha*, p. 90.
51 Jiang Jie, *Xibei Nonglin* Vol. III.
52 Harry A. Franck, *Wandering in North China*, New York, 1923, p. 400–401.
53 Bauer and Liu, *Rural Conditions . . .*, p. 25.
54 F. H. Nichols, *Through hidden Shensi*, p. 230.
55 Joint Committee of Rural Reconstruction, *Shaanxisheng Nongcun Diaocha* 1934, pp. 145–50.
56 Of the men of marriageable age (i.e. older than 15) 75 percent had married, as against 96 percent of the women, according to a 1936 survey, Jiang Jie, *Xibei Nonglin* Vol. III, p. 109.
57 *Zhongguo Jingji Nianjian 1934*, E204–205.
58 *Zhongguo Jingji Nianjian Xubian 1935*, N461–463; *Xibei Xiangdao* 1936, p. 374. Figures on wasteland and on land tax receipts for 1933 show agricultural decline especially in west Guanzhong, *Caizheng Nianjian* 1935, p. 2100–5.
59 *Laodong Nianjian* 1933, states that the price of dry land in the plains went down by 43 percent between 1931 and 1933, and that of slopeland by 36 percent. During the famine land prices were extremely low. *Shaanbao Yuekan* Vol. 1 no. 6 quotes 9 *yuan* per ha of dry land and 160 *yuan* per ha of irrigated land. The annual wage of an agricultural labourer, besides board and lodging, was 40 to 60 *yuan* during the early 1930s, short-term labourers were sometimes paid as much as 0.50 to 0.70 *yuan* per day in newly developed irrigation areas, and 0.20 *yuan* or so elsewhere, *Minguo 24-nian Mianchan Tongji*, pp. 112–18. By 1936, land prices had gone up again to the 1927 level of 100 to 400 *yuan* per ha of dry land and 700–1500 *yuan* per ha of irrigated

land, Jiang Jie, *Xibei Nonglin* Vol. III; Xiong and Wang, *Shaanxisheng Tudi Zhidu Diaocha Yanjiu*, Wugong, 1941.

60 *Shaanxi Shiye Kaocha*, Shanghai, 1933, p. 87.

61 JCCR, *Shaanxisheng Nongcun Diaocha* 1934.

62 *Shaanbao Yuekan* Vol. I no. 6 (Dec. 1932), pp. 804–6.

63 Jiang Jie, *Xibei Nonglin* Vol. III, p. 76. A 1940 survey of 17 villages in 3 counties found few landowners holding over 6 ha. 70 percent of the farmland was owned by farmers holding less than 3 ha. A decade later, during the communist Land Reform it would appear that less than 10 percent of the total farmland in Guanzhong could be redistributed from landlords and rich peasants to poor peasants and the landless, *Shaanxisheng Tudi Gaige Ziliao Huibian* Vol. I, Oct. 1951, pp. 4, 23.

64 *Mizhixian Yangjiagou Diaocha*, Beijing 1957; *Jigucun Enzhouji*, Beijing 1964; J. Myrdal, *Report from a Chinese Village*; Mark Selden, *The Yenan Way in Revolutionary China*, London 1972.

65 *Zhongguo Jingji Nianjian 1934*, G 264; Xiong and Wang, *Shaanxishang Tudi Zhidu Diaocha Yanjiu* Xibei Nongxueyuan, 1941, pp. 27–31.

66 *Dagongbao* Febr. 16, 1931; *Xin Zhongzao Banyuekan* Vol. II no. 1–2 (July 1932).

67 *Shaan Xi Bei* 16 Sept.–3 Oct. 1936.

68 *Binzhou Xin Zhigao* (1929), p. 109.

69 *Zhongguo Jingji Nianjian 1934*, G264; *Shaan Xi Bei* 16 Sept.–3 Oct., 1936.

70 'Private gangs of those with political or military power, together with local evil gentry, force peasants to sell. Official organizations, such as the Agricultural College, and the North China Relief Society (which during the disaster bought land on a large scale, on which it now has built an orphanage) have also forced people to sell their land. The Longhai Railroad Bureau, the Weihui Ditch Water Conservancy Bureau, the Xi'an–Fengxiang Highway etcetera have all done the same.' Ma Yulin, *Wugongxian* . . . pp. 36, 41. The author is refering to Wugong county.

2 COMMUNICATIONS AND TRANSPORT

1 'In the transportation sector . . . the common fact that China's economy changed only little in the first half of the 20th century has tended to be obscured, pushed out of sight by the disproportionate attention and space devoted to the small modern sector of the economy in official word and deed, in the writings of Chinese economists, in the yearbooks and reports . . .', Albert Feuerwerker, *Economic Trends in the Republic of China 1912–1949*, p. 73.

2 According to a travelogue writer, 'the words soldier–labour seem incompatible in China', Harry A. Franck, *Wandering* . . ., p. 367.

3 Harry A. Franck, *Wandering* . . ., pp. 367–71.

4 O. J. Todd, *Two Decades in China*, pp. 28–9, 220.

5 Harry A. Franck, *Wandering* . . ., p. 393.

6 P. R. Bohr, *Famine in China and the Missionary*, Harvard 1972, pp. 65–8; Deng Yunte, *The North China Famine of 1920–1921*, pp. 7–10.

7 O. J. Todd, *Two Decades* . . ., p. 257 lists these highways, their length and width.

8 O. J. Todd, *Two Decades* . . ., p. 27.

9 *ibidem*, p. 277.

10 'What I saw and heard in Xi'an', *Zhongguo Jianshe* Vol. XIV no. 4 (1936), pp. 116–17; 'Conditions of communications in the Northwest', *Xibei Ziyuan* Vol. I no. 9 (1940), pp. 78–9; *Xibei Lunheng* Vol. X no. 6 (1942), pp. 30–1; *Shaanxi-sheng Tongji Ziliao Huibian* Vol. III (1943) and IV (1944), pp. 65–6.

11 Huang Baikuei, 'The development of coal mining in Hancheng', *Kaifa Xibei* Vol. I no. 6 (1934), pp. 39–41 estimated in 1934 that after construction of the Tongguan–Hancheng railway the cost of coal from the Hancheng mines would drop from 32 *yuan* per ton to 9 *yuan* per ton on the Xi'an market, because of lowered

transport costs; Yang Hucheng, *Xibei Guofang Jingjizhi Jianshe*, n.p. 1938, p. 13 calculated that a railroad Xianyang–Tongchuan–Baishui–Hancheng (250 km long, 85 pound standard track) would cost US $10,000,000; Kang Yongfu, 'Coal mining in Shaanxi and Gansu and proposals for its improvement', *Xibei Lunheng* Vol. IX no. 9 (1941), p. 31–43; Bai Yinyuan, 'Present situation and future of construction of Shaanxi', *Shaanzheng* Vol. VIII no. 1–2 (1946), p. 12–21.

12 *Shaanxisheng Tongji Ziliao Huibian* Vol. III (1943); Ma Yulin, *Wugongxian Tudi Zhiduzhi Yanjiu* 1936, p. 6; *Xibei Jianshe Kaochatuan Baogao* (1943), Taibei 1968, p. 96.

13 'What I saw and heard in Xi'an', *Zhongguo Jianshe* Vol. XIV no. 4 (1936). Truck transport costs were about 0.45 *yuan* per ton/km, Bauer and Liu, *Rural Conditions* . . . pp. 33–4 stated in 1934 that freight on goods by bus from Fengxiang to Xi'an was twice as expensive as by native cart. In 1940, truck transport was over 50 percent more expensive per ton/km than the animal-drawn rubber-tyred cart (which cost 6 yuan per ton per day), *Xibei Ziyuan* Vol. 2 no. 1, pp. 45–60.

14 O. J. Todd, *Two Decades* . . ., pp. 353, 357.

15 Sha Fengbao, 'Report of a preliminary investigation of animal husbandry in the region along the Wei River in Guanzhong, Shaanxi', *Xibei Nonglin* Special Issue, Wugong 1936; *Shaanxisheng zhi Nongye Jianshe* 1942.

16 Wu Guoan, 'The postal transport system and the resources of the Northwest', *Xibei Ziyuan* Vol. 2, no. 1, pp. 45–60.

17 Longhai Tielu Guanliju, *Shaanxi Shiye Kaocha*, Shanghai 1933, pp. 310–16; *Shaanxisheng Tongji Ziliao Huikan* no. 2 (1942), pp. 31–5. In 1942, the number of ships on the Yellow River section was estimated to be over one thousand, on the Wei River section 450. Perhaps half of these had a capacity below 10 tons.

18 The extension and improvement of river transport in Guanzhong was included in the Second Five-Year Plan, but apparently with no success, *Shaanxi Ribao* Oct. 30, 1956.

19 Xibei Yanjiushe (ed.) *Kangzhan Zhongdi Shaanxi*, n.p. 1940, pp. 63–4.

20 Ling Hongxun, *Zhongguo Tielu Zhi*, Taibei, 1963, pp. 210–11; *Xibei Ziyuan* Vol. 1 no. 4, pp. 78–9.

21 Expectations about the development of the Weibei coalfield ran very high. In 1956, the coal mines of Tongchuan were expected to have an output of 6 million tons by 1960. In 1957, they came close to 1 million. *Shaanxi Ribao* 9 Aug. 1956; 6 Feb. 1958. The 1958 target was set at 2 million tons.

22 *Shaanxi Ribao* 23 Feb. and 27 Apr. 1957. The 1957 output of the coal mines in Tongchuan was 900,000 tons, *ibidem* 6 Feb. 1958.

23 In intermediate years, the increase was (1953 = 100) 1954:154, 1955:252, 1956:351, *Shaanxi Ribao* 15 July 1956. In 1957, the average number of waggon loads was 300 per day, *ibidem* 28 Sept. 1957. The 92 percent increase mentioned by *Shaanxi Ribao* 23 Jan. 1958: probably refers to intra-Shaanxi transport only.

24 World Bank, *China: socialist economic development* Vol. II, Washington, 1983, p. 153.

25 'The problem this year is that motive power is only one-quarter of what is needed for transport. For instance along the Shaanxi–Sichuan road, and along the Xi'an–Lanzhou road, the volume of goods has increased by 60 percent, but the motive power not even by 8 percent', *Shaanxi Ribao* 23 Apr. 1955.

26 *Shaanxi Ribao* 15 July 1956, *Shaanxi Ribao* 17 and 28 Sept. 1957; 1 Jan. 1958; oral communication.

27 According to Audrey Donnithorne, in 1957 it was found cheaper to send fertilizer from Nanjing to Chongqing by railroad via Baoji–Chengdu rather than ship it by the Yangzi River, Audrey Donnithorne, *China's Economic System*, New York 1967, p. 267. In its first year the Baoji–Chengdu railway handled one million tons of goods, a.o. large quantities of food grain were transported from Sichuan to the disaster areas of Honan and Hebei provinces, *Shaanxi Ribao* 28 Sept. 1957.

28 *Shaanxi Ribao* 23 April 1955; 7 Nov. 1956; 15 Jan. 1957; 23 Jan. 1958.

29 *Shaanxi Ribao* 23 Apr. 1955.

30 *Shaanxi Ribao* 7 Nov. 1956. For some improved roads, such as Weinan–Hancheng, average speed was stated to reach 40 km/h, *Shaanxi Ribao* 10 Nov. 1956.

31 In an example from south Shaanxi, transport from Zhenba to Xixiang and back (about 80 miles) used to take 5 or 6 days with human porterage and cost 140 *yuan* per ton. After construction of a highway, transport by truck took half a day and cost 26 *yuan* per ton, *Shaanxi Ribao* 28 Sept. 1957.

32 *Shaanxi Ribao* 5 Dec. 1957. According to other sources, early in 1957 6,400 kilometers of roads 'could be passed' by car, and another 2,000 kilometers by horse-cart only. Moreover, there were 800 kilometers of mountain footpaths, *Shaanxi Ribao* 3 Jan. 1957.

33 In 1956 it had been planned to extend Shaanxi's highway network from 4,895 km at the end of 1955 to over 9,000 km at the end of 1957, *Shaanxi Ribao* 30 Oct. 1956.

34 *Shaanxi Ribao* 30 Apr. 1956.

35 That is, short of imports from foreign countries. The first Chinese truck factory was set up in northeast China in 1957. It produced 4.5 ton-trucks. In 1957, capacity of truck transport in Shaanxi increased by only 7.5 percent over 1956, *Shaanxi Ribao* 14 Jan. 1957.

36 According to an editorial, the resultant diminished transport capacity had had negative effects on the flow of goods between villages and cities. The remaining transport carts could not cope with the tasks assigned by higher authorities, *Shaanxi Ribao* 18 Apr. 1956.

37 *Shaanxi Ribao* 7 Nov. 1956 and 15 Jan. 1957.

38 *Shaanxi Nongxun* 1955 no. 2, p. 1; no. 3, pp. 11–12.

39 *Shaanxi Ribao* 30 Oct. 1956.

40 *Xi'an Ribao* editorial, 16 Sept. 1958. According to official figures, freight carried over highways and by railways increased by 82 and 35 percent in 1958 over 1957. The People's Communes had to 'organize an appropriate number of specialized transport corps, and also transport reserve corps' which would 'undertake the collection and dispersal of supplies for the railways and trunk highways', Shaanxi Provincial Work Report 1958, *Shaanxi Ribao* 22 June 1959.

41 Audrey Donnithorne, *China's Economic System*, N.Y., 1967, p. 260; Philip W. Vetterling and James J. Wagy, 'China: the transportation sector, 1950–1971', in U.S. Congress JEC., *People's Republic of China: An Economic Assessment*, Washington D.C. 1972, 147–81; Albert S. Peterson, 'China: transportation developments 1971–1980', US Congress JEC, *China under the Four Modernizations* Part I, Washington D.C. 1982, pp. 138–70.

42 *Shaanxi Prov. Serv.* 31 Dec. 1983.

43 For a description of the native Guanzhong donkey and Qinchuan oxen see H. Epstein, *Domestic Animals of China*, London 1969, pp. 10–11, 113–14.

44 *Xinhua* 18 Oct. 1974; *Shaanxi Prov. Serv.* 29 Dec. 1977; *Shaanxi Ribao* 20 June 1981 and 12 Sept. 1984; *Zhongguo Jingji Nianjian 1983*, p. V 170. According to one source, building of the Xi'an–Yan'an railway was discontinued for some time 'because it might not be of great economic significance as the area was thought to lack underground minerals . . . Very recently it was discovered that large deposits of coal, oil, natural gas, arenaceous quartz and bauxite are located in the area' *Beijing Review* 13 Oct. 1980; *Shaanxi Ribao* 5 Dec. 1983.

45 *Shaanxi Ribao* 1 Oct. 1983. In 1980, China had 110,000 buses; 73 percent of its major roads were paved, *Zhongguo Jingji Nianjian 1981*, pp. 101, 110.

46 Shaanxisheng Keming Weiyuanhui Shuiliju (ed.), *Guanqu Nongtian Jiben Jianshe*, Beijing, 1976, p. 20.

47 World Bank, *China: Socialist Economic Development*, p. 365.

48 *Shaanxi Ribao* 20 June 1981.

49 In an unprecedented move, the factory was closed down on the orders of the provincial government, to be opened again after several conditions had been met by management and workers, *Shaanxi Ribao* 15 Nov. and 23 Dec. 1983.

50 *Zhongguo Jingji Nianjian 1983*, p. v 166; *Shaanxi Ribao* 20 June 1981.

51 *Shaanxi Ribao* 20 June 1981.

52 This is in line with the forecasts made by the World Bank Report, *China Socialist Economic Development*, p. 297.

53 *Shaanxi Ribao* 1 Oct. and 12 Dec. 1983; 3 Jan. 1984. Within Xi'an municipality, the volume of passenger transport increased by 84 percent between 1981 and 1982, *Zhongguo Jingji Nianjian 1983*, p. v 170.

54 *Shaanxi Ribao* 7 Feb. 1984.

55 *ibidem* 5 Oct. 1984.

3 THE GROWTH OF XI'AN AND INDUSTRIAL DEVELOPMENT

1 Wang Chongren, *Gudu Xi'an*, Xi'an, 1981; Shaanxisheng Bowuguan (ed.), *Xi'an Lishi Shulüe*, Xi'an, 1959; Ma Zhenglin, *Fenghao – Changan – Xi'an*, Xi'an, 1978; Tan Manni, 'The Thirty Centuries of Xi'an', *China Reconstructs* May 1982; *Xi'an Wenwu Shengji*, Xi'an, 1959; China International Travel Service, *China Travel, Xi'an*, Beijing, 1978. Of the Qin dynasty capital in Xianyang on the North bank of the Wei River nothing is left. Fragments of the Han dynasty Changan city wall (26 km in circumference) and Weiyang palace, and of the Tang dynasty city wall (36 km in circumference) can still be seen in the rural outskirts of Xi'an. The two pagoda's of Xi'an date back to the seventh century A.D. The traditional population figures of Changan during the Han (550,000) and the Tang dynasties (over 1 million) may have been exaggerated, Li Zhiqin, 'Xi'an Gudai Hukou Shumu Pingyi', *Xibei Daxue Xuebao* 1984 no. 2, pp. 45–51. The best description of the city walls has been given by Bishop, 'The walls of Changan', *Antiquity* 1938 no. 12.

2 'Sanyuan is one of the largest and most important cities in Shaanxi. Commercially it is an annex of Xi'anfu, much of the commerce which really belongs to the latter being transacted here to avoid the official exactions of the provincial capital. For the same reason most of the trade to and from Gansu passes through Sanyuan', E. Teichman, *Travels of a consular officer in Northwest China*, pp. 82–3.

3 Rhoads Murphy, *The Fading of the Maoist Vision: City and Country in China's Development*, New York, 1980.

4 C. S. Liu, chairman of the National Economic Council in the Northwest, to overseas students, Nien-li Liu, 'A tour from Nanking to the Northwest of China', *The China Review* Apr/June 1935.

5 *Zhongguo Jingji Nianjian Xubian 1935*, N 461–463; *Laodong Nianjian* Vol. 1 (1933), p. 56–58.

6 George A. Young, *The Living Christ in Modern China*, London 1947, p. 116.

7 Precise figures for 1930 through 1940 are given in 'The importance of land tax in Shaanxi's finance and its abuses', *Xibei Ziyuan* Vol. 1 no. 2 (1940), pp. 16–18. In 1936–8, yearly receipts were 17 million dollars.

8 *Caizheng Nianjian* 1935, pp. 1993, 2100–5, 2243–4, 2347–9. The opium fines were used mainly to cover the expenses of the military administration. For a comparison with other provinces, see Hung-mao Tien, *Government and Politics in Kuomintang China 1927–1937*, Stanford, 1972, p. 155. See also Bauer and Liu, *Rural Conditions . . .*, pp. 6–11.

9 Xu Fang, *Xibei Jiaofei Zhanshi Gaiyao*, Changan, 1936.

10 Quoted in *The China Review* Apr.–June 1935, p. 25.

11 'Political customs in Changan county', Chen Gengya, *Xibei Shichaji*, Shanghai 1936, p. 445; Rev. F. S. Russell, 'The Railway Comes to Sian', *The Herald* of the Baptist Missionary Society 1935, p. 55.

12 The thermo-power station had an electricity-generating capacity of only 750 kW at first, and 2,750 kW from 1937 onwards, *Xibei Ziyuan* Vol. 1 no. 2 (1940), p. 31. Large mills such as the Dahua cotton mill and the Huafeng and Chengfeng flour mills had their own sources of power. The total electric-generating capacity in Xi'an added up to 7,850 kW during the 1936–49 period, 2,300 kW of which with the First Power Station, *Xi'an Ribao* 7 July and 7 Sept. 1957. The water works was not yet finished in 1937, and completed only in 1946. The cotton mill and the machinery factory (which made agricultural implements, steam road rollers and measuring scales) had 120 and 130 labourers, *Zhongguo Jianshe* Vol. xiv no. 4 (1936), pp. 114–16.

13 *Caizheng Nianjian 1935*, p. 2347–2349; Sun Gehui, 'The problem of balancing our province's budget after the changes in the system of receipts', *Shaanzheng* Vol. 8 no. 1 (1947), p. 40.

14 *Zhongguo Jianshe* Vol. xiv no. 4 (1936), p. 114–15; *Xibei Ziyuan* Vol. 1 no. 2 (1940), p. 31.

15 Kang Yongfu, 'Coal mining in Shaanxi and Gansu and proposals for its improvement', *Xibei Lunheng* Vol. ix no. 9 (1941), pp. 31–43. Fu Anhua, 'The industrial situation in the Northwest', *Xibei Ziyuan* Vol. 1 no. 1 (1940), p. 45.

16 Xibei Yanjiushe (ed.), *Kangzhan Zhongdi Shaanxi*, n.p. 1940, p. 48–50.

17 Wu Yong, 'The problem of material production and supply in the Northwest during wartime', *Xibei Ziyuan* Vol. 1 no. 3 (1941), pp. 54–67, gives a list of some twenty major export products in 1936 and 1937. Total value of imports and exports during 1934–7 (opium excluded) was as follows:

	Exports	Imports	
1934	14.9	54.0	(million *yuan*)
1935	19.3	28.5	„
1936	29.9	29.7	„
1937	15.6	53.4	„

Source: *Kangzhan Zhongdi Shaanxi* 1940, pp. 61–2.

18 Dang Manzhen, 'Zhongguo Gongchandang Shi Ruhe Dadui Diyici Fangong Gaohcaodi', (How did the Chinese Communist Party beat off the first anti-communist campaign?) *Jiaoxue yu Yanjiu* 1981 no. 3, pp. 14–21.

19 Hsi-sheng Ch'i, *Nationalist China at war*, Ann Arbor 1982, pp. 80, 105.

20 Gunther Stein, *The Challenge of Red China*, New York 1945, p. 41.

21 *Kangzahn Zhongdi Shaanxi* 1940, p. 88–9, 126–9.

22 Hung-mao Tien, *Government and Politics* ... p. 30; Ma Jianzhong, "Factional struggle in the Shaanxi Provincial Guomindang", *Xi'an Wenshi Ziliao* Vol. 4 (1983) p. 88–101.

23 George A. Young, *The Living* ..., p. 166, 177–178. Actually, Hu Zongnan established this 'Northwestern Youth Labour Camp' in Xianyang in summer of 1939, from where it was moved to Zi'an's suburbs in spring 1940, Ma Zhenglin, *Fenghao – Changan – Xi'an*, p. 119. A Western delegation visited the camp in 1944, Gunther Stein, *The Challenge of Red China*, pp. 36–8.

24 *Kangzhan Zhongdi Shaanxi*, p. 54, 228–230.

25 *Price indexes in Xi'an 1937–40* (June 1937 = 100)

	Dec. 1937	June 1938	Dec. 1938	June 1939	Dec. 1939	June 1940
Foodstuffs	93	81	82	78	159	311
Clothing	106	117	162	149	378	605
Metal goods	163	188	232	274	529	551
Building materials	120	115	125	129	280	341
(weighted index	105	102	117	117	252	397)

Source: Zhao Lunyuan, 'About the war-time price control', *Xibei Ziyuan* Vol. 3 no. 1, pp. 71–6.

The 'general price index' used in this source is unweighted and does not reflect household consumption. A weighted index (foodstuffs 6, clothing 2, other 2) has therefore been added by me; it may understate the increased burden of housing rent, and of salt.

26 See footnote 25 and Han Qingtao, 'The problem of production and sales of edible salt in the Northwest', *Xibei Ziyuan* Vol. 1 no. 3 (1940), pp. 54–67.

27 Fu Anhua, 'The industrial situation in the Northwest', *ibidem* Vol. 1 no. 2, pp. 31–7.

28 'Heavy bombings of Sian created a great wave of refugees, that carried Baoji's population swiftly to 60,000 in the summer of 1939', George Hogg, *I see a New China*, Boston 1944, p. 45. Before the railroad reached Baoji in 1938, its city population had been less than ten thousand.

29 George A. Young, *The Living . . .*, p. 197.

30 Fu Anhua, 'The industrial situation in the Northwest', *Xibei Ziyuan* Vol. 1 no. 1, p. 43–58; George Hogg, *I see . . .*; *Kangzhan Zhongdi Shaanxi*, pp. 53–7.

31 According to Arthur N. Young, *China's wartime finance and inflation 1937–1945*, Cambridge 1965, p. 351, retail market prices in Xi'an developed as follows:

(Jan.–June 1937 = 1.00)

Year	1938		1939		1940		1941	
Month	6	12	6	12	6	12	6	12
	1.32	1.60	2.19	3.00	4.46	7.75	10.95	21.88

Year	1942		1943		1944		1945	
Month	6	12	6	12	6	12	6	12
	37.7	71.8	206	301	468	794	2671	2458

32 Zhao Lunyuan, 'About the wartime price control', *Xibei Ziyuan* Vol. 3 no. 1, pp. 71–6.

33 'Past and present of banking in Shaanxi', *Xibei Ziyuan* Vol. 1 no. 6 (1941), pp. 20–5; Zhongguo Xian Yinhang Nianjianshe, *Zhongguo Xian Yinhang Nianjian*, Shanghai, 1948, pp. 165–11.

34 Sun Gehui, 'The problem of balancing our province's budget after the changes in the system of receipts', *Shaanzheng* Vol. 8 no. 1–2 (1947), pp. 40–2.

35 Li Zhongzhi, 'Xibei Gonghe Yundong Shulüe' (Synopsis of the coop movement in the Northwest), *Xibei Daxue Xuebao* 1983 no. 3, pp. 28–35. George Hogg, *I see . . .*, p. 45, 66–68.

36 Ma Zhenglin, *op. cit.*, p. 33; *Xibei Jianshe Kaochatuan Baogao*, p. 305.

37 Wang Feng, 'Tongguan Meitian Zibenzhuyi Fazhan Diaocha' (An investigation of the capitalist development of the coalfields of Tongguan), *Shaanxi Shida Xuebao* 1984 no. 1, p. 90–95.

38 Li Zixiang, 'Private industries in the Rear area during the war', *Jingji Zhoubao* Vol. 2 no. 6 (1946), pp. 9–12 and no. 7, pp. 14–17.

39 See chapter on cotton production, Xie Jianyun, 'Flour industry in Xi'an', *Xibei Tongxun* Vol. III no. 1 (July 1948), pp. 13–14, and Bai Yinyuan, 'Present situation and future of construction of Shaanxi', *Shaanzheng* Vol. VIII no. 1–2 (1946).

40 *Xibei Jianshe Kaochatuan Baogao*, Taibei, 1968, pp. 28, 48, 57, 305–12.

41 Chen Cheng-siang, 'Population Growth and Urbanization in China 1953–1970', *Geographical Review* Vol. 63 (1973), p. 66.

42 The Huanglongshan resettlement area, which was used for animal husbandry and forestry, had been occupied in part by the communists, *Xibei Jianshe Kaochatuan Baogao*, pp. 289–91; Gunther Stein, *The Challenge of Red China*, NY 1945, pp. 41–50. There were also some small reclamation areas on the Wei River banks and in the Qinling mountains, none of which attracted many settlers, *ibidem* and Wu Chunke, 'Introduction to collective farms of refugees in Meixian and Fufeng', *Zhongnong Yuekan* Vol. 7 (Dec. 1947), pp. 51–5.

43 Of the remaining one-third, 27,000 relief recipients lived in Yongshou county, which had been recaptured from the communists, *Shaanxisheng Tongji Ziliao Huikan* no. 5, p. 166. In 1939, only 3,000 war refugees were on relief in Xi'an; in the counties, relief was provided mostly by individuals or missionary societies, Wang Depu (ed.) *Shaanxi Minzheng Gaikuang*, Relief Section, p. 1–4.

44 *Xi'an Lishi Shulüe*, p. 123; Ma Zhenglin, 'An investigation of a fundamental way of solving present and future problems of water resources, seen from the historical water supply of Xi'an', *Shaanxi Shida Xuebao* 1981 no. 4.

45 *Xibei Jianshe Kaochatuan Baogao*, p. 394–404.

46 Wang Depu (ed.), *Shaanxi Minzheng Gaikuang*, 1940; Ren Fu, 'Survey of the implementation of public health programs for women and children in Xi'an during 1940', *Xibei Lunheng* Vol. 9 no. 3 (1941), pp. 54–6.

47 *Shaanxisheng Tongji Ziliao Huikan* no. 5.

48 *Xibei Ziyuan* Vol. 1 no. 4 (1940), pp. 170–1; *Xi'an Ribao* 9 July 1957. Infant mortality was not included in the death rate.

49 H. R. Williamson, *British Baptists in China 1845–1952*, London 1957, p. 191.

50 Bai Yinyuan, 'The present situation and future of construction of Shaanxi', *Shaanzheng* Vol. VIII no. 1–2 (1946), p. 12–21.

51 Xie Jianyun, 'The May inflation in Xi'an', *Jingji Zhoubao* Vol. VI no. 22, 27 May 1948.

52 We have provincial budgetary data only for the first half of 1946, Sun Gehui, 'The problem of balancing our provincial budget after the changes in the system of receipts', *Shaanzheng* Vol. VIII no. 1–2 (1947), p. 40–2.

53 Albert Feuerwerker, *Economic Trends in the Republic of China 1912–1949*, Michigan, 1977, p. 90.

54 Xie Jianyun, 'The May inflation in Xi'an', *Jingji Zhoubao* Vol. VI no. 22, 27 May 1948.

55 Ma Zhenglin, *Fenghao – Changan – Xi'an*, Xi'an 1978, pp. 118–119, and personal communications to author. A somewhat less peaceful transition of power in Guanzhong has been suggested by a communist participant, Gao Mianchun, 'Cong Aozhan Guanzhong dao Lanzhou Dajie' (From the fierce battle for Guangzhong to the great victory at Lanzhou), *Shehui Kexue* (Lanzhou) 1982 no. 1.

56 *Zhongguo Jingji Nianjian 1983*, v p. 169; Yuan Ke, 'We love Xi'an', *Xi'an Ribao* 20 May 1958.

57 Productivity per labourer in industry in 1952 was 80 percent up on 1950, Zhang Shuyun, 'Is it a dogma to say that achievements are most important?' *Xi'an Ribao* 7 Sept. 1957. Between 1952 and 1956, despite new investments in modern production facilities it rose only by 40 percent, *ibidem*.

58 Thirteen banks were put under State guidance. Most capital had gone, however, and only 24.8 billion RMB (about US$1,500,000) remained, Dang Runyi, 'Jiefang Qianhou Xi'an Jinrongye Shilüe' (Historical abstract of the banking business in Xi'an before and after liberation), *Shaanxi Ribao* 29 Feb. 1984. In 1951, a joint public-private loan bureau was set up by Xi'an city, with the aim of collecting capital from both public and private banks, *Qunzhong Ribao* 25 Mar. 1951.

59 *Qunzhong Ribao* 11 and 28 Oct. 1950; 8 Jan. and 11 and 12 Feb. 1951. 1 catty of wheat gave 0.67 catty of wheat flour, which was sold in bags of 40 catties.

60 *Qunzhong Ribao* 25 Oct. 1950.

61 *Qunzhong Ribao* 11 Jan. 1951.

62 *Qunzhong Ribao* 4 Oct. 1950.

63 It was renamed the Northwest People's Cotton Textile Company, *Shaanxi Ribao* 29 Feb. 1984.

64 *Qunzhong Ribao* 30 Jan. 1951. A history of the Xianyang Cotton Textile mill describes how the working-day was reduced to 11 hours in 1950 and to 10 hours in 1951, and one day off every 7 days instead of 10 days, *Shinian Xinsuan Shinian Tian –*

Shaanxi Diyi Mianfang Zhichang Zhuangjian 10-nian Shihgao (mimeograph), Xi'an 1959.

65 *Qunzhong Ribao* 20 and 22 Feb. 1952.

66 Ren Ziyang at the Political Consultative Conference, *Shaanxi Ribao* 2 June 1957.

67 'Have living conditions of the workers improved after liberation or not?' *Shaanxi Ribao* 27 November 1957. The Xi'an average wage in State enterprises in 1956 was stated to be 15.3 percent higher than in 1955, about 30 percent higher than in 1952–3, and 53 percent higher than in 1950. *Xi'an Ribao* 2 and 3 Oct. 1957, *Shaanxi Ribao* 27 Nov. 1957.

68 Letter to the editor, *Shaanxi Ribao* 23 Oct. 1956.

69 *Shaanxi Ribao* 29 Sept. 1956; 9 July 1957.

70 Rhoads Murphey, *The Fading of the Maoist Vision: City and Country in China's Development*, New York, 1980, p. 70.

71 Although Murphey, *ibidem* p. 80, proposes that in the Chinese setting it meant 'additional emphasis on industry as opposed to trade, suppression of bourgeois consumerism and high life-styles and reorientation of city economies to expedite their serving of the countryside with both goods and services'. Certainly the last item was a Chinese concept.

72 Clifton W. Pannell *in*: Laurence J. C. Ma and Edward W. Hanten (eds), *Urban Development in Modern China*, Boulder Co., 1981, pp. 120–1.

73 G. W. Skinner, 'Vegetable supply and marketing in Chinese cities', *China Quarterly* no. 76 (December 1978), pp. 758–9.

74 Wu Zhenfeng, *Shaanxi Dili Yange*, Xi'an, 1981.

75 A plea for the incorporation of Xianyang was rejected, Yang Zhongguang et al. 'Guanyu Fahui Xi'anshi Jingji Zhongxin Zuoyongdi Diaocha' (Investigation concerning the development of the central function of the economy of Xi'an municipality), *Caimao Jingji* 1983 no. 10, pp. 60–4.

76 *Xi'an Ribao* 9 June 1957.

77 *Zhongguo Xinwen* 16 Nov. 1957.

78 *Zhongguo Jingji Nianjian* 1983, v p. 169 (GVIO expressed in 1980 prices); Li Tingbi, 'Xi'an has shaken off its backward aspect', *Shaanxi Ribao* 10 Sept. 1957; *Zhongguo Xinwen* 16 Nov. 1957; Zhang Shuyun, 'Is "achievements are most important" a dogma?' *Xi'an Ribao* 7 Sept. 1957. Local industry's (including handicrafts) gross output value rose by 136 percent between 1952 and 1957 to 370 million *yuan*, 'Municipal Government Work Report for 1957', *Xi'an Ribao* 5 June 1958.

79 Gross Industrial Output Value of Shaanxi Province rose by 149 percent during 1952–7, *Shaanxi Diyige Wunian Jihua Qijiandi Caizheng Mianmao*, Xi'an, 1958.

80 Liu Geng, 'Report on major work done since 1957 and the tasks for Xi'an', *Xi'an Ribao* 5 June 1958. Of the total capital investment in Shaanxi province of some 350 million *yuan* during 1953–1957, 73 million *yuan* was financed through public bonds, *Shaanxi Diyige Wunian Jihua Qijiandi Caizheng Mianmao*, Xi'an, 1958.

81 Qian Hua et al., *Qinianlai Woguo Siying Gongshangyedi Bianhua, 1949–1956-nian*, Beijing, 1957.

82 See source of Table 15, p. 228–229.

83 In June 1955, Xi'an *shi* had carried out the socialist transformation of the private wholesale establishments of food, cotton cloth, edible oil, coal, tea, and salt, *Xinhua News Agency* 29 June 1955.

84 *Shaanxi Ribao* 9 Jan. 1957; Wang Taixi, *Xibei Daxue Xuebao* 1984 no. 4, p. 94.

85 *Xi'an Ribao* 20 Aug. 1958.

86 *1954-Nian Quanguo Geti Shougongye Diaocha Ziliao*, p. 236.

87 *Xi'an Ribao* 5 June 1958.

88 *Shaanxi Ribao* 27 Oct. 1956.

89 *Shaanxi Ribao* 22 and 23 Aug., 11 and 17 Oct. 1956.

90 *Shaanxi Ribao* 13 Oct. 1956.

91 *Shaanxi Ribao* 7 Jan. 1957. According to the authorities, 42,000 peasants returned to their village from Xi'an during December 1956–April 1957. 'Because Xi'an does not need so many construction workers . . ., commodity supply and housing situation is tight; . . . they are needed in their village', *Shaanxi Ribao* 28 Apr. 1957.

92 Editorial, 'Educate the peasants not to flock blindly into the cities', *Shaanxi Ribao* 16 March 1957.

93 *Shaanxi Ribao* 22 March 1957.

94 *Gongshang Jingji* 19 Oct. 1957, translated in *Survey of China Mainland Press* no. 1678 (Dec. 1957), p. 31; *Shaanxi Ribao* 15 Nov. and 5 Dec. 1957.

95 *Shaanxi Ribao* 5 June 1958.

96 *Xi'an Ribao* 20 Nov. 1958.

97 *Xi'an Ribao* 1 and 14 Nov. 1958, editorials.

98 Liu Geng's speech at Second Meeting of Third Congress of People's Representatives, *Xi'an Ribao* 20 Nov. 1958.

99 *Xi'an Ribao* 5 Sept. 1958.

100 Christopher Howe, 'Industrialization under conditions of long-run population stability: Shanghai's achievement and prospect', in C. Howe (ed.), *Shanghai: Revolution and Development in an Asian Metropolis*, Cambridge, 1981, p. 187.

101 K. I. Fung, 'Urban Sprawl in China: Some Causative Factors', in Laurence J. C. Ma and Edward W. Hanten (eds), *Urban Development in Modern China*, Boulder Co., 1981, pp. 194–221.

102 Industrial and City Construction Bureau of the Xi'an Municipal People's Committee, 'Xi'an shi Chengshi Jianshe Gongzuozhongdi Jige Wenti' (Some problems of urban construction work in Xi'an municipality), *Chengshi Jianshe* 1957 no. 2, pp. 1–4.

103 Xinhua reporter, 'Change the style of inappropriately large city planning of Xi'an', *Xi'an Ribao* 25 May 195?.

104 Xiong Zhengping, *Xi'an Ribao* 25 May 1957. Rents had been lowered in December 1956, *Shaanxi Ribao* 2 Dec. 1956.

105 *Shaanxi Ribao* 30 Apr. 1957.

106 Fang Shanshou, 'Gongkuang Zhuzhai Shejidi Neirong yu Xingshi Wenti', *Jianzhu Xuebao* 1959 no. 3; Guojia Jianshe Weiyuanhui, 'Chengshi Jianshebu Guanyu Chengshi Kuihua Jixiang Kongzhi Zhibiaodi Tongzhi', *Fakui Huibian 1958* 1–6, pp. 180–2.

107 See above, note 101.

108 Hans Schenk, 'Notes on urban spatial planning and development in China', *Eastern Horizon* Vol. 11 no. 2 (1972).

109 'Xi'anshi Chengshi Jianshe Gongzuozhong Jige Wenti (Some problems of the urban construction work in Xi'an municipality)', *Jianshe Yuekan* 1957 no. 12; in 1956, the average per capita living space in 175 Chinese cities was 3.5 square meters, Kojima Reiitsu (ed.), *Chūgoku no Toshika to Nōson Kensetsu*, Tokyo, 1978, p. 60.

110 Liu Wenwei's Speech at the People's Political Consultative Conference, *Shaanxi Ribao* 23 March 1957.

111 Gu Duojing, '"Gutou" he "Rou" di Touzi Bili Guanxi Wenti' (Problems of the relative investment ratios between 'bones' and 'meat'), *Jianshe Yuekan* 1957 no. 10.

112 Kojima Reiitsu (ed.), *Chūgoku no Toshika to Nōson Kensetsu*, pp. 70–4.

113 By 1979, industrial plants in Xi'an discharged 300,000 tons of polluted water every day. Of these, only 60,000 tons were treated by natural settling. 17,000 hectares of farmland, which had been irrigated with untreated water for many years, had severely polluted soil, *Turang* no. 5 (Oct. 1979), p. 184; *Shaanxi Provincial Service* 26 June 1978. The underground water has high levels of nitrogen, Dong Fakai, 'Xi'anshi Dixiashui Dan Wurandi Huanjing Shuiwen Tantao' (Probe into the environmental hydrogeology of pollution by nitrogen of the underground water of Xi'an municipality), *Huanjing Kexue* Vol. v no. 2 (1984), pp. 35–8.

114 Of the housing stock of Xi'an, about 60 percent was owned by (which as a rule also means: constructed by) production units, and most of the remainder by the Municipality, Laurence J. C. Ma and Edward W. Hanten (eds), *Urban Development*, p. 224.

115 *Shaanxi Ribao* 7 June 1957.

116 *Xi'an Ribao* 5 Sept. 1958.

117 *Xi'an Ribao* 3 Nov. 1958. A production target for 1958 had been handed down of 130,000 tons, *Xi'an Ribao* 2 Sept. 1958; a month later, it had been raised to 150,000 to 180,000 tons, *Tongji Gongzuo* no. 19 (Oct. 1958), pp. 15–16. The first large steel mill was completed at the end of 1958.

118 *Xi'an Ribao* 30 Sept. 1957; *Shaanxi Nongye* no. 2 (Nov. 1961), p. 28–9; Yang Tingliang et al., *Jinri Xi'an*, Xi'an, 1957.

119 Official data for Shaanxi province reported drought in 1959, but also an increased production of grain and commercial crops. Gross income from agriculture and sidelines rose by 12 percent over 1958 and by 50 percent over 1957. Gross industrial production value rose by 48 percent over 1958 and by 150 percent over 1957 – but the political conclusion drawn in 1960 was that the agricultural 'front' should be reinforced using all available means, Fang Zhongru, *Qianfang Baiji Jiaqiang Nongye Zhanxian*, Xi'an, 1960.

120 *Jieyue Liangshidi Xianjin Jingyan*, Xi'an 1960.

121 E. B. Vermeer, 'Income differentials in rural China', *China Quarterly* March 1982.

122 *Jieyue Liangshidi Xianjin Jingyan*, Xi'an, 1960, p. 17.

123 *Ibidem*.

124 See appendix on demographic developments. 1959 was the worst drought year since 30 years in Guanzhong. Early in 1960, sweet potatoes were recommended as a drought-resistant, high yield crop. Fengxiang county's famous breweries started to make liquor without grain. The green fertilizer sown area had risen in 1959, but then went down to maybe one-half in 1961. Grain output figures published for Shangluo Special District (South of Guanzhong) show good harvests in 1958 through 1960 (resp. 348, 355, and 335 thousand tons) and bad harvests in 1957 and 1961 (257 and 267 thousand tons), while Yan'an and Yulin Special Districts had good harvests in 1959 and 1961 (500,000 tons) a harvest of 450,000 tons in 1960, and bad harvests of 380,000 resp. 400,000 tons in 1962–3. Although Shangluo's 1960 grain harvest was 20,000 tons lower than during the previous year, it exported 25,000 tons, ten times as much as in the previous two years. Within Guanzhong, although droughts and low yields of rice and maize were reported for 1959 in Hancheng and Zhouzhi counties, the 1959 foodgrain output of Dali county (extreme east of Guanzhong) was quite normal (143,000 tons), and from Longxian county (extreme west of Guanzhong) and Qianxian county quite good harvests were reported. Probably, the 1959 grain harvest was not much below that of 1958, but the 1960 grain harvest was. At the time, it was stated that the 1960 grain harvest of Shaanxi province was larger than the 1957 one (which had been a bad harvest year, with a total foodgrain output of 4,523,000 tons), although Shaanxi was twice ravaged by a serious drought lasting 100 days. Nevertheless, the grain saving campaigns started already early in 1959, and were stepped up during the winter of 1959–1960. In Guanzhong in 1961, the spring was rather dry, and August was wet; the next year, spring was very dry, and so was June. 10-day precipitation and soil humidity data for Guanzhong have been given in *Zhongguo Turang*, Beijing 1980, p. 269; p. 278 provides water consumption data for Wugong's wheat and cotton in 1957, 1962 and 1963. Fang Zhongru, *Qianfang Baiji Jiaqiang Nongye Zhanxian*, p. 2–3; Shaanxisheng Nonglinting, *Shaanxisheng 1959 – nian Mianhua Fengchan Jishu Jingyan Huibian*, Xi'an 1960, p. 2; idem, *Shaanxisheng 1959 – nian Lianghsi Fengchan Jishu Jingyan Hiubian*, Xi'an 1960; 'Dui Shaanxi Guanzhong Diqu Zengzhong Ganshudi Yijian', *Shaanxi Nongye Kexue* 1960 no. 2, p. 52–53; 'Fazhan Lufei,

Zengchan Liangmian', *Shaanxi Nongye* 1962 no. 3, p. 1–3 and no. 1, p. 11–13 *Shaanxi Nongye* 1962 no. 2, p. 1 and 7; *Shaanxi Nongye Kexue* 1960 no. 1, p. 10 and 34; no. 3, p. 121; no. 4, p. 183; *Jieyue Liangshidi Xianjin Jingyan* p. 13 and 152–155; *Hong Qi* 1961 no. 7, p. 8–11; Xibei Nongxueyuan, *Guanghuidi Shinian, Shaanxisheng Qianxian Fenghuo Renmin Gongshedi Chengzhang*, p. 43–48. *Shaanxi Ribao* 18 Nov. 1960 and 4 Feb. 1958; Renwen Zazhi (ed.), *Shaanxi Jingji Tantao*, Xi'an 1984, p. 16.

125 *Xibei Nongxueyuan Xuebao* 1959 no. 1, several articles; *Xibei Daxue Xuebao* Dec. 1958, p. 1–24; *Jianzhu Xuebao* 1958 no. 12, p. 12–13.

126 Editorial, *Xibei Nonglin* no. 1 (Jan. 1960), p. 63.

127 *Shaanxi Ribao* 14 June 1980.

128 The size of the 1958 foodgrain harvest is not mentioned in this source. Contemporary figures vary; a revised figure of 7.1 million tons was carried by the Shaanxi Ribao of 1 October 1959, but this was still an unlikely 30 percent higher than the record harvest of 1956. I assume that in comparing 1962 with 1958, an estimate of the 1958 foodgrain output has been used which is about equal to the 1956 harvest of 5.4 million tons. At least earlier *wheat* output figures had been very close, viz. 2,460,000 tons in 1956 and 2,500,000 tons in 1958, *Shaanxi Ribao* 2 Nov. 1956 and *Renmin Ribao* 30 May 1958. The 22 per cent decrease is close to the all-China average.

129 Zheng Zhicheng, 'Gaijin Gongzuo Tigao Jingji Xiaoguo', *Lilun Tansuo*, March 1980; *Shaanxi Jingji Tantao*, Xi'an, 1983, p. 293.

130 Tao Xiong and Wen Qun, 'Lanzhoushi Renkou Fazhan Qushi Fenxi' (Analysis of the development tendencies of the population of Langzhou municipality), *Xibei Renkou* 1980 no. 1.

131 *Shaanxi Ribao* 26 Feb. 1982; *Renmin Ribao* 2 May 1957; *Shaanxi Ribao* 18 July 1957; in 1960, a record 348 *yuan* per capita output value was reached (112 *yuan* more than the 1956 provincial figure), Ju Xiuzhen and Liang Naizhong, 'Shaanxisheng Renkou Xianzhuang Yu Kongzhi Tujing' (The present situation of the population of Shaanxi province and prospects for its control), in *Xibei Gesheng Renkou Wenti Lunji*, Shenzhou Press reprint, Hongkong 1981.

132 According to the *Shaanxi Ribao* 7 May 1983, in Shaanxi Province 1,980,000 more people depended on commercial grain consumption in 1981 than in 1963. Foodgrain rations increased from 501,000 tons to 978,000 tons. I assume the average ration (241 kg) to have been as low as 200 kg after the food crisis. Thus, in 1963, non-agricultural population may have been about 2,500,000 people. A peak figure of 3,600,000 people in 1960 has been reported in private communication. In the neighbouring province of Henan, the urban population dropped by 30 percent; Henan was much more seriously affected than Shaanxi, however, with a death rate of 39.6 per 1,000 in 1960 or 25.5 above the previous year. To put it more bluntly, 1.3 million people in Henan were killed by the post-Leap crisis in 1960, Lin Furui and Zhen Daikuang, *Henan Renkou Dili*, Henan, 1983, pp. 106–7, 115, 184. This publication gives no details on refugees from Henan in other provinces such as Shaanxi.

133 Wang Taixi, 'Xi'anshi Geti Jingjidi Lishi he Xiankuang' (History and present situation of the individual economy in Xi'an municipality), *Xibei Daxue Xuebao* 1984 no. 4.

134 See graph B. 1968 was the nadir of Shaanxi's industrial and agricultural production, due no doubt to the disturbances and lack of government control during the Cultural Revolution. The per capita output value in that year was only 216 *yuan*, as against 416 *yuan* two years later and 236 *yuan* in 1956, Ju Xiuzhen and Liang Naizhong, 'Shaanxisheng Renkou Xianzhuang Yu Kongzhi Tujing' (The present situation of the population of Shaanxi province and prospects for its control), in *Xibei Gesheng Renkou Wenti Lunji*, Shenzhou Press reprint, Hongkong 1981.

135 *Zhongguo Jingji Nianjian 1981*, IV, pp. 309ff; *Shaanxi Ribao* 8 Sept. 1984.
136 *Shaanxi Ribao* 23 Nov. 1981, 19 March 1982 and 25 Jan. 1984; *Dili Zhishi* 1984 no. 5; *Xinhua*, Eng. 17 July 1984.
137 *Shaanxi Ribao* 4 and 7 Nov. 1981; 14 June 1980; 13 July 1984.
138 Huo Jizhao, 'Jiben Jianshe Bixu Jiangjiu Touzi Xiaoguo' (In capital construction one must pay attention to investment results), *Shaanxi Ribao* 14 June 1980; Zheng Zhicheng, 'Gaijin Gongzuo Tigao Jingji Xiaoguo' (Improve work and raise economic results), *Lilun Tansuo* 1980 no. 3; *Shaanxi Ribao* 25 Apr. 1984.
139 *Ibidem* and *Shaanxi Ribao* 15 and 19 Nov., 23 Dec. 1983, 4 Mar. and 6 Apr. 1985.
140 *Shaanxi Ribao* 17 and 27 Apr. 1983, 27 Jan. and 17 May 1984.
141 Yang Zhongguang e.a., 'Guanyu Fahui Xi'anshi Jingji Zhongxin Zuoyongdi Diaocha', *Caimao Jingji* 1983 no. 10, pp. 60–4.
142 The article has been available to this author only through a non-confidential publication in which some of the financial data appear to have been blotted out. It was originally carried by *Lilun Tansuo*, March 1980.
143 *Zhongguo Jingji Nianjian 1981*, IV pp. 306–9 and 1982, VIP. 168.
144 Yang Hongzhang, 'Can the problem of unemployment be solved'?, *Shaanxi Ribao* 25 Nov. 1981.
145 In 1982, the employment situation was as follows:
Shaanxi urban and state employees, 1982

	state controlled organizations	township- or collectively controlled units
Total, of which:	2,586,000	499,000
Industry	1,151,000	256,000
Building, Mining, Surveying	285,000	81,000
Agriculture, Forestry, Water Conservation	85,000	10,000
Transport and Communications	146,000	30,000
Commercial and Food Services, Material Supply	287,000	82,000
Other	632,000	40,000

Source: *Zhongguo Tongji Nianjian 1983*, p. 127
146 Shaanxisheng Fangzhi Gongye Gongsi, 'Fahui Qiyexing Gongsidi Youyuexing', *Jingji Guanli* 1981 no. 10, p. 41–44; Zheng Yinbai, 'Yubiandian Chengtao Shebei di Zhizao Jidi', *Zhongguo Jingji Nianjian 1983*, VI p. 69–70.
147 One of the largest coal mine sites of China, yet to be developed, is the mine at Binxian. Reserves were estimated to be 9 billion metric tons of raw coal (steam), on a 1,170 square kilometer area. Seams are 8 to 15 meters thick, *China Business Review* May–June 1980.
148 In 1984, the Northwest power network was scheduled to deliver 1 billion kWh to Sichuan, and also some electricity to Shanxi and Henan. The Ankang Power Station will supply 2.8 billion kWh a year in 1990, *Shaanxi Ribao* 16 Jan. 1982, 19 Nov. and 27 Dec. 1983, 1 and 26 Febr. 1984. Unless it is connected with other networks, the Northwest Power Network will have a considerable over-capacity of electric power, *Liaowang* (Beijing) 24 Feb. 1984.
149 *Shaanxi Provincial Service* 10 Feb. 1984. FE/W1275 A11.
150 *Shaanxi Ribao* 17 May 1984.
151 For a less specified list of the 2,586,000 employees in State organizations and enterprises and in collective urban units see note 145.
152 Cheng Yunyi and Lin Yanjie, 'Gan Hanshanju Fazhan Hanzuo Nongyedi Tujing' (Prospects for development of dry crops in the dry upland and mountain areas), *Nongye Jingji Wenti* 1983 no. 10, p. 39–43; *Nongcun Gongzuo Tongxun* 1983 no. 12, p. 5; *Shaanxi Ribao* 27 Apr. 1983. For recommendations on the use of the subsidies, see

Wang Delian, *Shaanxi Ribao* 12 Dec. 1983; *Zhongguo Jingji Nianjian* 1982, vipp.
170–171. 1983 was a very prosperous year for north Shaanxi, *Shaanxi Ribao* 7 and 11
Sept. 1984.

153 Fan Jun, 'Xi'anshi Nandajie Gaijian Guihua Bitanhui Zongshu' (Report on the
planning contest for reconstruction of Nanda Street in Xi'an municipality),
Jianzhu Xuebao 1982 no. 10.

154 *Shaanxi Ribao* 31 Aug. 1979 9 Nov. 1983.

155 *Rural Health in the PRC*, NIH Publ. no. 81–2124 (1980), pp. 96–120.

156 In Xi'an municipality, average rural per capita income was 207 *yuan* in 1981 and
254 *yuan* in 1982, *Zhongguo Jingji Nianjian 1983*, v pp. 169–70. In 23 counties on the
hanyuan, it was 189 *yuan* in 1982, *Shaanxi Ribao* 17 Nov. 1983. In the whole of Shaanxi
province, average per capita rural income was 137 *yuan* in 1978 and 222 *yuan* in
1982, *Shaanxi Ribao* 19 Apr. 1983. A rural household survey of Shaanxi yielded
similar income figures, viz. 133 *yuan* in 1978, 177 *yuan* in 1981 and 218 *yuan* in 1982,
Shaanxi Ribao 27 Apr. 1983 (rural inflation rate in 1981 was 5 to 6 percent, *Shaanxi
Ribao* 2 May 1983). Although all these figures were stated to represent 'net income',
actually there were non-reported sources of income as well, and for private (as
against distributed collective) income, calculation of costs was defective, E. B.
Vermeer, 'Income differentials in rural China', *China Quarterly* no. 89 (March
1982), pp. 1–33.

157 *Shaanxi Ribao* 1 Oct. 1983.

158 *Shaanxi Ribao* 27 Oct. 1983 and 6 Sept. 1984. According to one source, average living
space per capita in Xi'an actually decreased to 3.4 square meters by 1978, *Xibei
Renkou* 1981 no. 1, p. 108.

159 'Has the living standard of workers been raised after liberation or not?', *Shaanxi
Ribao* 27 Nov. 1957; D. Reich e.a., *Raumplanung in China*, Dortmund, 1980, p. 282.
Zhongguo Jingji Nianjian 1983, iv p. 105.

160 Robert M. Field, 'Slow growth of labour productivity in Chinese industry,
1952–1981', *China Quarterly* no. 96 (Dec. 1983), pp. 641–64.

161 Robert M. Field, *ibidem*; *Zhongguo Jingji Nianjian 1981*, vi p. 18; *Zhongguo Tongji
Nianjian 1981*, pp. 265–6.

162 The average 1980 income in Xi'an of 41.60 *yuan* per month, and the dependency
rates were given by *Shaanxi Provincial Broadcasting Station* 8 March 1981.
41.60 × 1.92 = 79.87 *yuan* of average monthly wage in 1980, and
(41.60:1.68) × 3.06 × 75.77 *yuan* of average monthly wage in 1965. With a raised
cost of living of about 15 percent, the real wage then declined by about 10 percent
between 1965 and 1980. However, the 1980 figures given by this source seem to be
too high. In 1982, the average monthly wage in Xi'an was 79.43 *yuan*, 85 *yuan* for
employees in state enterprises and 61 *yuan* for employees in collective enterprises,
Zhongguo Tongji Nianjian 1983, p. 89. A city household survey (all with employees in
the state sector) gave an average per capita expendable income of 425.50 *yuan* in
1981 and 455.80 *yuan* in 1982, *Shaanxi Ribao* 27 Apr. 1983. Another survey of 46
households (all with employees in the Beida street market, 102 employees and 92
dependents) showed an average expendable income per capita of 28.60 *yuan* in 1980
and 33.38 *yuan* in 1983 (5.50 *yuan* resp. 6.93 *yuan* were saved!), *Shaanxi Ribao* 15 Feb.
1984. In all these data, non-monetary subsidies have not been taken into account.
Between 1980 and 1983, the dependency ratio decreased by 0.45 for peasants and
by 0.15 for employees, *Shaanxi Ribao* 11 Apr. 1984.

163 *Shaanxi Ribao* 2 May 1984.

164 Between 1978 and 1982, the work force in State-owned enterprises and organizations in Shaanxi was expanded by 371,000 people, i.e. by 17 percent, and in
collective enterprises by 122,000 people, i.e. by 42 percent; self-employed
individuals, a recent phenomenon, increased from one thousand to 28,000,

Zhongguo Jingji Nianjian 1983, v p. 168. According to the Provincial CCP First Secretary, Ma Wenrui, during 1979–82 875,000 people received an urban job, *Shaanxi Ribao* 19 Apr. 1983. The difference between these two sources is too large to be explained by retirements alone; probably the 875,000 figure includes short-term jobs and changes of employer.

165 Li Shixian 'Xi'andeng Shi Daqi Wuran yu Feiai di Guanxi' (Air pollution in Xi'an and other municipalities and its relation to lung cancer), *Huanjing Kexue* 1983 no. 5, pp. 58–9. Lung cancer incidence rates were between 40 and 55 per 100,000 in Yanliang, Jintai, Tongchuan and Baoji.

166 *Shaanxi Ribao* 5 Oct. and 13 and 15 Nov. 1981. Xi'an municipality used to have 4,700 ha of vegetable plots, but area and production have decreased because of diversion of land to other uses. Prices of vegetables were hiked up by 19 percent at the end of 1981. On the basis of an estimate, that 1 out of every 10 urban residents of Xi'an needed half a liter of milk per day, a daily need was projected of 81.5 tons of milk in 1981. Production costs of cow's milk on State farms was 0.34 yuan per liter. Both State farms and peasants were urged to produce more milk, *Shaanxi Ribao* 10 and 19 Aug. 1983. Daily milk supply doubled from 25 tons in 1980 to 47 tons in 1984, *ibidem* 8 May 1984.

167 For a description of the vegetable distribution system of the 1970s, see G. W. Skinner, 'Vegetable supply and marketing in Chinese cities', *China Quarterly* no. 76 (Dec. 1978).

168 Provincial Governor Li Qingwei's points of action, *Shaanxi Ribao* 9 Feb. 1984; complaints about urban life also reached the national press, *idem* 24 Mar. 1985.

169 Yang Zhongguang e.a. 'Guanyu Fahui Xi'anshi Jingji Zhongxin Zuoyongdi Diaocha' (Investigation concerning the development of the central function of the economy of Xi'an municipality), *Caimao Jingji* 1983 no. 10. pp. 60–4.

170 *Shaanxi Ribao* 3 Jan. 1984.

171 Wang Taixi, 'Xi'anshi Geti Jingjidi Lishi he Xianzhuang' (History and present situation of the individual economy in Xi'an municipality), *Xibei Daxue Xuebao* 1984 no. 4, pp. 94–101.

172 Kenneth R. Walker, *Foodgrain procurement and consumption in China*, 1984.

4 PHYSICAL ASPECTS OF A CHANGING COUNTRY

1 Dai Yingxin, *Guanzhong Shuili Shihua*, Xi'an, 1977; Chinese People's Association for Cultural Relations with Foreign Countries, Xi'an branch (ed.), *Famous Historical Places and Cultural Relics of Sian*, Xi'an, 1959. Of the 900 Han and Tang tombs still extant in 1957, 680 have been destroyed and levelled by farmland capital construction projects in subsequent years, so that by 1983 only 211 remained, of which 37 were in a well-preserved state. *Shaanxi Ribao* 18 Jan. 1984. For the Wei River and canal transport, see also Ma Zhenglin, 'Transportation on the Wei River and the Guanzhong grain transport canal', *Shaanxi Shida Xuebao* 1983 no. 4, pp. 92–102.

2 Ho Ping-ti, 'The loess and the origin of Chinese Agriculture', *American Historical Review* 75 (1969), p. 1–36, and *Huangtu yu Zhongguo Nongyedi Qiyuan*, Hongkong, 1969; R. Pearson, 'Pollen counts in North China', *Antiquity* 48 (1974), pp. 226–8; Li Huilin, 'The domestication of plants in China: ecogeographical considerations', in: David N. Keightley (ed.), *The Origins of Chinese civilization*, London, 1983. On the validity of Artemisia as an indicator of a semi-arid environment see Ho Ping-ti, 'The Paleo-environment of North China. A review article', *Journal of Asian Studies* Vol. XLIII no. 4 (1984).

3 'Because of felling of trees, much of the land lost its forest cover. Climate changed,

erosion increased, the ecological balance was disturbed, and many mountain areas became rocky and barren', Fang Xing, 'An investigation into the conditions of rise and decline of the capitalist sprouts in the Shaanxi area during the Qing dynasty', *Jingji Yanjiu* 1979 no. 12, pp. 59–66.

4 The Huanglongshan area was designated as a reclamation area by the Guomindang Government partly for strategic reasons. One thousand soldiers were to occupy this mountain stronghold. In 1937, already 28,000 civilian settlers had moved in from Henan, Xibei Yanjiushe (ed.), *Kangzhanzhongdi Shaanxi*, p. 13. In 1942, with 50,000 settlers who had reclaimed 14,000 ha of wasteland 'it seemed to be saturated', *Xibei Jianshe Kaochatuan Baogao*, Taibei 1968 (a 1943 survey), p. 289. In 1951, 1,300 families moved away because of infectious diseases, *Qunzhong Ribao* 5 Apr. 1951.

5 Wang Chengjing, *Shaanxi Tudi Liyong Wenti*, Shanghai, 1956, p. 10. The Baoji–Fengxian–Fufeng–Meixian reclamation area was used for settlement of war refugees under control of the North China United Relief Society. The Jianshan area covers the mountainous parts of Longxian–Qianyang Fengxian–Qishan–Linyou, Wang Depu (ed.), *Shaanxi Minzheng Gaikuang*, 1940, p. 7.

6 An., *Shaanxisheng zhi Nongye Jianshe*, n.p. 1942; Zhen Rong, *Zhongguo Senlin Shiliao*, Beijing, 1983 (1951 ed. reprinted), p. 234.

7 *Shaanxi Ribao* 23 Oct. and 4 Sept. 1956.

8 *Zhongguo Nongbao* Vol. 1 no. 6, Oct. 1950, p. 471; *Turang Zhuanbao* 1951 no. 26, pp. 91–4; *Qinzhuan Niu Diaocha Yanjiu Baogao*, Xi'an, 1958, p. 5.

9 Li Rui, *Huanghedi Zhili he Kaifa*, Peking, 1956; Deng Zihui, *Report on the multiple-purpose plan for permanently controlling the Yellow River and its water resources*, Peking, 1955. In 1955, 20,000 ha were afforested in Shaanxi, but by 1956 270,000 ha were planned to be afforested, *Shaanxi Ribao* 15 Nov. 1956.

10 Wang Chengjing, *Shaanxi Tudi Liyong Wenti*, pp. 45–50, 59–60. In the Qinling mountain belt the fruit tree area was to reach 54,000 ha by 1966, *Shaanxi Ribao* 17 Feb. 1958 and 15 Oct. 1956. In Guanzhong the main fruit trees were pears, apples, plums, grapes, jujubes and persimmons, Sun Yunwei (ed.), *Xibeidi Guoshu*, (enlarged ed.) Beijing, 1962, pp. 17–23.

11 *Nongtian Shuili* 1960 no. 8, p. 1; Shaanxi Nongye Dili, Xi'an, 1978, p. 18; *Shaanxi Jingji Tantao*, Xi'an, 1984, p. 74.

12 From 1950 till 1975, Shaanxi province afforested 2,750,000 ha, of which 750,000 ha of forests survived, *Shaanxi Ribao* 19 March 1982 and *Shaanxi Provincial Service* 30 Oct. 1976. 600,000 ha were afforested during 1966–75, an unknown amount of which survived, *Shaanxi Prov. Serv.* 28 Dec. 1975. According to the Shaanxi Provincial Investigation Group of Soil and Water Conservation to Australia, *Soil and Water Conservation of Shaanxi Province*, Xi'an, 1982 (mimeograph), 1,530,000 ha of 'soil conservation forests' were built. 300,000 ha of forest were planted each year in 1979, 1980 and 1981, *Shaanxi Ribao* 20 June 1981; 7 Jan. 1982.

13 Small natural forest areas of the Chinese pine (*yousong*) have been shown by Xu Huacheng e.a. 'Yousong Tianrandi Dili Fenbu he Zhongyuanqudi Huafen' (Natural geographic distribution of the Chinese pine and the division of the central plain districts), *Linye Kexue* 1981 no. 3. See also the forest maps in Liu Zhongming, 'The influence of the forest cover upon annual runoff in the Chinese loess plateau', *Dili Xuebao* 1978 no. 2, p. 114–16, and in Nie Shuren, *Shaanxi Ziran Dili* 1981, which also describes the natural vegetation of Guanzhong. The forest cover of the Huanglongshan has increased from 47 percent in 1965 to 65 percent in 1977, Zhou Houyuan and Cheng Liming, 'A study on the role of water conservation of the forest vegetation in Huanglongshan', *Linye Kexue* Vol. 18 no. 2 (1982); *Shaanxi Ribao* 6 Oct. 1983.

14 *Shaanxi Provincial Service* 25 June 1978.
15 See sections on irrigation and on erosion control.
16 Ma Zhenglin, 'An investigation of the fundamental way of solving present and future water resources from the historical water supply of Xi'an', *Shaanxi Shida Xuebao* 1981 no. 4, pp. 70–7. Falling underground water levels also occurred in adjacent Huxian county, *Shaanxi Prov. Serv.* 26 March 1978.
17 *Peking Home Service* 17 July 1980; *Shaanxi Ribao* 2 Oct. 1981; 3 Aug. 1983; *NCNA Chinese* 14 Aug. 1980; 24 Sept. 1981; *China Daily* 27 Feb. 1982; *Renmin Ribao* 19 Jan. 1981.
18 Liu Zhongming, *Dili Xuebao* 1978 no. 2, p. 114–116; *Shaanxi Ribao* 22 Feb. 1982; Zeng Yibing, 'Huanjing yu Shuizai-Xiqu Shaannan Ba Yiba Hongzai Jiaoxun' (Environment and flood disaster – take in the lesson from the great disaster in West and South Shaanxi on August 18), *Zhongguo Huanjing Kexue* 1983 no. 6, pp. 41–2.
19 Shaanxisheng Keming Weiyuanhui Nonglinju (ed.), *Nongye Kexue Jishu Shouce*, Xi'an 1973, p. 593; oral communication, *Northwest University*; Yunnan Linxueyuan, Shaanxisheng Shuitu Baochiju, *Shuitu Baochilin*, Beijing, 1975, pp. 58–76; Jan-Erik Gustafsson, *Water Resources Development in the People's Republic of China*, pp. 84–8.
20 *Nongcun Gongzuo Tongxun* 1980 no. 8, pp. 29–30.
21 Shaanxi Provincial Investigation Group of Soil and Water Conservation to Australia, *Soil and Water Conservation of Shaanxi Province*, Xi'an 1982; oral communication, *Chunhua County Agricultural Bureau* 1979. In 1978, several definitions appeared to be in use. The forest acreage was 4 percent, the forest cover (including orchards and trees lining roads etc.) was 9.6 percent, and the total area enclosed for forest was 24 percent, according to official county data.
22 Most recent of which are the 1981 Preliminary measures for forest protection and management, *Shaanxi Ribao* 14 Jan. 1982; *Qunzhong Ribao* 14 Feb. 1951.
23 *Renmin Ribao* 14 Nov. 1963.
24 *Shaanxi Provincial Service* 25 Feb. 1979; *Shaanxi Ribao* 18 Nov. 1983.
25 Based on official county data obtained during a regional survey in 1979.
26 1978 data were as follows:

	Longxian	Linyou	Qianyang	Total
Forest area (1,000 ha)	69.9	8.2	5.6	83.7
i.e. percentage of surface area suitable for afforestation	42%	4%	7%	17.9%
(1,000 ha)	23.3	60.9	22.7	106.9
of which already afforested (1,000 ha)	11.3	19.9	9.3	40.5
grass slope area (1,000 ha)	2.7	13.9	10.0	32.7
single roadside trees (no. per cap.)	71	13	49	

27 *Shaanxi Ribao* 22 Feb. 1982; Changwu county increased its forest cover from 2.3 percent in 1949 to 25 percent in 1983, *Shaanxi Ribao* 8 Oct. 1983. Taibai and Fengxian lie in the Hanshui River basin, but belong to Baoji prefecture; *Shaanxi Jingji Tantao*, Xi'an, 1984, pp. 91–100; data from my 1979 survey; ERTS satellite pictures. For a description of the Qinling mountain forest see Linyebu Diaocha Guihuayuan (ed.), *Zhongguo Shandi Senlin*, Beijing, 1981, pp. 128–49.
28 *Nongye Jingji Wenti* 1981 no. 1, p. 7; Li Zhankui e.a., 'Quickly change the passive situation of concentrated over-felling of the forests in our country's main forest areas', *Nongye Jingji Wenti* 1982 no. 1, pp. 9–12.
29 'Indiscriminate felling of trees and reclamation of pastures . . . continued and even worsened after liberation, in many places where the acreage under foodcrops was expanded to the total disregard of environmental consequences . . . Part of the existing farmland should be returned as quickly as possible to grazing grounds and forests', Tong Dalin and Bao Tong, 'Problems of the construction policy for the

Northwestern Loess plateau', *Renmin Ribao* 26 Nov. 1978; *Shaanxi Jingji Tantao*, Xi'an 1984, p. 97.

30 Speech of Zhang Chengxian, vice-minister in charge of the State Scientific and Technological Commission, *Beijing Domestic Service* 22 Feb. 1979.

31 Shaanxi Provincial Investigation Group of Soil and Water Conservation to Australia, *Soil and Water Conservation of Shaanxi Province*, mimeograph Xi'an 1982.

32 In 1956, a yearly silt transport of 320 million tons and 80 million tons was estimated for the Jing and Luo Rivers, 'Bei Luohe', *Huanghe Jianshe* 1956 no. 12; 'Jinghe', *Huanghe Jianshe* 1957 no. 1. Most recent official data on the Wei River and its tributaries are a little higher than that, as follows:

River	Station	Basin (sq. km.)	Yearly average silt content (kg/cu.m.)	Yearly average silt load (million tons)	Yearly eroded soil (ton/sq.km)
Jing R.	Zhangjiashan	43,216	171	306	7,081
Wei R.	Huaxian	106,498	42.8	406	3,812
Luo R.	Zhuangtou	25,154	118	91.3	3,629
(Yellow river at Longmen		497,561	33.4	1,120	2,300)

Source: Zhongguo Kexueyuan (ed.), *Zhongguo Ziran Dili, Dibiaoshui*, Beijing, 1981, pp. 72, 99. During the 'peach flood' in spring the Wei River silt load averages 3 to 56 kg. per cu.m., and during the summer flood 55 to 150 kg. per cu.m. of water, Shaanxisheng Geming Weiyuanhui Shuiliju (ed.), *Guanqu Nongtian Jiben Jianshe*, Beijing 1976, p. 180. See also Qian Ning and Dai Dingzhong, 'The problems of river sedimentation and the present status of its research in China', *paper* River Sedimentation Conference, Peking, 1980.

33 Zhongguo Kexueyuan (ed.), *Zhongguo Ziran Dili, Dimao*, Beijing, 1981, p. 182 distinguishes six degrees of erosion in the gullied Loess Plateau area.

34 See Huang Wenxi, *Soil and Water Conservation of the Yellow River Basin*, Studies on the Yellow River project 1946–1947) no. 5, n.p., 1948.

35 Ma Yongzhi and Wen Chixiao, 'Shaanbeizhi Turang Jiji Liyong' (The positive use of the soils of North Shaanxi), *Turang Zhuanbao* 1951 no. 26.

36 'Huanghe Zhongyou Shuitu Baochi Zuotanhui Zongjie' (Synopsis of the discussion meeting on water and soil erosion control of the Yellow river middle reaches), *Huanghe Jianshe* 1957 no. 9, pp. 1–4.

37 E. B. Vermeer, *Water Conservancy and Irrigation in China*, Leiden 1977, pp. 286–94.

38 In 1959 already some cautious notes were struck by specialists, e.g. Huanghe Shuili Weiyuanhui, 'Dui Huanghe Zhongyou Shuitu Baochi Gongzuo Zhongdi Jige Wentidi Yijian' (Opinion about some problems in the water and soil conservation control in the Yellow River middle reaches), *Nongtian Shuili* 1959 no. 11, and Zhen Chengren, 'Fanyouging Kuganjin Yingjie Xindi Shuitu Baochi Gaochao' (In the anti-rightist struggle we must welcome the new high tide of water and soil conservation), *Nongtian Shuili* 1959 no. 13.

39 Speech of Xin Shuzhi, *Shaanxi Ribao* 17 March 1957. For some descriptions of projects executed during this period, see Shaanxi Shuiliting (ed.), *Shaanxisheng Shuili Baochi Jingyan Jieshao* 2 Vols, Xi'an, 1958 and 1959. For techniques used, see the JPRS translations *Handbook of Water and Soil Conservation of the Middle Yellow River Loess Region*, Academia Sinica, Peking 1959, JPRS no. 19, p. 810; and *Water and Soil Conservation and Water Conservancy Measures*, Academia Sinica, Peking 1959 JPRS no. 17, p. 46.

40 E. B. Vermeer, *Water Conservancy and Irrigation in China*, Leiden 1977, pp. 288–9.

41 *Shaanxi Nongxun* 1955 no. 11, p. 50.

42 Tong Dalin and Bao Tong, 'Construction policies for the Loess Plateau', *Renmin Ribao* 26 Nov. 1978.

43 Qian Ning and Dai Dingzhong, *paper* at River Sedimentation Conference, Beijing 1980. The Sanmen reservoir was designed to have an eventual impounding capacity of 65 billion cubic meters of water at an elevation of 360 meters above sea level. This was to be reached in two stages in order to spread costs of resettlement and losses of farmland over a period of time. At 335 meters, the design capacity was 9.64 billion cubic meters.

44 *ibidem*, and Huang Wei, *Chunman Huanghe*, Beijing 1975, p. 36; for a picture of the reconstructed dam see *China Reconstructs* Vol. xxiii (1984) no. 7, p. 41.

45 *Personal communication*, Northwest College of Agriculture. Some of these were reaccommodated within their own county. The central government subsidized costs of moving and of initial installation, such as housing, tools, cattle etcetera. Settlers also went to Yinchuan. Some got work on State farms. *Shaanxi Ribao* 5 Nov. 1956, 26 Nov. 1959 and 7 May 1985.

46 *Shaanxi Nongye Dili*, p. 216.

47 Technical problems of constructing a reservoir at Longmenkou were deemed to be prohibitive at the River Sedimentation Conference in Beijing in 1980. The same reasons which were brought forward in 1933 for not constructing a hydro-electric power station there are still valid today: (1) heavy silt load, (2) lack of industrial demand, (3) long frost period, (4) cooperation between two provinces would be necessary, (5) there is much coal in Hancheng, for thermal power generation, (6) because Shaanxi is poor, it is difficult to find capital. Longhai Tielu Guanliju, *Shaanxi Shiye Kaocha*, Shanghai, 1933, p. 315. Also, some specialists feel that Yellow River water is more badly needed and economically more productive when used for irrigation in the North China Plain, Huang Pingwei, 'Agriculture and Water Conservation of the North China Plain', *paper* delivered in Australia, 1982.

48 *Shaanxi Ribao* 15 April 1983; *personal communication*, Northwest College of Agriculture and Hancheng County Agricultural Bureau; the first part of the Donglei project is to be completed in 1985, and will irrigate one-sixth of the farmland in the northern half of the Weinan prefecture, *Shaanxi Ribao* 3 May 1983.

49 Tao Ke, 'Shilun Shaanbei Qiuling Judi Titian Kuandu Wenti' (Discussing problems of width of terrace fields in the North Shaanxi hills), *Huanghe Jianshe* 1956 no. 10, pp. 45–7; Fang Zhengsan et al. (eds) *Huanghe Zhongyou Huangtu Gaoyuan Titiandi Diaocha Yanjiu*, Beijing, 1958.

In a 1966 article, the relation between various dimensions of loess terraces, based on 'experience of the masses' was given as follows (loss of land added by author):

Slope (degrees)	Surface slope length (meter)	Field width (meter)	Terrace embankment height (meter)	Slope of terrace embankment (degrees)	Loss of land (%)
10°–15°	6.9–9.3	6.2–8.1	1.5–2	74°–76°	10–13
15°–20°	6.7–8.3	5.4–6.8	2–2.5	72°–74°	18–19
20°–25°	6.5–7.8	4.9–5.8	2.5–3	70°–72°	24–26
25°–30°	6.5–7.7	4.3–5.0	3–3.5	68°–70°	33–35

Shaanxisheng Shuitu Baochi Gongzuozhan, 'Dzeyang Xiu Shuiping Titian', *Nongtian Shuili yu Shuitu Baochi* 1966 no. 1, pp. 28–9, 12–13.

50 State Council Directive dd. June 19, 1962, *Zhonghua Renmin Gongheguo Fakui Huibian*, Vol. xiii, pp. 198–9; Shaanxisheng Yulin Diqu Shuitu Baochizhan, *Shuiping Titian*, Beijing, 1974; Shaanxisheng Geming Weiyuanhui, Nonglinju (ed.), *Nongye Kexue Jishu Shouce*, Xi'an 1973, pp. 48–54; Shaanxisheng Geming Weiyuanhui Shuiliju

(ed.), *Guanqu Nongtian Jiben Jianshe*, Beijing 1956, p. 35; Huang Zili, 'Shaanbei Huangtu Gaoyuan Tudi Ziyuandi Heli Liyong' (Rational use of the soil resources of the loess plateau of North Shaanxi), *Ziran Ziyuan* 1985 no. 1, pp. 17–23.

51 Draft plan for conservation of the middle reaches of the Yellow River, *Renmin Ribao* 21 Nov. 1963; Zhao Mingfu's Conference speech, *Renmin Ribao* 14 Nov. 1963.

52 Shaanxisheng Baoji Shuitu Baochi Gongzuozhan, 'Poshi Titian Guodu wei Shuiping Titian Diaocha' (An investigation of the conversion of sloping terraces into level terraces), *Nongtian Shuili yu Shuitu Baochi* 1965 no. 3, pp. 1–4; Shaanxisheng Shuitu Baochi Gongzuozhan, 'Weibei Shanyuan Diqu Jianshe Wenchan Gaochan Nongtiandi Fangfa' (Methods to construct stable- and high-yield farmland in the mountain and plateau area north of the Wei river), *ibidem* 1965 no. 1, pp. 3–5.

53 Since the end of the 1970s, a method of sluicing-silting has been in use, whereby water is mixed with earth to form mud flowing to the dam site, Shaanxi Provincial Investigation Group of Soil and Water Conservation to Australia, *Soil and Water Conservation of Shaanxi Province*, Xi'an, 1982.

54 Shaanxisheng Shuitu Baochiju, *Shuitu Baochi*, Beijing, 1973, p. 7; *Nongye Jingji Wenti* 1980 no. 10, p. 33; Li Haiting, *Shaanxi Prov. Serv.* 25 June 1978. The total number of reservoirs in Shaanxi increased from over 1,000 with a storage capacity of 2.4 billion cubic meters in 1975 to 1,500 with a storage capacity of 3.9 billion cubic meters in 1980, *Shaanxi Prov. Serv.* 30 Oct. 1976 and *Shaanxi Ribao* 20 June 1981; a map showing all reservoirs with a storage capacity above 100 million cubic meters was carried by *Shaanxi Ribao* 18 Sept. 1984.

55 Yunnan Linxueyuan, Shaanxisheng Shuitu Baochiju, *Shuitu Baochi Lin*, p. 34.

56 Shaanshisheng Shuitu Baochi Gongzuozhan, 'Weibei Shanyuan Diqu Jianshe Wenchan Gaochan Nongtiandi Fangfa', *Nongtian Shuili Yu Shuitu Baochi* 1965 no. 1; Shaanxisheng Binxian Shuitu Baochizhan, 'Shaanxisheng Liquanxian Luoshanju Yinhong Mandidi Diaocha (Investigation of siltation of fields in the Luoshan area of Liquan county in Shaanxi province), *ibidem* 1965 no. 4, projected 1,100 ha of such fields in Liquan county, 2 percent of its farmland area; Draft plan for conservation of the Yellow River middle reaches 1964–80, *Renmin Ribao* 21 Nov. 1963.

57 According to experiments in Fuping county, silt-flooded fields showed a 15 to 25 percent increase in soil nitrogen content, and a 30 to 50 percent increase in organic matter (from 0.9–1.3 percent to 1.4–1.9 percent), depending on the thickness of the silt layer. A 10 to 20 centimeter thick layer appeared to be optimal. Shaanxisheng Shuitu Baochi Gongzuozhan, 'Shanyuan Diqu Jianshe Wenchan Gaochan Nongtiandi Yixiang Zuoshi' (Some measures for constructing stable- and high-yield farmland in the mountain plateau areas), *Nongtian Shuili Yu Shuitu Baochi* 1965 no. 7. An elaborate description of how to build 'damland', and how to protect it against flood, salinization and other hazards is given in: *Nongye Kexue Jishu Shouce* 1973, pp. 57–64.

58 See note 53 above. For roads, a maximal slope of 11 degrees has been recommended, Shaanxisheng Yulin Diqu Shuitu Baochizhan, *Shuiping Titian*, Beijing, 1974.

59 See note 53; *paper* on Chunhua county, National Conference on River Sedimentation, Beijing, 1980.

60 *Shaanxi Nongye Kexue* 1960 no. 2, pp. 71–4; it plowed 5 inch deep in average soil, *Shaanxi Ribao* 1 May 1955. 60,000 of such plows had been sold by 1957 in Shaanxi; instead of the norm of 10 ha, each plow was used on 1–2 ha only, *Shaanxi Nongxun* 1956 no. 5, p. 24. Many coops explicitly rejected the new plows, *Shaanxi Ribao* 22 Sept. 1957.

61 Plowing to a depth of 50 cm instead of 40 cm actually resulted in lower yields of wheat. 'The labour cost of plowing 1.5 foot deep is 5 times as costly as that of 0.6–0.8

foot deep. Plowing 1.2 foot deep is twice as costly . . . At present the most economical depth is 0.8–1.2 foot', 'Investigation into the most suitable plowing depth in large fields in Guanzhong', *Turang* 1975 no. 6, pp. 276–9.

62 Huang Ping-wei, 'Agriculture and Water Conservation of the North China Plain', paper 1982, p. 36; Experiments in the loess area showed that the steady state infiltrability of the soil varied a great deal, from 86 mm per day in so-called 'hard loess' to 580 mm per day in 'soft loess', a farm soil of high fertility. Improvement in this respect not only helps agriculture, but also reduces erosion, run-off and floods, Nanjing Turang Kexue Yanjiusuo (ed.), *Zhongguo Turang*, Beijing, 1978.

63 Figures based on data from County Agricultural Bureaus. In 1980, 295,600 tons of fertilizer (counted at 100% efficiency), mostly nitrogenous, were used in Shaanxi province, on an irrigated area of 1.35 million hectares, *Zhongguo Nongye Nianjian 1981*, pp. 65–7.

64 'Opinions on the present rural fertilizer problem', *Shaanxi Nongxun* 1958 no. 1, pp. 45–50; 'Developing green fertilizer on the *hanyuan*', *Shaanxi Nongye Kexue* 1960 no. 2, pp. 68–71; the green fertilizer crop area in Shaanxi rose from 11,000 ha in 1954 to 48,000 ha in 1959, but declined after the Great Leap Forward, 'Develop green fertilizer, increase production of grain and cotton', *Shaanxi Nongye* 1962 no. 3, pp. 1–3 and no. 1, pp. 11–13. In 1965, it had stabilized again at a level of 53,000 ha, *Shaanxi Nongye* 1965 no. 9, p. 6.

65 *Shaanxi Nongye* 1963 no. 2, pp. 19–23 and 1965 no. 9, p. 6.

66 *Oral communication*, Northwest Agricultural College 1979; Feng Shixiu, *Shaanxi Ribao* 16 Feb. 1982; Wugong county, *ibidem* 21 Feb. 1983; Zeng Xiangping, 'The Shaanxi provincial conference on long-term agricultural planning', *Nongye Jingji Wenti* 1982 no. 9; Hancheng County CCP Cttee, 'Jianshe Shanqudi Zhanlüe Zuoshi' (Strategic measures for the construction of mountain areas), *Nongcun Gongzuo Tongxun* 1983 no. 4.

67 *Nongye Kexue Jishu Shouce*, 1973; *oral communication*, Northwest Agricultural College. Intercropping (*hunzhong*) is different from 'row-cropping' (*taozhong*) which has been used with varying success on a very limited scale for wheat and cotton in areas where the growing season is short and no early-ripening varieties are available.

68 *Shaanxi Ribao* 12 May 1956; *Gongnong Qunzhong Shenghuo Zhuangkuang Diaocha Ziliao*, Xi'an 1958, p. 55; *Huanghe Jianshe* 1957 no. 9, pp. 1–4; *Shaanxi Ribao* 9 Feb. 1958. In 1960, it was stated that the water and soil erosion area put under control had increased from 8,000 sq.km. in 1956 to 60,000 sq.km. in 1960, *Nongtian Shuili* 1960 no. 8, p. 1.

69 *Shaanxi Nongye* 1965 no. 11, p. 6; *Nongtian Shuili yu Shuitu Baochi* 1965 no. 1, pp. 3–5. *Nongye Kexue Jishu Shouce* 1973, pp. 54–68; *Shaanxi Provincial Service* 30 Oct. 1976. Separate figures have been published for some counties, but not for Guanzhong.

70 See note 53 above.

71 The Committee considered that labour input could be increased to over 90 percent of all days, Zhonggong Shaanxishengwei Nongcun Gongzuobu (ed.), *Zhengqu Nongye Shengchan Dayuejin*, Xi'an 1958, p. 48. In view of the long period of frost and snow, this would mean a tremendous increase of labour not directly related to agricultural production.

72 In 1965, it was recommended that farmland capital construction teams should not include more than 20 percent of the labour force in the valleys and plains, and not more than 10 percent in the mountain areas. In Chengcheng county, their average size was eight people. 'Establish all-year-round capital construction teams, undertake farmland capital construction on a large scale', *Shaanxi Nongye* 1965 no. 11, pp. 11–13. See also E. B. Vermeer, *Water Conservancy . . .*, pp. 66–9.

73 See note 53 above; *Shaanxi Prov. Serv.* 22 Nov. 1975.

74 *Shaanxi Ribao* 4 May 1983.
75 See note 53 above.
76 This sand area is partly hilly, partly flat, and has a surface area of about 250 square kilometers. For a map see Nie Shuren, *Shaanxi Ziran Dili*, p. 55.
77 Official surveys of wasteland were made in 1932–5, and again in 1936. The resulting data showed 86,000 ha of public wasteland and 27,000 ha of private wasteland in Guanzhong, but were not the result of on the spot investigation, Zhen Wutai, 'Reclamation work in Shaanxi', *Xibei Ziyuan* Vol. I no. 4 (1940), pp. 110–15.
78 Bauer and Liu, *Rural conditions* . . ., p. 29.
79 Harry A. Franck, *Wandering* . . ., pp. 400–1.
80 'The social order is entirely destroyed . . . Not only the countryside but even 95 percent of the cities we visited are like ruins', Bauer and Liu, *Rural conditions*, p. 25.
81 Jiang Jie, 'Guanzhong Nongcun Renkou Diaocha' (An investigation of the rural population of Guanzhong), *Xibei Nonglin* Vol. III (July 1938), p. 54.
82 Bauer and Liu, *Rural conditions* . . ., p. 38.
83 See note 81 above. Between 1937 and 1939 measurement of private land was carried out and completed in Changan, Gaoling and Wugong counties; in 1939–1940 in Xianyang and Fufeng. Wang Depu (ed.), *Shaanxi Minzheng Gaikuang*, 1940.
84 Farmland area data were used for taxation purposes, both at the provincial and at county and village level. Before World War II, land survey by the government was effectuated only in the Jinghui and Weihui irrigation districts (as part of these irrigation schemes) and in the vicinity of Xi'an. Before 1940, only in one county, Xianyang, had taxation land revision been effectuated. The *baojia* chiefs of Xianyang reported a total of taxable land of 46,010 ha, as against 39,486 ha before 1937, and a population of 130,783 'gravemounds' (i.e. hearths), Wang Depu (ed.), *Shaanxi Minzheng Gaikuang*, Xi'an 1940. It met with considerable resistence from taxpayers, large and small. 'The degree of exactitude of the existing land records varies . . . From the side of the peasants there are doubts about the use of the metric system and the method of land measurement. Sometimes because it might be incorrect, but also because it might mean an increase of land tax even before they have received the benefits of irrigation. Generally after the revision of land measurement the vagrants in the area and those who have opposed paying taxes are not at all happy, because within the scope of the irrigation area there is no room for special classes', *Shaanzheng* vol. IX no. 7–8 (1946). An additional difficulty was presented by the existence of several sizes of the *mou* (with a variation of up to 8 percent), the *xun* ($2\frac{1}{2}$ *mou*) and the *dui* ($\frac{2}{3}$ *mou*), *Shaanxi Shiye Kaocha*, p. 85. During Land Reform in 1950, many 'hidden fields' were discovered. Subsequently, after the agricultural tax had been fixed for many years on the basis of output, there was little impetus for reappraisal of the farmland area of each collective. Assigned quotas might be lower, and yield achievement reports would look better if the farmland area was reported on the low side. The plain areas, however, were less likely to have much unreported farmland, because the construction of irrigated canals and roads entailed new surveying and measurement by state agencies (and reduced the farmland area as well).
85 'Strictly control the use of land for capital construction', *Renmin Ribao* 28 Nov. 1981. In 1958, the provincial government stipulated that a peasant household might not use more than 222 square meters for housing; in 1981 this decision was decentralized to the Prefectural level, which might set different limits for different areas such as mountains, plains, city outskirts and according to 'special characteristics of people's housing', *Shaanxi Ribao* 13 Nov. 1981. Part of this housing area, it might be pointed out, is used for raising pigs, chickens etc. or for other agriculture-related activities.

86 In Changan county, 2 percent of the farmland area was lost to other uses every year, according to a 1957 survey, *Shaanxi Ribao* 20 Sept. 1957; *Renmin Ribao* 24 Sept. 1957.

87 In Chunhua county, which lies outside the irrigated plain, the graveyard area was stated to be 88 ha in 1978, or 6 square meters per (live) inhabitant. In the 17 villages of the 1941 survey shown in Table 29 graves took 48 square meters or 8 times as much space as each live inhabitant.

88 In Chunhua county, with a population of 145,000, the settlement area was stated to be 4,950 ha in 1978, or about 1,000 square meters per household. In the 17 villages in the 1941 survey, 'houses and drying grounds' averaged 460 square meters per household (see Table 29).

89 A survey of 4 villages in Weinan and 5 villages in Fengxiang showed an average landholding of 21.1 *mou* resp. 14.8 *mou* in 1933, JCCR, *op. cit.*, pp. 17, 53. A 1936 population survey of over 1200 households in 6 counties (Sanyuan, Huxian, Pucheng, Huayin, Wugong and Fengxiang) showed an average landholding of 29.4 *mou*, with county averages between 12.3 *mou* in Sanyuan and 57 *mou* in Pucheng, see note 81 above. A 1936 financial survey of 1012 households in 6 counties (Zhouzhi, Jingyang and the four counties last mentioned above) showed an average landholding of 26.1 *mou*, with county averages of between 7.6 *mou* (Zhouzhi) and 50.1 *mou* (Pucheng), Nan Jianfang, 'Shaanxi Guanzhongqu Nongcun Jinrong Wentizhi Chubu Fenxi' (A preliminary analysis of the rural financial problems in the Guanzhong area of Shaanxi), *Xibei Nonglin* 1938. A 1941 land system survey of 231 households in 17 villages showed an average land-holding of 9.5 *mou* in Baoji, 17.4 *mou* in Wugong and 31 *mou* in Weinan, Xiong and Wang, *Shaanxisheng Tudi* . . . .

90 In 1936, land prices in the First District averaged 500 *yuan*/ha, in the Second District 825 *yuan*/ha, in the Third and Southern Districts, 2,300 yuan/ha. A survey of 85 farms showed a total of 213 plots with a total area of 84 ha, so average plot size was 0.4 ha, Ma Yulin, *Wugongxian Tudi Wentizhi Yanjiu*, Wugong 1936, p. 14, 27. In 1941, plot sizes varied between 0.57 ha and 0.13 ha in Wugong, between 0.67 ha and 0.14 ha in Weinan, and between 0.38 ha and 0.07 ha in Baoji; the average farm sizes in these three counties were resp. 1.18 ha, 2.15 ha, and 0.63 ha, Xiong and Wang, *Shaanxisheng* . . ., pp. 22–3.

91 *ibidem*, p. 24. The average distance between the farthest field of the farmer and his home was 0.96 km in Wugong, 0.84 km in Weinan and 0.90 km in Baoji.

92 Jiang Jie, 'Guanzhong Nongcun Renkou Diaocha', *Xibei Nonglin* Vol. III (July 1938), p. 64. The Henan provincial average was 481 inhabitants per village. Large villages were split up administratively in the 1930s, *Chongxiu Huxian Xianzhi*, 1933.

93 Michael Chisholm, *Rural Settlement and Land Use*, London 1979, p. 61. John L. Buck found an average distance between farmstead and farthest field of 1.1 km for the whole of China, varying from extremes of 0.5 km in the Sichuan Rice Region (where villages are not nucleated) to 1.8 km in the Spring Wheat Region.

94 Official sources gave exact figures of land transfers in Guanzhong as follows. Landlords owned 8 percent of all farmland, rich peasants 5 percent. 223,700 ha or 12 percent (including also land owned by temples, churches, schools and societies) was confiscated. It was distributed to 460,000 households with 2,020,000 people, viz. 82 percent of the landless rural labourers, 49 percent of the poor peasants and 7 percent of the 'middle peasants.' After that, the poorest 44.2 percent of the rural population owned 34.6 percent of all farmland, with an average 1 ha per household. The other farmers owned an average 1.5 ha per household. Shaanxhisheng Renmin Zhengfu Tudi Gaige Weiyuanhui (ed.), *Shaanxisheng Tudi Gaige Ziliao Huibian* Vol. I, pp. 4 and 23.

95 See E. B. Vermeer, 'Rural Economic Change and the Role of the State in China', *Asian Survey* Vol. XXII no. 9 (Sept. 1982).

96 Shaanxi province had 3.1 million rural households in 1950 and 4,978,000 rural

households in 1980. These were organized in 330,000 mutual-aid teams in 1953, 52,000 Agricultural Producers' Cooperatives in 1956 and 32,000 Higher Agricultural Producers' Cooperatives in 1957. People's Communes numbered 1673 in 1958, were combined into 681 enlarged People's Communes in 1959, and subsequently split up into about 2,500 People's Communes. In 1980, Shaanxi province had 2,523 People's Communes with 30,455 production brigades and 152,000 production teams. *Shaanxi Nongxun* 1957 no. 3 p. 17 and no. 10, p. 18; *Shaanxi Ribao* 20 Feb. 1957, 22 July 1959; *Zhongguo Nongye Nianjian 1981*, pp. 10–11.

97 Nongcun Gongzuobu, 'Guanyu Nongyeshe Tuixing Sanbao Zhidudi Yijian' (Opinion on the promotion of the 3-guarantee-system for agricultural cooperatives), *Shaanxi Nongxun* 1957 no. 3.

98 Data on the number of 'natural villages' in the counties of Guanzhong are scarce, because this concept was not used in administration either before or after 1949. Bauer and Liu, *op. cit.*, give village numbers of 21 counties in 1933. It seems that the number of production teams generally is 2 to 3 times as large as the pre-war number of natural villages. E.g. Weinan county (2500 production teams) was reported to have 1,100 natural villages in 1933 and 1,408 natural villages in 1952. Huxian county (2,000 production teams) had 480 natural villages in 1936. Wugong county (1500 production teams) had 615 natural villages in 1936. Qianxian (1,900 production teams) had 830 natural villages in 1983. Bauer and Liu, *Rural Conditions . . .*; Jiang Jie, *Xibei Nonglin* Vol. III; (1938), p. 64; *Nongye Shuishou Zhengce Wenxian Ji*, Xi'an, 1952; *Yikao Pinxiazhong Nong Guanhao Caiwu*, Xi'an, 1973; *Shaanxi Ribao* 7 Jan. 1984.

99 'How to divide cultivation areas', *Shaanxi Ribao* 8 May 1956.

100 Yeh Yu, Jinghui Irrigation District Management Bureau, *Shaanxi Ribao* 9 Apr. 1956.

101 *Nongye Kexue Jishu Shouce*, p. 45.

102 Shaanxisheng Geming Weiyuanhui Shuiliju (ed.), *Guanqu Nongtian Jiben Jianshe* 1976, p. 11.

103 *Xinhua News Agency* 5 Mar. 1974.

104 *Peking Home Service* 12 Nov. 1977.

105 'Model' descriptions of Xingping county were given in Shuili Dianlibu Shuili Si (ed.), *Shanqu Daqing Jingyan Huibian*, Beijing, 1974, pp. 64–72; in *Guanqu Nongtian Jiben Jianshe* 1976, pp. 5–6, and in the local press. Later it was reported that 'a counterrevolutionary revisionist line had been carried out . . . Revolution and production were seriously damaged . . . The county became a notorious severely stricken disaster area', *Shaanxi Provincial Service* 13 June 1978; Ren Dingfang, 'The problem of very large differentials in income from land and the price scissors', *Jingji Lilun yu Jingji Guanli* 1984 no. 4, pp. 6–10.

106 *Guanqu Nongtian Jiben Jianshe*, pp. 194–5.

107 'Some places adopted the method of contracting an average amount of land. As a result, land was used in a rather fragmentary way. The average amount of land contracted by each household was 11 plots, in hilly land 15 plots. The average area contracted by each household was 0.5 ha. This . . . caused inconvenience in irrigation, applying fertilizer, popularizing new techniques, utilizing farm machinery, and preventing diseases and insect pests', China's Rural Development Research Centre, 'At a new historical starting point – a summing-up report on an investigation of 100 villages in 1983', *Renmin Ribao* 1 Aug. 1983.

108 The 1983 regulations expressly forbade use of the land which was allocated to rural households, for housing, graves, soil digging, brickmaking, sales of sand and gravel, and mining. 'If peasants don't listen, the collectives should take the land back', *Shaanxi Ribao* editorial 10 Dec. 1983. In Qianxian county, 1,517 households had to return 30 ha of illegally occupied land in 1983, *ibidem* 28 Dec. 1983.

5 WATER CONSERVANCY AND IRRIGATION

1 Investigators of the Longhai Railroad Bureau listed many reasons why a hydroelectric power station should *not* be built at Yumenkou or upstream at the Hukou falls, *Shaanxi Shiye Kaocha*, Shanghai, 1933, p. 315. O. J. Todd proposed a hydroelectric power station at Hukou, and water lifting projects irrigating Shanxi farm fields at Yumenkou, 'Preliminary Report on Hydroelectric Development in Shanxi', O. J. Todd, *Two decades in China*, Beijing, 1938, pp. 561–72. (1935). During and again after the war, the Investigation Group for Permanent Control of the Yellow River (under Zhang Hanying) and the Yellow River Water Conservancy Committee (under Li Fudu) proposed to build a 150 meter-high dam 7 km. north of Yumenkou, but pointed to the complex geology of the site at Shimen. The project would generate electricity and irrigate farmland both in Shanxi and in Guanzhong, and also benefit flood control and navigation. *Huanghe Shuili Weiyuanhui Zhanhou 5-nian Jianshe Jihua*, 1942 (secret); Huanghe Zhiben Yanjiutuan, *Huanghe Shangzhongyou Kaocha Baogao* 1946, pp. 55, 91–2, 97.

2 O. J. Todd, *Two decades*, pp. 123–4, 127–9.

3 Charles E. Greer, *Chinese Water Management Strategies in the Yellow River Basin*, Ph.D.Diss. University of Washington, 1975.

4 *ibidem*; E. B. Vermeer, *Water Conservancy and Irrigation in China*, Leiden, 1977; Deng Zihui, *Multi-purpose plan for controlling the Yellow River and exploiting its water resources*, FLP, Beijing, 1955.

5 Qian Ning and Dai Dingzhong, 'The problems of river sedimentation and the present status of research in China', paper delivered at the International Symposium on River Sedimentation, Beijing 1980; Huang Pingwei, 'Agriculture and Water Conservation of the North China Plain', paper delivered in Australia, 1982; oral communications; *Shuili Fadian* 1983 no. 1, pp. 6–8; *Interview* with Head of Shaanxi Provincial Agricultural Bureau, 1979.

6 *Zhongguo Shuili Shigao* Vol. 1 (Beijing, 1979), pp. 59–60; Dai Yingxin, *Guanzhong Shuili Shihua*, Xi'an, 1977.

7 The main water source was the Jing River, which – at least nowadays – has an average flow of 22 m^3 sec in May and 36 m^3 sec in June; one cubic meter per second might suffice to irrigate 1,000 to 1,500 ha, *ibidem*, p. 125. The present-day Jinghui Ditch has an intake volume of 25 cubic meters per second.

8 Dai Yingxin, *Guanzhong Shuili Shihua*, pp. 49–55; Huang Shengzhang, *Lishi Dili Lunji*, Beijing, 1982, pp. 111–23; *Dili Zhishi* 1975 no. 2.

9 *Shaanxi Nongye Dili* 1978, p. 210.

10 *ibidem*, p. 209.

11 500 mm to 600 mm of rain fell from 1 August to 25 August 1981. Yet the peak flow of the Hanshui wasn't a record high, and was considerably lower than the 1964 flood. In the two counties of Fengxian and Taibai alone, damage was over one hundred million *yuan*. Part of Xianyang was flooded when a 6,000 cu.m./sec. flood of the Wei River burst through its dikes. A flow of 8,000 cu.m./sec. would have wiped out many high buildings of Baoji city, *Shaanxi Ribao* 5 Nov. 1981, 22 Feb. 1982, 19 Sept. and 10 Nov. 1983; *Shaanxi Jingji Tantao*, pp. 91–10. In 1983, a 30,000 cu.m/sec. flood of the Hanshui submerged the entire city of Ankang, *ibidem* 3 Aug. 1983.

12 *Shaanxi Ribao* 13 Jan. 1984 and 8 May 1984. See chapter 40.

13 The Jing, Luo and Wei Rivers (at Huaxian) have a yearly average silt content of 171, 118, and 43 kg respectively per cubic meter of water, Zhongguo Kexueyuan (ed.), *Zhongguo Ziran Dili, Dibiaoshui*, Beijing, 1981, p. 99. The silt content is highest during the summer flood peak period. The Wei river has an average silt load of 3 to 56 kg per cubic meter of water during the 'peach flood' in spring, and an average of 55 to 150 kg per cubic meter of water during the summer flood, Shaanxisheng

Geming Weiyuanhui Shuiliji (ed.), *Guanqu Nongtian Jiben Jianshe*, Beijing, 1976, p. 180.

14 The Jinghui and Luohui irrigation districts generally do not take water in when silt content is higher than 15 percent; lining of canals, however, has increased velocity and therewith silt tolerance. Peasants dig out the silt, and usually accept a higher silt load for small canals and ditches.

15 Prof. Li of the Northwest College of Agriculture, 1979. This is 60 percent of the total underground water resources in Guanzhong, which amount to 5.9 billion cubic meters, of which Weinan and Xianyang Prefecture each have 2.3 billion, and Baoji Prefecture and Xi'an have 0.83 resp. 0.46 billion, Nie Shuren, *Shaanxi Ziran Dili*, Xi'an, 1980, pp. 198–220, maps.

16 Originally planned to divert water from the Jing River, it drew its water (estimated as 1.8 cu. m. per sec.) from several springs which had been hit accidentally while cutting through the mountains, L. C. Ch'ang, 'Soil Regions in the Wei-Ho Valley, Shensi', *Soil Bulletin* 1935, p. 16.

17 'Insuring Shensi against famine', editorial, *The Chinese Economic Monthly*, June 1924.

18 O. J. Todd, *Two decades in China*, p. 327, 491–492, 500–501, 507–508. $700,000 was donated by the Sino-Foreign Relief Commission ($400,000 of which from American donors, $300,000 from Chinese donors), and $400,000 had been pledged by the Shaanxi provincial government.

19 Liu Zhongrui, *Shaanxisheng Shuili*, 1947; Shaanxi Jinghuiqu Guanliju (ed.), *Jinghuiqu Baogaoshu*, n.p. 1934, has a complete description and maps; *Jinghuiqu Shinian* n.p. 1942 (handwritten) and Shaanxisheng Shuiliju (ed.) Jinghuiqu Shiwunian, n.p. 1947. For completion of the branch canals, another $135,000 was donated in 1933 by the Beijing and Shanghai Sino-Foreign relief organizations, and in 1935 the National Economic Committee donated $248,000 for the same purpose.

20 Charles E. Greer, *Chinese Water Management* . . .; Li Yizhi, *Xibei Shuili* III Vols (manuscript); Li Yizhi's heritage became a matter of discussion in 1957, *Shaanxi Ribao* 5 June 1957.

21 *Shaanxi Shuili Jibao* Vol. VII no. 2; Sun Shaozhong, *Shaanxisheng Xinxing Guangai Shuili Tongji*, Xi'an, 1944, p. 29.

22 Shaanxi Jinghuiqu Guanliju, *Jinghuiqu Baogaoshu*, n.p., 1934.

23 Liu Zhongrui, 'Irrigation work and the peasants' psychology', *Shaanzheng* Vol. IX no. 7–8 (1947), pp. 13–15.

24 This was a difficult job, because existing land records often were not too exact. During revision of land measurement old *mou* were reconverted into standard *mou*, which meant that the number of *mou* increased by 12 to 20 percent. Land tax sometimes increased as a consequence, even before peasants had received the benefit of irrigation. Liu Zhongrui, 'Irrigation work and the peasants' psychology', *Shaanzheng* Vol. IX. no. 7–8 (1947), pp. 13–15.

25 In the 1933 plan, the Luohui Ditch was to irrigate 35,000 ha. Then it was found that the normal flow of the Luo River was not sufficient to provide 15 cubic meters per second, so it was decided to shorten the Ditch route and reduce the irrigated area. Before the war, although Chaoyi had salt pans, the quality of the salt was low because it contained too much gravel, and the Government did not permit it to be sold officially. Li Yizhi decided to use the Luohui Ditch water to overflow the salt banks and improve the soil. When after 1938 the import of salt from Shanxi stopped, the exploitation of the Chaoyi salt banks was formally approved by the Government. The Ministry of Revenues and its related organizations and the official salt merchants invested in salt pan development, so the plan of flooding the salt banks had to be abandoned. In 1935 the gentry of Chaoyi repeatedly petitioned to the county government to insist on reverting to the 1933 plan, in order to increase the irrigated area of Chaoyi, and they offered to provide all extra common labour.

The Luohui project office gave in, and changed the route again. At the end of 1937, four-fifths of the tunnel section had been completed, but then technical difficulties brought the project to a standstill. The revised 1942 plan was executed in 1946–1947. Only after 1949 was the project completed. Jingluo Gongchengju, *Luohuiqu Guangai Jihua*, 1947; (anonymous), *Luohuiqu Zongganqu ji Geganqu Zhengli Gongcheng Jihua Shu*, 1945 (manuscripts). A most elaborate description of the Luohui Ditch engineering project is given in Shuiliju (ed.), *Shuili Gongcheng Jihua Huibian*, Nanjing, 1937, pp. 1–46.

26 Xibeijun Zhengweiyuanhui Shuilibu (ed.), *Shaanxidi Guangai Guanli*, Xi'an 1952, p. 30. Feuds might eventually be settled by People's Courts, *Shaanxi Ribao* 3 June 1955.

27 'In the Jinghui Ditch Irrigation District only the main canal had been built using concrete, for the remainder old bricks from demolished village temples had been used. Therefore its projects were of inferior quality and during the war against Japan one didn't have the strength for repairs', 'Fourteen years of the Jinghui Ditch', *Shaanzheng* Vol. VII no. 11, 31 July 1946.

28 Zhou Shijin, 'Irrigation management and water fee standards in the irrigation districts of Shaanxi province', *Shaanzheng* Vol. VII no. 11 (1946), pp. 14–16.

29 The 1946 water fee standards have been given in Liu Zhongrui, *Shaanxisheng Shuili*, 1947, p. 5.

30 'Provisional Regulations for Irrigation Management in Publicly-owned Ditches', *Shaanxi Guangai Guanli*, pp. 39–48; *Qunzhong Ribao* 13 Jan. 1951.

31 'Jiefang Qianhoudi Shaanxi Shuili Shiye' (Water conservation work in Shaanxi before and after liberation), *Qunzhong Ribao* 27 Feb. 1951; *Renmin Ribao* 20 Dec. 1951.

32 These proposals concerned improving techniques, pest control, irrigation, variety improvement etc. and did not go into organizational problems, *Zhongguo Nongbao* 1954 no. 3.

33 The Jinghui Ditch was extended to Gaoling county, and its irrigated area (but not its intake volume) was increased from 50,000 ha in 1955 to 60,000 ha in 1956 and 80,000 ha in 1962. It received 4 million *yuan* of state investment in 1951 through 1956, and its 1956 yields were quite good (viz. cotton 665 kg/ha, wheat 2,350 kg/ha and maize 2,440 kg/ha. *Shaanxi Tudi Liyong Wenti*, p. 42; *Shaanxi Ribao* 9 Apr. 1956, 12 Sept., 13 and 26 Nov. 1957; *NCNA* 9 Apr. 1962. The Weihui Ditch irrigated area surpassed 40,000 ha in 1955, and was again expanded by 7,000 ha in 1956, *Shaanxi Ribao* 23 Jan. 1956.

34 *Shaanxi Ribao* 7 Aug. 1956.

35 *Shaanxi Tudi Liyong Wenti*, p. 58.

36 Ban Zili, Government Work Report, *Qunzhong Ribao* 9 Jan. 1954. Betweeen 1949 and 1955, about 20,000 new waterwheels had been supplied to the Shaanxi farmers. Each irrigated an average 0.8 hectare, *Shaanxi Ribao* 2 June 1955.

37 *Shaanxi Ribao* 28 Apr., 16 May and 14 Aug. 1956.

38 Examples of this total approach appear in Shaanxi Nonglinting (ed.). *1955-nian Shaanxisheng Nongye Zengchan Jingyan Huibian*, Xian, 1955; idem, *Shaanxi Guanzhong Mianhua Zengchan Tujing*, Xi'an 1954; 'Shaanxisheng Wunianlai Xiaomai Zengchan Qingkuang' (Situation of the production increase of wheat in Shaanxi province since the last five years), *Shaanxi Nongxun* 1955 no. 8, pp. 11–18, and 'Jiji Fazhan Nongye Shengchan, Wei Shixian Diyige Wunian Jihua Jianshe Jihua Er Fentou' (Positively develop agricultural production, fight for the realization of the first 5-year plan), *ibidem* no. 10, pp. 13–17, and 'Quanmian Guihua, Jiaqiang Lingdao, Wei Shixian Dui Nongyedi Shehui Zhuyi Gaizao Er Fentou' (Plan comprehensively, strengthen leadership, fight for the socialist transformation of agriculture), *ibidem* no. 12, pp. 21–8.

39 *Shaanxi Ribao* 29 Jan. 1956.

40 E. B. Vermeer, *Water Conservancy and Irrigation in China*, Leiden, 1977.

41 Bai Zhimin, '1958-nian Dafengshou Er Fentou' (Fight for a great harvest in 1958), *Shaanxi Ribao* 10 Dec. 1957.

42 Zhao Baiping's speech in Zhonggong Shaanxi Shengwei Nongcun Gongzuobu (ed.), *Zhengqu Nongye Shengchan Dayuejin, Xuexiyu Xuanchuan Ziliao*, II Vols., Xi'an 1958, pp. 39–62.

43 Editorial, *Shaanxi Ribao* 1 Jan. 1958.

44 *Renmin Ribao* 15 May 1958.

45 We have no separate statistics on Guanzhong. Irrigated area figures for Shaanxi province have been given as follows (ha):

1949: 224,000   1953: 380,000   1957:   649,000   1965   805,000
1950: 252,000   1954: 363,000   1958: 1,667,000   1973: 1,067,000
1951: 301,000   1955: 393,000   1959: 1,777,000   1975: 1,178,000
1952: 326,000   1956: 549,000   1962: 1,300,000   1978: 1,467,000

It should be pointed out that the definition of irrigated area has changed over the years. The 1965–73 figures refer to *effectively* irrigated area. Sources: Committee on the Economy of China, *Provincial Agricultural Statistics for Communist China*, Ithaca New York, 1969; *NCNA* 18 Febr. 1962; *Shaanxi Nongye Dili*, 1978; *Shaanxi Nongxun* 1955 no. 10; *Shaanxi Provincial Service* 11 Dec. 1973 and 3 Jan. 1978.

46 *Shaanxi Ribao* 14 June 1980; Shaanxi Provincial Work Report, *Shaanxi Ribao* 22 July 1959; *NCNA* 9 Oct. and 29 Nov. 1961.

47 Shaanxi Water Conservancy Bureau, 'Irrigation Administration in Shaanxi Province', *Nongtian Shuili yu Shuitu Baochi* 1964 no. 5, pp. 1–6 (JPRS 1,005).

48 'Fourteen years of the Jinghui Ditch', *Shaanzheng* Vol. 7 no. 11 (July 1946), pp. 10–13; *Shaanxi Guanzhong Mianchan Zengchan Tujing*, 1954, pp. 17–22; *Zhongguo Nongbao* 1954 no. 3; 'Secondary salinization and salt accumulataion of the soil in Luohui irrigation district', *Turang Xuebao* Vol. 13, no. 1 (March 1965), pp. 59–65; *Shaanxi Nongye Kexue* no. 1, Jan. 1959.

49 Xu Yian and Yue Ye, 'Experience of planned use of water', *Zhongguo Nongbao* 1964 no. 6, pp. 35–9 (JPRS 10,010); 'Irrigation administration in Shaanxi province', *Nongtian Shuili yu Shuitu Baochi* 1964 no. 5; Luo Yanwu, *Shuili yu Dianli* 1966 no. 2.

50 According to Shaanxisheng Shuili Kexue Yanjiusuo (ed.), *Qudao Fangshen*, Beijing 1976, pp. 4–5, seepage losses of the Jinghui, Weihui and Luohui Ditches were respectively 41.5 percent, 65 percent, and 40.7 percent of their water intake volume of 245, 335, and 121 million cubic meters of water.

51 *Shaanxi Ribao* 13 July 1957; Shaanxisheng Geming Weiyuanhui Shuiliju (ed.), *Guanqu Nongtian Jiben Jianshe*, Xi'an, 1976, pp. 182–92; V. A. Kovda, *Soils and natural environment of China* (JPRS 5967), p. 313; Deng Guoyan, 'Secondary salinization and salt accumulation of the soil in the Luohui irrigation district', *Turang Xuebao* Vol. 13 no. 1 (March 1965), pp. 59–65 stated that 50 percent of the Luohui district had a ground water salinity of between 1 and 3 grams per liter, 40 percent between 3 and 10 grams per liter, and 3 percent between 10 and 50 grams per liter. By 1982, Dali county had 438 km of drainage ditches of more than 10 meters wide, *Shaanxi Ribao* 21 Feb. 1982.

52 *Shaanxi Ribao* 10 July 1983 and 8 Jan. 1984; oral communications.

53 *NCNA* 25 Oct. and 23 Dec. 1961, 17 Nov. 1962; *Shaanxi Nongye* 1964 no. 11, pp. 20–1; Wu Zhenfeng, *Shaanxi Dili Yange*, Xi'an 1980, p. 39; rural electrification trial-started in Zhouzhi in 1958. By 1963, 3,500 km. of 10 kV lines had been built, and rural use was 46 million kWh, *Shaanxi Ribao* 16 Oct. 1984.

54 J. Humlum, *I Kina*, 1972, pp. 108–10; *Guanqu Nongtian Jiben Jianshe*, p. 185.

55 *Shaanxi Provincial Service* 11 Dec. 1973, 2 and 10 June 1976. In 1965, however, the irrigated area served by the 23,000 pump wells had been calculated on the basis of 6 to 7 hectare per well, *NCNA* 10 Sept. 1965.

56 *Shaanxi Provincial Service*, 28 Sept. 1970, and *NCNA* Eng. 23 Dec. 1970. 'The task of enlarging the irrigated area of Shaanxi by 230,000 ha this year was fulfilled. This figure is equivalent to approximately half of the total water conservancy construction work done during the 20 years since liberation. Yet investment was only one-third of the amount used during that period'; see also *Shaanxi Ribao* 16 Sept. 1984.

57 *I Kina*, p. 102; Wu Zhenfeng, *Shaanxi Dili Yange*, p. 39; actually no more than 35 cu.m./sec. was drawn from the Wei River, *oral communication*.

58 *Shaanxi Nongye Dili*, and *oral communication*, 1979. A picture of the Baojixia Ditch near its water intake is given in Wang Yongyan and Zhang Zonghu (eds), *Loess in China*, Xi'an, 1980.

59 Shaanxisheng Shuili Kexue Yanjiusuo (ed.), *Yumidi Guangai*, Xi'an 1976, p. 44; *Zhongguo Nongye Dili Zonglun*, Beijing 1981; *Shaanxi Nongye Dili*, p. 164.

60 *Shaanxi Nongye Dili*, p. 152.

61 *NCNA* 21 Nov. 1976.

62 *Shaanxisheng Shuitu Baochiju (ed.)*, *Shuitu Baochi*, p. 7 *Nongye Jingji Wenti* 1980 no. 10, p. 33; Li Haiting, *Shaanxi Provincial Service* 25 June 1978; *Shaanxi Provincial Service* 30 Oct. 1976; *Shaanxi Ribao* 20 June 1981.

63 Data from county Agricultural Bureaus, 1979.

64 *NCNA* 20 Oct. 1974; *Shaanxi Ribao* 31 Dec. 1983; oral communication. Its pump capacity is 120,000 kW. For a picture see Wang Yongyan and Zhang Zonghu (eds), *Loess in China*, Xi'an, 1980.

65 The Shitouhe project consists of a 104 meter high earth dam (the highest in China) across the Shitou River, a reservoir capable of holding 120 million cu.m of water, and two main canals. One goes east, along the mountainside, and irrigates 15,000 hectares in Meixian. The other goes west, and crosses the Wei River via an aqueduct. Along its course 4 hydro-electric power stations with a generating capacity of 54 MW will be built, *Shaanxi Qingnian* 1979 no. 5, pp. 44–5.

66 *Zhongguo Nongye Dili Zonglun*, pp. 166–8.

67 Requests at the Provincial People's Congress, *Shaanxi Ribao* 3 May 1983. In the second phase, flow would be expanded to 60 cu.m./sec.

68 Feng Shixiu, *Shaanxi Ribao* 21 Feb. 1982.

69 *Shaanxi Ribao* 14 Jan. and 1 May 1984, 16 Jan. 1982.

70 *Shaanxi Ribao* 16 Jan. 1982.

71 The average initial investment of pumping equipment *alone* per hectare of irrigated farmland varied between 1,500 and 2,500 *yuan*. Some examples: in Xingping county, where 5,000 wells were drilled between 1969 and 1973, deep wells needed an average investment of some 10,000 *yuan* each, irrigating 6 ha each. In Chunhua county, deep wells (for drinking water) cost 30,000 *yuan*, and ordinary wells with an average depth of 50 meters about 8,000 *yuan* each, irrigating 4–5 ha each. In Qianxian county, 2,410 wells were drilled with an average depth of 20 meters in the south, and 40 meters in the north, at a cost of between 4,000 and 10,000 *yuan*. A pumping station in Wugong, built in 1973, with a flow of 460 m³/h, and a total lift of 108 meters (primary pump height 42 meters) needed an investment of 120,000 *yuan*. All costs without labour. Shuili Dianlibu (ed.), *Shanqu Daqing Jingyan Huibian*, pp. 64–72; data from local agricultural cadres, 1979. The Provincial Agricultural Bureau estimated average costs at 10,000–20,000 *yuan*, *interview* 1979.

72 This has been a nationwide phenomenon. Recent examples from Shanxi and from Henan provinces showed the capacity of feeder lines and of reservoirs to be two or three times as large as necessary, partly because new facilities would undercut older existing irrigation systems, Caizhengbu Nongye Caiwusi (ed.), *Nongye Zijin Shiyong Xiaoyi Diaochaxuan*, Beijing, 1983, pp. 116–17.

73 *Shaanxi Ribao* 9 Nov. 1957.

74 *Shaanxi Ribao* 6 May 1984.

75 Data from local Agricultural Bureaus, 1979.

76 e.g. Sun Hongliang, 'Tiaozheng Shengchan Jiegou, Fahui Ganzuo Nongyedi Zengchan Qianli' (Adjust the production structure, develop the potential for production increase in dry land farming), *Nongye Jingji Wenti* 1984 no. 6, pp. 34–7, 62.

77 Caizhengbu Nongye Caiwusi (ed.), *Nongye Zijin Shiyong Xiaoyi Diaochaxuan*, Beijing, 1983, pp. 60–1 and 66–70.

78 Provincial water fee standards were:
(a) in natural flow irrigation areas 0.008 *yuan* per cu.m. of water in winter, spring and autumn; in summer 0.015 *yuan* (at the inlet).
(b) in pump irrigation areas, 0.015 to 0.017 *yuan* per cu.m. of water. Out of this sum, maintenance costs of the feeder canals and management personnels' salaries were paid. This last item used to be paid by the collectives before decollectivization. Now an extra maintenance fee was added of 0.001 *yuan* per cu.m. of water for the feeder canals and about 0.004 *yuan* per cu.m. of water for the management personnel, to be paid by each water-using household, *Shaanxi Ribao* 30 June 1983.

79 C.C.P. First Secretary Ma Wenrui's speech at the Provincial Rural Work Conference, *Shaanxi Ribao* 25 Jan. 1984.

80 Li Guozheng, 'We must stress accumulation within agriculture', *Shaanxi Ribao*, 19 Oct. 1983.

81 Instead of 160,000 teams, nowadays 5,220,000 rural households have to be considered in statistical work in Shaanxi, *Shaanxi Ribao* 22 Dec. 1983.

82 The press, however, carried examples of successfully built irrigation projects 'in spite of the *dabaogan* system', see e.g. *Shaanxi Ribao* 7 Jan. 1984.

83 *Nongcun Gongzuo Tongxun* 1984 no. 2, p. 43–4; *Nongye Jingji Wenti* 1981 no. 1, p. 7, 1982 no. 1, pp. 9–12; *Shaanxi Ribao* 20 Feb. 1984 describes five different ways of contracting out wasteland.

84 A recent example from Qishan county carried in *Shaanxi Ribao* 15 June 1984 described how a special unit of 45 county cadres investigated 1,321 cases of theft and damage of water conservancy installations and suppressed the 'evil wind of destroying water conservancy facilities'. A small number of criminals were handed over to the judicial authorities.

85 Zhou Xiao, 'Some aspects in the improvement of our country's agricultural production conditions', *Tongji* 1984 no. 4, p. 33.

86 *Shaanxi Ribao* 25 Aug. 1984. The present water supply situation of Xi'an is very tight, see Chapter 3.

87 *Shaanxi Ribao* 6 Nov. 1984.

6 CULTIVATION PRACTICES, RISING YIELDS AND AGROTECHNICAL CHANGE

1 Zhang Qipeng, *Dongxiaomai Zaipei Jishu Yanyu*, Xi'an, 1957.

2 F. H. King, *Farmers of Forty Centuries*, Emmaus, Pa., 1911; John L. Buck, *China's Farm Economy*, Shanghai, 1930 and *Land Utilization in China*, Nanking, 1937; Pearl Buck, *The Good Earth*, London, 1931.

3 Lack of education was stressed by Jiang Jie, 'Guanzhong Nongcun Renkou Diaocha' (Investment of the rural population of Guanzhong), *Xibei Nonglin* Vol. III, July 1938. The use of opium (and the easy profits from its cultivation) were blamed by Tsui Pingzi, 'Shaanxisheng Tudi Liyong Wenti' (Problems of soil use in Shaanxi province), *Xibei Ziyuan* Vol. I no. 6 (1940), and by missionaries. The Rev. H. Payne wrote in 1932: 'Unless the character of the native Shensi people changes, they are doomed to extinction. They are improvident, fond of good food, when the harvests

allow it, and worst of all they are handicapped by opium', *letter* to Miss Bowser, BMS Archives. O. J. Todd thought that Shantungese peasants could dig 3 times as much earth per day as the Shaanxi peasants, and blamed the latter's general physical condition for this, *Two Decades in China*. Endemic diseases were blamed for the 'short size and stupidity' of the Guanzhong population, and especially of second- and third-generation settlers from outside, *Xibei Jianshe Kaochatuan Baogao*, p. 404. Economic-psychological causes for peasant 'laziness' have been given also, such as lack of willingness to work outside one's village, the great dependency on rainfall and the lack of tools, labour power and fertilizer needed to achieve more intensive farming, e.g. in articles on the Jinghui irrigation district in *Shaanxibei* 16 Sept.–3 Oct. 1936, and Xibei Junzheng Weiyuanhui Shuilibu (ed.), *Shaanxidi Guangai Guanli*, Xi'an, 1952, p. 12.

4 *Shaanxi Nongye Dili* 1978, p. 154. 'Summer fallow of wheat fields, such as in Guanzhong, is rare in our country.'

5 L. C. Ch'ang, 'Soil Regions in the Wei-Ho Valley, Shensi', *Soil Bulletin* 1935, pp. 11–17, map; T. Y. Tschau et al., 'Bericht über die Bodenkartierung des Weiho-Tales, Shensi', *Soil Bulletin* 1935 no. 9; Ma Rongqi and Wen Qixiao, 'Shaanbeizhi Turang Jiji Liyong' (Positive use of the soils of North Shaanxi), *Turang Zhuanbao* 1951 no. 26, pp. 73–98, map; Shaanxisheng Turang Pucha Jianding Liyong Guihua Weiyuanhui, 'Zanni Shaanxi Turang Fenlei Xitong' (A temporary draft of a classification system for Shaanxi's soils), *Turang Tongbao* 1959 no. 1, pp. 23–7; Zhu Xianmo, *Loutu*, Beijing, 1964; Shaanxisheng Geming Weiyuanhui Nonglinju (ed.), *Nongye Kexue Jishu Shouce*, Xi'an, 1973; Zhongguo Kexueyuan Nanjing Turang Yanjiusuo (ed.), *Zhongguo Turang*, Beijing 1978, pp. 145–59, 268–9, 277–8, 442–7, 460, 573–85, maps.

6 *NCNA Eng.* 19 Apr. 1978.

7 Chemical analysis of field soil samples taken in Wugong and Jingyang counties, according to T. Y. Tschau et al., 'Bericht über die bodenkartierung des Weiho-Tales, Shensi', *Soil Bulletin* 1935 no. 9.

	Depth (cm)	N	P_2O_5	K_2O	Org. Matter (%)
Wugong	0–30	0.081	0.17	2.22	0.91
	30–60	0.052	0.17	2.04	0.80
Jingyang	0–36	0.048	0.22	2.44	0.71
	36–66	0.024	0.16	1.92	0.35
	66–100	0.028	0.16	1.81	0.38

8 Paul W. Wilm, *Die Früchtbarkeit und Ertragsleistung Nordchinas bis 1949*, Wiesbaden, 1968, p. 152–62.

9 With an output increase of 250 to 300 kg. of wheat per hectare, an extra 7 to 8.4 kg. of N would be withdrawn (on the basis of 2.8 kg. of N per 100 kg. of wheat). Using manure, at 30 percent effectiveness, 23.5 to 27.7 kg. of N should be applied per hectare. In terms of manure containing 0.3 percent of N, this would mean 7,750 kg. to 9,250 kg. of manure per hectare, Wang Dexuan, *Xiaomai Gaochan Zaipei Jishu*, Xi'an 1978.

10 Paul W. Wilm, *Die Früchtbarkeit*, p. 137.

11 *Ibidem*, pp. 134–5. He based his findings on 26 samples of farm compost taken in Hebei and Shandong during 1929–36, and on ten samples of farm compost enriched with city nightsoil.

12 Sha Fengbao, 'Shaanxi Guanzhong Yan Weihe Yidai Xumu Chubu Diaocha Baogao' (Report on a preliminary investigation of animal husbandry in the region along the Wei River in Guanzhong, Shaanxi province), *Xibei Nonglin* Special Animal Husbandry Issue, 1937?, p. 33–84. His survey covered 25 counties along the Wei River.

13 *ibidem.*
14 Paul W. Wilm, *Die Früchtbarkeit* . . ., p. 138.
15 Zhang Qipeng, *Dongxiaomai*, p. 4; *Shaanxi Nongye* 1965 no. 9, pp. 4–8.
16 Paul W. Wilm, *Die Früchtbarkeit* . . ., p. 105; *Shaanxi Jingji Tantao*, Xi'an 1984, pp. 34–5.
17 'Guanzhong di Lüfei', *Nongbao* Vol. IX (1944), pp. 288–94.
18 'Dadou Zai Guanzhong', *Nongbao* Vol. IX (1944), pp. 230–3.
19 Yuan Hong, 'Shaanxhisheng zhi Xiaomai Zaipeifa' (Wheat cultivation methods in Shaanxi province), *Shaanzheng* Vol. VII no. 11 (July 1946).
20 Anon, *Shaanxisheng zhi Nongye Jianshe*, n.p., 1942.
21 *Shaanxisheng zhi Nongye Jianshe*, 1942.
22 *Shaanxi Xiaomai*, Xi'an, 1947, pp. 20–7 gives data on the wheat area and production of every county in Shaanxi for the years 1941 through 1946, and of Shaanxi province for 1936 through 1946. The Shaanxi wheat sown area and output data are also included in Bai Yinyuan, 'Shaanxi Jianshe zhi Xiankuang yu Jianglai', (Present situation and future of construction in Shaanxi) *Shaanzheng* Vol. VIII no. 2 (1946), p. 14.
23 Local officials and village leaders had to strike a balance: depressing output figures alleviated tax and obligatory sales duties, raising output figures proved good performance in increasing production, *Shaanxi Ribao* 23 Jan. 1958. During the Great Leap, the latter option was preferred, but during the early 1960s again peasants and officials chose to be cautious in reporting of output.
24 *Shaanxisheng zhi Nongye Jianshe*, 1942.
25 *Shaanxi Xiaomai*, 1947, pp. 27–30.
26 *Shaanxi Ribao* 9 Nov. 1957.
27 For instance, eastern Guanzhong generally has less precipitation and more heat. In 1954 precipitation was abundant, and Weinan prefecture achieved an average yield of 1,778 kg per hectare, *Shaanxi Ribao* 20 May 1956.
28 I assume the Guanzhong average wheat yield to be 15 percent higher than the Shaanxi average. Guanzhong had about 70 percent of the sown wheat area of Shaanxi during the 1940s, 1950s and 1970s. According to one source, Guanzhong produced 85 percent of Shaanxi's total wheat output in 1957, *Shaanxi Ribao* 25 Sept. 1957. This would mean 20 percent higher yields than the Shaanxi average. Other data, both for 1957 and for earlier and later years, give much smaller differences, however. If underreporting is included, yield figures would be higher.
29 Jingji Ziliao Bianji Weiyuanhui (ed.), *Basheng Nongcun Jingji Dianxing Diaocha*, Beijing, 1957, p. 87.
30 The high prices of manure, and difficulty in procuring it from peasants, were given as a major reason for the low yields on the 86 state farms in Guanzhong, *Xibeiqu Guoying Jixie Nongchang Jingying Guanli Cankao Ziliao*. Xi'an, 1954, pp. 1–16, and 'Shaanxisheng 1954-nian Nongchang Gongzuo Zongjie ji 1955-nian Gongzuo Yijiandi Baogao' (Synopsis of the State Farm work in Shaanxi in 1954 and report on opinions on the work for 1955), *Shaanxi Nongxun* 1955 no. 1, pp. 28–33. This issue also lists unit yields of the various crops of all state farms in Shaanxi during 1952–4.
31 *Shaanxi Ribao* 17 July 1957.
32 *Shaanxi Ribao* 9 May 1956.
33 Letters from readers, *Shaanxi Ribao* 20 Aug. 1956; *Shaanxi Ribao* 30 Aug., 4 Sept. 1956 and 17 March 1957.
34 Directive of 3 Aug. 1956, *Shaanxi Ribao* 11 Sept. 1956.
35 *Shaanxi Ribao* 17 March 1957.
36 *Shaanxi Ribao* 14 Jan. 1957, and letter from reader, *Shaanxi Ribao* 11 Apr. 1957. Prices paid for dirt from walls and chimneys were raised to 1.50 *yuan* per cart, and

nightsoil was also raised in price. 40 cart-loads per year is an unusually large amount; generally one pig is reckoned to produce 2 cart-loads per month.

37 *Shaanxi Nongxun* 1957 no. 11, pp. 20–2.

38 *Shaanxi Ribao* 6 Nov. 1957.

39 In 1957, 81 percent of the live pigs were raised by peasants in the mountainous or semi-mountainous areas of Shaanxi, which then had half the population and 63 percent of the cultivated area of Shaanxi, Zhonggong Shangluo Diwei Xuanchuanbu (ed.), *Shanqu Shehui Zhuyi Jianshe Jianghua*, Xi'an, 1958, pp. 8–9.

40 *Shaanxi Ribao* 15 Nov. 1957; 'Dui Muqian Nongcun Feiliao Wentidi Yijian' (An opinion on the present problem of rural fertilizers). The figure for pig-manure production given here perhaps needs some explanation. 'Manure' in the present context does not mean excrements alone: these make up only about a quarter of the whole, the rest being earth which is mixed with the animal products before application. Pig-excrements constitute about 8.6% per day of the beast's weight ($\frac{2}{3}$ urine, $\frac{1}{3}$ solids). At an average weight of 75–100 kg., we get a daily output of about 7.5 kg.; this, mixed with earth in the appropriate proportion, results in a fertilizer production figure of some 35 kg, *Shaanxi Nongcun* 1958 no. pp. 45–50.

41 Editorial, *Shaanxi Ribao* 18 Dec. 1957; *Shaanxi Ribao* 11 and 25 Sept. 1957.

42 An interesting example of propaganda was the 'Three-character Classic of Pig-raising', edited by the Provincial Animal Husbandry Department, Shaanxisheng Nonglinting Xumuju (ed.), *Yangzhu Sanzi Jing*, Xi'an, 1958. A similar 'classic' on cattle raising had been published by the same department, *Yangniu Sanzi Jing*, Xi'an, 1957.

43 Shaanxisheng Sanyuan Yizhi Nongye Xuexiao (ed.), *Nongye 'Bazi Xianfa' Jianghua*, Xi'an, 1960, p. 14.

44 *Shaanxi Nongye* 1961 no. 1, p. 18.

45 During Land Reform, in Weinan prefecture, a quarter of the rural population (651,159 people out of 2,368,000) received '60,795 ha of farmland, 91,568 houses, and 16,281 draught animals'. Assuming an average household size of four persons, only one out of every ten of these households came to own an ox. Shaanxisheng Renmin Zhengfu Tudi Gaige Weiyuanhui (ed.), *Shaanxisheng Tudi Gaige Ziliao Huibian* Vol. 1, pp. 63–80. The total number of draught animals was 167,000, or only 1 for every 3 households, in Weinan prefecture in 1949. Pucheng county, a dry-land area with extensive farming, had only 36,580 head of cattle for its 108,700 ha of farmland, or about 2 for every 3 households. In the mountainous northwest Guanzhong, Longxian, Qianyang and Linyou counties together had 85,802 draught animals for a farmland area of 132,500 ha (and a rural population of 192,338). Data from local Agricultural Bureaus and *Qunzhong Ribao* 18 Feb. 1951.

46 *Qunzhong Ribao* 18 Feb. 1951.

47 *Qunzhong Ribao* 12 and 18 March, 11 Apr. 1951.

48 Provincial People's Committee directive, *Shaanxi Nongxun* 1955 no. 2, p. 1; Editorial, *Shaanxi Ribao* 8 Jan. 1956.

49 *Shaanxi Nongxun* 1955 no. 3, pp. 11–12.

50 Qinchuan Niu Diaochadui (ed.), *Qinchuan Niu Diaocha Yanjiu Baogao*, Xi'an, 1958.

51 Editorial, *Shaanxi Ribao* 10 Jan. 1957. The condition of draught animals was described by the Head of the Animal Husbandry Bureau as 'generally exhausted and emaciated', in an interview, *Shaanxi Ribao* 18 Feb. 1957.

52 *Shaanxi Ribao* 16 Feb. 1957.

53 Shaanxi Provincial Government Work Report, *Shaanxi Ribao* 4 Feb. 1958; *Shaanxi Ribao* 9 May 1956.

54 *Qinchuan Niu Diaocha Yanjiu Baogao*, Xi'an, 1958.

55 *Shaanxi Ribao* 11 Sept. 1957; *Shaanxi Nongcundi Shehui Zhuyi Jianshe* Vol. 11, Xi'an 1958, p. 87.

56 Up till spring 1957, 60,000 of such ploughs had been sold to the Shaanxi peasantry, *Shaanxi Nongxun* 1957 no. 5, p. 24; *Shaanxi Nongye Kexue* 1960 no. 2, pp. 71–4; *Shaanxi Ribao* 1 May 1955 and 28 Jan. 1956.

57 Shaanxisheng Nongyeting (ed.), *Xiaomai Zengchan Jingyan*, Xi'an, 1957, *Wugongxian Gandi Xiaomai Zengchan Jingyan*, Xi'an, 1957.

58 Sha Fengbao, 'Report of a preliminary investigation of animal husbandry in the region along the Wei River in Guanzhong, Shaanxi', *Xibei Nonglin* Wugong, 1936; Qinchuanniu Diaochadui (ed.), *Qinchuanniu Diaocha Yanjiu Baogao*, Xi'an 1958. According to a handbook of the early 1970s, a castrated bull weighed 400 to 450 kg, a cow 170 to 350 kg. A span of castrated bulls might plow 1 to 1.5 *mu* ($\frac{1}{15}$-to $\frac{1}{10}$-hectare) per hour, or one-third to a half hectare per day, with a depth of 4.5 inches. A single ox might pull a 1-ton cart over 35 to 50 kilometers per day, *Nongye Kexue Jishu Shouce*, 1973, p. 652. It was further improved during the 1970s, and the bulls and cows offered for export nowadays weigh an average of 615 resp. 500 kg, and can pull 398 and 252 kg, respectively China National Animal Breeding Stock Import and Export Corporation, *Breeding Livestock and Poultry of China*; H. Epstein, *Domestic animals of China*, London 1969, pp. 10–11.

59 Examples of cropping systems used in Guanzhong in the 1950s were (3 year) wheat + maize→peas + fallow→wheat. (5 year) peas→wheat→wheat→barley or rape→wheat + maize. (6 year) cotton→wheat + maize→peas + summer-sown maize→wheat + maize→wheat + maize (irrigated areas). (10 year) alfalfa and wheat interplanting→alfalfa→autumn grain→wheat (3 years)→maize→ peas→wheat (3 years).

60 Huang Jilin, 'A preliminary research into insect-damage to crops in Wugong', *Xibei Nonglin* Vol. IV (1936), pp. 1–10.

61 *Shaanxisheng zhi Nongye Jianshe*, 1942. Shaannong no. 7 was further improved, because it lost its kernels too easily.

62 Liu Dundao, 'Xibeiju Tuiguang Fanzhijian Linian Laizhi Fanzhi Tuiguang Gongzuo' (Breeding and popularization work of the Northwest Region Breeding and Popularization Station since its beginning), *Xibei Nongbao* Vol. II (1947) no. 6, pp. 222–8; Shen Xuenian et al., 'Benyuan Nongchang Zuijin Yucheng zhi Sange Youliang Xiaomai Pinzhong' (Three superior newly-bred wheat varieties from our college's agricultural farm), *ibidem*, pp. 260–9, mentioned *Xinong no. 30* as the most productive variety, with an average yield of 2,760 kg/ha during 1943–7. It also had a better resistance against smut.

63 *Shaanxi Ribao* 13 and 17 Sept. 1957.

64 Shaanxisheng Nonglinting (ed.), *Shaanxisheng Zhuyao Nongzuowu Youliang Pinzhong Zhi*, Xi'an, 1964, pp. 1–10, 42–3; Shaanxisheng Nonglinting (ed.), *Wugongxian Gandi Xiaomai Zengchan Jingyan*, Xi'an, 1957, pp. 2–3, 13–14; 'An inspection tour of wheat in Guanzhong in 1956', *Zhongguo Nongbao* 1956 no. 15, pp. 5–6; *Shaanxi Nonglin* 1960 no. 16, p. 13; a description of 15 more or less common wheat varieties in Guanzhong around 1961 is given by Jin and Liu, *Zhongguo Xiaomai Pinzhongzhi*, Beijing, 1964, pp. 198–9. At that time, especially the Dali area still had its own varieites *Dali 52* (lutescens Al.) and *Sanyuehuang* (alborubrum Körn).

65 *Shaanxi Nongye* 1961 no. 3 (Dec.), pp. 16–17, and 1963, no. 2, pp. 40–1.

66 Virgil A. Johnson and Halsey L. Beemer Jr (eds), *Wheat in the People's Republic of China*. A trip report of the American wheat studies delegation, CSCPRC Report no. 6, NAS, Washington D.C., 1977, p. 31.

67 Shaanxi Nonglinting, 'Guanyu Xunsu Tigao Wosheng Xiaomai Danwei Mianji Chanliangdi Jige Yijian' (Some opinions on rapidly raising the unity yield of wheat in one province), *Shaanxi Nongye* 1964 no. 9, pp. 6–11. Damage was reduced to some extent by replanting empty spots. In 1965, it was estimated that 15 to 20 percent of the wheat fields had no sprouts, *Shaanxi Nongye* 1965 no. 9, p. 4. Treatment was

discussed in 'Wosheng Jige Zhuyao Dixia Haizhongdi Fangzhi Banfa', *Shaanxi Nongye* 1963 no. 9, pp. 33–4.

68 Wang Yu, 'Jianyi Zhongshi Yanjiuhe Tuiguang Kangxiubing he Kangdaofudi Apodeng Xiaomai Liangzhong' (A proposal for stressing research on and popularization of the superior rust- and lodging-resistant Apo-variety of wheat), *Shaanxi Nongye* 1965 no. 5, p. 22.

69 'Apo is probably too tall or weak-strawed for highly fertilized irrigated production . . . It has high yield but apparently poor grain quality', Johnson and Beemer, *Wheat* . . ., p. 39.

70 Fufeng county (mostly dry land) was an example of this. The wheat area sown to *Bima no. 1.* had been reduced, and the area sown to *6028* had been expanded to 45% between 1959 and 1961. The new variety was not liked, however. 'Our problems with *6028* are (1) it has less resistance against cold, (2) it loses kernels easily, (3) the plant provides 375–600 kg of fodder per ha less than *Bima no. 1* does, (4) stalks suffer from *heifenbing* [black mildew?], with an average loss of 10.5 percent, (5) grains are smaller and of a lesser quality than *Bima no. 1.*' In 1962, the area sown to *6028* was reduced to 21 percent, and that of *Bima no. 1* expanded again to 66 percent. *Shaanxi Nongye* 1962 no. 9, p. 6.

71 *Shaanxi Nongye* 1964 no. 10, p. 16. Wugong, Jingyang and Pucheng were the key point counties for agricultural research in west, central and east Guanzhong.

72 The adulteration rate of good seeds was estimated at 20 to 30 percent, *Shaanxi Nongye* 1964 no. 9, pp. 6–10.

73 *Shaanxi Nongye* 1965 no. 9, pp. 4–8 gave a characteristic of the 1965 wheat harvest (which was excellent, the Guanzhong average yield being over 50 percent higher than in 1964), in which lack of good seeds was singled out as one of the four major deficiencies in wheat production (the other three being lack of fertilizer, dead sprouts, and wasteful harvesting methods).

74 *Plant Studies in the People's Republic of China.* A trip report of the American Plant Studies Delegation, Washington D.C. 1975, pp. 62–3.

75 Wang Dexuan, *Xiaomai Gaochan Zaipei Jishu*, Xi'an, 1978, p. 61.

76 Johnson and Beemer, *Wheat* . . ., pp. 39, 61; *Nongye Kexue Jishu Shouce*, Xi'an, 1973, pp. 254–9, describes two dozen varieties then in use.

77 *Oral communication*, Northwest Agricultural College, 1979.

78 Pucheng county Agricultural Bureau, 1979, and *Shaanxi Ribao* 30 Dec. 1983.

79 *Shaanxi Ribao* 19 Mar. 1955, 12 Apr. 1956; 'Guanzhong Pingyuan Diqu Yumiming Fasheng Guilüji Fangzhi Zhenglüedi Shangque' (Discussion on the periodicity of the cornborer in the plain areas of Guanzhong and the strategy of combating it), *Shaanxi Nongye,* 1964 no. 7, pp. 15–26; *Nongye Kexue Jishu Shouce,* 1973; Johnson and Beemer, *Wheat* . . ., 1974; Wang Dexuan, *Xiaomai Gaochan Zaipei Jishu,* Xi'an 1978, p. 122–124; *oral communications,* Northwestern College of Agriculture, and County Agricultural Bureaus, 1979; *Shaanxi Ribao* 5 Feb. 1983.

80 *Shaanxi Ribao* 22 Nov. 1981 and 9 June 1984.

81 *ibidem* 1 Sept. 1984; figures for 1964 and 1972 have been derived from *Shaanxi Jingji Tantao, p. 335; Shaanxi Nongye Dili,* pp. 200–3; however, a contemporary source stated that the 1964 grain harvest was lower than the 1963 harvest, *Shaanxi Nongye* 1965 no. 3, p. 8.

82 Su Xianzhong, *Yumi Zaipei Zhishi,* Xi'an, 1976; *Shaanxi Nongye Dili,* 1978; *Zhongguo Nongye Nianjian 1980.*

83 Absolute figures for Shaanxi are 779,000 ha in 1955, 800–867,000 ha in 1965, 944,000 ha in 1975 and 1,077,000 ha in 1980. Report on Agricultural Work, *Shaanxi Nongxun* 1955 no. 2, p. 10; *Shaanxi Ribao* 3 Apr. 1956; *Qinchuan Niu Diaocha Yanjiu Baogao,* 1958; *Shaanxi Nongye* 1965 no. 1, p. 5; *Shaanxi Nongye Dili,* 1978, p. 36; *Zhongguo Nongye Nianjian 1981; Yumidi Guangai,* Xi'an, 1976, p. 44.

84 Su Xianzhong, *Yumi Zaipei Zhishi*, Xi'an, 1976, p. 8; *Nongye Kexue Jishu Shouce*, 1973, pp. 262–7.

85 *Shaanxi Ribao* 3 Apr. 1956; Shaanxisheng Nongyeting, *Zaliang Zengchan Jingyan*, Xi'an, 1957; 'Guanzhong Pingyuan Diqu Yumiming Fasheng Guilüji Fangzhi Zhenglüedi Shangque' (Discussion on the periodicity of the cornborer in the plain areas of Guanzhong and the strategy of combating it), *Shaanxi Nongye* 1964 no. 7; Shaanxisheng Shuili Kexue Yanjiusuo (ed.), *Yumidi Guangai*, Xi'an, 1976; *Yumi Zaipei Zhishi*, Xi'an, 1976; *Xiqin Yumi Gaochan Jingyan*, Xi'an, 1977; *Shaanxi Ribao* 1 Mar. 1982.

86 In 1981, 35 million *yuan* of relief funds was received from the national government. Shaanxi exported 67,000 ton of pork in 1981 and probably more than that in 1982. In 1982, it had become the first in goat-milk production in China; 14,000 tons of milk powder were produced. During the early 1980s Guanzhong supplied about 50,000 goats per year to other provinces. *Shaanxi Ribao* 2 Oct. 1981, 27 Jan. and 25 Feb. 1982, 20 May 1983.

87 See my 'Income differentials in rural China', *China Quarterly* no. 89 (March 1982), pp. 13–14, 18, 16.

88 *Shaanxi Ribao* 23 Nov. 1981, 27 Mar. and 5 May 1983, 8 and 26 Jan., 27 Mar., 6 and 10 May 1984. The per capita food grain production in north Shaanxi averaged only 225 kg. during 1978–1980, *Shaanxi Ribao* 9 Dec. 1981; *Renmin Ribao* 19 Jan. 1981. In 1982, village grain stocks had to be replenished first.

89 *Xinhua* 6 Feb. 1979. Shaanxi Agricultural Development Plan.

90 'The central government has decided to supply Shaanxi with grain. We must strive to diminish this by stabilizing our grain area. The *hanyuan* must become a "second granary"'. Report on the work of the Shaanxi Provincial People's Government, *Shaanxi Ribao* 7 May 1983. In 1980, 1981 and 1982, per capita food grain production in Shaanxi was 267 kg, 265 kg resp. 320 kg, *Shaanxi Ribao* 23 Jan. 1981, and 26 Feb. 1982; *Zhongguo Jingji Nianjian 1980*, p. 306–309. The all-China average in those years was about 325 kg; *Shaanxi Ribao* 16 Sept. 1984.

91 Shaanxi Statistical Bureau, 'Report on the economy of 1982', *Shaanxi Ribao* 27 Apr. 1983.

92 *Shaanxi Nongye Dili*, p. 36.

93 In the 1983 grain year (Apr. 1983–March 1984) the State requisitioned 1,645,000 tons of grain, 504,000 tons more than the State levy on Shaanxi, and bought an additional 175,000 tons, *Shaanxi Ribao* 27 March, 6 and 10 May, and 13 July 1984. In Aug. 1984, the provincial government decided to use an extra 50,000 tons of grain for increasing alcohol production, 'in order to alleviate the farmer's difficulties in selling grain', *ibidem* 13 Aug. 1984. In January 1985, it decided to allocate 100,000 tons of grain per year to animal feed industries, *ibidem* 13 Jan. 1985.

94 *Shaanxi Ribao* 6 March 1984 and 3 Apr. 1985. One should consider, though, that less than 10 percent of Shaanxi's food grain output is made up by rice, as against 45 percent for China; thus, its milling losses are relatively less than China's.

95 'Fazhan Lüfei, Zengchan Liangmian' (Develop green fertilizer, increase grain production), *Shaanxi Nongye* 1962 no. 3, pp. 1–3; 'Caomuxi' (Sweet clover), *Shaanxi Nongye* 1963 no. 12, p. 19–23; 'Tantan Guanzhong Xiabo Fei' (On the application of fertilizer in summer in Guanzhong). *Shaanxi Nongye* 1964 no. 6, p. 1–3; *Nongye Kexue Jishu Shouce*, Xi'an 1973; *Shaanxi Ribao* 16 Feb. 1982; *Shaanxi Nongye Dili* 1975, p. 158–9; Weinan prefecture sowed 40,000 ha to green fertilizer crops in 1979, *Shaanxi Ribao* 27 Aug. 1979. In 1966 and 1978, green fertilizer crops were sown on 275,000 resp. 287,000 ha in Shannxi, *China Report (Agriculture)* 1979, 57: 34; *Shaanxi Jingji Tantao*, Xi'an 1984, p. 34–35.

96 Shaanxi produced 250,000 tons of pork in 1981; of this amount, the State bought 174,000 tons, 67,000 tons of which were exported. In Xi'an, per capita consumption was one kilogram per month, which was twice as much as in 1957. 1982 pork

output fell by 10 percent (in contrast, national output rose by 10 percent). *Shaanxi Ribao* 27 Jan. and 19 Mar. 1982; 8 Mar. and 5 May 1983.

97 'Of the meat consumption in Shaanxi, 94.5 percent is pork. Although supply is plentiful nowadays, there are some problems: (1) Pig breeds are mixed and impure, with too much fat . . . mainly crosses between the *neijiang* pig and the Parkland pig. Their lean meat content is only 40 to 44 percent. (2) Fodder industry must be developed. (3) Pig improvement stations must be established' *Shaanxi Ribao* 18 and 28 Nov. 1983. (The *neijiang* breed originates from Sichuan province; it is black, with very short snout, a broad head, a curved back, deep belly and short legs. It weighs about 120–140 kg.)

98 *Nongye Kexue Jishu Shouce*, p. 95.

99 Human excrement contains about as much nitrogen as pig excrement, but more of it gets lost. The population of Guanzhong has numbered over 10 million since the 1960s.

100 *Shaanxi Ribao* 19 Mar. and 20 Sept. 1957; Du Shouqian, *Gezhong Huaxue Feiliaodi Xingneng he Shiyongfa*, Xi'an, 1957.

101 *Shaanxi Nongye* 1962 no. 6, p. 29.

102 *Shaanxi Ribao* 9 July 1973, 24 and 30 Dec. 1975, 3 Feb. 1976.

103 *Shaanxi Ribao* 4 Feb. 1977.

104 *Interview* with Head of the Shaanxi Provincial Agricultural Bureau, Xi'an, 1 Sept. 1979.

105 *Shaanxi Ribao* 1 Mar. 1982.

106 *NCNA Eng.* 5 June 1977 and *Shaanxi Prov. Serv.* 15 Oct. 1973.

107 *Shaanxi Nongxun* 1957 no. 6, p. 58.

108 *Shaanxi Nongye* 1962 no. 10, p. 11. This means only 120 ha per tractor.

109 *Shaanxi Nongye* 1964 no. 10, pp. 40–2; Li Shenan, 'Xiangdi Nongye Jixiehua Zuoye Chengbendi Jige Wenti' (Some problems of lowering costs of mechanized operations in agriculture), *Renmin Ribao* 30 June 1964. A 'standard hectare' was ploughed 20 to 22 centimeters deep; with greater or lesser depths, charges were adjusted accordingly. The fuel costs alone of ploughing a standard hectare were over 9 *yuan*.

110 *Shaanxi Nongye* 1962 no. 10, p. 11 and 1965 no. 11, p. 34; earlier, there had been great problems with maintenance and quality of the tractors in Pucheng *Shaanxi Nongye Kexue* 1960 no. 2, p. 72.

111 *Nongye Kexue Jishu Shouce* 1973, pp. 507–10; oral communication.

112 *Shaanxi Nongye Dili*, p. 156.

113 *Interviews* with Mr Kang, Chief of Baoji Regional Agricultural Bureau, with Mr Huo, Chief of Xianyang Regional Agricultural Bureau, with Chief of Weinan Regional Agricultural Bureau, and with Chief of Agricultural Reclamation Bureau, Aug.–Sept. 1979.

114 Directive dd. 29 Aug. 1958; it was also included in the '8-point charter' of 1956.

115 *Shaanxi Nongye Kexue* 1960 no. 2, pp. 71–4; Shaanxisheng Keming Weiyuanhui Shuidianju (ed.), *Guanqu Nongtian Jiben Jianshe*, 1976, pp. 153–5.

116 *Oral communications*, 1979; *Shaanxi Nongye Kexue* 1959 no. 9; *Turang* 1975 no. 6, pp. 276–9.

117 According to official data, in 1962 Shaanxi's 1,256 tractors used an average of 14 liters per hectare (1.5 gallons per acre), *Shaanxi Nongye* 1962 no. 10, p. 11. The Dongfanghong-75 model, with four shears, when ploughing 0.7 foot deep used 12 liter per hectare, *Turang* 1975 no. 6, p. 276–279. The 1962 figures probably included gasoline used in going to and from the fields.

118 Shaanxisheng Nonglin Kexueyuan Tufeisuo Turangshi, 'Guanzhong Diqu Datian Shiyi Shengeng Shendudi Tantao' (Discussion of the fitting ploughing depth on the large fields of Guanzhong region), *Turang* 1975 no. 6, pp. 276–279.

119 Wang Dexuan, *Xiaomai Gaochan Zaipei Jishu*, Shaanxi, 1978, advocated a ploughing

depth of 1.2–1.5 feet, or over. According to him, increasing ploughing depths over 0.5 feet showed the following wheat yield increases: 0.8 feet 25 percent, 1 and 1.3 feet 33 percent, 1.5 feet 43 percent, 2 feet 51 percent; *Guanqu Nongtian Jiben Jianshe*, a 1976 publication by the Shaanxi Provincial Bureau of Water Conservation and Electric Power seemed to favour a depth of 1.5 feet in irrigated areas, pp. 149–51).

120 *Nongye Kexue Jishu Shouce* 1973, p. 72.
121 *Shaanxi Ribao* 15 Nov. 1981 28 Nov. 1983; see Table 47.
122 *Zhongguo Nongye Nianjian 1980; Shaanxi Ribao* 20 June 1981 and 27 Apr. 1983.
123 At the end of 1983, there were 30,000 privately-owned tractors and power tillers on the *Weibeihanyuan, Shaanxi Ribao* 17 Nov. 1983.
124 *Interview* with Head of Shaanxi Provincial Department of Agriculture, 1 Sept. 1979.

7 COOPERATIVES, LAND REFORM AND COLLECTIVIZATION

1 Bauer and Liu, *Rural Conditions . . .,* pp. 3–15, 103–4, 115.
2 'The work of agricultural cooperativization in Shaanxi', *Xibei Ziyuan* Vol. 1 no. 2 (1940), pp. 61–2; Guomin Jingji Jihua Weiyuanhui (ed.), *Shinianlai zhi Zhongguo Jingji Jianshe*, Taibei, 1971.
3 In 1939, the Committee provided 750,000 *yuan* in agricultural coop loans directly, 5,000,000 *yuan* through various banks, and 3,500,000 yuan jointly with the banks (in a 2:8 ratio). The banks independently lent 1,700,000 *yuan*, Shaanxi Hezuo Shiye Guanliju, *Shaanxisheng Hezuo Shiye Gaikuang*, Xi'an 1942, pp. 1–3, 52; *Kangzhan Zhongdi Shaanxi*, pp. 11–13.
4 George Hogg, *I See a New China*, Boston 1944, describes the influx of industrial labour into Baoji, where 104 'indusco's' with 1,280 members had been formed in summer 1939. Competition from Shanghai- and Japan-made textiles brought their number down to less than half before the end of the year. In 1940, there were 539 indusco's in Shaanxi, with 7,414 members. In spring 1942 their number had been reduced to 362 in the Northwestern provinces, with an average loan capital (from bank and government) of only 11,644 *yuan* per coop – enough to buy no more than one-and-a-half bales of cotton, or one hundred sacks of flour at that time, according to Hogg's observations. Wu Yong, 'The problem of material production and supply in the Northwest during wartime', *Xibei Ziyuan* Vol. 1 no. 3 (1940), p. 65.
5 *Shaanxi Hezuo Shiye Gaikuang*, 1942, p. 51.
6 *Xibei Jianshe Kaochatuan Baogao*, Taibei, 1968, p. 198 (this is a 1943 survey undertaken under the leadership of Warren Kuo); Zhongguo Xian Yinhang Nianjianshe, *Zhongguo Xian Yinhang Nianjian*, Shanghai, 1948.
7 Xibei Yanjiushe (ed.), *Kangzhan Zhongdi Shaanxi*, 1940, p. 232.
8 *Qunzhong Ribao* 7 Oct. 1950.
9 *Qunzhong Ribao* 22 Nov. 1950.
10 One such case concerned salt farmers in Chaoyi, who lost their right to exploit salt fields, and came *en masse* to Xi'an in protest against this reinforcement of the State monopoly. The authorities did not know how to handle this situation, *Qunzhong Ribao* 8 Oct. 1950.
11 Report originally carried in *Qunzhong Ribao, Xi'an*, 19 July 1950; Zhongguo Jingji Lunwenxuan Editorial Committee, *1950-Nian Zhongguo Jingji Lunwen Xuan* Vol. II, Beijing, 1951, pp. 64–71.
12 *Qunzhong Ribao* 5 Oct. 1950.
13 According to official data, in 1950 the grain tax burden of the Guanzhong farmers averaged 18.86 percent of their gross agricultural income. For the different 'classes', the actual tax burden had varied between 4 and 29 percent: for landlords 29.33

percent, for rich farmers 16.42 percent, for middle farmers 13.12 percent, for poor peasants 7.7 percent, for hired hands 4 percent. Areas where Land Reform had been carried through, had paid only 50 to 60 percent of their dues (as against 80 percent for not-yet-Reformed areas), because of a lesser inclination or capability to pay taxes than before; this was a cause for government worry, *Qunzhong Ribao* 13 Nov. 1950 and 15 Jan. 1951.

14 Agriculture and Forestry Bureau, 'Report on the situation of agricultural production in Shaanxi province in the first half year', *Zhongguo Nongbao* Vol. 1 no. 6 (Oct. 1950), p. 470–2.

15 Shaanxisheng Renmin Zhengfu Tudi Gaige Weiyuanhui (ed.), *Shaanxisheng Tudi Gaige Ziliao Huibian* Vol. II, Xi'an 1951, p. 149–150.

16 *Qunzhong Ribao* 19 Oct. 1950, 19 and 31 Jan. 1951.

17 *Shaanxisheng Tudi Gaige Ziliao Huibian*, Vol. I, pp. 4, 23, 53, 63 and 81.

18 In 1954, 2.34 percent of the population did not receive voting rights, 'those who have been deprived by law, had such rights suspended, or are mentally ill', *Qunzhong Ribao* 26 Sept. 1954.

19 *Shaanxisheng Tudi Gaige Ziliao Huibian*, p. 67.

20 *Qunzhong Ribao* 31 Jan. 1951.

21 *Shaanxisheng Tudi Gaige Ziliao Huibian*, p. 163.

22 *Qunzhong Ribao* 30 Jan. 1951.

23 *Qunzhong Ribao* 7 Oct. 1950.

24 According to investigations of several counties in Guanzhong, in 1949 the summer grain tax had been 13.35 percent, 16.4 percent if local surtaxes were included, and 18.86 percent of agricultural income if the grassland tax was included as well. Moreover, the farmers contributed shoes, timber, and transportation work to the army (albeit voluntarily). In 1950, the grassland tax had been abolished, and the summer grain tax amounted to 14.88 percent (of which 1.94 for local surtaxes), *Qunzhong Ribao* 15 Oct. 1950 and 15 Jan. 1951.

25 Northwest Finance Department, *Qunzhong Ribao* 15 Jan. 1951.

26 *ibidem.*

27 In Weinan Special District alone, 1949 grain tax arrears amounted to 11,000 tons, of which one-half was recovered in 1950, *ibidem.*

28 Xibei Caizhengbu, *Nongye Shuishou Zhengce Wenjian Ji*, Xi'an, 1952. Under the 1952 regulations for northwest China, agricultural tax was based on per capita yearly income of households. 26 grades of income were used, with progressive rates from 5 percent for those with an income below 95 kg of food grain to a maximum of 30 percent for incomes above 845 kg of food grain. At 175–95 kg, 10 percent was to be paid, at 275–305 kg 15 percent and at 425–455 kg 20 percent. Tax exemption was given to those earning less than 75 kg.

29 Jiang Yan et al., Gongnong Qunzhong Shenghuo Zhuangkuang Diaocha Ziliao, Xi'an, 1958, pp. 53–63.

30 *NCNA* 25 Feb. 1953, 14 Aug. and 2 Nov. 1954.

31 *NCNA* 13 Dec. 1954.

32 *Shaanxi Ribao* 21 Apr. 1955.

33 Wu Lao, *Shaanxi Ribao* 9 Apr. 1955.

34 Editorial *Shaanxi Ribao* 25 Apr. 1955.

35 *ibidem* 26 Apr. and 14 June 1955.

36 *Shaanxi Nongxun* 1955 no. 1, pp. 1–2.

37 *Shaanxi Ribao* 2 and 30 Jan., 6 and 8 Apr., 5 May 1956.

38 Benefits of early cooperativization have been described in *Basheng Nongcun Jingji Dianxing Diaocha*, Beijing, 1957. For their management, see a.o. *Dzenyang Zuohao Nongye Shengchan Hezuoshede Jingying Guanli*, Xi'an, 1955, and *Weinan Quanqu Qige Nongye Shengchan Hezuoshe Jingying Guanlide Chubu Jingyan*, Xi'an, 1954, and *Dzenyang*

Zuzhihe Lingdao Lianshe, Xi'an, 1956. Many positive aspects are given in *Shaanxi Nongcunde Shehui Zhuyi Jianshe*, 2 Vols, Xi'an, 1956–8.

39 *Shaanxi Ribao* 4 Jan. 1956.

40 Zhang Desheng's speech, *Shaanxi Ribao* 8 Apr. 1956.

41 *Shaanxi Ribao* 11 and 13 May, 9 Oct. 1956.

42 *Shaanxi Ribao* 4, 13 and 25 Apr., 21 July 1956.

43 'Two problems in present rural work', *Shaanxi Ribao* 8 Aug. 1956. The other serious problem during cooperativization was how to protect and raise cattle.

44 *Shaanxi Ribao* 19 and 21 Apr. 1956.

45 *Shaanxi Ribao* 24 Oct. 1956.

46 E.g. *Shaanxi Ribao* 17 Apr. and 30 Oct. 1956; investigation of Red Star Coop in Dali, *Shaanxi Ribao* 26 Oct. 1956 and 28 Nov. 1956; experiences of the 5 Stars Coop in Xianyang, *Shaanxi Ribao* 7 and 8 Dec. 1956.

47 *Shaanxi Ribao* 20 Feb. 1957; 'How to accomplish this year's summer harvest preparation and distribution in the agricultural cooperatives', *Shaanxi Ribao* 9 May 1957; 'On the problem of the size of HAPC's,', *Shaanxi Ribao* 18 June 1957.

48 *Shaanxi Ribao* 12 and 21 Sept. 1957.

49 Bai Zhimin's Speech of 16 Nov. 1957, *Shaanxi Ribao* 10 Dec. 1957.

50 Zhonggong Shaanxi Shengwei Xuanzhuanbu, *Renmin Gongshe Tongsu Jianghua*, Xi'an, 1958.

51 *Shaanxi Ribao*, 22 July 1959.

52 Fang Zhongru, *Qianfang Baiji Jiaqiang Nongye Zhanxian*, Xi'an, 1960, p. 15.

53 Shi Xiangsheng, 'Guanyu Konggu he Fazhan Renmin Gongshedi Jige Wenti' (Some problems in strengthening and developing the People's Communes), *Renmin Ribao* 14 Mar. 1960.

54 Vice-governor Zhao Baiping's speech to county chiefs, Zhonggong Shaanxi Shengwei Nongcun Gongzuobu (ed.), *Zhengqu Nongye Shengchan Dayuejin*, Xi'an, 1958, p. 49.

55 Zhonggong Shaanxisheng Nongcun Gongzuobu (ed.), *Zhengdun Renmin Gongshe Shidian Gongzuodi Jingyan*, Xi'an, 1959.

56 *Shaanxi Ribao* 4 Nov. 1959; the same was repeated in an editorial of *Shaanxi Nonglin* 1960 no. 1, p. 63.

57 The mess-hall in the Fenghuo People's Commune in Liquan county was described as having been closed for lack of fuel, but then reopened on the demand of its two dozen of participating households. It was cut down in size. It lowered its p.c. average supply standards from 15 kilograms to 14 kilograms of grain per month (differing amounts were supplied to old people, young people and to labourers). It brought food to the fields during the busy season, and to sick people at home, Zhang Kuang, 'Yaidixin village manages a good mess hall', *Renmin Ribao* 29 Aug. 1959. At the end of 1959, support for mess halls was waning, 'Establish more mess-halls and manage them well', *Shaanxi Ribao* editorial, 8 Nov. 1959 and 4 Nov. 1959. The '100,000 Red Flag units and 1,000,000 Red Flag hands' labour emulation campaign started by the provincial government in March 1960 was directed mainly at industrial workers, *Renmin Ribao* 29 March 1960; Fang Zhongru, *Qianfang . . .*, 1960.

58 Dwight H. Perkins, 'Research on the Economy of the People's Republic of China: A Survey of the Field', *Journal of Asian Studies* Vol. XLII no. 2 (Feb. 1983), pp. 345–71.

59 In 1983, 30 percent of the rural population of Shaanxi had a primary school education, 23 percent a lower or higher secondary school education; about 30 percent of the youngsters had not attended or had dropped out of primary school, *Shaanxi Ribao* 11 Apr. 1984.

60 *Shaanxi Prov. Serv.* 10 Jan. 1979, as cited in FBIS CHI 79–12.

61 *NCNC Ch.* 4 Feb. 1979.

62 'During the Cultural Revolution, over 2,000 Party and government cadres were killed or driven to death. We have changed the class status (*chengfen*) of over 60,000 people wrongly classified as landlords or rich peasants. We have lifted the caps of over 110,000 landlords and rich peasants who are under long-term labour surveillance. We have separated over 15,000 small pedlars and merchants and handicraft labourers from the capitalists, merchants and industrialists', Ma Wenrui's speech at the 6th CCP Shaanxi Provincial Congress, *Shaanxi Ribao* 19 Apr. 1983.

63 Zhang Yutong, 'Zhengshe Fenkai yu Renmin Gongshe Jingji Tizhi Gaige' (The separation of government and commune and reform of the economic system of People's Communes), *Jingji Yanjiu* 1984 no. 5, pp. 25–9.

64 *Shaanxi Ribao* 22 Jan. 1982.

65 Zhang Guoning, 'Xiaomai Lianchan Daolaodi Fengbo' (The upsurge of the labour-output connection in wheat), *Nongcun Gongzuo Tongxun* 1981 no. 6 and Shaanxisheng Nongwei, Weinan Diwei Nonggongbu Lianhe Diaochazu, 'Si Maqian Guxiangdi Xixun' (Happy news from the old homeplace of Si Maqian), *Nongye Jingji Wenti* 1981 no. 10, p. 21–27.

66 Ding Wenfeng et al., 'Zhenxing Nongyedi Biyou zhi Lu' (The only way for promoting agriculture), *Xibei Daxue Xuebao* 1982 no. 1. The Fenghuo Brigade was separately described in *Nongye Jingji Wenti* 1981 no. 4.

67 Hu Yaobang during his visit to Baoji, *Shaanxi Ribao* 13 Nov. 1984. The peasants wanted to apply the *dabaogan* system, it should be permitted, and he added that local cadres should not be afraid that this would be considered a transgression or mistake.[67]

68 Criteria applied were, for instance, that a 'specialized household' should obtain more than 65 percent of its output value from specialized production and also have a commodity rate higher than 80 percent. For 'keypoint households', requirements were lower, viz. 50 percent. Huang Hanzhong pointed out that these regulations were not beneficial for supporting the development of the 'two kinds of households' in grain or forestry, and were meaningless in some other sectors such as medicinal herbs or bee-keeping. Instead, he proposed a set of qualitative and quantitative criteria, which should take into account both the development process and the level achieved, and differentiate between sectors of production. 'Guanyu Nongcun Zhuanyehu Ruogan Wentidi Tantao' (Discussion of some problems about rural specialized households), *Nongye Jingji Wenti* 1983 no. 12 pp. 27–31. The issue of definition has been decided by the central government at the end of 1984.

69 If the household enterprise originated from sidelines, it would be called a 'keypoint household' once the sideline enterprise had reached a certain scale; if it was based on a contract with the collective it would be called a 'specialized household', Rural Finance Office of the Policy Research Bureau of the Shaanxi Provincial CCP Committee, 'Investigation of the keypoint households and specialized households', *Nongye Jingji Wenti* 1983 no. 2, pp. 40–6.

70 *Nongcun Gongzuo Tongxun* 1984 no. 1, p. 13; *Shaanxi Ribao* 18 June 1984.

71 The Shaanxi cloth and confection wear industry had 17,400 employees, in almost 1,000 enterprises, with an output value of 150,000,000 *yuan*. Productivity per labourer was 27 percent below the national average. Products generally did not stand up to market demands, *Shaanxi Ribao* 7 Nov. 1981 and 7 Feb. 1982.

72 *Shaanxi Ribao* 15 Mar. 1981, 15 Aug. 1983, 7 Jan. and 11 Aug. 1984.

73 Agronomic Office of the Policy Research Bureau of the Shaanxi Provincial CCP Committee, 'Investigation report of the specialized villages in Qianxian', *Shaanxi Ribao* 12 Apr. 1984. For its specialized collective markets, see Yang Wenhan et al., 'A good form of opening rural circulation channels – an investigation of the specialized market in Qianxian', *Shaanxi Ribao* 4 Sept. 1984.

74 Policy Research Bureau of the Shaanxi Provincial CCP Committee, 'An investigation into household sidelines of members of collectives in Changan county', *Nongye Jingji Wenti* 1982 no. 5. In 1983, Shaanxi had 23 million egg-laying chickens, which produced 109,000 tons of eggs; this was one-third more than in 1982, *Shaanxi Ribao* 14 Dec. 1983. Sales became more difficult, as the state bought only a small percentage of the increasing output.

75 Rural Finance Office of the Policy Research Bureau of the Shaanxi Provincial CCP Committee, 'Investigation of the keypoint households and specialized households', *Nongye Jingji Wenti* 1983 no. 2, pp. 40–6.

76 *Shaanxi Ribao* 6 Apr. 1984.

77 *ibidem.*

78 P. J. A. Gorissen and E. B. Vermeer, *The Development of Milk Production in China in the 1980s*, Pudoc Wageningen, the Netherlands, 1985, pp. 28–9, 54–6; Hou Buxiang and Wang Guangzu, 'Shaanxi Naishanyang Ji Ruzhipin Kongyedi Fazhan he Buju' (The development and spread of milk goats in Shaanxi and of the dairy industry), *Shaanxi Caijing Xueyuan Xuebao* 1982 no. 3, pp. 27–35.

79 Dong Jichang, Secretary of the Shaanxi Provincial CCP Committee, 'Positively support and guide the healthy development of the "two kinds of households"', *Nongcun Gongzuo Tongxun* 1984 no. 1, pp. 13–15.

80 *ibidem* and *Shaanxi Ribao* 4 and 26 Jan. 1984.

81 Shaanxi Provincial CCP Secretary Ma Wenrui's speech at the Provincial Rural Work Conference, *Shaanxi Ribao* 25 Jan. 1984; Provincial Governor Li Qingwei's Points of action, *ibidem* 9 Feb. 1984.

82 Investigation of 28 grain-producing specialized households by the Weinan Prefectural Agricultural Bureau, *Shaanxi Ribao* 4 June 1984.

83 *Shaanxi Ribao* 3 Sept. 1984.

84 *Shaanxi Ribao* 31 Aug. 1984.

85 Weinan Prefectural Committee, 'An investigation of the improvement of the land contract system', *Shaanxi Ribao* 31 Aug. 1984. In a Weinan village, the land price was obtained in the following way: all land was divided into four classes, each with three grades. Per grade a fixed price was set, with the wheat price (0.166 *yuan* per .5 kg) × the average production of that grade of land × 3 times the yearly obtained output value as the land price. For problems of grading of farmland (factors being terrain, soil texture, fertility, irrigation, accessibility etc.), see Juxian CCP Committee, 'Grade and appraise farmland and issue certificates to stabilize land contract relations and to encourage peasants to increase work and investments', *Nongye Jingji Wenti* 1984 no. 3, pp. 29–32.

86 *Shaanxi Ribao* 7 Sept. 1984.

87 Du Runsheng, 'Lianchan Chengbaozhi he Nongcun Hezuo Jingjidi Xin Fazhan' (The production contract system and the new development of the rural cooperative ecnonomy), *Renmin Ribao* 7 Mar. 1983.

8 COTTON AND COTTON TEXTILE PRODUCTION

1 During 1934–8, Shaanxi's cotton area averaged 267,000 ha, of which 248,500 ha in Guanzhong. In 1975, cotton area was about 260,000 ha, of which 248,500 ha in Guanzhong, Li Guozhen (ed.), *Shaanxi Mianchan*, pp. 2–13 and *Shaanxi Nongye Dili*, pp. 38–9.

2 According to the Northwestern Agricultural College cotton could be sown if the temperature of the 5–10 cm top soil layer had been above 12°C for more than five continuous days. Sowing on dry fields, which warm up quickly in spring, generally is some days earlier than on irrigated fields, *Shaanxi Ribao* 6 Apr. 1956. Cotton is

harvested between 10 Oct. and 22 Oct. because the staple is longest then, *Shaanxi Nongye* 1963 no. 9, pp. 17–19.

3 *Shaanxi Nongye* 1965 no. 2, p. 31.
4 *Shaanxi Nongye Dili*, p. 76. See also *Nongye Kexue Jishu Shouce*, pp. 23–4.
5 *Shaanzheng* Vol. VII no. 11, 31 July 1946, p. 10–13; *Shaanxi Nongye Dili*, p. 76.
6 *Shaanxi Nongye Dili*, p. 172.
7 Richard A. Kraus, *Cotton and Cotton Goods in China, 1918–1936*, pp. 39–40.
8 *Ibidem*, pp. 2, 42, 48.
9 The cotton acreage in 1938 was more than double that of 1937 in Xingping, Baoji, Fufeng, Longxian and Chunhua in the West, and also in Jianyang, Huayin, Pucheng and Baishui, *Shaanxi Mianchan*, pp. 4–13.
10 Bauer and Liu, *Rural Conditions . . .*, p. 35.
11 Tsung-han Sheng, 'Food production and distribution for civilian and military needs in wartime China 1937–1945', in Paul K. T. Sih (ed.), *Nationalist China During the Sino-Japanese war, 1937–1945*, N.Y., 1977, pp. 172–3.
12 Chen Gengya, *Xibei Shicha Ji*, 2 Vols, p. 445.
13 *Letter* from F. S. Russell to Miss M. E. Bowser, dd. 8 March 1935, BMS Archives London.
14 The counties were Xingping, Zhouzhi, Huxian, Meixian, Qishan, Wugong, Fufeng, Fengxiang, Baoji, Jianyang, Longxian and more to the north, Changwu, Binxian and Yaoxian.
15 In 1936, opium consumption in Dali was estimated to be over 10,000 *liang* (ounces) per month, *Xibei Xiangdao* 1936, p. 374; Zhang Yangming, *Dao Xibei Lai*, pp. 102–5.
16 *Qunzhong Ribao* 20 Feb. 1951.
17 Their location was Changan, Dali, Weinan, Sanyuan, Lochuan, Wugong, Baoji, Binxian, and Xi'an.
18 Wang Depu (ed.), *Shaanxi Minzheng Gaikuang* 1940, pp. 1–13.
19 The cotton acreage in the eleven counties west of Xi'an, where a poppy eradication campaign was conducted during 1937–1939, increased from about 21,000 ha in 1936 and 1937 to 27,000 ha in 1938 and about 25,000 ha in 1939 and 1940, Li Guozhen (ed.), *Shaanxi Mianchan*, pp. 4–11.
20 *USDA Cotton price statistics*, Washington D.C., 1946.
21 Hu Jingliang, *Zhongguo Mianchan Gaijin Shi*, Chengdu, 1943, p. 15.
22 *ibidem*, pp. 25, 31, 41–2 and Li Xiaosu, 'Shaanxi may become the cotton textile centre of the Northwest', *Xibei Tongxun* no. 6 (Aug. 1947), pp. 9–12.
23 *Shaanxisheng Zhi Nongye Jianshe* 1942, pp. 6–10.
24 Its production of Stoneville no. 4 seeds grew from 860 kg in 1942 to 7,300 kg in 1945 and 115,800 kg in 1946, Liu Dundao, 'Breeding and popularization work by the Northwest Popularization and Breeding Station in recent years', *Xibei Nongbao* Vol. II no. 6 (1947), pp. 215–17.
25 *Minguo 24-nian Mianchan Tongji*, pp. 112–18.
26 Huang Jilin, 'A preliminary investigation of insect-damage to crops in Wugong', *Xibei Nonglin* Vol. 4 (1936), pp. 1–10.
27 See chapter 5c.
28 R. A. Kraus, *Cotton and Cotton Goods in China 1918–1936*, pp. 39–42.
29 *Zhongguo Jingji Nianjian 1936*, Vol. 3, N.126.
30 For the 1931–1933 period see *Laodong Nianjian 1933*, pp. 635–39.
31 See table 58.
32 *Kangzhan Zhongdi Shaanxi*, pp. 60–66.
33 Wu Yong, 'The problem of material production and supply in the Northwest during wartime', *Xibei Ziyuan* Vol. 3 no. 1, pp. 54–67.
34 In 1937 Shaanxi produced 58,000 ton of cotton, or 10.7 per cent of the China total.
35 *Zhongguo Jianshe* Vol. XIV no. 4 (1936), p. 114.

36 *Shaanxi Shiye Kaocha*, Shanghai 1933, p. 99; *Zhongguo Jingji Nianjian 1936* Vol. III, N 126; *Xibei Xiangdao* 1936 (June–Dec.), pp. 242–244; *North China Herald* 7 Aug. 1935.

37 *Minguo 24-nian Mianchan Tongji*, pp. 112–18; Shaanxi Shiye Kaocha, pp. 311–15.

38 The Weinan cotton packing factory could pack 750 bales per day. It employed over 1,000 workers in 1936, and had an export volume of 1,000 tons, *Xibei Xiangdao* 1936 June–Dec., pp. 242–4. The Xianyang factory packed 40,000 bales in 1936, with over 3,000 labourers. The Tongguan factory could pack 200 bales a day. All used modern machinery, packing bales of 250 kg. *Xibei Ziyuan* Vol. 1 no. 1 (Oct. 1940), pp. 43–58 and No. 2, pp. 31–7.

39 *Zhongguo Jianshe* Vol. XIV no. 4 (1936), p. 114 and *Caizhong Nianjian* 1935, pp 2243–4, 2347–9.

40 Bauer and Liu, *Rural Conditions . . .*, pp. 48–9.

41 Fu Anhua, 'The industrial situation in the Northwest', *Xibei Ziyuan* Vol. 1 no. 1 (1940), pp. 43–58.

42 Sha Fengbao, 'Report of a preliminary investigation of animal husbandry in the region along the Wei River in Shaanxi', *Xibei Nonglin* Special Issue on Animal Husbandry, 1936.

43 In 1940 Longxian had almost 1,000 ha of flax, producing about 600 tons, Fu Anhua, *Xibei Ziyuan* Vol. 1 no. 1 (1940), p. 52.

44 Fu-ting Koh and Yin-yuan Wang, 'The production and prices of cotton in Shensi', *Economic Facts* no. 18 (March 1943), p. 71–80, cited sown acreage figures of about 240,000 hectares in 1940 and in 1941, and an output of 57,000 tons in 1941.

45 'Fourteen years of the Jinghui Ditch', *Shaanzheng* Vol. 7 no. 11 (July 1946), pp. 10–13.

46 Relative prices (April 1937 = 100) were 1,058 for cotton and 2,875 for wheat in April 1942, and 5,543 resp. 12,917 in April 1943, Yin-yuen Wang, 'Price Margins of imported raw materials and manufactured goods in Sian, Shensi', *Economic Facts* no. 27 (Dec. 1943).

47 Fu-ting Koh and Yin-yeun Wang, 'The Production and Prices of Cotton in Shensi', *Economic Facts* no. 18 (March 1943), pp. 71–80.

48 Min Naiyang, 'Shaanxi Cotton Situation', *Fangzhi Gongye* 1947, pp. 111–13; Zhen Hongxu, 'The fate of cotton in Shaanxi', *ibidem*, pp. 19–11.

49 'Representatives of the cotton districts came to the provincial authorities to complain. They presented the following estimate of costs of production made per ha: seeds 15,000 *yuan*, hired labour for weeding 157,500 *yuan*, fertilizer 72,000 *yuan*, ploughing 30,000 *yuan*, sowing 36,000 *yuan*, ginning 120,000 *yuan*, picking 105,000 *yuan*, eradicating stems 52,500 *yuan*, mixed expenses in the village 75,000 *yuan*, interest on capital 315,000 *yuan*, water fee 45,000 *yuan*, land tax 105,000 *yuan*, altogether 1,140,000 *yuan*. At 300 kg per ha, production costs per kg are 3,800 *yuan*. But the present price is 2,800 to 3,000 *yuan* per kg', Zhen Hongxu. 'The fate of cotton in Shaanxi', *Fangzhi Gongye* 1947, pp. 19–11.

50 Xie Jianyun, 'The fate of the cotton farmers in Shaanxi', *Jingji Zhoubao* Vol. 6 no. 13 (March 25, 1948), p. 264.

51 Meng Ruo, 'The drama of cotton farmers in Shaanxi', *Jingji Zhoubao* Vol. 7 no. 21 (Nov. 25), 1948.

52 *Ibidem*.

53 'What I saw and heard in Xi'an', *Zhongguo Jianshe* Vol. XIV no. 4 (1936), p. 114.

54 *Kangzhan Zhongdi Shaanxi*, p. 55. Food was provided by the employer.

55 See note 57.

56 Li Xiaosu, 'Shaanxi may become the cotton textile centre of the Northwest', *Xibei Tongxun* no. 6 (Aug. 1947), pp. 9–12; *Xibei Jianshe Kaochatuan Baogao*, p. 305; Fu Anhua, 'The industrial situation in the Northwest', *Xibei Ziyuan* Vol. 1 no. 1 (Oct. 1940), pp. 31ff; *Kangzhan zhongdi Shaanxi*, p. 32.

57 *Xibei Jianshe Kaochatuan Baogao*, p. 305.

58 Sun Hanwen, 'Record of a trip to West Shaanxi', *Xibei Lunheng* Vol. 9 no. 2 (1941), pp. 68–72.

59 Li Xiaosu, 'Shaanxi may become the cotton textile centre of the Northwest', *Xibei Tongxun* no. 6 (Aug. 1947), pp. 9–12 gives data on individual mills.

60 Zhongguo Kexueyuan Jingji Yanjiuso (ed.), *1954-nian Quanguo Geti Shougongye Diaocha Ziliao*, Beijing, 1957, p. 228.

61 This calculation ran as follows: the Northwestern Region had 96,000 spindles, needing (at 150 kg per spindle) 14,400 tons of cotton. The 28 million population (a substantial undercount, the 1953 census gave a figure of 38 million, EBV) used for its clothes and quilts 10,500 tons of cotton. So in total the Region used 25,000 tons, and could export 49,000 tons per year, *Qunzhong Ribao* 19 Oct. 1950.

62 *ibidem.*

63 Cotton output was 444,000 ton in 1949, 693,000 ton in 1950 and 1,350,000 ton in 1952, *Renmin Ribao* 1 April 1953.

64 During 1928–36 the wheat:cotton price ratio had been 8.33:1 in the USA, and 9.02:1 in Shanxi province, Li Debin 'Cotton price and cotton production in our country after liberation', *Beijing Daxue Xuebao* 1980 no. 2, pp. 49–54.

65 *Qunzhong Ribao* 2 Feb. and 31 March 1951.

66 *Qunzhong Ribao* 11 Oct. 1950, 17 Feb. and 8 March 1951; GAC Directive on the grain:cotton price ratio, *Renmin Ribao* 1 April 1953. All ratios were based on medium-grade, ginned cotton. Commercial departments could vary according to quality (distinction being made between 12 grades) and according to season.

67 *Qunzhong Ribao* 9 Oct. 1950; *Shaanxi Ribao* 18 Oct. 1956.

68 *Shaanxi Ribao* 18 Feb. 1957. 11th grade cotton fetched 0.78 yuan per kg; 3rd grade $\frac{7}{8}$ inch cotton fetched 1.54 yuan per kg, *Shaanxi Ribao* 22 Apr. 1955.

69 This is an average of prices in the provinces of Shandong and Sichuan, Li Debin, 'Cotton price and cotton production in our country after Liberation, *Beijing Daxue Xuebao* 1980 no. 2, pp. 49–54.

70 *Shaanxi Ribao* 4 Jan. 1956.

71 *Qunzhong Ribao* 31 March 1954.

72 Chu-yuan Cheng, *China's Economic Development: Growth and Structural Change*, Boulder 1982, pp. 203–4.

73 Nicholas Lardy, 'State Planning and Marketing Policy and Peasant Opportunities', unpublished paper, 1983.

74 *Shaanxi Ribao* 22 Apr. 1955. In 1956, from end August till begin September the Shaanxi Provincial Agricultural Products Purchase Bureau paid 2 million yuan in advance on cotton purchases in Weinan Special District (which had a cotton cultivating population of 2,720,000 people) to be used for the most urgent daily needs of the peasants, *Shaanxi Ribao* 11 Sept. 1956.

75 *Shaanxi Ribao* 28 Apr. 1955.

76 *Shaanxi Ribao* 21 and 22 Apr. 1955.

77 *Shaanxi Ribao* 27 Feb. and 2 Apr. 1956.

78 *Shaanxi Ribao* 18 Feb. 1957.

79 *Shaanxi Ribao* 12 March 1957.

80 *Shaanxi Ribao* 18 Oct. 1956. Alexander Eckstein has pointed out that it would be misleading to consider the price differential as a measure of quasi-tax. Since the 'free' market is small and all of the repressed, excess demand tends to be concentrated in this narrow market, prices in it were almost certainly above the levels at which they would have been if there had been no fixed purchase arrangements, *China's Economic Revolution*, Cambridge, 1977, p. 119.

81 *Shaanxi Ribao* 22 Nov. 1956.

82 *Shaanxi Ribao* 11 March 1957.

83 *Shaanxi Ribao* 22 Sept. 1957.
84 *Shaanxi Ribao* 21 Apr. 1957, 19 Apr. and 21 Aug. 1956.
85 *Shaanxi Ribao* 23 March 1957.
86 *Shaanxi Ribao* 20 Feb. 1957.
87 Xi'an had 375,000 spindles and 10,800 machine looms by the end of 1957, *Shaanxi Ribao* 29 June and 16 Nov. 1957.
88 *Shaanxi Ribao* 17 Nov. 1956, 30 Dec. 1957, 3 Feb. 1958.
89 In 1957, almost 300 million meters of cotton cloth were exported from Shaanxi, *Shaanxi Ribao* 26 Dec. 1957.
90 *Shaanxi Ribao* 23 March 1957.
91 *Shaanxi Ribao* 16 March 1957. *Shaanxi Ribao* 9 March 1957, mentions a wage of 0.08 *yuan* per kg.
92 *Shaanxi Ribao* 21 March 1957.
93 'The local cadres called upon the brigade members (in a village in Lintong) to *buy* cloth to wear. In this way the problem of labour shortage could be solved, and it would benefit both the State and the members. Their calculation ran as follows: 5 kg of ginned cotton can be spun into 4.25 kg of yarn, and woven into 120 feet of local cloth, with a value of 26.40 *yuan*. Of this, ginning cost is 1.20 *yuan*, salary for the weaver plus his lodging and food is 6 *yuan*, leaving only 19.20 *yuan* (of profit). This can be set against 90 feet of cloth from the factory', *Shaanxi Ribao* 9 March 1957. This calculation disregards the opportunity costs of labour and qualitative differences of cloth.
94 Directive on the unified purchase of cotton, *Shaanxi Ribao* 22 Sept. 1957.
95 *Shaanxi Ribao* 9 Dec. 1957.
96 *Shaanxi Ribao* 29 Jan. 1956. This was 6 times the 1956 output figure.
97 'Until the end of December, 85,500 tons of cotton were purchased by the State . . . If we reckon its quality to be 2 grades higher than average this alone increases the income of the peasants by 13.5 million *yuan*', *Shaanxi Ribao* 28 Dec. 1957. One should consider, however, that part of the qualitative and quantitative increase of purchased cotton may have been due to the fact that less cotton could be retained by the peasants for their own use.
98 The 1980 Agricultural Yearbook of China gives (pp. 35–6) revised official cotton figures for China as follows:

Acreage (1,000,000 ha)	Production (1,000 tons)	Average Yield (kg/ha)
1957 5.8	1,640	285
1958 5.5	1,969	353
1959 5.5	1,709	308
1960 5.2	1,063	203
1961 3.9	800	210
1962 3.5	750	217
1963 4.4	1,200	270

For Guanzhong there are no reliable figures for the 1959–62 period.

99 *Jingji Guanli* 1981 no. 10.
100 By 1980, only 60 percent of the cotton raw materials used was produced in Shaanxi itself. From 1966 through 1978, investments in the textile industry constituted only 1.14 percent of the total industrial investment in Shaanxi. In 1981, capacity was 910,000 spindles and 22,700 looms, *Shaanxi Ribao* 4 Oct and 7 Nov. 1981.
101 'The situation and experiences in the improvement of cotton cultivation techniques in the Jinghui irrigation district of Shaanxi province in 1953'. *Zhongguo Nongbao* 1954 no. 3, pp. 24–26.
102 A cartful held 500 to 750 kg of manure mixed with earth, containing about 0.3 percent whole nitrogen.

103 See chapter 6h.

104 *Shaanxi Nongye Kexue* 1959 no. 7, pp. 289–91, and 1960 no. 5, p. 224.

105 *Shaanxi Nongye Kexue* 1960 no. 3, p. 123. In 1963 and 1964, 53 and 58 percent of Guanzhong's cotton fields were affected by dead sprouts; 69,000 ha and 47,000 ha (i.e. 20 to 25 percent of the total cotton area) had over 50 percent of dead sprouts. High humidity (>90 percent) and low temperature (15–20°C) are most conducive to this phenomenon, *Shaanxi Nongye* 1965 no. 2, p. 31.

106 *Zhongguo Nongbao* 1954 no. 3, pp. 24–6.

107 *Map* of distribution of Miridae in Shaanxi, Sept. 1956, Provincial Agricultural Bureau; 'Miridae in the cotton areas of Guanzhong', *Xibei Nonglin* 1954 no. 5, pp. 19–21.

108 Shaanxisheng Nonglinting, *Shaanxi Guanzhong Mianchan Zengchan Tujing*, Xi'an, 1954, pp. 2–17.

109 *Qunzhong Ribao* 26 Apr. 1953.

110 'The Northwest Agricultural College thought that cotton sowing could be antedated to 5 April on dry fields and to 10 April on irrigated fields. This goes for average years.' (one can sow if the temperature of the top-soil layer has been above 12°C for more than 5 continuous days.) 'In Chaoyi, cotton had to be planted from 5 April onwards, and be finished within 7 days. Close planting should be applied everywhere, 90,000 stems per ha in irrigated areas and 105,000 in dry areas', *Shaanxi Ribao* 6 Apr. and 9 Sept. 1956.

111 *Shaanxi Ribao* 1 Oct. 1956.

112 *Shaanxi Ribao* 4 Apr. 1957.

113 *Nongye Kexue Jishu Shouce*, p. 359; personal communication.

114 Xu Yian and Yue Ye, 'The experience of planned use of water in the irrigation districts of Shaanxi province', *Zhongguo Nongbao* no. 6, June 1964, pp. 35–9.

115 Dept. of Water Conservation, Shaanxi, 'Irrigation administration in Shaanxi province', *Nongtian Shuili yu Shuitu Baochi*, no. 5 Nov. 1964, pp. 1–6; Liu Zhongrui, *Shaanxisheng Shuili*, Xi'an, 1947, pp. 2–6.

116 Liu Zhongrui, *Shaanxisheng Shuili*, p. 5; Xibeijun Zhengweiyuanhui Shuilibu (ed.), *Shaanxi di Guangai Guanli*, Xi'an, 1952, pp. 25–8, 46.

117 July is the month when cotton usually has the largest need for additional water in Guanzhong; precipitation averages 100 mm, as against a water need of about 150 mm. During its growth period of April–August cotton needs about 400 mm of water, most of which is supplied by precipitation. Jinghui irrigation district experimental station, 'The influence of deep-plowing, close-planting and heavy fertilization on the water need of cotton', *Nongtian Shuili* 1960 no. 6, pp. 18–19; 'Experiences in cotton irrigation in the Jinghui irrigation district', *Nongtian Shuili yu Shuitu Baochi* 1964 no. 1, pp. 19–21.

118 See chapter 5e.

119 A subdivision of the cotton acreage according to administrative regions showed the following figures: Baoji Special District (19 counties) 33,000 ha, i.e. 5 percent of its dry farmland area, Weinan Special District (10 counties) 113,000 ha, i.e. 12 percent of its dry farmland area, Xianyang/Changan Directly Controlled District (7 counties and municipalities) 13,000 ha, i.e. 10 percent of its dry farmland area, *Shaanxi Guanzhong Mianchan Zengchan Tujing*, p. 24.

120 *Shaanxi Nongye Kexue* 1959 no. 6, p. 223 and 1960 no. 3, p. 104. The exact increase figure given was 97.3 percent, as against only 38.7 percent in the main irrigated areas over this same period.

121 Shaanxisheng Nongyeting, *Shaanxisheng Zhuyao Nongzuowu Youliang Pinzhongzhi*, Xi'an, 1964, pp. 223–31; *Shaanxisheng Mianhua Liangzhong Jingsimian he Wuyiqimian*, Xi'an, 1957.

122 Shaanxisheng Nonglinting (ed.), *Mianhua Zengchan Jingyan*, Xi'an 1957, pp. 13–14, 31–4.

123 *Shaanxi Nongye Dili*, p. 76; *Nongye Kexue Jishu Shouce*, pp. 210–12, 250, 281–4; personal communication.

124 The foodgrain prices mentioned in Tables 68 and 69 are state purchase prices, paid by the State for regular sales within the assigned quota. These made up most, but not all, sales to the State. Above-quota sales commanded substantially higher prices. Grain sold on the free markets (which in some periods were legally allowed but only to a certain degree) might fetch an even higher price. For a price-comparison with cotton (which could legally be sold only to the State) there is another complicating factor, in that in return for cotton sales the State allocated extra quantities of chemical fertilizer at the regular price – from 1978 on, 80 kg of chemical fertilizer for every 100 kg of cotton. There are no data on the size of illegal cotton sales. In 1979, the price of above-quota wheat was 44.80 *yuan* per 100 kg, and of free market wheat 56.00 *yuan* per 100 kg in Guanzhong.

125 Li Debin, 'Cotton price and cotton production in our country since liberation', *Beijing Daxue Xuebao* 1980 no. 2, pp. 49–54, points out that in the U.S.A. the wheat:cotton exchange rate averaged 8.3 to 1 during the 1928–36 period, and 14.8 to 1 during 1968–76.

126 *ibidem*, and Zhang Ruhai, *Nongchanpin Jiage Wenti Yanjiu*, Shanghai, 1984, pp. 18–24, 38. The value of a labour day was arbitrarily calculated as 0.80 *yuan*, however, both for 1965 and for 1975–7. Also, in the 1970s more of the agricultural produce was sold at above-list prices than in the 1960s. Tax (4 to 5 percent) was included in costs.

127 Wu Yongxian, 'An evaluation of the economic benefits of growing cotton in the dry area of Wugong county', *Jingji Yanjiu* no. 10, Oct. 1963, pp. 27–36.

128 In Wugong county, good harvests with an average output of 400 to 600 kg per ha were obtained in 1965, 1966, 1972, 1974, 1977 and 1978; bad harvests with an average output of 200 to 250 kg per ha occurred in 1975 and 1976, and several times during the 60s (data from county Agricultural Bureau).

129 During the 60s and 70s, standard chemical fertilizer (18–20% N) was sold at 180 *yuan* per ton, urea (46% N) at 450 *yuan* per ton. In many areas, chemical fertilizer could be obtained only through barter, in exchange for grain and cotton produced above the state-assigned quota. Manure mixed with earth (with a nitrogen content of 0.2–0.3 percent) sold for about 2 *yuan* per ton.

130 Li Debin, 'Cotton price . . .', *Beijing Daxue Xuebao* 1980 no. 2, p. 51–53.

131 One such exception was Wugong county in western Guanzhong, which usually is very responsive both to government policies and to agrotechnical developments, owing to the presence of the Northwest Agricultural College. Wugong expanded its cotton acreage in 1979 and again in 1980, but it fell back subsequently to the previous level.

Wugong county cotton acreage, production and yield 1947–1982

	(ha)	(ton)	(kg/ha)		(ha)	(ton)	(kg/ha)		(ha)
1947	2,222	429	193	1974	4,670	1,900	407	1979	6,400
1957	3,135	1,220	389	1975	4,800	1,240	258	1980	6,670
1958	3,330	1,125	338	1976	4,800	1,000	208	1981	5,335
1962	2,770	–.–	–.–	1977	4,770	2,700	570	1982	4,667
1966	4,070	2,350	578	1978	4,770	2,900	615		

Sources: *Shaanxi Mianchan* 1947; *Jingji Yanjiu* no. 10, Oct. 1963; *Shaanxi Ribao* 20 Nov. 1981 and 21 Feb. 1983; data from Wugong county Agricultural Bureau.

132 *Shaanxi Ribao* 22 July 1981.

133 *Shaanxi Ribao* 5 Nov. 1981; *Renmin Ribao* 19 Jan. 1981; *Xinhua* 14 Aug. 1980.

134 'Before 1966, Shaanxi province had been basically self-sufficient in oil crops. Since then, production stagnated. In 1980, production was increased to 110,000 tons . . . 2.4 times as much as in 1979. In 1981 it will increase again', *Shaanxi Ribao* 27 Nov. 1981.

135 'Wugongxian, on the basis of a scientific agricultural regionalization, has restricted its cotton area on the uplands where heat resources are limited, but expanded its oil crops there . . . to 2,700 ha', *Shaanxi Ribao* 20 Nov. 1981.

136 In Qianxian cotton yields averaged 255 kg per ha over the 1949–75 period. The 1976 yield was only 86 kg per ha, the 1978 and 1979 yields were 375 resp. 450 kg per ha. The cotton acreage was reduced from 10,500 ha in 1979 to 7,000 ha in 1980. *Nongcun Gongzuo Tongzuan* 1980 no. 7; personal communication.

137 Bai Jinian, 'Reallocation of crops speeds up agricultural development', *Nongcun Gongzuo Tongxun* 1981 no. 2, p. 14. The plans for commercial grain and cotton bases had already been worked out early in 1979, *Shaanxi Prov. Serv.* 23 Jan. 1979.

138 *Shaanxi Ribao* 7 Jan. 1982.

139 The Dali county government spent almost one million *yuan* on this program, expanding its cotton acreage by 6,000 ha.

140 *Shaanxi Ribao* 21 Feb. 1982.

141 The floods destroyed 6,000 ha, and inundated a further 9,800 ha, of which 5,300 ha yielded no harvest at all, *Xinhua* 24 Sept. 1981. Weinan prefecture had a cotton acreage of 177,000 ha in 1955 and 132,000 ha in 1973, *Shaanxi Ribao* 21 Apr. 1955 and 9 Apr. 1974.

142 *Shaanxi Ribao* 13 March 1982.

143 *Shaanxi Ribao* 1 and 6 May 1984. In the same year, several textile factories clashed with the State Commercial Department, which in 1982 had purchased a lot of below-standard cotton which factories could not but refuse. Causes of the bad quality were a neglect of state grading standards, mixing of yellow and white cotton wool, acceptance of 'sentiment cotton' and 'relations cotton' (which was accepted because of close relations between village cadres and the factory leadership) and lack of inspection of storage. Of the 1982 harvest, 16,000 tons had been stored underground in the cotton-producing counties for more than 8 months. Economic losses were more than one million *yuan*, *Shaanxi Ribao* 30 Aug. 1984.

9 AN EXPLORATION INTO REGIONAL INEQUALITY

1 Siebert defines the concept of a region as 'an intermediate category between an aggregate economy with no spatial dimension and a highly disaggregated economic system defined as a set of spatial points'. H. Siebert, *Regional economic growth: theory and policy*, Scranton Pa., 1969, p. 16.

2 See Harold Brookfield, *Interdependent Development*, London 1975, for a synopsis of the views of D. C. North, R. E. Baldwin, J. M. Gilmour, and M. H. Watkins on export-based economic development.

3 J. Friedmann, *Regional development policy: a case study of Venezuela*, Cambridge Mass. 1966, p. 16.

4 *Shaanxi Nongye Dili*, Xi'an, 1978, p. 216; *Turang Xuebao* Vol. xiii no. 1 (1965).

5 This flood received little publicity at the time. For strategic reasons (it was a defense area near Tongguan) the Nationalist Government denied its occurrence, so that no official investigation by relief organizations could be undertaken, George Hogg, *I see a New China*, Boston, 1944, p. 132; *Pingmingxian Zhi*, 1943. Later, relief was provided though, *Shaanxisheng Zhengfu Gongbao* no. 816 13 Sept. 1942). The danger areas along the lower Wei and Huang Rivers have been occupied by State Farms in the 1958–1962 period and taken into extensive cultivation.

6 In summer 1981, 1.4 million ha were calamity-stricken, with 11.8 million people, *Shaanxi Ribao* 7 May 1983.

7 *Shaanxi Ribao* 13 Nov. 1981; *Renmin Ribao* 28 Nov. 1981. See chapter 4f.

8 Rev. F. S. Russell, 'The Railway Comes to Sian', *The Herald* of the Baptist Missionary Society, London ed. 1935, p. 55; *Memorandum of the Forward Movement in*

Shensi, Dec. 1936, BMS Archives; Chen Gengya, *Xibei Shichaji*, Shanghai, 1936, p. 445.

9 *Xibei Xiangdao* June–Dec. 1936, p. 374 (Luohui Ditch); *Shaanxibei* 16 Sept. 1936 (Jinghui Ditch); *Shaanxi Shuili Jibao* Vol. xii no. 2 (1938), p. 30 (Weihui Ditch). See chapter 5 c.

10 In 1934, the production value of opium in Guanzhong was 13 million *yuan* (equal to the *total* export value, minus opium, of Shaanxi province). Most opium was exported. Xibei Yanjiushe (ed.), *Kangzhan Zhongdi Shaanxi*, n.p. 1940, pp. 60–2. See chapter 8 b.

11 Sun Hanwen, 'Record of a trip to west Shaanxi', *Xibei Lunheng* Vol. ix no. 2 (1941), pp. 68–72. Fu Anhua, 'The industrial situation in the Northwest', *Xibei Ziyuan* Vol. i no. 1 (1940), pp. 43–58. See chapter 3 b.

12 Zhen Hongxu, 'The fate of cotton in Shaanxi', *Fangzhi Gongye* 1947, pp. 19–11. See chapter 8 d.

13 In Guanzhong, cotton production and acreage went down within 4 years to about one-third of the pre-war average, but much less so in the counties near Xi'an. Jingyang, Sanyuan, Gaoling and Changan counties produced 35 percent of Guanzhong's cotton during 1934–8, but 47 percent of it during 1941–5; their cotton acreage rose from 29 percent to 39 percent of Guanzhong's total during the same periods; calculated from Lu Guozhen (ed.), *Shaanxi Mianchan*, n.p. 1947. The northern counties lost much of their traditional wheat exports because of this change-over from cotton to wheat in the counties along the Wei River and south of it. See chapter 8 d.

14 *Shaanxibei* 16 Sept.–3 Oct. 1936; 'What I saw and heard in Xi'an', *Zhongguo Jianshe* Vol. xiv no. 4 (1936), p. 114–114.

15 According to the Provincial Relief Society, 1.9 million people left their village for an unknown fate. *Zhongguo Nongcun Jingji Ziliao*, pp. 774–7. 780,000 people fled to other provinces, *Shaanxi Nongye Dili*, Xi'an 1978, p. 5. See chapter 1 c.

16 In 1939 alone, Shaanxi province received over 100,000 refugees, Zhen Wutai, 'Reclamation work in Shaanxi', *Xibei Ziyuan* Vol. i no. 4, pp. 110–15. Wang Depu (ed.), *Shaanxi Minzheng Gaikuang*, n.p., 1940, Land Administration Section p. 7 and Relief Section p. 1, states that by 1940 20,000 war refugees had been resettled in reclamation areas, but that the Jianshan area alone might accommodate 250,000 settlers. By the end of 1942, the Huanglongshan area had 50,000 settlers and the Jianshan area 12,00 settlers, *Xibei Jianshe Kaochatuan Baogao*, Taibei 1968, pp. 289–90.

17 *Communication* from the Director of State Farms and Reclamation, Shaanxi province, 1979. *Shaanxi Ribao* 26 Nov. 1959, mentioned also Weinan and Dali for Sanmen refugees. See chapter 4 c.

18 *Shaanxi Ribao* 28 Oct. 1956 and 15 Nov. 1957.

19 *Shaanxi Ribao* 8 Feb. 1979. Hereby, urban youngsters were sent down to the country on a semi-permanent basis.

20 According to a survey of migration in 7 counties, during the past 3 decades, on average, 1 to 2 percent of the population moved in or out every year, with an about equal number of immigrants and emigrants. *Data* collected in 1979 from local Agricultural Bureaus. None of these counties, it should be said, is near Xi'an.

21 The quote is from Vice-governor Xie Huaide's comment in *Shaanxi Ribao* 13 Nov. 1981. Under the 1981 rules, agricultural land is recompensated with 4 to 8 times (depending on size) the annual production value, and for every ha of vegetable plot an additional 3,000 to 5,000 *yuan* is paid. As the collectives around Xi'an had rented out some 170 ha during 1978–80, at the above-quoted price they must have earned a tremendous – though illegal – amount. It appears that past visitors to suburban communes were unaware of this source of income. A legal commentator

maintained that willful obstruction and extortion against state organizations in need of agricultural land could be dealt with by law, *Shaanxi Ribao* 23 May 1983.

22 Hua Nianlun, 'The Shaanxi Provincial Party Committee severily punishes "Land tyrants" and "Land masters"', *Renmin Ribao* 23 Feb. 1984.

23 I offer two examples, one in the west and one in the east of Guanzhong. Chaoyi county (which since 1960 has been incorporated in Dali county) had 60,000 ha of farmland with an agricultural population of 180,000 in 1956. Four agricultural regions should be distinguished: the dry uplands, the Luohui irrigation distrct, the sandy stretches along the Yellow River (later to be occupied by a state farm) and the '*shawan*' (sand-bowl) which was inhabited by sheep-tending nomad Muslims. Shaanxisheng Nongyeting (ed.), *Shaanxisheng Chaoyixian Jishu Tuiguangzhan Shi Zenyang Tuiguang Nongye Jishudi*, Xi'an, 1956; Sha Fengbao, 'Report of a preliminary investigation of animal husbandry in the region along the Wei River in Guanzhong, Shaanxi', *Xibei Nonglin*. Special issue on animal husbandry, n.p., 1936. Wugong county, which has a farmland area of 34,000 ha, was recently described as consisting of 'three worlds': the low-lying plain near the river, heavily irrigated and densely populated, the medium plain which has a medium-level production of foodgrain, cotton and oil crops, and the high plain which is still underdeveloped. 'Ideas of agricultural specialists on the transformation plan of Wugong country', *Shaanxi Ribao* 13, 21 and 28 Feb. 1983; see *Loutu*, Xi'an, 1964, pp. 17–18 for a cross-section of Wugong.

24 Feng Shixiu, 'Development of the dry uplands', *Shaanxi Ribao* 16 and 21 Feb. 1982; 'Ideas of agricultural specialists on the transformation plan of Wugong county', *Shaanxi Ribao* 13 and 21 Feb. 1983.

25 Bai Jinian, 'Reallocation of crops speeds up agricultural development', *Nongcun Gongzuo Tongxun* 1981 no. 2, p. 14; *Shaanxi Ribao* 27 Nov. 1981, 7 Jan. and 3 March 1982. See chapters 6 g and 7 f.

26 e.g. with Fenghuo in Liquan county and with Qianjin in Wugong county, *Kuzhan Sannian Gaibian Shaanxi Mianmao*, Xi'an, 1958, pp. 9–10.

27 *Shaanxi Nongye* 1964 no. 10, p. 16. Wugong, Pucheng and Jingyang counties were the most important centres for agroscientific research at that time; 'On Agroscience Stations', *Shaanxi Nongye* 1964 no. 11, pp. 5–6.

28 In the minds of politicians and common people alike, immediate associations have been nurtured between counties and products. Nowadays Meixian county stands for apples, Liquan for pears, Fengxiang for *gaoliang*-based alchohol, Huaxian for bamboo, Xunyi for sugar, Dali for peanuts, Chunhua for reforestation. Some of these associations date back to the pre-war period. Specialization of crops has not gone very far, however, because of the policies of self-reliance and autarchy. For present-day specialization, see maps 30 and 20.

29 'All the famine relief efforts only touch the margin . . . There is grain outside but the difficulty is to get it up. For the great mass of refugees nothing can be done. Meanwhile soldiers are going east, commandeering the few remaining carts and animals', Rev. E. W. Burt, *The Herald* of the BMS, 1930, p. 42. See chapter 1 d.

30 *Xin Shaanxi* Vol. 1 no. 1, pp. 9–10; Li Qinfen and Song Zheyuan, *Xibeijun Jishi (1924–1930 nian)*, Hongkong, 1978 (reprint), pp. 447–52; *Xibei Ziyuan* Vol. 1 no. 4, pp. 78–9.

31 'I asked peasants and local officials for a solution of the famine problem. Officials would answer: 'communications are bad, one cannot send relief grain to faraway places . . .' Peasants said: 'formerly each family would have some savings, so that it could tide over the disaster year. But nowadays it is different', Luo Linzao, 'Xibei Nongmin Fuyedi Zhongyaoxing', *Shi Huang* Vol. II no. 3 (1934), p. 25. See chapter 1 e.

32 *Zhongyang Ribao* 27 and 28 Jan. 1938; Jiang Jie, 'Guanzhong Nongcun Renkou Diaocha' (Investigation of the rural population of Guanzhong), *Xibei Nonglin* Vol. III (July 1938); JCRR, *Shaanxisheng Nongcun Diaocha*, 1934; *Zhongguo Nongcun Jingji Ziliao*, pp. 774–7. See chapter 1 c.

33 See chapter 2 a.
34 *Shaanxi Ribao* 15 July 1956.
35 *Xibei Xiangdao* June–Dec., pp. 119, 242–4, 374; *Zhongguo Jingji Nianjian Xubian*, Shanghai, 1935, pp. N 461–3.
36 E. Teichman, *Travels of a consular officer in Northwest China*, p. 81.
37 See chapter 2 b.
38 Ren Fu, 'Investigation of the general condition of 9 counties in Guanzhong, Shaanxi', *Xibei Lunheng* Vol. IX no. 4 (1941), pp. 53–6. See also Table 71, which shows four counties with railroad connections (Wugong, Weinan, Hancheng, and Pucheng) and three counties without.
39 Glover and Simon found a very high correlation ($R^2 = 0.83$) between the density of the road network, population density and income per capita in 113 nations in 1968, *Economic Development and Cultural Change* Vol. 23, pp. 453–68.
40 The sparsely populated counties call for an extra explanation. Chunhua has the status of an 'old liberated area'. In spite of its dire poverty it gets preferential state support, also in the form of highway construction subsidies. The peasants of Hancheng live almost exclusively in the southeastern parts of the county, near the county capital which has a fairly large population of miners and industrial labourers. To the west and north the Huanglongshan mountains occupy most of Hancheng. The very uneven distribution of population and farmland explains the combination of high rural income and low highway density.
41 Total capital of the registered industries was 69 million *yuan* (1940 value). Only five had a capital of over 5 million *yuan* and over 500 Hp of motive power: the Dahua textile factory in Xi'an, the Shenxin 4th textile factory in Baoji, the Xianyang textile factory, the Tongchuan Cement factory and the Caijiapo Tool factory, *Xibei Jianshe Kaochatuan Baogao*, pp. 305–22. A list of factories established during 1906–39 shows cotton, machinery, railway supplies, flour, matches, chemicals and paper as major industries. The percentage of indigenous versus outside capital varied according to different branches of industry, *Kangzhan Zhongdi Shaanxi*, pp. 23–50. See chapter 3 b.
42 Li Xiaosu, 'Shaanxi may become the cotton textile centre of the Northwest', *Xibei Tongxun* no. 6, Aug. 1947, pp. 9–12. Sun Hanwen, 'Record of a trip to Shaanxi', *Xibei Lunheng* Vol. IX no. 2 (1941), pp. 68–72.
43 Fu Anhua, 'The industrial situation in the Northwest', *Xibei Ziyuan* Vol. I no. 3 (1940), pp. 31–7; Xie Jianyun, 'Flour industry in Xi'an', *Xibei Tongxun* Vol. III no. I (July 1948), pp. 13–14. One sack weighs 24 kg.
44 Fu Anhua, *ibidem*. The cotton packing season ran from October till June. Major oils were rapeseed oil, sesame oil, peanut oil, castor oil, varnish oil, and cotton seed oil.
45 *Xibei Xiangdao* June–Dec. 1936, p. 119 mentions an output in Fengxiang alone of only 40,000 litres of alcohol per year. During the war, however, the number of distilleries went up to over 60. Production methods of linen and woolens were very backward. Paper was produced on the basis of hemp, waste shoes, bark, rags, and leftovers from cloth. Pucheng made high-quality paper. Fengxiang produced about 300,000 quires per year, most of which were exported to Gansu province. Newspapers in Xi'an had their own paper mills. Zhu Baoding, 'The paper handicraft and industry in the Northwest', *Xibei Tongxun* Vol. II no. 12, (June 1948), pp. 14–15, and Fu Anhua, *ibidem*, pp. 51–8.
46 See chapters 3 b and 8 d. In 1947, the 8 modern cotton mills had 80,000 spindles and 2,500 looms; the small-scale mills had 3,700 looms in Xi'an, Baoji and Sanyuan alone; cottage industrial size may best be indicated by the predicted expansion of the modern cotton mills (which planned to enlarge their market share) to 300,000 spindles and 10,000 looms within 10 years after 1947. In 1981, Shaanxi's textile industries had 22,700 looms, *Shaanxi Ribao* 4 Oct. 1981.

47 (In 1956, average rural net income increased by 21 percent. One-quarter came from sidelines). 'However, 19 percent of all people had *decreased* income. What kind of people? (1) '. . . (2) those peasants pursuing other occupations: industrial labourers, small pedlars, handicraftsmen, families going into sideline production. Altogether this is about 10 percent of the coop members, (3) . . .', Jiang Yan et al., *Gongnong Qunzhong Shenghuo Zhuangkuang Diaocha Ziliao*, Xi'an, 1958, pp. 53–63; Fang Zhongru, *Qianfang Baiji Jiaqiang Nongye Zhanxian*, Xi'an, 1960, pp. 2 and 15; *Xinhua* 6 Feb. 1979; *Shaanxi Prov. Serv.* 24 Mar. 1981.

48 Zhongguo Kexueyuan Dili Yanjiusuo (ed.) *Zhongguo Sheng (qu) Dili*, Beijing, 1977, pp. 71–74; *Zhongguo Jingji Nianjian 1981*, Beijing, 1981, pp. 306–9.

49 *Shaanxi Ribao* 7 Nov. 1981 and 5 May 1983 (cotton industry), 7 Feb. 1982 (ready made clothing industry), 17 Apr. 1983 (lack of profits); Wang Ziyi et al., 'Qianyi Shaanxi Jinggongye Fazhan Wenti' (A superficial opinion on the problems of development of Shaanxi's light industry), *Shaanxi Shida Xuebao*, 1984, no. 4, pp. 26–30 (light industry). For a general appraisal see chapter 3f.

50 For total employment figures in Shaanxi province see chapter 3, tables 20, 21 and note 145.

51 Good examples of these are the investigation of Dali county industry over the period 1970–9, *Shaanxi Ribao* 28 Aug. 1979, and the story of the state brick factory in Liquan county which went bankrupt and was handed over to a private contractor, who fired people, instituted piece-rate wages and tripled productivity, *Shaanxi Ribao* 26 Dec. 1984.

52 Peasants contract labourers are also used in coal mines (3,750 people in 1982). High productivity, low wages, easy to lay off, no social security, no dependents and other 'advantages' of this category have been put forward, *Shaanxi Ribao* 14 May 1983.

53 63 percent of the total production value of these enterprises was produced in just one-fifth of the counties of Shaanxi province, most of which in the irrigated areas of Guanzhong, *Shaanxi Ribao* 5 Aug. 1979. In 1980, gross income from this source constituted 58% of the total rural income in Changan, and 34% in Huxian, *Shaanxi Ribao* 29 Nov. 1981. In the rural areas of Xi'an in 1982 gross income from this source was 249 million yuan, *Shaanxi Ribao* 8 Apr. 1983, at that time maybe one-fifth of the Shaanxi provincial total.

54 In 1971, gross production value was 16 million *yuan*; in 1982 it was 127 million *yuan*, with a profit of 21 million *yuan*. *Renzhen Zhixing Dangdi Nongcun Jingji Zhengce*, Xi'an 1972, pp. 29–35; *Shaanxi Ribao* 26 May 1983.

55 Zhao Tianzhen, 'How to manage village and zhen-enterprises well', *Shaanxi Ribao* 15 June 1984; *Shaanxi Ribao* 10 May 1984.

56 Report on the Shaanxi Provincial Government Work, *Shaanxi Ribao* 7 May 1983.

57 'An investigation into household sidelines of members of collectives in Changan county', *Nongye Jingji Wenti* 1982 no. 5. 'An investigation of keypoint households and specialized households', *ibidem* 1983 no. 2. According to a survey of Heyang county, in 1983 3.5 percent of the rural households were engaged in industrial or commercial work alone, *Shaanxi Ribao* 15 June 1983.

58 *Shaanxi Ribao* 23 Feb. 1957 and *Shaanxisheng Tongji Ziliao Huikan* no. 1–5 (1940–5), Xi'an.

59 See tables 65 and 71.

60 *Shaanxi Ribao*, 19 Apr. and 15 June 1983; see chapter 3g, tables 24 and 25, and below, p. 414.

61 See Table 24.

62 SSB Report on the economy of Shaanxi, *Shaanxi Ribao* 27 Apr. 1983.

63 An example is the case of the Weinan Regional Cotton Mill. The female workers asked for a fixed 5-year contract, so that their job would be guaranteed. They

complained about their living conditions, because there was only 2 square meters of living space per worker. Even so, out of the 1,600 workers, 500 had to live in guesthouses or neighbouring peasant homes, *Shaanxi Ribao* 22 Nov. 1981.

64 See e.g. a factory history published by the Shaanxi First Cotton Mill in 1959. In 1949 the working hours for the 1,343 labourers were reduced from 12 to 11 hours, with one day off every week. In 1951 there was a further reduction to 10 hours. In 1952 the national labour regulations were put into effect: 8 hours a day (and a nightshift of $6\frac{1}{2}$ hours). Illiteracy was reduced from over 70 percent to below 10 percent. '*10 Years of bitterness, 10 years of sweetness*' – a 20-year history of the Shaanxi First Cotton Mill, Xi'an, 1959 (in Chinese, mimeographed).

65 Kang Yongfu, 'Coal mining in Shaanxi and Gansu and proposals for its improvement', *Xibei Lunheng* Vol. IX no. 9 (1941), pp. 31–43.

66 *Jigucun Enzhouji*, Beijing, 1964, describes a village in Fuping county. *Mizhixian Yangjiagou Diaocha*, Beijing, 1957 (and also J. Myrdal and Mark Selden) are based on experiences in north Shaanxi mountain areas. *Zhongguo Nongcun Jingji Ziliao* II Vols, Shanghai, 1934, pp. 772–3, 783.

67 See e.g. figures on wasteland and land tax receipts for 1933, *Caizheng Nianjian 1935*, pp. 2100–5. The lack of draught animals, of manure and of agricultural implements and also a reduced market demand especially affected western Guanzhong.

68 The price for a wife was at least 100 *yuan* (about 2 year's full wages). Jiang Jie, 'An investigation of the rural population of Guanzhong', *Xibei Nonglin* Vol. III (July 1938).

69 In Long Bow village, poor peasants held 3 *mou* per person, middle peasants 6.4 *mou*, W. Hinton, *Fanshen*, p. 699.

70 Official statistics in county averages of household size and landholding for 23 counties in 1933 show low household averages (2.5–4.5 persons) in a few irrigated counties with much employment outside agriculture, and for most other counties household averages of 5 to 7 persons, with average landholdings ranging from 25 to 60 *mou*. *Manuscript* Shaanxi Civil Administration Bureau, 1934, Land Reform Office Archives, Taipei.

71 Ma Yulin, *Wugongxian Tudi Wenti zhi Yanjiu*, Xi'an, 1936, pp. 17–32, based on a survey of 3,000 households. See chapter 4 f, tables 30 and 31.

72 Hsiong Baiheng and Wang Dianjun, *Shaanxisheng Tudi Zhidu Diaocha Yanjiu*, Wugong, 1941. As landlords and tenants were so few in number, the sample was rather small: 32 tenant farms.

73 'The Luohe Valley counties are regarded as a rather good region for development because the region has never been given so extensively to poppy cultivation and because the farmer's organization for self-defence is strong . . . The districts west of Xi'an are certainly worse. All the banks shun them.' Bauer and Liu, *An investigation of rural conditions in Shaanxi*, Nanjing, 1934, p. 15 (mimeographed).

74 Jiang Jie, 'An investigation of the rural population of Guanzhong', *Xibei Nonglin* Vol. III (July 1938), pp. 53–4, 102, 126, 156.

75 *Xijing Ribao* 28 Sept. 1936.

76 *Shaanxi Shuili Jibao* Vol. VII no. 2 (Dec. 1942), *Shaanxidi Guangai Guanli*, Xi'an, 1952. 'Irrigation administration in Shaanxi province', *Nongtian Shuili yu Shuitu Baochi* no. 5 (Nov. 1964), pp. 1–6.

77 Gaoling, Jingyang and Sanyuan received an average of 20 *yuan* per capita of the total rural population during 1935–41; most counties received an average of less than 5 *yuan* per capita. Shaanxi Hezuo Shiye Guanliju, *Shaanxi Hezuo Shiye Gaikuang*, Xi'an, 1942, p. 21, 51.

78 Ma Yulin, *Wugongxian . . .*, pp. 36, 41. The author refers to Wugong county. He may have his figure of 2,000 *mou* wrong; in another publication he states that the 'certain VIP from Xi'an' bought over 700 *mou*, Ma Yulin, *Shaanxi Shixi Diaocha Riji*, 1936, p. 61.

79 An Yongqing and Yu Chengzhong, 'Preliminary report of an investigation of the peasants' burden in Guanzhong during war-time', *Xibei Nongbao* Vol. 1 no. 3 (1946), p. 46. 35,431 families were surveyed in Weinan, Baoji, Jingyang and Wugong.

80 *ibidem*, pp. 110–15. In July 1940, the price of a recruit was in the range of 200 to 1,000 *yuan* in Guanzhong, but less than 100 *yuan* in the Ankang region. This may reflect both a lower standard of living and a greater willingness to be recruited. At the time the *yuan* still had one-quarter of its 1937 value; 100 *yuan* would buy 300 to 400 kg of wheat.

81 In 1957, half of Shaanxi's population lived in the mountains. They had 63 percent of the cultivated area, 69 percent of the large domestic animals, 81 percent of the pigs, 94 percent of the sheep and goats. Yearly production value of the 'special mountain products' (medicinal herbs etc., *ex*cluding varnish, tea, tong-oil, apricots etc. and mineral resources) reached 48 million *yuan*. Shaanxi Provincial Agriculture and Forestry Bureau (ed.), *Shanqu Qunzhong Zenyang Gao Linfuye Shengchan*, Xi'an 1957; Shangwei CCP Propaganda Department (ed.), *Shanqu Shehui Zhuyi Jianshe Jianghua*, Xi'an, 1958.

82 At the end of 1958, most mountain districts still had no accountants, *Shaanxi Nongxun* 1958 no. 3, p. 7.

83 World Bank, *China: socialist economic development*, Table 1-4, p. 98. Under the new definition of the 1982 census, 19 percent of Shaanxi's population was urban.

84 *Shaanxi Ribao* 8 Jan. 1982; *Shaanxi Qingnian* 1979 no. 3, p. 31, no. 6, p. 27, no. 10, pp. 19–20 and no. 12, pp. 2–3.

85 Data from Regional Agricultural Bureaus, 1979.

86 See chapter 3.

87 'The situation of production increase, distribution and members' thought in four Higher Agricultural Producers' Cooperatives', *Shaanxi Ribao* 1 Jan. 1957.

88 This survey came close to the official figures of 137 *yuan* in 1978 and 222 *yuan* in 1982 (computed from *Shaanxi Ribao* 19 Apr. 1983). Inflation percentage (computed from a national survey which gave corresponding figures of 134 *yuan* in 1978 and 270 *yuan* in 1982, *Shaanxi Ribao* 15 June 1983) may be too low.

89 *Shaanxi Ribao* 7 Sept. 1984 and 17 Feb. 1985.

90 See e.g. Qiao Junwu, 'Employment opportunities for the superfluous rural labour force on the *Hanyuan*. An investigation of Heyang county', *Shaanxi Ribao* 15 June 1983 and Yang Hongzhang, 'Can the problem of unemployment be solved?', *Shaanxi Ribao* 25 Nov. 1981.

10 CONCLUDING OBSERVATIONS

1 *Shaanxi Jingji Tantao*, p. 31.

2 Wang Shaowu and Zhao Zongci, 'Zhongguo Xiaji Diwen Lenghai' (Damage by low temperatures in the summer season in China), *Ziran Ziyuan* 1985 no. 1, pp. 54–69.

3 Guojia Tongjiju (ed.), *Zhongguo Tongji Zhaiyao* 1984 and *Caiwu yu Kuaiji* 1984 no. 9, p. 12 show national budgetary income and expenditure and state investments from 1950 through 1983.

4 Zeng Kuihao et al., 'Fahui Shaanxi Nongye Youshi Jige Wentidi Qianyi' (A superficial opinion about some problems of developing the outstanding situation of Shaanxi's agriculture), *Shaanxi Caijing Xueyuan Xuebao* 1982 no. 3, pp. 15–20.

5 *ibidem*.

6 'One must hold on to grain production', *Shaanxi Ribao* 30 Mar. 1985.

7 Randolph Barker and Radha Sinha (eds), *The Chinese Agricultural Economy*, Boulder, 1982, p. 200.

8 Jon Sigurdson, 'Rural Industrialization in China', in U.S. Congress Joint Economic Committee, *China: A Reassessment of the Economy*, Washington DC, 1975; Dwight Perkins (ed.), *Rural Small-Scale Industry in the People's Republic of China*, Berkeley, 1977; Christine Pui Wah Wong, 'Rural Industrialization in China', in Randolph Barker and Radha Sinha (eds), *The Chinese Agricultural Economy*, p. 137–46.

9 Zhou Xuetong, 'Fangshou Fazhan Xiangzhen Qiye Jinkuai Gaishan Xianji Caizheng Zhuangkuang' (Give a free hand to the development of rural enterprises, and remedy the financial situation of county governments as soon as possible), *Shaanxi Shida Xuebao* 1985 no. 1, pp. 17–21.

10 Dernberger, Rawski and Barker in *The Chinese Agricultural Economy*, pp. 2, 101 and 132.

BIBLIOGRAPHY

CITED WESTERN-LANGUAGE BOOKS

Academia Sinica, *Water and Soil Conservation and Water Conservancy Measures*, Peking, 1959, JPRS transl. no. 17,046.

Academia Sinica, *Handbook of Water and Soil Conservation of the Middle Yellow River Loess Region*, Peking, 1959, JPRS transl. no. 19,810.

R. Barker and R. Sinha (eds), *The Chinese Agricultural Economy*, Boulder Col. 1982.

Max Bauer and Gaines Liu, *Rural Conditions and Cooperative Movement in central Shensi*, Economic Council Manuscript, Nanjing, 1934.

P. R. Bohr, *Famine in China and the Missionary*, Harvard, 1972.

John L. Buck, *China's Farm Economy*, Shanghai, 1930.

John L. Buck, *Land Utilization in China*, Nanking, 1937.

S. Chandrasekhar, *China's population, census and vital statistics*, Hongkong, 1960.

Cheng Chu-yuan, *China's Economic Development: Growth and Structural Change*, Boulder Co., 1982.

Ch'i Hsi-sheng, *Nationalist China at war: Military defeats and political collapse, 1937–1945*, Ann Arbor, 1982.

China Christian Yearbook 1931, Shanghai, 1931.

China Handbook 1950, New York, 1950.

Chinese People's Association for Cultural Relations with Foreign Countries, Xi'an branch (ed.). *Famous Historical Places and Cultural Relics of Sian*, Xi'an, 1959.

The Chinese Yearbook 1936–1937, Shanghai, 1938.

The Chinese Yearbook 1944–1945, Shanghai, 1946.

Committee on the Economy of China, *Provincial Agricultural Statistics for Communist China*, Ithaca N.Y., 1969.

Deng Yunte, *The North China Famine of 1920–21*, Peking, 1922.

Deng Zihui, *Multi-purpose plan for controlling the Yellow River and exploiting its water resources*, FLP Beijing, 1955.

Audrey Donnithorne, *China's Economic System*, New York, 1967.

R. Dumont, *Révolution dans les campagnes chinoises*, Paris, 1957.

R. Dumont, *Chine surpeuplée, tiers monde affamée*, Paris, 1965.

Alexander Eckstein, *China's Economic Revolution*, Cambridge, 1977.

H. Epstein, *Domestic Animals of China*, London, 1969.

Albert Feuerwerker, *Economic Trends in the Republic of China 1912–1949*, Ann Arbor, 1977.

Harry A. Franck, *Wandering in Northern China*, New York, 1923.

P. J. A. Gorissen and E. B. Vermeer, *Development of milk production in China in the 1980s*, Pudoc, Wageningen, 1985.

Charles E. Greer, *Chinese Water Management Strategies in the Yellow River Basin*, Ph.D. Diss.Un. of Washington, 1975.

Jan-Erik Gustafsson, *Water Resources Development in the People's Republic of China*, Royal Institute of Technology, Dept. of Land Improvement and Drainage, publ. no. 1035, Stockholm, 1984.

521

William Hinton, *Fanshen, A Documentary of revolution in a Chinese village*, Harmondsworth, 1972.

George Hogg, *I see a New China*, Boston, 1944.

C. Howe (ed.). *Shanghai: Revolution and Development in an Asian Metropolis*, Cambridge, 1981.

J. Humlum, *I Kina 1972*, Copenhagen, 1974 (Gyldendal).

Virgil A. Johnson and Halsey L. Beemer, Jr. (eds), *Wheat in the People's Republic of China. A trip report of the American Wheat Studies Delegation*, CSCPRC Report no. 6, NAS, Washington DC, 1977.

David N. Keightley (ed.), *The Origins of Chinese Civilization*, London, 1983.

V. A. Kovda, *Soils and Natural Environment of China*, transl. by JPRS no. 5967.

Richard A. Kraus, *Cotton and Cotton Goods in China 1918–1936*, New York 1980.

Nicholas Lardy, *Agriculture in China's Modern Economic Development*, Cambridge, 1983.

Laurence J. C. Ma and Edward W. Hanten (eds), *Urban Development in Modern China*, Boulder Co., 1981.

William H. Mallory, *China: Land of Famine*, New York, 1926.

J. Myrdal, *Report from a Chinese Village*, New York 1972.

Guides Nagel, *Chine*, Genève, 1977.

F. H. Nichols, *Through Hidden Shensi*, London, 1902.

Dwight H. Perkins (ed.), *China's Modern Economy in Historical Perspective*, Stanford, 1975.

D. Perkins and S. Yusuf, *Rural Development in China*, World Bank, Washington DC, 1984.

Plant Studies in the People's Republic of China. A trip report of the American Plant Studies Delegation, CSCPRC Washington, D.C., 1975.

D. Reich e.a., *Raumplanung in China*, Dortmund, 1980.

Rural Health in the People's Republic of China, NIH Publ. no. 81–2124, Washington D.C., 1980.

Rhoads, Murphey, *The Fading of the Maoist Vision: City and Country in China's Development*, New York, 1980.

Mark Selden, *The Yenan Way in Revolutionary China*, London, 1972.

James E. Sheridan, *Chinese Warlord – the Career of Feng Yü-hsiang*, Stanford, 1966.

Paul K. T. Sih (ed.) *Nationalist China during the Sino-Japanese war, 1937–1945*, New York, 1977.

Gunther Stein, *The Challenge of Red China*, New York 1945.

Eric Teichmann, *Travels of a Consular Officer in Northwest China*.

Hung-mao Tien, *Government and politics in KMT China 1927–1937*, Stanford 1972.

O. J. Todd, *Two Decades in China*, Association of Chinese and American Engineers, Peking 1938.

M. B. Ullman, *Cities of Mainland China: 1953 and 1958*, U.S. Bureau of Census, International Population Reports, Series P-95 no. 59, Washington D.C., 1961.

U.S. Congress JEC, *China under the Four Modernizations*, 2 Vols, Washington D.C., 1982.

E. B. Vermeer, *Water Conservancy and Irrigation in China*: Social, Economic and Agrotechnical Aspects, Leiden, 1977.

Kenneth Walker, *Food grain procurement and consumption in China*, Cambridge, 1984.

Wang Yongyan and Zhang Zhongu (eds), *Loess in China*, Xi'an, 1980.

Huang Wenxi, *Soil and Water Conservation of the Yellow River Basin*, Studies on the Yellow River project (1946–1947) no. 5, n.p. 1948.

H. R. Williamson, *British Baptists in China 1945–1952*, London, 1957.

Paul W. Wilm, *Die Früchtbarkeit und Ertragsleistung Nordchinas bis 1949*, Wiesbaden, 1968.

World Bank, *China: Socialist Economic Development*, 3 Vols, Washington D.C., 1983.

Wu Yuanli, *The Spatial Economy of Communist China*, New York, 1967.

Arthur N. Young, *China's wartime finance and inflation 1937–1945*, Cambridge, 1965.

George A. Young, *The Living Christ in Modern China*, London. 1947.

Bibliography 523

CHINESE LANGUAGE

Bai Dizhou, *Guanzhong Fangyin Diaocha Baogao*, Beijing, 1954.
Baoji Diqu Xingshu Nongyeju, *Baoji Diqu Wei-Bei-Yuanqu Sanxian Baogao*, n.p., 1979.
Beijing Shida, *Turangxue Ji Turang Dilixue Cankao Ziliao Jianjie*, Beijing, 1957.
Cai Pingfan, *Shaanxi Geming Jiyao*, Taipei, 1962.
Cai Pingfan, *Shaanxi Geming Xianlie Shilüe*, Taipei, 1962.
Caizhengbu, *Caizheng Nianjian 1935*, n.p., 1935.
Chen Gengya, *Xibei Shicha Ji*, Shanghai, 1936.
Chen Qiaoyi (ed.), *Zhongguo Liuda Gudu*, n.p., n.d.
Chen Wannan, *Xixing Riji*, n.p., n.d.
Chen Zhengmo, *Zhongguo Geshengde Dizu*, Shanghai, 1936.
Dai Yingxin, *Guanzhong Shuili Shihua*, Xi'an, 1977.
Deng Yunte, *Zhongguo Jiuhuang Shi*, Shanghai, 1937.
Dinghao Jiti Jiaoliang Hetong, n.p., 1956.
Ditu Chubanshe, *Shaanxisheng Ditu*, Beijing 1973, 1976.
Dongguangzhuang Handi Xiaomai Bianxiezu, *Dongguangzhuang Handi Xiaomai*, Beijing, 1978.
Dongya Yanjiusuo, *Beizhi Guangai Yu Yushiye Diaocha*, n.p., 1941.
Du Shouqian, *Gezhong Huaxue Feiliaode Xingneng He Shiyongfa*, Xi'an, 1957.
Fang Zhengsan et al. (eds), *Huanghe Zhongguo Huangtu Gaoyuan Titiandi Diaocha Yanjiu*, Beijing, 1958.
Fang Zhongru, *Qianfang Baiji Jiaqiang Nongye Zhanxian*, Xi'an, 1960.
Feng Hefa (ed.), *Zhongguo Nongcun Jingji Ziliao*, Shanghai, 1933?
Feng Hefa (ed.), *Zhongguo Nongcun Jingji Ziliao Xubian*, Shanghai, 1935.
Fu Jiaojin, *Shaanxisheng*, Shanghai, 1934.
Gongchandang Shaanxisheng Weiyuanhui Bangongting, *Shaanxi Nongcunde Shehui Zhuyi Jianshe*, 2 Vols, Xi'an, 1956–1958.
Guanzhong Bahui Weizhi Zongtu, n.p., 1938.
Guomindang Zhongyangdangbu Guomin Jingji Jihua Weiyuanhui, *Shinian Lai Zhi Zhongguo Jingji Jianshe*, Zhongguo Caijing Ziliao Huibian nr. 20, Taipei, 1971.
Guoshiguan (ed.), *Xibei Jianshe Kaochatuan Baogao*, Taipei, 1968.
Han Tao (ed.), *Xibei Tequde Zhanshi Zong Dongyuan*, Shanghai, 1938.
Han Xiangang, *Xibeide Qihou*, Xi'an, 1950.
He Bingdi (Ho Ping-ti), *Huangtu Yu Zhongguo Nongyede Qiyuan*, Hong Kong, 1969.
He Hanwei, *Guangxu Chunian (1876–79) Huabeide Da Hanzai*, Hong Kong, 1980.
Henansheng Dizhiju Shuiwen Dizhi Gongcheng Dizhidui, *Dixia Feishui*, Beijing, 1979.
He Qingyun, *Shaanxi Shiye Kaocha Ji*, Taipei, 1983.
Hou Renzhi, *Zhongguo Gudai Dilixue Jianshi*, Beijing, 1962.
Hu Jingliang, *Zhongguo Mianchan Gaijin Shi*, Chengdu, 1943.
Hu Yuanmin, 'Xibei Shengchan Xianzhuang Ji Gaijin Banfa', in *Jingji Qingbao Congkan*, Dishiliu Ji, n.p., 1943.
Huanghe Shuili Weiyuanhui Wunian Zhanhou Jianshe Jihua, n.p., 1942 (secret).
Huanghe Zhiben Yanjiutuan, *Huanghe Shangzhongyou Kaocha Baogao*, n.p., 1946.
Huang Shengzhang, *Lishi Dili Lunji*, Beijing, 1982.
Huang Wei, *Chunman Huanghe*, Beijing, 1975.
Jianchi Jiben Luxian, Shiduo Gaochan Wenchan – Hanyuan Shanqu Nongye Gaochan Wenchan Shili, Xi'an, 1974.
Jiang Yan et al., *Gongnong Qunzhong Shenghuo Zhuangtai Diaocha Ziliao*, Xi'an, 1958.
Jieyue Liangshide Xianjin Jingyan, Xi'an, 1960.
Jin Shanbao and Liu Dingan, *Zhongguo Xiaomai Pinzhong Zhi*, Beijing, 1964.

Jingi Ziliao Bianji Weiyuanhui, *Basheng Nongcun Jingji Dianxing Diaocha*, Beijing, 1957.
Kojima Reiitsu (ed.), *Chúgoku no Toshika to Nôson Kensetsu*, Tokyo, 1978.
Kuzhan Sannian Gaibian Shaanxi Mianmao, Xi'an, 1958.
Lan Mengbo, *Xi'an*, Taipei, 1957.
Laodong Nianjian 1933, n.p., 1933.
Li Guozhen, *Shaanxi Mianchan*, Xi'an, 1949.
Li Qinfen and Song Zheyuan, *Xibei Jun Jishi (1924–1930 Nian)*, Hong Kong, 1978.
Li Rui, *Huanghede Zhili He Kaifa*, Beijing, 1956.
Li Wenzhi, *Zhongguo Jindai Nongyeshi Ziliao*, Beijing, 1957.
Li Yizhi, *Xibei Shuili*, 2 Vols, n.p., 1940.
Liang Shanchang, *Baishui Xianzhi*, Taipei, 1976 (reprint of 1925 ed.).
Liaoning Caijing Xueyuan Nongye Caiwu Kuaiji Jiaoxue Yanjiuzu, *Shengchandui Jingji Huodong Fenxi*, Beijing, 1965.
Lin Furui and Chen Daiguang, *Henan Renkou Dili*, Henan, 1983.
Ling Hongxun, *Zhongguo Tielu Zhi*, Taipei, 1963.
Liu Chao, *Xibei Xumu Ye*, Shanghai, 1955.
Liu Dongsheng, *Huangtude Wuzhi Chengfen He Jiegou*, Beijing, 1966.
Liu Peigui, *Xi'an Shixi Diaocha Riji*, n.p., n.d.
Liu Zhongrui, *Shaanxi Guangai Shiye Zhi Shiji Wenti*, n.p., 1942.
Liu Zhongrui, *Shaanxisheng Shuili*, Xi'an, 1947.
Longhai Tielu Guanliju, *Shaanxi Shiye Kaocha*, Shanghai, 1933.
Ma Yulin, *Shaanxi Shixi Diaocha Riji*, n.p., 1936.
Ma Yulin, *Wugongxian Tudi Wenti Zhi Yanjiu*, n.p., 1936.
Ma Zhenglin, *Fenghao–Chang'an–Xi'an*, Xi'an, 1978.
Neizhengbu Tongjisi, *Minguo Shiqi Nian Ge Shengshi Hukou Diaocha Tongji Baogao*, Nanjing, 1931.
Ni Xiying, Shanghai, 1936.
Nie Shuren, *Shaanxi Ziran Dili*, Xi'an, 1980.
Nie Shuren, *Shaanxi Ziran Jingji Dili Gaikuang*, Xi'an, 1955.
Nie Yurun and Li Tai, *Dalixian Xinzhi Cungao*, 2 vols, Taipei, 1970 (reprint of 1937 ed.).
Nongfubu, *Shaanxisheng Nongcun Diaocha*, Shanghai, 1934.
Nongyebu, *Nongye Shengchan Huzhuzu Cankao Ziliao, vol. I*, Beijing, 1952.
Quandang Quanmin Ban Jiaotong Jingyan Huibian, n.p., 1959.
Quanguo Jingji Weiyuanhui Shuiliju, *Shuili Gongcheng Jihua Huibian*, Nanjing, 1937.
Qianhua et al., *Qinianlai Woguo Siying Gongshangyede Bianhua 1949–1956 Nian*, Beijing, 1957.
Qianxian Kexue Jishu Weiyuanhui, *Qianxian Kexue Yanjiu Jishu Gexin Ziliao Huibian*, Qianxian, 1960.
Qinchuan Niu Diaochadui, *Guanzhong Lü Diaocha Yanjiu Baogao*, Xi'an, 1959.
Qinchuan Niu Diaochadui, *Qinchuan Niu Diaocha Yanjiu Baogao*, Xi'an, 1958.
Qingniantuan Shaanxisheng Gongwei Xuanchuanbu (ed.), *Kaizhan Huzu Hezuo Yundong*, Xi'an, 1952.
Renmin Jiaoyu Chubanshe, *Zhongguo Jingji Dili*, n.p., 1953.
Renzhen Zhixing Dangde Nongcun Jingji Zhengce, Xi'an, 1972.
Rui Qiaosong, *Zuguode Da Xibei*, Shanghai, 1955.
Shaanxi Diyige Wunian Jihua Qijiande Caizheng Mianmao, n.p., 1958.
Shaanxi Diyi Mian Fangzhichang, *Shinian Xinsuan Shinian Tian – Shaanxi Diyi Mian Fangzhichang Chuangjian Ershi Nian Shigao*, Xi'an, 1959.
Shaanxi Hezuo Shiye Guanliju, *Shaanxi Hezuo Shiye Gaikuang*, Xi'an, 1942.
Shaanxi Jinghuiqu Guanliju, *Jinghuiqu Baogaoshu*, Xi'an, 1934.
Shaanxi Liping Kenqu Diaocha Baogao, n.p., 1939.
Shaanxi Quansheng Chengzhenxiang Zizhiqi Tuyu, n.p., 1978.

Shaanxi Renmin Chubanshe (ed.) *Nongye Shengchan Hezuoshe Baogong Baochan Baotouzi Wenda*, Xi'an, 1956.

Shaanxisheng Bowuguan, *Xi'an Lishi Shulüe*, Xi'an, 1959.

Shaanxisheng Dixiashui Gongzuodui, *Nongyong Jingquan*, Beijing, 1978.

Shaanxisheng Fupingxian Chengguan Gongshe Jigucun Cunshi Bianxiezu, *Jigucun Enzhou Ji*, Beijing, 1964.

Shaanxisheng Geming Weiyuanhui Nonglinju (ed.), *Nongye Kexue Jishu Shouce*, Xi'an 1973, 1975.

Shaanxisheng Geming Weiyuanhui Shuidianju (ed.), *Guangai Yongshui*, Beijing, 1977.

Shaanxisheng Geming Weiyuanhui Shuiliju (ed.), *Guanqu Nongtian Jiben Jianshe*, Xi'an, 1976.

Shaanxisheng Guoshu Yanjiusuo, *Shaanxi Guoshu Zhi*, Xi'an, 1978.

Shaanxisheng Hezuo Shiye Guanliju, *Shaanxisheng Hezuo Shiye Gaikuang*, n.p., 1942.

Shaanxisheng Jiansheting, *Shaanxisheng Jianshe Tongji*, Xi'an, 1935.

Shaanxisheng Kaogu Yanjiusuo, *Shaanxi Tongchuan Yaozhou Yao*, Beijing, 1965.

Shaanxisheng Kexue Jishu Xiehui, *Shaanxi Nongmin Kexuejiade Zhihui He Fengge*, Xi'an, 1961.

Shaanxisheng Linyeting, *Shanqu Qunzhong Zenyang Gao Linfuye Shengchan*, Xi'an, 1957.

Shaanxisheng Nonglin Kexueyuan Linye Yanjiusuo, *Shaanxi Linmu Bingchong Tuzhi*, Xi'an, 1977.

Shaanxisheng Nonglinting, *Guanqu Mianhua Fengchan Xian*, Xi'an, 1959.

Shaanxisheng Nonglinting, *Shaanxi Guanzhong Mianhua Zengchan Tujing*, Xi'an, 1954.

Shaanxisheng Nonglinting, *Shaanxisheng Yijiuwujiu Nian Liangshi Fengchan Jishu Jingyan Huibian*, Xi'an, 1960.

Shaanxisheng Nonglinting, *Shaanxisheng Yijiuwujiu Nian Mianhua Fengchan Jishu Jingyan Huibian*, Xi'an, 1960.

Shaanxisheng Nonglinting, *Shaanxisheng Zhuyao Nongzuowu Youliang Pinzhong*, Xi'an 1958.

Shaanxisheng Nonglinting, *Yangzhu Sanzi Jing*, Xi'an, 1958.

Shaanxisheng Nonglinting, *Yijiuwuwu Nian Shaanxisheng Nongye Zengchan Jingyan Huiyi*, Xi'an, 1955.

Shaanxisheng Nongye Jishu Tuiguangchu, *Shaanxisheng Xiaomai Liangzhong Tuiguang Gongzuode Jidian Jingyan*, n.p., n.d.

Shaanxisheng Nongyeting, *Mianhua Zengchan Jingyan*, Xi'an, 1957.

Shaanxisheng Nongyeting, *Shaanxisheng Chang'anxian Xiaomai Fengchan Jingyan*, Xi'an, 1957.

Shaanxisheng Nongyeting, *Shaanxisheng Chaoyixian Jishu Tuiguangzhan Shi Zenyang Tuiguang Nongye Jishude*, Xi'an, 1956.

Shaanxisheng Nongyeting, *Shaanxisheng Fangzhi Xiaomai Xijiangchong Jingyan Jieshao*, Xi'an, 1957.

Shaanxisheng Nongyeting, *Shaanxisheng Mianhua Liangzhong "Jingsimian" He "Wuqiyimian"*, Xi'an, 1957.

Shaaxisheng Nongyeting, *Shaanxisheng Wugongxian Handi Xiaomai Zengchan Jingyan*, Xi'an, 1957.

Shaanxisheng Nongyeting, *Shaanxisheng Xiaomai Liangzhong Shi Zenyang Tuiguang Pujide*, Xi'an, 1957.

Shaanxisheng Nongyeting, *Shaanxisheng Yijiuwuliu Nian Jinghui Guanqu Mianhua Da Mianji Fengchan Jingyan*, Xi'an, 1957.

Shaanxisheng Nongyeting, *Shaanxisheng Yijiuwuliu Nian Xiaomai Qianjin Fengchan Jingyan*, Xi'an, 1957.

Shaanxisheng Nongyeting, *Shaanxisheng Zhuyao Nongzuowu Youliang Pinzhong Zhi*, Xi'an, 1964.

Shaanxisheng Nongyeting, *Xiaomai Zengchan Jingyan*, Xi'an, 1957.

Shaanxisheng Nongyeting, *Youliao Zuowu Zengchan Jingyan*, Xi'an, 1957.

Shaanxisheng Nongyeting, *Zaliang Zengchan Jingyan*, Xi'an, 1957.

Shaanxisheng Qixiangju Qixiangtai Yanjiusuo, *Shaanxi Jin Wubainian Hanlao Guilüde Yanjiu Ji Weilai Hanlao Shide Chubu Tantao*, Xi'an, 1978.

Shaanxisheng Renmin Jingcha, *Zai Baowei Shehui Zhuyi Jianshede Zhanxianshang*, Xi'an, 1956.

Shaanxisheng Renmin Zhengfu Nonglinting Shuiliju, *Shaanxisheng Nongtian Shuili Gaikuang*, Xi'an, 1951.

Shaanxisheng Renmin Zhengfu Tudi Gaige Weiyuanhui, *Shaanxisheng Tudi Gaige Ziliao Huibian*, Xi'an, 1951.

Shaanxisheng Sanyuan Yizhi Nongye Xuexiao, *Nongye Bazi Xianfa Jianghua*, Xi'an, 1960.

Shaanxisheng Shuidianju, *Guangai Gongcheng Guanli*, Xi'an, 1979.

Shaanxisheng Shuili Kexue Yanjiusuo, *Qudao Fangshen*, Beijing, 1976.

Shaanxisheng Shuiliju, *Jinghuiqu Shiwu Nian*, Xi'an, 1947.

Shaanxisheng Shuiliju Jishu Weiyuanhui, *Shaanxisheng Jinghuiqu Guanqu Mianhua Guangai Jingyan Jieshao*, Xi'an, 1957.

Shaanxisheng Shuili Kexue Yanjiusuo, *Yumide Guangai*, Xi'an, 1976.

Shaanxisheng Shuiliting, *Shaanxisheng Shuitu Baochi Jingyan*, Xi'an, 1959.

Shaanxisheng Shuiliting, *Shaanxisheng Shuitu Baochi Jingyan Jieshao*, 2 Vols, Xi'an 1958, 1959.

Shaanxisheng Shuitu Baochiju, *Badi Fanghong Yu Zhiyan*, Beijang, 1976.

Shaanxisheng Shuitu Baochiju, *Badi Liyong*, Xi'an, 1977.

Shaanxisheng Shuitu Baochiju, *Shuitu Baochi*, Beijing, 1973.

Shaanxisheng Shuitu Baochiju, Xibei Huanghe Gongchengju, *Zenyang Xiu Titian*, Xi'an, 1957.

Shaanxisheng Weibei Hanyuan Dixiashui Kaifa Liyong Zonghe Yanjiu Bangongshi, *Shaanxisheng Weibei Hanyuan Dixiashui Kaifa Liyong Zonghe Yanjiu Ziliao Huibian*, Xi'an, 1978.

Shaanxisheng Weiyuanhui Nonglinju, *Siji Nongye Kexue Shiyanwang Jishu Shouce*, n.p., 1978.

Shaanxisheng Yan Weihe Guanzhong Yidai Gexian Nonghu Ji Gengdi Tongji Biao (Zhailu 1934 Nian Shiyebu Tongjiju Baogao), n.p., n.d.

Shaanxisheng Yulin Diqu Shuitu Baochizhan, *Shuiping Titian*, Beijing, 1974.

Shaanxisheng Zhengfu, *Shaanxisheng Zhi Nongye Jianshe*, n.p., 1942.

Shaanxisheng Zhengfu Tongjishi, *Shaanxisheng Tongji Shouce*, Shanghai, 1944.

Shaanxisheng Zhengfu Tongjishi (ed.), *Shaanxisheng Tongji Ziliao Huikan*, 5 Vols, Xi'an, 1941–1945.

Shaanxisheng Zonggonghui, *Gongye Qiye Dagao Qunzhong Yundongde Jingyan*, Xi'an, 1959.

Shaanxi Wenxian She, *Shaanxi Wenxian, Yi Zhi Ershisi Qi Hedingben*, n.p., 1976.

Shuili Dianlibu (ed.), *Jijing Buju Ji Waqian Peitao*, Beijing, 1974.

Shuili Dianlibu Shuilisi (ed.), *Shanqu Daqing Jingyan Huibian*, Beijing, 1974.

Shuili Dianlibu Shuilisi (ed.), *Shuili Guanli Gongzuo Jingyan Huibian*, Beijing, 1973.

Shuili Dianli Chubanshe (ed.), *Zhongguo Shuili Shigao*, Beijing, 1979.

Su Xianzhong, *Yumi Zaipei Zhishi*, Xi'an, 1976.

Sun Shaozong, *Shaanxisheng Xinxing Guangai Shuili Tongji*, Xi'an, 1943.

Tian Weijun and Bai Xiuyun, *Chongxiu Qishan Xianzhi*, Taipei, 1976 (reprint of 1935 ed.).

Wan Tingshu and Hong Liangji, *Chunhua Xianzhi*, 2 vols, Taipei, 1976 (reprint of 1934 ed.).

Wang Chengjing, *Shaanxi Tudi Liyong Wenti*, Shanghai, 1956.
Wang Chengjing, *Xibeide Nongtian Shuili*, Shanghai, 1950.
Wang Chongren, *Gudu Xi'an*, Xi'an, 1981.
Wang Depu, *Shaanxi Minzheng Gaikuang*, Xi'an, 1940.
Wang Dexuan, *Xiaomai Gaochan Zaipei Jishu*, Xi'an, 1978.
Wang Dianzhong et al. (eds), *(Xuxiu) Shaanxisheng Tongzhigao*, 122 Vols, n.p., 1934.
Wang Gongliang, *Xibei Dili*, Nanjing, 1936.
Wang Ruqing, *Shaanxi Xiangxian Shilüe*, n.p., 1935.
Wang Wang (ed.), *Xin Xi'an*, Kunming, 1940.
Wang Yong and Mao Naiwen, *Zhongguo Dixue Lunwen Suoyin*, Beijing, 1934.
Wang Yong and Mao Naiwen, *Zhongguo Dixue Lunwen Suoyin Xubian*, Beijing, 1936.
Weinan He Chaoyi Liang Nongcun Jinrong Gongzuo Jingyan Huibian, Beijing, 1958.
Wu Zhenfeng, *Shaanxi Dili Yange*, Xi'an, 1980.
Xiang Huai and Wang Senwen, *Xutongguan Xianzhi*, Taipei, 1969 (reprint of 1817 ed.).
Xibei Daxue Dilixi 'Shaanxi Nongye Dili' Bianxiezu, *Shaanxi Nongye Dili*, Xi'an, 1979.
Xibei Daxue Lishixi, *Zhengguo Qu*, Xi'an, 1976.
Xibei Gesheng Renkou Wenti Lilun, Hong Kong, 1981.
Xibei Junzheng Weiyuanhui Caijing Weiyuanhui, *Xibei Tu Techan Gaikuang*, Xi'an, 1951.
Xibei Junzheng Weiyuanhui Caizhengbu, *Nongye Shuishou Zhengce Wenjianji*, Xi'an, 1952.
Xibei Junzheng Weiyuanhui Shuilibu, *Shaanxide Guangai Guanli*, Xi'an, 1951?
Xibei Nongxueyuan, *Guanghuide Shinian; Shaanxisheng Qianxian Fenghuo Renmin Gongshede Chengzhang*, Beijing, 1960.
Xibei Nongxueyuan Chubanshe, *Xibei Nonglin Shikan*, n.p., n.d.
Xibei Shinian Jianshe Jihua Shuili Bumen Chugao, n.p., 1943–44.
Xibei Shuili Kexue Yanjiusuo, *Xibei Huangtude Xingzhi*, Xi'an, 1959.
Xibei Yanjiusuo (ed.), *Kangzhan Zhongdi Shaanxi*, n.p., 1940.
Xibeiqu Guoying Jixie Nongchang Jingying Guanli Cankao Ziliao, Xi'an, 1954.
Xiqin Yumi Gaochan Jingyan, Xi'an 1977.
Xinhua Shishi Congkan She, *Shengchan Jiuzai*, Beijing, 1950.
Xingshengyuan Nongcun Fuxing Weiyuanhui, *Zhongguo Nongcun Diaocha Ziliao Wuzhong – Shaanxisheng Nongcun Diaocha*, n.p., 1934.
Xiong Boheng and Wang Dianjun, *Shaanxisheng Tudi Zhidu Diaocha Yanjiu*, Wugong 1941.
Xu Daofu (ed.), *Zhongguo Jindai Nongye Shengchan Ji Maoyi Tongji Ziliao*, Shanghai, 1983.
Xu Fang, *Xibei Jiaofei Zhanshi Gaiyao*, Chang'an, 1936.
Xu Ying, *Kangzhan Zhongdi Xibei*, Shanghai, 1938.
Yanan Nongcun Diaochatuan, *Mizhixian, Yangjiagou Diaocha*, Beijing, 1957.
Yang Hucheng, *Xibei Guofang Jingji Zhi Jianshe*, n.p., 1938?
Yang Ruiting and Huo Guangjin, *Pingmin Xianzhi*, Taipei, 1969 (reprint of 1932 ed.).
Yang Tingliang, *Jinri Xi'an*, Xi'an, 1957.
Yejin Gongyebu Wuhan Kancha Gongsi, *Nongcun Jianyi Cetufa*, Beijing, 1978.
Yijiuliu'er Nian Ziran Quhua Taolunhui Lunwenji, Beijing, 1962.
Yijiuliuling Nian Quanguo Dili Xueshu Huiyi Lunwenji, Shaanxisheng Ziran Quhua (Cao'an), n.p., n.d.
Yi Junzuo, *Xibei Zhuangyou*, Taipei, 1949.
Yikao Pinxiazhong Nong Guanhao Caiwu, Huxian Xinxiang Dadui Minzhu Licai Jingyan, Xi'an, 1973.
Yunnan Linxueyuan Shaanxisheng Shuitu Baochiju, *Shuitu Baochi Lin*, Beijing, 1975.
Zhang Guangye and Zhou Huashan, *Woguode Pingyuan*, Beijing, 1978.

Zhang Qipeng, *Dongxiaomai Zaipei Jishu Yanyu*, Xi'an, 1957.

Zhang Renjian, *Kaifa Xibei Shiye Jihua*, n.p., 1933.

Zhang Ruhai, *Nongchanpin Jiage Wenti Yanjiu*, Shanghai, 1984.

Zhang Yangming, *Dao Xibei Lai*, Shanghai, 1937.

Zhao Baozhen, *Hu Xianzhi*, Taipei, 1969.

Zhao Baozhen and Duan Guangshi, *Chongxiu Huxian Xianzhi*, 2 vols, Taipei, 1969 (reprint of 1933 ed.).

Zhao Benyin and Cheng Zhongzhao, *Hanchengxian Xuzhi*, Taipei, 1976 (reprint of 1925 ed.).

Zhao Puyuan, *Binzhou Xin Zhigao*, Taipei, 1969 (reprint of 1929 ed.).

Zhao Shoushan, *Wei Fanrong Xingfude Mingtian Er Fendou*, Xi'an, 1956.

Zhongguo Dili Xuehui Yijiuliuyi Nian Dimao Xueshu Taolunhui Lunwen Zhaiyao, n.p., n.d.

Zhongguo Dili Yijiuliuwu Nian Dimao Xueshu Taolunhui Wenji, Beijing, 1965.

Zhongguo Disanci Renkou Puchade Zhuyao Shuzi, n.p., 1982.

Zhongguo Jingji Nianjian, n.p. 1934, 1935, 1936, 1980, 1981, 1982, 1983.

Zhongguo Kexueyuan (ed.), *Zhongguo Ziran Dili, Dibiaoshui*, Beijing, 1981. idem (ed.), *Zhongguo Ziran Dili, Dimao*, Beijing, 1980.

Zhongguo Kexueyuan Dili Yanjiusuo, *Nongyong Yangban Ditude Bianzhi*, Beijing, 1964.

Zhongguo Jingji Nianjian Xubian, n.p., 1935.

Zhongguo Kexueyuan Dili Yanjiusuo, *Zhongguo Sheng (Qu) Dili*, Beijing, 1977.

Zhongguo Kexueyuan Dili Yanjiusuo Jingji Dili Yanjiushi (ed.), *Zhongguo Nongye Dili Zonglun*, Beijing, 1981.

Zhongguo Kexueyuan Jingji Yanjiusuo, *Yijiuwusi Nian Quanguo Geti Shougongye Diaocha Ziliao*, Beijing, 1957.

Zhongguo Kexueyuan Nanjing Dizhi Geshengwu Yanjiusuo, *Shaanxi Lantian Gongwangling Gengxinshi Puru*, Beijing, 1978.

Zhongguo Kexueyuan Nanjing Turang Yanjiusuo, *Zhongguo Turang*, Beijing, 1978.

Zhongguo Laodong Nianjian, n.p., 1934.

Zhongguo Nongye Kexueyuan Shaanxi Fenyuan, *Shaanxisheng Yijiuwujiu Nian Xiaomai Zengchan Jige Zhuyao Wentide Fenxi*, Xi'an, 1960.

Zhongguo Nongye Nianjian 1980, 1981, 1983, 1984, Beijing, 1981, 1982, 1984, 1985.

Zhongguo Xian Yinhang Nianjianshe, *Zhongguo Xian Yinhang Nianjian*, Shanghai, 1948.

Zhonggong Shaanxisheng Nongcun Gongzuobu, *Zhengdun Renmin Gongshe Shidian Gongzuode Jingyan*, Xi'an, 1959.

Zhonggong Shaanxi Shengwei Nongcun Gongzuobu, *Weinan Zhuanqu Qige Nongye Shengchan Hezuoshe Jingying Guanlide Chubu Jingyan* Xi'an, 1954.

Zhonggong Shaanxi Shengwei Nongcun Gongzuobu, *Zenyang Zuohao Nongye Hezuoshede Jingying Guanli*, Xi'an, 1955.

Zhonggong Shaanxi Shengwei Nongcun Gongzuobu, *Zenyang Zuzhi He Lingdao Lianshe*, Xi'an, 1956.

Zhonggong Shaanxi Shengwei Nongcun Gongzuobu, *Zhengqu Nongye Shengchan Da Yuejin*, Xi'an, 1958.

Zhonggong Shaanxi Shengwei Nongcun Gongzuodui, *Tamen Shi Zenyang Banhao Shengchanduide*, Xi'an, 1964.

Zhonggong Shaanxi Shengwei Xuanchuanbu, *Renmin Gongshe Tongsu Jianghua*, Xi'an, 1958.

Zhonggong Shangluo Diwei Xuanchuanbu, *Shanqu Shehui Zhuyi Jianshe Jianghua*, Xi'an, 1958.

Zhonggong Zhongyang Xibeiju Nongcun Gongzuodui, *Xibei Diqu Nongye Wenchan Gaochan Jingyan Jieshao*, Xi'an, 1964.

Zhongguo Baike Nianjian, n.p., 1980, 1981.

Zhongguo Caizheng Jingji Chubanshe, *Banhao Nongcun Daigou Daixiao Dian*, Beijing, 1975.

Zhonghua Mianye Tongjihui, *Zhongguo Mianchan Tongji*, Shanghai, 1935.

Zhou Yishi, *Zhongguo Gonglu Zhi*, Taipei, 1957.

Zhu Shaozhou, *Shianian Lai Zhi Shaanxi Dizheng*, n.p., 1946.

Zhu Xianmo, *Loutu*, Beijing, 1964.

INDEX